CHARISMATIC NATIONS

At the core of nationalism, the nation has always been defined and celebrated as a fundamentally cultural community. This pioneering cultural history shows how artists and intellectuals since the days of Napoleon have celebrated and taken inspiration from an idealized nationality, and how this in turn has informed and influenced social and political nationalism. The book brings together telling examples from across the entire European continent, from Dublin and Barcelona to Istanbul and Helsinki, and from cultural fields that include literature, painting, music, sports, world fairs and cinema as well as intellectual history. *Charismatic Nations* offers unique insights into how the unobtrusive soft power of a culture inspired by the national interacts with nationalism as a hard-edged political agenda. It demonstrates how, thanks to its pervasive cultural and 'unpolitical' presence, nationalism can shape-shift between Romantic insurgency and nativist populism. This title is also available as Open Access on Cambridge Core.

JOEP LEERSSEN was educated in the Netherlands, Germany, Ireland and Canada and held the chair of European Studies at the University of Amsterdam until 2022. His award-winning works on the comparative history of cultural nationalism (*National Thought in Europe* and the *Encyclopaedia of Romantic Nationalism in Europe*) are widely regarded as authoritative.

0.1 Yvonne (Madeleine Lebeau) in the film *Casablanca* (1942).

CHARISMATIC NATIONS

A Cultural History of Nationalism in Europe from 1800 to the Present

JOEP LEERSSEN

CAMBRIDGE
UNIVERSITY PRESS

CAMBRIDGE UNIVERSITY PRESS

Shaftesbury Road, Cambridge CB2 8EA, United Kingdom

One Liberty Plaza, 20th Floor, New York, NY 10006, USA

477 Williamstown Road, Port Melbourne, VIC 3207, Australia

314–321, 3rd Floor, Plot 3, Splendor Forum, Jasola District Centre, New Delhi – 110025, India

103 Penang Road, #05–06/07, Visioncrest Commercial, Singapore 238467

Cambridge University Press is part of Cambridge University Press & Assessment, a department of the University of Cambridge.

We share the University's mission to contribute to society through the pursuit of education, learning and research at the highest international levels of excellence.

www.cambridge.org
Information on this title: www.cambridge.org/9781009667159

DOI: 10.1017/9781009667142

First published 2026

A catalogue record for this publication is available from the British Library

Library of Congress Cataloging-in-Publication Data
NAMES: Leerssen, Joseph Th. (Joseph Theodoor), 1955– author
TITLE: Charismatic nations : a cultural history of nationalism in Europe from 1800 to the present / Joep Leerssen, University of Amsterdam.
DESCRIPTION: Cambridge, United Kingdom ; New York : Cambridge University Press, 2026. | Includes bibliographical references and index.
IDENTIFIERS: LCCN 2025033306 (print) | LCCN 2025033307 (ebook) | ISBN 9781009667159 hardback | ISBN 9781009667142 ebook
SUBJECTS: LCSH: Nationalism – Europe – History | Nationalism – Social aspects – Europe – History | Nationalism and literature – Europe – History | Nationalism and the arts – Europe – History | Europe – Civilization – 19th century | Europe – Civilization – 20th century | Europe – Civilization – 21st century
CLASSIFICATION: LCC JC201 .L44 2026 (print) | LCC JC201 (ebook)
LC record available at https://lccn.loc.gov/2025033306
LC ebook record available at https://lccn.loc.gov/2025033307

ISBN 978-1-009-66715-9 Hardback

Voor Ann

Contents

List of Figures *page* xi
List of Tables xiv
Acknowledgements xv

Introduction 1
The Culture of Nationalism 1
Cultural Production: Artists and Intellectuals 3
Dissemination, Canonicity, Remediation 5
The Self-Distinguishing Nation and the Cultivation of Culture 8
Culture and the Nation in History 12
Methodological Nationalism as a Historical Problem 14
The Nation's Short History and Long Memory 15
The Nation as Contingency: Working Definitions 17
Outline of the Book 20

PART I MEMORY AND POWER

1 The Romantic Spell 27
Strong Feelings, Deep Memories, Long Distance 27
The Rhine to Landsberg Prison, 1814–1925 27
Strasbourg to Casablanca, 1792–1942 31
Agincourt to D-Day, Novgorod to Leningrad 33
From Reverence to Charisma 35
Civic Religion and History-Makers 35
Hero-Worship: Carlyle to Weber 38
Charismatic Leaders, Charismatic Nations 41
'Beyond Politics': The Unpolitical Nation 44

2 Becoming Something, Unmaking Empires 49
Versailles, Berlin, Belfast, Odessa 49
States, Subjects, Secret Societies 51
Uprisings 55
1848 and the End of the Congress System 57
The Nation-State and the Unmaking of Empires 61

PART II ROMANCING THE NATION

3 Romantic Prophets: Inspired Poets Inspiring People 67
At the Dawn of History: Original Genius 67
An Apparition from the Past 68
Sublime Liminality and Visionary Inspiration 71
Channelling the Nation 72
The Voice of the Nation 76
The Poet as Role Model 79
Imagined, Embodied and Affective Communities 81

4 Manuscripts Found in the Attic 83
Antiquaries and the Literary Past 83
Archaeology in the Archives 86
The European Republic of Philology 88
Literary Histories, National Identity 93
Entangled Roots 95
Contested Heritage 100
The Nation Goes Epic 105

5 Ancestral Voices 109
Heroic Balladry 109
Flashback: Ossian in the Balkans 113
The Nation as Author 115
A Window on Mythology 118
The Roots of Identity 124
Making the Nation Personal: Self-Renamings 130

6 Languages, States, Races 133
Mother Tongue, Fatherland 133
Macro-nationalism and Pan-movements: German as a Sliding Scale 138
Etic and Emic: Which Differences Matter? 140
Matryoshka Scalarity 143
Historical Permanence versus Social Outreach 146
Celts, Aryans, Turanians: Max Müller and Race 149

7 History Related 158
Walter Scott Moves On from Ossian 158
Between History and Legend: Facts, Fiction and Fakes 164
The Long Tail of the Historical Novel: Epic, Sentimental, Juvenile 169
National History, National-Historical Myths, National Memory 175

8 The Image and the Presence 183
City Academies and Academic History Paintings 183
From Classical to National: History and Imagination 185
The Nazarenes and the Mural 187

The Past as a Magic Mountain: Goslar 191
Sentimental Historicism 194
Remediations and Mass Commodification 197
A Repertoire 199

9 In Tune: Concerts, Choirs 203
How a Wunderkind Became Hungarian 203
'Gypsies', Rhapsodies and the National Turn 207
Audience, Participation, Festivals 211
Appendix: 'National' Rhapsodies, 1840–1940 222

PART III ADAPTING TO MODERNITY

10 People in the Present 227
Festive Culture, Urban Reticulation, Embodied Communities 227
The City as Showcase: Modernity, Memory, Belonging 232
Narratives of Timelessness, Rustic Spectacles 235
The Tube and the Dirndl: *Plein-air* Painting and National Costume 240
Exhibiting the Nation: World Fairs and Nation-Branding 247
Henrik Ibsen and the Theatre 256
Arts and Crafts in *Fin-de-siècle* Nation-Building 260

11 Culture Mobilized 264
Public Opinion, Public Rancour 264
Political Professors: Fichte to Fustel 268
Kultur, War, Propaganda 279
National Identity at Stake 287
Dulce et Decorum 291

12 The Long Tail 295
Romantic Afterlife in a Modern Century 295
Democracy and Ethnocracy 302
Nationalism after Decolonization 306
The Nation at the Movies 310
Cold-War Asymmetries 315
Meanwhile, outside Europe 322
Epic Nationalism: Outrage into Charisma 326
Diffusion Condensed 330

Summing Up 333
The Wave and the Turbulence 333
Shape-Shifting, Thin-Centred, Soft-Powered 334
The Presence of the Past 336
National Culture Transnationally Pursued 337
Cultural Entanglement, Political Localism 338

Transnational and Intimate: Scalarity and Affect 340
Charisma, Disenchantment, Narcissism 341
Small Government, Big Flags 343

Notes 347
Bibliography 375
Index 419

Figures

0.1	Yvonne (Madeleine Lebeau) in the film *Casablanca* (1942).	*page* ii
I.1	Cultural production schematized.	4
I.2	The dynamics of culture in nineteenth-century nationalism.	7
I.3	The cultivation of culture in nation-building.	10
1.1	Germania monument at Niederwald near Bingen.	28
1.2	Yvonne (Madeleine Lebeau) in the film *Casablanca* (1942).	31
1.3	Claude Joseph Rouget de Lisle singing 'La Marseillaise' (Isidore Pils, 1849; Musée historique de Strasbourg).	32
1.4	Mustafa Kemal Atatürk depicted twice on the Monument of the Republic, Gezi Square, Istanbul (1928).	42
2.1	Opening page of Emmanuel Sieyès's *What Is the Third Estate?* (1789).	50
2.2	Statue of Byron in Athens (Henri-Michel Chapu and Alexandre Falguière, 1896).	56
2.3	Seating plan of the Frankfurt National Assembly (1848).	58
3.1	Title-page vignette for James Macpherson's *Fingal* (1762).	70
3.2	Frontispiece to Emile Debraux's *Chansons nationales* (1822).	78
3.3	Tomb of Rosalía De Castro, Santiago de Compostela (Jesús Landeira, 1891).	79
4.1	Title-page vignette for Melchiorre Cesarotti's Italian version of Ossian (1763).	85
4.2	A timeline of 540 nineteenth-century text editions.	90
4.3	The correspondence network of Jacob Grimm.	92
4.4	August Heinrich Hoffmann von Fallersleben in the garb of a wandering student.	97
4.5	The differently oriented correspondence networks of Ernst Moritz Arndt and Prosper Mérimee.	104
5.1	Frontispiece and title page of the 1824 edition of Vuk Karadžić's anthology.	111
5.2	A mind-map of relations between genres in popular culture and specialisms in knowledge production.	120

5.3 'QAnon Shaman' Jacob Chansley during the 2021 Capitol riots. 124
5.4 A mind-map showing how Romantic nationalism sees the connections among cultural fields. 126
6.1 Title-page vignette for the Grimms' *Deutsches Wörterbuch* (1854). 136
6.2 Millennium Church, Csikszereda, Romania (designed by Imre Makovecz, completed in 2003). 156
7.1 *Slavín* memorial in the Vyšehrad cemetery, Prague. 168
7.2 Memory into memorabilia: souvenirs in the tourist gift shop at the Regensburg Walhalla. 182
8.1 Allegory of Germania (Philipp Veit, 1848; Germanisches Nationalmuseum, Nuremberg). 188
8.2 *Joan of Arc in Armour at the Siege of Orléans* (Jules Lenepveu, 1874; Panthéon, Paris). 189
8.3 *Yermak's Conquest of Siberia* (Vasilij Surikov, 1895; State Russian Museum, St Petersburg). 191
8.4 *Wilhelm I as Refounder of the Reich* (Hermann Wislicenus, 1885; Imperial Manor, Goslar). 193
8.5 *And When Did You Last See Your Father?* (William Frederick Yeames, 1878; Walker Art Gallery, Liverpool). 196
8.6 *The Goddess Saraswati* (Raja Ravi Varma, 1896; Maharaja Fateh Singh Museum, Vadodara). 198
8.7 History painting, history writing and the historical novel. 199
8.8 *'Birchlegs' Skiing Across the Mountains with the Infant King* (Knud Bergslien, 1869; Holmenkollen Ski Museum, Oslo). 202
9.1 *A Matinee Performance by Liszt* (Josef Danhauser, 1840; Alte Nationalgalerie, Berlin). 204
9.2 Liszt's concert tours across Europe, 1818–1886. 206
9.3 Bust of the choral conductor and composer Josep Clavè in the art nouveau Palace of Catalan Music, Barcelona. 214
9.4 Participants in the Latvian national song festival in traditional dress, 2023. 220
10.1 The spirit of Schiller exhorting a dejected Germany (Carl Jäger, 1859). 229
10.2 Shifting proportions of national-historical and rustic themes in 4,500 academic paintings, 1760–1910. 237
10.3 Newspaper coverage of Frédéric Mistral's Nobel Prize for literature (1904). 239

10.4 *The Reaper* (Kanutas Ruseckas, 1844; Lithuanian Art Museum, Vilnius). 242
10.5 Jindřich Fügner in the Sokol club's national Slavic uniform. 244
10.6 Sigmund and Anna Freud in Austrian country dress. 245
10.7 A landmark left by the 1911 world fair in Rome: lighthouse donated by Argentina to the host city as a 'beacon of the Latin world'. 249
10.8 Poster for the Romanian cabaret at the 1889 Paris Exposition Universelle (Jules Chéret). 253
10.9 Art nouveau posters for national events: the Barcelona Floral Games (1908, Ramón Casas) and the Sokol sports festival in Prague (1912, Alphonse Mucha). 261
11.1 The philosopher Johann Gottlieb Fichte on parade as a member of the Prussian Landwehr (1862 engraving after Carl Zimmermann, 1813). 269
11.2 French/German ethnotypes around 1914. 276
11.3 The pedantic Professor Knatschke as drawn by 'Hansi' (1912). 277
12.1 National commemorative monuments per decade and country. 296
12.2 Latvian postage stamp (1932). 299
12.3 Polish pavilion at the 1939 New York World's Fair. 300
12.4 Monument to the Portuguese Discoveries, Belém, Lisbon (António Pardal Monteiro and Leopoldo de Almeida, 1960). 301
12.5 Production of films with national-heroic content per decade. 326
12.6 Eurasian geographic distribution of 100 epic-heroic national action movies since 1990. 329
12.7 A visual metaphor for the alternating states of latency and salience in the cultural history of nationalism. 332
13.1 Phases of national movements between communicative diffusion and localized activism. 339

Tables

6.1 Types of minority language cultivation in nineteenth-century Europe *page* 148
9.1a Chronological list of nationally themed rhapsodies, 1846–1899: interactively accessible at e-rn.ie/rhapsodies 222
9.1b Chronological list of nationally themed rhapsodies, 1900–1913: interactively accessible at e-rn.ie/rhapsodies 223
9.1c Chronological list of nationally themed rhapsodies, 1915–1940: interactively accessible at e-rn.ie/rhapsodies 224
12.1a National-heroic movies in Europe, 1909–1914 310
12.1b National-heroic movies in Europe, 1918–1929 311
12.1c National-heroic movies in Europe, 1930–1939 312
12.2a National-heroic movies in Western Europe, 1950–1960 317
12.2b National-heroic movies in Western Europe, 1961–1987 317
12.3a National-heroic movies in Central and Eastern Europe, 1946–1962 319
12.3b National-heroic movies in Central and Eastern Europe, 1966–1979 319
12.3c National-heroic movies in Central and Eastern Europe, 1980–1989 320
12.4a National-heroic movies in India, 1949–1991 323
12.4b National-heroic movies in India, 2000–2022 324

Acknowledgements

This book summarizes a decades-long research project based on the materials collected in the *Encyclopedia of Romantic Nationalism in Europe*, hereinafter referred to as ERNiE. The aim of the ERNiE project was to document the history and lingering presence of the many cultural assertions of national identity in Europe over the last two centuries. To capture the data here analysed, so dispersed and diffuse, took much effort and expertise coming from many different specialisms; my own role, also as the author of this book, was mainly to act as a comparatist, a connector of dots. In 'connecting the dots' I was aided by a digital work environment, 'Nodegoat' (also the operating basis for the online version of ERNiE), which allowed me to do justice to the complex interrelations of the historical data in all their great quantity and multimedial diversity. Many visualizations in this book are graphic renderings of data managed in Nodegoat.

I want to express my deep, abiding thanks to my many fellow researchers: those who contributed their independent research either to ERNiE or to the book series *National Cultivation of Culture* (Leiden: Brill); and to my colleagues, research assistants and student assistants, both within the University of Amsterdam and further afield. This book draws on their input, and has benefited from the collegiality and friendship, more deeply and widely, and more gratefully, than can be captured in mere source-referencing footnotes. To list them all would amount almost to an autobiography. Like any autobiography, the following roll call must be partial: my gratitude is, quite literally, boundless.

I came to nationalism studies in mid-career, on the basis of working hypotheses developed during my work on Irish cultural self-awareness. In that transition I was stimulated by many Irish friends and supportive colleagues, such as Claire Connolly, Ann Dooley, the late Tom Dunne, Roy Foster, Luke Gibbons, Margaret Kelleher, Ian McBride, Clare O'Halloran, Harry White and (like me 'honorary Irishmen' by association) Guy Beiner and Murray Pittock. An institutional Irish support base was provided over the years by the Long Room Hub at Trinity College Dublin: thank you, Caitriona Curtis, Eva Muhlhause, Jane Ohlmeyer, Eve Patten.

A very special place in my grateful memory is kept by my late friend Rolf Loeber, who as a social psychologist with an abiding interest in Irish cultural history opened my eyes to the possibility that ambitious, large-scale, long-term empirical projects were in fact feasible; the husband-and-wife collaboration between him and his wife Magda Loeber-Stouthamer was a formative inspiration.

Another demonstration that longitudinal, wide-ranging studies need not deter even the historical humanities came from my late Amsterdam colleague, the great comparatist John Neubauer. His work on the literary history of Central and Eastern Europe was a true, direct inspiration. It broadened my horizon from the north-west of Europe in a decade when contacts were once again established across a vanished Iron Curtain; many of the collaborators that John brought together would later become valuable associates of the Romantic Nationalism project. This cohort of researchers from Europe's ex-communist countries found an invaluable hub in the Central European University in Budapest; particularly enriching were my contacts there with Balázs Trencsényi. In my exploratory work on the national movements of Central and Eastern Europe, which started with Ingrid Merchiers's fine thesis co-supervised by Raymond Detrez and myself, the intellectual expertise, support and kindness of Miroslav Hroch were precious. In the post-Hroch generation, those who broadened my horizons eastwards and south-eastwards included Miloš Řezník and Dalibor Dobiaš in Prague; Sándor Hites in Budapest; Marijan Dović and Marko Juvan in Ljubljana; Pavle and Ivana Šekeruš in Novi Sad; Diana Mishkova in Sofia; and Paschalis Kitromilides and Christina Koulouri in Athens.

In Europe's north and west, my continuing interest in the history of the philological and ethnographic sciences profited immensely from the insights and the comradeship of Mary-Ann Constantine, Terry Gunnell, Diarmuid Ó Giolláin and Tom Shippey. A Nordic network took shape from Reykjavík to the Baltic, with friends and colleagues including Pertti Anttonen, Benedikte Brincker, Sveinn Yngvi Egilsson, Tim van Gerven, Rasmus Glenthøj, Simon Halink, Jón Karl Helgason, Ruth Hemstad, David Hopkin, Kristina Jõekalda, Linda Kaljundi, Toms Ķencis, the late Kristin Kuutma and Per Øhrgaard. In Britain, Joanne Parker and Ian Wood shared my interest in medievalism, which also profited from the research networks around Patrick Geary and Hedwig Röckelein. Comparative historiography was given a massive impetus and stimulation by the work, vision and organizational teamwork of Stefan Berger. Among historians, these Dutch and Flemish names stand out: Matthijs Lok, Niek van Sas, Eric Storm, Jo Tollebeek, Maarten Vanginderachter and Tom Verschaffel. Alpita de Jong's fine doctoral thesis, co-supervised with Philippus Breuker, acquainted me at an early stage with the Frisian movement, a salient case close to home. Congenial spirits in the field of literature were Goffe Jensma, Frits van Oostrom and the late Pieter Steinz.

New to the field of nationalism studies, I encountered kind, inspiring and authoritative colleagues at the London School of Economics: the late Anthony Smith, John Breuilly, John Hutchinson, Jon Hearn; the collegiality of the Association for the Study of Ethnicity and Nationalism and the editorial team around the journal *Nations and Nationalism* (thank you, David Landon Cole and Seeta Persaud!) remain a shining example to the world of learning. Collegiality was also the defining characteristic of NISE at Antwerp, which, thanks to the work of Eva Bidania, Luc Boeva, Hanno Brand, Elly Broes, Andreas Stynen and Kas Swerts, brought together inspiring colleagues from all corners of Europe, from Darius Staliunas in Vilnius to Johannes Koll in Vienna and, last but by no means least, Xosé Manoel Núnez Seixas in Santiago de Compostela.

In Paris, Anne-Marie Thiesse soon turned from an inspiring authority into a dear friend. Much do I owe to her work, her sparkling and erudite conversation and her hospitality. She also unlocked collegial networks to me in the south: Antonino de Francesco in Milan and Ferran Archiles and Xavier Andreu Muralles in Valencia. This is also the place to acknowledge the collegiality and generosity of Ramón Maiz in Galicia, Magi Sunyer in Catalunya, and the enriching intellectual presence of Francesca Zantedeschi.

That all these contacts across Europe could find a hub in Amsterdam is thanks largely to what was then a thriving, interdisciplinary culture of internationally oriented historical humanities at the University of Amsterdam. Within European studies, the culture of nationalism had been a research focus since the days of Bram Boxhoorn, Lily Coenen, Manet van Montfrans, the late Wim Roobol, Menno Spiering and Fernando Venâncio; that tradition has been continued by such colleagues as Alex Drace-Francis, Krisztina Lajosi, Yolanda Rodríguez Pérez, Roel Schuyt, Guido Snel and Michael Wintle, with talented PhD students who taught me more than I taught them: Usman Ahmedani, Tim van Gerven, Rutger Helmers, Josip Kešić, Kasper van Kooten, Ayşenur Korkmaz, Enno Maessen, Tymen Peverelli, Janette Verrijzer-Sampimon and Marija Sniečkutė. Bob van der Linden came to inspire us, with good humour and erudition, to broaden our horizons beyond Europe.

Elsewhere in the Faculty of Humanities, there were sympathetic and collaborative colleagues in Germanic, Jewish, Romance, Scandinavian and Slavic studies, and in Dutch literary history there was the pioneering work of Marita Mathijsen and the many younger scholars inspired by her; from among them, Lotte Jensen has gone on to become an authoritative voice in the field. Jan Rock led the team of research assistants and student assistants of the 'Study Platform on Interlocking Nationalisms', set up in 2008, as the successor of the late Anne Hilde van Baal; he and Stefan Poland became indispensable editorial assistants in the ERNiE project, which was supported by a dedicated and cheerful staff of student assistants, notably Nanne van der Linden and Eva Supèr. Faculty support I received from the deans Aafke Hulk, José van Dijck and Frank van Vree. The faculty's greatest strength I found to be its administrative, library and IT support staff: thank you, Tatjana Das, the late Letje Lips, Wendy Pezarro, Nienke Rentenaar and Silvain Smit. Outstanding among them all was my go-to fixer and mate, Paul Koopman. I fondly recall the weekly lunches with my friend and colleague the late Arthur Mitzman, historian and Michelet biographer.

I thank the institutions whose largesse made the enterprise feasible and enabled this book to appear in Open Access: the Dutch Research Council, the Royal Netherlands Academy of Arts and Sciences and the European Federation of Academies of Sciences and Humanities. I also thank the places of refuge where, as a guest researcher over the past decades, I was able to develop and refine my planning of this cultural history of European nationalisms: Harvard University (especially its Department of Celtic Studies, which hosted me as Erasmus Lecturer), Magdalene College, Cambridge, the Lichtenberg-Kolleg at the University of Göttingen, the University of Toronto (in particular Ann Dooley and Paul Stevens), the École normale supérieure in Paris, the Royal Netherlands Institute in Rome and the Netherlands Institute for Advanced Studies.

For technical support, my warms thanks go to Pim van Bree and Geert Kessels for assisting me with their fine 'Nodegoat' data management environment; Mark Dodemont of studiododemont.be, who improved the graphic design of the illustrations; Pierke of isbnindex.nl, for the index; and Ray Ryan at Cambridge University Press, for shepherding this book into print.

My greatest, steadiest and most joyful source of strength has been my family, its generations past present and future. Above all, my dear wife Ann Rigney, constant soulmate and best of colleagues.

Introduction

The Culture of Nationalism

To understand nationalism properly we should see it as more than a political doctrine or social movement. The nation, after which nationalism names itself and which it invokes as its supreme guiding principle, seems to be above politics. It is invoked not as one of those socio-economic or political principles or allegiance patterns that run across society – the way in which stability is invoked by conservatives, free enterprise by liberals, class by socialists, labour by social democrats, or religion by Christian democrats – but as something that transcends those particular interests; the nation is considered to unite rather than divide society. The nation is felt to be politically uncontentious, something to which everyone, regardless of political hue, can feel and express allegiance. Accordingly, nationalism is a shape-shifting, flexible presence in the political landscape; it can hyphenate itself with other political movements of the left, centre, or right, effortlessly adapting itself to the political climate of the decade. It appears as anti-Napoleonism in the 1810s, as anti-absolutism in the 1830s and 1840s, as chauvinistic patriotism in the decades around 1900, and nowadays as a key ingredient in ethnopopulism. The nation can be invoked as vindication by practically any politician – dictators as different as Stalin and Salazar; Italian leaders as different as Mazzini, Mussolini and Berlusconi; and in the post-imperial tradition of Britain and France, political leaders as different as Churchill, Gandhi and Boris Johnson, as De Gaulle, Bourguiba and Le Pen.

In order to get this shifting political force field into focus we need to understand nationalism as the political application of a fundamentally cultural concept. The nation that is invoked as a political ideal is, from the days of Napoleon onward, seen as a community held together by a shared culture and expressing its identity culturally. The nation is as commanding and all-pervasive a presence in the field of cultural production as in those of social and political relations, and its prominent spokespersons are artists and intellectuals as much as politicians or economists. Culture is central to the nation and central to our understanding of nationalism as a historical force.

In this book, I chart not only a history of this culture of nationalism, from Romantic medievalism beginning around 1800 to national-heroic action movies from the 2000s, but also a cultural history of nationalism.[1] Culture does not just, as the old-fashioned expression has it, hold up a mirror to society, reflecting political nationalism in the spheres of learning, literature, the arts, and leisure-time amusement. It does all that, but it is in the first instance a blueprint, a scenario, inspiring and articulating agendas and ambitions for the future, disseminating them in alluring forms across platforms and media (prestigious as well as popular ones), and as such it is an active participant in political developments and exercises an autonomous historical agency. In the well-known 'phase model' of Miroslav Hroch, which identifies stages in the development of national movements in Europe, the initial stage, 'Phase A', is cultural in nature. It does, undeniably, come first (at least within Europe), preparing the subsequent stages of social demands and mass mobilization; and it has left lasting, deep, widespread traces. Europe (and not Europe alone) has been dominated over the past two centuries, and continues to be dominated, by a culture of nationalism. This culture is a generally ambient ('unpolitical') repertoire of tropes and references; it frames the way in which we see history and society, past and future. Much as the nation is seen fundamentally as a cultural community, culture itself, in all its manifold fields and expressions, can function as the habitat of nationalism, its conceptual hatching-ground, its rhetorical amplifier and its communicative platform. Culture, in other words, ensures the social presence and the political prevalence of nationalism. It aids the conceptualization as well as the propagation of the idea that nations are natural, timeless entities and that as moral instances they justify the policies that are pursued in their name. Nationalism, in this definition, is a politically influential cultural repertoire; and this book sets out to chart that repertoire and its development since 1800.

The cultural repertoire of nationalism does not in itself explain the course of history, and readers should not expect this book to provide such an explanation. What I attempt, in the following pages, is to explain the repertoire itself; to chart it across cultural fields, across countries and over the decades, in its proliferating and mutating development; to document and disentangle its historical adaptability and its protean, multifarious, ongoing presence.

By now, the word 'culture' may begin to sound like a mantra. Sharpening my usage of the term is necessary.

In a bare-bones semantic distinction, culture is everything in human life that is not 'nature'. In that contradistinction, culture refers to those behavioural or communicative practices by which humans deliberately shape, control, adjust and modify their physical environment and their physiological processes. In this anthropological meaning, culture ranges from agriculture to the building of dikes and dwellings, from clothing and fashion to food preparation and table manners, from the societal regulation of mating and procreation to wedding parties and baby showers, from the grinding of lenses to the manufacture of ink and photocopiers. Culture also involves sharing memories and keeping them alive by means of writing, ritual or the symbolic dedication of spaces; it involves dancing, music and telling stories from nursery rhymes to epic and cinema; it includes the recitation of prayers and debating the international rule of law. Etcetera; this list serves only to give the reader an idea. Of course, not all of this is relevant for our present purposes. Some of this culture is 'deep': ancient, widespread and anthropological, such as the domestication of the dog; some of it is rarefied, a by-product of modern Western commercialism and leisure-time entertainment. In the following pages, samples of 'culture' will range across that entire spectrum, from 'deep' things such as language, cultural memory and narrating the past to classical music concerts, action movies and postage stamps.

Culture is all over the place; how can we save this book from being all over the place? In the following clarifications I will attempt to present a more fine-grained understanding of the 'culture of nationalism'.

Cultural Production: Artists and Intellectuals

Culture involves not only artistic production and philosophical reflection but also knowledge production. Scholarly and scientific insights may at first sight appear as the systematic explanation of independently existing, objective facts of life – oxidization, gravity or ancient Egyptian hieroglyphs. But these discoveries occurred at specific historical moments, were made possible by historically specific circumstances; and whatever wider reverberations they had turned them into specific historical events. In the humanities in particular, scholarly advances dovetail with infrastructural innovations: the exploration of the world and its cultures under colonial auspices; the reinventorization of old archives after 1780; the widening platform of printed books thanks to wood-pulp paper and automated printing presses; the post-1800 restructuring of university faculties and departments. On the timeline of those historical changes, we can map developments in knowledge production (such as the collecting of folk tales and folk ballads and the re-edition and dating of ancient epics), as well as developments in literature and the arts (the rise of the bestseller author and of the historical novel, the national turn in history painting and history writing, the neo-Gothic taste in architecture). In this book I will treat cultural production as the joint operation of artistic production (in aesthetically valorized genres such as the visual arts, fiction/drama and music) and knowledge production (in the world of scholarship), with institutional, socio-political and technological changes functioning as an enabling ambience or context.[2]

This two-pronged approach to cultural production is complemented by the fact that culture invariably reflects upon itself: literature, the arts and music are pursued in an ambience of literary, artistic and musical criticism, with periodicals and public lectures dedicated to those critical reflections; history writing is accompanied by reviews and by educational discussions about the pedagogical uses of the past. The importance of culture (which frequently means its importance for the nation) is a constant point of reflection among those who are involved in artistic or scholarly production. I therefore schematize cultural activities in a triad of artistic production, knowledge production and critical reflection, as visualized in Figure I.1.

The individuals involved in cultural production are, then, artists and intellectuals. They are the 'protagonists', as Miroslav Hroch calls them, of national movements in their early stages of consciousness-building. Their work is what forms the core corpus of this book. Indeed, the texts and artworks produced by these artists and intellectuals are themselves historical

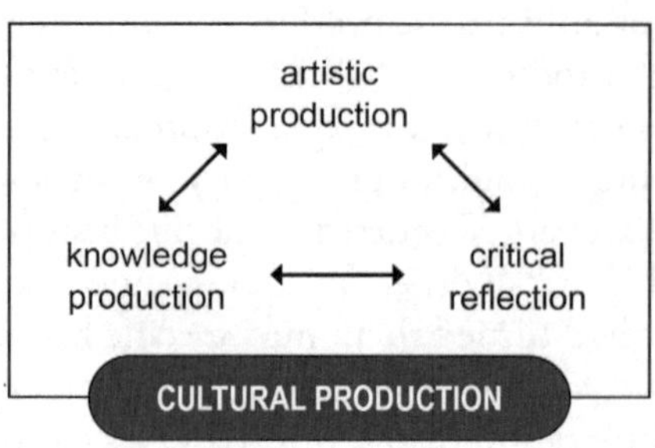

Figure I.1 Cultural production schematized as the interplay of artistic production, knowledge production and critical reflection.

actors: they are productive as well as being produced, procreative as well as created – for example 'La Marseillaise' and statues of Joan of Arc in France, the *Kalevala* in Finland and Hendrik Conscience's novel *De Leeuw van Vlaenderen* (1838) in Flanders.[3]

The artists and intellectuals who produced the culture of nationalism cannot really be laid along the measuring tape of 'elite' versus 'popular masses'. The 'intelligentsia' (as Hroch calls them elsewhere, those who 'speak for the nation') ranged from fretful tutors in private households and bohemian artists starving in garrets to members of the high nobility, urbanites, *salonnières* and countryfolk, and included country parsons, doctors and schoolmasters who, highly educated, were in close contact with rural-peripheral communities. For them, the nation was, precisely, something that united society across the divides of class and locality thanks to a common heritage and cultural allegiance.[4]

Dissemination, Canonicity, Remediation

In the history of cultural production and dissemination since 1800, we shall notice a long-term trend towards mass-reproduced media. A new 'technical reproducibility' of culture was identified in 1935 by Walter Benjamin (Benjamin 1963). More generally, the past centuries were characterized by increased quantitative production at decreasing costs, resulting in cheaper availability and greater market penetration. A typical example is the lower price and increased production and availability of printed books after the introduction of woodpulp paper and the mechanized printing press – involving widening circles of readership; or the reproduction of opera arias as sheet music for amateur choirs. For Pierre Bourdieu, these supply-and-demand factors play a crucial role in the symbolic value of cultural products. Culture that is in short supply and involves great expense (such as a ballet performance at Covent Garden, or a rare antique) will be more exclusive and accordingly more highly valorized. Conversely, culture that is readily available to great numbers of people (hence the word 'popular') will have less exclusivity or prestige. I will rely on Bourdieu's distinction between 'restricted' and 'unrestricted' cultural production when discussing these dynamic shifts: over time, the nation's identity and self-articulation will come to rely increasingly on 'popular' media such as postage stamps, characterized by 'unrestricted' production.[5]

Bourdieu's criterion is also relevant when tracing the dynamics between 'high' and 'popular' culture. Artists and intellectuals of the Romantic generation draw on folk tales and folksongs, *fin-de-siècle* design is inspired by popular-traditional crafts; conversely, hitherto prestigious genres such as the historical novel become popular reading for boys, and history paintings end up as engraved or lithographed illustrations in school textbooks. No sooner does one try to apply a distinction between 'high' and 'popular' culture than the entanglement between them becomes obvious. Status and canonicity were, however, important elements for the influence that high-status culture could exercise, and mass popularity was a measure of its social penetration; ignoring such historical factors would be unwise.

We can usefully apply Bourdieu's notion of *prestige* here. Some cultural practices play into a societal mechanism whereby elites affirm and perpetuate their higher standing in the social order. Such culture involves, in Bourdieu's analysis, 'distinction'; it is prestigious and belongs to what is generally distinguished as 'high culture' from the less prestigious 'popular culture'. High culture is in turn linked to the idea of *canonicity*. This is at work when a set of cultural expressions or memories are credited with persistently enduring merit or importance, and as such deemed to have a particular pedagogical, society-reaffirming value. As such, high culture is not ephemeral, and even though its social catchment area may be narrow, restricted to the privileged apex of society, its endurance over time renders its importance more considerable than more widespread but ephemeral cultural fashions. The centuries-long cultural presence of the patriotic speeches in Shakespeare's *Henry V* are a case in point. *Henry V* also illustrates another element of canonicity: its capacity for remediation. In Chapter 1, we shall encounter an important instance of how those patriotic speeches were reprised in Lawrence Olivier's 1944 film version of the play. Canonical works are particularly apt at being adapted into new media as these emerge: certain plays and novels, thanks to their canonicity, are chosen to be reworked into operas, movies, comic strips and musicals, and that adaptability is both a result and a measure of their canonicity. Again, readers will encounter repeated instances in the course of this book.[6]

Cultural production is itself only one of at least three ways in which culture makes its presence felt historically. Culture is not only produced, it is also received. People inhabit cities suffused with architectural and monumental markers of history and nationality. People read books (from poetry to collections of folk tales and treatises on myths and archaeology); and they also read book reviews and periodicals dedicated to reviewing and criticism; they go to exhibitions, festivals, concerts and public lectures, and the success of this or that author or work before a more-or-less

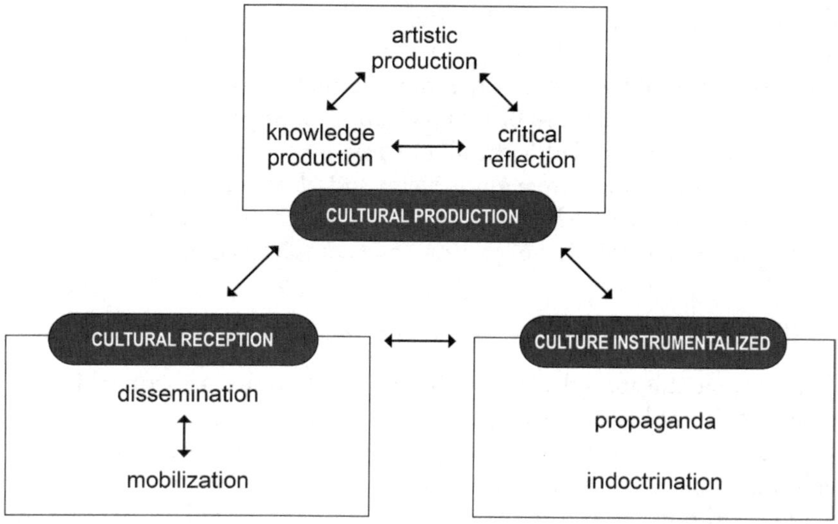

Figure I.2 The dynamics of culture in nineteenth-century nationalism.

appreciative audience *matters*. Successful cultural producers may even convey a direct national-political message to their audiences, as Thomas Davis did in Ireland, 'La Marseillaise' in France, Jacob Grimm and Ernst Moritz Arndt in Germany, the *Kalevala* in Finland, Liszt's rhapsodies in Hungary, Taras Shevchenko's verse in Ukraine and Vuk Karadžić's philological work in Serbia. Ultimately, such work may be instrumentalized by governments for political propaganda and culture may become a tool for national politics. The dynamics of the 'culture of nationalism' may accordingly be schematized more fully, as shown in Figure I.2.

This schematization visualizes a good many feedback loops between culture as produced in different fields and as received/disseminated in different modalities. Such feedback loops – all elements simultaneously experience influences from others and in turn exercise influences upon them in their nesting mutual relations – are par for the course in a complex system,[7] involving things as diverse as a Walter Scott novel, a choral festival in Tallinn in 1897 or in 1989, the unveiling of a commemorative statue of Dante in Florence in 1862, Wagner using the ancient German *Nibelungenlied* for an operatic German *Gesamtkunstwerk*, the Norwegian folk tale of Peer Gynt, Frisians commemorating the seventeenth-century poet Gysbert Japikx, Irish activists playing national sports and taking evening classes in the Gaelic language, the restored imperial manor of Goslar being decorated with murals illustrative of German history and the

German fairy tale of Sleeping Beauty. All these things (we shall encounter them in the course of this book) hang together, and in their hanging together they establish, both at the international and at the national level, what I here call the culture of nationalism. It is important not to reduce that to a mere glop called 'culture' but instead to envisage how intricate such connections and interactions were; and also (for this is a historical study) to examine which ones came first, which ones later: that alone requires a disentanglement of 'culture' as a complex system.

The Self-Distinguishing Nation and the Cultivation of Culture

The fact that culture reflects upon itself – is self-aware – is crucial for the type of cultural history attempted here. The mere presence of a certain set of cultural practices (e.g. having domesticated, house-trained dogs, or lighting bonfires on certain occasions) may characterize a society or population without necessarily playing a nation-defining role. I here follow the classic argument of Ernest Renan, in his seminal lecture 'Qu'est-ce qu'une nation?' of 1883, that whatever elements play a role in marking and identifying a nation as such can do so only provided the people concerned are ready to acknowledge them as being meaningful. (More on this in Chapter 11.)

What makes culture, or a given cultural practice, meaningful is, precisely, this reflective self-awareness. Owning dogs, or tying one's shoes with shoelaces, or eating one's food with fork and knife, or speaking a certain language, can be an unreflected, ingrained habitus, as unconsciously performed as blinking one's eyes or drawing breath.[8] However, the fact that one speaks one language rather than another can, in a confrontational setting, become deliberate, a conscious choice, made for identifiable reasons; and those reasons may have to do with asserting one's separate identity or maintaining a cultural continuity with previous and future generations. At that moment, language use becomes reflected, conscious, meaningful. So too for other cultural practices. One may wear a kilt merely because it looks cool to show off one's calves, but it may also be motivated by a self-identification with the specific tradition that it stands for (i.e. its *meaning*). Singing songs together may be just an assertion of togetherness ('Happy Birthday', 'For He's a Jolly Good Fellow'), but it can also be much more meaningful, as a symbol of the continuity of togetherness joyfully or respectfully asserted: 'Previous generations sang the national anthem at their moments of joy, pride or anguish, and as I sing it I am mindful of that fact.'

We can infer at the outset that turning a cultural habit into a conscious cultural choice presupposes that there are alternatives – such as other languages or articles of clothing competing in a given setting, and a sense that the habitual language or dress is no longer the only, default option. In other words, the sense that one's habitual cultural practices are exposed to, and are competing with, other ones, is a strong motivator for attaching an added, consciously experienced meaning and importance to them. Nationality becomes meaningful once it is exposed to the presence of foreignness – the *Fremderfahrung*, as Hugo Dyserinck called it. Hence in this book I follow Walker Connor's definition of the nation as a 'self-distinguishing culture group'[9] – not only as a 'self-identifying' group that chooses to identify as a nation, on the basis of whatever shared culture is considered meaningful (the point already made by Renan), but also as a group that performs that self-identification in the process of articulating its distinctness from others.*

This helps us to sharpen our focus on the types of culture that are meaningful in the nation's articulation of its distinctness. To begin with, it means that we can no longer invoke 'culture' as the generic thing that establishes a national identity. The culture that establishes a national identity is a highly specific and restricted subset of culture: it is culture that is aware of itself and that is consciously experienced as being meaningful for one's national self-distinguishing.

Such consciously experienced culture is a historical praxis, a choice made in specific, datable circumstances. That alone should alert us that the nation can never be 'timeless'. Speaking Basque in the town of Guernica was unremarkable in 1800; in the 1950s it was an act of defiance. Culture as such may be of long standing, almost perennial, and difficult to plot on a timeline; but the self-conscious cultivation of culture to enable a national self-distinguishing is a firmly historical process. I shall return to this ambivalent chronology further on.

All these considerations make it possible to array a specific set of cultural practices as being meaningful for national self-distinguishing and as operative elements in a 'culture of nationalism'. We can, empirically

* The notion of 'articulation' will be encountered repeatedly in this book. It has been used for the process of identity-formulation in nation-building in studies like Suny & Kennedy 2001 and Sampimon 2006; more specifically I also take my cue from Stuart Hall, who in turn took his cue from Antonio Gramsci (see Solomos 2014). Articulation as used here involves a discursive act that brings a new idea into expression and into social circulation; more specifically, the idea involved concerns the 'hinged' connections (neither rigid nor disjointed) between social elements (such as the nation, or, in Hall's analysis, race).

intensity of cultivation →

fields / media of culture	1: Recollection: salvage, retrieval, inventory	2: Production: recycling, perpetuation	3: Propaganda: instrumentalization
Language	dictionaries grammars [L1]	orthography standardization / dialect debates purism [L2]	language planning language activism language education [L3]
Discourse	editions of ancient literary texts editions of ancient laws editions of ancient documents [D1]	historical drama, poetry, novels national history-writing literary history / criticism Bible / world classics translated [D2]	history education historical pageants commemorations literary festivals / awards [D3]
Artefacts, material culture	monumental remains symbolically invested sites [A1]	monument protection restorations exhibitions [A2]	monuments public space dedications historicist architecture decorative arts / design [A3]
Performative practices	oral literature proverbs, superstitions pastimes, dances folk music, folklore collecting [P1]	rustic/realist literature traditional sports / pastimes national music folklore displays [P2]	traditionalist events / festivals (sports, folklore) [P3]
Sociability	associations, congresses, city academies; publishing ventures, reading societies, book clubs, periodicals [S]		
Institutions	museums, libraries, archives, university departments/chairs, government agencies [I]		

Figure I.3 The cultivation of culture in nation-building.

and phenomenologically, select from the historical record such cultural practices as were consciously invested with symbolic meaningfulness for national identity; and we can establish, for each of these, the degree of intensity to which they were 'cultivated' as such in the political articulation of a national identity. This results in a matrix that I call the 'cultivation of culture', shown in Figure I.3. In this matrix, the horizontal rows capture relevant cultural practices as inventorized according to their field or medium of expression (language, texts, material artefacts and performative practices). The vertical columns distinguish three degrees of intensity in cultivation, ranging from mere 'recollection' (a salvaging drive to record, inventorize and document culture that is considered to be under pressure or eroding) to downright propaganda instrumentalization, with a middle category for culture produced, recycled and disseminated as being nationally inspired or inspiring.[10]

To explain the schema:

- The preoccupation with **language** (top row of Figure I.3) moves from dialectology and linguistics (L1) by way of concerns with orthography, standardization and purism (L2) to the instrumentalization of language as a marker of national identity (L3: activism, language planning and state-planned language education).
- The field of textually communicated culture (**discourse**, second row) embraces artistic and knowledge production. The leftmost

'Recollection' column (D1) involves the rediscovery, salvage and printed publication of ancient texts, from epics to laws and ancient charters. Historical novels and dramas, national history writing including literary history, and the field of cultural criticism follow in the middle row (D2). What is also marked here is how many emerging, minoritarian and often newly literate language communities symbolically claim their place in the modern world by translating and appropriating great classical texts (the Bible, Shakespeare, Homer) in their vernacular. On the right (D3) we encounter how nation-building makes use of national history education, the staging of historical pageants and commemorations and the self-celebration of the national literature by means of festivals and awards.

- In the third row, material culture (**artefacts**) is salvaged by archaeologists and in the antiquarian identification of important sites (A1). The protection and restoration of artefacts follows in the next stage (A2), together with the establishment of dedicated national museums. The past is also evoked in history paintings. Such material culture becomes a carrier of national propaganda (A3) when commemorative statues are used to mark public spaces and when public buildings are put up using nationally historicizing architecture, often reinforced by means of decorative arts. Traditional dress is also among the material artefacts gaining national meaningfulness.
- Immaterial culture (**performative practices**) moves, in the fourth row, from folkloristic collections of oral literature and performed traditional music, dances, sports and customs (P1) to their revival as a middle-class pastime and their celebration in rustic literature and rustic genre painting; the composition of national music belongs here as well (P2); and festival culture can turn all of these into mass events with an identity-affirming or propagandistic purpose.

For good measure, the grid also includes two categories that can accommodate initiatives in civil society or government policy enabling a national cultivation of culture: **sociability**, associational life and journalism; and **institutions**, museums, libraries and archives.

As a sorting grid, this matrix captures most of the cultural events and practices that I have encountered over the past twenty-five years as meaningful elements in the emergence of national movements across Europe. It is of course highly artificial, like drawing a longitude/latitude grid across the world map: it does not describe the world as it is, but it makes it possible to situate places and trajectories across its varied and irregular surface.

Applying the parameters of the 'cultivation of culture' differentiates 'culture' into an identifiable set of discrete points where cultural practices intervene in society and in history. That makes it possible to write a cultural history of nationalism – a historical analysis of nationalism that is properly cultural, and a cultural analysis of nationalism that is properly historical.

Culture and the Nation in History

I hope, then, not just to elucidate the development of nationalism by approaching it from a cultural history perspective but also to throw some light on cultural history (the arts, literature, memory and knowledge production) by aligning its developments with the political climate of nationalism. Of course, just as there was a good deal of nationalism outside the realm of culture, there was a great deal of culture outside of nationalism. Many artists and intellectuals were dedicated anti-nationalists: liberal cosmopolitans or internationalist socialists. Many others were conflicted: Heinrich Heine, while deeply, romantically attached to his cherished native country, was repelled by the chauvinistic nationalism of his German contemporaries and satirized them mercilessly. Such voices I find edifying and personally inspiring, but they are not my topic here.

That being said, in focusing on the culture/nationalism overlap I hope to mediate between two tendencies in nationalism studies that have for too long been at loggerheads: traditionalism and modernism.* For modernists, nationalism is a by-product of the modernization process, and its application to pre-modern societies is considered an anachronism, almost like calling Nebuchadnezzar II anti-Semitic. For traditionalists, it is patently obvious that the societies that developed nationalist aspirations in the nineteenth century did so in continuation of similar aspirations that were operative in those same societies centuries previously and with which they identify by asserting a historical continuity. As in any dilemma properly speaking, both sides, though incompatible, are perfectly correct. And both suffer from blind spots.

* I use 'traditionalism' as an umbrella term for various anti-modernist tendencies also, variously, labelled primordialism or perennialism. The literature is vast and tangled, and surveyed in Özkirimli 2000, Lawrence 2005 and the various contributions to Breuilly 2013. A classic flashpoint were the 'Warwick debates' (Gellner & Smith 1996).

Many modernists, concentrated as they are in the fields of historical sociology and social or political history, are reluctant to acknowledge the agency of anything that is not part of the social, economic, technological and political modernization process. From this perspective, the prime mover of history and of social or political movements is the contestation of power distribution, and such things as culture are either shrugged off as mere inconsequential pastimes or rhetorical window-dressing, or else reductively explained away as the mere by-product of 'underlying' socio-economic or political power contestations.[11]

Traditionalists take culture much more seriously but tend to downplay the importance of the modernization process – as if the shift from monarchical systems to popular sovereignty, or scientific progress, or the technological and institutional revolutions of the period 1750–1850, did not really matter. Nor is there much discussion among traditionalists of how modernity affected the production, reception and status of culture, its shift to popular, unrestricted productivity and its cultivation as a nationally meaningful rallying point. While culture is given its proper importance, it tends to be invoked glop-like, as the invariant, transgenerationally maintained lifestyle by which a given society has always maintained its own specific identity. The assertion is frequently encountered that, just because the notion of nationalism had not yet been coined in 1600, that doesn't mean the thing itself (like gravity or oxidization) was not operative.

That last argument is, by the way, something I wish to dispel. Ideologies are not like physical laws. Women's suffrage was not really a 'thing' under the T'ang dynasty, although gravity and oxidization were: ideologies are society-specific, as is the discourse in which they are articulated and make sense; and in the decades around 1800 (the watershed period or *Sattelzeit*) European society changed fundamentally, and with it the discourse that made new ideologies, such as nationalism, thinkable and sayable.*

With that assertion, readers will think, and for good reason, that I have nailed my colours to the mast of modernism. Not quite, though; for I see culture as a separate, autonomous social agent, unlike many modernists who see national movements as wholly socially and politically determined.[12]

* These decades around 1800 are known, after the coinage by Reinhart Koselleck, as the *Sattelzeit* or 'watershed period', a historical tipping point marked by concurrent drastic changes in the social order, demographics, the economy, state relations, technology and culture. This brusque acceleration of modernity fundamentally affected people's experience of time and history. Koselleck 1988, Motzkin 2005, Williamson 2018. For the cultural repercussion: Fritzsche 2004.

Methodological Nationalism as a Historical Problem

Methodological nationalism can for my present purposes be defined as the uncritical reliance on the contours and catchment of the present-day state as the most meaningful and valid framework for the analysis of historical processes.[13] To some extent this involves a tunnel vision whereby phenomena are primarily, if not exclusively, registered as taking place within a given national context (with a concomitant marginalization of transnational and border-straddling phenomena), and the causes for these phenomena are sought primarily within that same national context (with a concomitant marginalization of border-crossing patterns of cause and effect, influence and interaction). Such methodological nationalism threatens social and political historians especially, since the archives they rely on for their work have often been assembled and administered by public authorities and hence foreground in their organization those state-political categories that were in force as these archives were being organized.

That this national compartmentalization needs to be counterbalanced by a comparative, cross-border approach has been obvious for the past decades, with the work of Miroslav Hroch and of Anne-Marie Thiesse standing out as shining examples. To some extent this book can be seen as the extension, by a cultural and intellectual historian, of Hroch's work as a social historian.[14] I was convinced – and I aim to demonstrate in the following pages – that Hroch's 'Phase A' of national-cultural consciousness-raising did not emerge gradually out of older cultural-patriotic traditions. Its emergence was brusque, marked by the coinciding moments of the Romantic revolution and the discovery of Indo-European language relations; and this in itself marks an important historical inflection point. Moreover, as a comparatist I was especially intrigued by the transfers and influences that I saw unfold between different cultural communities within Phase A and as part of the cultural consciousness-raising that persisted even in Phases B and C; and it is here that I found the work of the cultural and literary sociologist Thiesse especially inspiring. Her pioneering analysis of 'cultural transfers' between national movements in different countries allowed her to identify a specific – and transnational – agency for intellectuals and for knowledge production, and a set of common concerns. As Thiesse has demonstrated, European nationalism, like European literature, should be studied as a multinational phenomenon from a transnational point of view (as Hugo Dyserinck phrased it).[15]

The challenge remains that, since the scholar's working environment (archives, national libraries, university departments) was established by the modern state, our working assumptions may be slanted and determined by the national purview of those states who organized our working field for us. It is still counter-intuitive to see that pre-1815 Danish literature is to a significant extent written in German, or to trace the history of the pre-1830 Low Countries in a continuous shuttle search between Dutch and Belgian archives. One side-effect of this is that the *Sattelzeit* or watershed around 1800 is also to some extent a filtering threshold in the historian's own expertise and field of vision (given their familiarity with archives differently ordered pre- and post-1800): traditionalists on the whole tend to neglect the analysis of post-1800 events, while modernists rarely study the pre-1800 centuries as closely as they deserve. This plays into a tendency of both approaches to gravitate towards their own archival bubbles; they look for their lost car keys under the street lamps either on one side of the road or on the other.[16]

The Nation's Short History and Long Memory

While the advent of modernity is an indispensable precondition for the development of the nationalist ideology, culture sits uneasily astride the *Sattelzeit* that marks the acceleration of modernizing process around 1800. The iterative, feedback-looped notion of culture means that certain cultural practices drawn on in the development of nationalist thought (e.g. language and a repertoire of literary texts and historical memories) do indeed date from well before the rise of nationalism by many centuries; but the cultivation of those cultural things, their recycling with the added investment of being meaningful markers of a separate identity, is something that very much part of post-1800 modernity.[17] The *Nibelungenlied* and the *Chanson de Roland*, as texts, are of medieval vintage; their redissemination and canonization as national German and French classics is strictly a nineteenth-century process.

Given this dual timescale on which the cultivation of culture operates (a modern cultivation of more ancient culture) it may be said that nationalism has a modern, post-1800 history that draws on an old, pre-1800 legacy. It is in this sense that I present the approach taken here as a reconciliation midway between modernist and traditionalist approaches. It is also meant as a way of moving on beyond the 'invention of tradition' model. Traditions (authentic, manipulated or faked) are, all of them, sites of memory, *lieux de mémoire*, and should be analysed in their reception trajectory rather than in the conditions of how they came into being.[18] Yes, to be sure, the Romantic century recreated the past in its own image, and in the process produced much that was meant to look authentic but was in fact a latter-day contrivance. To take it at face value would make us fall victim to anachronism. But merely to denounce this way of recreating the past as a mere humbug to hoodwink the credulous public may just be one-upmanship. We must ask ourselves, as with all forms of historicist artistic and knowledge production (fake, misguided or faithfully accurate), what their driving force was, what repertoire they drew on, what purpose they hoped to serve, and how contemporaries (not latter-day historians) reacted to it. Whether accurately documented or falsely imagined, the nation's collective cultural memory was drawn upon in marshalling the past to inspire contemporary cultural productivity in the arts, literature and learning.[19]

While accepting anachronism as a fact of life, certainly in the Romantic century, we should nonetheless realize that the 'short history, long memory' ambivalence of the cultivation of culture creates one overriding anachronism that has bedevilled our proper understanding of the nation as such, and which, though widely current as 'a truth universally acknowledged', should not be exempt from critical inquiry. The culture of nationalism asserts, and is predicated on the a priori supposition, that the nation is ancient, and that it stands as an ancient, transgenerationally enduring presence amidst the turmoil and vicissitudes of unstable states.* Most modern states evoke in their national symbolism a pretended continuity from ancient, pre-modern (feudal or tribal) polities, and some (Greece, Ireland, Israel) saw or see themselves, quite anachronistically, as ancient, primordial polities newly reconstituted.

* The words 'nation' and 'state' are often used interchangeably. In phrases such as 'the national debt' or 'the nation's capital', the reference is clearly to a debt shouldered by a state, or a city functioning as the centre of a state. In this book, the word 'state' is used in the strictly political sense: it refers to a polity exercising a monopoly on legitimate violence, with the sovereign power to raise taxes, to wage war and to administer justice. I use 'nation' in its strictly socio-cultural sense: a society whose degree of internal communication is noticeably and significantly higher than with external non-members (Lévi-Strauss 1963, 296); more specifically, to a society that transgenerationally maintains its internal communicative cohesion by means of a shared culture: language or historical practices and memories (a 'cultural group'); more specifically still: to a self-distinguishing cultural group (as per Connor 1978).

The hyphenated notion of the 'nation-state' refers to the idealized Venn diagram where there is a seamless overlap between the state and the nation. The congruence between nation and state in the notion of the nation-state is, of course, more aspirational than real (Roobol 1998). It is a shorthand invocation asserting that the state represents, and is organically rooted in, a citizenry that is more than a mere population and that self-defines as a nation. This view sidelines the existence of minorities or cross-border populations. A problematic confusion ensues when 'the national interest' is invoked, with the nation as a moral community justifying the expediency of the state.

As this book will demonstrate, the appropriation of a national antiquity by the modern state is the fundamental, axiomatic basis of nationalism. It denies the extent to which the nation has been imagined or reimagined in recent history, as the outcome of volatile processes of self-distinguishing. In the words of Karl Deutsch (invoking a 'rueful European saying'), a nation is 'a group of persons united by a common error about their ancestry and a common dislike of their neighbors'. As such, it is a rather unstable, contentious foundation to base states on.[20]

The Nation as Contingency: Working Definitions

An interesting attempt to transcend the ambivalence between the nation's short history and its long memory was made by Anthony Smith with his 'ethno-symbolist' approach. For Smith, nationalism was a politically performative mobilization of ethnic identity, and he was, later on in his career, increasingly ready to acknowledge that that ethnic identity was itself (re-)constituted as part of this performative self-articulation. Much valuable research has come out of the ethno-symbolist approach (e.g. John Hutchinson's study of Irish cultural nationalism); but nonetheless, ethno-symbolism harbours a risk of backsliding into ethnic essentialism and into what Rogers Brubaker has aptly termed 'groupism'. I take that term to mean that social behaviour (and culture) are seen as a variable output that is produced by an a priori given social group. The group is thus seen as the fixity and as the engendering agent for various social and cultural practices. Brubaker rightly criticizes this one-way line of thinking, pointing out that many groups constitute themselves through – come into being as a result of – the actions they collectively perform or the causes they identify with. Groups can emerge out of ad hoc lifestyle choices such as riding a Harley-Davidson motorcycle; and the historian who studies the history of nations and national self-articulations will notice much the same thing. Whether people collectively self-distinguish as Samogitians or Lithuanians, as Macedonians, Estonians or Walloons, is a historical contingency; ethnogenesis is happening and revising itself all the time. The cause, the act of identification, shapes the group, not vice versa. The same goes for that 'ethnicity' at the heart of ethno-symbolism; yet many in the tradition of ethno-symbolism see the ethnie as a social fixity producing culture and are reluctant to see it as a historical contingency culturally produced – as, in Hugo Dyserinck's words, 'a mental concept acquiring a transitory actualization in space and time'.[21]

Avoiding groupism and taking a constructivist approach safeguards us from historical anachronisms and forces us to acknowledge the open-ended variabilities and the never-ending contestations of history. As John Hutchinson has pointed out, the agenda of cultural nationalists was not necessarily 'state-seeking'; their primary concern was nation-building, that is, the consolidation of national communities as persistent moral-collective entities.[22] How this panned out in the course of political history was highly contingent, and even the patterns of self-distinguishing the nation were anything but fixed. The self-identifications that were historically operative in Ulster, Flanders or Savoy at successive moments (say: 1640, 1740, 1840 and 1940) are documented, historical givens, but over time they show radical breaks and shifts. To see behind them, in all their contradictory discontinuity, the agency of a single, persistent group ('the nation'), identified as such from a present-day vantage point: that is a questionable leap of faith. It is one that is habitually asserted by those who believe in the ideological tenets of nationalism (the belief that behind the vicissitudes of history there is a transhistorically constant agent called the nation), but it is nonetheless an act of faith, an article of belief, a metaphysics of nationalism. As Brubaker put it:

> we should not ask 'what is a nation?' but rather: how is nationhood as a political and cultural form institutionalized within and among states? How does the nation work as practical category, as classificatory scheme, as cognitive frame? What makes the use of that category by or against states more of less resonant or effective? What makes the nation-evoking, nation-invoking efforts of political entrepreneurs more or less likely to succeed?[23]

In this book, I trace a history of self-positionings, ideas and repertoires, rather than the history of groups, or nations, or societies in which those ideas and repertoires circulated. I am not even overly bothered by how 'representative' those ideas or repertoires were for society at large at any given moment in time; that I leave to social historians. I am more interested in their longevity and adaptability over time: their persistence amidst shifting circumstances. That persistence and adaptability is a measure of the influence of culture – its influence on other, emerging and developing culture, as well as on political institutions – which to me appears at least as relevant as raw mobilizing power. (The distinction between influence and power is something I shall return to in the course of this book.) What I trace is how those ideas and repertoires reproduced themselves, in what media or cultural fields, with what rhetoric or endorsement; how they *worked.*

On that basis I offer three conceptual definitions on which this books rests.

- Nations are the result of collective acts of political self-distinguishing (i.e. a self-identification as being collectively separate from others) performed on the basis of a cultural self-characterization.
- Nationalism is a political agenda working towards the social and political recognition of the nation; it is, as such, the political application of a cultural sense of identity.[24]
- The culture of nationalism is the celebration of the nation (defined in its language, history and cultural character) as an inspiring ideal for artistic production and a meaningful category for knowledge production; and the instrumentalization of that cultural productivity in political consciousness-raising.

That last definition echoes, in slightly expanded form, my definition of 'Romantic nationalism' in earlier work on the subject.[25] In this book, the reader will encounter repeated references to Romanticism and explanations of why it enjoys a privileged relationship with the ideology and culture of nationalism. Nationalism emerged during the Romantic movement, among intellectuals and artists profoundly influenced by it. It accordingly exhibits some hallmarks typical of Romanticism (further explored in Chapter 3): its idealism (the assumption that pragmatic reality is informed by a transcendent world of abstract ideas, national identity being one of these), its reliance on intuitive knowledge, its resistance to disenchantment, its charismatic heroes, and the power of affect and enthusiasm. In nineteenth- and early-twentieth-century Europe, cultural nationalism is practically coterminous with Romantic nationalism and what I call its 'long tail'.

The emergence of Romanticism explains both the starting date and the geographical purview of this book. The starting date is the *Sattelzeit*, the watershed decades around 1800; the area is Europe, in particular the fault-lines and border zones among the European empires as shaken by the democratic revolutions and the reign of Napoleon. I do take into account the long memories at work that reached back across 1800 into a far deeper past, but I focus on their cultivation in the context of the modernizing nineteenth and twentieth centuries.

The time-curve of Romanticism and of Romantic nationalism is like a wave: a fairly sudden onset, relatively precisely datable, cresting to a burgeoning high point that is then followed by a protracted, tapering run-off with occasional eddies and aftermaths. As a result, it is far less easy to be precise about the end-point of my working period. The 'long tail' of Romanticism was overlaid by opposing movements (positivism and realism in the nineteenth century, a technocratic and/or anti-lyrical avant-garde modernity in the twentieth); it is also marked by resurging neo-Romantic currents and undercurrents (*fin-de-siècle* symbolism, 1960s counterculture), finding expression in newly emerging media such as folk museums and epic or rustic-idyllic movies. That 'long tail' also characterizes Romantic nationalism; it will be flagged repeatedly in the book's chapters and specifically in the closing one.

The focus will on the whole be European, since the legacy of Romantic nationalism cannot claim to have general, worldwide (trans-European) applicability; that it became part of a global circulation of ideas and did not leave Japan, India, Persia, or other continents altogether uninvolved, is recognized in principle and gestured at wherever the reminder seemed opportune; but the further exploration of those extra-European dimensions I leave to better qualified scholars. The European working field itself is here defined as it was in the *Encyclopedia of Romantic Nationalism in Europe*, as the polygon marked out by the metropolitan catchment areas of Reykjavík, Seville, Athens, Tbilisi, Kazan and St Petersburg.[26]

Outline of the Book

Chapter 1, 'The Romantic Spell', begins *in medias res* and traces the ongoing potency of Romantic historicism in the political imagination of the two World Wars. Two specific legacies of Romanticism are identified: the idea that the nation is a transcendent principle deserving our devotion and loyalty and the paradox that the nation, while commanding our political allegiance, it is itself not political or contentious but, rather, 'unpolitical'. This twofold legacy explains the title of this book, *Charismatic Nations*.

Chapter 2, 'Becoming Something, Unmaking Empires', gives a background outline of how, between the French Revolution and the Treaty of Versailles, the nation gained force as a constitutional principle in political history, and how nationalism, despite its lack of actual political clout or mobilizing power, was eventually capable of replacing empires with nation-states.

Following this, the cultural history of nationalism is traced in Chapters 3–8, which run more or less parallel across the long nineteenth century. Each addresses one of the cultural fields mapped in Figure I.3 and analyses how it was cultivated in a national sense.

Chapter 3, 'Romantic Prophets: Inspired Poets Inspiring People', deals with the poetics of Romanticism and the idea that the transcendent identity of the nation required inspired voices to channel it and to spread its inspiration.

Chapter 4, 'Manuscripts Found in the Attic', discusses the rise of historicism: the cultivation of the past and the desire to turn it, and the nation's ancient roots, into an inspiring contemporary presence.

Chapter 5, 'Ancestral Voices', analyses how the Romantic interest in popular and oral traditions deepened into an ethnography of the nation's mythologies, world-view and fundamental character or *Volksgeist*.

Chapter 6, 'Languages, States, Races', discusses the problematic but ubiquitous attempt to map languages onto language areas and to map states onto those. Much as languages have an uneasy scalar position between dialects and language families, so too states can fission or expand in order to embrace more or less broadly circumscribed language groups. The chapter discusses the logic whereby wider Germanic and Indo-European aggregations make nationalism shade into racism.

Chapter 7, 'History Related', deals with narrative representations of the national past. The rise and decline of the Romantic historical novel is discussed, and its lasting impact on cultural memory – which became increasingly divorced from history writing as the latter turned towards academic, archive-based factualism.

The visual imagery of the national past is the topic of Chapter 8, 'The Image and the Presence'. The heyday of Romantic-academic history painting is traced from its beginnings by way of the Nazarenes to the ubiquitous dominance of the large-scale historical mural. An analysis of the German history murals of Goslar shows how high academicism, paradoxically, morphs into a decorative art form as, towards the end of the nineteenth century, academicism declines and avant-garde movements take over.

Chapter 9 turns to music, not only as a high-Romantic art form experiencing a national inflection (the sample case here being Franz Liszt, who, after an early cosmopolitan life, rediscovered his Hungarian roots and celebrated them in his rhapsodies) but also as a convivial platform for joint performance and rousing patriotic choruses. Choral gatherings and mass concerts become the prototype of participatory festival culture in general.

In many cultural fields and genres, developments across the century marked a shift from what one might call 'past to peasant'. The medievalism and historicism that marked the Romantic novel and academic painting gave way, or were overlaid by, a greater interest in the contemporary peasantry, in a shift that moved by way of post-Romantic sentimentalism towards something called, both in literature and in the visual arts, 'realism'. For those wishing to evoke the nation's essential character, the 'timeless' countryfolk, rather than tribal or medieval forebears, were now held up as characteristic and recognizable representative types. Paradoxically, this folkloristic turn took place during a period of accelerated, technology-driven and urbanizing modernity, and a shift towards 'unrestricted', commercially driven, mass-appeal cultural media.

That paradox is explored in Chapter 10, 'People in the Present', which traces the interaction between the modern city and the timeless country from world's fairs to the art theatres of the *fin-de-siècle*. The chapter concludes by outlining how the new modern and decorative arts (Arts and Crafts, art nouveau) functioned as carriers of progressive national revival movements in Europe's sub-imperial capitals, from Dublin and Barcelona to Prague and Riga; and how their anti-imperial emancipation agenda was uneasily poised between progressive cosmopolitanism and nativist essentialism.

Chapter 11, 'Culture Mobilized', covers the same period, the half-century prior to 1914, but this time as a period of increasingly contentious international relations characterized by the developing force of public opinion. Patriotic humanities scholars acquired a new role as public intellectuals, to justify the ways of history to men. The French–German debates over Germany's annexation of Alsace-Lorraine in 1871 are placed in the time frame of what Wolfgang Schivelbusch has identified as a 'Culture of Defeat' – both countries repeatedly experienced the bitterness and rancour of lost wars between 1804 and 1918, with 1871 as a hinge moment for French revanchism and German triumphalism.[27] The debates of 1871 are seen as the breeding ground, paradoxically, both of Ernest Renan's seminal and still authoritative 'voluntaristic' theory of national identity and of a type of chauvinistic propaganda that reached almost hysterical levels in 1914. The fervent jingoism of the Great War, fomented and rationalized by learned disquisitions from prestigious academics, marks the zenith of nationalism as a force in European relations.

Chapter 12, 'The Long Tail', starts with the universal adoption of the principle of the nation's right to self-determination,[28] which, applied in the Paris peace treaties of 1919, was meant to stabilize international relations and which turned the central tenet of nationalism into a cornerstone of international law. The chapter traces how, in a European continent divided into ethnoculturally defined nation-states, the culture of nationalism continued to be operative. The newly established democracies slid (partly because of an unresolved ambiguity between civic and ethnic definitions of the nation) from parliamentary and constitutional governance towards authoritarianism and dictatorships. Meanwhile, new cultural media emerged, such as cinema. This medium is surveyed to explain the remarkable survival of nationalism across the totalitarian dictatorships and devastating wars of the mid-century, and across the internationalist and anti-totalitarian recoil that dominated the post-1945 decades. It is suggested that this survival, and the renewed contemporary dominance of nationalism as an ideology, is due in large part to its ability to shift back and forth between anodyne and virulent states, latency and salience. The alternation between those states served to proclaim the nation's charisma both as a merely cultural (unpolitical) feel-good factor and as a political imperative, a commanding, inspiring validator for belligerent heroism.[29]

Finally, 'Summing Up' draws some more general inferences that are relevant for a historical theory of nationalism and national movements. In tracing nationalism across its more antagonistic manifestations and towards populist 'ethnocracy', the chapter suggests that the experience of the nation's charisma could act as a palliative against political and social disenchantment, but may erode the rule of law and derail into national narcissism.*

* Source references are given in endnotes; footnotes are used for occasional side comments or more theoretical reflections on analytical concepts. Unless otherwise indicated, all translations and paraphrases from other languages are mine.

PART I

Memory and Power

CHAPTER 1

The Romantic Spell

Strong Feelings, Deep Memories, Long Distance

The Rhine to Landsberg Prison, 1814–1925

After the Great War, a former volunteer in the Bavarian army recollected his experience of August 1914 – the railway transport from Munich to the Western Front along the Rhine, and the initial charges on Flemish battlefields.

> Finally, the day came when we left Munich in order to start fulfilling our duty. Now for the first time I saw the Rhine as we were riding towards the west along its quiet waters, the German river of all rivers, in order to protect it against the greed of the old enemy. When through the delicate veil of the dawn's mist the mild rays of the early sun set the Niederwalddenkmal [Niederwald Monument] shimmering before our eyes, 'Die Wacht am Rhein' [The Watch on the Rhine] roared up to the morning sky from the interminably long transport train and I had a feeling as though my chest would burst.

What set the soldiers singing was a huge statue near Bingen overlooking the Rhine, erected to celebrate the unification of the German Reich in 1871 following their victory in the war against France in 1870–1871. Finished in 1883, the statue was a cherished landmark: the huge, imposing figure of a personified victorious 'Germania' goddess, twelve meters high, standing out on a lofty terraced setting overlooking the steep banks of the Rhine, visible from far away as part of the picturesque landscape (Figure 1.1). The Germania figure had become (and still is) a popular tourist destination. Its universal acceptance as a symbol of the German nation is demonstrated by the fact that in 1893 the chocolate manufacturer Stollwerck had exhibited a three-meter-high chocolate model of it at the Chicago World's Fair.

On the plinth of the monument, the full text of 'Die Wacht am Rhein' was engraved on bronze plates. That song had been the semi-official anthem

Figure 1.1 Germania monument at Niederwald near Bingen (drawing by Nikolai von Astudin, 1920). ERNiE imagebank

of the 1870–1871 war, and it was now reprised by the passing soldiers, with its refrain 'Dear Fatherland, you may rest assured, firm and faithful stands the Watch on the Rhine.' Indeed, the outbreak of the war in 1914 was said to have been greeted with fervent joy by the men who sang 'with feelings as though their chests would burst' as they made their way to the fields of Flanders. Although some historians now query the ubiquity and fervour of that widely reported war enthusiasm, there were singing crowds, and there were many patriotic postcards from the early war years depicting merry soldiers singing 'Die Wacht am Rhein' in front of the Germania statue, keeping a felt experience in circulation like the one attested to in this wartime memoir – an influential one, at that, because the 1914 volunteer reminiscing here was Adolf Hitler, and the quoted passage is from *Mein Kampf*.[1]

What was it that raised the soldiers' spirits? The singing and the heaving chests were inspired not by a calculated endorsement of realpolitik or of strategic war aims but by remembered glories, a nationally iconic landscape in the sunrise, a lavish statue that had become a landmark for all passers-by to admire, and a song that was familiar to and singable by everybody. And behind it all lay the collective sense that, as a nation, the singers were facing an 'old enemy' – that this war was the latest instalment in something transgenerational, an eternally renewed national challenge.

The same affects return in the continuation of Hitler's reminiscences. Against the terror and courage of the battlefield is set the inspirational value of an old song.

> Then at last came a damp, cold night in Flanders through which we marched silently, and when the day began to emerge from the fog, suddenly an iron salute came whizzing over our heads towards us and with a sharp report the small bullets struck between our rows, whipping up the wet earth; but before the small cloud had dispersed, out of two hundred throats the first hurrah roared a welcome to the first messenger of death. But then it began to crackle and roar, to sing and howl, and with feverish eyes each one of us was drawn forward faster and faster over turnip fields and hedges till suddenly the fight began, the fight of man against man. But from the distance the sounds of a song met our ears, coming nearer and nearer, passing from company to company, and then, while Death busily plunged his hand into our rows, the song reached also us, and now we passed it on : 'Deutschland, Deutschland über alles, über alles in der Welt!' (Hitler 1939, 214).

Is this even genuine? Is it the recall of an authentic, factual experience, or is it embellished grandstanding? It matters little: this is how Hitler's purple prose invokes national traditions in order to make the past relatable and inspirational. Hitler presents the events to his readers in terms that to him, and them, meaningfully suggest themselves. The cultural references that he uses to tie his narrative and his experience together were immediately familiar to all his readers, a clear and immediate presence in their minds and in their cultural frame of reference. But their chronology and combination is telling.

The Rhine's picturesque, quintessential Germanness, and the need to defend it against an 'old enemy': these had been tropes ever since the Napoleonic Wars of 1806–1815, especially in E. M. Arndt's seminal *The Rhine, Germany's River, but Not Germany's Boundary* (1813a). The two songs that are name-checked as being spontaneously sung and shared by the comrades-in-arms are from the 1840s. 'Die Wacht am Rhein' was written in 1840 by one Max Schneckenburger, defying France and its expansionism by asserting that the German nation was ready to defend its quintessential river in arms. 'Das Lied der Deutschen' (The Song of the German People, known from its opening line as 'Deutschland, Deutschland über alles') was penned in 1842 by August Heinrich Hoffmann von Fallersleben, yearning in exile for his country's unification. The Niederwald Monument celebrating the victory of 1871 had been erected in 1883.[2]

All these dates, 1813, 1840, 1842, 1871 and 1883, are simultaneously recalled and invoked as a single compound – indeed, in the root sense of the term, a 'commonplace' – in a narrative that, set in 1914, was written down in 1925 while Hitler was serving a prison sentence at Landsberg. These dates 'hang together' culturally, not only in their recall but also in their gestation. They were not isolated offshoots of different circumstances at separate historical moments. As I shall argue in greater detail towards the close of this book (Chapter 11), these successive moments of crisis were experienced, even at the time, as a concatenated, ongoing and iterative whole; and it is that iterative whole that formed the memoryscape and the *Weltanschauung* of Hitler's reminiscences. Arndt's tract on the cultural geopolitics of the Rhine had been echoed in many reprints across the nineteenth century and, let it be stressed, also as war propaganda (a pocket edition was distributed to soldiers in 1914–1918); Schneckenburger's song was written under Arndt's shadow and with his endorsement, with reactivations in 1870, 1883 and 1914. To see these as momentary cultural flare-ups triggered separately by the different political crises of 1814, 1840, 1870 and 1914 is to deny their ongoing presence and persistent, mashed-up availability as a cultural repertoire. Indeed, it is this cultural persistence that made it possible to experience the very different crises punctuating the century from 1814 to 1914 as an ongoing struggle between a timeless Germany and its 'old enemy'. Both Germany and France, as states, had gone through repeated, drastic regime changes in those 100 years, but the enduring cultural repertoire made it feel as if it was always the same France, always the same Germany (nations, indeed, rather than states), in an ongoing struggle.

Nor do the iterative and self-stoking reverberations end there. By 1925–1927, when Hitler wrote *Mein Kampf*, 'Das Lied der Deutschen' had become Weimar Germany's national anthem. Propagandistic reports that it had been sung in battle led to the 'Myth of the Battle of Langemarck', about the heroism displayed on 10 November 1914 as a result of the anthem's inspiring power. Hitler's account obviously resonated with that myth. Initially reported in a propagandistic despatch from the Oberste Heeresleitung (supreme army command), and intended to raise the morale of the home front, the Langemarck myth developed into a memory cult after 1918. Veterans and revanchists gathered to commemorate their heroism in a war whose ruinous outcome they could not come to terms with, and the recall of Langemarck became a veritable cult among revanchists in the Weimar Republic in precisely the years when *Mein Kampf* was written. There were mass commemorations and fresh monuments and memorializations, which persisted into the Third Reich. In 1943, a Flemish contingent within the Waffen-SS was formed under the name Sturmbrigade Langemarck.[3]

Strasbourg to Casablanca, 1792–1942

As to 'Die Wacht am Rhein', modern readers are probably most familiar with that song from the movie *Casablanca* (1942). In Rick's café, the song is chauvinistically belted out by a new generation of German soldiers, Nazi officers this time. It is, however, drowned out as 'La Marseillaise' is defiantly, triumphantly intoned by a united chorus of refugees from all over Europe. Among the many stranded nationals, all trying to escape from Nazi tyranny, one young Frenchwoman, Yvonne, stands out. Jilted by Rick, she has become dissipated and promiscuous and has been degrading herself with Germans; but she now finds her true moral compass and identity as, tearfully and passionately, she sings the anthem that is hers more than anyone else's, and concludes with a shouted 'Vive la France!' (Figure 1.2).

The tears were not just acted: the French actress Madeleine Lebeau, who played the Yvonne character in the Hollywood studio, had in real life lived the plight of the fictional *Casablanca* refugees. She and her Jewish husband, Marcel Dalio (who played a croupier in Rick's café), had been forced to flee Nazi-occupied France and on dodgy passports had wandered from Lisbon via Mexico and Canada to Hollywood. The role and the actress merged in the very real passion of this scene. Madeleine Lebeau, too, in a bitterly ironical twist of twentieth-century history, experienced that 'feeling as though my chest would burst'.[4]

Figure 1.2 Yvonne (played by Madeleine Lebeau) tearfully shouting 'Vive la France!' after singing 'La Marseillaise' in the film *Casablanca* (1942). Wikimedia Commons

Figure 1.3 Claude Joseph Rouget de Lisle singing 'La Marseillaise' (Isidore Pils, 1849; Musée historique de Strasbourg). Wikimedia Commons

The power of 'La Marseillaise' to inspire such passion is almost proverbial. Composed by Charles Joseph Rouget de Lisle in Strasbourg on the eve of the Battle of Valmy (1792), it became an icon of popular defiance and battle-readiness. The Romantic historian Jules Michelet canonized the moment of its creation (Figure 1.3) as an almost metaphysical, spiritual moment of self-realization:

> Rouget de Lisle, for he it was, burst into the room, wrote it all down, music and words. He returned singing the stanza 'Come, children of the fatherland!' (*Allons enfants de la patrie!*). It was like a burst of light from the sky. Everyone was moved, excited, all recognized the song even as they heard it for the first time. They all knew it, they all sang it, all of Strasbourg, all of France. The world, for as long as there will be a world, will forever sing it.

To the Romantic transcendence of this magic moment, Michelet adds an explanation of his own: in its combination of battle fury and magnanimity, this song is more than a mere rhetorical contrivance. It is a direct manifestation of the very soul of the French nation. 'Such indeed was the soul of France, moved by imminent combat, violent against its obstacle, yet wholly magnanimous, with a youthful and naive grandeur; even at the height of anger, above anger.' That sublime rhetoric is vintage Michelet, who habitually saw in the glories of Revolutionary events the glory of France itself. But precisely in that oft-repeated flourish, Michelet proves himself a Romantic. He constantly extrapolates from the concrete to the metaphysical, from event-based factualism to the transcendent. And while history is a series of concrete events, the informing power that drives and experiences it – the nation, the 'soul of France' – is transcendent, metaphysical, eternal.

That rousing power of 'La Marseillaise' makes it the mother of all national anthems.* Indeed it was – and in a historical sense too.[5]

People who, at moments of crisis, invoke the nation in a national anthem, attune themselves to the superhuman power that the nation is held to possess. The ecstatic fervour that can result, the 'feeling as though one's chest might burst', is what in this book I call *charisma*.

Agincourt to D-Day, Novgorod to Leningrad

There is something poignant and uncomfortable in the realization that the author of *Mein Kampf* and the defiant anti-Nazi refugees in *Casablanca* could both share the same affect: the charismatic fervour derived from dedication to one's nation and to the ideals that the nation stands for. National fervour is obviously an affect that can inspire very different ideologies and that can be found in many different countries. Let me briefly add, for good measure, examples from the other two main belligerents in World War II: imperial Britain and Stalin's Russia.

In 1944, around the time of the Normandy landings, Lawrence Olivier was commissioned to turn Shakespeare's *Henry V* into a government-funded, morale-boosting film.[6] The film was dedicated to the 'Commandos and Airborne Troops of Great Britain, the spirit of whose ancestors it has been humbly attempted to recapture'. That 'spirit of the ancestors' involves a set of cultural remembrances telescoping first 350, then 500 years back in history. The film's opening shots set the scene at William Shakespeare's own theatre in London. At the Globe, sometime in 1600, Shakespeare's play *The Chronicle History of King Henry the Fifth with His Battell Fought at Agincourt in France* is to be produced. That framing device is gradually abandoned and the play-as-staged-in-early-modern-London dissolves into the play-as-set-in-medieval-France. After the initial framing minutes, Olivier's *Henry V* moves from 1600 London to 1415 France.

First staged in 1600, a fraught year in Elizabeth I's reign, Shakespeare's history play recalled and celebrated an expedition during the Hundred

* A chronology of some sixty European anthems (e-rn.ie/anthems) shows that only two (anomalous ones at that) antedate 'La Marseillaise': the British 'God Save the King' (which dates back to the early eighteenth century and which celebrates the monarchy and its sovereign rather than a nation-state) and the Dutch 'Wilhelmus' (which dates back to the sixteenth). The 'Wilhelmus' gained its status as the official anthem of the Netherlands only in the course of the nineteenth century, and during that century had to wrest that status from an anthem composed in 1816, 'Those of Netherlandic Blood'. To all intents and purposes, then, 'La Marseillaise' is the prototype of all European national anthems.

Years' War that culminated in England's glorious victory at Agincourt (1415). *Henry V* is studded with rousing speeches, familiar and quotable sound bites, spurring on the combatants ('Once more unto the breach, dear friends, once more') and glorifying them as 'We few, we happy few, we band of brothers'. That last speech is a masterstroke of time-travel back and forth: for Shakespeare, in recalling 1415, is putting a prophecy into Henry's mouth foretelling how the battle of 1415 will be remembered and celebrated in the future.

And so the spirits of the Agincourt ancestors travel from 1415 through the Shakespearean amplification of 1600 into Olivier's 1944 film; in the process they canonize the Normandy landings as an iteration of England's heroic history. The battles were waged against France (in Henry V's time), against Philip II's Spain (in Shakespeare's time) and against Hitler's Germany, but England is always England.

A film that channelled memories from an even deeper past was Sergey Eisenstein's *Alexander Nevsky* of 1938. It was commissioned by Stalin at a precarious juncture, when Eisenstein was absolved from an ideological ban during the ongoing purges of the time and before the Molotov–Ribbentrop Pact, which imposed a brief truce between Nazi Germany and the USSR. In that year, Eisenstein filmed a historical novel in the patriotic 'defence of the fatherland' mode, culminating in the defeat of the Teutonic Knights in 1242 on Lake Peipus at the hands of the Russian leader Alexander Nevsky, Prince of Novgorod and Kiev. The stature of Alexander Nevsky in Russian historical consciousness had been assured by his canonization as a saint of the Russian Orthodox Church. In the post-Napoleonic nineteenth century, some fourteen Russian Orthodox churches had been built and dedicated to Alexander Nevsky around the edges of the empire: from Vilnius (1865) to Tbilisi (1871), from Łódż (1884) to Baku (1888), from Warsaw (1894) to Novosibirsk (1896) and from Tallinn (1900) to Yalta (1902), as well as in Paris (1861) and Belgrade (Serbian Orthodox, 1877). The national celebration of thirteenth-century Nevsky was as familiar to communist Russia as that of Henry V was to Britain. In the event, Eisenstein's film conformed to the ideological requirements of the time by combining a strong leader (Stalin-style) with idealized stalwarts from the common people. What united them was the German threat coming from the west.[7]

All these cases combine rousing war propaganda with elements that are both culturally produced and culturally disseminated: anthems, theatre, commemorations. The formula is strikingly similar across profoundly diverse ideologies (Fascist, republican–democratic, imperial, communist).

The culturally platformed appeal to nationality also encompasses countries and locations far apart in space – the placenames mentioned here reach from Hollywood to Novosibirsk and from London to Baku. And the cultural texts produced in a very short time span (*Mein Kampf*, 1925; *Alexander Nevsky*, 1938; *Casablanca*, 1942; *Henry V*, 1944) can effortlessly activate memories from a time span ranging from 100 to 150 years before (*Mein Kampf*, *Casablanca*) to five centuries (*Henry V*) or even seven (*Alexander Nevsky*). The process is obviously one of condensation, even compression. That is what the cultural element in nationalism does: it consists of a vast, diffuse set of symbols and references but can condense and pack all of that into a tight political punch, concentrating the nation's time and space into a single thing – timeless, topical, ubiquitous.

From Reverence to Charisma

Civic Religion and History-Makers

Love of one's country is a very ancient affect, and in the spectrum of human virtues and emotions it has since Cicero been linked to the concept of filial piety: we love our country the way we love our parents, with a sense of reverence and an acknowledgement of their superiority and our subservience. There is a religious, devotional element in this relationship between an individual and their country. In 1762, Jean-Jacques Rousseau's *Du contrat social* (The Social Contract) pinpointed it: 'Jamais État ne fût fondé, que la Religion ne lui servit de base' (never was there a state founded without religion having served as a basis). Religion and the state share protocols, ceremonies, hallowed spaces and a sense of permanence transcending the lives of individual people. They share cults: the churches have their saints, the states their Great Men, and statues, shrines and commemorative feasts honour both. For Edmund Burke, it is the superhuman longevity of the state and of its institutions that inspire awe and reverence. A social contract, yes; but one much more august than 'a partnership agreement in a trade of pepper and coffee, calico or tobacco, or some other such low concern'. It is a universal rather than a particular one, stretching over 'many generations', and for that reason it is to be looked upon with 'reverence':

> it becomes a partnership not only between those who are living, but between those who are living, those who are dead, and those who are to be born. Each contract of each particular state is but a clause in the great primeval contract of eternal society.[8]

Burke's sense of pious reverence towards the state as a sublime edifice of social permanence is still classical, rooted in the Ciceronian ethics of proper citizenship. In the course of the nineteenth century, this would morph into a tearful, chest-constricting pathos inspired by the nation.

Burke's assertion of the state's awe-inspiring stability responded to a rising tide of subversion: the quotation is from his *Reflections on the Revolution in France* (1790). That revolution put paid, much to Burke's dismay, to the time-hallowed endurance of the old order. As the French Revolution swept custom and tradition aside and rebooted the state, its new leaders felt that their position was like that of the early statesmen of the emerging states of classical antiquity, unburdened by established tradition and free to shape society as they saw fit. They started a new calendar and year-count, to begin with, and developed a personality cult of the strong political visionary. Robespierre considered himself a 'lawgiver' in the mode of the primordial legislator of ancient Sparta, Lycurgus. Napoleon was universally seen, in dread or admiration, as a superhuman Titan and crowned himself like a new Julius Caesar. His stature is strikingly expressed in the proto-Fascist art of his tomb in the Invalides, where he is depicted as dispensing laws, roads, canals, weights and measures, institutions – creating the state in a continuous act of superhuman willpower. The cult of personality around Stalin, Hitler, Ceauşescu *et hoc genus omne* is a direct continuation of this tradition. It combines omnipresence with absence: portraits are everywhere, mass rallies part of the pageantry repertoire, but with the Great Leader himself usually at a safe distance.[9]

As we shall see in Chapter 3, the decades that saw the political turmoil of Robespierre and Napoleon also saw the cultural onset of Romanticism. The most prominent philosopher of the time, Georg Wilhelm Friedrich Hegel, was deeply concerned with the historical turbulence of his times, and Napoleon loomed large in his thought. His *Lectures on the Philosophy of History* (delivered in the 1820s and published posthumously in 1837 and 1840) were primarily concerned with the rise and fall of states – the stability of the Burkean state was well and truly obsolete by now. Hegel argues that the self-perpetuating power and grandeur of the state (the thing that had so impressed Burke and the Burkean conservatives) was susceptible to drastic change, but only if that change emanated from outside its own order. Truly revolutionary and history-moving impulses are given from outside the state through the personal instrumentality of specifically 'clear-sighted' and powerful individuals who, though concerned with their individual vision rather than with their institutional context, at the same time actualize a higher, world-changing purpose. These order-changing supermen Hegel called by the ancient Greek name of ἥρωες, heroes: demigods, offspring of a divine/human couple, often mythically standing at the beginning of a dynastic lineage.

> Such [i.e. such as Julius Caesar] are all great historical men – whose own particular aims involve those large issues which are the will of the World-Spirit. They may be called Heroes, inasmuch as they have derived their purposes and their vocation, not from the calm, regular course of things, sanctioned by the existing order; but from … that inner Spirit, still hidden beneath the surface, which, impinging on the outer world as on a shell, bursts it in pieces, because it is another kernel than that which belonged to the shell in question. … Such individuals had no consciousness of the general Idea they were unfolding, while prosecuting those aims of theirs; on the contrary, they were practical, political men. But at the same time they were thinking men, who had an insight into the requirements of the time – what was ripe for development.

In other words: the order of things was made, and from time to time unmade and remade, by Great Men with a superhuman purpose and power. Their power to shape history, rather than to be shaped by it, was what made mutations in the world order possible: the downfall of existing empires, the rise of new ones. Hegel obviously had Napoleon in mind.

> This was the very Truth for their age, for their world; the species next in order, so to speak, and which was already formed in the womb of time. It was theirs to know this nascent principle; the necessary, directly sequent step in progress, which their world was to take; to make this their aim, and to expend their energy in promoting it. World-historical men – the Heroes of an epoch – must, therefore, be recognized as its clear-sighted ones; their deeds, their words are the best of that time.[10]

Alongside this political philosophy of history, Romanticism also created a poetic philosophy of history. The poetics of Romanticism (discussed more fully in Chapter 3) sets the creative spirit apart from the common individual. What makes the artist special is not just accomplished craftsmanship but also a power to reach higher states of awareness and to intuit transcendent truths. The *inspired* artist is the essence of Romanticism, and like the primordial lawgivers he, too, is traced back to the dawn of civilization. His typology goes back, by way of Ossian, to the mantic bards who explore liminal spaces and who, in Shelley's words, are 'the unacknowledged legislators of the world'. What they produce is, in Thomas De Quincey's distinction, a 'literature of power' rather than a 'literature of knowledge'.

This intuitive, visionary power means that the Romantic artist, heir to Homer and Ossian, can stand alongside political state-makers such as Robespierre or Napoleon, heirs to Moses, Lycurgus and Caesar. The Romantic artist in his 'literature of power' articulates the nation, brings it into being through his capacity to channel and capture its essence and to express its character in inspired, poetic language. Moses, Jesus and Muhammad founded religions; Lycurgus, Caesar and Napoleon established empires, states; Homer, Dante and Shakespeare can create civilizations, cultural communities, nations.

Hero-Worship: Carlyle to Weber

The twinning of political and cultural ἥρωες-supermen, initiators of new orders, was made explicit by Thomas Carlyle in his *On Heroes, Hero-Worship, and the Heroic in History* (1841). Carlyle provided a moral compass for a timidly secularizing world. What, if not religion, could make us good, and make us better people? Carlyle argued that we should realize the best in our humanity by trying to live up to the great ἥρωες and the example they set us. Hero-worship was the next best thing to the worship of a divine godhead.

For Carlyle, as for Hegel, 'heroes' is a word redolent with its original Greek root meaning: superhumans occupying an intermediate, indeed mediating position between humanity and the gods, often born from a union between a god and a mortal. Their awe-inspiring power provides their descendants with a lasting reservoir of moral pride and collective idealism. Hero-worship, accordingly, was held up by Carlyle as a just and necessary pedagogical principle, enabling individuals to rise above their mean level by emulating lofty examples.

Carlyle found some modern-day equivalents of the Greek Kadmos and Theseus figures, or the Hebraic Moses, in the powerful, history-changing cases of the prophet Muhammad and Frederick the Great of Prussia. (Hegel himself had identified three: Alexander the Great, Caesar and Napoleon.) Carlyle's history of the French Revolution, anti-French and anti-Revolutionary though it was, showed surprising respect for the strong, inspired leadership of Robespierre and Napoleon, capable of taming the forces of anarchic discord.[11]

Alongside such political history-changers, however, Carlyle recognized that the same role could be played by writers: hypercanonical writers such as Homer, Shakespeare and Dante, who provided the Greeks, English and Italians with a lasting cultural identity as strong as any religion or state. 'The Great Man here too, as always, is a Force of Nature. Whatsoever is truly great in him springs up from the inarticulate deeps.' Carlyle canonizes

Shakespeare into an essential cornerstone of the English presence in world history: an Everyman ('our poor Warwickshire Peasant, who rose to be Manager of a Playhouse, so that he could live without begging'), not a primeval mythical deity like Odin, and yet, 'in spite of the sad state Hero-worship now lies in', the most cherished cultural presence 'in this land of ours', for 'millionsof Englishmen'. More cherished and precious, even, than Britain's colonial empire in India.

> For our honour among foreign nations, as an ornament to our English Household, what item is there that we would not surrender rather than him? Consider now, if they asked us, Will you give up your Indian Empire or your Shakspeare, you English; never have had any Indian Empire, or never have had any Shakspeare? Really it were a grave question. ... should not we be forced to answer: Indian Empire, or no Indian Empire; we cannot do without Shakspeare! Indian Empire will go, at any rate, some day; but this Shakspeare does not go, he lasts forever with us; we cannot give up our Shakspeare![12]

One of the most important followers of Carlyle, Matthew Arnold, picked up this idea in his *Culture and Anarchy* of 1869. Arnold, like Carlyle, saw a new responsibility for public intellectuals in a secularizing age: to dispense life-lessons, to give ethical and intellectual guidance. Arnold located this responsibility primarily in the field of culture, which in his outlook almost takes the place that had been left behind by an evaporating religiosity. Culture for him was 'the best that is known and thought in the world' and a necessary ingredient in lifting humans above the level of mere cogs in a socio-economic machinery. He idealized the Greek world for the 'sweetness and light' of its culture – poetically indicating that the hard work of a beehive is not an end in itself but provides the world with honey (sweetness) and candlewax (light). This provides a saving grace without which Arnold's dour, pragmatic, wealth-obsessed Victorian contemporaries would become (his word) mere *philistines*. What society needed was public intellectuals ('critics') who could 'learn and propagate the best that is known and thought in the world'. What is more, it was ultimately through the instrumentality of culture that societies could become harmonious wholes, rather than merely transactional exchange networks. Indeed, culture was ultimately a necessary safeguard against social disintegration – hence the 'Culture and Anarchy' title of his book.[13]

Thus Carlylean thought accorded an increasing 'national' importance and authority for writers. Many, from Pushkin, Mickiewicz and Petőfi on, saw themselves as sacral prophet-figures, as champions articulating or channelling their nations' wishes, aspirations and collective imagination. Even where they themselves did not develop Romantic pretensions to become Heroes in the Carlylean sense, they did attract the hero-worship of their readers, who following their deaths proved quite ready to canonize them and to create a cult in their memory. By 1916, James Joyce sarcastically imputed to his adolescent persona Stephen Dedalus the ambition to 'forge in the smithy of his soul the uncreated conscience of his race' (*A Portrait of the Artist as a Young Man*); Joyce was by then already beginning to see through this lofty sentiment as a commonplace.

If we look at the cult of great heroes of the nation, we see that artists and writers feature surprisingly prominently – given their lack of political agency or actual raw power. Indeed, their lack of political power is compensated for by a surplus of cultural authority, and in the long run this may give cultural saints, as opposed to political leaders, a greater historical permanence; for political leaders are usually caught up in political struggles that leave political losers and victims in their wake, as well as hard feelings. Artists and writers are feel-good heroes. They serve as consensus figures and have fewer enemies. There were many, many statues erected to Lenin and Stalin in Russia between 1920 and 1990, but the ones to Pushkin and Rimsky-Korsakov have survived. In the historical portrait gallery of twentieth-century French banknotes, Napoleon makes only a fleeting appearance (and that only in his early-career status as general in the service of the Directoire); his presence on French twentieth-century banknotes is drowned out by a huge company of writers, painters and composers.[14]

Carlyle's notion of the hero-figure as an inspiration to society was followed and amplified by Emerson's lecture series on 'Representative Men' and in Nietzschean thought. It kept a cultural life in nineteenth-century historiography, where the organizational narrative model of arranging important developments under the rubrics of heroic 'Great Men' was notoriously predominant. 'Men' they were, of course; the shining exception being Joan of Arc, who was rediscovered by the Romantics after Schiller's play *Die Jungfrau von Orléans* and, celebrated by Michelet and his followers, became a national cult figure in France as a truly supernatural agency for the country's salvation, embodying (depending on the historian's secular or religious proclivities) either the transcendent, imperishable spirit of France or God's solicitude for that chosen nation.[15]

From the field of culture the Carlylean hero model returns to the field of politics around the end of World War I, when Max Weber introduced the notion of *charisma* into his analysis of political leadership (*Herrschaft*).

Weber distinguished three type of rule: dynastic and institutional (those two being the ones already operative in Burke's sense of state authority) and a third one, non-Burkean and close to that of Hegel's Heroes. To that third form of leadership, a mesmerizing, crowd-mobilizing force of personality, he gave the Greek name of *charisma*. The examples he gave were the Bavarian socialist leader Kurt Eisner (who had turned Bavaria from a kingdom into a republic), the American religious prophet Joseph Smith and the German poet Stefan George, who had gathered a cult-like coterie around himself.[16]

Tellingly, *charisma* was originally a theological term, denoting the gracious disposition of divinity that elicits joy among worshippers and attracts the warmth of their devotion. Weber's direct inspiration, the theologian Rudolf Sohm, had used it to explain how early Christians were motivated to endure and overcome massive repression. Early Christians were inspired, Weber argued, by the guidance of a leadership displaying

> a certain quality of an individual personality by virtue of which he is set apart from ordinary men and treated as endowed with supernatural, superhuman, or at least specifically exceptional powers or qualities. These as such are not accessible to the ordinary person, but are regarded as of divine origin or as exemplary, and on the basis of them the individual concerned is treated as a leader.

Weber died in 1920, before he could fully elaborate his theory of charismatic leadership, bequeathing little more than this thumbnail sketch to posterity. Brief though it is, it does betray the traces of Carlylean thought, which in the previous half-century had become widespread all over Europe. (In Germany, Carlyle had been revered for his hero-worshipping biography of Frederick the Great of Prussia – apparently one of the chosen books to provide reading material, until the very end, in Hitler's bunker in 1945.) The social acceptance of charismatic leadership is explained by Weber in Carlylean terms: 'It is recognition on the part of those subject to authority which is decisive for the validity of charisma. This is freely given and … consists in devotion to the corresponding revelation, *hero worship*, or absolute trust in the leader [my emphasis].'

Charismatic Leaders, Charismatic Nations

Historians have wondered if and how Weber's idea of charismatic leadership could be applied to the new leaders, totalitarian and otherwise, that emerged out of the Great War and after Weber's death in 1920. The mass appeal of Mussolini and of Hitler himself strongly suggests an analysis in

Weberian terms;[17] but the question 'What would Weber have thought of that?' is as moot as it is unavoidable. It does make sense, however, to place the fervour with which a charismatic leader is embraced in the context of what Wolfgang Schivelbusch (2004) has aptly termed a 'culture of defeat'. (For that reason, many scholars see a tension between the appeal of charismatic leadership and the actual 'routinized' running of state affairs.[18]) People unable to stomach the grinding mortification of a lost war, who find themselves in disarray or in parlous circumstances, will eagerly, and joyfully, embrace unexpected saviour-figures. The veterans who clung to their Langemarck myth, the people to whom Hitler's *Mein Kampf* appealed, found such a figure initially in the gruff paternal figure of Field Marshal von Hindenburg, last president of the Weimar republic and Bismarck lookalike. He had commanded at Germany's greatest victory in 1914–1918, the Battle of Tannenberg on the Eastern Front. He it was who, in an inquest conducted by the new Weimar authorities on the conduct of the war effort, launched the notorious 'stab in the back' legend; and he spread that myth also through his self-serving but massively popular book of reminiscences. It was Hindenburg most of all (more than the erratic fanatic Ludendorff) who leveraged, well before Hitler, Germany's post-1918 political bitterness into his political leadership and into a veritable cult of personality. Hitler's own upgrade from street fighter to chancellor was effected by the accolade from the august war hero Hindenburg (who, as an aristocratic general, scorned the Austrian corporal as a vulgar upstart).[19]

Following four years of total war, the generals of those wars emerged after 1918 with an almost Napoleonic aura of authoritative power, and many

Figure 1.4 Mustafa Kemal Atatürk depicted twice on two sides of the Monument of the Republic, Gezi Square, Istanbul (1928): as wartime general (left) and as postwar statesman (right). Wikimedia Commons: Ank Kumar (left), Julien Maury (right)

of them became state leaders. Alongside Hindenburg in Germany we see strongmen such as Mustafa Kemal Pasha (the future Atatürk) in Turkey (Figure 1.4), Horthy in Hungary, Metaxas in Greece, Piłsudski in Poland, Pétain in France; as well as the more complex figure of Mannerheim in Finland.[20] Their aura of military authority was envied by their more vulgar emulators, Mussolini in Italy and Hitler in Germany. Although they could not claim to have held any field command they also affected military uniforms and style. The cult of uniforms, salutes, parades, flags and insignia suffused these states' official display culture post-1918. That contributed to the general militarization of politics and to the decline of parliamentary and constitutional rule (civic and civilian as that was) in most post-1918 European states.

However, the charismatic leaders post-1918 were not just military commanders in a Napoleonic lineage (in Weberian terms they would have embodied 'institutional leadership', albeit embellished with a personal heroic aura). As the venerable Burkean empires crumbled in the Great War, the leaders that emerged in the vacuum they left behind were, predictably, of the 'charismatic' type, and many of them came from the cultural field as well. The new states arising from the wreckage of 1914–1918 were, certainly at first, represented highly effectively by men who had gained status as a result of their achievements in the field of culture, or at least outside the field of inherited or institutionally established lineages of power. They include Thomas Masaryk, public intellectual, lawyer and historian, who became the first president of an independent Czechoslovakia; Fridtjof Nansen, polar explorer and apologist for Norwegian independence, who became a highly respected international statesman; and Ignacy Paderewski, piano virtuoso and composer, who became the first prime minister of a newly independent Poland.[21] As charismatic leaders, they derived their political authority from cultural achievements.

So whom, Piłsudski or Paderewski, Mussolini or Masaryk, might Weber have been thinking of? It is far from easy to pinpoint the type of statesman that fits Weber's bill as a charismatic leader. With that, I return to the question of what or who it was that gave people that sense as if their chest would burst; and I return to the tears on Madeleine Lebeau's face in *Casablanca*. *Casablanca* attempts to build up an element of hero-worship around the figure of Viktor Laszlo, leader of the anti-Nazi resistance (played by the Austrian exile Paul Henreid). Laszlo is supposed to be one of the most redoubtable enemies of Nazi rule, and it is he who initiates the singing of 'La Marseillaise' and the collective multinational show of defiance. Ingrid Bergman goes dewy-eyed at seeing his rousing strength of character. However, his presence pales besides that of the brooding, Byronic Rick; next to Humphrey Bogart, Henreid is, in fact, a bit colourless. And it is neither Viktor Laszlo nor Rick who moves Yvonne to tears and to her defiant exclamation. That is the work of the song itself, the words and lyrics of 'La Marseillaise'; and what Yvonne exclaims is, accordingly, a passionate commitment, not to this or that leader, but to her national identity: 'Vive la France!'

This is what lies behind the title of this book. It is the nation itself (not the state or its leaders) that has become the most compelling charismatic force in politics.[22] It is the nation, as an abstraction, timeless and ubiquitous, that can rouse people into something that goes far beyond Burkean reverence. The ecstatic assertions of love and devotion that sent young men such as Hitler singing into battle, that made them enlist as they sang their respective national anthems, with feelings as though their chest would burst: all that was inspired by the nation, which had itself acquired charisma in the century after Burke and Napoleon.

'Beyond Politics': The Unpolitical Nation

An early example of charismatic leadership in Ireland was Charles Stewart Parnell, whose scandalous political downfall and untimely death in 1891 left a sense of tragic bereavement. It is generally accepted that in that political void, Douglas Hyde's lecture on 'The Necessity for De-Anglicising Ireland' (1893) started a process of cultural (rather than parliamentary–political) nationalism, calling for a reinvigoration of Ireland's traditional cultural pursuits: music, dance, sports and, most importantly, the declining Gaelic language. This cultural revival movement eventually radicalized and politicized, preparing the ground for the Easter Rising of 1916 and the Irish War of Independence (1919–1921). As far as Hyde himself was concerned, that radicalization and politicization was an unintended aberration. He denounced the growing politicization of the Gaelic League (the association that his lecture had kick-started and which he chaired). He went as far as withdrawing from its chairmanship over this very issue in 1910. But by 1903, under his guidance and presidency, the League had already declared a 'War on Anglicisation'; and in retrospect the move from Hyde's cultural revivalism and regenerationism towards a political rejection of English hegemony seems perfectly straightforward. That impression is confirmed, it would seem, by the fact that it was Douglas Hyde who was later chosen to become the first president of the independent Irish Republic. All in all, the developments seem a typical illustration of

Miroslav Hroch's model of how national movements develop from initial cultural consciousness-raising ('Phase A') to social and political activism.[23]

Hyde's 1893 lecture denounces and rejects the predominance of English culture in Ireland and calls for a return to the country's native Gaelic roots. Contemporary readers will be puzzled at Hyde's simultaneous assertion that this agenda of 'de-anglicisation' is in fact not political at all. For a discourse carrying such a – not altogether unpolitical-sounding – title, that comes as a surprise. Is it crafty rhetoric or blithe ingenuousness? Hyde concludes as follows:

> I would earnestly appeal to every one, whether Unionist or Nationalist, who wishes to see the Irish nation produce its best – and surely whatever our politics are we all wish that – to set his face against this constant running to England for our books, literature, music, games, fashions, and ideas. I appeal to every one whatever his politics – for this is no political matter – to do his best to help the Irish race to develop in future upon Irish lines, even at the risk of encouraging national aspirations, because upon Irish lines alone can the Irish race once more become what it was of yore – one of the most original, artistic, literary, and charming peoples of Europe.[24]

Readers will recognize the echoes of Matthew Arnold's *Culture and Anarchy*. Hyde argues that culture is a force of moral improvement and regeneration for a nation, and that this cultural mission is itself a moral one and therefore politically uncontentious. It ought to be endorsed by all morally upright people, whatever their party-political preferences. Strengthening the national culture is as unpolitical as denouncing child abuse and will be agreed upon by all: socialists, liberals or conservatives. The national culture and its improvement are seen by 1893 as a categorical imperative, a self-evident moral duty. This turns cultural nationalism from a political agenda into a virtue plain and simple – something above 'politics'.

Hyde was utterly sincere about this, as his 1910 resignation as president of his Gaelic League bears out. His came from a Protestant, English-descended background, and he saw a turn to Gaelic culture as joint venture for Ireland's two classes: the Protestant Anglo-Irish elite and the Catholic, Gaelic-descended (though no longer Gaelic-speaking) underclass and emerging petty bourgeoisie. Hyde's vision can be compared to that of the Fennomans in Finland, descended from a Swedish elite but now adopting Finnish culture and the Finnish language in an act of cultural self-rearticulation.

Twenty years after Hyde's lecture, the nationalist invocation of an 'unpolitical' nation was made more stridently in Thomas Mann's *Betrachtungen eines Unpolitischen* (Observations of an Unpolitical Man, 1918).

In the fervour of the 1914 moment, a wave of opinion-making had broken loose over Germany, with public intellectuals asserting to the general public the necessity and justness of Germany's belligerence and war aims (see Chapter 11). One of these volunteer propagandists was Thomas Mann. His justifications of Germany's wartime conduct were published in 1918 as 'unpolitical' observations (Mann 2012). That, again, may surprise a contemporary reader, and for two reasons. For one thing, as with Hyde, the book is nothing if not political – it is, in fact, war propaganda wrapped up in moral reflections. As with Hyde, it is 'unpolitical' (as we shall translate the German *unpolitisch* here) only in the sense that Mann claims to stay aloof from party politics, in fact following Wilhelm II's battle cry of 1914: 'Now I no longer recognize parties – I only recognize Germans!'.

The other startling thing about this book is that Mann is now known as a dignified, courageous opponent of the Hitler regime, who, though cherished and celebrated as a Nobel-prize winning novelist, preferred to exile himself rather than to live in a Nazi-ruled country. A wartime chauvinist, he? Yes: the liberal humanism for which Mann is now known and admired was a post-1918 conversion.[25] In his earlier years, Mann was a committed German patriot, who expressed his attachment to nationally German values in terms of the ethnotypes (ethnic stereotypes) that were commonplace around 1910 and that were becoming virulently xenophobic around 1914.* Germans, so the ethnotype goes, are earnest and profound,

* Ethnotypes are Europe-wide stereotypes identifying perceived 'national characters' in terms of their alleged temperamental proclivities (stingy Scots, passionate Italians, inscrutable Chinese). These ethnotypes have been studied over the past decades as tropes in comparative literary history by scholars in the specialist field of 'imagology'. Their insights (Beller & Leerssen 2007, Dyserinck 1988 and 2015, Florack 2000a and 2000b, and the website imagologica.eu) can here be summarized as follows:

- Ethnotypes are discursive formulae that, while pretending to refer to empirical reality, are in fact largely intertextual and without testable factual basis;
- they function largely as part of a self–other distinction, meaning that the ethnotype of the foreigner (hetero-image) is contrastively co-determined by a national self-image (auto-image);
- while they are formulated in ahistorical, anthropological terms, asserting invariant essential characteristics, they are in fact changeable over time (Spaniards as dour, severe and cruel in the seventeenth century, as warm-blooded and passionate in the nineteenth and twentieth).
- The accumulation of these changing images leads to a compounded ethnotype ('imageme') that comports contradictory temperamental profiles (English: stiff upper lip and hooliganism; French: convivial debonair charm and Cartesian rigidity; German: Romantics or technocrats); the ultimate cliché is that 'X is a nation of contrasts'.

Ethnotypes emerge around the mid-seventeenth century in the neo-Aristotelian poetical and encyclopaedic tradition, often aligning temperamental traits with the climatological circumstances of a given society, using 'hot' 'cold' or 'damp' as temperamental metaphors (Zacharasiewicz 1977). Ethnotypes then develop from ad hoc ethnocentric characterizations to become, in the course of the eighteenth century, a formalized frame to schematize perceived intercultural differences. The characterizations as applied to specific individuals (e.g. fictional characters) tend to be inflected by as opposed to the frivolous and superficial French and the cynically self-serving British. That, too, is how Mann defended the German war effort. 'Politics' in the republican, democratic sense was a French invention and boiled down to the transactional bickering between interested parties; while politics, British-style, was only a coldly calculating concern with economic advantage and power expansion. Germans, so Mann asserted, had no truck with those 'politics'. Instead, their sense of being part of a larger societal whole was profound, almost anthropological, based on the awareness of a deep, shared culture. In this context, the war was not a political thing but an engagement of the entire nation as a whole, including its spiritual values and culture. Mann, in seeing German *Kultur* as a set of spiritual values, opposed that profound, moral sense of national identity against French *civilisation*, which consisted of good manners polishing the mere surface of social relations. And in collectivizing the war into a totalizing national engagement beyond politics, Mann lifted his commitment to the German nation – and its war aims, and even its methods of submarine torpedo warfare, which Mann defended – out of the realm of politics and into what he terms 'unpolitics': it was a question of fundamental identity and as such a moral rather than a political principle.*

stereotypes concerning that individual's gender, class and/or age group; since 1918, ethnotypes have maintained their recognizability and are still drawn upon in, for instance, the nostrums of intercultural management; but in culture at large they tend to be deployed back-handedly, ironically/comically or as an ambient ethnocultural 'background noise' (Leerssen 2016c).

These characterizations together form a literary repertoire that is drawn upon, in the nineteenth century, to underpin the alleged temperamental parameters of the nation's character or *Volksgeist*. They become more pronounced in situations of friction and antagonism.

* I use the slightly un-idiomatic translation 'unpolitical' (rather than 'nonpolitical' or 'apolitical') to highlight what is, fundamentally, an oxymoron: that a national ideology can claim to be removed from politics. Mann's use of *Unpolitischen* is close to how Alain Badiou uses the idea of *metapolitics* (Badiou 2005), a word that has, however, complex and unfortunate conceptual entanglements (Camus 2019, Teitelbaum 2019). Mann did engage positively with the notion of metapolitics as used in 1940 by the political maverick Peter Viereck; see Viereck 2004, li–lxi, 'Thomas Mann on Metapolitics'. Badiou sees metapolitics as an attitude regarding social relations or the position of humans in the world, which, while not itself deriving from a political *parti pris* or forming part of a political philosophy, can inform one's political outlook and values. As such it is close to the notion of a 'moral' position, in the root sense of that term (derived from *mores*, manners and customs): a set of ingrained societal and behavioural patterns, and the ethical valorization of these as being proper or improper.

An attachment to, and advocacy for, one's nation can be unpolitical in that it can be seen as a moral virtue ('amor patriae'), compatible with very different, mutually incompatible political doctrines (conservatism, liberalism, socialism etc.). Nationalism can thus be generalized and 'moralized' into an unpolitical rather than political stance; while informing political choices, it can be encountered among people of very different political persuasions. As we shall see, this political/unpolitical ambivalence explains the power of nationalism to oscillate between 'hot' (salient, political) and 'banal' (latent, unpolitical) states (as per Billig 1995). It also chimes with Michael Freeden's widely accepted contention that nationalism is a 'thin-centred' ideology (Freeden 1998), not propounding its own vision of society or of how to shape it, but rather a meta-ideology capable of inflecting and 'flavouring' political doctrines.

These national-characterological ethnotypes couch historically specific social or political structures in a generic, anthropological assertion that 'that is just how people are'.

Here, then, is a conundrum. On the one hand, commitment to the nation is being generalized into a general human virtue, like fidelity to one's spouse, or kindness to children, or being true to one's identity. On the other hand, it is a powerfully strong mobilizing – and antagonizing – force, capable of inspiring battle courage in soldiers and strenuous defiance in civilians.[26] 'Die Wacht am Rhein' can be sung en route to battle or as a jolly convivial outburst in Rick's café. Much of this book will deal with this ambivalence, so characteristic of nationalism. Both in culture and in politics, the idealized, charismatic nation can be a mellow feel-good factor, or bestow moral edification, or justify bitter antagonism, often in rapid alternation.

CHAPTER 2

Becoming Something, Unmaking Empires

Versailles, Berlin, Belfast, Odessa

> What is the Third Estate? EVERYTHING.
> What has it been in the political order so far? NOTHING.
> What does it demand? To become SOMETHING.
>
> Emmanuel-Joseph Sieyès, *Qu'est-ce que le tiers-état?*, 1789

The formative moments in the emergence of the nation as a political principle were 1789 (Versailles) and 1808 (Berlin).[1] In June 1789, delegates of the French Third Estate gathered in Versailles as the French Revolution was forming in the air. That 'Third Estate' was a container term for those who were neither prelates nor noblemen. In the words of the seminal pamphlet by Emmanuel Sieyès, *Qu'est-ce que le tiers état?*, the Third Estate had always been 'Everything' in socio-economic terms, had amounted to 'Nothing' in the running of the state, and now demanded, politically, to 'become Something' (Figure 2.1). As the political events of mid-1789 unfolded, this Third Estate constituted itself into a mandate-giving representative body. That body christened itself, at the suggestion of the same Sieyès, the Assemblée nationale, and thereby gave the word *nation* a new political meaning. The nation was the Something that the Third Estate aspired to become. Their *assemblée* was the rump continuation of a meeting of the Estates General that, convoked by King Louis XVI, had disbanded when Louis found the delegates too fractious and rebellious. The First and Second Estates (clergy and nobility) obeyed the king's dissolution of the Estates General and disbanded, but the Third Estate vowed to remain in session until they had given France a constitution. It was this decision that formed the actual beginning of the French Revolution; the storming of the Bastille took place almost a month later (14 July). In August 1789 the Assemblée nationale voted for the abolition of feudalism and enacted the Declaration of Human and Civil Rights. In the space of two months, the nation had definitely managed to become Something.

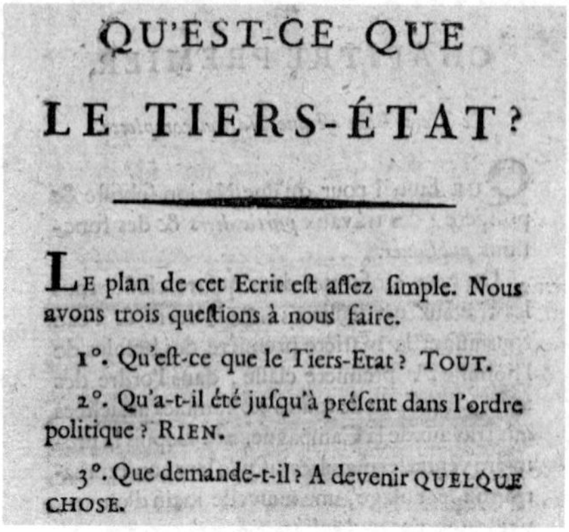

QU'EST-CE QUE

LE TIERS-ÉTAT?

LE plan de cet Ecrit eſt aſſez ſimple. Nous avons trois queſtions à nous faire.

1°. Qu'eſt-ce que le Tiers-Etat? TOUT.

2°. Qu'a-t-il été juſqu'à préſent dans l'ordre politique? RIEN.

3°. Que demande-t-il? A devenir QUELQUE CHOSE.

Figure 2.1 Opening page of Emmanuel Sieyès's *What Is the Third Estate?* (1789). Wikimedia Commons

In 1808 in Germany, the nation also became Something; in this case, it became the principle that was called upon to fill the void left by the imploding Reich. Following the imposition of Napoleonic overlordship, the thousand-year-old empire (formally known as the Holy Roman Empire of the German Nation, *das Heilige Römische Reich Deutscher Nation*) had abolished itself in 1806. At that juncture, the celebrated philosopher Johann Gottlieb Fichte held public lectures (*Reden an die deutsche Nation*, 1808), in which he addressed the bereft 'Deutsche Nation'; he implicitly redefined them as the subsisting body politic of the now-defunct empire. He, too, tried to turn the nation into Something: a continuity principle,[2] a cultural community, autonomously existing as such on the basis of a common language, a common past and shared values. That nation, now culturally rather than constitutionally defined, was to become the focus of the political loyalty and aspirations of the German Romantic generation. Fichte's *Reden* followed and consolidated a line of argument already thought out by Schiller in 1797, when territorial losses had begun to threaten the millennial fabric of the Holy Roman Empire:

> Can the German, with head held confidently high, take his place among the nations? Yes he can! The German Reich and the German nation are two different things. The Germans' majesty never rested on the head of their monarch. Outside the realm of the political, Germans have established a dignity unto themselves, and even were the Empire to go under, that German dignity would remain unimpeached. It is a moral quantity, residing in the nation's culture and character, which is independent of its political vicissitudes.[3]

This emergence of the nation as a political Something was provoked, in France and in Germany, by constitutional crises requiring a redefinition of the relations between the state and its taxpayers. But there was a new force at work as well, and it was operative in various places along the edges of the European monarchies and empires: people were rejecting state rule altogether because it was considered an alien imposition. A separatist, republican rebellion took place in Ireland in 1798; an anti-Ottoman secret society was founded by Greek merchants in Odessa in 1814. Both invoked the right of the people to secede from, or to rise against, a government they considered tyrannical. In that respect they were both inspired by the American and French Revolutions of 1776 and 1789 and by the notion of popular sovereignty. But in these cases, popular sovereignty was invoked to secede from states whose governments were denounced not only as despotic but also as a foreign yoke (English and Turkish, respectively) on their own nation (Irish, not English; Greek, not Turkish). The aim was not to reform the state but to secede from it; and unlike the Founding Fathers in the United States, they aimed not to start a new state afresh but rather to re-establish an ancient one that in the course of history had been vanquished and conquered.

Belfast to Odessa: the European span does not get much wider, either in space or indeed in time. Those two cities have remained flashpoints in Europe's national conflicts ever since. Everywhere along the tectonic faultlines of Europe, the seismic tremors were noticed, along the grinding edges of the British, Spanish, French, Habsburg, Romanov and Ottoman Empires. The political seismographs register violent regime changes and internal conflicts, fluttering between sullen disaffection and open rebellion. In the Southern Netherlands (present-day Belgium) anti-Austrian resistance was distributed evenly between radical and traditionalist factions; in the Balkans, Serbian and Romanian resistance against Ottoman rule was no less vehement than in Greece; in the Tyrol, the enforced transfer from Austria to Bavaria in 1805 was hotly resented and led to a rebellion; in Scandinavia, where in 1809 Finland was moved from Sweden to Russia and in 1814 Norway was moved from Denmark to Sweden, both Norway and Finland strove to maintain constitutional liberties in the process; in Spain, the Carlist wars affected the Basque and Catalan *fueros* (local autonomies) and provoked regionalist consciousness-raising.

States, Subjects, Secret Societies

The epicentre of all this was Napoleon, who vanquished and abolished ancient realms and created new ones at will. In the span of a few years, he put an end to the Papal States and to the Venetian, Swiss and Dutch republics; conquered Spain and Naples and humiliated Prussia; reduced and annexed sovereign German lordships, temporal and ecclesiastical; and drove the venerable Holy Roman Empire to self-abolish as he crowned himself an Emperor of the French. And then his own empire crashed and burned – not once, but twice. First at the Battle of Leipzig (1813), which sent him off to Elba, and then again at Waterloo (1815), which sent him off to St Helena.

The European state system staggered out of the Napoleonic upheavals with a desperate need for, above all else, stability. The congress system devised by Austria's chancellor Clemens von Metternich attempted to provide this. The balance of power in Europe was regulated by diplomats who at crisis moments would convene to work out solutions, first at the Congress of Vienna (1814), then at further follow-up congresses. The one at Aachen (1818) was notable for taking repressive measures (such as censorship) against democratic activism and aspirations. This persecution of 'demagogues' affected many of the Romantic intellectuals who had supported the insurrection against Napoleonic hegemony: the pamphleteer and versifier Ernst Moritz Arndt, the theologian Friedrich Schleiermacher, the gymnastics organizer Friedrich Ludwig Jahn, the folksong collector Werner von Haxthausen, the student activist Hans Ferdinand Maßmann. For indeed the Napoleonic period had left Europe sharply divided ideologically: the restored monarchical governments aimed above all to return to their old authoritative positions and abhorred the French *liberté, égalité, fraternité* as a sinister force of anarchism and upheaval. A 'democrat' in their understanding of the word was a fanatical *sans-culotte* itching to unleash the *terreur* of the guillotine. But many populations in Europe, though they had come to abhor Napoleon as a warmongering despot, had tasted the benefits of a state that was based not on the privileges of the aristocracy but on a constitution with citizens' equality before the law. After an anti-Napoleonic honeymoon period of 1813–1817, that friction between princes and peoples became apparent again. The reinstated monarchs, who had initially agreed to rule constitutionally rather than absolutely, tended to ignore the constitutions they had half-heartedly accepted, to whittle them away or even to abolish them.[4]

Signs of unrest at this reactionary trend flared up at various points on the European map. As early as 1817, a commemorative feast at the Wartburg Castle, bringing together students who had seen military action in 1813, turned into an act of defiance; in its wake, a participating student activist murdered a writer who was seen as an advocate of reactionary absolutism, and this in turn triggered the repressive measures of the Aachen Congress. Semi-private societies, modelled on the German Tugendbund (an anti-Napoleonic organization in Prussia in 1808–1809) and on the template of masonic lodges, kept the idea of patriotic civic empowerment alive.* As they were regarded with increasing suspicion by the authorities, these organizations retreated into discreet obscurity and in the process acquired the aura of sinister secret societies. At the Polish-Lithuanian University of Vilnius, now under Russian rule, a group of liberal-minded intellectuals was active in the early 1820s, with a visible outer layer known as the Philomaths harbouring a more radical inner circle, the Philarets. They were disbanded and harshly sentenced by the Russian authorities in 1823; but they were a first sign that the Polish intelligentsia would not abide by the continuing dismemberment of what once had been a separate realm (the united Kingdom of Poland and Grand Duchy of Lithuania). Ex-Philarets in exile who would continue their advocacy for a separate Polish nationality were the poet Adam Mickiewicz and the historian Joachim Lelewel. The university itself was closed down after the Polish Uprising of 1831. (Ironically, its books were distributed among newly founded universities in the Ukraine, which would later on become seedbeds of Ukrainian nationalism.) Meanwhile Russia itself had experienced the shock of the Decembrist revolt of 1825, which hastened the tsar's paranoid withdrawal into reactionary absolutism. At the same time, however, Russia's geopolitical rivalry with the Ottoman Empire (which had been excluded from Metternich's congress system) developed into a semi-mystical mission to re-establish Christianity in Jerusalem and Istanbul; disaffected subjects of the Ottoman sultan were welcomed and supported in Russia on the basis of their shared orthodox religion. Macedonians, Bulgarians, Romanians and Greeks could find refuge and succour in Moscow or Odessa, and it

* The notion of *amor patriae*, dedication to the native land, is much more widespread than the ideology of nationalism, which it antedates by many centuries. In the eighteenth century, the moral principle of love of the fatherland had gained a political meaning: it referred to an anti-aristocratic agenda. The ethos of chivalry (revolving around dauntlessness in battle, self-control and courtesy in social intercourse and fealty to the liege) had become threadbare in the century of Louis XV and the Four Georges, and a new, civic ethos had arisen alongside the rising middle classes. This revolved around accountability, probity, reliability and selfless dedication to the public welfare. Those who, as part of this ethos, rejected the aristocratic honour code and instead endorsed a bourgeois code of civic virtue, called themselves patriots, because they saw *amor patriae* as a higher ideal than loyalty to the king. This ethos of political patriotism politicized the ideal of love of the fatherland and drove the democratic revolutions of 1776 and 1789.

Patriotism, though largely ingested by nationalism as that ideology developed after Napoleon, has ever since denoted a civic virtue: selfless dedication to one's country. As such, it is still used now; it has also become a euphemism for national chauvinism. (Brubaker 2004a, 2004b, Venturi 1971, Viroli 1995.)

is in the latter city that another secret society with nationalist aims was founded: the Greek Filiki Eteria (Φιληκη εταιρια: literally, 'Friendly Society').[5] Pushkin, in provincial exile from Moscow, became an early sympathizer and was enrolled as a member. The euphemistic high-mindedness of that name recalls the German Tugendbund ('Virtue Association') and the Philomaths and Philarets ('Friends of Science'/'Friends of Virtue'). Similarly, the groups behind the Decembrist revolt of 1825 called themselves the 'Union of Salvation' in 1816, morphing into a 'Society of True and Loyal Sons of the Fatherland' in 1817 and into a 'Union of Prosperity' in 1818. These were obviously what Tolstoy had in mind when, at the end of *War and Peace*, he mentions Pierre Bezukhov's project for a reformist association:

> 'And what position [Nikolai Rostov asks] will you adopt toward the government?'
>
> 'Why, the position of assistants. … We join hands only for the public welfare and the general safety.'
>
> 'Yes, but it's a secret society and therefore a hostile and harmful one which can only cause harm.'
>
> 'Why? Did the Tugendbund which saved Europe … do any harm?'*

Meanwhile, in Italy, where absolute rule had been restored in the Kingdom of Naples and the Papal States, a group called the Carbonari resisted; there were imitators of that resistance in restoration France, the Charbonnerie. In time the Carbonari would evolve into the Young Italy movement led by Mazzini and Garibaldi. That, in turn, would inspire a number of national reform movements across the century, from Junges Deutschland to the Young Turks.[6]

In Germany, anti-absolutism initially took a more coded, cultural form: a cult of Schiller commemorations in the 1820s recalled how that great poet had celebrated the unification and revolt of the Swiss cantons under Wilhelm Tell (see Figure 10.1) and how he had passionately asserted the right to freedom of thought in his *Don Carlos*. A popular song, 'Die Gedanken sind frei', had been published in Achim von Arnim and Clemens Brentano's anthology *Des Knaben Wunderhorn* in 1808, and it remained a widespread, subversive inspiration well into the twentieth century: it was distributed in the *Commersbuch* student songbooks (see

* *War and Peace* (Tolstoy 1869), 'First Epilogue: 1813', chapter 14. It should be recalled that Tolstoy's original plan had been to write the tale of a convicted Decembrist couple, Pierre and Natasha, returning from their Siberian exile in 1856; this plotline changed into the novel we now know, chronicling the experiences of the decades preceding 1825. In 1868, Tolstoy wrote further draft outlines of a sequel to *War and Peace* under the working title *The Decembrists*. See Feuer 2008, Trigos 2009.

Chapter 9), played by Sophie Scholl to her imprisoned father in 1942, and sung by demonstrators in blockaded Berlin in 1948.[7]

The anti-Napoleonic restoration tried to obliterate the memory of democracy; but the memory was kept alive in semi-clandestine cultural form. It would become a programme not just of political emancipation but of national liberation.

Uprisings

The Metternich system was rocked on its foundations by a number of revolts. The earliest of these (Serbia in 1816; Greece and Romania, masterminded by the Filiki Eteria, in 1822) were anti-Ottoman in character and took place in the Turkish-ruled Balkans; as such, they could still be seen as external to the congress system's remit. But the ongoing decline of that alien Islamic empire would nonetheless affect Europe deeply. A wave of sympathy for the Greek cause – philhellenism – swept across Europe in the 1820s, and provided a coded outlet for anti-Metternich feeling among progressives. Some young men took active service to support the Greek cause, but most foregrounded was the cultural and moral–intellectual support, expressed in poetry, painting (Delacroix) and philology (Claude Fauriel editing collections of Greek insurrectionist songs in 1824). The symbolic culmination came when the Romantic poet Byron, who had become famous with dramatic poems set in the Ottoman-ruled Levant, embarked for Greece and died in besieged Missolonghi in 1824 (Figure 2.2).[8]

Finally in 1832, the European powers, despite their ingrained mistrust of popular sovereignty, came down on the side of the Greeks and agreed to sponsor the establishment of an independent Greek kingdom: this took the place of the Hellenic Republic of 1822, the first new European state in the century of nationalism.*

The Hellenic Republic was followed by Belgium. In 1830, liberal anti-restoration revolts broke out in many European states. In France, the reactionary autocrat Charles X was replaced by the constitutional 'bourgeois

* This did nothing to end the continuing irritant of the vacuum left by shrinking Ottoman power. The Balkans would become the arena for a geopolitical battle between the Habsburg and Romanov empires, each striving to establish its sphere of influence in the region and it coastlands, something that culminated eventually in the fateful shooting at Sarajevo in 1914. In Northern Africa, the decline of Ottoman imperial power led to the colonial-expansionist scramble of France, Spain and Italy on the southern shores of the Mediterranean, with France and Britain involved because of the Suez Canal, and Germany's Wilhelm II trying to gain a German foothold in Morocco and Anatolia as part of his ambition to make Germany a world power. For transnational surveys in diplomatic history, see Bridge & Bullen 2004 and Wilson 2003.

Figure 2.2 Statue of Byron in Athens (Henri-Michel Chapu and Alexandre Falguière, 1896): the Greek goddess of fame pulls the dying poet heavenwards. Wikimedia Commons

king' Louis-Philippe. Revolts in Brunswick, Hanover and Saxony enforced constitutional changes. But the Southern Netherlands went further: rechristening themselves 'Belgium', they formally seceded from the United Kingdom of the Netherlands and its reactionary king Willem I and proclaimed a separate state. After some geopolitical balancing between neighbouring Germany and France, Belgium was internationally recognized, under a king from the German house of Saxe-Coburg-Gotha, brother-in-law to the future English queen Victoria and son-in-law to the French king Louis-Philippe. The country's neutrality was internationally guaranteed – something that would become a *casus belli* when German armies, singing 'Die Wacht am Rhein' and on their way to defend that river against the perfidious French, invaded the country in 1914.

In 1830, again, the French and Belgian examples inspired an uprising in the Russian portion of partitioned Poland. Like the Greek one, it triggered a wave of sympathy among European progressives. Its own battle slogan ('For our freedom and yours') played into this sense that the cause of defending the people's ('national') liberty against autocratic rule was a universal one. Indeed, the uprising was triggered by the refusal of Polish officers to be deployed for the intended repression of the Paris and Brussels revolts. The Polish Uprising was doomed, and henceforth the tsar became a despised symbol of tyranny and oriental despotism among European progressives everywhere. (He would in 1848 send troops to repress the anti-Habsburg revolt in Budapest, following the logic of the Metternich system.) A renewed Polish uprising in 1863 was equally unsuccessful, with many participants and sympathizers being sent to Siberia, but the cause of Poland was by now firmly accepted by liberal European opinion, thanks in no small part to its artists and intellectuals in exile: Mickiewicz, Lelewel, Chopin. The internationalism of the freedom fighters of 1830 became a universalist messianism: the sufferings of Poland were sufferings on behalf of Europe's liberty generally. The Polish anthem 'Not Yet is Poland Lost' was adapted to become that of Croatian nationalists as well.[9]

1848 and the End of the Congress System

Belgium apart, it was only in the Balkans that the cause of national self-determination made any headway during this time, and that was largely thanks to the decrepitude of the Ottoman Empire. In the mid-century decades, Serbia and the Danubian provinces gained in autonomy and Greece began a process of territorial expansion. Elsewhere in Europe, national movements failed to wrest power from the state but, in the process of trying, gained influence and public sympathy for their principles. Sociability increased – choirs, athletic societies, book clubs and cultural societies with periodicals – and increasingly became platforms for the proclamation of national ideals. The political secret societies of yore were evolving into grass-roots cultural associations. Europe was now replete with self-defining nations with memories of ancient (feudal or pre-modern) autonomy. As their historical consciousness deepened (discussed in Chapter 7), these erstwhile realms and fiefdoms were beginning to chafe at the their contemporary subaltern and disempowered positions: Iceland, Norway, Ireland, Catalonia, Bohemia, Poland, Croatia, Hungary, Bulgaria. And in Germany, philologists and historians refused to acquiesce altogether to the abolition of the Holy Roman Empire with its vestiges of deep tribal–ancestral traditions. Its abolition was felt as an irksome and wrongful truncation of historical continuity, and a *Reichsidee* subsisted culturally as a vaguely felt nostalgia.[10]

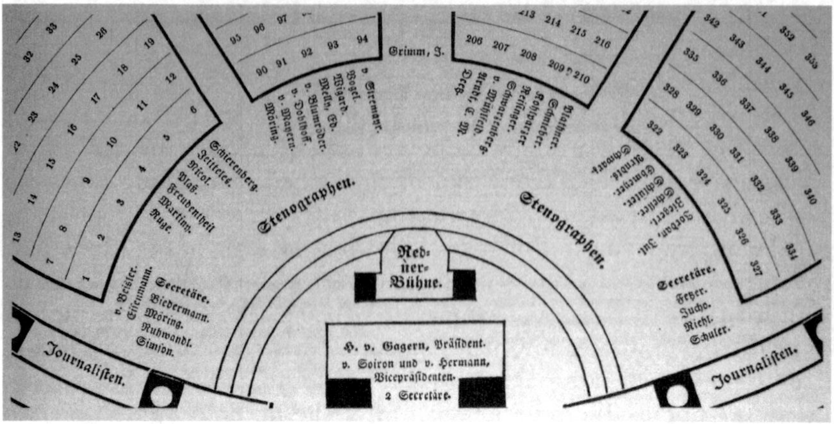

Figure 2.3 Seating plan of the Frankfurt National Assembly (1848). Jacob Grimm occupies an impartial seat of honour, centrally in the front row. ERNiE imagebank

A revolutionary upheaval came in 1848, when activists attempted to unify Germany politically by means of a Nationalversammlung (National Assembly) in the Free Imperial City of Frankfurt. (The patriotic Germans, by now habituated into a firm dislike of everything French, would have been aghast had they realized that they owed both the template and the name of this National Assembly to Emmanuel Sieyès.) The Nationalversammlung, in which intellectuals of the Romantic generation – Jacob Grimm, Ernst Moritz Arndt, Ludwig Uhland – took pride of place (Figure 2.3), failed to realize these unifying aims; the delegates had little or no standing with the autocratic German princes, were split between a radical left and a traditionalist right wing, and were divided even on the question as to which lands of the former Holy Roman Empire, north and/or south of the Alps, were to be included as 'German' in the new, national sense. But what they did achieve was to revive and turbocharge the dormant *Reichsidee*, the notion that the abolition of the Holy Roman Empire was merely a suspension, an interregnum, and that the Reich was in abeyance, awaiting its future revival and reconstitution.[11]

One imperial crown land that had been invited to attend, Bohemia (under Habsburg rule), used the occasion to firmly opt out of this once-and-future *Reich*. Its invited representative, the Czech historian František Palacký, declined the invitation, stating that as a Slav and as representative of the Czech Slavs of Bohemia, he had no reason to come to Frankfurt to join a German national love-in. Palacký and fellow Slavs even set up a rival to the Frankfurt Parliament in Prague: the Slavic Congress. It was attended by Czechs, Slovaks, Slovenians, Croatians, Serbian, Bulgarians, Sorbians and Poles, who proclaimed the unity of all Slavic nations in Europe, and their ambition to 'become Something'.[12]

Both the Slavic and the Frankfurt assemblies foundered in the disordered revolutionary events of 1848. That year saw the overthrow of kings Louis-Philippe of France and Ludwig of Bavaria. Habsburg power tottered (and Metternich's career finally ended) as Hungarian nationalists, inspired by the poet Petőfi and led by Lajos Kossuth, rose in arms to claim self-determination.[13]

All these revolutions failed – only in France was a republic established, and it was soon to be hijacked by Napoleon III. The Habsburg regime post-1848 strenuously discountenanced any form of nationalist activism in its many non-German provinces, Slavic and Italian. And with Metternich gone and France (briefly) a republic, the old congress system of 1813 broke down.[14]

A war between Russia and the weakened Ottoman Empire soon followed, with some of the heaviest action taking place on the Crimean peninsula. It saw France and the United Kingdom intervene, strange to say, on the Turkish side, worried as they were about Russian expansionism around the shores of the Black Sea. The Ottoman Empire had enacted its Tanzimat reforms in 1837 and was modernizing; Russia, on the other hand, had proved itself to be ruthlessly autocratic. It was now moot who the true oriental despot was. The Crimean War of 1853–1856 signalled the beginning of an uneasy jockeying for position between the European powers, each seeking to strengthen its position through shifting and constantly renegotiated alliances.

In those unsettled circumstances, Italy was able, with covert support from France, to finally achieve a united statehood in 1861 under the rule of the King of Sardinia, Vittorio Emmanuele – much to the disgust of the original republican instigators of the Risorgimento, Mazzini and Garibaldi. Bismarck engineered the rise of Prussia to become a major European power with a cunning combination of diplomacy and carefully calibrated wars: against Denmark (1864), against Austria (1866) and finally against France (1870). Now it was time for Denmark, Austria and France to live through their own 'culture of defeat'. In Denmark, dreams of becoming the centre of a Scandinavian Union evaporated, and the country settled into post-imperial domestic disenchantment. In France, revanchist resentment against Germany grew over the loss of Alsace-Lorraine; during the toxic and relentlessly protracted Dreyfus affair, anti-Semitism mixed with ultramontanist Catholicism and reactionary conservatism to spawn something for which the journalist Maurice Barrès coined the word *nationalisme*. He introduced the term in an article in *Le Figaro* in 1892 ('La querelle des nationalistes et des cosmopolites'), and it was thenceforth used to define a system of thought centred on the exaltation of the national idea and anti-cosmopolitanism. His trilogy of novels *Les déracinés* (1897), *L'appel au soldat* (1900) and *Leurs figures* (1902) continued to exhibit this combination of xenophobia, chauvinism and conservatism, which also found an outlet in the movement/newspaper *L'Action française* (cofounded by Barrès in 1899). Barrès's impact on public opinion was acknowledged by his election to the Académie française in 1906.[15]

Austria's defeat by Prussia in 1866 forced it to marshal its inner resources and to make concessions to its minority nationalities, especially the Hungarians; it reinvented itself as a 'dual monarchy', consisting of an autonomous Hungarian Kingdom in personal union with an Austrian Empire. Over the next decades, the dual monarchy cultivated the idea of a *Vielvölkerstaat*, a multi-ethnic empire where all nationalities would happily coexist in common loyalty to a paternal monarch. (This model was attractive to moderate Irish nationalists, who wanted to achieve a similar autonomy for their country in an imperial British setting.) Strauss's operetta *Die Fledermaus* (1874) accordingly contained ballet music combining a Viennese waltz, a Hungarian csardas, and a Bohemian polka yoked with a Polish mazurka.

This operetta model cast a golden sheen over what in hindsight became known as the *belle époque*. Younger sons from German dynasties (Wittelsbach, Saxe-Coburg-Gotha, Hohenzollern and Battenberg) were placed on the thrones of the newly created kingdoms of Greece, Romania and Bulgaria. Alongside the princes of Serbia and Montenegro from the native dynasties of Obrenović and Njegoš, their courts, set in Ottoman-style or neo-Gothic palaces, presented to western onlookers a theatrical and slightly gimcrack aspect, summarized in the notion of 'Ruritania' or 'operetta state'.* At the same time, a fairy-tale glamour began to be attached to the queens of the European monarchies, who represented

* The Ruritanian moniker derives from the name of the fictitious kingdom in Anthony Hope's romance fantasy *The Prisoner of Zenda* (1894), with its king Rudolf V. The 'operetta' statelet recalls the statelet of Pontevedro in Léhar's *Die Lustige Witwe* (1905), with its grand-duchess Hanna Glawari. Other such fictitious Balkan monarchs are General Antonio Molara of Laurania in *Savrola* (1900) by none other than young Winston Churchill; Theodosius II in Marcel Proust's *A l'ombre des jeunes filles en fleurs* (1914/1919); and Muskar XII of Syldavia in Hergé's Tintin album *Le sceptre d'Ottokar* (1939). See Goldsworthy 1998 and Daly 2020.

the sentimental 'soft power' of their dynastic houses: Queen Louise of Prussia of revered memory, (young) queen Victoria, Empress Sissi, Queen Elisabeth of Romania (a poet under the pen name of Carmen Sylva, née von Wied); such soft power was also wielded by the gender-bending, extravagant Ludwig II of Bavaria.[16] The iconography of 'Disney Princesses' and the continuing appeal of sentimental monarchy kitsch derives from the twin ancestry of Grimm's fairy tales and these Romantic queens – witness the design of the castle of Disneyland, modelled after Ludwig of Bavaria's Neuschwanstein.

Underneath this Ruritanian glamour, geopolitical wars in the Balkans would continue, with Austria annexing Bosnia-Herzegovina to thwart Serbian expansionism, Bulgaria achieving independence in 1878, Greece eating progressively into Ottoman territory, and the newly independent states jostling for territory.

This continued until the very eve of the Great War. In March 1914, Prince Wilhelm of Wied mounted the wobbly throne of a newly created Principality of Albania; less than four months later, the Habsburg archduke Franz Ferdinand was shot in Sarajevo. In August, young Adolf Hitler passed the Germania monument on the Rhine as a member of the Bavarian forces deployed on the Western Front.

The Nation-State and the Unmaking of Empires

Russia's defeat by Japan in 1904 presented a similar crisis for the Russian empire to that which Austria had experienced in 1866. In 1905, Russia's autocracy was relaxed and we see a drive towards autonomy accelerate in the empire's western provinces: Finland, Estonia, Lithuania, Ukraine. Once again, achieving national autonomy was a question of opportunism, making use of the weakening of imperial power following a defeat. The final opportunity presented itself when the Russian empire collapsed into revolution in 1917, with its minority nationalities on the periphery achieving autonomy; many of them (Ukraine, Armenia, Georgia) were later eaten up by the new Bolshevik USSR, but Finland, the Baltic states and Poland maintained their independence, Poland and Lithuania immediately entering into hostilities over the city of Vilnius. At the Paris Peace conference, the American president Woodrow Wilson introduced the principle of 'national self-determination' as a cogent principle that served to dismember the vanquished Ottoman and Habsburg Empires. The nation had definitely become Something: if you were a nation, you were entitled to an autonomous state. By 1918, many provincial peripheries of Europe's empires, from Helsinki to Novi Sad and from Gdańsk to Trieste, were freed from their imperial subservience and achieved independence. Of the western minority nations, only Ireland was able to fight the battle-weary British Empire into a standoff and an uneasy compromise, which left the issue of Ulster/Northern Ireland unresolved and sparked a civil war in the newly independent Irish Free State. In France and neutral Spain, the Catalans, Basques and Bretons were left out of the Wilsonian principle of the 'self-determination of peoples'. And the application of that principle to non-European populations in the imperial peripheries and colonies was even more haphazard and ill-considered.

As Robert Gerwarth (2016) reminds us, the armistice of 11 November 1918 did not end the hostilities of that war. Not only was there the standoff between Poland and Lithuania over the city of Vilnius, there were ongoing armed conflicts in Finland, between Greece and Turkey, in Ireland, in Fiume/Rijeka (where Gabriele D'Annunzio set up the first Fascist statelet of Europe), and around irregular militias in Germany's lands and former possessions. Now Germany, Hungary and Turkey experienced their 'culture of defeat' and developed a rancorous nationalism that bitterly refused to come to terms with the indigestible truth: that the war had been lost.

1918 was the crowning achievement of many national movements in Europe. All the new nation-states of 1918–1920 benefited from the defeat of their former overlords and all of them could trace their emergence back to a nineteenth-century movement. And in all cases, that movement had begun with, and relied on, the *cultural* identity of the nation, its separate and authentic language, history and folk life as asserted in the crisis moments of Europe's empires. As a political force, nationalism from 1805 on had failed and failed again, except in a few countries such as Greece and Belgium; but it failed better every time. As an outlook, it had indoctrinated and saturated all of Europe by 1900. That outlook held that the state should ideally be based on the sovereignty of the people; that that people should ideally be bonded by a common culture; and that therefore, as people with a common culture deserved a sovereign state of their own, each state should ideally be a nation-state, embody the nation's essential identity and rest on the nation's common culture: one state (and not more than one) for each nation. The political sovereignty of the state was derived from the unpolitical, cultural identity of the nation.

Even during the high point of 1848 and in the Polish Uprisings of 1831 and 1863, the mobilizing power of nationalism was limited to relatively small insurgency units aided by street barricades in the cities. After 1848, it became increasingly clear that real mobilizing power was wielded by social reformists and revolutionaries defined by class rather than by ethnicity, and that it was the state itself that could most successfully harness national sentiment to its armies and propaganda machinery. The influence of nationalism lay, then, less in its power to overthrow the state than in the ability to convince the state of its ideals. Nationalism wielded more influence than power; it shaped the outlook, the self-image and the institutions of existing and emerging states by persuasion rather than coercion, by cultural allure rather than clout, by bestowing charisma rather than by enforcing authority.

PART II

Romancing the Nation

CHAPTER 3

Romantic Prophets
Inspired Poets Inspiring People

At the Dawn of History: Original Genius

At the core of the Enlightenment, with its firm belief in the steady, progressive rationalization of human affairs, we also encounter a new preoccupation with the past. What was it that, at the dawn of history, had sparked human civilization, or human civilizations, and launched them on their course of historical progress? Critics such as William Duff (*An Essay on Original Geniuses*, 1767) and Robert Wood (*An Essay on the Original Genius and Writings of Homer*, 1776) began to re-read Homer in search of clues, and instead found a conundrum. How could it be that, out of nothing, and without the benefit of having examples to emulate, Homer, primordial poet, could have achieved such an immediate benchmark status from which all classical standards were derived? Where did his 'original genius' come from, from whom had he learned his craft? What was there before this literary Big Bang?

In 1720s Naples, an as yet obscure Giambattista Vico had developed a model suggesting that each civilization originated with its own separate 'Big Bang'. His treatise *Scienza nuova* argued that, in a concentrated act of self-articulation, societies would burst upon the scene of world history and become civilizations by formulating, all at once, their mythology, legal system and foundational epic texts. The *Scienza nuova* was an intellectual time bomb: scarcely noticed through most of the eighteenth century, it would became all-important fifty to a hundred years after its appearance. In Vico's view, the gods of the original mythological pantheon were interchangeable with the mythologized early monarchs of those ancient epics that celebrated their heroic acts at the dawn of recorded history. The idea caught on. In Denmark, for example, the historiographer royal Peter Frederik Suhm approached early Scandinavian history in this way, tracing the descent of medieval rulers from a patriarchal ancestor Odin, raised by his descendants to the ranks of the gods; Suhm saw the Edda (and the sagas of the Edda's continuation) as the early historical documentation of the Nordic peoples.[1]

People began to realize, also, that history shows more than one 'original genius'. After Homer, there were, in modern times, Dante and Shakespeare. This emerging theory of original geniuses, readers will recognize, was a run-up to Hegel's and Carlyle's identification of the cultural hero-figure (Chapter 1). But the most important original genius to come to Europe's attention was discredited by 1800 and is now somewhat obscure: Ossian. It was Ossian who helped detonate Vico's time bomb. And it was Ossian who allowed every nation in Europe, even peripheral ones, to identify themselves as ancient civilizations, in terms of their own vernacular roots and their own ethnocultural origins.[2]

An Apparition from the Past

Around 1760, the literate public was dazzled by the rediscovery of Ossian, an original genius now retrieved from oblivion. Ossian, a fourth-century bard who had been active in Caledonia (Scotland) in the darkest Middle Ages, had remembranced the decline of his native heroic society in elegiac dirges in Gaelic (the Celtic language of the Scottish Highlands). These elegies were now scattered across dispersed manuscripts or else remembered orally, as ballads. At the behest of the Edinburgh literati, a fieldworker, James Macpherson, had gathered these scattered oral and manuscript sources and published them in English as *Fragments of Ancient Poetry Collected in the Highlands of Scotland* (1760). The impact was sensational. Macpherson was charged to inquire further, and in the course of the 1760s he offered his readers the epic cantos he had reconstructed from the fragments into which they had been broken up. The titles were *Fingal* and *Temora*. They soon came under a cloud of suspicion and were later dismissed as forgeries; but not until they had enjoyed immense fame for a while as the Northern European counterparts to the *Iliad* and the *Odyssey* and had profoundly and lastingly shaken the poetic, the aesthetic and the cultural-historical outlook of literate Europeans.

Ossian was from the outset presented to the reading public as an original genius. The classical mottos on the title pages of the 1760 collection of *Fragments of Ancient Poetry* and of the 1762 *Fingal* both highlight the role of the 'bard' as the chronicler of the heroic deeds of the nation's patriarchal ancestors, in the 'primitive' Homeric mode.*

* The mottos are taken, respectively, from Lucan's *Bellum civile* (I: 447–448) and from Virgil's *Aeneid* (I: 641–642). The Lucan motto reads in translation: 'You too, O Bards, who in your praise-songs conveyed into a distant afterlife the strong and battle-hardened deeds, you can now in safety pour forth plentiful songs'. The Virgil motto, 'Fortia facta patrum' ('the strong deeds of

Hugh Blair's *Critical Dissertation on the Poems of Ossian, the Son of Fingal* (1763) made this the dominant frame in which Ossian was read: Ossian was a voice from the 'infancy of societies', like the skaldic bards investigated by Nordic antiquaries. Blair accordingly places him in a northern Celtic/'Gothic' tradition. Thenceforth, as Blair's dissertation was prefixed to every subsequent Ossian edition, Ossian became, proverbially, the 'Homer of the North'.

This in turn led to a great fission in the self-image of European literature. Madame de Staël's summation, in her seminal *On Literature in its Relations to Social Institutions* (1800), is typical: it sees European literature as a dual tradition. One is Mediterranean, classical, rooted in ancient Greece and in the Roman empire; its mainspring is Homer. The other is northern, Romantic, rooted in Ossian. And she extends the dualism further: literature in the Mediterranean–classical tradition is temperamentally sanguine, realistically descriptive, and suited to societies with strong social conventions; whereas literature in the northern–Romantic mode is temperamentally melancholic, metaphysically contemplative, and suited to societies with a strong tradition of individualism. We seen the germ here of that temperamental dualism that later informed Thomas Mann's ethnotypes, discussed in Chapter 1: the opposition between the superficial French and the contemplative Germans. Ossian is more, then, than a literary curiosity; as a northern Homer, and as figurehead and fountainhead of a non-classical, north European tradition, he triggered a veritable paradigm shift in Europe's literary and cultural self-awareness.

Ossian is even made to look like Homer (or like an Old Testament prophet), in line with his status as a primordial poet-chronicler of the epic Olden Days. His garb from the outset is represented as a crossover between a classical toga and a biblical cloak. His long flowing beard also fits this 'hoary sage' role pattern. Indeed, Ossian's dress code has been iconographically fixed in dozens of paintings and has since then influenced the standard of how we see bards, druids and even wizards: from Merlin to Getafix, Gandalf and Professor Dumbledore. The 'original genius' iconography appears as early as the engravings that were used as vignettes

the ancestors') is a truncated version of 'and in gold are graven the doughty deeds of her [Dido's] sires, a long, long course of exploits traced through many a hero from the early dawn of the race' (Fairclough trl., Virgil 1916, 306–307). There is an unmistable political undertone in the first motto (from Lucan). Macpherson was active very shortly after the devastating 1745 rebellion, which had led to the severe repression and proscription of Highland culture; he appears to signal a hope that a new tolerance for Gaelic literature may now be forming and the bards' celebration of their ancestral glories can once again be safely presented.

Figure 3.1 Title-page vignette for James Macpherson's *Fingal* (2nd ed., 1762, engraving by Wale and Taylor). ERNiE imagebank

for the title page of *Fingal* (Figure 3.1) and for Melchiorre Cesarotti's Italian edition of the *Poesie di Ossian* (1763), itself the source for many other European translations.[3]

What is depicted in Figure 3.1 is the scene of Ossian's last elegy, the mournful culmination of a doleful series. The ageing bard, close to death, is alone on a windswept heath, with craggy mountains in the background. His harp, hung in a tree in an overt echo of Psalm 137, is set humming by the wind blowing through it. In a reverie he senses the presence of the ghosts of the past playing upon its strings with invisible fingers. He beholds the fair Malvina, daughter of Toscar, and Toscar himself, and all the other dead heroes of the past in a spectral apparition. Ossian addresses them:

> I am alone at Lutha: my voice is like the last sound of the wind, when it forsakes the woods. But Ossian shall not be long alone, he sees the mist that shall receive his ghost. He beholds the mist that shall form his robe, when he appears on his hills. … The dark wave of the lake resounds. Bends there not a tree from Mora with its branches bare? It bends, son of Alpin, in the rustling blast. My harp hangs on a blasted branch. The sound of its firings is mournful. – Does the wind touch thee, O harp, or is it some passing ghost! – It is the hand of Malvina! … The aged oak bends over the stream. It sighs with all its moss. The withered fern whistles near, and mixes, as it waves, with Ossian's hair. … The blast of the north opens thy gates, O king, and I behold thee sitting on mist, dimly gleaming in all thine arms. Thy form now is not the terror of the valiant: but like a watery

> cloud; when we see the stars behind it with their weeping eyes. … Beside the stone of Mora I shall fall asleep. The winds whistling in my grey hair, shall not waken me. – Depart on thy wings, O wind: thou canst not disturb the rest of the bard. The night is long, but his eyes are heavy; depart, thou rustling blast.[4]

This fey, spooky scene strongly affected the wig-wearing literati of the 1760s. Goethe translated this piece to include it in his *Sorrows of Young Werther* (1774), the book that is said to have triggered a wave of copycat suicides; and there are good reasons why this of all scenes was chosen to be the title-page vignette and 'brand image' for the entire work.

It is no exaggeration to say that in this fragment, we see the germ of what was to explode across Europe as the Romantic movement. The main effects of Ossian, which we will survey in what follows, were twofold: the idea of visionary inspiration; and the turn towards vernacular, nativist historicism in cultural and national consciousness. As we shall see, both of these made themselves felt, not only in literary culture ('Romanticism') and in scholarship, but also in public opinion ('Romantic nationalism').

Sublime Liminality and Visionary Inspiration

Ossian's awesome and oppressive setting is one of the strongest manifestations of a new aesthetic that had been developing in the preceding decades. People no longer appreciated only the Beautiful, the *locus amoenus*, the park-like landscapes of Tuscany with their gentle, pleasurable aspect; what was now beginning to emerge was an alternative mode of appreciating the world, one well outside the comfort zone of the Beautiful. Austere mountain ranges, thunderstorms at night, battlefields, stormy seas, dark forests and craggy coastlines – places that would be the opposite of pleasant or pleasurable, that impress and awe onlookers with their unforgiving grandeur and render them aware of their vulnerability and mortality. This 'pleasure mixed with horror' was now identified as (a neologism) the Sublime. Edmund Burke had juxtaposed the two, the Sublime and the Beautiful, in a youthful essay in 1745, and Ossian – as we can see from the fragment quoted here – laid it on with a trowel.[5] The Sublime, thus turbocharged, would dominate the aesthetics of Romanticism and would also inform the nascent genre of the Gothic. When we shiver pleasurably in our cinema seats or on our sofa at the sight of Dracula's bat-circled castle in the eerie moonlight, we are following a tradition that started in 1760.

It was not just the external setting that proved influential: it was the way in which the setting sets the scene. The sublime landscape is also *liminal* – by which I mean that we are in a shadow zone between two worlds, a threshold (for that is the Latin root meaning of *limen*) full of ambiguities both spatial and ontological. The liminality effect, too, is used unstintingly. In space, the setting is between light and darkness (moonlight at night) and between heaven and earth (a mountain top under a lowering sky). Ontologically, we are between the embodied, material world of the living and the ghostly, spectral world of the dead. And it is in this liminal situation that Ossian, himself scarcely alive any more and aware of his impending death, and in a dreamlike reverie between consciousness and unconsciousness, summons from the spirit world the presence of the dead, passing on their memories to future generations who might otherwise forget. The strongest manifestation of that communication between the living and the dead is the ghostly sound of the harp, set vibrating either by the wind or by the spectral fingers of dead heroes.

This, too, was to be a seminal influence on the slowly forming poetics of Romanticism. The Romantic poets saw themselves as highly sensitive souls, attuned to the unspoken emotive charge of the situation, intuiting it and being able to express this intuition and inspiration in words. They saw themselves, their own souls, as Aeolian harps. Hence the constantly reoccurring theme of the breeze or wind that touches the poet or is perceived through waving grass or swaying tree-boughs, and that communicates a sense of transcendence to the sympathetic poet. The word 'inspiration' is central to Romanticism, and central to that word is its Latin root, *in-spiro*, 'breathing into', a *spir*-it infused by blowing air; much as God did when breathing life and a soul into Adam shaped out of clay (Gen. 2:7). And that breeze-borne inspiration would reach the poet very often in liminal situations: on beaches, in moonlight, in mist or fog, at dusk. All that is Ossianic.[6]

Channelling the Nation

Romantic poets see themselves surrounded by mystery and darkness and use their creative intuition to 'tune in' to that. 'Humanity is surrounded by infinity, by the mystery of divinity and of the world' – that is how Ludwig Uhland begins his 1807 essay 'On the Romantic'. This tension-filled juxtaposition of the mundane and the transcendent is one of the most salient and all-pervasive characteristics of the Romantic generation of lyrical poets. Novalis had metaphorically phrased the Romantic oscillation between the humdrum and the sublime as a mathematical operation, analogous to raising a figure's exponent to a higher power by squaring it (in German: *potenzieren*, so that 4 becomes 16) or logarithmically bringing it down to its root integer (in German: *logarithmisieren*, so that 25 becomes 5). As Novalis wrote,

> Romanticizing something is to raise it to a higher power. The lower self becomes its higher self, much as we ourselves are such an exponential succession. … If I give the everyday a higher sense, give the well-known a mysterious aspect, vest the familiar with the dignity of the unfamiliar, then I romanticize it; and conversely so, when I logarithmically bring down the higher, unknown, mystical and infinite into a common expression.

The poetics of 'inspiration', both in Wordsworth's Preface to the *Lyrical Ballads* and among his German contemporaries, are well known as one of the salient features of Romanticism. Poetry (and art in general) can, in this romantic view, electrify the world, *potenzieren*; enchanting and enrapturing it, as poetry itself results from enchantment and rapturous inspiration.[7]

This constant habit of *potenzieren* is the hallmark of Romantic idealism, its tendency towards epiphany: seeing reality in terms of its underlying essential principles, its Platonic ideas. The skylark apostrophized by Shelley is not an actual bird but a manifestation of the spirit of soaring creativity: 'Hail to thee, blithe spirit! Bird thou never wert.' When Wordsworth hears a Highland reaping-woman sing, or Keats a nightingale, those songs immediately become transcendent, generalized into a spirit of enchantment far beyond the time and place of the specific setting.

Ossianic manticism feeds into a Romantic revival of Platonic idealism, manifested also in the philosophy of Hegel, which loomed large over the entire following century. Hegel's influence has been seen as politically pernicious by thinkers as different as Karl Popper (who aligns Plato, Hegel and Marx in his *The Open Society and its Enemies*, 1945) and Peter Viereck (*Metapolitics*, 1941). That alignment, while suggestive, is not unproblematic, and in any case it cannot be wholly derived from the after-effects of Ossianic poetics. Nonetheless, Ossian's poetics of visionary inspiration did leave a specific political legacy. The power Ossian ascribed, in the teeth of Enlightenment rationalism, to poetic intuition and to non-cerebral rapture survived into the nineteenth century.

The poetics of visionary and creative power gave a new collective, 'national' authority to poets, artists and those who created from visionary inspiration. Their public personas developed from what Shelley called 'the unacknowledged legislators of mankind' into figures who, having the power of being inspired, also had the power to inspire others: the prophetic voices of the nation's needs and aspirations. Victor Hugo would proclaim 'The Poet's Function' in 1840:

> Nations! Hark to the poets! Hearken the sacred dreamer!
> In your darkness, which without him would be complete,
> his brow is the only thing illumined.
> Of the future which penetrates the shadows, only he can discern
> in their dark outlines, the germ which is not yet opened.
> Though a man, he is mild as a woman. God whispers to his soul as
> to the forests and to the waves.[8]

The power to intuit the deeper meaning of things behind their appearance became a Romantic habit of epiphany. Michelet and Carlyle use it constantly. At every turn, concrete historical events or occurrences would be represented in terms of what they really stood for: the spirit of France, the principle of Liberty or Chaos. Michelet defines the French Revolution as 'the advent of Law, the resurrection of Right, the response of Justice' ('l'avènement de la Loi, la résurrection du Droit, la réaction de la Justice'). Carlyle sees 'The Great Man [as] a Force of Nature'. We also see it applied to the way people begin to see the relationship between state and nation. The state is the material expression, the nation its informing, essential quiddity.

The French Revolution had unleashed a torrent of turgid, swollen political rhetoric and grandstanding upon the world – all the new politicians grandiosely modelling themselves upon the orators and heroes of ancient history; and Napoleon himself, notoriously, carried a pocket edition of Ossian with him on his campaigns. (He also carried a lot of other stuff around with him, including a zinc bathtub, and Ossian's sonorous dirges may have been used as a night-time soporific.) When Prussia had been reduced to a French puppet state, it was the intellectuals and poets (Arndt, Fichte, the Grimm brothers, Görres) who campaigned for a national resurrection. Typically, the resurrection was initially spiritual (cultural, literary, philosophical, moral: unpolitical) and was only in the second instance state-oriented. Finally, general Gneisenau urged king Friedrich Wilhelm III him to arm his subjects, form militias, and harness the force of public opinion. Friedrich Wilhelm dismissed this as a fictitious pipe dream, 'mere poetry', at which Gneisenau retorted that poetry was an indispensable and underrated force in social relations; 'the future of the throne is based upon poetry'.[9]

That, in the event, was what ensued. In March 1813 Friedrich Wilhelm issued his manifesto *An mein Volk*, militias were formed in which the ageing philosopher Fichte and the young poet Theodor Körner volunteered, and at Leipzig in October that year the earlier defeats of Jena and Austerlitz were reversed. Napoleon, weakened by his Russian campaign, was vanquished and sent to Elba. Napoleon himself had intuited something like this, sensing the power of literature, when in 1807 he kept his implacable critic Madame de Staël banned from Paris, telling her to stick to her knitting; because in her salon, she could 'make politics by talking literature, morality, arts, anything'.[10]

Prussia's national mobilization of 1813, driven by poets and literati and accompanied by a great deal of patriotic verse, left its own 'long tail' of cultural memory.[11] It was celebrated for the next 150 years as the glorious moment of national harmony between intellectuals, monarchs and generals and the active involvement of the *Volk* in the destiny of the state. Young Theodor Körner died of his wounds; as a martyr-poet, he became a role model for all young poets who would become the saviours of their nation henceforth. A line from his poem was so memorable that it was quoted in Berlin's sports palace in 1943 when Goebbels declared total war: 'Then, *Volk*, arise, and storm, break loose!'[12]

Pre-1914, Körner had inspired poets everywhere in Europe. His biography, written by his father, was translated into many European languages; the English one (1827, dedicated to Prince Albert) was noticed especially in Ireland. Alessandro Manzoni dedicated an ode to him; Irish Romantics translated him, and Lydia Koidula adapted a play by him into Estonian. The type of the 'national poet' emerged in his wake. Many of these are now cherished canonical figures: Petőfi, Mickiewicz, Thomas Davis, even (in the European colonies of Cuba and Bengal) José Martí and Rabindranath Tagore. Poets, dealing lyrically with intimate affects, now became public figures. When Ireland's poet-critic Thomas Davis died at a young age in 1846, his fellow poet Samuel Ferguson wrote a 'Lament for Thomas Davis' (1847) that glorified him as nation-builder, sowing the seeds of a future harvest, and as the nation's prophet (foreteller, forerunner):

> Young husbandman of Erin's fruitful seed-time,
> In the fresh track of danger's plough!
> Who will walk the heavy, toilsome, perilous furrow,
> Girt with freedom's seed-sheets, now?
> Who will banish with the wholesome crop of knowledge
> The daunting weed and the bitter thorn,
> Now that thou thyself art but a seed for hopeful planting
> Against the Resurrection morn?
>
> ....

Oh, brave young men, my love, my pride, my promise,
'T is on you my hopes are set,
In manliness, in kindliness, in justice,
To make Erin a nation yet;
Self-respecting, self-relying, self-advancing –
In union or in severance, free and strong –
And if God grant this, then, under God, to Thomas Davis
Let the greater praise belong.[13]

The Voice of the Nation

Lyrical poetry (i.e. emotion-centred and driven by visionary inspiration) became a prominent vehicle for the expression and propagation of national ideals after 1800. The new lyricism was more direct and homelier in its diction than its stately eighteenth-century forerunners: Wordsworth had propagated the use of 'language really used by men' as the proper way to express a 'spontaneous overflow of powerful feeling' and had turned to the simple, oral-performative metre of the ballad (rum te-tum te-tum te-tum) much as the German poets after Goethe had discovered the simplicity of the *Lied*. This had the added advantage that such verse could be easily set to music and performed as, indeed, a ballad or a song. Many Romantic ballads and verses in fact owe their popularity not to to the printed page but to vocal performance – as we shall discuss in Chapter 9. Sentimental lyricism became chamber music for domestic use (the *Lieder* of Schubert, often setting verse by Goethe, or Thomas Moore's 'Last Rose of Summer'); while patriotic verse such as *Die Wacht am Rhein* was performed by choirs as public proclamation.

The long-standing affect of 'love of the fatherland' was a popular theme for this generation of poets. Initially it was sentimental, referring merely to the attachment to one's native place, the pangs of homesickness (or exile, or emigration), and the joy of returning after an absence. Walter Scott's 'Breathes There the Man' set the tone and became a household invocation in the course of the century.

Breathes there the man, with soul so dead,
Who never to himself hath said,
'This is my own, my native land!'
Whose heart hath ne'er within him burn'd,
As home his footsteps he hath turn'd
From wandering on a foreign strand!

(*Lay of the Last Minstrel*, Canto VI)

The idea that homesickness is a universal human affect, and that it comes naturally to people to spontaneously love their homeland, meant that an important political conclusion was being drawn from an intimate emotion. In the climate of the Revolutionary and Napoleonic Wars it gained a fresh political edge. Love of the fatherland, from being a general moral virtue, a type of social altruism, now became the stalwart defence of one's own nation against foreign threats. The poem 'England and Spain; or, Valour and Patriotism' (1808) by the seventeen-year-old Felicia Hemans is a case in point, celebrating the two anti-Napoleonic allies and the campaign in which her brother was serving. At the same time, the Romantic climate also meant that poets began to thematize the vernacular diversity of Europe's cultural geography; 'national' in this sense could refer to the local colour specific to different countries. This 'national' taste fed the success of Robert Burns in Scotland and inspired the Irish melodies of Thomas Moore. Again, the work of Felicia Hemans, dating largely from the period 1810–1835, is a good example. While some of it is English-patriotic, sometimes in the militaristic and sometimes in the moral mode, her work is equally preoccupied with evocations of the culture of her adopted fatherland of Wales, with Walter-Scott-inspired scenes from Scottish history, with philhellenic celebrations of Greece, and with appreciative solidarity poems about the admirable medieval and modern champions defending the national liberties of Switzerland, Spain and Italy. If a common denominator is to be found here, it lies in the climate of the anti-Napoleonic wars and the post-Napoleonic restoration, linking poetic feeling to the local colour of scenery and historical memories and to the liberation of the nation from tyrants (especially foreign ones). She also wrote verse in praise of Körner; and in her collected works all this was grouped together under the rubric 'national'.[14]

In Germany, Ernst Moritz Arndt used the form of the *Lied* for anti-French propagandistic purposes, militaristic rather than lyrical. Arndt was particularly successful with his song 'What is the German's Fatherland?', which in stanza after stanza asks, rhetorically, whether the German's fatherland is located here (along the Rhine), there (near the Alps), or somewhere else (the coast). The refrain answers: 'Nay! That it cannot be, the German's fatherland is greater than this.' Finally, the answer is given: it is 'wherever the German language is spoken. That is must be! That, bold German, you may call yours! That is the German's fatherland!' It became Germany's answer to 'La Marseillaise' for a while, and it was particularly popular as a choral anthem; we shall encounter it again in Chapter 6.

Figure 3.2 Frontispiece to Emile Debraux's *Chansons nationales* (1822). ERNiE imagebank

No less inspiring across Europe were the songs of Pierre Béranger, who in the restoration climate of the post-Waterloo decades kept a more populist nationalism alive in France. Like the *goguettier* Émile Debraux, his songs would recall the glorious memories of Napoleon's great victories, the moments when France stood proud and tall (Figure 3.2). These songs were written in opposition to the oppressive restoration regime of the Bourbons, which demonized the very memory of Napoleon, and both poets spent time in prison over their songs of former national glory. Arndt, too, fell under a political cloud after 1818 as the Metternich regime tightened its censorship and mistrust of 'demagogues' grew. But this only enhanced the reputation of Arndt and Béranger as stalwart and courageous defenders of their national glories against the dynastic power of autocratic monarchs.

And so the public status of poets could be semi-clandestine, rebellious or state-endorsed (establishment poets such as Tollens in Holland or Oehlenschläger in Denmark). The most 'Romantic' ones were those who were persecuted or insurrectionary activists such as the Hungarian Petőfi,

Figure 3.3 Tomb of Rosalía de Castro in the Pantheon of Illustrious Galicians, Santiago de Compostela (sculpture by Jesús Landeira, 1891). The figure offering a bouquet represents her husband, the historian Manuel Murguía. ERNiE imagebank

the Pole Mickiewicz, the Bulgarian Hristo Botev and the Ukrainian Taras Shevchenko. An in-between category included Felicia Hemans in England, Thomas Davis in Ireland, France Prešeren in Slovenia, Karel Hynek Mácha, Jan Kollár and Ľudovit Štúr in the Czech and Slovak lands, Almeida Garrett in Portugal, Jacint Verdaguer in Catalonia, Guido Gezelle in Flanders, Henrik Wergeland in Norway, Johan Ludvig Runeberg in Finland, Lydia Koidula in Estonia. The topics of their verse could range from the overtly nationalistic, with a deliberate propagandistic intent, to more lyrical effusions whose main nationalistic effect lay in their demonstration that the vernacular language could be used for serious, ambitious literary purposes. Cases in point are the long dramatic poem in Occitan, *Mirèio*, which earned its author, Frédéric Mistral, the 1904 Nobel Prize (the event depicted in Figure 10.3); and the Galician verse of Rosalía de Castro, whose tomb is shown in Figure 3.3.[15]

The Poet as Role Model

Poets themselves adopted a Romantic self-image and became Romantic-nationalist role models. Körner as a soldier-poet was celebrated as a martyr to the national cause both inside and outside Germany, but his type of role model is in fact one of several templates. Three other 'poetic stances' besides the soldier-hero-martyr poet (Petőfi, Botev) can be seen, and these may be linked to Byron, Wordsworth and Scott respectively.

Byronism was one of the most pervasive and enduring repercussions of the Romantic movement for European (and indeed global) culture. It was inspired less by Byron's actual poetry (which is often glibly satirical and if anything classicist in its orientation) than by his poems' protagonists and indeed his own self-dramatization. The Byronic hero (and Byron himself in his Byronic pose) is a solitary, morose, brooding character, virile but misanthropic, whose capacity for tender feeling has been scarred by bitter experiences. Rick, he of the eponymous café in *Casablanca* as played by Humphrey Bogart, is probably the most powerful twentieth-century embodiment of a Byronic hero. Haughtily averse to social niceties, he leads a wandering existence and stands apart from the crowd because his ideals are too lofty, his passions too intense and his manners too rough-hewn to fit into modern conventions. Heroes such as Manfred and Childe Harold are of this type, and Byron's own restless, scandal-ridden wanderings were seen as expressions of this passionate, intriguing ('Romantic') character. What appealed especially was that in his anti-bourgeois nonconformism, Byron evinced sympathy for the outlaws and warlords of harsher, non-civic societies and adhered to an honour-and-shame ethos that was disappearing in the modernization process. Thus Byronism glorified the lawless peripheries of Europe, from the Balkans to the Andalusia of Mérimée's *Carmen*, and his poetry became the great beacon for a solidarity between the ethos of the cynically Romantic rebel-poet (emulated by the likes of Pushkin, Heine and Prešeren) and the emerging national cultures in Europe's late-imperial borderlands with their outlaws and brigands ('klephts' in Greek, 'hajduks' in the Slavic languages). This function was hugely strengthened, of course, by Byron's active philhellenism and his death in Greece (1824) as a supporter of the anti-Ottoman insurrection there.[16]

The Wordsworthian stance is that of the inspirational retreat into the idyll of the countryside and proximity to nature. This idyllic lyricism gives a voice to the rural peasantry and creates a conduit from spontaneous folk art into high literature. In national movements whose language was just emerging from the stigmatized register of mere peasant *patois* into the ambitions of a literate, public-sphere status, such poetry could be a nationalist inspiration (e.g. the Galician verse of Rosalía de Castro or, in the Catalan language, verse by Verdaguer and Teodor Llorente). One lyrical trope that is common to a number of Romantic poets from subaltern cultural communities is that the lost beloved is deified ('potenziert') into an inspiring muse-figure or even into a personification of the yearned-for nation: thus with Nikoloz Baratashvili's conflation of Princess Dadiani and his subjected Georgian homeland, or with Jan Kollár's *Slavy Dcera* ('Daughter of Slava', 1824), Auguste Brizeux's Breton *Marie* (1832) and (through the Kathleen Ní Houlihan trope) W. B. Yeats's idolatry of the unattainable Maud Gonne.

Walter Scott brought into circulation the role model of the wandering minstrel voicing cultural memories, especially through his popular poem 'Lay of the Last Minstrel'. It appeared in 1805, just when the cult of Ossian as a 'bard' had died out, and provided an alternative Romantic model in its stead (see Chapter 7). It presents an emotional, incident-rich ('Romantic') tale of olden days; the frame-setting, however, is that of an Ossianic poet who has outlived the glories of his former days but who can awaken old tales through his rapt inspiration, taking his audience into the fictional world of long-vanished deeds and passions. This, too, was a role model; and the verse of Adam Oehlenschläger and Esaias Tegnér (in Denmark and Sweden) and the cult of 'troubadours' and 'bards' singing of the nation's glorious, colourful past cannot be understood without Scott's post-Ossianic prototype. It also explains why the historical narrative poem maintained great popularity alongside the new genre of the historical novel.[17]

Thus the register of the Romantic poet is situated between the soldier and the outlaw (Körner and Byron), between the aristocratic past and the contemporary peasant (Scott and Wordsworth). In all cases, the poet enjoys a privileged status as the voice of their nation (or of that nation's aspirations) and as having, through the power of inspiration, an intuitive understanding of the transcendent principles informing contemporary affairs.

Imagined, Embodied and Affective Communities

Benedict Anderson's classic *Imagined Communities* (1983) has given us a powerful template aligning the rise of nationalism (or rather, of the 'imagined community' self-defining as a nation) with that of 'print capitalism': individuals would, thanks to modern mass-distributed novels and periodicals, become amalgamated into a readership, all readers at the same moment experiencing and being involved in events and narratives that lay far outside their domestic ken. The point stands, but we can add to it. Ann Rigney has shown how mass festivities in numerous Scottish towns around the centenary of Robert Burns (1859) created a sense of national cohesion that was not mediated over long distances by the distribution of printed matter but was experienced in a direct physical co-presence of people: alongside the 'imagined community' there was also the 'embodied community', and other studies of the festive culture of the nineteenth-century confirm this sense that 'embodied' togetherness was as important as its virtual, imagined counterpart. This embodied co-presence specifically appears to have involved the oral or choral performance of lyrical poetry, and often celebrated poets as the common focus of the crowd. The poet could be a cherished historical one, as in the commemorative festivals celebrating Shakespeare, Camões, Dante, Pushkin, Petrarch – the 'original geniuses' of their countries' literary tradition. Or else, specifically in subaltern nations, much more recent memories could be evoked of recent champions of their nation's literacy and literature: Conscience in Flanders, Mickiewicz in Poland (the statues erected in his honour were torn down by the Nazis and re-erected after the war), Mácha in Prague, Prešeren in Slovenia, Wergeland in Norway, Moore in Ireland, and Schiller in nineteenth-century Germany. In each case, the statues rendered the revered poet a firm presence in the city's streetscape; but the statue was also a venue for commemorative gatherings, proclamations, cantatas, wreath-layings. That praxis of embodied community-gathering still continues: I saw in pre-COVID Rome how the many Filipino and Filipina domestic workers in that city would gather convivially, on their free Saturday evenings, around the statue of the national hero José Rizal on Piazza Manila, often placing flowers there as a sign of affection and connection. And in the nineteenth century, when freedom of association was not yet the self-evident civil right it is nowadays, the funerals of poets would provide a legitimate occasion for mass demonstrations asserting the nation's common identity around a shared lyrical core. Such occasions were often redolent with allegorical pathos. At the funeral of the Czech activist writer Karel Havliček Borovský, the poet Božena Němcová laid a wreath in (or on) his coffin; in popular retellings of this event, that wreath was soon mythologized into a crown of thorns, as a mute protest at the dead poet's prosecution by the Habsburg authorities.[18]

Such gatherings, and the singing of cherished songs and anthems on public occasions, were a powerful manifestation of a type of literature that did not owe its social outreach to 'print capitalism' but that, as Romantic lyric, spoke directly, without mediation, from heart to heart and was performatively reactivated from generation to generation. 'La Marseillaise' and 'Die Wacht am Rhein' were the tips not of an iceberg but of a sea of heaving and crunching pack ice.

CHAPTER 4

Manuscripts Found in the Attic

Antiquaries and the Literary Past

Ossian's appeal to the late-Enlightenment reading public lay not only in his uncanny settings and spooky scenes but also in the remarkable tale of his retrieval: snatched from oblivion in a remote corner of the Old World, where his memory lingered among balladeering Highlanders in desolate mountain ranges and in almost-illegible manuscripts. The mission of James Macpherson seems almost like an Indiana-Jones-style quest for lost treasures. A difference between the two is that the fictitious Indiana Jones is an archaeologist, a scholarly specialism that did not yet exist in Macpherson's day. Those who investigated antiquities were called antiquaries, and they had a wide remit: 'antiquities' included material remains (be they from the medieval, the classical or the prehistoric past) and whatever could be found in ancient manuscripts, be they ballads, genealogies, law texts or chronicles. Macpherson was an innovator in that he searched for antique remains in living oral poetry.[1]

Another difference is that antiquaries had no academic or professional standards to go by. They were learned, dedicated amateurs, usually with a steady independent income, and although there were some fledgling associations (a Society of Antiquaries was established in London in 1707 and another one in Edinburgh in 1780) they worked largely on their own and on whatever material they happened to come across. They were also often carried away by their enthusiasm: their interpretations of the past were, more often than not, over the top, unchecked by sceptical reservations or by factual background knowledge. They had no qualms about tracing the origin of the Irish and Scottish Celts back to Carthaginians or Phoenicians. In the eighteenth century, before solid comparative linguistics, antiquaries frantically tried to read Gaelic with the help of Greek and Hebrew dictionaries. In his novel *The Antiquary* (1816) Walter Scott drew the portrait of such an amateur scholar of the Macpherson generation with affectionate irony; fondly, because Scott was himself an antiquary at one remove. He worked on ancient ballads and minstrelsy, on Scottish legal and social history, on the country's ancient manners and customs, and he hoarded material remains of the past at his museum-mansion at Abbotsford. And he was a proud, card-carrying member of the Scottish Society of Antiquaries. But Scott's *Antiquary* also signalled that this type of antiquarianism was a thing of the past. In the next century, the investigation of the past would split up into the scholarly disciplines of archaeology, philology, and the studies of folklore and mythology. The undisciplined imagination with which antiquaries had approached the past was no longer suitable to these new, respectably academic offshoots, and it became the characteristic feature of a Romantic literary genre of which Scott was the first and foremost practitioner: the historical novel (on which, see Chapter 7).[2]

Cesarotti's Italian edition of Ossian carried, besides the frontispiece that we have seen in the previous chapter (Figure 3.1), another vignette on its title page (Figure 4.1). It shows a dapper man, obviously an 'amateur gentleman' rather than a menial, wearing a hat – probably against the sun, because the surroundings look more Italian than Highland Scottish. He is digging with a spade around some half-buried objects; a marble slab next to him carries a quotation from Horace (Epistles I.6:24–25), 'Whatever lies buried below ground, time will bring to light'. The gentleman is clearly an archaeologist, and his work is to unearth the remains of the past. That is what was famously going on in Cesarotti's Italy at the time: the ruins of Pompeii were being uncovered in these very decades, and caused a sensation. Word had spread to Germany as a result of J. J. Winckelmann's letters 'on the discoveries at Herculaneum' published in 1762 and 1764.* This is an altogether different frame for reading Ossian from the 'ghosts on a moonlit mountain top'. Ossian was an antiquarian sensation.

The juxtaposition of Ossian with Homer, which we noticed in Chapter 3, is not just a typological one (both were sublime original geniuses relating the heroism of the ancestors in epic form) but also a historical one. With Ossian, Scotland (and, by extension, Northern Europe in general) is

* Winckelmann 2011. The development of a new archaeology in the Romantic decades after the Pompeii excavations has been charted for France by Blix (2008), who traces a dual impact: on the one hand a more consciously scientific modus operandi (in line with Winckelmann's critique of the treasure-hunting methods of the 1760s), on the other hand an exotic-historicist fascination with the resurgence of lost memories and with the historical strangeness of the material brought to light. As we shall see in this chapter, a similar technical/Romantic duality affected philology, which as another successor discipline to old school antiquarianism was a scholarly sibling of archaeology: one oriented towards texts, the other towards material artefacts. For subsequent cross-currents between archaeology and nationalism: Diaz-Andreu & Champion 1996 and e-rn.ie/archaeology.

Figure 4.1 Title-page vignette for Melchiorre Cesarotti's Italian version of Ossian (1763). National Library of Scotland

rediscovering its ancestral antiquity. Until then, classical and biblical antiquity had held the monopoly on Europe's most ancient cultural memories; that monopoly was now broken. The impact of Ossian was that Northern Europe could opt out of this Mediterranean, biblical/classical ancestral antiquity and look back on its own cultural roots. That pattern was reinforced by the fact that at the same time Nordic antiquities, rooted in the Edda and the *Heimskringla*, were being reactivated by Scandinavian antiquaries. The result was that for a while, the 'Gothic' (Scandinavian) and 'Celtic' antiquities of Northern Europe were being lumped together; the trend had been set by Paul-Henri Mallet's *Monuments de la mythologie et de la poésie des Celtes, et particulièrement des anciens Scandinaves* (1756). By that time, the Swiss antiquaries Bodmer and Breitinger had also retrieved a manuscript of the *Nibelungenlied*, which they presented to the reading public as 'Chriemhild's Revenge' (*Chriemhilden Rache*), commenting that, although it fell short of the Aristotelian rules for tragedy, it could stand, as an epic poem, beside the pre-Aristotelian epic poet Homer.[3]

All this dealt a huge blow to the still prevalent classicism of the time. Until then, the cultural rearview mirror had reached back to the periods of humanism and the Renaissance and then, bypassing the dark and scantily known Middle Ages, had focused on the biblical and classical periods – the recourse to which had allowed those humanists and their Renaissance successors to emerge from Europe's medieval benightedness. Now, however, Northern Europe's vernacular, non-classical ancestry could be traced back further along native lines towards an origin, and an original genius, of their own. And the Middle Ages themselves became something more than a centuries-long night-time of impenetrable barbarism: the Middle Ages now became a literary Pompeii, a continuum for the nation's buried cultural heritage, with chivalric and epic heroes such as King Arthur and Siegfried the Dragon-Slayer appearing in a favourable, prestigious light. These philological discoveries not only inspired the medievalism of the Romantic century but also necessitated a new, national form of literary history writing. Literary history had to be rewritten and to accommodate in its opening chapters these newly discovered materials: ancient, heroic, vernacular.[4]

Cesarotti himself was quite sensitive to this 'shock of the old'. In his annotations to Ossian and his Homer translations, he instilled a great many of Vico's theories of cultural history, notably that each civilization articulates its cultural self-awareness, and marks its emergence into history, in a primordial Big Bang where laws, epic-heroic poems and religious myths are almost undifferentiated. These notions in turn found their way into the German translation of Ossian (which followed the Italian version rather than Macpherson's English one). We may even surmise that it is through the intermediary stepping-stone of Cesarotti's Ossian that Vico's ideas began to spread in the Republic of Learning.[5]

Cesarotti's Ossian presentation triggered a veritable paradigm shift in European literary history, which outlasted the brief fame of Ossian himself. It triggered a form of literary archaeology (digging around to see what submerged things could be brought to the light of day). The treasures found by Macpherson led to a gold rush; and the Klondike of that literary gold rush were libraries and archives – which, as it happened, were now beginning to make their riches publicly available.

Archaeology in the Archives

Libraries are like sponges: they soak up available books and texts circulating in the marketplace, and that ingestion is by and large a one-way process. Libraries siphon off the marketplace: they are predicated on acquiring and keeping stuff. Over the decades and centuries – as institutions, libraries can be very long-lived – dispersed materials drift from private ownership into library collections. The oldest of these are monastic libraries and court libraries, with college/university and municipal libraries following in the later Middle Ages. The public had only limited access to these.

But periodically, sponges get squeezed, and then their accumulated storage either trickles out or gushes out profusely. Sometimes, libraries are opened to the public: Florence's Biblioteca Laurentina was opened to scholars in 1571, and Louis XIV opened the Bibliothèque du roi to the public in 1692. A major squeeze occurred with Henry VIII's dissolution of the monasteries. The monastic libraries of medieval England were plundered by the king's officials, and a great number of ancient manuscripts circulated among private owners (John Leland, William Camden, Matthew Parker, Lawrence Nowell, Robert Cotton) before finally settling down, once again, in other libraries: Matthew Parker's books became the library of Corpus Christi College, Cambridge, and Robert Cotton's library, donated to the nation in 1700, was merged with the Sloane, Harley and Royal libraries to form the British Museum's library in 1757. It was here that an inquisitive Danish scholar, Grímur Jónsson Thorkelin, located the sole surviving copy of the *Beowulf* epic in 1786–1787. A first edition was published in Copenhagen in 1815. Literary archaeology was beginning to bring long-lost manuscripts back to the light of day.

At precisely this time, a great library squeeze was underway in Europe. As in Henry VIII's day, it targeted, at least initially, monastic libraries. The process began with the suspension of the Jesuit order in the 1770s. In Lisbon, this meant that the Jesuitical Ajuda library was transferred to a new, state-run teaching institution; and it was here that the oldest surviving medieval manuscript of vernacular love songs came to light: the *Cancioneiro da Ajuda*. A first edition was published in Paris in 1823.

After the Jesuits, under Emperor Joseph II, the libraries of contemplative orders such as the Benedictines were targeted; then came the nationalization, by the authorities of the French Republic, of monastic and noble libraries in France; and then came the libraries, in the German lands, of those church establishments that were annexed by Napoleon or (in the great Reich reshuffle of 1803) were placed under the control of temporal lords.* In France, the Bibliothèque de l'Arsenal was formed in Paris, incorporating many former monastic libraries from the metropolitan area, and the former Bibliothèque du roi and Bibliothèque mazarine became public research institutes. In Germany, the huge libraries and archives of formerly self-governing ecclesiastical establishments were transferred to the court libraries of Vienna, Munich and Stuttgart, and as part of that transfer they were inventorized and recatalogued. The Munich court library swelled to become one of the largest in Europe, a process mirrored at slightly smaller

* The Habsburg emperor had been forced to acquiesce to the French annexation of all lands of the Holy Roman Empire west of the Rhine (1797). The lords of those lands, formally liegemen of the emperor, had to be recompensed. This was achieved in 1803 by a huge reshuffle, which assigned to these claimants many free cities or lordships that until then had been fiefs held directly by the emperor ('Reich-immediate'). They were, as a result, 'mediatized': no longer immediately under the Empire, but with a liegelord as a new interposed, intermediate layer between the lordship and the Empire, giving orders and collecting taxes. Many of these Reich-immediate fiefs had been ecclesiastical lordships; in that case, the phraseology was that they were 'secularized' rather than 'mediatized'. The reshuffle was a fatal blow to the Burkean sense (see Chapter 2) of the age-old, awe-inspiring immutability of the Reich, which was in fact disbanded shortly after.

scale at the Württemberg Library in Stuttgart. Finally, when Napoleon annexed the Papal States in 1808, even the mother of all libraries at the Vatican was placed under the bureaucratic management of French civil servants. And men of letters descended in great numbers on these newly accessible hoards, made many discoveries and laid the basis for many a scholarly career. In Munich, soon to become the capital of a Napoleon-created kingdom, the court librarian Johann Christoph von Aretin encountered, with some wistfulness, an old document about Charlemagne in the mediatized library of Freising Abbey. He published it in 1803 with a nostalgic preface linking, quite aptly, the simultaneous overhaul of ancient libraries and overthrowing of ancient monarchies.

> It is now a thousand years ago that Charlemagne founded the German empire. I alert my readers to this fact, not to draw their attention to the remarkable changeability of things during that timespan, or to make them ponder the recent events which have appeared to threaten that very empire with an overthrow after its millennial existence; rather, I would mark a literary jubilee of that great occurrence, and an occasion presented itself when I could consult a remarkable ancient German manuscript in the most ancient abbey of Weihenstephan near Freising, and which with all the literary treasures of the Bavarian monasteries has been lodged in the Munich court library.[6]

One of the biggest finds was in Rome. The Vatican library, now under Napoleonic administration, was inventorized by a librarian called Gloeckle – notorious for his drunkenness and known in Rome as *il porco tedesco* – together with the literary historian J. J. Görres; what they found was the old collection of the Palatinate counts on the Rhine, which had been taken from Heidelberg in 1622 as war booty and presented to the pope. This 'Biblioteca palatina' turned out to be packed with long-lost classics from medieval German literature: chivalric romances, *Tristan*, *Reynard the Fox*, *Lohengrin* (of which Görres himself would bring out an edition in 1813) and much besides. Görres sent an open letter to the *Heidelbergische Jahrbücher der Literatur* in 1812, hoping to raise subscriptions for a printed edition of all these classics. Two centuries later we can still sense the breathless excitement of these thrilled bookworms.[7]

The European Republic of Philology

When we look at the text editions that came out between 1800 and 1840, we see that they include practically all the 'classics' that now feature in the opening chapters of literary history books. Besides the Portuguese *cancioneiros*, *Reynard*, *Beowulf*, the *Nibelungenlied* and *Lohengrin*, the list includes the French *Chanson de Roland* (discovered in the mid-1830s in the Bodleian library by Francisque Michel), the Russian/Ukrainian *Lay of Prince Igor's Campaign*, the Dutch *Legend of Saint Servatius*, the Irish *Annals of the Four Masters* and Deirdre/Cuchulain tales, and many others. Literary histories were, quite literally, being rewritten and traced back to their vernacular and tribal origins rather than to classical antiquity.

Friedrich Schlegel gave a name to the scholars who were doing this work. Rejecting the speculative waywardness of the old-school antiquaries, he called for a systematic comparative-historical method, and in his diaries began to call this line of work *philology*. In doing so he revived an old Latin word for 'erudite bookworm', which, however, had been given a trenchant new importance in Vico's *Scienza nuova*. There, Vico had compared two forms of knowledge production, one dealing with the nature of things and the other with the meaning of things. The former Vico called philosophy, the latter *philologia*. The underlying meaning of that term was a preoccupation with *logos*, the language-empowered faculty of human cogitation. Schlegel applied this in his Viennese lectures on ancient and modern literature (1812, published 1815). What makes humans different from animals, Schlegel argues, is language (with each human society developing their own language: see Chapter 6). The primary function of language, besides communication, is commemoration: the articulation of memories and their formulation into something that is more than a fleeting state of mind. Once these memories take the form of crystallized narratives recalling important events and figures from a past that is longer than a human lifespan ago, such a society has a culture: it is no longer a band of grunting cavepeople but on its way to becoming a civilization. The primal role of literature, for Schlegel, is to encapsulate collective (he calls them 'national') memories.

> What appears important above all else for a nation's development and indeed its spiritual existence is that a people should have great national memories, which mostly reach back into the dark times of its first origins, and which it is the great task of literature to maintain and to celebrate. Such national memories, the finest inheritance that a people can boast, offer advantages that cannot be matched by anything else. When a people finds itself exalted and ennobled in their feelings by their possession of such a great past, of such memories from ancient days, in short: of such a poetry, we must admit their higher standing in our esteem. … Remarkable deeds, great and fateful events do not suffice in themselves to gain our admiration and to sway the judgement of posterity. A nation's value depends on its clear awareness of its deeds and destinies. This self-awareness of a nation, as articulated in contemplative and descriptive works, is its history.[8]

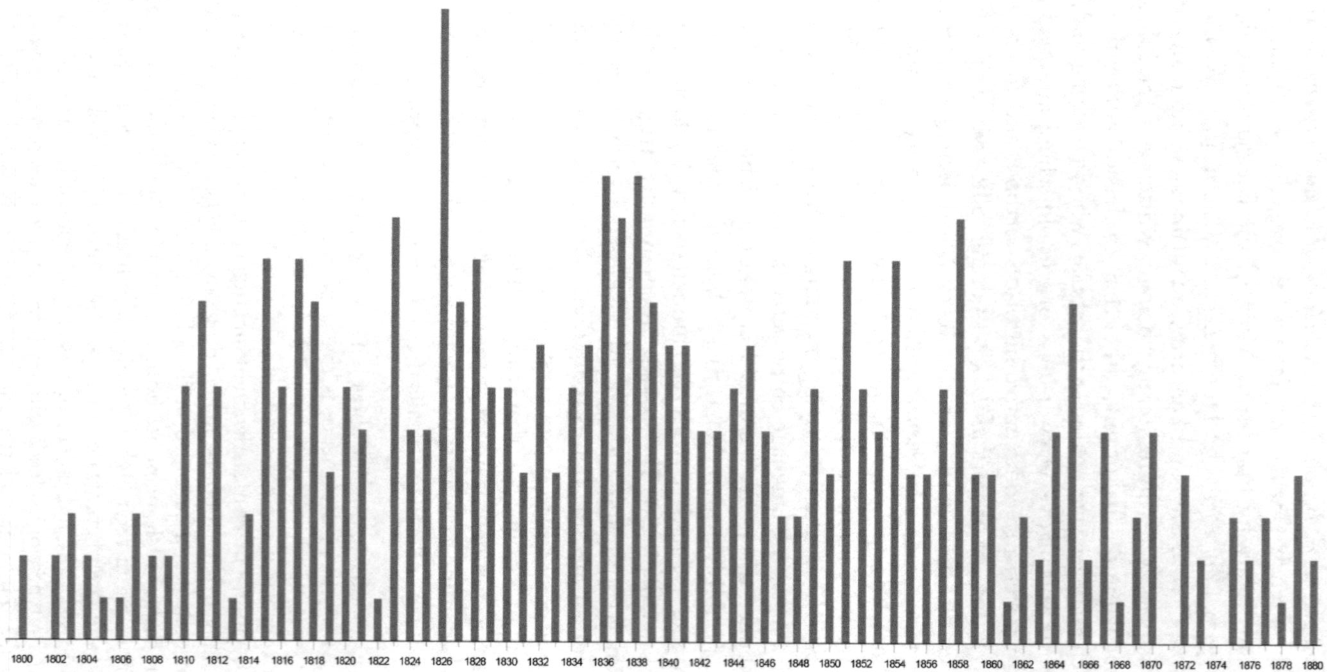

Figure 4.2 A timeline of 540 nineteenth-century text editions (e-rn.ie/editions).

Schlegel in fact updates Vico for the new century. He combines the textual investigation of ancient literary history with a sense of comparative historical linguistics and with what he calls 'Völkergeschichte'; as such, he is also one of the great harbingers of a new philology, which takes over from the antiquaries of the preceding generations.[9]

The takeover was effected by a wave of re-editions of vernacular classics. The *Encyclopedia of Romantic Nationalism in Europe* lists some 500 editions of ancient texts over the century,* with productivity peaks in the 1820s, the late 1830s and the 1850s (Figure 4.2). Productivity after 1860 consists mainly of re-editions of the initial harvest and of belated text discoveries in comparatively poorly archived cultural communities.

The striking thing about this rediscovery of nations' vernacular roots was that, while it served to set off these nations against each other as each having their own, distinct cultural mainsprings, it was an almost pan-European enterprise. It was not just that German libraries yielded medieval texts to local (German) philologists, while French and Portuguese ones proved, in separate but parallel developments, fertile working grounds for their local users; far from it. Those users travelled to libraries outside their own countries (as we have encountered, or will in the following pages: Thorkelin in the British Museum, Michel in the Bodleian, Grimm in Paris, Görres in Rome, and Hoffmann von Fallersleben in Vienna and Valenciennes). Their rediscoveries were part of a development that all of them in their different countries recognized as a joint, multinational concern. The contacts between them, whether amicable or competitive, were intense, and they were keenly aware of each other's work. The epistolary network of Jacob Grimm (13,000 letters, Figure 4.3) casts a dense, far-flung web over all of Europe; it can be confidently said that it enmeshes everyone involved in such enterprises, if not directly, then at most at two degrees of separation. Anyone who was active in philology in the nineteenth century exchanged letters with Grimm or, failing that, with someone else who did.[10]

The intensity and spread of this network is deeply meaningful for our understanding of Europe as a unified intellectual space. The philologists were the last representatives of the old Europe-wide Republic of Learning. The modernization of the university system, with humanities faculties and historical and philological departments, was a development that took place

* The new generation of textual scholars applied the expertise of classical philology to vernacular, mostly medieval texts. An important conduit in transferring the expertise of the classical philologists on to the medieval source material of the new philologists was Karl Lachmann, an eminent classicist and long-standing ally of Jacob Grimm. He prepared editions of medieval German as well as ancient Latin texts.

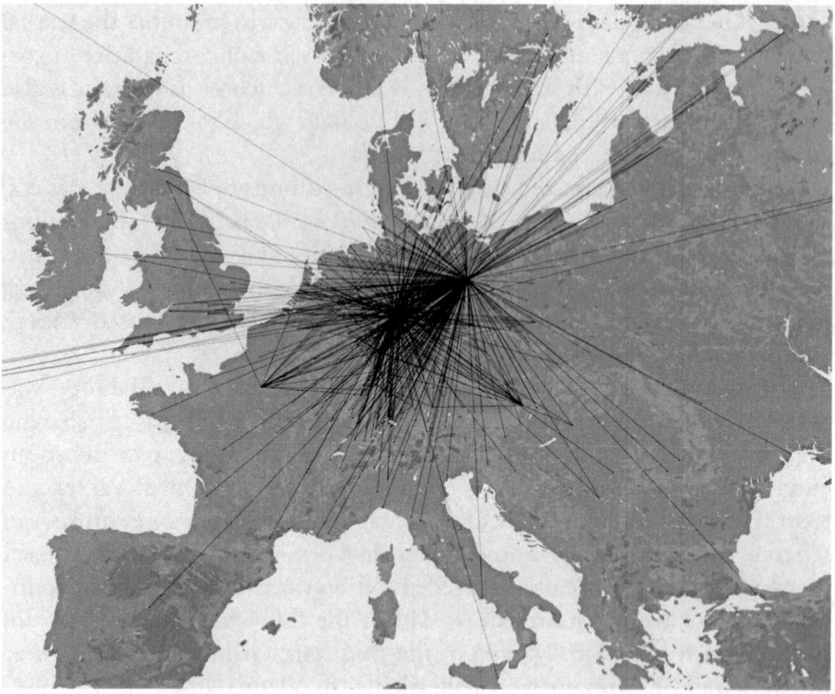

Figure 4.3 The correspondence network of Jacob Grimm (e-rn.ie/grimmnetwork).

all over Europe; so was the establishment of national academies, libraries and archives, along with the professionalization of whose who worked in all those new types of institutions. And while those working environments might be compartmentalized by state, the people working in them were in mutual contact, constantly exchanging information, aware of each other's work. The fact that so many agents in a 'cultivation of culture' crop up in parallel forms in different countries is, then, not a matter of happenstance or parallel responses to similar circumstances: they are the systemic, Europe-wide manifestation of a transnational communicative network and a homogeneous intellectual space. Different though Europe's states were in their governance and in their socio-economic states of development, the philologists and scholars, from Anders Sjögren in St Petersburg to Alexandre Herculano in Lisbon, were part of a single intellectual continuum.

The 'cultivation of culture', of which this new type of knowledge production forms part, is itself an important aspect of 'Phase A' of national movements as theorized by Miroslav Hroch: the phase of national consciousness-raising. The later phases (B and C) of those national movements – social demands and political activism – may pan out differently according to the local conditions of the various European societies, regions and countries. But unlike those later phases, Phase A is very strongly transnational. Musical, literary and artistic fashions spread, and so does scholarship and knowledge production. Ossian, Herder, Byron, Scott, Grimm: the influence of these names reaches far beyond their country of origin or their place of work. Nothing in this cultivation of culture takes place in national isolation.[11]

Literary Histories, National Identity

Ironically, the editions of national classics, supported though they were by a pan-European intellectual vogue, had a deeply nationalizing effect on their readership. Culture and literature were now seen as historical traditions carried, specifically, by the nation over the centuries. In some instances the nation-building effect was announced in so many words as a deliberate intent at the forefront of the philologists' mind. The most famous example is the preface given by Friedrich Heinrich von der Hagen to his edition of the *Nibelungenlied* (1807). Von der Hagen was evidently trying to come to terms with a crisis: the abolition of the Holy Roman Empire and the Napoleonic hegemony over the German lands.

> [I]n present-day Germany, torn by destructive tempests, the love of the language and literature of our virtuous ancestors is alive and active, and it seems as if people seek in the past and in its poetry what is so grievously declining today. And this need for comfort is the last remaining sign of the imperishable German character, which, raised above all servility, will sooner or later always break foreign bonds and, wiser and chastened, will retrieve its inherited nature and liberty.
>
> ...Nothing can afford a German heart more comfort and true edification than the most immortal of all heroic lays, which from long oblivion re-emerges in vital and rejuvenated form: the song of the Nibelungs, undoubtedly one of the greatest and most admirable works of all periods and nations, grown and matured wholly from German life and sensibility, and pre-eminent for its sublime perfection among the admirable remains of our long-forgotten national poetry – comparable to the colossal edifice of Erwin von Steinach [i.e. Strasbourg Cathedral]. No other lay can so move and grip a patriotic heart, delight and fortify it.

Twenty-five years later, the preface of Jan Frans Willems's edition of the Flemish Reynard tale used the occasion to upbraid his countrymen for their adoption of French culture:

> Our Flemish Reynard surpasses all other poems on that theme. ... in a word, it is by far the best poem (Dante's *Divina commedia* excepted) which has come down to us from the Middle Ages. And it is a Belgian one! And the Belgians know it not! And the editing of it was left to Germans! ... May this, my edition of the more ancient part of *Reynard the Fox*, contribute to the revival of our once-cherished language, at a time when our country is being inundated by French trash![12]

Ancient literature is now becoming a national heirloom, and an argument in the imperative to maintain the nation's cultural continuity. France, in its 'culture of defeat' after 1871, gives the most heightened examples of this nationalization of the literary heritage. The *Chanson de Roland*, first published in the 1830s, gained fresh national symbolism in the traumatic events of 1870–1871. Much as Von der Hagen in 1807 had taken comfort from the death-defying heroism of the Nibelungen heroes, so too in 1870 Léon Gautier turned to the stalwart Roland, killed on the medieval battlefield of Roncesvalles while covering the army's retreat to his 'douce France'. Gautier wrote his preface

> wrapped up in sadness and with tears in my eyes, during the siege of Paris, in those lugubrious hours when we might have thought that France was in its death-throes. And so what is the *Roland*? It is the tale of a great defeat for France, from which France has risen gloriously and which has been fully atoned for. What could be more topical? The defeat so far is the only part we have lived through, but this Roncesvalles of the nineteenth century has its own glory ... It cannot be, really, that she should die, that France of the *Chanson de Roland*, which is still our France ... where were they, those boastful invaders, when our *Chanson* was written? They roamed in savage bands through the gloom of nameless forests; all they knew was how to plunder and kill.

As Gautier wrote his preface, and during the siege of Paris, Charles Lenient taught a lecture course at the Sorbonne on 'La poésie patriotique en France', and Gaston Paris lectured at the Collège de France on '*La Chanson de Roland* et la nationalité française'.[13] When in 1875 Gaston Paris and his father Paulin Paris founded the Ancient French Texts Society, its philological aims were also presented as a 'national enterprise':

> The *Société des anciens textes français* is a national enterprise ... it needs the support of all those who understand the importance of tradition, all those who realize that the strongest bond keeping a nation together is piety towards our ancestors, all those who are vigilant about the intellectual and scientific standing of our country amidst other peoples; all those who love, throughout all the centuries of its history, that *douce France* for which one could already die such a good death at Roncesvalles.[14]

'Roncesvalles' echoes through the period of French revanchism, 1871–1914, much as *Nibelungentreue* would haunt German history in the twentieth century. If we want to understand what made Churchill and Stalin commission cinematic recalls of Henry V and Alexander Nevsky, here are the origins of that national historicism.

Entangled Roots

As the new philologists gradually professionalized into state-salaried archivists, librarians and professors (of history, philology, archaeology), they became civil servants of the state. The antiquaries had been gentlemen of leisure; the new professionals acquired not only a professional, academic work ethos but also a sense that their knowledge production was a service to the nation. When, in 1846 and 1847, Jacob Grimm called together two countrywide congresses of *Germanisten* (German philologists, including legal and cultural historians), the gathering showed how the new post-antiquarian university disciplines were now positioning themselves as a useful helpmeet to the nation's identity. They manifested this with the same patriotic arguments that we have encountered in the later manifesto of the Society of Ancient French Texts: the importance of tradition and of ancestral piety, and the vigilant safeguarding of one's country's intellectual and scientific standing amidst other peoples. Concretely, the *Germanisten* proceedings revolved around an assertion that Schleswig-Holstein had always been, and should once again become, German; a call for the ancient Germanic liberty of trial by jury (an oblique dig at arbitrary monarchical government); and the need for a proper German dictionary. The 1846 meeting was held in St Paul's church, Frankfurt; two years later, no fewer than thirty-one of the participating *Germanisten* would meet again in the same spot, this time as delegates of the 1848 Frankfurt National Assembly.[15]

Germany was in the forefront of the new philology, establishing benchmarks for all of Europe in many fields. The presiding genius was Jacob Grimm, together with his (slightly more withdrawn and amiable) brother Wilhelm. Nowadays known mainly as the collectors of fairy tales (*Kinder- und Hausmärchen*, literally 'Wonder Tales for Children and the Household', 1812–1815), the Grimms were also the instigators of the huge lexicographical enterprise of the 'German Dictionary' (*Deutsches Wörterbuch*, 1852–1961) and collectors of German legends (*Deutsche Sagen*, 1816–1818). Jacob himself edited ancient German texts and legal customs, extrapolating from the latter a generalized ethnography of public mores and their enforcement ('German Legal Antiquities', *Deutsche Rechtsaltertümer*, 1828); we will encounter, further on, his German mythology and his history of the German language and its dialects (*Geschichte der deutschen Sprache*, 1848). The breadth of these interests recalls the antiquarians of yore, and indeed Grimm could be prone to flights of fancy in interpreting his material; but his data management was thorough and rigidly systematic. No amateur he: he was a legal scholar by training and had been a librarian in his first employment. That he was firmly part of the new comparative-historical paradigm is manifested triumphantly in his comparative grammar of the Germanic languages, the *Deutsche Grammatik* (1824–1836), in which he went as far as formulating linguistic 'laws' (regularities in historical consonantal shifts*). It was the first time such 'laws'/regularities had been observed in human culture rather than inanimate nature. Among fellow philologists, this gave Grimm a scientific stature comparable only to that of Newton. In addition, he was involved in momentous political crisis moments. When Jacob and Wilhelm were dismissed as professors at Göttingen University in 1837 for refusing to acquiesce in the arbitrary autocracy of the incoming King of Hanover, they became martyrs to the cause of academic freedom, and Jacob was a delegate in the Frankfurt National Assembly of 1848.[16]

The Grimm-style German 'new philology' inspired scholars in Spain and Portugal (Hermann Böhl de Faber and Carolina Michaëlis de Vasconcellos). At Oxford, the Anglo-Saxonist Kemble and the Sanskritist Max Müller were Grimm adepts. Even French philology in France was inspired deeply by Grimm's pupil Friedrich Diez, to the point that the manifesto of the Ancient French Texts Society complained of 'Germany being the European country where ancient French texts are printed most'.[17]

Also, Jan Frans Willems invoked Grimm when he chided Belgium for its neglect of its Flemish-language roots. Indeed, the 'Flemish Movement' – one of Europe's best-documented national movements – leaned heavily on German intellectual aid in its cultural insurgency against the dominance of French. A stalwart supporter of the Flemish cause was the poet-philologist and political activist August Heinrich Hoffmann von Fallersleben, a larger-than-life figure mainly known as the author of the 'Deutschland, Deutschland über alles' anthem (Figure 4.4).[18] Hoffmann was a fervent adherent of the Grimm school of philology and made a name for himself as a canny investigator of archives and libraries (he edited two volumes

* Grimm aligned two sets of consonantal shifts between language clusters. One set marked a difference between the Germanic languages and other Indo-European ones (English/Dutch **h**eart/**h**art, **f**oot/**v**oet and **th**ree/**d**rie as opposed to Latin/Greek **c**or/**κ**αρδια, **p**es/**π**ους and **tres**/**τ**ρια. The other set marked a difference, within the Germanic languages, between German and the others: **Pf**eife, Hi**tz**e, Rau**ch** against **p**ipe/**p**ijp, hea**t**/hi**tt**e, ree**k**/roo**k**.

Figure 4.4 August Heinrich Hoffmann von Fallersleben in the garb of a nationally minded wandering student: Dürer-inspired hairstyle, beret, unstarched collar, tight waistcoat. The full portrait also shows a walking stick and a drinking gourd. ERNiE imagebank

of ancient German 'treasure troves', *Fundgruben*, published in 1830 and 1837). In the many places he visited on his philological quests, he invariably sought out kindred spirits who, like him, were inspired by the glories of the vernacular literary tradition. This made him a 'networking' mediator among the various national revival movements that these kindred spirits were involved in. A hub of these was formed around the Vienna librarian and philologist Jernej Kopitar. While on a visit there, Hoffmann joined the *Stammtisch* or regulars' table at the inn where the Slovenian Kopitar gathered intellectuals from the Slavic minority populations of the Habsburg Empire – a typical instance of the intensive private and convivial networking among these Romantic scholars.[19] While in Vienna, Hoffmann also got wind of the possible whereabouts of a long-lost medieval German manuscript – somewhere near Ghent, in Flanders, where Jan Frans Willems had edited the Flemish Reynard.

Hoffmann immediately hastened from Vienna to Ghent, in the process boarding one of the very first steam trains to run on the newly opened railroad north from Brussels. He and Willems then travelled from Ghent to the public library of Valenciennes, where the French authorities, who had closed down the ancient monastery of St Amand des Eaux, were rumoured to have lodged its collection of books and manuscripts. They hit the jackpot: what they retrieved was the long-lost ninth-century *Ludwigslied*, one of the most ancient poetic texts in vernacular German. Only a few months later, their edition of the manuscript appeared in print (*Elnonensia*, 1838).

Hoffmann was familiar with Flanders and its literary history; he had been editing ancient Flemish texts since 1833 in a series called *Horae Belgicae*. Indeed, it is to this German's editorial work that Dutch and Flemish literature owe many of the first printed versions of their medieval heritage. But by 1838, when Hoffmann visited Ghent, the climate was shifting. We have seen how Jan Frans Willems in 1835 was already chafing at the pronounced francophilia of the newly independent Belgian state and the marginalization of Flemish culture in that state. Hoffmann was fêted by Willems in a convivial club of Flemish-minded intellectuals called, tellingly, De taal is gansch het volk – 'The language is, entirely, the nation' – and Hoffmann, impressionable and enthusiastic as ever, now started to support the Flemish emancipation cause with his accustomed fervour. That same year, he wrote a firebrand introduction to yet another text edition (*Altniederländische Schaubühne*, 1838), in which he vehemently denounced the fact that on his railway journey from Brussels, passing through Flemish territory, he had heard announcements only in French. His denunciation of the general retreat of Flemish before the hegemonic French language was a fervent endorsement for the emerging Flemish movement; though possibly it was also somewhat embarrassing.[20]

Hoffmann did not only feel solidarity with a marginalized language; as a nationalistic German, he felt a proprietorial paternalism towards it and wanted to place the small sister language under the protection and tutelage of the older brother. If Belgium wanted to have a bilingual regime with a metropolitan language alongside the local Flemish, he asked, why then should that metropolitan language be the alien French? Why should it not be, rather, the more closely related and more easily understood German? And he continues, in a remarkable mash-up of different variants of 'German' and Netherlandic:

> Feminglandish is a *Niederdeutsch* language and conveys just like *Plattdeutsch* a familiarity and understanding of High German (*Hochdeutsch*). If German Belgium were to give up its own language and literature, then the High German language would have a more natural, and therefore more justified

> claim than that non-German, French language. If at some future date the educated classes of German Belgium were to speak and write High German, and to that extent take part in the German-language literary production, then this would not be a great marvel, any more than that ever since the sixteenth century the Nether-Germans in Germany's northern lands (the lower Rhine, Westphalia, Lower Saxony and on the hither shores of the Baltic Sea) speak and write High German, and add their intellectual cooperation to German literature as much as the inhabitants of the regions where Upland-German (*Oberdeutsch*) is spoken, even though *Niederdeutsch* has remained their native tongue.[21]

This tendency to fold the Low Countries into a greater German whole played itself out in other fields than mere linguistic confusion. Hoffmann had, indeed, looked on the Low Countries with an acquisitively greater-German eye since 1820; and he was the poet who in his 'Deutschland, Deutschland über alles' had proclaimed that his aspirational, beloved Germany should stretch 'from the Meuse [i.e. Namur-Liège] to the Niemen [Königsberg], from the Belt [Kiel, Schleswig] to the Adige [southern Tyrol]'. That was put forward as a programme of popular unification and emancipation; but it also implied territorial expansionism at the cost of neighbouring states and linguistically mixed populations. In the event, the association with greater-German nationalism was to prove a mixed blessing for the Flemish movement. German nationalists supported Flanders as a bulwark against encroaching French culture and repeatedly (in 1848, and fatally in 1914 and 1940) made the Flemish cause their own. This meant that after 1918, Flemish activism was tainted with the notion of uncivically betraying, with the aid of the German military occupiers, their country, Belgium; and ever since 1944, the Flemish movement has carried the guilty burden of its wartime sympathy, and widespread collaboration, with the Nazis.[22]

There was one great irony in this. What Willems and Hoffman found in the Elnon manuscript in Valenciennes was not just the most ancient contemporary copy of a vernacular German poem but also the most ancient contemporary copy of a vernacular French poem: on the same page as the 'Ludwigslied', and written in the same hand, is the ancient French 'Hymn to Saint Eulalie'. The nearby monastery of St Amand, where the manuscript was produced and was kept until the French Revolution, had been founded in Merovingian times in the transition zone between the German-speaking and the Latinizing branches of the Frankish tribes. At that period and in that area, proto-German and proto-French coexisted and intermingled. Their peaceful literary coexistence in this ninth-century manuscript is a quiet reproach to the growing national chauvinism of the nineteenth-century philologists. A century after the manuscript's discovery, its home region, between Ghent and Valenciennes, was torn up by the French–German gash of the Western Front.

Contested Heritage

In providing the modern nation with its 'own' cultural heritage, the past was not so much rediscovered as reappropriated. That reappropriation was to a large extent anachronistic, since the materials claimed as a national heritage themselves dated from a prenational (feudal or even tribal) past. That one should feel proprietorial towards one's heritage is to a certain extent understandable. Modern countries such as England and Egypt may cherish and feel stakeholders in the ancient monuments located on their soil, such as Stonehenge and the Pyramids of Giza; in that privileged sense of being uniquely associated with them it matters little that the builders of those monuments had no familiarity with the country's modern inhabitants. But the literary heritage presented a problem. Manuscripts as 'portable monuments' were transnationally dispersed across libraries and discovered by a roaming band of philologists; and they were written in idioms that were the forerunners of a palette of various modern languages current in different countries.[23] As a result, they could become contested among different appropriations. The successor traditions to these medieval texts had fanned out into groups of different nationalities, each of which felt that they, and they more than any other, were the true heirs.

Thus Thorkelin thought that the *Beowulf* text he had discovered was a Danish poem, for the action is located along the Saxon coastlands that were Danish territory around 1800; nearby coastal tribes that the poem mentions are the Frisians, Angles and Geats, all of them known to Danish antiquarians. Small wonder that Thorkelin presented *Beowulf* as 'a Danish poem in the Anglo-Saxon dialect'. *Beowulf* was thereby placed under a double mortgage: a scholarly one (since Thorkelin's version was error-ridden) and a political one (in that the text was claimed by German, Danish and English scholars as culturally theirs). It took decades of debate for the English view to become dominant: that the Angles and Saxons, having migrated across the North Sea, had become the tribal ancestors of England, and that *Beowulf* was an Old English poem recalling events from before the Anglo-Saxon migration. That debate was further muddied by German philologists who argued that, since the Saxons were a German tribe, this was in fact a German poem casting light on the mores of the Saxon contemporaries of Charlemagne. In 1839 and 1859, editions appeared calling *Beowulf Das älteste deutsche, in angelsächsischer Mundart erhaltene Heldengedicht* and *Das älteste deutsche Epos*. The subtitle of the 1839 edition (by Heinrich Leo) offers full disclosure as to its approach: 'The most ancient German heroic poem, in the Anglo-Saxon dialect, considered in its contents and in its relations to history and mythology: A contribution to the history of the ancient German mentality'. The preface to the 1859 edition (by Karl Simrock, a Grimm adept) voiced sentiments such as this: 'As has already been pointed out, the *Beowulf*, though handed down in Anglo-Saxon, is in its foundations a German poem. In addition, the following comments clarify that its plot-line (*Mythus*) is a German one, which has left many traces amongst us. All this increased my wish to reappropriate this poem into our language.' Simrock hopes 'to bridge a thousand-year old division and to renew for this poem, that emigrated away along with the Angles and Saxons, its native domicile [*Heimatrecht*] amongst us.' It is no coincidence that these editions appeared at a time when a strenuous German–Danish struggle was underway over ownership of Schleswig-Holstein – including precisely the coastlands where *Beowulf* was set.[24]

Within England, the assertion of *Beowulf*'s Englishness did much to strengthen a sense of Anglo-Saxon roots, rejecting the country's other cultural source traditions – Celtic and Norman French. The marriage of Victoria, from the Hanover dynasty, to Albert, Prince of Saxe-Coburg-Gotha, symbolically enshrined this sense of Saxon–Germanic affinity at the apex of society. Intellectuals such as Carlyle vociferously expressed a 'Saxonism' that dominated the mid-century. It was even projected across the Atlantic Ocean, where the ideal type of the WASP (White Anglo-Saxon Protestant) shored up the ideology of manifest destiny and a sense of a westward-expanding Anglo-Saxon world empire. The echoes of that ideology would inform Winston Churchill's notion of the north Atlantic community of 'English-speaking peoples'.[25]

The effect of these contesting appropriations in fanning national rivalries and national chauvinism is shown best by the most protean literary heirloom of them all: the satirical fables around Reynard, the canny, Machiavellian fox, who outwits the tooth-and-claw aggression of Isengrim the Wolf, the lumbering overbearing bearishness of Bruin the Bear, and the harsh arrogance of Noble the Lion, reigning monarch of the animal kingdom. The poem was known from early modern popular 'chapbook' printings in Dutch, in Low German and in English, and wily foxes were widely proverbial and featured in the fables of La Fontaine. The fables' literary standing had been raised by Goethe's new verse rendition, *Reineke Fuchs*, and French antiquarians had published early French versions – possibly the very oldest ones. It looked as if the French version was the original one, from which later versions had branched off.[26]

But when a young Jacob Grimm in 1805 was on a bibliographical mission to the French National Library (as an assistant to his mentor, the legal scholar Savigny), he could not help wondering at the fact that even in these oldest French versions, the animal's names tended to sound German: Isengrim, Reynard's wife Hersinde, even Reynard himself, the sarcastically named 'Reinhart' (pure-heart). And so Grimm began to hunt for the occulted Germanic roots of this *Roman de Renard* (much as Simrock would later discern *Beowulf*'s fundamentally German *Mythus* underneath the Anglo-Saxon language). His hunch was that there had been a lost prototype somewhere in the Flemish–French borderlands (where the tale is set, and where Hoffmann von Fallersleben and Willems would, thirty years later, find the German–French Elnon manuscript). He began to ply Dutch colleagues at Leiden with requests for information. Shortly after, the library of Comburg Abbey was transferred to Stuttgart, and in the process a manuscript was found that contained a previously unknown early Flemish version of the Reynard fable.

Grimm's fox-hunt would last almost thirty years; only in 1834 did he bring out his majestic text edition *Reinhart Fuchs*, with a 200-page introduction to the High German text (discovered by Gloeckle and Görres in the Vatican Library) and other versions discovered in the former monastic library of Comburg, the former episcopal library of Kolocza, and elsewhere. It was a feisty assertion of the seniority of the German Reinhart over the French Renard. The French staked their claim with Dominique Martin Méon's *Roman de Renard* (1826), followed by Paulin Paris's *Les aventures du maître Renard* of 1861. The fox-hunt turned into a trench war.

That battle was also between two modes of editing ancient texts, 'diplomatic' or 'critical'. The French editions were 'diplomatic' in that they based themselves on the best and most ancient available manuscript, noting marginally how other versions diverged from it; and this played out in favour of French seniority. Grimm's way of editing was, however, 'critical', something he had learned from the renowned classical philologist Karl Lachmann. This method compared the available versions on the basis of their mutual resemblances and differences and schematized these variants into a type of 'family tree' of forking paths, known technically by the Latin term *stemma*. The *stemma* guided the philologist back towards the common root of all these diverging branches, an *Urtext* or underlying text-type that, while it might not have been expressed as such in any single version, formed the best starting-point for them all. And as it happened, the *Urtext* or *Mythus* for Reynard and *Beowulf* would turn out to be German (or Germanic, which for Grimm and his adepts – Hoffmann, Simrock – amounted to much the same thing).[27]

The choice between diplomatic or critical editing was also generational: the diplomatic mode harked back to the antiquarian tradition, while the critical mode was philological. And in the French–German philological bickering, it also became nationalized. The French denounced the obscurantist flim-flam of the German X-ray approach to texts; the Germans denounced the facile and superficial French obsession with appearances. The reader may discern here, once again, the ethnotypes that suffused the war propaganda of Thomas Mann (Chapter 2). Even scholarly method became an expression of national character and of national incompatibilities.

Over the century, the Franco-German appropriation war ground on. One edition followed another, and contemporary national values were projected onto the medieval material itself. Reynard himself was fitted into the prevailing ethnotypes. For the French, Renard was a nimble, sardonic charmer full of Gallic wit, and the episodes involving gross or obscene acts had all been added to the charming French original by vulgar German elaborators with their coarse sense of harsh, low-comic pranks. For Grimm, Reinhart was a moralistic Frankish animal epic harking back to the prehistorical days of tribal-totemic belief in animal magic, and the gross or obscene episodes had been spliced into it by *oh-là-là* French pornographers, frivolous and immoral as the French are known to be.

The tendency of philological traditions to fission along national lines is illustrated by the mid-century epistolary networks of Ernst Moritz Arndt (for most of his life professor at Bonn) and the Paris-based writer and inspector of antiquities Prosper Mérimée (some 4,000 letters in all, Figure 4.5); both were contemporaries of Grimm. Arndt's network faces north-east, while that of Mérimée faces south-west. Between Paris and Bonn there is a dead zone of non-communication, running from London and Valenciennes/Saint-Amand-les-Eaux (where the Elnon manuscript had been written) to Venice, in an uncanny foreshadowing of the Western Front in 1914–1918.

In this 'ground zero', Flanders, a very early Reynard version was discovered, written in, of all languages, Latin. But that did nothing to defuse the terms in which the contesting appropriations were now fought. Grimm kept on questing for older Netherlandic-Germanic versions antedating the ones that were coming to light. In 1830, though, when

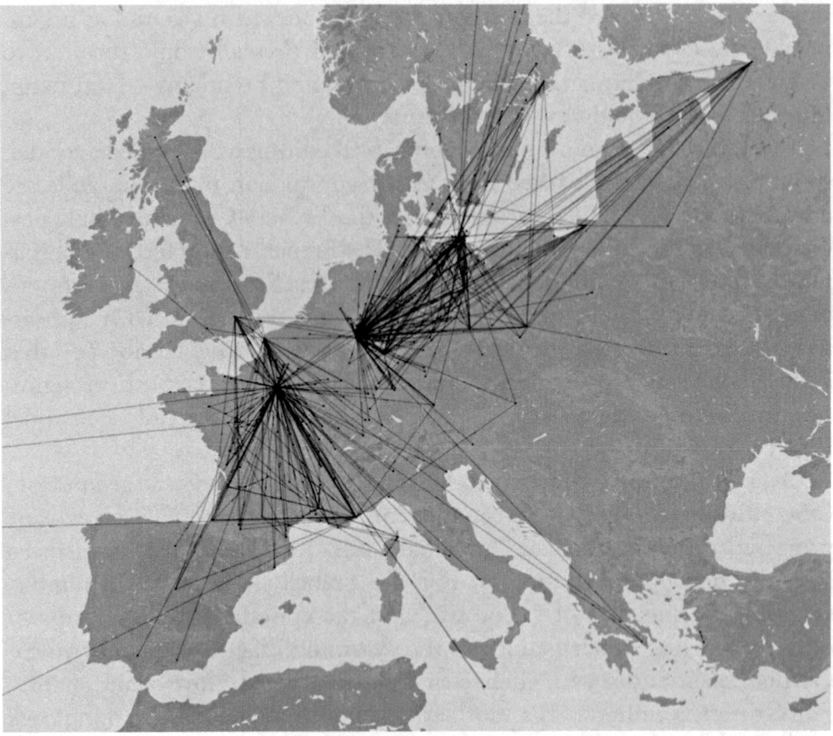

Figure 4.5 The differently oriented correspondence networks of Ernst Moritz Arndt and Prosper Mérimée (e-rn.ie/arndtmerimee).

Flanders seceded from the Netherlands, he gave up hope; for the new state, Belgium, exhibited a strong affinity with France. Grimm (a cantankerous character at the best of times) voiced bitter resentment towards the stolid indifference of the Dutch and the traitorous francophilia of the Catholic Flemings, which now seemed to preclude any possible discovery of a Flemish *Ur*-Reynard. In a review of 1830 he vented his spleen at the Belgian secession:

> The Catholic, formerly Spanish, then Austrian Netherlands offer a warning example of how the neglect of the native language weakens all love of the fatherland. Any nation that surrenders the language of its ancestors is degenerate and without firm footing. The present revolution in the Netherlands cannot be attributed to a properly patriotic movement but merely reflects the long-established influence of French manners and the plotting of priests. Common folk from Antwerp to Brussels and Ghent still

> speak Netherlandic. The almost-extinct nationality of the Belgians might have been rekindled by closer ties with Holland; but the tremendous torrent of events now threatens to sweep away all that remains of it.[28]

These reproaches were later to be quoted by none other than Jan Frans Willems when he edited his Flemish Reynard in 1836, praising the fox fable as the crown jewel of Netherlandic literature and denouncing its obscurity as a standing reproach to the hegemony of French in Belgium. That edition, of the long-lost Flemish version, presented a double irony. Grimm's own *Reinhart Fuchs*, appearing after thirty years of painstaking preparation in 1834, proved to be still premature; for in 1835, that selfsame Belgium that Grimm had accused of a lack of true patriotism had acquired an important manuscript from the estate of a British bibliophile, which contained, among other foundational Flemish texts, the long-sought-after *Reynaert*. The boost that this gave to Flemish self-esteem in the new Belgium can be imagined; and Grimm embraced Willems as the long-sought philological soulmate and his fellow worker in the Low Countries. Willems died soon after Hoffmann von Fallersleben's visit, however, and Grimm dedicated a heartfelt eulogy to this absent friend when he opened the *Germanisten* Congress in 1846.[29]

Reynaert has ever since remained a trump card in the Flemish rejection of francophone dominance in Belgium, and the character attributed to him here was again a projection of a national self-image. Reynard as framed in Flemish terms is beset by many authoritarian figures claiming dominance over him; unable to challenge their brute force, Reynard instead uses his wiles as a trickster to outwit them. The fox continued to be all things to all nations competing for his appropriation.

The Nation Goes Epic

These foundational texts have all become hyper-canonical. *Beowulf*, the *Chanson de Roland*, the *Nibelungenlied*, *Reynaert*, the *Lay of Prince Igor's Campaign*: they take pride of place in the opening chapters of national literary history books and anthologies, they form part of national school curricula and they have, in the root sense of the word, been canonized as being foundational to their nations' cultural-historical presence.

The hallmark of canonicity is the fact that a text is regularly adapted and recycled into different updated retellings, often in different genres or media ('remediation'). The public cannot, literally, get enough of it, and besides the many reprints and new editions (spurred on by professional rivalry between 'diplomatic' and 'critical' editors and by the discovery of additional manuscript fragments), there were numerous literary spin-offs: retellings in contemporary language for the general public or for juvenile readers; or adaptations as stage plays, as operas, as novels and, in the twentieth century, as films and graphic novels. Britain rediscovered King Arthur, King Alfred and Queen Boudicca. In post-1870s France, Sarah Bernhardt starred in a patriotic theatre play, *La fille de Roland*; in Germany, the Nibelungen generated some forty poetic and theatrical adaptations, culminating, of course, in Richard Wagner's operatic *Ring* cycle; in 1916 a volume of propagandistic war poetry was published under the title *Nibelungentreue: Kriegsgesänge*, signalling a robust politicization of the epic for nationalistic and militaristic purposes.[30]

It was in the nineteenth century that the notion of a 'national epic' became current; previously, epics such as the *Iliad* had been seen as simply classical and nationally unspecific. By the 1840s, it became commonplace to see each literary tradition begin with an epic foundation. Goethe had wryly pointed this out: 'Each nation owes it to its self-esteem to possess its own epic'. As the *Oxford English Dictionary* (1933 edition, under 'Epic') puts it:

> The typical epics, the Homeric poems, the Nibelungenlied, etc., have often been regarded as embodying a nation's conception of its own past history, or of the events in that history which it finds most worthy of remembrance. Hence by some writers the phrase *national epic* has been applied to any imaginative work (whatever its form) which is considered to fulfil this function.

For Jacob Grimm, the peculiar power of the epic was that it makes no concessions to the modern reader, forcing that reader into mental time-travel to the days of yore:

> Lyrical poetry, arising as it does out of the human heart itself, turns directly to our feelings and is understood from all periods in all periods; and dramatic poetry attempts to translate the past into the frame of reference, the language almost, of the present, and cannot fail to impress us when it succeeds. But the case is far different with epic poetry. Born in the past, it reaches over to us from this past, without abandoning its proper nature; and if we want to savour it, we must project ourselves into wholly vanished conditions.[31]

'Projecting oneself into wholly vanished conditions' (*uns in ganz geschwundene umstände versetzen*) – that imaginative time-travel into the past and directly experiencing it as it must have felt at the time: that may provide us with a pithy definition of historicism, which the rediscovery of epic did much to engender. The remediations and adaptations should also be understood, then, as bridges across the historical gap between the epic Then and the national Now.

It is still a sobering surprise to realize that these national epics had dropped out of cultural memory more or less completely for so many centuries and that their currency as texts was achieved largely in the post-Napoleonic decades. The presentations of the oldest texts in the national canons are mostly a product of, or at least initially marketed as part of, the Romantic movement; and the philological bookworms were as much part of that Romantic movement as the idealistic poets.

Those poets did their nationally epic thing, too – Romanticism wasn't exclusively about the lyrical intuition of Higher Things, it was also about the epic evocation of Olden Things. Foundational epics were freshly composed as part of a Romantic-national literary agenda. In many cases, these newly written epics originate in nations experiencing an existential crisis. Jan Frederik Helmers's *De Hollandsche Natie* (1812) dates from the Netherlands' Napoleonic occupation and annexation. In Sweden, the national poetry of Esaias Tegnér was fed by regrets about that country's loss of its Finnish possessions (*Svea*, 1811; *Frithiofs Saga*, 1825). Similarly, there are various mythical and historical plays and poems by the Danish national poet Adam Gottlob Oehlenschläger, starting with *Vaulundur's Saga* (1805) and culminating in the heroic-epic poem *Hrolf Krake* of 1828. As in the Dutch case of Helmers, Oehlenschläger's work reflects a nation with a great past sinking to second-rank status: Denmark lost its Norwegian dominions after Waterloo and saw Schleswig-Holstein threatened by an increasingly powerful German neighbour.

Whereas Dutch, Swedish and Danish were the established official languages of long-standing sovereign states, national epics were to become particularly popular in languages newly emerging as literary vehicles, particularly in Central and Eastern Europe. In a number of emerging literatures, in languages until then seen as uncouth dialects, poets were inspired by these discoveries and by the taste of literary historicism to *become* their nations' Homers. The Slovak language, overshadowed on all sides (in Bohemia by Czech and German, in Hungary by Magyar), declared its presence in the epic poems of Jan Hollí (*Svatopluk*, 1833; *Cirillo-Metodiada*, 1835).* Jan Kollár, another Slovak, though writing in Czech, produced the

* These poems intervened in a thorny antiquarian debate – showing, once more, how porous the borders between literary and learned writing were at the time. The lives of the ninth-century 'Apostles of Eastern Europe', St Cyril (after whom the the Cyrillic alphabet had been named) and St Method, had been given fresh topicality by the Czech scholar Josef Dobrovský. He had in his Old Church Slavonic grammar of 1822 (*Institutiones linguae Slavicae dialecti veteris*) and in a German-language

remarkable sonnet cycle *Slavy dcera* ('The Daughter of the Goddess Slava', 1824), which has formed a national-Romantic inspiration to all Slavic languages and literatures.

For the Hungarian, Polish, Slovene and Ukrainian languages, likewise at that moment outside the repertoire of established literary praxis, the verse epics *Zalan futása* ('Zalan's Flight', 1823, by Mihaly Vörösmarty), *Konrad Wallenrod* (1828, by Adam Mickiewicz), *Krst pri Savici* ('The Baptism on the River Savica', 1836, by France Prešeren) and *Hajdamaky* ('The Outlaws', 1841, by Taras Shevchenko) became the very foundation of subsequent national literatures. What is more, they were written as such. The very choice of a marginalized minority language for an ambitious and extensive heroic poem is in each of these cases already a blatant cultural–political signal. They were national both in theme and in ambition – in that the poet dealt with a foundational episode in the nation's early history. The case of Prešeren's *Baptism on the Savica* may stand for the others: it deals with the Slovenes' transition from ancient paganism to Christianity. (Figures straddling the transition from tribal paganism to Christianity were a favourite Romantic theme: the Gaulish princess Norma in Bellini's 1831 opera; the Lithuanian Princess Birutė; the Batavian maiden Hermingard in Aarnout Drost's 1832 novel.) Prešeren's poem describes the defeat of the last pagan chieftain at the hand of the Christian armies and his discovery that his even his beloved has become a Christian; written in the metre of Slovene folksong, the poem traces a crucial and tragically dignified moment of transition in the nation's collective history. It is this quality that gives it its epic character. In turn, this epic scale has ensured for the poet (a cosmopolitan intellectual, whose literary sensibility resembles Heine's ironic *Weltschmerz* more than Macpherson's sublime sentimentalism) his stature as the founding father of his country's national literature. Prešeren's statue is prominent in the central square of Slovenia's capital Ljubljana.

In this process, the epic slipped its antiquarian moorings in the 'manuscript found in an attic' mode. Indeed, not all nationalities in Europe had manuscript-stocked attics, or ancient libraries or archives with dormant primordial texts. What they had instead was a thriving oral-performative culture, and alongside the national epic rose the oral epic. That will be the topic of Chapter 5.

brochure of the following year (*Cyrill und Method, der Slawen Apostel*) strengthened Moravian (i.e. Central European) claims on the missionary and linguistic work of these saints, who originally hailed from the Macedonian lands in the Orthodox-rite Byzantine Empire. Hollí followed Dobroský's appropriation of the saints to the Latin-rite region by emphasizing that the saints had been invited into Moravia by the local Prince Svatopluk.

CHAPTER 5

Ancestral Voices

Heroic Balladry

The philological project of editing epics from ancient manuscripts was flanked by a concurrent vogue for materials taken down from oral performance. The prototype appeared in Vienna in 1814. It was a Serbian anthology, sponsored by the Vienna court librarian and Slavic philologist Jernej Kopitar (whom we encountered in Chapter 4 as a contact of Hoffmann von Fallersleben). Kopitar had taken a young man under his wing who had taken refuge in Vienna from the anti-Ottoman warfare in the Pashalik of Belgrade. This man, Vuk Karadžić, had the unique advantage of being both highly literate and intimately acquainted with the oral literature traditions of his home region. At Kopitar's behest, he published a collection of Serbian folksongs, *Srpske narodne pjesme*, in 1814.[1]

In this initiative Kopitar took his cue from Jacob Grimm, who was beginning to make a name for himself as a philologist and as a collector of oral literature. Jacob and Wilhelm had tangentially collaborated on the seminal collection of German balladry *Des Knaben Wunderhorn*, edited by Achim von Arnim and Clemens Brentano. The Grimms' collaboration with Arnim/Brentano's family–friends network (the so-called Bökendorf Circle) had continued when the brothers followed through with that benchmark of benchmarks: their collection of folktales and fairy tales (in the original: *Kinder- und Hausmärchen*, 'Wonder Tales for Children and the Household', 1812–1815). The Grimms were shifting the frame in which oral literature was collected and read. Formerly, folk literature had been read sentimentally, as representing the artless, homely pastimes of naive but virtuous rustics; but starting with the Grimms, such texts were also read ethnographically, as the unmediated cultural expression of the unlettered masses, who, thanks to their lack of exposure to polite learning, had kept their native cultural heritage intact in unadulterated, authentic, albeit rough-hewn form.

Grimm had met Kopitar after joining the Hessian delegation to the Congress of Vienna in a secretarial capacity. In Vienna, Grimm had elaborated his new, more ethnographical approach to folk literature in a convivial circle that met during the Congress in 1814: the 'Wollzeiler Circle'. Its members had drawn up a questionnaire to be distributed to wide circles of possible respondents, developing a similar one that had already been drawn up by Brentano for the *Wunderhorn* project in 1806.* Karadžić's anthologizing work was sparked off when Kopitar presented that questionnaire to him.[2]

In turn, Grimm was fascinated by this voice from what was still the Ottoman-dominated part of Europe. He went to the trouble of learning Serbian, entered into direct correspondence with Karadžić, reviewed his work and published a translation of his Serbian grammar in 1824.

Authentic and rough-hewn: that is what Karadžić's collection certainly was. It came from a part of Europe where late-Enlightenment, genteel sentimentalism was thin on the ground. Instead, there were violent altercations between local warlords and outlaws and their capricious and harsh Ottoman rulers. A follow-up volume appeared in 1815, when the second Serbian insurrection against the Ottomans broke out, and in it were hard-bitten martial ballads based on recent events. Grimm was delighted with this unexpected contribution to his folkloric–philological agenda from an unexpected corner of Europe. He would support a new expanded edition that appeared in Leipzig in three volumes in 1823–1824.

The combination of linguistic and folkloric interests characterizes both Grimm and Karadžić. The latter would become the 'Serbian Grimm' and would go on to collect further oral material. He would also reform the Serbian language and alphabet, lessening its dependence on the old liturgical language and adapting it to modern circumstances and usage.

* Personal overlaps between the Bökendorf Circle and the Wollzeiler Circle were, besides Grimm, Werner von Haxthausen (host at the Bökendorf estate, and himself a folksong collector) and Joseph van Laßberg (future husband of Haxthausen's niece Jenny von Droste-Hülshoff, with whom Wilhelm Grimm had flirted at Bökendorf). The rural, estate-based Bökendorf ambience was more domestic and familial than the urban sociability of the inn-based Wollzeiler Circle; the shift marks an early stage of the professionalization, or at least the de-domestication, of literary studies. At Bökendorf, the core members were from a tight-knit aristocratic background: Arnim and Savigny (who introduced his protégés, the Grimms, to the group) were Brentano's brothers-in-law through his sisters Bettina and Kunigunde. The role of women in these convivial/domestic learned circles is noteworthy and stands out against the masculine exclusiveness of professional university careers. Suggestive parallels to the female-connected Bökendorf circle are the networks around Lady Llanover in Wales (Fraser 1968) and the Tengström family in Helsinki (Eiranen 2019). The role of *salonnières* and salons in intellectual history, as nodal points in networked connections, invites further investigation (as per Watson 2022).

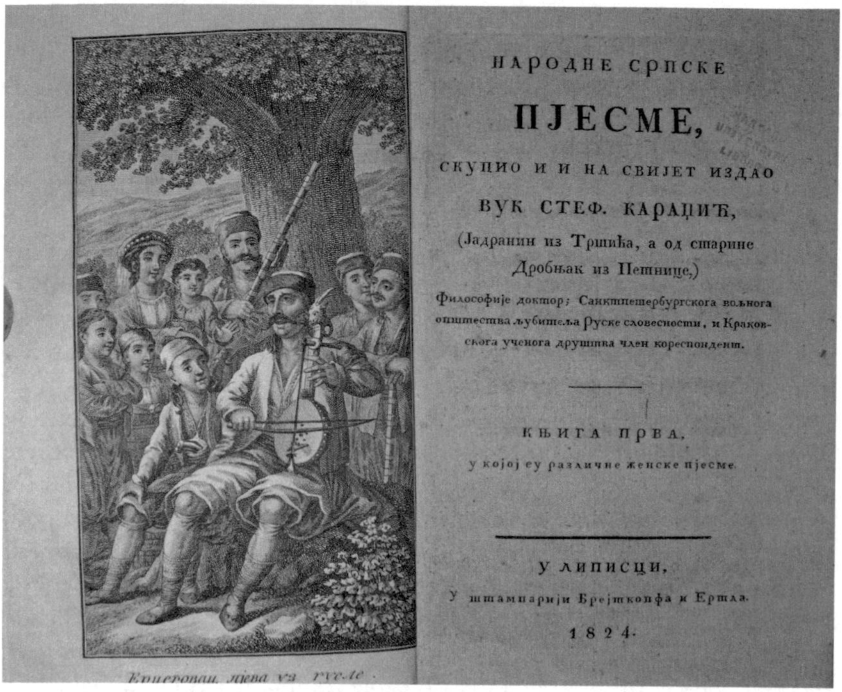

НАРОДНЕ СРПСКЕ

ПЈЕСМЕ,

СКУПИО И И НА СВИЈЕТ ИЗДАО

ВУК СТЕФ. КАРАЏИЋ,

(Јадранин из Тршића, а од старине
Дробњак из Петнице,)

Философије доктор; Санктпетербургскога вољнога
општества љубитеља Руске словесности, и Краковскога
ученога друштва члан кореспондент.

КЊИГА ПРВА.

у којој су различне женске пјесме.

У ЛИПИСЦИ,

У штампарији Брејткопфа и Ертла.

1824.

Figure 5.1 Frontispiece and title page of the 1824 edition of Vuk Karadžić's anthology. ERNiE imagebank

The Serbian heroic balladry collected by Karadžić reached a European readership on the wings of the Serbian insurrection; meanwhile, Byron had published his stirring poems of passionate violence in Europe's wild, Turkish-dominated outlands. The *Srpske narodne pjesme* were just that: songs of the nation (*narod*), nothing like the juvenile and domestic (*Kinder- und Haus-*) context where the Grimms' fairy tales came from.

The frontispiece to the 1824 Leipzig edition of Karadžić's collection (Figure 5.1) shows the setting for this type of oral-performative literature: a seated singer with his one-string fiddle (*gusle*) to accompany his rhythmically chanted ballad. He stares into the middle distance in something that is either concentration, a poetic 'flow' or a Romantic rapture that, Ossian-style, captures the collective imagination; we are reminded, incongruously, of the painting in which an impassioned Rouget de Lisle sings 'La Marseillaise' before enraptured listeners (Figure 1.3). The 'abstracted staring gaze' can be encountered repeatedly in many illustrations in this book, from Ossian to Liszt. In most cases it signifies inspired rapture. In this specific instance it may also connote blindness. Vuk Karadžić's main informant, the *guslar* Filip Višnjić, had gone blind at an early age as a result of smallpox. In many societies, the visually impaired made a living as performing poets/musicians. Their physical blindness was, in the popular imagination, often linked to their literary gifts, for example in Irish folklore (Ó hÓgáin 1982). The blindness of Homer and Tiresias added classical prototypes; Višnjić became known as the 'Serbian Homer'. Around the *guslar* (to return to the frontispiece of Karadžić's anthology), and under the tree of what is apparently a village setting, various representative members of the community (different genders and ages) are listening to his song, united in their rapt attention as an 'affective community'; one of them is a martial young man with a rifle.

This picture of the performer as, literally, the voice of his *narod*, reciting the traditional literary heritage for a contemporary audience, quickly became iconic. In part it suited the post-Ossianic idea of the inspired poet as the voice of his nation – the *guslar* shown here is the modern equivalent of Ossian, and both are 'bards'. There was also a contemporary context for this appeal: in these years there was a widespread philhellenic interest in the klephtic songs of insurrectionary Greece, and it had repercussions far afield. Claude Fauriel's philhellenic *Chants populaires de la Grèce moderne* appeared in 1825; and that book in turn inspired the Irish collection of James Hardiman, *Irish Minstrelsy* (1834), which retrieved anti-English balladry from the preceding century. Hardiman prefaced it with a firebrand introduction, citing Fauriel's example and arguing that the position of Ireland under British rule was similar to that of Greece under Turkish rule – explosive stuff, in a year that saw Athens established as the capital of an independent Greece.[3]

Popular songs, including those that were folkloristically retrieved, became the public carriers and platforms of popular discontent and national aspirations. The outlaws and rebels (*hajduks*) celebrated in these songs became Byronic hero-figures with a nationally inspiring value. One century later, the *guslar* was cited as the most important cultural claim to independence for the southern Slavic nations. In 1917, when American geographers were preparing the Paris Peace Conference and deliberating how to apply the principle of the 'self-determination of peoples', the echoes of Karadžić's frontispiece of 1822 were still reverberating in a book with the indicative title *The Frontiers of Language and Nationality in Europe*:

> The *pjesme* voices Serbia's national aspirations once more in the storm and stress of new afflictions. Its accents ring so true, that the geographer, in search of Serbian boundaries, tries in vain to discover a surer guide to delimitation. From the Adriatic to the Western walls of the Balkan ranges,

> from Croatia to Macedonia, the *guzlar*'s ballad is the symbol of national solidarity. His tune lives within the heart and upon the lips of every Serbian. The *pjesme* may therefore be fittingly considered the measure and index of a nationality whose fibre it has stirred. To make Serbian territory coincide with the regional extension of the *pjesme* implies the defining of the Serbian national area.[4]

The European spread of this heroic balladry ran through the conduit of the works of a young woman of letters, Therese von Jacob (her pen name, based on her initials, was 'Talvj'), whose translation of *Volkslieder der Serben* appeared in 1825. Talvj had been recommended to Kopitar and Grimm by none other than Goethe himself, who used the occasion to recall that he himself had, in fact, already translated one of these ballads forty years previously.

That was part of what made Goethe so awe-inspiring and so irritating to his younger literary contemporaries: the fact that he had always already been there and done all that – all those things that were subsequently being discovered as new and exciting. Since his debut in 1770s he had consistently been ahead of the literary curve; and in 1775 he had, in fact, translated a southern Slavic ballad, *Hasanaginica*.

Flashback: Ossian in the Balkans

The ballad in question, on the tragic fate of the wife of the warlord Hasan-Aga, had been noted down in 1770 by a Venetian traveller and geographer, the priest Alberto Fortis. Fortis had undertaken a field trip to Dalmatia, the eastern coastlands of the Adriatic sea, then under Venetian control but adjacent to Ottoman-dominated territory. His *Viaggio in Dalmazia* (1774) contained, next to the description of cities and regions, the full text of *Hasanaginica*, in the original Croatian with an Italian translation on the facing pages. It caused a furore. Goethe got hold of a German prose translation and cast it into metrical form, using the ten-syllable metre that was also used in the original Croatian ballad. The text was published in Herder's classic edition of multinational *Volkslieder* (1778, later retitled *Stimmen der Völker in Liedern*, 'the voices of nations in their songs'). From there, *Hasanaginica* went viral across Europe, with versions in English, French and Russian being penned by the likes of Walter Scott, Prosper Mérimee and Alexander Pushkin.[5]

This first wave of European popularity was as yet in the sombre, Ossianic, sentimental mode that dominated the 1770s. Indeed, Ossian's shadow is all over *Hasanaginica*'s reputation and spread. Fortis was in fact an associate of Cesarotti, the Vico-inspired translator of Homer and Ossian, and his Dalmatian voyage had been sponsored by the great Scottish champion of Ossian's authenticity, Lord Bute. (The 1778 English version of Fortis's book, *Travels into Dalmatia*, is dedicated to Bute.). It looks as if an Ossianic bug had spread in Venice: here, too, antiquaries were hunting for ancient, lost literary treasures. Like Edinburgh, the Venetian metropolis had wild highlands in its geographical backyard, inhabited by a population that seemed to Venetians alien and primitive. Situationally, the Scottish model that had led to the discovery of Ossian could inspire fieldwork in the Dalmatian uplands. But fieldwork it was indeed: not a search amidst library shelves for lost manuscripts, but (as with Macpherson) a voyage into remote lands to note down orally performed traditions.

The Ossian model could obviously inspire folklore research as well as philology. Indeed, the scandal of Ossian had the effect of breaking down the division between literary epic and oral tradition. Initially, Ossian was exposed as fraudulent because written originals were not forthcoming and people were unwilling to credit 'savage Highlanders' with maintaining, orally and over many centuries, an epic tradition. But that crux could be turned on its head. If indeed Ossian was not the 'northern Homer' he had been reputed to be, could it not be that Homer himself had been a sort of 'Mediterranean Macpherson'? Was not Homer's own method closely akin to what Macpherson had done – cobbling together oral ballad material into an epic whole? Were there not oral-performative ('rhapsodic') sources providing Homer with the building blocks of his *Iliad* and *Odyssey*? Was Homer not the compiler, rather than the creator, of his epics? This was the notorious 'Homeric question' that hit Europe in the 1790s; it had been anticipated by Herder's reflections on the authenticity of Ossian and by the discovery of *Hasanaginica*.[6]

By the early nineteenth century some consensus had been reached that 'foundational' epic texts were perhaps not that Big Bang out of nowhere that they had previously been imagined to be: that they were the crystallization of an earlier, orally circulating body of heroic ballads sung by 'rhapsodes', not unlike the *guslar* on the title page of Karadžić's collection. The Golden Age of ancient literature was preceded, as Thomas Love Peacock put it, by an Iron Age. This hugely raised the status of balladry and oral literature. Philologists began to look for the moment when national literatures (in written, formalized form) emerged from their oral-formulaic, folkloric run-up; contemporary performances such as the Serbian ones were a case in point and were aligned with other, older cases such as the medieval Provençal *troubadours*. Claude Fauriel, first professor of *littératures étrangères* at the Sorbonne, studied the origins of both troubadour poetry and oral Greek balladry (spawning his philhellenic *Chants populaires de la Grèce moderne* of 1824). In both cases, he was trying to chart the transition from oral-performative to written-literate stages of national literatures.[7]

No wonder the framing of oral literature shifted from sentimental to national-historicist, as the two-stage reception of *Hasanaginica* shows. Forty years after Goethe, Karadžić's collection included the *Hasanaginica* once more.* By now, however, the frame in which those texts were read was no longer sentimental and Ossianic; it had shifted to a Byronic register, with its harsh evocation of violent passions under Ottoman tyranny. In addition, the status of oral literature had shifted as well. The Grimm brothers by 1812 had begun to consider fairy tales as very serious business indeed: the last vestiges of ancient legends and sagas (much as Macpherson had seen his Highland balladry as the broken remains of an ancient epic). And the collecting of oral-performative, traditional literature became a twin discipline to the textual scholarship of philology. The Grimms and Karadžić were players in both fields. The idea of 'oral epic' was born – something that, like 'national epic', might have seemed a self-contradictory term a few decades previously.

The Nation as Author

Epic and oral literature had in common anonymity and an unclear provenance. It was this that opened up the suspicion of forgery. (More on that in Chapter 7.) When Prosper Mérimée, in his collection *La guzla* (1824), cashed in on the vogue for the balladry of Balkan outlaws, he included, among his French translations, some counterfeits of his own as well as a patently fabricated story of how he had 'noted these down' from oral recitation; Hoffmann von Fallersleben later on 'edited' traditional Flemish ballads that turned out to have been his own confections. Both men later tried to brush these off as mere playful Romantic pranks.[8]

Another way of dealing with this murky uncertainty was to proclaim the diffuseness of the provenance as a virtue: ancient epics were the

* When compiling his own anthologies, Karadžić felt obliged to include *Hasanaginica*, even though he had never heard it performed: it was too famous to leave out (see Vaillant 1939). The reason for this anomaly may be that the domestic tragedy of Hasan-Aga's wife and her harsh fate belongs to a genre that was usually performed among women and that Karadžić relied largely on more masculine sub-genres. For this gender division in Serbian oral-performative poetry, see Vidan 2003.

product of the nation's collective imagination at the very moment when it was beginning to find a voice of its own. The ancient bards, rhapsodes and myth-tellers were mere mouthpieces of the nation at large, and their anonymity was therefore fitting. The Grimms went so far as to argue that the medieval chivalric texts with known authors (Wolfram von Eschenbach, Gottfried of Strasbourg etc.) were already beginning to lose the vigour of the truly archaic, authorless texts, were beginning to pander to the courtly taste of the elite and were exposed to the pernicious influence of a French-based, Europe-wide taste for romance rather than rough-hewn, native epic.[9]

For those cultural communities that had historically been unable to build up a textual documentary archive of their own, or whose literary output had obtained no access to the printing press, it was a good second best to have access to heroic balladry and oral epic. Such literature documented the vigorous character and ancient traditions of the nation, even in the absence of written documentation. The ripple effects of the Grimms' oral researches spread far and wide. In Russia and its Baltic provinces, *byliny* (ballads) and *skazki* (folktales) were a matter of interest (collected by Pavel Rybnikov and by Alexander Afanas'ev in the 1860s). In Ireland, Norway, Finland, the Baltic, the Balkans, the work of the Grimms was picked up. Inspired by the Grimms, Thomas Crofton Croker collected Irish fairy legends, which the Grimms then translated into German as *Irische Märchen*. In Norway, Asbjørnsen and Moe collected their *Norske Folkeæventyr*. But nowhere was the impact as powerful as in Finland.[10]

Long a Swedish province, Finland had been ceded to the Russian Empire in 1811, and Finnish culture was better off as a result of the transfer. Its cultivation was allowed under Russian rule because this weakened the old ties with Sweden. The local elite, traditionally Swedish-speaking, turned to Finnish as a way out of the predicament that, no longer Swedish, they could never become Russian. What is more, there was now an open border with Karelia to the east and with the hinterland around St Petersburg, where similar, related vernacular cultures could be encountered. Fieldwork and ballad-collecting was done among the local populations, largely in the eastern parts of Finland, and a rich harvest of oral-formulaic poetry was noted down. The heroes of these lays and ballads were already known from legends, and one of the foremost collectors, Elias Lönnrot, spliced the ballads together into a coherent legendarium involving the deeds and fates of a focused set of mythical protagonists. Indeed, the tales bordered on myth in that many of the incidents bespoke a magical world-view full of supernatural incidents and a fluid non-demarcation among humans, animals and objects.[11]

In fact, Lönnrot did exactly what Macpherson had tried to do. But whereas Macpherson was still working in the paradigm of discrete heroic epics created by a single, individually known original genius, Lönnrot (who anyway was more candid about the provenance of his diffuse source material) presented his *Kalevala* more in the mode of a thematically integrated legendarium of ancient Finnish traditions involving ancestral figures and memories as told in formulaic verse by rustic performers. The result was nonetheless immediately hailed as 'the Finnish national epic', once again demonstrating the philological proximity between folklore and high literature. Grimm's comments on the epic quoted in Chapter 4 (to the effect that it required its readers to mentally project themselves into wholly vanished circumstances) were made, in fact, in a paper 'Über das finnische Epos' presenting the *Kalevala* to the Prussian Academy in 1845; and in it Grimm drew a direct line from Finland to Serbia:

> In Serbia the faithful memory of the people, especially old blind men, preserved a body of songs, each of which contains fifty, a hundred or even 500 or 1000 lines in the purest and most easy-flowing language; if one were to integrate those which belong together … one could form entire cycles amounting to minor epics.[12]

Finnish culture received a huge boost from the *Kalevala*; its publication day is still a national holiday in contemporary Finland. It put Finland, literally, on the European map, stimulated the fennicization of the Swedish-speaking Finnish elite and stimulated the organization of Finnish-language cultural and academic life. And it had a knock-on effect of its own: the German-speaking bourgeoisie of present-day Estonia was inspired to delve into the country's own vernacular culture, closely related to Finnish. An Estonian who studied theology in Helsinki notified the local learned society of Tartu of the appearance of the *Kalevala*; this galvanized an already emerging interest in similar Estonian lays; and before long these were compiled in the Estonian 'national epic', the *Kalevipoeg*.[13]

The pattern even caught on outside Europe. In North America, Henry Schoolcraft collected Ojibwe material, very much in the Grimm mode. He had privileged access to this cultural tradition because his wife Jane was of Ojibwe descent and informed many of the works published under Henry's name. Also in North America, loosely circulating heroic legends were forged together into a literary whole in Henry Longfellow's *The Song of Hiawatha* (1855). It was consciously inspired by Lönnrot's *Kalevala* and shared its metre (a trochaic tetrameter prevalent in Finnish oral poetry), and for its theme it drew on Schoolcraft's *Algic Researches* (1839); its publication triggered in turn Schoolcraft's *The Myth of Hiawatha* (1856, dedicated to Longfellow). In the background, there were also (to some extent misidentified) cultural memories of a historical Hiawatha, cofounder of the Iroquois Confederacy.[14]

What made these epics truly 'national' was their inspirational value for contemporary audiences. The texts became classics, and as we saw in Chapter 4, that canonical status was demonstrated most of all by the wealth of remediation that these heroic epics inspired. Hiawatha and his beloved Minnehaha resonated through sentimental American culture in countless paintings and porcelain figurines; and it was to have been the basis for a nationally American opera by Dvořák (who abandoned the project and instead used it as an incidental, tangential inspiration for his symphony *From the New World*). Parts of the *Kalevala* were set to music in many compositions by Jean Sibelius, and it inspired illustrations, paintings and murals by the art nouveau artist Akseli Gallen-Kallela. The streetscapes of Helsinki are suffused with references to the characters of the *Kalevala*, in the names of streets, buildings and businesses. And the cultural backbone of Finland shifted decisively towards a mythical, idealized 'Karelia', an undefined rustic region remote from Swedish modernity and uncertainly straddling what is now the Russian-Finnish border. The *Kalevala*-driven fennicization of Finland as an emergent nation also meant that this Finland claimed descent from a Karelia that would always be, fatally, contested with the neighbouring Russian Empire, leading to repeated frictions and hostilities.[15]

A Window on Mythology

The retrieval of epic, be it as literary text or as folkloric material, is a way of trying to delve into to the deep primordial antiquity, the primeval roots even, of the nation's literature. For Grimm, both epic and folklore were expressions of the deepest strata of the nation's self-articulation and *Weltanschauung*. Ancient epic and folklore offer us glimpses of how the nation experienced the world at very ancient moments of its emergence into history, and before it experienced the influences of other cultural traditions. Grimm used law in a similar ethnographic manner, studying ancient legal customs about ownership, kinship, trespass and punishment, in order to retrieve, almost anthropologically, the German nation's primal ethics and self-regulations.[16]

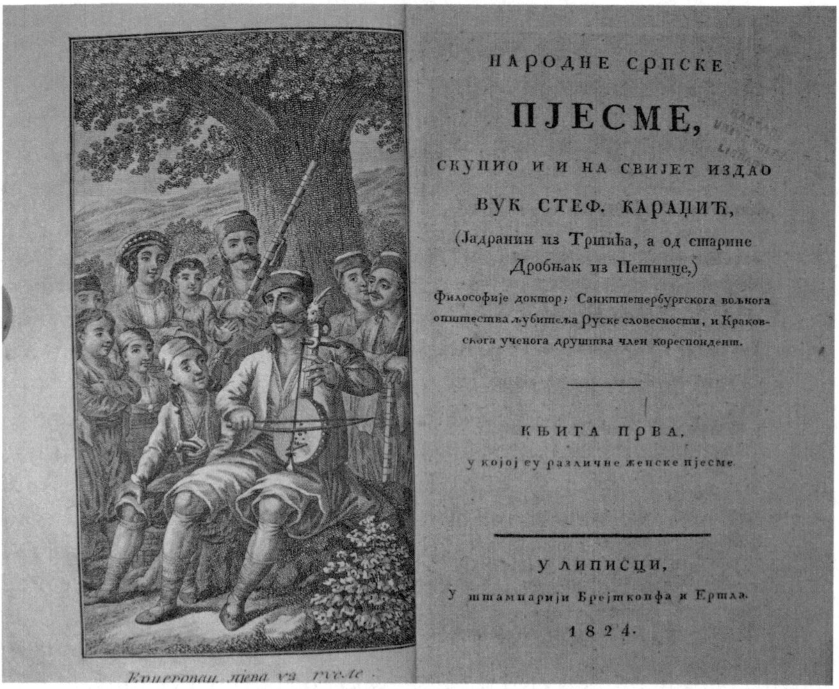

At this point we must briefly ask ourselves what precisely the orality was that philologists were beginning to investigate. The word 'folklore' did not yet exist – that word was consciously coined later to cover the field of 'popular culture' – but an interest in unwritten texts and oral-performative culture was on the rise everywhere. From the beginning it covered various genres.

- Ballads both heroic and sentimental were included (the former shading into what became known as 'oral epic').
- The study of melodies arose later and became the object of ethnomusicology. The study (and revival) of folk-dances branched off from this, as well as more generally the ethnographic study of manners, customs and popular practices.
- Wonder tales were a central concern; in the Grimmian approach, their study feeds into that of supernatural folk beliefs, soon aligned with the study of ancient myths.

This cluster of practices and concerns, usually grouped together as the study of 'folklore' or 'traditional/oral culture', would map out as shown in Figure 5.2.

Grimm's *Deutsche Mythologie* of 1835 was an extension of his work on the comparative grammar and history of the Germanic languages. He was hampered by the fact that there was no written corpus of German myths comparable to the Graeco-Roman or Scandinavian ones. In trying to establish what the original German system of myths had been, Grimm wanted to complement the Scandinavian myth texts with German material, and this he found in fairy tales and customs – in other words: folklore – mythologically deciphered. In his attempt to unlock oral traditions as a window on ancient myths, Grimm was applying a method (comparative-historical) that he practically patented; we have already seen him apply it to ancient literary texts and to linguistic relations. This approach examines concrete data (such as variant manuscripts, different versions of a folktale or a superstition, legal verdicts or consonants in different languages) as variable instances each of which reflects in its own way an underlying pattern, word-root or *Stoff*. The variant 'expressions' are multiple, but through their family resemblances they can be reconciled into an underlying pattern. It was in applying this method of 'comparing expressions to elaborate the underlying type' that Grimm had been able to come up with his archaeology of words and consonantal shifts.[17]

For Grimm, the comparative-historical method becomes a type of structuralism of 'types' generating 'expressions', foreshadowing the Saussurean

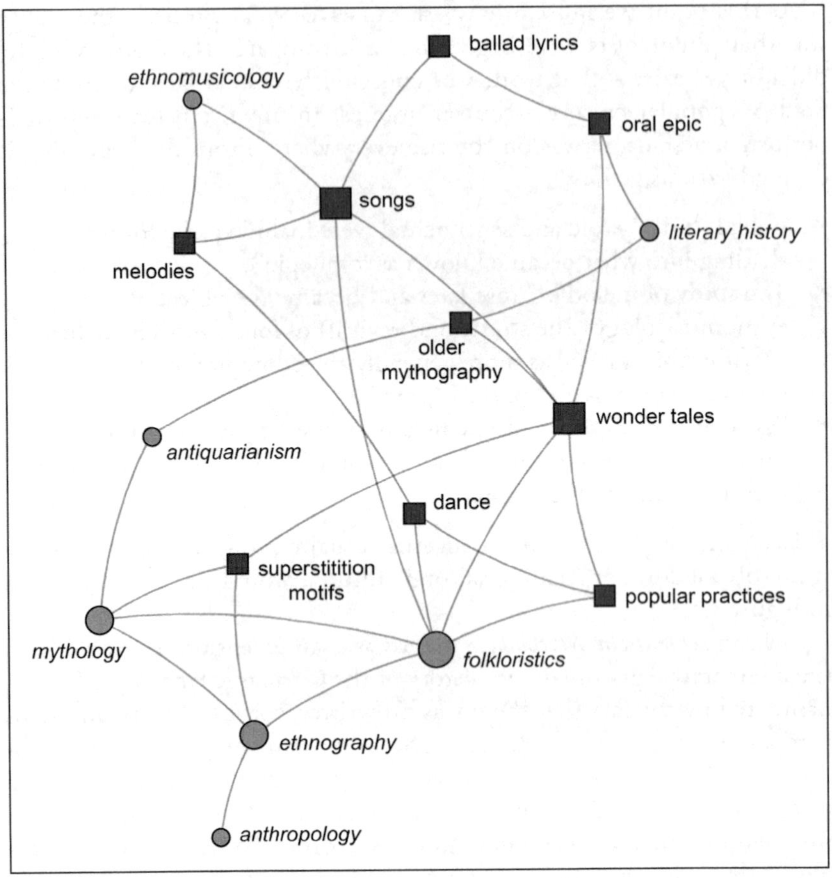

Figure 5.2 A mind-map of relations between genres in popular culture (square nodes) and specialisms in knowledge production (round nodes).

notion that different speech acts – *paroles* – express an underlying language, *langue*. Grimm's critical edition of the Reinhart material, going from the variants to the *Stoff*, exemplifies the operation of this model in the field of animal epic. In Grimm analyses of folklore materials (popular wonder tales), the motifs themselves were apparent as parts of a structure underlying the tales' different versions; but the motifs could themselves be aligned to suggest something deeper still, something of which they were themselves the expression. In aligning folklore motifs comparatively Grimm began to go beyond the epic/folklore divide and to drill down to what he considered the deepest, and most formative layer in a nation's expression of its world-view: its mythology.[18]

'Mythology' traditionally meant two things: either a collection of tales (*muthos* being the neutral Greek word for a tale, a plotline motif or an anecdote) or else a belief system – a pagan theology describing the deities, their acts and mutual relations, against the background of a cosmogony of how the world took its present shape.[19] In the Romantic period, mythology developed a third meaning. Alongside the anthology (a collection of supernatural, traditionally transmitted tales) and the theology (a pagan belief system), 'mythology' also became a form of philology: the scholarly, academic investigation of myths. This trifurcation can be observed neatly in the core area from which the rediscovery of vernacular mythologies fanned out all over Europe: Denmark. Following Edda editions and re-editions in the later eighteenth century, N. F. S. Grundtvig addressed, philologically, what he called *Nordens Mytologi* (the Edda-derived set of tales); Rasmus Nyerup analysed the Edda as *Skandinavernes hedenske Gudelære*, a pagan belief system; and Nyerup's study, published in 1806, cantilevered out of the more historical/antiquarian work of Fredrik Suhm, *Om Odin og den hedniske Gudelære og Gudstjeneste udi Norden* (1771), which treated the Edda as an originally secular historical account whose protagonists were in later treatments raised to divine status.[20]

Like the Greek and Roman mythologies, this Nordic material was authentically documented in ancient texts. But the mythological spin-offs elsewhere in Europe had little or no written sources to work from. Instead they drew their information from oral praxis and traditional folktales, as the run-up to Lönnrot's *Kalevala* shows. Interest in Finnish oral literature had been evinced early on by Swedish intellectuals at the University of Åbo (Turku). Christfried Ganander's *Mythologia Fennica* (1789) was a dictionary-style list of deities from folk religion illustrated with stanzas from Finnish folk balladry; the book already included such names as Ilmarinen and Väinämöinen, important figures in the later *Kalevala* compilation.

Slavic mythology, which emerged around the same time, moved in the same literary–folkloric–pagan triangle. Unlike the Finnish case, it drew on a dispersed variety of source traditions and different intellectual centres (Russian, Bohemian, Croatian); only in the mid-century, as the ideology of pan-Slavism took hold, did it converge into a common Slavic *matière* (Konrad Schwenck, *Die Mythologie der Slawen*, 1853). Folklore and oral material became available as folktales (*skazki*) were collected; an early researcher was the Russian army officer Andrej von Kayssarow, who published his *Versuch einer slavischen Mythologie in alphabetischer Ordnung* in Göttingen in 1804.*

For all this, Grimm's *Deutsche Mythologie* provided a Europe-wide benchmark. Fairy tales and popular superstitions were decoded as a trickled-down residue of ancient superstitions, involving supernatural beings (dwarves, giants and elves) and reflecting ancient socio-cultural patterns such as curses, cures, rites of passage, seasonal festivals and shamanism. Supernatural beings such as dwarfs and elves, in particular, Jacob Grimm saw as things handed down from pagan times and reflecting pre-Christian beliefs and, yes, myths. Once identified as such, these mythical elements could be encountered in an astounding variety of cultural expressions.

Myths, then, are something always in the background, rather than manifestly present in solid documentation. But for all its vagueness, mythology is omnipresent in the nineteenth-century imagination; although it never quite solidified into an academic discipline, it generated enormous quantities of popular infotainment, collections of myths and legends aimed at the general public as a form of cultural archaeology for leisure-time reading. As the ancient pursuit of 'antiquarianism' fissioned into archaeology, linguistics and folklore, the study of vernacular mythologies came to rest, or rather wobble, on a tripod of archaeological, philological and folkloric-ethnographical approaches. These methods and fields of expertise were not easy to reconcile. As a result, mythology became both ubiquitous and vague, a diffuse and speculative background to other forms of knowledge production. Mythology was invoked to provide background 'explanations' for folktales, for epic, for archaeological remains, for the social history of Europe's ancient tribal societies.

Accordingly, mythology often reverts to the genre of a quasi-scholarly anthology of ancient wonder tales; it enriches not so much the field of

* I mention in passing some developments from the Polish/Baltic and southern Slavic areas. In Poland-Lithuania, Slavic mythological interest was inspired by the Nordic Edda rediscovery: Joachim Lelewel, in the earliest stages of his turbulent career as a historian and radical activist, gave Polish-language accounts of the Edda at Vilnius University. Lelewel, too, dovetailed the antiquarian with an ethnographic approach: his treatise on Polish-Lithuanian folk customs *Winulska sławiansczyzn* (1816) opened mythological sight-lines later explored by his student in Vilnius, Teodor Narbutt. Slavic mythology was adopted into Grimm-style philological scholarship when eighteenth-century writings by the Polish cleric and antiquarian Adam Naruszewicz were republished in Leipzig in 1836 as *Mythologia Słowiańska*, followed in 1842 by the more speculative philosophical treatise of the Slovak-Austrian Ignaz Johann Hanusch, *Die Wissenschaft des slawischen Mythus, im weitesten, den altpreussische-lithauischen Mythus mitumfassenden Sinne* (Vienna 1842). In the southern Slavic lands under the Habsburg Crown, an eighteenth-century antiquarian tradition was academically consolidated by Gregor Krek, Professor of Slavic Mythology at Graz, in his *Über die Wichtigkeit der slavischen traditionellen Literatur als Quelle der Mythologie* (1869).

academic knowledge production as that of artistic inspiration. Literary raconteurs or visual artists make grateful use of the mythographers' harvest: the proto-Czech prophetess Libuše, the Celtic Rhiannon or Manannan Mac Lír, or the Lithuanian love goddess Milda. The most outstanding example is the reception history of the Edda in German culture. The dual-track, scholarly-cum-cultural recyclings culminate in the popularizing retellings by the Germanist Andreas Heusler (*Urväterhort*, 1904), the poet/novelist professor Felix Dahn (*Walhall*, 1885) and, of course, the operatic-dramatic treatment by Richard Wagner in *Der Ring des Nibelungen*.[21]

In the post-Wagner century, the pattern is aptly illustrated by the fantasy world of J. R. R. Tolkien. As a philologist, Tolkien was a true scion of the Grimm school, doing work on the *Oxford English Dictionary*, editing medieval texts such as *Sir Gawain and the Green Knight*, and looking for archaic elements in *Beowulf*. In his fascination with Old English texts, he was constantly (again like Grimm) reaching for the unspoken, mythological or archetypical traces of something underlying even ancient epic. Tolkien bitterly regretted the fact that England had no mythology of its own (much as in Grimm's envy of the Scandinavians). In response, he created a fictional legendarium *faute de mieux*. True to the Grimm model, Tolkien's philological celebration of a mythologized Englishness moved from linguistic history and language derivations (his Middle-Earth cosmogony) to legends (the *Silmarillion*) and epic and chivalric romance (*The Lord of the Rings*), with some folk-rustic hobbits thrown in for good measure. Companiable hobbits for homely folklore, aristocratic Gondor for chivalric romance, grim dwarves and Rohan warriors for epic, vanished Númenor for sagas, eternal elves for myth: it is all there, and all is held together by Tolkien's linguistic framework. For as he famously stated, the history of his Middle-Earth was an explanatory narrative frame for him to trace the branching developments of the fictional languages he fabricated.[22]

Another offshoot in the twentieth century was the resurgence of neo-paganism. For those who saw Christianity as a regrettable Mediterranean/Roman/Semitic adulteration of the stalwart native morality of the Germanic Northern Europeans, ancient myth became an object of fond nostalgia; Grimm and his adepts Felix Dahn and Max Müller had repeatedly stressed the integrity of the religious and moral world-view of their Germanic ancestors, while rejecting Roman Catholicism as a hypocritical perversion. For the *Germanisten* of the post-Grimm generation, the pagan Saxon leader Widukind becomes a tragically doomed tribal hero, sadly overcome by the Rome-supported imperial power politics of his Frankish opponent Charlemagne. That pagan-friendly tendency ran wild

Figure 5.3 'QAnon Shaman' Jacob Chansley during the 2021 Capitol riots. Associated Press / Alamy Stock Photo

in certain factions of National Socialism – notably Himmler's SS and its cultural department, the Ahnenerbe. With the resurgence of an identitarian alt-right in post-1989 Europe, this tradition sprang back to life, often recycling – naively or knowingly – Ahnenerbe material. At the same time, a new-age type of neopaganism began to flourish, which in some manifestations (though by no means in all) harked back to a Nazi-tainted iconography, sometimes in knowing sympathy with the underlying ideology, sometimes naively, sometimes quasi-naively as a 'dog whistle'. This repertoire of Germanic neopaganism, including runic and Nordic ornamental symbols, was also proclaimed in heavy metal rock music ('viking metal', which itself can shade into 'National Socialist black metal').[23] And it showed up on the bare chest of the 'QAnon Shaman', a colourful participant in the storming of Washington's Capitol in January 2021 (Figure 5.3). Wearing a horned bison headdress and carrying an American flag, he displayed on his bare chest three Germanic neopagan tattoos: the 'Valknut', the 'Yggdrasil' Tree of Life, and the 'Mjölnir' Hammer of Thor.

The Roots of Identity

Many myths relate how the world came into being and came to be populated with gods and heroes. Chronologically, their narratives form a prequel to those of the heroic epics. For that reason, myths (as pagan religions) were held to date back to the very earliest literary products of a nation, something that came into being as that nation was going through its cultural ethnogenesis. If, in the Grimmian logic, each cultural expression emanates from an underlying cultural type, then mythology, itself a type underlying the later expressions of epic and folklore, must be the expression of the nethermost bedrock of the nation's position in the world (that is to say, its very identity), a 'type underlying all other types', a cultural archetype.* There was a word for that archetype, and it had been coined by Grimm's mentor, the legal scholar Carl von Savigny: *Volksgeist*, the nation's spirit or essence.[24]

For Savigny and Grimm, two immediate emanations of the *Volksgeist* were the nation's language and its legal customs. Grimm studies the two conjointly in his great, now neglected *Rechtsaltertümer* or 'legal antiquities', propped up by four massive volumes of documentation inventorizing the rulings of medieval case law: the *Weisthümer* (1840–1863). In it he analyses the historical vocabulary and the conceptual history of fundamental legal and societal principles such as 'right', 'ownership', 'crime' and 'freedom', aiming to show how the German social, moral and legal order developed in tandem with its verbal articulation, almost in tandem with the language itself. In that he proves himself the adept of his teacher Savigny, even though he chose not to follow the profession of law. It had been Savigny who had rejected Napoleonic law as an artificial, technocratic instrument of conflict and power management, an alien imposition on a Germany whose native law system had organically developed in accordance with the moral outlook of the people, a direct expression of their (as he coined the word) *Volksgeist*.

Grimm remained a lifelong adherent of this organicist notion of law. At the *Germanisten* conferences of 1846 and 1847 he included legal scholars alongside philologists and historians in the discipline of 'Germanisten': all three groups were concerned with historical manifestations of the German identity. In sum, the Romantic successors to old school antiquarianism could address three fields of deep, anthropological culture that offered them access to the nation's primordial essence or *Volksgeist*: deep antiquity and ancient history;** mythology; and language as the nation's cultural

* I use the word 'archetype' in its Platonic meaning and without buying into the speculative pitfalls conjured up by C. G. Jung and Mircea Eliade. 'Archetype' was used in German *Naturphilosophie* to mean a fundamental blueprint for life forms (as per Darwin's later idea that there was an 'ancient progenitor, the archetype as it may be called, of all mammals'; quoted in Richards 2018, 2). It was also used in the philological stemmatology of Karl Lachmann in the sense of the *Urtext*, an ideal-notional original text at the point of incipience for all later variants.

** The German term for such (non-classical) ancient history was *Völkergeschichte* ('ethnohistory' or 'tribal history'), i.e. history as seen in terms of ethnicities (as opposed to states or institutions) in their mutual relations. In France and England, this approach fed into questions about the racial ethnicity of the nation's ancestral populations (Celtic, Frankish, Saxon etc.). In Germany, its great harbinger was Arndt (*Versuch in vergleichender Völkergeschichte*, 1843). A fuzzy term, *Völkergeschichte* had been used pre-1800 for an international form of antiquarianism; after the 1840s, it drifted out of the academically professionalizing historical discipline and became part of the repertoire of quasi-scientific racial thought; see Krügel 1914 and Leerssen 2025.

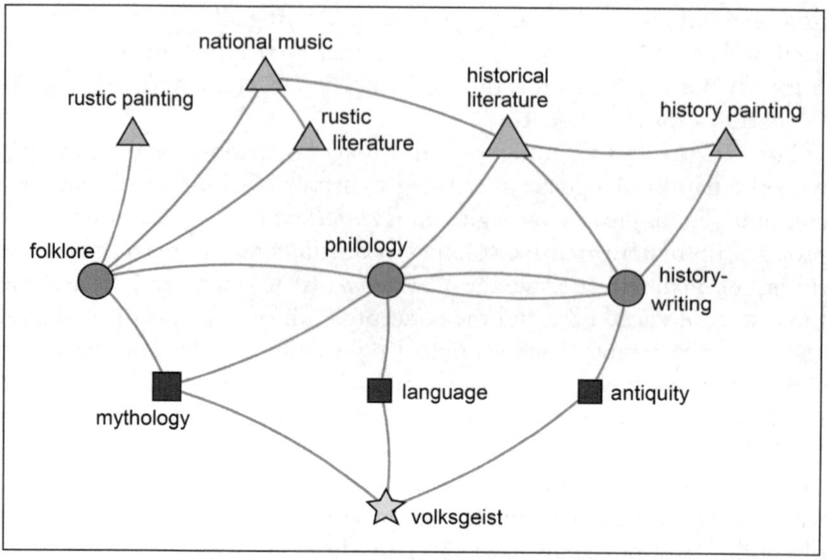

Figure 5.4 A mind-map showing how Romantic nationalism sees the connections among cultural fields.

operating system. Those fields are somewhat haphazardly divided among the scholarly disciplines of the ethnohistorian, the philologist and the folklorist, and they inspire a nation's art in various media of expression. This is shown schematically in Figure 5.4.

The triangular nodes (top tier of Figure 5.4) represent genres of artistic production and their intermedial connections; the round nodes (second tier) represent fields of knowledge production, their interdisciplinary relationships, and how they informed artistic production. The square nodes represent 'deep culture' (ancient, primordial or ambient) emanating from the fundamental spirit of the nation or *Volksgeist* (star-shaped node at the bottom), and how they are studied by the scholarly disciplines. The scheme also suggests how knowledge production takes up an intermediate, intellectual position between artistic cultural production and the 'deep' anthropological culture that fundamentally characterizes the nation. Only lyrical poetry, as we saw in Chapter 3, can directly intuit the *Volksgeist* without any intermediary or intellectual aid, thanks to its powers of visionary inspiration.

In critical writings of the nineteenth century, we frequently encounter the notion that a nation's language is directly linked to the nation's character, spirit or essential identity, both philosophically and in more commonplace contexts. Philosophically, the Platonic idea of language as *logos* was inflected by Herder's insight that the essence of language is its capacity for diversification. For Plato, the *logos* is the specifically human intellectual capacity to schematize and formulate one's sensations and thoughts into a rational position, and this is done with the tool of language, its lexical concepts and its grammatical order. Language is not a mere code system for communicating one's ideas but a human operating system allowing one to conceptualize and articulate one's thoughts in the first place. This language-as-*logos* concept was originally anthropological in the general sense, a factor that set humans (as animals endowed with sapience) apart from 'brute' beasts; we still encounter it in full force in Friedrich Schlegel's Vienna lectures of 1812: 'Spirit and language are so indivisible, as are thought and word, that, if we consider thought to be the specific privilege of humans, we must also consider the word (in its primal meaning and dignity) to be a human's inner nature.'[25] But on top of that, Herder had powerfully argued that what made human language special was also its power of proliferating diversification, its multiplicity, allowing societies in very different circumstances to each have their own *logos*, and if necessary their own 'fifty words for snow' (to quote a hackneyed phrase). The end result of this merger between Platonic idealism and Herderian diversity we see in the linguistic anthropology of Wilhelm von Humboldt, witness his *Latium und Hellas* (1806):

> Most of the circumstances that accompany the life of a nation (residence, climate, religion, political constitution, manners and customs) can be seen separately from it, and one can, even in the case of intense interaction, distinguish between the influence they exerted and the influences they were exposed to. But one aspect is of a wholly different order, and that is language. It is the breath, the very soul of the nation, appearing everywhere in tandem with it, and (whether it be considered as something that has exerted historical influence or else undergone it) setting the limits of what can be known about it.[26]

Humboldt was to return repeatedly to this idea that language is both *ergon* (something performed, an impact) and *energeia* (something enabling the performance, an impetus). Language is both the expression of, and the formative impulse behind, a nation's identity (e.g. in Humboldt's 1836 treatise 'On the Diversity of Human Language and Its Impact on the Mental Development of Humankind'); in due course this was to debouch into the famous Sapir–Whorf hypothesis and, anecdotally, played into the ambient ethnotypes of the century explaining national differences based on the nations' innate 'characters' (see note 2 in Chapter 1).

The association between native language and national identity was also a powerful poetical trope. In his song 'What is the German's Fatherland?' (see Chapter 3), E. M. Arndt answered his title question not only linguistically (wherever the German language is spoken; more on that in Chapter 6) but also characterologically and morally: 'That is the German's fatherland, where a clasped hand is as good as an oath, where faithfulness shines from the sparkling eye and love speaks warmly in the heart.' This ethnotype of forthright honesty is highlighted by contrasting it with the specious deceitfulness of the French foe – for Arndt wrote this song in 1813, while the German lands were still under Napoleonic hegemony: in the German's fatherland 'French frippery is scornfully swept aside, every Frenchman is called a foe and each German called a friend.'* The apposition of the positive self-image and the sneering image of the Other's innate character is glaringly illustrated here, hinting more generally at the ease with which nationalistic self-celebrations can derail into a character assassination of foreigners.[27]

The invocation of language as *Volksgeist*-determined is most strenuously made when that language is under threat, and will be encountered at its most explicit among subaltern cultural communities; I will cite a Flemish, an Irish and a Corsican example. Flemish nationalists, resisting the hegemony of French in post-1830 Belgium, are a case in point. Conscience in his novel *The Lion of Flanders* (1838) coined the slogan *Wat Wals is, vals is* ('If it is French, it is false'), and as we have seen, a patriotic-Flemish association in Ghent called itself De Taal is gansch het Volk – 'The language is, entirely, the nation' or 'The language wholly marks the nation.' That phrase had been lifted from a poem by Prudens Van Duyse, who in turn referred to Buffon's famous 'Le style, c'est l'homme même' ('A man's style bespeaks his very personality'). In Van Duyse's words: 'The style wholly bespeaks the man – Buffon, those are your words: the language wholly marks the nation.'[28] Grimm was to repeat the sentiment in 1846: 'What is a *Volk*? A *Volk* is the totality of people speaking the same language.'

* Arndt was notorious for his anti-French invective and indeed went on record stating that 'national hatred' was a moral imperative. Here is a sample from 1814: 'So what, in general, is the individual Frenchman vis-à-vis the faithful, upright, honest, and manly German? An empty, hollow, doll-like, formless and vacuous nobody without force, meaning, or character, an elegant lackey, a bending servant, a dressed-up monkey, a preening Jew, with a petty, half-leering and half-awkward rakish mien, a pitiful wight who does not even have the strength of personality to acknowledge his sins, but always pretends that he cannot live up to the power of his conscience.' (Arndt 1813b, 22–23). The many ethnotypical diatribes in Arndt's writings were collected during the Nazi years into a reverential anthology entitled *Deutsche Volkwerdung* ('German Ethnogenesis': Arndt 1934).

Indeed, in commenting on the Frenchification of Belgium, including Flanders, Grimm had in 1830 stated that giving up one's language was tantamount to giving up one's essential nature: 'Any *Volk* that relinquishes the language of its ancestors is degenerate [*entartet*] and anchorless [*ohne festen Halt*].' Anchorless implies that the language and its permanence are what provide a fixed, firm position for a nation in the world. Degeneracy connotes more than merely depravity or corruption: such a nation is denatured, out of touch with its inner nature and *Volksgeist*. Without its native/ancestral language, a nation, in Grimm's view, has no ethical footing in the world anymore.[29]

In the mid-nineteenth century, the Irish nationalist poet and journalist Thomas Davis echoed the same sentiments:

> The language, which grows up with a people, is conformed to their organs, descriptive of their climate, constitution, and manners, mingled inseparably with their history and their soil, fitted beyond any other language to express their prevalent thoughts in the most natural and efficient way. To impose another language on such a people is to send their history adrift among the accidents of translation – 'tis to tear their identity from all places – 'tis to substitute arbitrary signs for picturesque and suggestive names – 'tis to cut off the entail of feeling, and separate the people from their forefathers by a deep gulf – 'tis to corrupt their very organs, and abridge their power of expression. … A people without a language of its own is only half a nation. A nation should guard its language more than its territories – 'tis a surer barrier, and more important frontier, than fortress or river.[30]

And this is how Salvatore Viale renounced the Frenchification of Corsica in 1857 in his 'On the use of the native language in Corsica' (*Dell'uso della lingua patria in Corsica*):

> And as regards love of country, which is the most powerful and necessary affection in the citizen, it should be noted that the language of a people is the complex expression of its way of thinking and feeling, of its domestic and civil customs; it is the repository, in a certain way, of its traditions, its history, its literature, all of which the homeland largely consists of. Therefore, in changing their language, a people loses their identity, or rather their personality, indeed they themselves contribute to divesting themselves of it; they therefore lose that self-esteem and awareness, that faith in themselves, in which their value lies.[31]

These instances from various corners of Europe are multiplied. The notion that the fundamental personality of a nation is encoded in its own language is, in the aftermath of Romanticism, one of Europe's great cultural commonplaces. If mythology and ancient pagan belief systems bring us close to the ethnographic bedrock of the nation, the language is not only the nation's proper, fundamental 'operating system' but also the container of its cultural legacies, traditions and memories. It is the main guarantor not only of its distinct position vis-à-vis other nations in the proximity of space but also of its historical permanence in the vicissitudes of time. And, more than that, the language articulates and bespeaks the nation's essential *Volksgeist*.

The discourse of national identity habitually and almost in passing asserts formulaic characterizations – ethnotypes – as 'truths universally acknowledged': contemplative Germans, gallant French, Slavs either long-suffering or intransigent. These are not trivial asides or anecdotal parenthetical proverbs; they operate in a discourse that is suffused with invocations of the nations' underlying temperamental proclivities, and these in turn ultimately boil down to something like a blueprint or genome, something that is so fundamental as to be almost nameless. That ineffable archetype is the perspectival vanishing point on the cognitive horizon of Romantic philologists, mythologists and folklorists. It is metaphysical: something beyond the practical or material things that are open to empirical investigation. It is gestured at by such terms as 'identity', '*Volksgeist*', 'national character', the 'spirit of the nation', and it is seen as the informing principle of the nation's *mores* and culture as well as the validator of the repertoire of ethnotypes. Felix Dahn summarized it in a five-line motto he composed for Alldeutscher Verband; it was to be repeatedly reproduced, sometimes in truncated form.

> Man's highest good is his nation.
> The nation's highest good is its right.
> The nation's spirit lives in its language.
> Faithful to the nation, to its right and to our language
> Has this day found us, will each day find us.[32]

Making the Nation Personal: Self-Renamings

A remarkable phenomenon occurred across Europe as the modernizing states were perfecting their administrative grip on their population records. Family names became, after Napoleon, a far more fundamental part of a person's civic identity than they had been heretofore, although their spelling remained, for most of the century, fluid (my own ancestors show up in records up to 1914 as Lerschen, Lerssen, Lersen and other tentative approximations). For members of minority cultures in multinational states, the gap between the native and the administrative rendering of the name could be considerable and could signify alienation between the state and its minority cultures. In various places we accordingly see a trend to 'nativize' name-forms in a deliberate rejection of official administrative usage in the hegemonic language. Sometimes this was merely a question of orthography and was retroactively imposed as new ways of spelling were established and modern standards replaced older ones: Franz Prescheren has become France Prešeren, Paul Schaffarik has become Pavol Šafárik, and the fact that Edmond de Valero morphed into the Irish statesman Éamonn De Valera is the result of a gradual adaptation to Gaelic standards as these crystallized. But De Valera's wife, Sinéad De Valera née Ní Fhlannagáin, replaced her birth name (Jane Flanagan) with its nativist, Gaelic form in a deliberate act of self-renaming, in line with a widespread movement: Douglas Hyde himself, when writing in Gaelic, used the name-form Dubhghlas de h-Íde. A similar process spread in Finland, where Swedish name-forms were fennicized: Axel Gallen to Akseli Gallen-Kallela, Zacharias Forsman to Sakari Yrjö-Koskinen, and Einar Lönnbohm becoming the poet Eino Leino. Many Jews Hebraized their names: Eliezer Perlman and Asher Ginsberg became Eliezer Ben-Yehuda and Ahad Ha'am, David Ben-Gurion had been born as David Grün. In Hungary, many cultural activists Magyarized their names: Schedel to Toldy, Petrovics to Petőfi, Hunsdorfer to Hunfalvy, Blum to Virág, in order to signal their patriotic identification with their country (many Budapest Jews also adopting the gesture). In the 1880s a Central Name-Magyarization Society was established, encouraging people to undergo 'national baptism'. A third crest in this wave of transnominations occurred in the period 1920–1945.[33] The trend took a specific form among Czechs and Slovaks. They adopted given names of an archaic, Slavic nature, involving elements such as -slav or -mir: for example, the sports organizer Miroslav Tyrš, born Friedrich Tirsch. Among the followers of the Slovak leader Ľudovit (born Ludwig) Štúr, entire groups would undertake a pilgrimage to the historically symbolic site of Devin Castle and there choose a Slavic given name by way of 'national baptism'.[34]

To some extent this activism took place on the old battle-line between the private and public spheres: names being both intensely personal and also a way of positioning oneself in society. In pre-independence Ireland, controversies ensued as to whether Gaelic name-forms could be displayed on shop-signs or used for addressing letters through the Royal Mail; this more public form of national name-contestation would of course become sharply visible in the later politics of city names, from Irish Dún Laoghaire (formerly Kingstown) to Indian Chennai (Madras). But at the same time, this was an intensely private, even intimate matter, an interiorization of the national ideal at the most fundamental level of self-identification. Private to public: what we note here is a fluid, small-to-large 'multiscalarity' that is particularly pronounced in language politics. Territorial multiscalarity will be discussed in Chapter 6.

CHAPTER 6

Languages, States, Races

What is a *Volk*?

A *Volk* is the totality of people speaking the same language.

Jacob Grimm, address as chair of the Germanisten Congress, 1847

Mother Tongue, Fatherland

In 1812, Jacob Grimm fired the opening volley in a lifetime of hostilities with the Danish linguist Rasmus Rask. At stake was the status of German in Schleswig-Holstein and the status of the Danish language as such. Grimm asserted that the hegemony of German over Danish was a historical inevitability – 'it would be foolish for a mere 1.5 million people to think that they could close themselves off from the unstoppable influx of a neighbouring, closely related language spoken by 32 million and set alight for practically all time by the greatest intellects' – and he comforted the hapless Danes with the notion that 'the domination of German letters is not a dishonour, as the dialect speakers of Lower Saxony and East Frisia can confirm'. He then concludes on a note of pathos. His assertion of linguistic patriotism was, he asserts, not only necessary (on the basis that the Danes were trying to oppress the German language in Schleswig-Holstein) but also a spontaneous overflow of powerful feeling: 'Is it not right, o ye Germans, that you should cherish and value the language which you sucked in as an infant from your mother's sweet murmurings, together with her milk?'[1] And so the deep physical and emotional intimacy between an infant and a nursing mother justifies blatant linguistic irredentism; and the process of one language ousting another in Schleswig-Holstein, viewed from the moral high ground, is simultaneously justified (for German vis-à-vis Danish) and denounced (for Danish-vis-à-vis German).

Language is, as we saw in Chapter 5, a deeply rooted element of what makes humans human; but it is also the primal ambience for societal communication. As such, its public function and status have long been an object of intellectual reflection and public policy-making – going back to Francis I's Ordinance of Villiers-Cotterêts of 1539 (followed by Du Bellay's *Défense et illustration de la langue françoyse* of 1549) and Henry VIII's ban on Gaelic in English-ruled Ireland in 1543. Since language is a shared thing, owned in common by all who use it, language policies are always a matter for public debate.[2] In this chapter we shall trace how that public importance became a national one, a key issue in the self-distinguishing discourse of national identity.

Spelling reforms invariably elicit clashes: the 'ABC war' in 1820s Ljubljana, for instance. How should the Latin alphabet, used in Catholic–Slavic countries, render that widespread Slavic consonant that we hear at the beginning of the name of Tchaikovsky? The Cyrillic alphabet has a single letter for it, ч (Чайковский), but German needs four ('Tschaikowsky'). For Slovenian literati (Slovenian was just finding its way into mass-circulation print) the choice went between the Hungarian solution <cs> (as in *csardas*), the Polish solution <cz> (as in Mickiewicz) and the Czech use of a diacritical hook (as in the name for that little hook, 'haček'). Conservative Catholics resisted the haček because, invented as it had been by the humanist reformer Jan Hus (burnt at the stake as a heretic in 1415), it smacked of Protestantism. Thus this minute choice was heavily burdened with international, political and generational allegiances, and therefore heavily debated. In the event, the haček won out, witness the now-standard spelling of such names as Prešeren; but it still comes as a surprise, when reading early-nineteenth-century sources in emerging or subaltern languages, how fluid and variable the competing orthographies and alphabets were. The states that gained their sovereignty in the twentieth-century present their history and their historical figures in the spellings that were subsequently standardized, and thus they project the nationality that eventually crystallized out of historical contingencies back into the past, as if history had been experienced in the form in which contemporary nation-states remember it. The ABC war in fact took place in a city that called itself, at that time, by the German place-name Laibach; one of the participants, the philologist Kopitar, was then called Bartholomäus but now carries the given name Jernej. Again, the Slovak antiquary who spelled his own name as Schaffarik is now known as Šafařik of Šafárik (depending on whether he is invoked by his Czech or his Slovak heirs). The fluidity of the protonational past is hidden from view as it is anachronistically presented in the nationally crystallized form that emerged from it – as if it had ever been thus.[3]

Across Europe and across the centuries we encounter a public and intellectual investment in language standards, spelling norms and the purist rejection of foreign loanwords; the invocation of 'mother's milk' by Grimm was in fact a quotation from the seventeenth-century language enthusiast Schottelius. The long process of state formation in post-1300 Europe is accompanied, throughout its course, by reflections on the state's linguistic regime – whether non-state ('minority') languages are to be tolerated or discountenanced, and how to ensure public standards for the state language. In this lengthy process, a shift occurred between 1770 and 1810.[4]

Johann Gottlieb Herder realized that the formative anthropological role of language lay not just in its capacity for articulating and ordering our thoughts and facilitating human sapience but also in its capacity for diversification. Language is, in fact, a proliferation of different languages, each in their different ways articulating and ordering our thoughts and facilitating human sapience in different cultural communities – 'nations', as they were soon to be called. As we saw in Chapter 5, languages became the specific markers – carriers, even – of separate national identities.

Following the fall of the Holy Roman Empire of the German Nation, German intellectuals realized that the most important remaining thing they, as 'the German Nation', still had in common was in fact the German language – we have encountered Arndt's stance. As the lexicographer Campe phrased it in the preface to his 1807 German dictionary:

> Let me in conclusion commit myself to the firm opinion that in this time, full of impending doom, or even in recent years circling towards absolute downfall, there is nothing more needful, urgent or meritorious for our lamented German nationality that the cultivation – the development, purification and consolidation – of our excellent language. The language is the only remaining tie which holds us together as a nation, is at the same time the only remaining reason to hope that the name of Germans will not altogether disappear from the annals of mankind; the only thing which renders the possibility of a future reunification into an independent polity conceivable.[5]

It became, following Fichte's 'Addresses to the German Nation', a matter of pride that of all the Germanic tribes that had swarmed over the European landmass during the fifth-century migration period, the Germans had stuck to their ancestral language. The Vandals and Visigoths in Spain, the Ostrogoths and Longobards in Italy, the Franks and Burgundians in France: they all had adopted the Vulgar Latin of their conquered countries, in time switching over to Romance languages. Not so the Germans

Figure 6.1 Title-page vignette for the Grimms' *Deutsches Wörterbuch* (1854). ERNiE imagebank

(with some tribes, as Grimm noted, still occupying their premigration homelands). That linguistic tenacity was seen as fidelity to the ancestral inheritance and as giving the Germans a moral edge over the French and Italians. 'A nation that abandons its ancestral language is degenerate and anchorless', Grimm wrote in 1830, meaning that it has lost its rootedness in its inherited identity and character. For the Grimms' greatest enterprise, the dictionary of the German language (*Deutsches Wörterbuch*), the chosen motto was 'Im Anfang war das Wort' ('In the Beginning was the Word'; Figure 6.1). That opening phrase of the Gospel according to John, as translated by Luther, was used both metaphysically and anthropologically. It referred to the Word as a Platonic *logos* but also, more specifically, to the German language as the very bedrock of a German identity – in line, again, with what we saw in Chapter 5.[6]

Grimm reverted to the register of Romantic–sentimental pathos in his inaugural lecture (1830) at the University of Göttingen. It was, ironically, delivered in Latin, but it presented an intellectual blueprint of his national commitment. The lecture is entitled *De desiderio patriae*. That translates as 'Of homesickness', which alerts us to one of the crucial turns of thought in this piece. Grimm conflates the notions of desire and love, *desiderium* and *amor*, and he leads us from one to the other deliberately and purposefully. For it is *amor patriae*, rather than *desiderium*, that presides over his closing sentence:

> For in this time of turmoil and change through which there is foreshadowed for us, whether we are aware of it or not, the passage from our traditional ways into a new order, we must hold fast the pure and holy love of our country; for while that love lasts we may even yet be saved, unless the anger of Heaven itself should be against us. Let us then be united in the common purpose to guard like men the honour and liberty to which we are born, with eyes afire and hearts beating high whenever we hear spoken the beloved name of our native land.[7]

Love of the fatherland for Grimm is a primal instinct tugging at the heartstrings and inspiring homesickness when one is abroad. As an affect it is as intimate and as universal as that bond between infant and breastfeeding mother, and as such it proves that love of the fatherland is 'naturally human', neither a socially inculcated political virtue nor a matter of pragmatic expedience. It is the non-negotiable tie that links us to our *Art*, our collective nature, to those who are close and dear to us; it accompanies us throughout our life's experiences. And it is intimately bound up with the native language, which in and of itself defines for the German speakers their own homeland. Grimm's scholarly Latin contains a hard-edged, Arndt-like political conclusion: 'But our own language, which is the surest foundation upon which our state can rest, we must cultivate and perfect, and not doubt that the limits of its life and power will also be the boundaries of Germany itself.' And that would include, obviously, Schleswig-Holstein.

In 1848, as a delegate to the Frankfurt Nationalversammlung (National Assembly; see Figure 2.3), Grimm urged persistence in the flagging Schleswig-Holstein war against Denmark;* he threw his great scholarly prestige behind this belligerence. As he had elaborated in his own attempt at *Völkergeschichte*, his *Geschichte der deutschen Sprache* of 1848, and now brought forward in the National Assembly, the Danish dialects of Jutland betrayed a pre-Danish, German substratum in that territory. From that he concluded that a return of those territories into a greater Germany was historically preordained and inevitable. The Danish isles, he felt, were best left to Sweden. Holland, too, would ultimately find its way back to the German bosom from which it had regrettably detached itself a few centuries ago: 'A reversal of the Dutch to the German language … I consider, over the next centuries, to be a probability which will redound to the benefit of all German peoples. … It stands to reason that the Netherlander would rather become German than French.'[8] Language is, then, a cornerstone both of Romantic–sentimental anthropology post-Herder and of nascent nationalist ideology, oscillating between the tender recall of infancy and the hard-bitten demand for geopolitical expansion. Grimm's meanderings between etymological antiquarianism, sentimental

* The National Assembly was implicated in the first Schleswig-Holstein War, since Prussian troops were deployed on behalf of the German Confederation (of which Schleswig and Holstein formed part). Prussia was dissuaded by Russia, France and the UK from pursuing the war (Truce of Malmö, 26 August 1848). The refusal of the Frankfurt National Assembly to ratify that truce (in line with Grimm's motion) led to severe polarization and was one of the causes of the parliament's fracture in the revolutionary events of September 1848.

affect and territorial expansionism fully echo the *Völkergeschichte* and the political agenda of Ernst Moritz Arndt, who sat beside him in the Frankfurt National Assembly. Arndt had patented the territorialization of language in his song 'What is the German's Fatherland', for which he was given a spontaneous, ovational vote of thanks by the Assembly delegates (see Chapter 9).[9]

This political territorialization of language, extrapolating from language (as a communicative ambience) to language area (a communicatively homogeneous homeland) and thence to state expansionism, is a fundamental characteristic of Romantic nationalism.[10] In the second half of the nineteenth century, it forms the cornerstone of almost all manifestations of irredentism, when the presence, outside the state's borders, of fellow nationals (usually identified as such by their language, more rarely by religion) inspires a policy of expanding the state so as to aim for maximum inclusion and to gather all members of the nation/language community into a single homeland. The nation's division across different states is felt to be unnatural and undesirable. The geopolitical problems arising from this nostrum are obvious, and they play out along two axes. What to do with border zones, such as Schleswig-Holstein, where there is a mixed bilingual population? And what is, ultimately 'a' language? Where do different dialects group together into 'a' single language or else fall apart into separate 'different' languages? These issues were addressed by the vociferous identity politics of such men as Arndt and Grimm, and it is here that philologists, in particular, played a political role in the fluid years after Napoleon's downfall.

Macro-nationalism and Pan-movements: German as a Sliding Scale

The Germanic language family has diversified into different standard languages over the past centuries. Norwegian has established itself, in two competing variants, as a language distinct from both Danish and Swedish; Faroese has claimed linguistic specificity on the coat-tails of the Icelandic national revival. In the Netherlands, an uneasy bi-stability has been maintained since 1840 between a common Netherlandic (written) standard and two main (orally based) variants, Flemish and Dutch; Luxembourgish and Afrikaans have become state languages in the course of the twentieth century, and regiolects such as Scots, West Flemish, Low Saxon and Limburgish have at different moments claimed a subsidiary distinctness and recognition. The particularism of minor variants requesting separate recognition can be juxtaposed with an opposite tendency: to group together large family groups as single, compound wholes. The followers of the two tendencies are known as 'splitters' and 'lumpers'.[11]

The 'lumpers' in this process were the German philologists of the Romantic generation: Grimm, Arndt, Hoffmann von Fallersleben and their later adepts, Simrock and Dahn. They saw all variants as mere variations within a greater German language. When Grimm viewed the future convergence of Dutch into German as something beneficial for all German peoples, he apparently included the Dutch themselves in that aggregation of future beneficiaries. That, indeed, is characteristic of the elasticity with which Grimm uses the notion of 'German'. We have seen an egregious example in the case of Hoffmann von Fallersleben in Chapter 4, where the 'German' language as used from Luther to Goethe (*Hochdeutsch*, 'High German') can also subsume 'Niederdeutsch' variants that are either regiolects (Low Saxon) or the languages of neighbouring states (Dutch and Flemish). A future merger of all these variants into a greater German whole is then presented as natural and proper – both linguistically and politically. Arndt in 1831 asserted it as the Germans' 'right and duty to see Holland and Switzerland joined to the ancient German lands in a new life'. Arndt hastens to add that there should be no forcible annexation or enforced union; but precisely how that reintegration process should be driven forward, and by whom, is glossed over in a contorted, weaseling word salad: 'as Germany, a united whole, will present itself in such a new, rejuvenated guise, they [the Swiss and the Dutch] could not reasonably refuse acknowledging that as a matter of common sense they should accept an invitation to that effect.' And he adds, with greater clarity and more menace: 'But this should be held up to them, if necessary on the point of a rapier: that the Swiss can no longer hire themselves out as mercenaries to combat or even subjugate their fellow Germans, or that the Dutch should remain in a position to throttle and block the Rhine, that vital German artery.'[12] In the Frankfurt National Assembly of 1848, much of the deliberation was taken up with geolinguistic questions concerning German borderlands such as the Low Countries, the southern Tyrol and, most of all, Schleswig-Holstein. It was in this context that Grimm asserted, on philological grounds, the right for Germany to include not only Schleswig-Holstein but all of Jutland and prophesied the future merger of Flanders and the Netherlands into the greater German whole.

That, then, is how the 'lumpers' use the term 'German' in an expansionist sense. Grimm uses it thus in the *Deutsche Grammatik*, the *Geschichte der*

Deutschen Sprache and the *Deutsche Mythologie*, where it refers essentially to all the living German languages and dialects spoken on the European continent south of Scandinavia. In this scheme, German, as the centre and default of that linguistic continuum, becomes almost tantamount to 'Germanic'. And what in the first half of the nineteenth century seemed like the visionary musings of Romantic poets and philologists became part of an expansionist policy, not only regarding Alsace-Lorraine in 1870–1871 but also in the direction of the Low Countries and Denmark, as the German war aims in the two World Wars make clear.

Broadly speaking, the opposition between lumpers and splitters maps onto the distinction between aggregationist and separatist nationalism; the former, aiming to unify large groups, lead into pan-movements such as Pan-Germanism or Pan-Slavism, while the latter tend to claim a separate status for smaller self-distinguishing nationalities such as Flemings or Slovenians. The two intersect, for Flemings are comprised in the larger Germanic category, Slovenians in the Slavic one, as nesting dolls are inside a matryoshka.

In this nesting matryoshka model, sometimes a wider, sometimes a narrower ethnolinguistic category is seen as the one that matters. In Flanders, some lumpers followed a Pan-German logic and placed themselves under the aegis of a greater German whole; other people saw Flemish as an independent, separate sibling language of Dutch; and some splitters even wanted to develop a separate linguistic standard for it based on the outlying dialects as spoken near Ypres. In Scandinavia, Danish anxieties over the possible loss of Schleswig-Holstein to an expanding Germany favoured a reframing of their identity as 'Scandinavians', drawing on the cultural kinship and (it was hoped) the political solidarity of Sweden–Norway. But amidst this Pan-Nordic unification ideal, in Norway a rivalry developed between two variants of a Norwegian language standard, and the leading Norwegian playwright Bjørnstjerne Bjørnson later embraced Pan-Germanism.[13]

So how and why do people, in formulating the relation between language and national identity, opt for one or another of the matryoshka's nesting shells? How and why do they decide which linguistic differences are decisive and which are inconsequential?

Etic and Emic: Which Differences Matter?

Practically all new states that came into being around 1918 owed their independence to an ethnolinguistic national movement in the preceding decades. From Iceland to Bulgaria and from Finland and Norway to

Luxembourg and Bohemia, advocacy for 'national languages' had dominated public consciousness-raising since the mid-nineteenth century. Everywhere, minority populations had claimed their status as distinct nations by asserting that what they spoke was a separate language.

Not, emphatically, dialects. 'Dialects' was a word colloquially used for subsidiary variants within a language, characterizing a regional variation at best, never a separate nationality. Languages, on the other hand, are demarcated by differences between one another, much as adjoining countries are, and each ideally maps onto its own nation-state. As philologists began to see relations in terms of branching family trees, the status of 'a language' derived in large part from having an early historical branch-off point. Lithuanian famously obtained great prestige from the recognition that its descent from Indo-European antedated and bypassed the spit into Slavic, Celtic, Germanic and Romance clusters. The stature of Catalan and Occitan was raised by their status as siblings, rather than offshoots, of French and Castilian Spanish, all of these claiming their own independent derivation from Vulgar Latin (see Chapter 10). The often-encountered formula that Irish, Albanian, Slovenian, Galego and Frisian are 'ancient' languages (which, strictly speaking, is nonsensical: how can one language be more 'ancient' than another, since all descend equally from the primal origins of human speech?) is a debased echo of this family tree schematization. 'Ancient' means, in fact, being an 'early branch': a variant whose taxonomic separateness was established early on, as attested by certain archaic (hence 'authentic', non-derivative) features.

But the discussion was anything but cut and dried. Linguistic descent is a tangled mycelium, not a neat pedigree. Linguists now roll their eyes at the very idea of distinguishing between the levels of 'dialect' and 'language'. There is no clear-cut criterion that makes the taxon 'language' qualitatively or objectively different from the taxon 'dialect'. As the oft-repeated quip has it, languages are dialects with an army and a navy:[14] they are classified as such as a result of that contingent happenstance called state formation. The cases of Afrikaans and Luxembourgish bear this out. Local idioms, originally classed as dialects (a variant of Dutch among the Boers of Southern Africa, and 'Moselle-Franconian' in Luxembourg, respectively), they received state-initiated recognition as official languages in 1923 and 1975, in the context of their (relatively recent) state independence.

But while the distinction between a language and a dialect has no underlying, objective foundation ('etic', i.e. as part of specific, empirically measurable, language-intrinsic features), it does, as the recognition of Afrikaans and Luxembourgish shows, have a real-world presence. People attach a real-world meaning ('emic') to whatever causes them to apply that distinction.*

Where 'a' language begins or ends is historically floating and somewhat arbitrary, and 'emic' rather than 'etic'. Witness the language that used to be called Serbo-Croatian. It embraces, as Slavicists know, a number of interpenetrating regiolects and dialect groups.** Important divisions ran through the populations using this language/dialect cluster: between the Ottoman and Habsburg Empires (and Venice), between Orthodox and Roman Catholic Christianity, and between the Cyrillic and Latin alphabets. There was only a limited history of communicative interaction between Belgrade, Ragusa (present-day Dubrovnik) and Zagrab/Agram (present-day Zagreb). Cross-communitarian interaction intensified in the nineteenth century, however, and crystallized in the Vienna Literary Agreement of 1850, when assorted intellectuals – each prominent in their respective communities, with Vuk Karadžić among them – signed a declaration asserting the unity of their dialects under a single standard. In the declaration's preamble, the signatories express their dismay at the diffraction caused 'not only by alphabets, but still by orthographic rules as well'.[15]

From this integrationist high point, the last half-century has witnessed a relapse into 'splitting' particularism. After the break-up of Yugoslavia, the Serbo-Croatian language lost its unitary status; Croatia and Serbia as separate successor states put forward separate linguistic standards for 'their' Croatian and Serbian languages. And with the further dismemberment of Serbia, we have witnessed how Bosnian and Montenegrin have cultivated a divergent linguistic standard from rump-Serbian: for example, by introducing new letters into their state-sanctioned alphabets.[16]

In all this contested fluidity, one linguistic aggregate remained firmly outside the Serbo/Croatian lumping and splitting: Slovenian. It profited

* Emically – at the experiential level – it is possible to specify how and why the distinction between the concepts 'language' and 'dialect' tends to be applied, connotationally and almost stereotypically. The concept of 'language' (as opposed to dialect) is used [a] for official state languages, [b] for regiolects with a line of descent that is generally recognized as being other than that of the state language and [c] for regiolects that are used in long-distance communication (print, mass media) and as vehicles for a Habermassian 'public sphere' (literature, educational or religious institutions, usage between strangers in the social setting of public spaces). By contrast, 'dialects' (in the *patois* sense, as opposed to 'language') are seen as confined to face-to-face communication – primarily oral rather than written – in private or small-scale communitarian settings. This emic distinction roughly mirrors the one between *Gesellschaft* and *Gemeinschaft*: languages are seen as media of interaction in a historical or modern 'society', while dialects are seen as media of interaction in a traditional 'community'. On etic and emic: Harris 1976, Olivier de Sardan 1998, Barnard 2002, Sahlins 2017.

** These are distinguished by their way of forming the interrogative pronoun. They are called Čakavian, Kajkavian and Štokavian, the last one comprising three subvariants (Ekavian, Ikavian and Ijekavian).

from the philological trump card of the 'early branch-off' and independent descent from Old Slavonic, as demonstrated by its archaic and unique feature of the 'dual number'. In 1808, Jernej Kopitar's *Grammatik der Slavischen Sprache in Krain, Kärnten und Steyermark* grouped together the Slavic dialects spoken (and to some extent written) in Styria, Carniola, Carinthia and the Prekmurje region; and he proposed a new ethnonym for these populations: Slovenec. He also asserted the separate and indeed senior position of their language among the Slavic ones. It was, Kopitar argued, independently descended from Old Church Slavonic and had maintained a basic feature of the ancestral *Ur*-language: Slovenec alone had kept the archaic 'dual number', known to educated Europeans from its lingering traces in Homeric Greek and already noted in Kopitar's 1808 grammar. The *dualis*, which refers to 'a pair' as something that is neither singular nor plural (as in trousers, scissors or twin siblings), has since remained a trump card in the particularism of Slovenian vis-à-vis neighbouring South-Slavic regiolects. Slovenian remained outside the Vienna Declaration on the unity of Serbo-Croatian. Its symbolic prestige ensured for Slovenia a separate status among the southern Slavs who united into Yugoslavia after 1918 and divorced out of Yugoslavia after 1991. If present-day Slovenia as a state can boast an army and an (admittedly diminutive) navy, this is due to the fact that Slovenian has long been recognized as 'being a language rather than a dialect' – on the grounds, ultimately, of its *dualis*.[17] And so the dictum that 'a language is a dialect with an army and a navy' can be turned on its head: you get to have your own army and navy if you speak a language rather than a dialect.

Matryoshka Scalarity

Thus we encounter the competing forces of splitting (centrifugal particularism, Slovene) and lumping (centripetal aggregationism: Serbo-Croat, South-Slavic). One of the most intractable problems in the negotiations of linguistic identity was and is that of scalarity: how variants of language could be aggregated from the small local regiolect to the large macro-family.

The linguistic 'family tree' model saw the great linguistic families (Slavic, Germanic, Romance, Celtic) as great sub-trunks of the Indo-European tree, subdividing from the level of the family to that of 'languages' (branches) and then further into 'dialects' (boughs and twigs). But the distinction between these successive levels (trunk, branch, bough and twig; language family, language and dialect) was open to debate and subject to ideological agendas.

Accounts of the number of Slavic languages have varied wildly. In 1756, Andrija Kačić-Miošić enumerated eleven of them, erroneously including Albanian; the eminent Göttingen antiquary August Schlözer identified eight, including the obscure and extinct Polabian. In the early 1820s, the no less eminent philologist Josef Dobrovský saw all Slavic languages as dialect offshoots of one common, ancient language, Old Church Slavonic. He distinguished two main groups, with Russian being uneasily assigned to either one or the other. The now-current tripartite division of southern, western and eastern clusters was consolidated only later. Within these clusters, the taxonomy has remained tentative, with certain small variants (Sorbian) enjoying separate status and other pairs, such as Czech and Slovak, and Bulgarian and Macedonian, counted either together as one or separately as two, as the case might be, and some, such as Kashubian or Rusyn, either being overlooked (by outsiders) or else strenuously asserted (by their speakers).[18]

And so, as the outer twigs of the family tree were being uncertainly counted, there was a tendency to revert it all back to the tree-trunk. Were these variants not all part of a single macro-language? The Slovak Jan Herkel argued this in his *Elementa universalis linguae Slavicae e vivis dialectis eruta* (Buda 1826), proposing a common Slavic literary language and an 'Unio in Litteratura inter omnes Slavos, sive verus pan-slavismus' (A unified literacy for all Slavs, indeed a pan-Slavism). Other Slovak intellectuals, the poet Jan Kollár and the antiquarian Pavol Šafárik, had also opted for this linguistic holism; and so 'Pan-Slavism' was born. It manifested itself politically with a Pan-Slavic Congress in Prague in 1848, which got caught up in the revolutionary events of that fateful year (see Chapter 2); and it inspired the paintings of Alphonse Mucha a century later.

The complex history of Pan-Slavism can only briefly be summarized here.[19] The initial stage culminated in the 1848 Prague Congress and ended when that congress, and the city of Prague, got embroiled in the armed conflicts around the 1848 revolutions. The pre-1848 Slavic activists (we have encountered Palacký, Šafárik and Kollár) consisted primarily of intellectuals in the Habsburg Empire. Opposing the Habsburgs' imperial, arbitrary government, they mistrusted the autocracy of the Russian tsar even more; they were themselves mistrusted by the Hungarian nobility (who used 'Pan-Slavism' as a scare word) and to some extent by the more aristocratically minded Polish gentry of Galicia – although the 1831 uprising had unleashed a wave of Slavic solidarity. After the failure of the 1848 revolution, a regrouping of Slavic-minded activists looked to Russia, where at the same time a 'Slavophile' tendency was taking hold.

Denouncing Western European influences, Slavophiles saw Russia as the natural leader of all Christian Orthodox Slavic nations. Pan-Slavism was revived in an 1867 congress held in Moscow and became noticeably more Russian-oriented. This Pan-Russianist tendency continued in force in the mid-twentieth century, spurred on by the German attack of 1941; a Pan-Slavic Committee was formed in Moscow in 1941 and published a monthly periodical from 1943. Following Russia's victory, in 1945 a

> Pan-Slav Congress in Sofia, which had been called by the victorious Russians, adopted a resolution pronouncing it 'not only an international political necessity to declare Russian its language of general communication and the official language of all Slav countries, but a moral necessity.' Shortly before, the Bulgarian radio had broadcast a message by the Metropolitan Stefan, vicar of the Holy Bulgarian Synod, in which he called upon the Russian people 'to remember their messianic mission' and prophesied the coming 'unity of the Slav people'.[20]

Readers will easily discern here the roots of Vladimir Putin's Ukrainian policies and the influential stance of the Russian Orthodox Church under its Metropolitan Kirill.

Although another Pan-Slavic Congress was held in Belgrade in 1946, chaired by Tito, Yugoslavia opted out of this frame in 1948. Instead, Tito fell back on an alternative, subsidiary pan-movement, South-Slavism or Yugo-Slavism. It had developed out of earlier antecedents (the 'Illyrian' movement of the 1830s; the successful self-positioning of Croatia under Jelačić after 1848) and had been marked by an ambivalent position astride Habsburg and Russian orientations – the former strongest in Catholic Slovenia and Croatia, the latter in Orthodox Serbia, Montenegro and Bulgaria.

The scalar vacillation in pan-movements was driven by the political application of linguistic lumping or splitting. Pan-Slavism assumes the ideal notion of a single Slavic macro-language, with merely secondary (dialectal) differences. Particular emancipation movements will accord even minor etic features a decisive emic (difference-making) importance and, as a result, multiply the number of self-distinguishing Slavic languages – as in the case of Slovak (which came to achieve a position of its own in the course of the nineteenth century) and, latterly, Montenegrin. Three of these Slavic languages would become, or remain, the official languages of independent states: Russian, Polish and Bulgarian. Eight (or seven, depending on how you count Serbo-Croatian) would become co-official languages of federal states: Czech and Slovak in Czechoslovakia; Slovenian, Macedonian and Serbian/Croatian in Yugoslavia; and (intermittently and grudgingly) Ukrainian and Belarusian in the USSR. Sorbian and other smaller variants would subsist as regional minorities. In the century after Versailles, newly self-distinguishing languages would begin to assert their presence, such as Rusyn (in the Carpathian borderlands where Poland, Slovakia and Ukraine meet).

Also in the century after Versailles, the political organization of the self-distinguishing nations and nation-states of Europe did, despite two World Wars and other upheavals, more or less settle down. The break-up of the Habsburg, Romanov and Ottoman Empires saw new states emerge, each with its language now constitutionally enshrined as the 'national' one.* After 1918, linguistic minorities in the new states of Central and Eastern Europe were given some protection under League of Nations regulations. In 1992 the Council of Europe established a Charter for Regional and Minority Languages to which most European states are signatories. As a result, all these minority languages now assert their individuality and their right to maintain themselves under the European charter, and in almost any European country there is an ongoing debate about linguistic diversity. Language is, in short, the mother of all identity politics issues.

Historical Permanence versus Social Outreach

It is not for nothing that philologists, who more than anyone else reflect on variations within languages and on differences and similarities between them, are at the forefront of the lumpers, tending to merge regions and nations into macro-groups (Pan-Slavism, Pan-Germanism, Pan-Celticism). Linguists and philologists are, if nothing else, masters of language. They deal with languages as dexterously as a magician does a deck of cards. For men such as Josef Dobrovský, Jernej Kopitar, Rasmus Rask and Jacob Grimm, Slavic or Germanic really were a single language. Icelandic, Old Saxon and Frisian were as insignificantly different for Rask as Church Slavonic, modern Russian and medieval Czech were for Dobrovský. They corresponded in whatever language came in handy, or (in the case of Kopitar) in a macaronic welter of mashed-up Latin, German and smatterings from various other idioms that all coexisted in his word-soaked brain.[21]

Such philologists see through centuries of language transformation as if these were merely superficial shifts of complexion. On the family tree

* For the victorious allies, the Wilsonian principle was implemented less vigorously and old states were not dismembered on the altar of the 'self-determination of peoples'. Welsh, Scots Gaelic, Flemish, Faroese, Greenlandic, Basque, Catalan, Breton, Frisian and Saami remained in their accustomed position vis-à-vis their superimposed state languages. As a result, language movements continued in their respective states that varied between mild regionalist and fervent nationalist levels.

of language relationships, they automatically trace the present-day leaves and twigs back to the primordial branches and trunk and even to the tree's hypothetically reconstructed prehistoric root system. They read with X-ray eyes, discerning the ancient, skeletal roots of words through their modern appearances, immediately sensing how the English *gate* relates to the Nordic *gata* or the German *Gasse*, how the Gaulish name-ending -rix signified royal status, as in the Latin *rex* or the Gothic -ric, and how Theodoric of Verona could later, in German texts, come to be called Dietrich von Bern. The resemblance between English *daughter*, German *Tochter*, Greek θυγατηρ and Sanskrit *duhitr* would be as predictable to them as the multiplication table. Their expertise of deep linguistic scanning foreshortens the passage of time, as it were: for philologists the tribal Dark Ages were right next door, just a few sound-shifts away. And the tribes of yore were, for them, a recent past, still discernible in their traces. Surely any child could see that the tribe of the Catti mentioned in Tacitus map onto present-day Hessia, or Gaelic *leabhar* and Welsh *llyfr* were both derived from Latin *liber*, 'book', a mere millennium and a half ago.

At the 'lumped' aggregation level of the language family, historical and linguistic distances are both abolished, and macronationalism can see modern societies as the continuation of the tribal constituents of an original common ethnicity. This is why the ancient Cimbri and Teutones of Jutland are still a present force in the *Völkergeschichte* and the geopolitical thought of Jacob Grimm. The fifth-century Burgundians of the *Nibelungenlied*, domiciled between Xanten and Worms on the Rhine, are identified as a tribe that was midway in their migration towards the Bourgogne from their ancestral origin Bornholm (originally *Burgundaholmr*, obviously).

In looking at the function of language, philologists gravitated to a historicist rather than social emphasis: language is the thing that can be traced as a filiation across time, and it is the thing that ensures that successive generations belong to the same communicative tradition. In nineteenth-century language politics, the philologically inspired view would therefore aim for orthographic and lexical standards that did the greatest justice to the language's historical antecedents and that would ensure the legibility of the literary heritage by modern readers.

An opposing view emerged around the mid-century; we encounter it particularly among popular educationalists, authors and activists. Their priority was to spread and facilitate literacy and to ensure that even people with low literacy rates and using modern sociolects and regiolects could easily learn a common standard. After 1848, a new generation of language activists drew their experience from social life, folklore and education, rather than from ancient manuscripts and archives. Their frame of reference was much more society-specific. In emphasizing the communicative, present-day bonding power of the language, they opted for standardizations that were more reformist and closer to the usage of present-day speakers, and for a stricter systematization of spelling rules so as to achieve higher literacy rates more easily.

These two opposing viewpoints played themselves out in language standardization debates all over Europe. The prototype is that of Greek, where originally a 'purified' (*katharevousa*) form of the historical language was cultivated, challenged later by a more 'demotic' alternative. In Serbia, conservative intellectuals defended the traditional language as liturgically endorsed in the Orthodox Church against the innovations proposed by Vuk Karadžić. In Ireland, the need to salvage and retrieve the old literary language opposed a turn towards the contemporary 'speech of the people' (*cainnt na ndaoine*).[22]

On the whole, it may be said that the philologically based, historicist standard came first, followed at a later stage by the demotic alternative. What is more, the historicist–philological standard tends to prevail among lumpers, favouring an aggregationist, more inclusive view of different variants, while modern demotic standards are more specifically prescriptive and favour 'splitting' with competing standardizations for different variants (e.g. Valencian and Balearic alongside Catalan), or competing lexical and orthographic standards (Slovak, Norwegian, Breton). These tendencies are shown schematically in Table 6.1.

The two coexist, of course, the latter being an overlay on the former, not its replacement. But on the whole, over the nineteenth century, language communities tended to diffract into increasingly fine-grained, smaller and hence more numerous aggregates. As the number of self-distinguishing languages (each with its own language area) has grown, the length of the

Table 6.1 *Types of minority language cultivation in nineteenth-century Europe*

1800–1845	Post-1845
Historicist–philological	Vernacular–social
Literature-oriented	Speech-oriented
Fluid standardization	Stricter standardization
Lumpers	Splitters

borders between them has increased – and with it, the potential for problematic demarcations and borderline contestations.

The historical dimension declines in prominence, then, as the contemporary social one increases. What remains constant is the undiminishing importance of the territorial dimension, the automatic conceptualization of language as being tantamount to a 'language area' and the need to establish clear and fixed boundaries between these. That territorialism would become a cornerstone of the post-1918 nation-state system; and the state-resisting, state-breaking and state-aspiring forces of language assertion would remain a constant in the century after Versailles.

Celts, Aryans, Turanians: Max Müller and Race

Pan-movements such as Celticism were aggregationist from a minority position, rather than hegemonically expansionist or irredentist. The self-defining 'Celts', whether as speakers or as a 'race', never seriously contemplated turning their kinship into a serious nation-building programme – not even a language revival programme, for the Celtic languages are too tenuously related to be mutually intelligible; nor can they provide a shared communicative ambience. What they share is a sense of marginalization and cultural decline in their respective countries. Their political programme was, at best, to strengthen each other's positions in their respective states by acts of cultural solidarity and the joint assertion of their independent descent and 'ancient' roots. This sense of deep linguistic–mythical roots is asserted, logically enough, in folkloristic displays involving folk dances, folk dress, bagpipes and music, annually at the Interceltic Festival in Lorient (Brittany). And there is a huge statue of the mythical figure Breogán, known from Irish Gaelic legend, in the harbour of La Coruña celebrating the Celtiberian roots of Galicia.[23]

Pan-Celticism began in the 1820s as a literary collaboration between Welsh and Breton intellectuals and poets. The learned clergyman Thomas Price supported the efforts of the Breton lexicographer Le Gonidec to make a Breton translation of the New Testament. The scheme was funded by the British Foreign Bible Society (BFBS), an association established in 1804 and dedicated to the Protestant mission of making the Scriptures directly available to (potential) believers everywhere, and in their own languages.*

* The BFBS spread rapidly: by 1816 there were numerous branches across the UK and a network of some forty-nine associated societies had spread across Europe (with German-speaking cities heavily represented). Sponsored translations included Armenian, Finnish, Polish, Russian, Latvian,

The aims of the BFBS did not envisage the stimulation of anything like a national consciousness or cultural nationalism and were conceived only in terms of Protestant evangelism. Even so, we see an opportunistic working relationship take place between BFBS sponsorship and many activists in 'Phase A' cultural consciousness-raising; among them were the Serbian Vuk Karadžić and the Breton Le Gonidec, but also the Albanian Fan Noli. They opportunistically made use of the BFBS agenda to bankroll their philological or literary interests. In Mérimée's supernatural tale *Lokis* (1869), the narrator, Professor Wittembach (a spoof on the type of the pedantic German philologist) sets out for the Lithuanian countryside to prepare a new gospel translation into the obscure local language called 'Zhumaitic' or 'Zhmoud' – a language, as the knowledgeable Professor Wittembach observes, 'possibly closer than even Lithuanian to Sanskrit'. Mérimée knew full well what he was lampooning; the background details he furnished to his tale were in fact well-informed. Professor Wittembach's 'Žmudaitic' language is close to the local name for the dialect of Samogitia, an important Lithuanian region: Žemaitiu.[24]

Le Gonidec's Bible translation, banned as it was by the Catholic authorities in Brittany, was no great success – anecdote has it that Price was reduced to fobbing off excess stock for use in Wales. But the notion of Breton–Welsh kinship took hold. Price, who was involved in the influential coterie around the Welsh-minded Lady Llanover near Abergavenny, launched, in the 1820, the idea of reviving an ancient Welsh literary festival, the eisteddfod. Thanks to the support of Lady Llanover and her network, the idea bore fruit; in fact it was the germination of what today is the highly prestigious and popular Welsh National Eisteddfod. And Price was mindful of his, and his country's, Breton connections. In 1838, the year of Le Gonidec's death, his successor La Villemarqué headed a Breton delegation to take part in that year's Eisteddfod. La Villemarqué plagiarized Lady Charlotte Guest's work on medieval Welsh poetry to produce his own fanciful *Les bardes bretons du VIe siècle*, and the notion of a Celtic–Arthurian unity between Wales and Brittany was firmly established. The Welsh institutions of the eisteddfod and the Gorsedd (a neo-bardic council) were

Estonian, Lithuanian, Moldavian and modern Greek. Estonian, curiously, was specified as a twofold language with different translations envisaged for Livonia and Courland. In the case of Lithuanian, dialect differences were additionally complicated by the fact that the Lithuanian lands with their long-standing Catholic tradition were partitioned between Prussian- and Russian-governed parts (imposing, respectively, a Protestant and an Orthodox religious regime). Many more European languages would follow in the course of the century; and many, many more again from among the native languages in the British Empire, from the Indian subcontinent to Canada (Howsam 1991).

copied in Wales and later also in the intermediate region of Cornwall, which likewise looked back upon a 'Celtic' past. The word 'Celtic' was in these years gaining currency as the technical appellation for the language family of which Breton, Welsh and Cornish formed part. The term had been retrieved from classical usage a century before to refer to the extinct Gaulish language and contemporary Breton.

The Gaelic languages were also included in this 'Celtic' complex: Gaelic in its Irish, Scots and Manx variants. It was only in the 1820s that philologists would establish that this Celtic language family did in fact form part of the Indo-European complex. Being 'Celtic', and as such an independently descended archaic western outrider of the Indo-European complex, hugely raised the status of Welsh, as we can see from the international, prestigious outreach of the 1830s Eisteddfods of Abergavenny. At these events, German scholars competed for essay prizes. Addresses were read out from Sir Walter Scott, Thomas Moore, Robert Southey and Lamartine; the Eisteddfod even reached out in 1838 to the Calcutta tycoon Dwarkanath Tagore (grandfather of the poet Rabindranath and instigator of the 'Bengal Renaissance'), then visiting Britain, as a 'fellow Aryan'. The hub for this international outreach was Christian Bunsen, Prussian ambassador in Britain as of 1842 and brother-in-law to Lady Llanover. Bunsen had philological interests, had learned Persian and Sanskrit and was aware that the westernmost and easternmost branches of the Indo-European 'Aryan' language complex were both under Britain's imperial dominion.[25]

The Celtic languages were fully placed on the map in 1854, when the German scholar Johann Caspar Zeuss published his august *Grammatica Celtica* and the French critic and scholar Ernest Renan published *La poésie des races celtiques*. The latter book, and a visit to the Llandudno Eisteddfod of 1864, would inspire Matthew Arnold's Oxford lecture series on 'The Study of Celtic Literature'. By this time, the comparative philology of Celtic antiquity in Indo-European contexts was firmly established as a British imperial enterprise, and scholars noted the ethnographic and ancient legal similarities between Celts and Indians. One of these was the institution of the hunger strike. An ancient Irish bardic hunger strike was thematized in W. B. Yeats's play *The King's Threshold* of 1905; it would suggest a powerful political pressure tactic for Mahatma Gandhi, suffragettes and Irish nationalists.[26]

Hunger strikes were far from the minds of the Breton–Welsh Celticists of the mid-century as they toasted their benevolent cultural kinship at festive banquets. Pan-Celticism never developed a common separatism but merely acted as an echo chamber that strengthened the national movements in the various Celtic regions. And for the Pan-Celts taking cultural comfort in each other's kinship and proximity, the Sanskrit word 'Aryan' only had the lustre of ancient Brahminic prestige and carried a sense that they, peripheral on the Atlantic fringe of Europe, were enmeshed in a great world civilization.

That sense of connection was fed by Bunsen and, though him, by his protégé Max Müller. Friedrich Max Müller was Mérimée's Professor Wittembach in real life and probably the most celebrated adept of the Grimm school of comparative philology. A sanskritist and translator of the Rig-Veda (for which he could draw on the resources of the East India Company), he became (aided by Bunsen) a professor at Oxford; thanks to his public lectures and popularizing books on Indo-European languages and comparative mythology, his name became a household word. Like Bunsen, he made his career in a Victorian England that was deeply committed to its Anglo-Saxon connections with the 'German cousins'; he was naturalized as a British citizen in 1855 and towards the end of his life was even appointed to the Privy Council.[27]

It was Müller, with his interest in comparative religion, who most famously worked out the deep connections between language, mythology and the cultural DNA of the 'Aryan nations'. For Müller, mythology *was* in fact a form of language: natural occurrences such as rain, thunder and fertility were given names as proper nouns, but these were also personal names that could, as deities or personified forces of nature, explain their functions in a mythical narrative.

For mythologists and comparative religionists such as Müller the cultural unity of the Indo-Europeans was not just linguistic but also a matter of collective *Weltanschauung*, involving parallel gods and goddesses and similar reflections on relations between the physical and the metaphysical. And in turn this fed in to a more racial–ethnic view of what these nations were. We have seen how Ernest Renan spoke of 'La poésie des *races* celtiques'; and the word 'race' was used more and more freely to refer to the ethnicity of the speakers of related languages (see also Douglas Hyde's use of racial phraseology). It was, to be sure, often used loosely and metaphorically, not yet in the hard, genetic–biological sense that racists would come to deploy. Even so, scientific racism was gestating in these very decades, drawing on the comparative zoology of Darwin and on the white supremacism of Arthur de Gobineau (*Essay on the Inequality of the Human Races*, 1835). In the year before Max Müller's death, Houston Stewart Chamberlain, a French-educated Englishman who had married into the anti-Semitic Richard Wagner family, would bring these source traditions together into a hard-core racist theory (*The Foundations of the Nineteenth*

Century, 1899). Between them, they gave 'Aryan' (for Müller still a neutral term, shorthand for 'Indo-European') a very bad name indeed.[28]

By that time Müller had sharply distanced himself from the equation between language family and race. His famous denunciation is often quoted:

> To me an ethnologist who speaks of an Aryan race, Aryan blood, Aryan eyes and hair, is as great a sinner as a linguist who speaks of a dolichocephalic dictionary or a brachycephalic grammar. It is worse than a Babylonian confusion of tongues – it is downright theft. We have made our own terminology for the classification of languages; let ethnologists make their own for the classification of skulls, and hair, and blood.[29]

But that bluster from the moral high ground is a tad self-serving. Müller is waxing wroth at things he himself had been very prone to. His own 'Lectures on the Science of Language' (1861–1864) had constantly mashed up linguistic and ethnic nomenclature, and it was precisely when discussing mythology that the two registers became inextricably entangled. Müller had propounded a cultural/mythological connection between the 'Aryan races' as much as a linguistic one: 'a family likeness between the sacred names worshipped by the Aryans of India and the Aryans of Greece'. 'In the hymns of the Rig-Veda we still have the last chapter of the real Theogony of the Aryan races.'[30]

Aryan races – *ipse dixit*. Müller is throwing stones from inside a glass house of his own making. In truth, the conflation between the family trees of languages and of races was in fact almost unavoidable, and in the decades around 1900 the discourse of 'race' drew indiscriminately on ethnography, social Darwinism and comparative linguistics. A deep proclivity towards racialism was at work in comparative philology, although those proclivities were operative elsewhere as well, and not all philologists fell for them – it would be reductive to suggest that 'all roads lead to Auschwitz'. That being said, the entanglements between ideas of nationhood and notions of race run too deep, far and wide to be ignored.

As a Sanskritist, Müller did not use the term 'Aryan' lightly; he knew what it stood for in its original, Sanskrit and Vedic meaning; and he coined a different ethnonym (alongside 'Semitic', of course) to designate the Aryan's defining other. That word he took from the ancient Iranian epic, the *Shahnameh*, in which the hostile territory to the north of Iran is identified as 'Turan'. The name had been sporadically used in a territorial sense for the lands east of the Caspian Sea. The word will be known to most readers from the name of the opera character of Princess Turandot, for she features as such in the ancient Persian tale on which that opera's libretto is ultimately based: as a princess from the Turanian north. The Caspian–Bactrian area north of Iran began to draw the attention of the British Empire around the mid-century, when the colonial spheres of imperial Russia and British India began to edge closer to each other and the two empires faced each other in the Crimean War.

As comparative linguistics elaborated the taxonomy of the Indo-European linguistic family tree, a concept was created to categorize non-member languages such as Finnish, Hungarian and Turkish. Tentative models for a Ural-Altaic group of languages were in the air, and on the basis of a suggestion from Bunsen, Max Müller in 1855 posited the existence of a 'Turanian' language family. The background of the Crimean War is evident from the title of Müller's book: *The Languages of the Seat of War in the East, with a Survey of the Three Families of Language, Semitic, Arian and Turanian*. Müller included in his Turanian group 'those languages spoken in Asia or Europe not included under the Arian and Semitic families, with the exception perhaps of the Chinese and its dialects'; he correlated their agglutinative grammar (the concatenation of subordinate clauses into long compound words) with their tribal–nomadic lifestyle, as distinct from 'state or political languages' with settled institutions and a more sentence-structured grammar.[31] In short, he perpetuated precisely that conflation between language and race which he would later denounce in others. In 1870, Müller also gave a physiological–ethnological profile of the Turanian race: yellow-skinned, slant-eyed, with large jawbones.

'Turanian' became a very useful container term for languages that fell outside both the Indo-European and the Semitic clusters, largely in the penumbra of the Russian Empire. Müller asserted that languages as widely distinct as Hungarian and Finnish could be traced back conclusively to this common 'Turanian' source. This model got considerable traction in Hungary, which gained new confidence after its constitutional emancipation of 1867 and which was now preparing to celebrate the millennium of the arrival of the ancestral Magyars. The name of 'Huns' and of their leader Attila, abhorrent memories in most of Europe, for Hungarians recalled the proud martial days of their horse-riding tribal forebears; and their roaming origin in the plains of Central Asia fitted neatly into Max Müller's Turan. Hungarian nationalists had sought refuge in Istanbul after the failure of the 1848 insurrections and returned after 1867; they, as well as students who, from anti-Slavic sentiment, felt sympathetic to the Ottoman side in the Russo-Turkish war of 1875–1878, were particularly drawn to the idea that the Turkic and the Magyar nations shared a common homeland in the steppes of Central Asia.[32]

Turkish-Hungarian connections were personified in Ármin Vámbéry. He had settled in Istanbul in the 1850s as a private tutor, had published a Turkish dictionary in 1858, and had become so deeply assimilated into Ottoman society that he was able to travel incognito between Trabzon, Tehran and Samarkand as 'Reshit Efendi' (1861–1863; he published his experiences as *Travels in Central Asia*, 1864). He was also used by the British Foreign Office as an agent to counteract Russian influence in the region. In later publications he defended a Turanian model whereby the Turks were the direct descendants (and the Hungarians a side branch) of the Turanian tribes of Central Asia (*Uigurisch-Türkische Wortvergleichungen*, 1870; *Die Primitive Cultur des Turkotatarischen Volkes*, 1879; *Der Ursprung der Magyaren*, 1882). The 1893 deciphering of the Orkhon inscriptions, discovered in Mongolia in 1889, as being in a form of Old Turkic provided a boost for the Turkish historical consciousness to look for their pre-Ottoman, tribal roots in Central Asia and 'Turan'.

Young Turk reformers, organized in the Committee of Union and Progress (1906), occasionally referred to their ethnicity under its 'Turanian' appellation: thus Halide Edib Adıvar in her utopian-regenerationist novel *Yeni Turan* ('Young/New Turan', 1912). Since a number of the Young Turk activists had ties with the Turkic populations around the shores of the Caspian Sea and among the Tatars of Russia, the notion of a Turkish ethnicity did not stop at the Ottoman borders. Important go-betweens were the Baku-born, Russian-educated Azeri Hüseyinzade Ali (1864–1931), who later took the family name 'Turan', and Yusuf Akçura (1876–1935), of Volga-Tatar descent, raised in Turkey but a Turkic–Muslim activist in imperial Russia between 1904 and 1910 and, following his return from there, editor of the newspaper *Türk Yurdu* ('Turkish homeland', as of 1911). 'Turanian' became a term with which to refer to an ethnic Greater Turkey stretching beyond the Anatolian peninsula into Central Asia, and possibly, quite wistfully and romantically, into a de-territorialized and transhistorical ethnic ideal. Ziya Gökalp's poem of 1911 became a classic.

The feelings pulsating in my veins are the deep echoes of history.
I read the distant and near triumphs of my beautiful, noble, and glorious race.
I read them not on the pages, but on the resonances of my heart.
I read them, understand them, and revere them in my veins.

I read them not on the pages because Attila, Genghis,
These chiefs that crowned my race with victory,
Are slandered in those dusty bindings.
Traduced in foul company;

Yet Caesar and Alexander are honoured!
Yes, in my pulses,
My heart recognizes the enduring Oghuz Khan.
Who remained unknown to scholars.

He lives in my veins in all his greatness and glory
Oghuz Khan, this is what makes my heart sing:
The homeland of the Turks is neither Turkey nor Turkestan
The homeland is that great and eternal country: Turan.[33]

Turan thus became something that Max Müller would have recognized: a myth – not just in the sense of a fictitious fancy inspiring politics, but in the ethnographic sense of deriving the nation's deepest origins from primordial *Ur*-forces – of the legendary ancestral patriarch, Oghuz Khan, father of all the Turkic tribes from Tashkent to Anatolia. These ancestral legends were later complemented by a fancifully revived shamanistic religion, Tengrism.[34]

Turan was a poetic way of referring to what was in fact Pan-Turkism, attempting in post-Ottoman Turkey to connect with ethnic kin from Xinjiang to Turkestan. It inspired Enver Pasha's support for the Basmachi rebellion in Turkestan in 1921–1924, and later the fanatical nationalism of the Grey Wolves. That ethno-nationalism is now mainstreamed in ultra-patriotic Turkish films and television series celebrating heroes from the olden days of the ancient Turkic tribes; and it is, more trivially, still behind the *douze points* solidarity between Turkey and Azerbaijan at Eurovision Song Contests. In Hungary, Turanism provided an attractive alternative to the Finno-Ugric linguistic model, since nationalistically minded Hungarians preferred to align themselves with the warlike, conquering, horse-riding races of Central Asia rather than with the placid, subjugated Finns. Hungarian decorative arts and design developed a specific Central Asian orientalist style, invoking yurt tents and Turkic motifs (Figure 6.2).[35]

Figure 6.2 Millennium Church, Csikszereda, Romania (designed by Imre Makovecz, completed in 2003). Wikimedia Commons

Both in Turkey and in Hungary, Turanism – discredited though it is as a linguistic category – remains an inspiring identity frame for ethnic nationalists in search of Eurasian connections. The Central Asian 'Nomadic Games', hosted in 2018 by Kyrgyzstan, was attended by a roll-call of heads of state/government who represented not only a rogues' gallery of despotic and/or corrupt regimes, but also the outline of a new, Turan-derived nativist alliance in the twenty-first century: Messrs Erdoğan of Turkey, Nazarbayev of Kazakhstan, Aliyev of Azerbaijan, Mirziyoyev of Uzbekistan – and Hungary's Viktor Orbán.[36] Thus the logic of pan-movements can fold nativism into internationalist, (con)federative frameworks of mutual support.

CHAPTER 7

History Related

Walter Scott Moves On from Ossian

By 1803, Macpherson's Ossian was thoroughly discredited as a rank forgery. In English culture, the position of 'Bard of the Nation' had fallen vacant and was now increasingly allocated to Shakespeare. North of the Scottish border, however, Walter Scott was beginning his literary rise. He edited ancient ballads from the Scottish–English borderlands (*Minstrelsy of the Scottish Border*, 1803) and on that basis created an original narrative ballad, 'The Lay of the Last Minstrel' (1805). Although the setting is late-to-post-chivalric rather than primitive antiquity, and the poet figure is a 'minstrel' rather than a 'bard', the stage is still set in the Ossianic mode: we are at the tail-end of an era. The profession of minstrelsy has lost its standing, and the minstrel himself is old and decrepit. Indeed, as Scott himself phrases it in Ossianic diction, 'the last of all the Bards was he': a relic of the past.[1]

> The way was long, the wind was cold,
> The Minstrel was infirm and old;
> His withered cheek, and tresses gray,
> Seemed to have known a better day;
> The harp, his sole remaining joy,
> Was carried by an orphan boy.
> The last of all the Bards was he,
> Who sung of Border chivalry;
> For, well-a-day! their date was fled,
> His tuneful brethren all were dead;
> And he, neglected and oppressed,
> Wished to be with them, and at rest.

The wandering poet is invited to perform for the noble Buccleugh family, for whom he, quite literally, channels the past in rapturous, Ossianic inspiration (not unlike the *guslar* on the Karadžić frontispiece, Figure 5.1):

Amid the strings his fingers strayed,
And an uncertain warbling made –
And oft he shook his hoary head.
But when he caught the measure wild,
The old man raised his face, and smiled;
And lightened up his faded eye,
With all a poet's extacy!

Again, that fixed stare into a space of inspiration, as with Ossian and the Serbian *guslar*. The minstrel recalls the past, and whatever is not solid memory is supplied by the imagination.

In varying cadence, soft or strong,
He swept the sounding chords along;
The present scene, the future lot,
His toils, his wants, were all forgot;
. . .
Each blank, in faithless memory void,
The poet's glowing thought supplied;
And, while his harp responsive rung,
'T was thus the Latest Minstrel sung.

What then follows is the tale of a baronial feud of bygone days; but at the ending we return to the frame story and the aged performer. The fate of this wandering bard is much more cheerful than that of Ossian. The grateful duchess provides him with a little cottage under the castle walls to live out his days, and here he performs his ancient songs for appreciative passers-by.

There sheltered wanderers, by the blaze,
Oft heard the tale of other days;
For much he loved to ope his door,
And give the aid he begged before.
. . .
The aged Harper's soul awoke!
Then would he sing achievements high,
And circumstance of Chivalry,
Till the rapt traveller would stay,
Forgetful of the closing day.[2]

Scott's minstrel both echoes and bypasses Ossian, and that in two ways. To begin with, as Ann Rigney has noted, the minstrel manages to turn his pastness into gainful employment, in almost a prefiguration of what Scott was to become himself: a voice from the past, recalling bygone deeds but with a huge appeal to present-day audiences. Antiquity becomes historicism: pastness obtains a function in the present.[3]

The other innovation that Scott introduces is his deft use of a layered perspective. The frame story is already set in the past (somewhere in the later seventeenth century) and at this past moment the minstrel recalls an even earlier historical episode: we approach the past telescopically, through a frame story containing a ballad relating the past events. This is an early sign of Romantic historicism: unlike antiquaries, the historians of Scott's generation were acutely aware of their source dependency, the fact that they gained access to the past by way of sources that were themselves part of the past. A few decades later, the historian Leopold von Ranke would turn this awareness – how to cope with one's source dependency – into a keystone of his scholarly method. He devised an entire methodology of 'source criticism' (*Quellenkritik*) and in addition fixed a cognitive point on the horizon: to get an 'immediate', umediated sense of the past as it had actually been experienced at the time, liberated from its im-mediation in third-party informants.* This approach parallels the philological attempt to critically compare different manuscript variants to arrive at a putative *Urtext*, the text as it must have been imagined at the moment of its creation.[4]

For academic scholars (historians such as Ranke, philologists of the Lachmann school), this source dependency is a problem to be dealt with; Scott, however, turns it into a virtue, an attractive narrative strategy. Paradoxically, he makes his evocation of the past more realistic by explicitly evoking the tunnelling trajectory one has to perform between Now and Then, the many generations and transitions that separate us from a receding Long Ago. In *Old Mortality* (1816), the days of the Covenanting wars (1679) are approached through a survivor (nicknamed 'Old Mortality') who maintains the graves of the fallen, striving to stave off their oblivion. This stratagem renders the past truly exotic: alien and alluring at the same time, something approached in an enticing game of disclosure and deferral.

Scott does the same for Scotland itself. He always approaches the most colourful destinations in that country from a starting point of

* Ranke wanted to apprehend every historical period *unmittelbar zu Gott*, 'immediately under God'. That idea was informed by the constitution of the old Reich, where some fiefs would be *reichsunmittelbar*, held directly (immediately) under the emperor rather than from some intermediate liegelord. (It should be remembered that he proffered this idea to an audience including King Max II of Bavaria in 1854; Ranke 1906.) It chimes with his famous historicist principle that the past should be understood *wie es eigentlich gewesen*. Often naively misunderstood to mean 'the past as it actually was', Ranke's use of *eigentlich*, as counterpart to *uneigentlich*, and as a parallel to *unmittelbar*, indicates 'the past on its own terms', i.e. empathetically, undistorted by external interpretative frames. See Hardtwig 1997, Braw 2007.

familiar domesticity and reaches them by way of successive stages, each with increased exotic strangeness. In *Rob Roy* (1818), the English narrator moves first to the mansion of his rough-hewn relatives in Northumberland; then, in a daring escape, across the border to the unknown and adventurous setting of Glasgow; and finally to the haunts of the wild Highlander, Rob Roy McGregor himself, around the shores of Loch Katrine. The mechanism is most noticeable in the novel that turbocharged Scott's literary career, *Waverley* (1814). It marked Scott's transition from dramatic poems set in the past (*The Lay of the Last Minstrel, Marmion, The Lady of the Lake)* to the genre of historical prose fiction. Scott had become a celebrity as a poet and was in 1820 given the title of baronet. He sought to avoid the stigma of being a mere novelist (the novel was at that time considered a trivial pastime, and not serious literature at all), so that *Waverley* was published anonymously, and subsequent novels were stated to be 'by the author of *Waverley*'. It was only after those 'Waverley novels' had become a literary sensation, and well and truly redeemed from the stigma of triviality, that Scott owned up to his authorship in 1827. Those novels had meanwhile also become considerable money-spinners; Scott was the first bestseller author in history, turning writing into a business model.

The title hero of *Waverley* also approaches Scotland, and the Scottish Highlands (where the core of the action is located), in telescoping stages. He is sent from his native England to Dundee and stays with a family friend in Perthshire, close to the Highlands. From there he accompanies Highlanders to their home north of Stirling, and it is here, at the residence of the MacIvor clan, that he encounters the true heart of Scottish exoticism. The acme of that exoticism is reached in Chapter XXII, entitled 'Highland Minstrelsy': the attractive sister of his Highland host, Flora, takes him to a wild and remote glen. There, near a picturesque waterfall, she plays the harp for him and performs an ancient Scottish ballad. Waverley's progress up the glen, following Flora, is a transition from reality into romance: the countryside becomes wilder and more sublime at each turn and step, and the hero, who feels like a 'knight of Romance', falls under the spell of the almost supernatural (quite literally 'enchanting') Flora. It will not surprise the reader that what Flora finally delivers is Ossian pure and simple: a ballad by 'Rory Dall, one of the last Highland bards', beginning 'Mist darkens the mountain, night darkens the vale, but more dark is the sleep of the son of the Gael!'[5]

This is how Scott latches onto the Ossianic legacy. As Waverley, starting out from 'life as we know it', ventures into the world of Highland minstrelsy, he also moves out of modernity. Scott hammers this message home in the urgent topicality of the novel's politics. Its subtitle, *'Tis Sixty Years Since*, recalls a moment still within living memory for its readers: *Waverley* is set during the 1745 coup d'état of the exiled pretender to the British throne, Bonnie Prince Charlie (scion of the ousted Stuart dynasty), supported by his adherents in the Scottish Highlands. This 1745 Rebellion posed, briefly, a threat to the Hanover dynasty, established on the throne only since 1715; its failure and bloody suppression broke the political power and independence of the Scottish Highland clans. Like any civil war, it left traumatic memories, unresolved conflicts and divided loyalties in its wake. It is at this critical historical juncture that Scott sets his *Waverley*. The political divisions between Hanover and Stuart are superimposed on the novel's oppositional scheme between Now and Then, familiar and exotic, England and Highlands, Anglo-Saxon and Celtic, reality and romance. Waverley is a junior officer in the British army, the MacIvor clan and Flora are adherents of the Stuart pretender. The enchantment that Flora exercises over Waverley makes him join the rebels and their doomed cause, with potentially tragic results.

This makes the novel also a political allegory. Waverley's escape from his rebellious Stuart entanglement is a return from poetry and romance to a more prosaic form of realism – a dis-enchantment. (He marries a woman of an altogether more sensible disposition than the firebrand revolutionary Flora.) We now usually see the concept of disenchantment in Weberian terms, as a rationalization and secularization process working in tandem with modernity; but enchantment is not exclusively a religious principle, and it makes sense to see Romanticism, an anti-rationalist and anti-Enlightenment paradigm in cultural history, as an attempt to salvage the forces of enchantment; a cultural re-enchantment.*

Scott balances the contradictory impulses of disenchantment and (re-)enchantment, the coming-of-age novel and the historical romance. Waverley's predisposition to headlong romantic enchantment is a symptom of his immaturity, and he needs to outgrow it. And with that, Scott also gives his verdict on the 1745 rebellion, still a very precarious topic in

* Max Weber defines the term in *Wissenschaft als Beruf* (1919) as the historical process of discarding magical thinking; but to see history as a long process of disenchantment was heralded earlier in Romantic literature, witness Friedrich Schiller's poem *Die Götter Griechenlands* (1788), which expresses nostalgia for a time the world was still suffused with a sense of divinity, 'when the gods were more like humans, and humans more like gods' (see Lehmann 2009). After Romanticism, with its penchant for re-enchantment, disenchantment again becomes a prominent literary theme, as in Balzac's *Illusions perdues* (1837–1843), Dickens's *Great Expectations* (1861) and Flaubert's *L'éducation sentimentale* (1869).

Scottish public affairs. The Stuart rebels had romance and poetical allure on their side, with their chivalry, courageous loyalty and colourful traditions; but they were also linked to Scotland's past rather than to its future. Progress and a sense of practical realism demanded an accommodation with the new, Hanoverian dispensation. Thus, while the interest of the characters and the action undoubtedly lies with the Highlanders and Stuart rebels, the narrator firmly endorses the Hanoverian status quo.

What Scott created, then, was a hybrid genre, uniting the excitement of the romance and the realism of the novel. He reflected on this himself in his article on 'Romance' for the 1824 *Encyclopaedia Britannica*. The central action of *Waverley* is firmly of a 'romantic' nature, evoking medieval chivalric romance, featuring passionate characters and exciting incidents in colourful settings, exotic because of the distance both in time and in space. The authorial voice (the narrator), however, and the framing of the action, are much more in the mode of psychological realism, following the genre of the novel (rather than the romance) as it had been practised by Samuel Richardson and Jane Austen, establishing a rapport between narrator and reader on the basis of of shared (modern, middle-class, sensible) values and experiences. Scott wraps a romance into a novel. In the opening chapters of *Waverley*, Scott admits in so many words that he had been inspired by Cervantes, realistically evoking a romantic, starry-eyed hero: the delusional Quixote, and the impressionable young Waverley.[6]

Scott is a master at setting up strong, almost overdetermined binary polarities and then mediating between them: between Scotland's fond clannish memories and its British, Hanoverian present; between heart and head; between first-love infatuation and mature married life; between enchantment and realism, romance and novel. He also mediated, uniquely, in the relationship between past and present. On the one hand the past is relatable, something where the modern reader is delighted to find points of familiarity or continuity; on the other hand the past is deeply alien, something that requires an act of the imagination to engage with. In *Ivanhoe* (1819) with its chivalric-medieval setting, points of recognition across the intervening centuries involve the history of dining, its changes and continuities. Scott explains the origin of the still common phrase 'seated above/below the salt'. He alerts the reader to the lexical dichotomy between livestock and the meat dishes prepared from them (oxen and cows are turned into beef, sheep into mutton, swine into pork), and he points out the ethnic and class associations of such words: Saxon/peasant for the farm animals, Norman-French/aristocratic for the company at the dinner table (*boeuf, mouton, porc*). Such things create a sense of familiarity across time. On the other hand, the novel revolves around thrilling scenes of lawlessness that render the chivalric Middle Ages truly alien territory: the armchair time-traveller encounters trial by combat, knights jousting, women to be burnt at the stake on the accusation of witchcraft, brigands laying siege to a castle. (Even so, Scott titillates the reader by hinting that the head of these brigands is none other than the familiar folk figure Robin Hood.)

In the hybridity of this genre, Scott can have it both ways: his evocation of the manners and customs of yesteryear has all the authority of the well-informed historian, but his narration of heroes and heroines trying to come to terms with challenging circumstances is pure fiction. This is, as Ranke would call it, the 'immediate', non-mediated experience of the past. The modern reader, through the power of the stimulated imagination, senses how it must have felt for Edward Waverley to have to choose between Rose Bradwardine and Flora MacIvor, or for Wilfred of Ivanhoe to reconcile his dutiful loyalty to his Saxon father with his fealty to his Norman liege lord, Richard the Lionheart; or his love for the fair Rowena with the undeniable but impossible chemistry between him and the beautiful, healing Rebecca. The emotional dilemmas and the exciting cliffhangers are such that any reader will breathlessly turn the pages and mentally engage with a bygone age vividly rendered, alive and present. In the process, the arresting anecdotes and glimpses of social manners provide an intellectually stimulating encounter with life as it was long ago. Readers immerse themselves in a history that is both past and present – and that may stand as a definition of Romantic historicism.

Between History and Legend: Facts, Fiction and Fakes

It is well known that not only leisure-time readers but also an entire generation of historians took inspiration from Scott. These Romantic historians show a specific set of characteristic traits. In their writing style, they deliberately emulated Scott's powers of 'bringing the past to life'. As a result, they deployed a variety of techniques that strictly speaking were proper to narrative fiction and that were a novelty for the historian's craft. These narrative strategies involve shifts of perspective, relating the events sometimes in the voice of an omniscient narrator, sometimes focused through the experiences of participants (deliberately selected by the historians as points of sympathetic identification). Also noticeable is an alternation between 'spectacle' and narrative. Spectacular writing evokes a scene or situation for the mind's eye, often even asking the reader to accompany the author's imagination into a situation that is then described as a tableau, with elements arranged in a quasi-visual, panoramic style. The panorama is static; the account is not about events or occurrences but a stage being set. The description of the successive events then becomes a narrative, and here literary techniques are used such as shifting focuses, back-and-forth juxtapositions between concurrent actions in different locations (the 'Meanwhile, back at the ranch' mode), and a dramatic characterization invoking stock characters calculated to evoke sympathy or antipathy: family fathers, haughty courtiers, calculating Jesuits, innocent maidens, stalwart young idealists. Those techniques are, properly speaking, dramatic, theatrical; but this turn towards the dramatic (the melodramatic, even) was made by historians under the novelistic influence of Walter Scott, and it later earned them the qualifications 'narrative' and 'Romantic' at the same time.[7]

Yet for all that, these authors were historians, and they took the scholarly part of their calling seriously. They, like the philologists, were living through a sea-change. History writing had been a genre of philosophical disquisition, dominated by the examples of Hume's *History of England* and Voltaire's *Siècle de Louis XIV*. History was, as the phrase had it, 'philosophy teaching by example': the past was studied as a dataset from which to distil what circumstances and decisions had led to the glories or failures of royal reigns or military campaigns. After 1790, the overhaul of libraries and archives and the Napoleon-induced crisis of universities affected this field of learning as much as literary studies. The newly assembled or reorganized archives made different perspectives on past events available, and the study of archival material became the historian's primary technique. Historians such as Augustin Thierry and Jules Michelet gained their professional experience in the Arsénal and other archives. At the University of Berlin, where Ranke used the *Seminar* as a dialogic training workshop for history students, a methodology of source criticism was instituted that privileged original archival sources above later-established accounts. Historians became professionally defined by their Rankean *Quellenkritik* or source criticism and by their reliance on archival, rather than secondary, material. This set them apart from the novelistic liberties that Scott, much to their envy, could take, but it also defined their calling as what was now becoming a profession and an academic discipline rather than a literary–philosophical pursuit. And in subsequent decades, like the professionalizing philologists, the historians, as civil servants in public employ, would write in the service of the nation-state.[8]

Meanwhile, on the far side of literary fiction, forgery was rife. As we saw in Chapter 4, the archives in these decades yielded unexpected treasures documenting the nation's forgotten vernacular literary history. These authentic relics of the past were highly prized and in great demand. Philologists competed, as in a gold rush, for the ancient materials that were coming to light: discoveries spoke to the imagination, could make careers, and provided the readers with a sensational feeling of connectedness with the national past. With such high value being set on ancient documents, is it to be wondered at that some of these were manufactured in order to meet the demand? Macpherson was remembered above all as a forger – not altogether fairly, but not quite unjustly either – and as a forger, too, he became a role model. The most egregious of all the forged 'ancient documents' that came onto the market were the 'Bohemian manuscripts', with the celebrated Czech philologist and antiquary Václav Hanka playing a key role. Found in the localities known as Königinhof/Dvůr Kralové and Grünberg/Zelená Hora, they contained legendary and literary material from medieval Bohemia, purportedly from the thirteenth and even the eighth/ninth centuries. Those materials furnished the Czech readership of the Romantic period (which was just beginning to develop a national self-awareness) with tales of epic, gratifying victories. Now subordinated under the Habsburg crown, Czechs were invited to look back on a proud and authentically Slavic history. The manuscripts dovetailed with legends and myths that had been written down in earlier chronicles and helped flesh out a glorified image of early Czech history. In particular the story of the founding of Prague, invoking legendary ethnic ancestors such as Krok, Cech and the princess/prophetess Libuše, was expanded with additional episodes and characters. In the years when *Beowulf*, the *Nibelungenlied*, the *Chanson de Roland* and the *Lay of Prince Igor's Campaign* were drastically realigning the literary–historical landscape of Europe, an additional discovery from the Czech lands was not in itself implausible, and Czech historians such as Palacký actually relied on these manuscripts for the medieval portions of their national histories. The sculptor Myslbek took inspiration from them for some of his public statues, and nationally minded writers such as Čelakovský and Erben also stood by the manuscripts. Philologists, however, habitually fixated on sources and provenance and mindful of the Ossianic imbroglio, were sceptical; there was considerable mistrust around the Bohemian manuscripts, which by some were denounced as fakes. The result was a decades-long controversy. Even when scholars argued, on the evidence, that the manuscripts were fakes, people rallied behind the revered figure of Václav Hanka and doubled down on their belief in the authenticity of the contents; all the more so since the Habsburg authorities had clamped down on Slavic–Czech nationalism after the fateful 1848 revolution (in which intellectuals including Palacký and Hanka himself had played an active part as participants in Prague's Slavic Congress).[9]

Following Hanka's death in 1861, his funeral helped to instil the legendary and romantically imagined past into the very cityscape of the Czech capital. Occurring as it did in the repressive post-1848 atmosphere, the funeral provided a rare occasion for a public demonstration of Czech patriotism. It became a mass event; Hanka was laid to rest on the Vyšehrad hill overlooking the river Vltava. Vyšehrad was the site where the mythical Krok, at the behest of his daughter, the prophetess Libuše, had established the castle of the primordial Czech royal lineage and where Libuše had foretold the rise of a great future city (Prague). Already in 1836 the nationalist-Romantic poet Karel Hynek Mácha had been buried here. Following the interment of Hanka in the same spot, Vyšehrad began to emerge as a patriotic pantheon, a shrine infused by the spirit of Libuše herself; re-enchanted in the here and now. As in so many other countries, nationalism was to some extent a cult of the dead, with public funerals providing rare instances of national demonstrations in an atmosphere where the public assembly was not yet an acknowledged part of civil liberty. Certainly in the case of nationalist leaders, whose death could be construed as a form of martyrdom, their funerals fulfilled a strong propagandistic purpose. The Czech poetess Božena Němcová placed what may have been a bouquet of flowers, a laurel wreath or a crown of thorns on the coffin of the persecuted nationalist poet Karel Havliček Borovský in 1856; she herself was buried at Vyšehrad in 1862. A central monument called *Slavín* was erected there in 1880 (Figure 7.1), and even under the shadow of the Nazi occupation, Alphonse Mucha, like so many other great Czech artists and public figures before and after him, was buried there in 1939.

Vyšehrad thus became 'hallowed ground': a site where medieval legend and modern nationalism meet, in a sort of timeless time-share. Figures of Romantic legend, poets, artists and historians (Libuše, Hanka, Němcová and Mucha) are all stakeholders in this *lieu de mémoire* (and as Pierre Nora pointed out in coining that phrase, a *lieu de mémoire* typically condenses a maximum of historical meanings and evocations into a single symbolic unit.) What nineteenth-century historicism brought back to life, that past 'on its own terms' as it was actually experienced, was not necessarily the past that was demonstrably, archivally factual. What was resuscitated was in many cases a legendary past, and those legends and myths are, as we have seen, fluid in their provenance. They can be medieval, recently invented, or somewhere between the two (heavily reworked, or elaborated with additional incidents, side characters or episodes).[10]

Figure 7.1 *Slavín* memorial in the Vyšehrad cemetery, Prague. ERNiE imagebank

The legends that appealed to the taste of Romantic historicism often negotiated the borderline between life, death and afterlife. Prevalent tropes were the 'last of the race' (Ossian's successors include Fenimore Cooper's Last of the Mohicans and Scott's Last Minstrel[II]), and the 'pagan princess at the dawn of history' – for example Libuše. Her legend was known from medieval sources even before the discovery of the forged manuscripts and had been given literary treatment, initially by German Romantics (Brentano, *Die Gründung Prags*, 1812; Grillparzer, *Libussa*, 1844). After 1848, she was reappropriated by the Czechs with a vengeance. Smetana's opera *Libuše*, used to celebrate the opening of Prague's opera house in 1881, culminates in her foretelling of Prague's greatness and has become the Czech national opera. The figure of Libuše became a favourite for paintings, statues and tile tableaux, and as a national icon her ontological status (non-historical, legendary) does not make the slightest difference. What was operative was the combination of feminine grace and lofty symbolism.

The national-Romantic imagination is full of female characters combining historical stature and maidenly charm. Scott's heroine Flora MacIvor, 'last of the Jacobites', who beguiles Waverley with her Highland minstrelsy, is an example: that almost preternaturally alluring *femme fatale* with her harp at a wild waterfall, who is among the last diehard loyalists to support Bonnie Prince Charlie. The opera composer Bellini created the figure of Norma, a Gaulish priestess, depicted at the moment when Christianity was about to drive out paganism. The princess Bogomila in France Prešeren's *Baptism at the Savica* is in a similar transitional position from paganism to Christianity, as is Libuše in Brentano's *Die Gründung Prags*. We could add the Lithuanian Princess Birutė (last of the pagan priestess-princesses, again), the Polish princess Wanda, the proto-Dutch Batavian heroine of *Hermingard van de Eikenterpen* (by Aarnout Drost, 1832) and Amaya, last descendant of the tribal god Aitor, in Francisco Navarro Valloslada's *Amaya o los vascos en el siglo VIII* (1879).[12] Some of these are purely fictional creations (Norman, Flora MacIvor, Hermingard, the Ossianic prototype Malvina); the others are legendary figures, whose true rise to fame occurred when they were reworked by nineteenth-century Romantics. Many of them became the pagan patron saints of popular girls' names: Aino in Finland, Milda in Lithuania, Wanda in Poland, Linda in Estonia, Maeve, Gráinne and Deirdre in Ireland, Angharad in Wales, Gudrun in Germany and its neighbouring countries, and even the Spanish-Argentinian name for the Falkland Islands, Las Malvinas: they all testify to the power of the past to re-enchant the present.

But the fact that this pattern was so obviously transnational and pan-European, like the influence of Scott or Romanticism itself, should not make us forget that the remembered past was always a specifically national past, a history dominated by the theme of the nation at crisis moments in its own particular existence. What Scott and the Romantic historians bequeathed to the succeeding generations was an overriding sense of history as, precisely, national history, recounted in episodes that were emblematic of the history of the nation's own, distinct identity and character.

The Long Tail of the Historical Novel: Epic, Sentimental, Juvenile

The historical novel has been described as history *faute de mieux* – an ersatz history writing for situations where the real thing was not a feasible option, much like Scott's Last Minstrel using 'glowing thought' to supplement the blanks in his memory. The novel could make up for gaps in the historical documentation with a fictional supplement, and as such was a particularly suitable stop-gap medium for scantily documented topics.[13] This played into an interest in the medieval period, not only in long-standing sovereign states such as Holland, Portugal or France, but equally for countries such as Flanders, Poland and Hungary (and of course Scotland), now subordinate under a higher crown but keenly aware of their erstwhile feudal, chivalric autonomy.

Novelists in the Scott tradition from those countries did important memory work (history *faute de mieux*) to recall and celebrate former glories, and their novels have become enshrined in their nations' literary histories. Like the Waverley novels, their evocations of the past became revered classics. Hendrik Conscience is proverbially known in Flanders as 'the man who taught his nation to read'. His historical novels have all become formative launching pad for powerful *lieux de mémoire*. Public statues in Flemish cities commemorate the medieval heroes that his novels rendered famous: Breydel and De Koninck in Bruges, Artevelde in Ghent. Most importantly, Conscience's evocation of the Battle of the Golden Spurs of 1302 rendered that Flemish victory over the French army at Courtrai a national high point *par excellence*; the heraldic emblem that furnished the novel's title (*De Leeuw van Vlaenderen*, 'The Lion of Flanders') is now the official flag of the Flemish region in Belgium, a song of that title is the Flemish Community's official anthem, and the battle's date, 11 July, is now a Flemish feast day and an occasion for nationalist manifestations. Something similar (familiar to us nowadays from the movie *Braveheart*) was at work for Henryk Sienkiewicz's evocation of the Battle of Grünwald, which forms the culmination point of his novel *Krzyżaci* (1900, 'The Knights of the Cross', i.e. the Teutonic Order). The novel evokes the long, bitter oppression inflicted by those feudal German tyrants until finally a glorious Polish-Lithuanian army defeats them in 1410. Much as Conscience's novel was itself inspired by a huge, historical painting of the Battle of the Golden Spurs (by Gustaaf Wappers, 1836), so too Sienkiewicz's novel was inspired by the vast history painting by Jan Matejko (1878). In another parallel to the Flemish case, the novel prepared the ground for turning the medieval battle into a galvanizing commemorative event. The 500-year commemoration in 1910 became a vast, fervently nationalistic festivity, followed by the erection of statues in diverse places and ultimately an equally fervent mass event at the next centenary in 2010. The other historical novels of Sienkiewicz (the 'Trilogy', 1884–1887, evoking the seventeenth-century wars against Cossacks, Swedes and Turks) remained fixed on school reading lists throughout the twentieth century.[14]

Conscience and Sienkiewicz (and the many other Scott adepts from Central Eastern Europe) diverged in one crucial aspect from their Scottish prototype. Scott was keenly aware of the ongoing dialectics of history and usually resolves the conflicts in his novels in a Hegelian type of 'sublation': the conflict, while being recalled and indeed enshrined, ensuring its availability for future recall, is at the same time seen as something that ultimately had to be overcome, with history providing a transcendence of the old enmities into a higher unity. (That is what the Hegelian term *Aufhebung*, sublation in its threefold meaning, stands for: to enshrine something for safe keeping; to abolish it as an active agency; and to lift it to a higher plane.) Ivanhoe marries his fair Saxon lady Rowena, but he will, as a courtier of the Plantagenet King Richard, be part of the merger of Saxon and Norman groups into a new, English identity. Waverley will marry Rose Bradwardine and, while wistfully mindful of the romantic memories of Flora and the Jacobite cause, point the way towards a viable Scottish participation in the United Kingdom. Scott personally helped perform that integration when he stage-managed the 1822 visit of George IV to the Scottish capital following his coronation. It was the first Hanoverian royal visit to Scotland, and there was a sense of awkwardness about the fraught historical relations between the Scots and the Four Georges. Walter Scott, entrusted with the organization of the event, sublated that tension by enshrining Highland culture into the very heart of the festivities, calling on all Highland chiefs to be present with all their traditional retinue and their accoutrements of kilts and bagpipes. Kilts and tartan (until then the uncouth dress of the delinquent, disaffected Highlanders, and frequently banned by law) were to be worn by the Edinburgh socialites as well, and even George himself was dressed up in that ultra-Scottish finery. It marked the beginning of the British royals' love affair with Scotland and its Highland culture: young Queen Victoria, George's successor, acquired Balmoral Castle around 1850, festooned it with neo-Gothic turrets and battlements, and turned it into a Romantic Highland theme park for the royal family.[15]

Scott, politically a conservative and no radical, opts for reconciliation between the parties whose historical conflicts he evokes. No such reconciliation can be found in Conscience or Sienkiewicz. For them, history is in the most fundamental sense unfinished business, and the ancestral battle against the oppressors is evoked to inspire its renewal in the present. Conscience concludes his *Lion of Flanders* with this clarion call to his readers: 'You, O Fleming, who have been reading this book, reflect (considering the glorious deeds which it contains) what Flanders used to be, what it is now, and especially, what shall become of it if you should forget the sacred examples of your forefathers!'[16] This is activist writing. Conscience's book is one of the trigger moments of the Flemish national movement, which came to see modern-day Belgium as a re-run of the medieval conflict between freedom-loving Flemish burghers and a haughty French (or French-speaking) elite. No sense of letting bygones be bygones, or moving on from the past: the past, on the contrary, is held up as an enduring model for the present, and the modern, novelistic side of Scott is abandoned for blood-and-guts epic. We have in Chapter 4 seen newly produced epic poems by Romantics such as Prešeren, Mickiewicz or Shevchenko complementing the ancient ones that had been philologically retrieved from oblivion or noted down by folklorists from oral-traditional performers. To that mix we can now add a third element: the historical novel-as-epic, prose fictions of ancient battles and heroism. The epic-heroic past as an inspiration for modern nationalism: that ran directly counter to what Scott had intended to achieve with his work, and it threw a long shadow over the twentieth century. In Slovenia in 2014, the controversial politician Janez Janša (his chequered career is a matter of record, as is his sympathy with far-right nationalism) published a historical romance *Beli panter* ('The White Panther') charting the mythical-heroic rise of a primordial Slovenian state, 'revealing the secret of the Slovenes' ethnic origins'. In 2021 Janša, back in power as Prime Minister after a spell in jail, was reported as using the panther symbol, which by then had become a trademark of extreme far-right groups in Slovenia, as a national 'brand' on cufflinks to be given out as diplomatic presents during the country's tenure of the EU presidency.[17]

Janša's 'White Panther' is closer to pulp fiction, closer to epic fantasy such as *Conan the Barbarian* or *Game of Thrones*, than to *Waverley*; it lacks any of the novelistic subtlety of Scott, or of Scott's successors in the literary genre of the historical novel (Manzoni, Tolstoy, Eco, Ghosh). If one were to point out a more congenial model, it would be Felix Dahn's *Ein Kampf um Rom* (1876), set among the Ostrogothic tribal kingdoms of Italy during the migration period, epic-heroic in spirit and breathing a fervent Germanic ethnic nationalism. The author was a highly regarded historian of the migration period, a leading academic, popularizer of Germanic myth, nationalist versifier and founding member of the *völkisch* Alldeutscher Verband. *Ein Kampf um Rom* became successful mainly as a juvenile novel, avidly read by adolescent and young-adult boys, many of whom would carry the Ostrogothic warrior ethic of Dahn's book into their post-1918 political careers.[18]

This appeal to young readers signals another mutation of the historical novel in its post-Scott afterlife. Its demise as a prestigious literary genre was repeatedly announced, and its dominance in the literary field was taken over by realistic and naturalistic novels set in the here-and-now; but the genre continued its tenacious existence in the margins of the literary marketplace, in unprestigious writing aimed at unprestigious readers such as women and boys.[19]

For women, there were 'bodice-rippers' from Georgette Heyer to the *Angélique* series by Serge and Anne Golon, reverting back firmly from the register of the novel to that of the romance. The light-entertainment historical romance, targeted specifically at female readers, still thrives, a prominent example being the Scott- (or at least Scottish-) inspired *Outlander* series by Diana Gabaldon. This feminine inflection of the historical novel tends to eschew national/patriotic affect, and significantly its locations and settings are less fixated on the author's or reader's own nationality – witness the many romancified recyclings of Jane Austen as rom-com costume drama, even in Californian or Indian settings, or the cheerfully heedless counterfactuality of Julia Quinn's *Bridgerton* romances (2000–2006) in their multiracially cast Netflix adaptation. Worthy of mention also is the remarkable genre of high-gloss romance featuring (historical) female royals as protagonists. The identificatory frame is largely that of gender, with a national-patriotic element being at best in the ambient background. At most, the historical-Romantic treatment of Queen Louise of Prussia and Empress-Queen Elisabeth of Austria-Hungary (Sissi) has played on their nationally inspirational value for their German and Austro-Hungarian subjects; but within Europe the genre on the whole tends to play into the monarchy as a glamorous institution rather than the nation as a political motivator.[20]

For boys, historical fiction was continued in an altogether more heroic and national vein. In the wake of Robert Louis Stevenson (*Kidnapped*, 1886; *The Black Arrow*, 1888) many adventure romances were set in the exciting glory days of the national past featuring increasingly juvenile heroes. The masculinity code for such boy-heroes firmly echoed the pedagogy of 'pluck', cheerful optimism and undaunted self-discipline, which would later find its most potent expressions in Rudyard Kipling's *Kim* (1901) and the Boy Scout movement partly inspired by that book. G. A. Henty (1832–1902) has become proverbial as an author for nationalist (or rather, imperialist) boys' fiction in English; his titles total well over 100 and range from *The Young Buglers, A Tale of the Peninsular War* (1880) to *By Conduct and Courage: A Story of Nelson's Days* (1905). In the Netherlands, there were tales of young boys joining the celebrated nation-building seamen of the 'Golden Age' as shipmates.[21] How tenacious this ethos was became clear in a parliamentary exchange in 2006 when the centre-right prime minister of the Netherlands, Jan-Peter Balkenende, championed a can-do mentality that he called a *VOC-mentaliteit*, an 'attitude like that of the East India Company': 'I fail to see why you are being so negative. Let's take heart from each other! Let's be optimistic! Let us say: Holland can do it again! That VOC mentality, looking beyond our frontiers, dynamism. No?!'[22] To invoke that colonial trading company as a role model was, to say the least, awkward; the incident has become notorious. The Verenigde Oost-Indische Compagnie (VOC, United East India Company, founded in 1602) had been the main entrepreneurial driving force in the establishment of Holland's colonial empire and had helped finance the country's war of independence against Spain. While its track record is now seen to have been mired in violent conquests, slave labour and slave trade, and a ruthlessly oppressive extractive economic colonial system, it was, during the late nineteenth century and the early twentieth (when colonialism was nothing to be ashamed of), a proud symbol of the country's political and economic rise to power – its so-called Golden Century. This is the memory that obviously came through here: a belated echo of Balkenende's conservative Protestant upbringing in the 1960s, when songbooks and juvenile fiction still unproblematically, unpolitically extolled the stalwart masculinity of colonial seafarers.

Besides the material aiming to instil a spirit of feisty, patriotic masculinity in the boys of the nation, there were also historical novels that had initially been targeted at an adult readership but that became, in the course of their subsequent career, juvenile or school reading. Besides Dahn, Scott and Sienkiewicz, this juvenile retargeting is also noticeable in Dumas's *The Three Musketeers*. We shall note in Chapter 12 how historical fiction post-Scott was also given a fresh lease of life in cinematic form. All this helped to maintain historical fiction as a powerful and popular frame for bringing the past (and by default that meant the national past) to life as an immersive and inspiring environment.*

* Some heroic fantasy is set in fictional places (*Conan the Barbarian*; *Game of Thrones*). Tolkien's seminal Middle-Earth is such a place, inhabited by dragons and elves as well as humans, but the Englishness of much of Tolkien's mythical imagination, and of his hobbits, is well known. There is, besides, a tenacious tradition of historical fiction set in ancient Rome and/or in the days of early Christianity – another tradition that nineteenth- and twentieth-century readers could easily identify with. That tradition runs from Chateaubriand's *Les martyrs* (1809) to Edward Bulwer-Lytton's *The Last Days of Pompeii* (1834) and Nicholas Wiseman's *Fabiola* (1854), thence to Lew Wallace's *Ben-Hur*

National History, National-Historical Myths, National Memory

Scott had shown the historians of this generation how to turn away from the palace-and-battlefield focus of earlier practitioners. Antiquarians had always been more inclusive in their interests: anything that might illustrate ancestral manners and customs was grist to their mill. That more societal focus was now also becoming the primary concern of historians; but what we would call 'society' they called 'the nation'. Not kings or generals, but the nation was the main actor in their narratives (as indeed it was for Scott, although he used fictional protagonists as proxies through which to focus the collective experience of 'national' crisis moments).

Friedrich Schlegel had, earlier in the century, seen philology as a twin specialism to *Völkergeschichte*, the history of peoples. He used that term still in an older sense, to refer to pre-state antiquity studied in a wide geographical ambit. The implied notion of *Volk* became more focused when the historian Leopold von Ranke applied it. His main analytical frame for the European past was the contentious coexistence of two ethnocultural spheres that he identified in his *Geschichten der germanischen und romanischen Völker* of 1824. Jacob Grimm echoed Ranke's view in his 1844 account of a voyage to early-Risorgimento Italy:

> All of Europe consists of only two *Völker*, Germans and Italians, whose external powers had been sundered from the earliest time on. The reasons for that split must be sought directly in their nature and temperament [*Sinnesart*] as well as in their history. … These two *Völker*, whose destinies have been so tightly entwined, have long harmed one another, and the two now need to reconcile.[23]

As we saw in Chapter 6, *Völkergeschichte* was used by Arndt and Grimm to vindicate German claims on disputed borderlands, notably Schleswig-Holstein and Alsace, but also the Low Countries. It was philologically and archaeologically argued that at some point in history those territories had been settled by populations whose language or ethnicity could be qualified as Germanic. That in turn was invoked as scientific proof that the areas in

(1880) and Henryk Sienkiewicz's *Quo Vadis* (1895). The film adaptations of many of these intersected with the Italian–Hollywood genre of the sword-and-sandal or 'peplum' movie (Schenk 2006, Dumont 2009; Italian cinema had some national-proprietorial interest in tales of ancient Rome). These peplum movies featured the battles of muscular strongmen such as Maciste, Samson, Hercules or Ursus, played by body-building lead actors; the genre harked back to heroic fantasy and itself provided a source tradition for the patriotic action thriller of more recent vintage. In the career of Arnold Schwarzenegger, we can trace the lineage: from the early peplum-style *Hercules in New York* (1970) by way of the fantasy *Conan the Barbarian* (1982) to the US-chauvinistic *Commando* (1985).

question should legitimately be reunited with Germany (or annexed by it, as would be the fate of Alsace-Lorraine in 1871; see Chapter 11).

'Ethnohistory' was more generally widespread. Everywhere, history was focused on the nation (an ethnic community) as the experiencing subject of temporal change, rather than on states or institutions. Scott himself had set the tone in *Ivanhoe*, which saw medieval English history as a long ethnic conflict between Saxons and Normans. *Ivanhoe*'s Europe-wide fame ensured that this ethnohistorical frame was adopted in other countries as well: the Scott fan Augustin Thierry applied it to France, which he saw as the battleground between Gaulish, Roman and Frankish ethnic traditions (*Lettres sur l'histoire de France*, 1827) – to the point even that cranial measurements were taken to see which 'race' had left its traces where in the nation's past. Taking Thierry's cue, the Belgian Flemish historian Joseph Kervyn de Lettenhove traced a long ethnic struggle between the Flemings and their neighbouring French-francophone hegemons (*Histoire de Flandre*, 1847–1850). Although Thierry and Kervyn influenced later popularizing raconteurs such as Henri Martin (*Histoire de France*, 1833–1883), Eugène Sue (*Les mystères du peuple*, 1849–1856) and Hendrik Conscience (*De Kerels van Vlaanderen*, 1870), this type of ethnohistory drifted away from the academically professionalizing historical discipline after 1850.

As history becomes, almost by default, national history, the nation as seen by historians both enacts and experiences the challenges of the changing times. Wars, catastrophes and revolutions are described as affecting the national collective; defeats in war are described as national tragedies, victories as glories that the entire nation can rejoice in. More than that: since historians usually narrate the history of their own nation, the collectivity of the nation unites both the nation in the past and the nation in the present – the historian's readership, that is. Readers are meant to identify with the nation whose past tragedies and triumphs are being held up to them. Libuše speaks to modern Czechs. Michelet, after relating a key moment of the French Revolution (the abolition of feudalism and estate privileges on 4 August 1789), cannot help himself from exclaiming 'Vive la France!' – like Madeleine Lebeau in *Casablanca* a century later.

> The night grew late, it was two o'clock. That night took away the immense and painful spell of the Middle Ages. The approaching dawn was that of liberty. After that marvellous night there were no more classes, but French people; no more provinces, but one France. *Vive la France!*[24]

There is a civic pedagogy at work here. In narrating to their readers the glories and tragedies of their ancestors, historians became instructors of the public concerning what was now *their* history, enacted and experienced by *their* ancestors. The opening phrase of the French schoolbook, evoking 'Nos ancêtres les Gaulois' *à la* Henri Martin and Ernest Lavisse, has become proverbial in this respect (to the point of being gently lampooned at the opening of each *Astérix* album). The educational implications of this shift came soon enough: history was made a school subject in most European countries in the course of the nineteenth century, and it was aimed specifically at instilling in young pupils a sense of moral-cum-civic identification with the fatherland.

As national history was given a place in school curricula, university departments now had the task of training not only young historians in the craft of archival fieldwork and source criticism, but also future history teachers at secondary and primary schools, and inspiring or helping to prepare the textbooks that were to be used at those schools. Historians became public intellectuals and opinion leaders, even *maîtres à penser* – witness the tumultuous scenes around Michelet at the Collège de France on the eve of the 1848 revolution. Many a historian became a 'nation-builder', such as Alexandre Herculano in Portugal or František Palacký in Bohemia. In Ireland, the most vehement ideological battles were fought over the past, with poets and activists (Tom Moore, Thomas Davis, John Mitchel) writing fiery anti-English popular histories in the teeth of the professional and professorial mainstream. In the Netherlands, conflicting Protestant and Catholic interpretations of the revolt against Spain led to confessional frictions. This friction intensified as the events of that revolt, which had unfolded in the 1570s and 1580s, were commemorated on their successive tercentenaries in the 1870s and 1880s. The battle over the moral meaning of the foundational Dutch Revolt for the present Netherlands fed into the establishment of separate school systems for the country's different denominations and a deep societal split along confessional lines that lasted into the 1950s. The past *mattered*.[25]

The outreach of Romantic history writing was noticeable everywhere. Commemorative events and public holidays, the placement and presence of public statues, the historical branding and ornamentation of public spaces (indoors and outdoors) in statuary, tile tableaux, reliefs, murals and paintings, not to mention street names: all of this drew on the colourful, immersive stories of the past that historians had learned to narrate and evoke – indeed, had brought to life, and with a vengeance – in the wake of Sir Walter Scott.

To be sure, the literary influence of Scott was on the wane. The canonicity of Scott was frequently asserted to be a thing of the past, but the decline was in fact much slower than those who tried to 'get over Walter Scott' would like to believe. Scott's afterlives lingered tenaciously in odd corners of the cultural field: tourism, historical re-enactment, the ambient taste for Romantic historicism as it percolated into the decorative arts, product design and popular culture. The historical novel lost its literary primacy but seeded traces of Romantic historicism all over the public spaces of Europe.[26]

Historians, too, tried to 'get over Scott'. They came to disavow their envy of Scott's narrative and evocative powers, and indeed disavowed Romantic history writing altogether. Figures such as Michelet and Thierry, Palacký and Herculano, became a bit of an embarrassment for their successors, were considered mere *littérateurs* rather than proper 'serious historians'. The real, 'serious' historians were now embarked on a rapid process of academic professionalization, consolidated into university departments, and developed a professional ethos privileging archival (unpublished) sources. As the archives themselves became state-curated records of public policies, historians became state historians, or else social historians, rather than the 'national historians' they had been heretofore – they chose to be 'national' no longer, either in their working frame or in their audience appeal. Post-Romantic historians mistrusted the rhetoric and enthusiasm, and indeed the entire taste for drama or narrativity, that had characterized the Romantic generation, and they pursued their professionalism in austere factualism, in quantitative methods in the mode of the developing science of sociology, and in debunking the over-interpretations of their immediate forerunners. A positivistic professional ethos of anti-enthusiasm set in, and a distrust of appearances and generalizations took hold of the profession. This positivistic habitus has continued to dominate history departments, although leftist historians have returned to a Romantic sense of empathy when describing the historical struggles of class, race, gender and other subaltern identities.

That shift towards scientism, positivism and factualism, and away from pathos, imagination and narrativity, occurred in the second half of the nineteenth century; it was marked by books such as Louis Bourdeau's *L'histoire et les historiens: Essai critique sur l'histoire considérée comme science positive* (1888). Ranke's historicism now hardened into a precept of dispassionate exactitude and strict reliance on attested facts. The narrative evocation of 'the story of the nation' was left to popularizers and school textbooks. These were usually not based on fresh archival research and hence failed to qualify as serious history writing, instead seen as recycling yesterday's news. But while they were ignored by the historical profession, they kept the Romantic legacy alive among the public at large. Michelet,

Palacký and Mitchel were reprinted in popular editions, as was Walter Scott, throughout the century and beyond, while the historical profession began to publish more and more for an academic peer group. Writing history for a larger or indeed 'national' audience was, at best, popularization. Historians claiming to be both professional and 'national', such as Treitschke, would pursue the latter role in their journalistic and controversial writings, as public intellectuals, rather than in their historiography.

In this development towards academic professionalization, historians lost their grip on the public imagination, and the public imagination continued to feel the allure of the Romantics. This was in part because Romantic history writing had broadcast and canonized stirring, heroic episodes of the past: things that became, properly speaking, myths – in the common modern sense of that word. These were key episodes from the nation's history, frequently retold, widely remediated into visual imagery, into popular landmarks and narratives. The German landscape in the course of the century became dotted with huge monuments that as tourist attractions kept the myths of their dedicatees alive: the huge Arminius monument near Detmold recalling the Battle of the Teutoburg Forest, the equally huge Kyffhäuser monument recalling the myth of Barbarossa as the Once and Future German emperor, Cologne Cathedral as a monument to the continuity from the medieval to the modern Empire.[27] France had its walk-in history book in the Panthéon, with its statues, murals and graves, the many landmarks restored by Viollet-le-Duc, Napoleon's tomb in the Invalides and the many, many statues of Joan of Arc. Here and there tourists could visit in-the-round panorama paintings recalling the heroic occasions of glorious battles: Waterloo, Sebastopol, the arrival of the Magyars in Hungary.[28] The Netherlands combined feudal-medieval and seventeenth-century bourgeois cultural history in its Muiderslot near Amsterdam. The Risorgimento told its story in the gigantic monument to Vittorio Emmanuele in central Rome. And so on, and so on. With all those landmarks and tourist attractions dotting the landscape, the narrative highlights of national history – national myths – had solidified themselves in the public mind without needing to rely on the archival research or textual production of card-carrying historians.

It is difficult to think of post-Romantic academic historians enjoying the same cultural stature as their Romantic forerunners – Michelet, Alexandre Herculano, František Palacký, Carlo Cattaneo, Alexandros Rangavis or Joachim Lelewel. Indeed, all the scholarly corrections made by professional academic historians on the basis of painstaking archival research failed to inspire or even instruct the public at large to the same extent as their heedlessly Romantic predecessors had done in their own, almost literary writings or through their general culture-historicist outreach. Indeed, as academic historians introduced non-national topics into school curricula after 1945 (world history, social and economic history) those changes provoked a slow-burning backlash. National feeling had placed national history on school curricula in the 1850s, and history could not discard national feeling with impunity in the 1980s. Policy makers and public intellectuals at the national conservative end of the political spectrum periodically issued calls to bring national narrative historicism back into the school curricula. The UK prime minister John Major stressed the importance of teaching Shakespeare; Michael Gove, a British Conservative politician, spoke as follows at the Conservative party Conference of 2010:

> One of the under-appreciated tragedies of our time has been the sundering of our society from its past. Children are growing up ignorant of one of the most inspiring stories I know – the history of our United Kingdom. Our history has moments of pride, and shame, but unless we fully understand the struggles of the past we will not properly value the liberties of the present. The current approach we have to history denies children the opportunity to hear our island story. Children are given a mix of topics at primary, a cursory run through Henry VIII and Hitler at secondary and many give up the subject at 14, without knowing how the vivid episodes of our past become a connected narrative. Well, this trashing of our past has to stop.[29]

In the Netherlands, a National Canon was drawn up in 2006, and a National History Museum proposed, with the avowed aim to bring society together around a shared set of narratives. A similar canon had been drawn up in Denmark; Flanders followed suit in 2021. Although academics were involved in the canons' elaboration, many professional historians voiced reservations.[30] There were flanking initiatives to recycle and publicize this new national historicism. In Denmark, the Netherlands and Flanders (the three countries that had defined national canons), there were television series (*Historien om Danmark*, 2017; *Het verhaal van Nederland*, 2022; *Het verhaal van Vlaanderen*, 2023) with explicitly national-narrative titles and, in Flanders, a nationalist conservative politician endorsing 'the logic of promoting Flemish identity'.[31] Public and commercial media such as cinema, television and musicals have since 2000 continued to recycle canonical national figures. Quiz election shows on 'the nation's greatest figure in history' were held in many European countries: in the UK (2002, '100 Greatest Britons'), in Germany (2003, 'Die größten Deutschen'), in Finland and the Netherlands (2004, 'Suuret suomalaiset' and 'De grootste Nederlander'), in Portugal (2007, 'Os grandes portugueses'), in Greece (2009, 'Megali Ellines'), and in Italy (2010, 'Il più grande italiano di tutti i tempi').

What fed that populist mass-media historicism? The answer must be sought in the lingering legacy of Romanticism. The Romantics, obsolete among their professional successors, continued to be read as *littérateurs*, and their thrilling narratives could continue to be reworked: not only in middlebrow historical fiction and tourist landmarks, but also in the decorative arts that proliferated across cities' public spaces in the second half of the nineteenth century to leave nostalgic traces deep into the twentieth. The historical murals that embellished the interiors of Europe's great public and historical buildings all depicted narrative episodes rendered famous in the Romantic national histories of the early part of the century. Schoolrooms in the Netherlands and other countries had been decorated with colourful lithographed posters: cheap, portable murals, intended to render the national histories taught in the classroom more vividly imaginable. Patriotic songs cherished the memories of the key scenes and actors of Romantic-historical vintage. And as soon as new media cropped up, these activated that same old repertoire of nationally canonical figures and episodes, the canonicty of which has been established by those Romantic historians now dismissed by their academic successors. New media: book illustrations and the revived art of the mural; grand opera (*I Lombardi*, *Les vêpres siciliennes*, *Libuše*); decorated household ware (Figure 7.2); waxworks; panoramas; and, as the century drew to a close, film, to be followed in the twentieth century by TV serials, musicals, graphic novels, re-enactment societies and theme parks.

Thanks to this widely diffused presence, the ingrained repertoire of the nation's history and heroes is both canonical and banal. Firmly Romantic in rhetoric and provenance, it has remained solidly part of a generalized cultural memory and continues to underpin a historicist sense of the nation's inner authenticity and outer distinctness. Under the twin pressures of international entanglement and demographic multiculturalization, that national-historical repertoire seems to be used increasingly as part of a nativist political agenda: the nation, following Michael Gove's ideal, as having an internally connected narrative and being externally an island.

In recent years we have tended to twin the concepts of history and memory. How the two relate to each other is a complex and interesting question; but the two both belong to a wider sense of history, memorably defined by Johan Huizinga as the 'mental form in which a cultural community takes account of its past'. Within that wider field of 'taking account of the past',

Figure 7.2 Memory into memorabilia: souvenirs in the tourist gift shop at the Regensburg Walhalla; the Walhalla was established in 1842 by the Bavarian king Ludwig I to honour 'great historical personalities of the German nation'. ERNiE imagebank

the term 'history' has been given a more restricted, professional meaning as 'history proper', as it is studied by academics in university departments, and with a gravitation towards the archive-based investigation of political and social topics. There, the legacy of Romantic historicism has been put aside. But there are other ways of taking account of the past: outside the university, people recall the past on the basis of what they encounter informally in the field of culture or what they remember from hearsay. All that gravitates towards a field now usually seen as collective or cultural memory. In that bifurcation between history and memory, the national narratives of Romantic vintage were abandoned by 'history proper' but continued in force as an informing presence in memory.[32]

CHAPTER 8

The Image and the Presence

City Academies and Academic History Paintings

The rise of history painting in Europe is intimately linked to the rise of academic art itself. Art academies had originated towards the end of the Middle Ages at city level, emerging from the guild system of the medieval municipalities and the private studios (workshops, *ateliers*) of recognized masters with their trainees. This *atelier* tradition persisted into modern times in osmosis with municipal art schools, where the master would often also teach and which would host exhibitions and broker commissions. Even in the nineteenth century, we see that travelling art students would seek their training at institutional academies surrounded by private studios. A European model of 'official' training establishments evolved in the course of the seventeenth and eighteenth centuries. The prototypes were in Renaissance Italy: Florence (1563), Perugia (1573) and, most importantly, Rome (1593). In 1648, the Académie royale de peinture et de sculpture was founded in Paris, later to become the Académie des beaux-arts; subsequent foundations were usually in metropolitan centres with strong ties to court life.*

In and between these academies, and in the wake of the Italian Renaissance and the baroque, a 'classicist' repertoire and set of techniques crystallized and converged into a pan-European style. The technique stressed lifelike verisimilitude, a finesse of unobtrusive brushstrokes and a mastery of perspective and anatomy. These were studied and applied in a set of genres that became standardized and were classified in a hierarchy of status. History painting counted as the most prestigious of all artistic genres, above the portrait, landscape or still life. History paintings were usually in the high, heroic or 'sublime' mode, ambitious in topic and on

* Nuremberg (1662), Antwerp (1663), Turin (1678), The Hague (1682), Berlin (1696), Vienna (1725), Stockholm (1735), Venice (1750), Genoa (1751), Naples (1752), Madrid (1754), Copenhagen and St Petersburg (1757), Leipzig and Verona (1764), Dresden and London (1768), Munich (1770), Düsseldorf (1773), Milan (1776), Palermo (1780) and Kraków (1818).

a large canvas, often involving complex, dramatic scenarios (battles, crisis moments known from classical or biblical literature) in settings that also required a mastery of anatomy, perspective, landscape and architectural design. The topics were taken from a repertoire that was strictly circumscribed by the horizons of ancient Greece, ancient Rome and the Bible. No distinction was made between fictional or historical themes: scenes from the *Iliad* or Euripides were mixed with those from Greek mythology and the Roman historians. Classical as it was, the repertoire was also timeless (ironic for something called 'history painting'), much like the commemorative statues, paintings and sepulchral monuments of saints, princes and prelates in churches.[1]

Besides being transhistorically timeless, the classicist repertoire was also transnational. Biblical and classical antiquity, the stories of Troy, Jerusalem, Athens and Rome (even including outriders such as Babylon and Carthage), were considered to be the shared heritage of all of modern Europe. Any localization was mostly at the level of court or metropolis. The equestrian statues of the condottieri Gattamelata and Bartolomeo Colleoni in Padua and Venice (mid-to-late fifteenth century) are modelled on the classical prototype statue of Marcus Aurelius (c. 175 AD), but they specifically honour champions of Italian city republics, Venice in particular. The seventeenth-century statue of Erasmus belongs to Rotterdam; Jeanne d'Arc was commemorated in the public spaces of Orléans and Rouen, the diocesan cities of her triumph and martyrdom, long before she became a nationally French saint.

This biblical/classical thematic repertoire never really went away. It remained prominent within history painting for as long as that genre endured, right up to the time of Lawrence Alma-Tadema; but it was overlaid by an additional repertoire: themes taken from medieval and early modern European history. Those themes, dealing with the period when the European state system crystallized out of its feudal antecedents, were usually known as 'national' as opposed to 'classical'.

The style of these paintings remained in the 'academic' mode, largely impervious to the great nineteenth-century artistic transitions of plein-air painting, realism and the avant-garde -isms. Conventional as they were, these history paintings tend to be overlooked or marginalized in those art histories that focus on the emergence of new modes of expression and on the search for originality and individualism. The style of late (Romantic) academicism has long been decried as kitsch, 'salon art' or *art pompier*, reflecting at best the century's bourgeois complacency and anxieties. A point of critical attention has traditionally been the genre's voyeuristic obsession with female nudity in 'respectable' (allegorical, orientalist, mythological or historical) contexts.[2]

From Classical to National: History and Imagination

In the course of the eighteenth century 'classical antiquity' was increasingly turned into 'ancient history'. It was seen not as the timeless foundation of civilization but as a period in human affairs with its historical dynamics of conflict and resolution, growth and decline (as per Gibbon's *Decline and Fall of the Roman Empire*, 1776–1789), and as a period in which visual evidence, often archaeologically retrieved (e.g. at Pompeii and in the Roman catacombs), provided welcome documentation to complement written sources. Indeed, as Francis Haskell has argued, the visual reproduction of archaeological material evidence about life in ancient times (coins, vases, statuary) provided a strong incentive to render the imagination of those distant periods itself a visual one, and one that could be evoked by visual means. In this shift, history painting developed into a representation of past events, rather than a 'classical' exemplum of timeless relevance. Ancient manners and events were depicted, visualizing what things must have been like – a stimulus to the viewer's historical imagination. This budding historicism was accompanied, from the late eighteenth century onwards, by a turn towards the vernacular past: themes were increasingly chosen from the post-classical history of the European nations. *The Death of General Wolfe* (1770) by Benjamin West, a glorification of the conqueror of Quebec expiring on the battlefield in 1759, is usually considered a turning point in the thematization of the national as opposed to the universal (classical or biblical) past.[3]

Another nationalizing trend was set in motion by dynastic and literary antiquarianism: monarchs would have their palaces adorned with portraits and acts of their forefathers, which in the cases of Britain and France might lead into the medieval and semi-legendary territory (Merovingian, Anglo-Saxon) that would subsequently be claimed for 'national' history.[4] Tellingly, the Romantic 'Nazarenes' (on whom more in what follows) found employment in adding historically reimagined portraits to the gallery of medieval and later emperors in the Kaisersaal in Frankfurt's Römer buildings. Visual and textual antiquarianism went hand in hand. Portraits (usually fanciful) of medieval kings and queens adorned, as woodcuttings, the pages of treatises by antiquarians such as Jean-Baptise de La Curne de Saint-Palaye; illustrations of ancient bards and Nordic heroes began to proliferate in the wake of Macpherson and his contemporaries. The Swiss–English painter Henry Fuseli depicted scenes from the *Nibelungenlied*, which had recently been re-edited. Again, the line between historical veracity and legendary fable was not easily drawn in these decades when historical source criticism was still in its infancy and the mythologies narrated by Suhm and Macpherson were often taken as historical fact.

By contrast, in the revolution-inspired works of Jacques-Louis David classical themes were used to allegorize and inspire contemporary, national affairs, holding up ancient Greek or Roman heroes such as Leonidas or the Horatii as models for the republican virtues of contemporary France. Thus national history could, even in the Romantic century, hark back to classical symbols. The tribal opponents who had resisted Roman expansionism in the first or second centuries AD, mentioned by Roman historians such as Tacitus or Livy, now became national heroes defending an independence understood, anachronistically, in terms of contemporary nation-building. Arminius the Cheruscan became a German inspiration, Vercingetorix a French one, and Boudicca an English one.

With the Parisian Academy of Fine Arts as an obvious starting ground, an increasingly recognizable, clearly characterized genre of national history paintings spread across Europe in the course of the nineteenth century by means of the tight, professional system of masters and pupils that formed the art world. David, his pupils Antoine-Jean Gros and Jean-Auguste-Dominique Ingres, and their pupils and pupils' pupils such as Paul Delaroche and Jean-Léon Gérôme, among them span the entire century (David died in 1825 and Gérôme in 1904) and fixed an iconography of sublime evocations of key moments in the nation's history. Their topics included court scenes, deathbed scenes, battle scenes and a number of genre scenes showing great historical figures (frequently other painters: Dürer, Leonardo) in domestic situations. At the same time, this choice canonized such national moments as being suitable for even the most prestigious of artistic expressions. Although the choice and treatment of topics is often Romantic (evoking the Walter-Scott-style *couleur locale* of the past and the pathos of history), the style is that of high, classical academicism: ambitiously striving for technically convincing verisimilitude through the mastery of brush technique, perspective, textures, human anatomy and physiognomy, and historical detail, often on a large canvas.[5]

The shared technique of academicism helps to explain the pan-European spread of history painting. Not only could artists from many countries assemble around masters in European 'hubs' such as Paris; the paintings themselves were also mobile. The exhibition of two prominent painters from the Antwerp historicist school, Édouard de Biefve and Louis Gallait, in nine German cities between 1842 and 1844 famously inspired a new departure for history painting in many parts of Germany, notably Bavaria. But usually it is the personal network, the filiations of masters to pupils, often through the hub of an internationally renowned academy, that adds up to a quasi-genealogical conduit carrying the spread of history painting across Europe. Even from remote countries with a modest local art scene, promising young artists would be sent (often thanks to sponsorship from wealthy, public-minded patrons) to train at academies and return to introduce the fruit of their training in their own countries: Theodor Aman was given funds by his Romanian patrons to travel to Paris, Norwegian painters such as Peter Nicolai Arbo trained in Düsseldorf, and Munich became the preferred training ground for aspiring painters from the Bohemian lands. All of them celebrated their own countries and their unique authenticity, be it in historical scenes (Aman), Nordic mythology (Arbo) or legend-infused landscapes (the Czechs); all of them did so in the universally current techniques and conventions of academicism.[6]

The Nazarenes and the Mural

In this Europe-wide urban-academic network, Paris remained, despite all the French regime changes between 1789 and 1871, a pre-eminent node for the academic depiction of national history, with in its wake the academies of Berlin, St Petersburg, Vienna, Antwerp and Düsseldorf. But special mention should be made, alongside Paris, of Rome as a central hub and hatching ground. Not only was the Papal Academy located there amidst the continuity from classical antiquity into Renaissance and baroque, but also various ateliers were set up in Rome by artists from different countries as meeting-grounds for their fellow countrymen, foreshadowing the rise of 'national' art institutes in that European metropolis. A sojourn in Rome (often facilitated by a Prix de Rome or a patronage scholarship) counted as the culmination of an artist's training and helped consolidate the city's function as a hub. Among these private ateliers and points of artistic congregation, none proved more influential than that of the German Nazarenes.[7]

A number of Romantically minded young painters found themselves excluded from the rolls of the Vienna academy in that city's Napoleon-inflicted decline after 1805. They decided to take up residence in Rome, now annexed by Napoleon, where they could make use of a recently secularized Franciscan monastery. Their nationally German hairstyles (long and parted in the middle, *à la* Dürer, in a rejection of the powdered wig; see Figure 4.4) earned them the nickname of 'Nazarenes'. In their residence at the San Isidoro church and monastery they lived amidst specimens of the ancient, now languishing, art of the fresco. It appealed to their religious earnestness, their cultural nostalgia and their anti-classicism. The fresco, with its bold colours and clear outlines, sidestepped the jejune artistic opposition between *disegno* and *colorito* and allowed them to express their spiritualism and their sympathy with late medieval and early Renaissance forms.

The Nazarenes obtained commissions to decorate Roman villas with frescos and gained lasting, Europe-wide influence. Their clearly outlined and brightly coloured style became the hallmark of the new, Romantic-historicist mural, which was institutionalized when their leader Peter von Cornelius was appointed to head the academy of Düsseldorf and then that of Munich. Düsseldorf and Munich as training grounds helped established the Nazarene mode as a standard for a great number of Romantic-academic painters of the period and the mural as a flagship genre. In Frankfurt's Paulskirche, the deliberations of the 1848 National Assembly were overlooked by a large allegory of Germania (Figure 8.1) by

Figure 8.1 Allegory of Germania (Philipp Veit, 1848; Germanisches Nationalmuseum, Nuremberg). Wikimedia Commons

Figure 8.2 *Joan of Arc in Armour at the Siege of Orléans* (Jules Lenepveu, 1874; Panthéon, Paris). Wikimedia Commons

the Nazarene Philipp Veit; she was depicted as an oak-wreathed female, foot-shackles undone, displaying on her robe the imperial escutcheon of the double-headed eagle and holding a sword and the national tricolour flag of 1813–1814.[8]

Throughout the century, many prestigious commissions were for mural decorations of restored or newly built palaces and government buildings everywhere in Europe, with Germany as 'ground zero'. This in turn helped consolidate the Nazarene, Romantic style in academicism: from Maclise's murals for the new Houses of Parliament in London to Jules Lenepveu's Joan of Arc cycle in the Parisian Panthéon (Figure 8.2); from Henri Leys's historical murals for the Antwerp City Hall to Ford Madox Brown's Pre-Raphaelite celebrations of craftsmanship and labour for the Manchester Town Hall. Within Germany, there are the sumptuous murals at Wartburg Castle, the city hall of Aachen, Munich's city hall and Neue Pinakothek, and the Imperial Manor at Goslar (more on which further on). As a result of such lavish, large-scale decoration, public buildings became an immersive experience, a time capsule where the visitor would be transported back to the settings, scenery and narratives of bygone ages – a form of mental time-travel that is the essence of historicism. Among them, these murals captured a selected iconography of historical episodes and helped canonize those episodes as historical myths.[9]

The grandiose style of history paintings was also used for prestigious topical affairs. Napoleon, and many nineteenth-century rulers after him, commissioned paintings of their coronations and of battles scenes from recent victories; these were done in the grand manner of the history painting and in the process propagandistically asserted the claim that 'history was being made' and that these coronations or battles were of lasting historical importance.[10] The nineteenth century produced a welter of battle scenes, some depicting events as long ago as the first-century battle of the Teutoburg Forest, others as recent as the Crimean War or the scramble for Africa (e.g. Marià Fortuny's *The Battle of Wad-Rass*, 1868). Academic history painters would become the recorders of their country's old and recent glories. Sixty-five years after David painted Napoleon's 1806 self-coronation 'from life' (having been invited to the occasion for the purpose), Anton von Werner was summoned to Versailles to witness the German imperial proclamation there in 1871, which he proceeded to depict in no fewer than three copies.

Those were state-sanctioned applications. More subversively, Eugène Delacroix painted his famous *Liberty Leading the People* only months after the 1830 revolution that it celebrates. The 'history' in such history painting is often of very recent vintage and signified 'importance' rather than 'pastness'. At the same time the nationalizing tendency is all-pervasive. The nation becomes the dominant frame for calibrating such general notions as historical importance, glory and liberty: it is always the nation's experience of history, the nation's glory and its liberty that are celebrated or extolled, with religion running a distant second. The Romantic-historicist preoccupation with early Christianity spawned a great number of history paintings evoking scenes of Christian martyrdom in Roman arenas. And there was, of course, a good deal of inter-nation solidarity, especially regarding the Greek and Polish struggles for national independence: Delacroix was a prominent philhellene, and many of his paintings denounced Ottoman tyranny.[11]

As Delacroix and his philhellenic paintings indicate, the turn to nationality could go in tandem with an altogether different taste for colourful exoticism: that of orientalism. Almost every painter of history paintings also tried his hand at odalisques, harems or bazaars. The tight conjunction between exoticism and historicism is not fortuitous: both are, in true Romantic fashion, attempts to render a world other than the straightforward here and now. In addition, a nationalist undercurrent is noticeable in both: while historicism bolsters the nation's rootedness in

Figure 8.3 *Yermak's Conquest of Siberia* (Vasilij Surikov, 1895; State Russian Museum, St Petersburg). Wikimedia Commons

the past, exoticism often bespeaks colonial ambitions, rooted as it was in Mediterranean expeditions from Napoleon's Egyptian campaign onwards. Maghrebinian scenes by French or Spanish painters are part of the colonial expansionism of both countries in Northern Africa. Orientalism in Russian painting is part of that country's oriental imperial colonialism in the Caucasus and Central Asia, overtly celebrated in Vasilij Surikov's huge canvas on the conquest of Siberia (1895, Figure 8.3).[12]

The Past as a Magic Mountain: Goslar

The history painters of the nineteenth century are overshadowed these days by names such as Monet, Van Gogh, Klimt and Picasso: those who innovated their style away from academicism and historicism. But we should not underestimate the influence of history painters at the time: through official commissions and through the teaching institutions of the visual arts, they were in a position to establish a pictorial canon of key moments and scenes from the nation's past, often displayed as murals on the walls of public buildings or reproduced as engravings, lithographs or photographs, also in book illustrations. And they were called upon to broadcast the nation's identity in high-prestige form. A telling example is the murals for the Imperial Manor at Goslar by Hermann Wislicenus. He had been a pupil at the Dresden Academy of the Nazarene Julius Schnorr von Carolsfeld and, while in Rome, of Peter von Cornelius; and as of 1868 he had taught at the Düsseldorf Academy.[13]

Goslar's palace of the medieval Hohenstaufen emperors had been restored once that city had come under Prussian rule in 1868, and the restoration works were rounded off by an ambitious programme of some forty historical murals in the main hall. Executed by Wislicenus in the late 1880s, these evoked scenes of German history from Charlemagne to the 1870 proclamation of the Second Reich. They were arranged 'in the round' in a narrative sequence that positioned Wilhelm of Prussia as the white-bearded avatar of the greatest Hohenstaufen emperor, Friedrich Barbarossa. Recurrent themes run through this sequence: the emperor's problems with insubordinate liegemen (the recalcitrant duke of Saxony and Bavaria foreshadowing recent frictions with the kings of Hanover and Bavaria) and with the papacy (foreshadowing the *Kulturkampf*, Bismarck's attempt to root out Papal ultramontanism in Germany). Thus an anti-Papal and anti-Guelph continuity from Hohenstaufen to Hohenzollern is constructed; in the process, the Habsburgs' long tenure of imperial dignity is written out of the story.

The entire cycle culminates in a huge centrepiece evoking 'history coming full circle'. Wilhelm I's re-establishment of the German empire is allegorically evoked as he and the Crown Prince ride on horseback towards the spectator (Figure 8.4). They are overseen by celestial spirits above them: their dynastic ancestors and their imperial predecessors, including Charlemagne and Barbarossa, and also the revered Queen Louise, Wilhelm's mother. In the wings, on the right and left, are the Hohenzollern royal household and the assembled German princes; Ludwig of Bavaria is even made to proffer the imperial crown. They are flanked on one side by Bismarck and Moltke (the victorious general of the 1870–1871 war) and on the other side by allegorical representations of Alsace and Lorraine, now reunited into the Reich. At their feet are allegorical figures of Father Rhine and the Muse of German Legend, holding an open book.

In this apotheosis, everything becomes a spectacle, with history, legend and allegorical symbolism merged into an eternal, timeless moment. That, indeed, is the overall effect as one enters Goslar's Kaisersaal: a magic mountain (like Barbarossa's Kyffhäuser, or the one where an elf queen entertains Tannhäuser) where time stands still, and all of history is suspended and simultaneously present. The effect is heightened by the shock-and-awe scale of the design: there is not a single surface that is not covered by heavily allegorical scenes visualizing historical episodes, and the visitor's field of vision is wholly occupied by them, as in a panorama or an Imax 3D theatre. Furthermore, these scenes are often of a legendary nature and even involve fairy tales: the Barbarossa legend is dovetailed with the tale

Figure 8.4 *Wilhelm I as Refounder of the Reich* (Hermann Wislicenus, 1885; Imperial Manor, Goslar). ERNiE imagebank

of Sleeping Beauty, depicted in numerous scenes as an allegory of the dormancy of the German Reich. The Muse of German Legend has good reason for sitting at the emperor's feet.

Wislicenus's hugely ambitious, densely layered and hyper-referential project was the grandiose culmination of a tradition that at the time of its completion was already beginning to be outflanked. The grand historical style, focusing on battles, coronations and crises at court, was no longer the only way to impress onlookers. Indeed, the academic style as a whole, including its flagship, the mural, was maintaining itself only in an increasingly isolated sanctuary, artificially nurtured by government commissions for high-prestige buildings.

A new avant-garde, deliberately defying the academic tradition, had announced itself when Gustave Courbet, rejected for an Academy Salon in the mid-1850, mounted a private exhibition that he entitled *Le réalisme* (more on this in Chapter 10). Amplified by other new developments (the rise of plein-air painting, of artists' colonies and of new, looser brush techniques), the visual arts embarked on an agenda of innovative experiment that thrived in a climate of *épater les bourgeois* and moved sharply away from the conformism of the academy; at the same time, this new artistic vanguard moved away from historical topics in favour of landscapes, contemporary social scenes and abstraction.

Friedrich Nietzsche's 1874 essay 'On the Use and Abuse of History for Life' marked a more generalized weariness with the monumental celebration of the past *à la* Wislicenus: historicism was pushed into the cultural margins by a more future-oriented, innovatory and critical approach to culture. Realism fed into Impressionism and the various secessionist and avant-garde movements of the *fin-de-siècle* and the twentieth century. All of these movements were united in their scorn for academic art, and art critics and art historians soon adopted that scorn.

Notwithstanding, historicism remained an inspiring modality in the late-emerging sub-imperial nationalities of Europe. In the Russian borderlands from Finland to Georgia, the state-sanctioned monumentalization of the past in academic painting had never been applied to subaltern cultural traditions. As new generations of artists emerged in these peripheries, fully sensitized to a more modern style and technique, they still felt the need to apply this to the retrieval and celebration of their national culture. Russian historicism flourished in an art nouveau style and was also used by Akseli Gallen-Kallela for Finnish mythological themes.[14]

Sentimental Historicism

Of course, history painting was more than bombastic murals. The historicism that was mentioned earlier, in the mode of Walter Scott, stressed not only the awesome and somewhat stilted grandeur of the past but also its relatable domesticity.

When setting the agenda for Romantic historicism, Scott had, uniquely, combined elements of alienation and recognizability in his evocations of history. His narrative focus was always on the domestic, private affects of his protagonists, while situating these in the grand sweep of historical crisis moments and transitions. He patented, as it were, the historicist dualism of empathy and exoticism. *Ivanhoe* (1819–1820) had evoked, in a sweeping historical canvas, the crisis of Plantagenet kingship during the crusading absence of Richard the Lionheart, amidst all the tensions of an ethnically divided, Saxon-versus-Norman medieval England; but it also depicted the private emotions of the protagonists, Wilfred of Ivanhoe and Rebecca.

That dualism had become the hallmark of the historical novel as such. In historical novels such as Tolstoy's *War and Peace*, Lampedusa's *The Leopard* and Eco's *The Name of the Rose*, Napoleon's Russian campaign needs its young Natasha Rostov, Garibaldi's Sicilian campaign its ageing Prince of Salina, and the theological showdown between Dominicans and Franciscans its *ingénu* Adso of Melk. These fictitious protagonists with their private, individual relatability allow the past to 'come to life', to be empathetically experienced, imaginatively at least, from within, as it must have felt at the time.

The vivid evocation of domestic familiarity amidst the sublime grandeur of historical distance was also attempted in Romantic history painting. Next to the grandeur of the battle and court scenes, we see the sentimental sub-genre of the 'historical genre painting'. Genre art was one of the lesser academic styles, evoking scenes from domestic home life, frequently also involving middle-class or peasant settings. As the scenic settings of Brueghel, Van Ostade and Vermeer had receded into the past, they had become defamiliarized, quaint: illustrations of bygone manners and fashions.[15] And this appealed to the many history painters who chose to take their topics not from the sublime or heroic register (battles, executions and coronations) but from the private lives of historical figures. And so we see various renditions of Charles V visiting Titian in his studio or Henri IV playing with his children. As the century progressed and Romanticism developed into Biedermeier or Victorian sentimentalism, this taste became more pronounced. William Frederick Yeames's *And When Did You Last See Your Father?* (1878) shows Cromwellian investigators, hunting for Cavaliers, interrogating a young boy, whose mother, the wife of the fugitive cavalier, looks on in anguished apprehension (Figure 8.5).[16] One can imaginatively immerse oneself in scenes such as these. The period detail, the lovingly rendered clothes, furnishings and interiors, are all meant to assist an emotional immediacy, helping the viewer to experience the past as it must have been experienced at the time.[17]

With the rise of realism this sentimental historicism also declines, along with the recession of the historical novel, which moved by way of Dickens's *A Tale of Two Cities* and baroness D'Orczy's *Scarlet Pimpernel*

Figure 8.5 *And When Did You Last See Your Father?* (William Frederick Yeames, 1878; Walker Art Gallery, Liverpool). Wikimedia Commons

to the unprestigious margins of the literary system: the female readers of Georgette Heyer, the juvenile readers of G. A. Henty. Despite occasional masterpieces, the genre of the historical novel as a whole became, as the telling German word has it, *gesunkenes Kulturgut*, a depreciated cultural heritage. And something similar befell academic history painting.

Painters such as Il'ja Repin and Theodor Aman, who had made their names as academic history painters, turned towards more contemporary themes and a looser style, abandoning the clear outline that had been the hallmark of the fresco and of its historicist-academic derivations. As the great talents moved to different registers, national history painting proper subsisted as a pale imitation of its former self. It drifted from the salon and from palatial public buildings towards the eye-candy glitter of fairgound attraction and mass entertainment. Alongside Wislicenus's Goslar murals, we see Árpád Feszty's huge panorama celebrating the Hungarian *Landnahme* by the Magyars (1894), part of an entire fashion for 360°-panorama paintings embellishing historical tourist destinations all around Europe, from Sebastopol to Waterloo. History paintings were used for diorama pavilions in world fairs; Yeames's *And When Did You Last See Your Father?* became a waxwork display in Madame Tussaud's. Only in a few cases do we see that avant-garde artists of the later century continue to treat historical topics in a modern register: Puvis de Chavannes's St Geneviève murals for the Panthéon (1874), Carl Larsson's *Midvinterblot* mural for Stockholm's National Museum (1915) and Alphonse Mucha's *Slavic Epic* cycle (1910–1928).[18]

Remediations and Mass Commodification

This is the irony, then: the most august genre of the academic tradition, the history painting, around 1900 becomes almost a decorative art, used to embellish public buildings or tourist attractions. Its scenes were found less and less on canvas and more and more in remediated form: as engravings or illustrations for popular periodicals or historical surveys or albums such as the German collection *Bildersaal der deutschen Geschichte* (1890), or collectible chromolithographs, or educational school plates. The mural turned, increasingly, from paint to stained-glass windows and ceramic or glass tiles (mosaics such as those of the Venetian firm of Salviati, or *azulejos* in Spain and Portugal, or the tile tableaux on the outside walls of Amsterdam's Rijksmuseum). Such media were also eminently suited to the fresco-derived style patented by the Nazarenes: a combination of bright colours and crisp outlines.[19]

That Nazarene style survived principally in the art of religious ultramontanism. There had always been a degree of Catholic fervour among the Nazarenes, and their art flourished most conspicuously in the altarpieces and pious lithographs and prayer cards distributed in their millions during the decades of ultramontanist devotionalism, showing ultra-saccharine, pastel-coloured madonnas, saints and biblical scenes. That this religious kitsch breathes and perpetuates the aesthetics of Nazarene Romanticism alerts us to the continuing, camouflaged subsistence of this school of academic painting. The same goes for the brightly coloured lithographs of Hindu deities popular among religious devotees and often encountered in Europe as restaurant decorations. These were pioneered by Raja Ravi Varma (1848–1906), a successful Indian painter and lithograph publisher, who had learned his craft from a German, Nazarene-influenced teacher and applied it towards Nazarene-style icons of Hindu deities and Indian national and mythological heroes (Figure 8.6).[20]

Far away from the salons and galleries, then, academic history painting left its traces – wherever, indeed, its celebratory piety and easy-on-the-eye style were suitable.* One such medium was that of the national currencies developed for newly independent countries after 1918. Artists such as Alphonse Mucha and the Latvian Rihards Zariņš, masters of decorative and graphic

* An interesting suggestion for this mass-reproduced diffusion of an academic style is made with regard to the female nudes of William Bouguereau. Merlijn Schoonenboom (2015) has traced the reception history and changing canonicity of Bouguereau nudes 'from art to kitsch and back again', especially in America, and suggests – plausibly to my mind – that the academic aesthetics of the female nude *à la* Bouguereau have been perpetuated in *Playboy*-style glamour photography.

Figure 8.6 *The Goddess Saraswati* (Raja Ravi Varma, 1896; Maharaja Fateh Singh Museum, Vadodara). ERNiE imagebank

arts, produced patriotic propaganda posters (another suitable medium with its preference for the bright-colours/clear-outline register) and would later provide their newly independent homelands, Czechoslovakia and Latvia, with designs for postage stamps and banknotes, often involving allegories, scenes from the nation's past, and portraits of the nation's heroes.[21]

This is the diffused, watered-down legacy of academic art. In the terminology of Pierre Bourdieu, the genre has moved from 'restricted' to 'unrestricted' culture (mass-produced, non-exclusive, widely and cheaply available, and accordingly without exclusiveness or prestige). In Michael Billig's terms it has become the genre of 'banal nationalism', merely ambient and unobtrusive after having once been the carrier of a definitive and explicit, 'hot' national agenda – yet (in spite of what the word 'banal' may suggest) wielding a huge influence, penetrating far and wide in society. Recalling David Lowenthal, we may also phrase it as a shift from the academy towards 'heritage' commodification. After its big splash in the early nineteenth century, history painting has become static noise, a vague background radiation in nations' public spheres.[22]

Sic transit? Not quite.

A Repertoire

The true importance of history painting comes to the fore if we align it not with the other visual arts but with the textual media of historicism: history writing and the historical novel. We have seen how the rise of the history painting involved an increasingly visualized understanding of the past seen in historical rather than antiquarian terms; we have also noted the influence of Walter-Scott-style historicism and how its marginalization occurred more or less in tandem with that of the historical novel. These are not fortuitous coincidences; they bespeak a meaningful cohesion between the three genres. These relate to each other in a complex triangulation, in which two of the three are textual (the historical novel and history writing), one visual; alternatively, two of the three belong to the field of cultural/artistic production (the novel and history painting), one to the field of knowledge production (history writing). Finally, two of the three are factually representative (history painting and history writing), one fictionally narrative (the novel) (Figure 8.7).

Against this background, we notice how very *discursive* history painting is. Much more so than landscapes, portraits or still life, it evokes a historical record and an intertext. We are meant to understand (or know first-hand) how the painting relies on accounts known from other, textual sources: histories mostly, but often also fictions (myths, epics or romances). The

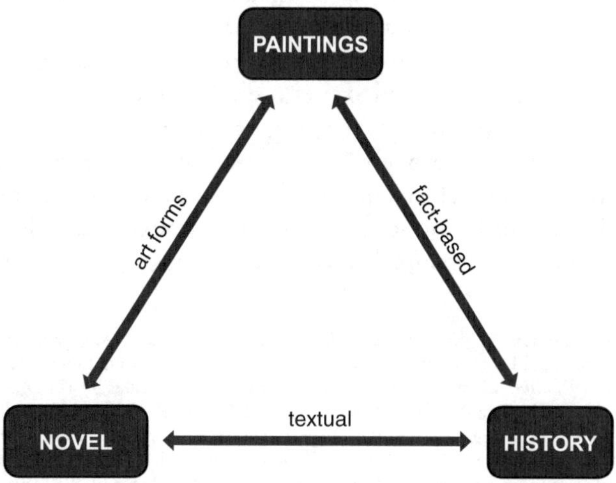

Figure 8.7 History painting, history writing and the historical novel.

Edda, *Iliad* and *Nibelungenlied* furnished themes as well as Joan of Arc or the conquest of Siberia.*

In other words, the past was mined by historians, novelists and painters, and each of the three took their bearings from the other two. Like historians and novelists, painters had to negotiate the problematic relationship between a truthful, documented representation of the past and the need to fill the gaps in the documentary evidence by means of informed guesses and the imagination. Whereas the novel relies mainly on the organizing principle of a fictional narrative, history writing (even narrative history) is organized around the constraints of the available archive and pre-existing knowledge.[23] In that negotiation, history paintings tended to gravitate to a documented rather than to a fictional past – based on existing knowledge, or on a known historiographical account. This means that history painting, although it is an art form, is quite close to historiographical knowledge production. It is, in a way, an illustration to history writing, transmuting the textual narrative into a spectacle and rendering accounts of the past, in the most literal sense of the word, imaginable.

The three genres parted ways after the death of Walter Scott in 1832. As history writing professionalized into the positivistic factualism of austere university departments, it was left to the art genres of the novel and painting to keep the Romantic sensation of the past alive. As they did so, they lost (as we have seen) artistic prestige and canonicity towards the end of the century; but they maintained their hold on the popular imagination. The public at large continued to imagine the past, and especially the Middle Ages, in the mode established by the Romantic generation; and novels and paintings helped to recycle and perpetuate that image.

The perpetuation was aided by reproducing and recycling Romantic evocations of the past in newly emerging media. Canonical narratives and themes had always been apt to move from one medium of expression (visual, textual or musical) to another: witness the importance of pictorial, theatrical and operatic spin-offs of historical novels. This also extended to new media as they emerged: waxworks and cinema in the nineteenth

* In the Romantic decades, medieval and early modern historical themes were usually taken from the painter's own national history, but Joan of Arc, Wilhelm Tell, crusading knights and scenes from Dante's *Divina Commedia* were internationally popular. In the French 'troubadour style', which flourished in the early decades after 1800 (also in historicist clothes design: Chaudonneret 1980; Mackrell 1998), medieval themes were often English. The reason may have been that themes such as the two doomed young princes in the Tower of London, painted by Delaroche (Bann 1997, 2006), had been made famous in Shakespeare's history plays (in this case, *Richard III*) and were thus indicative of a tendency to draw historical topics from an international literary canon. Delaroche also took medieval themes from Walter Scott's *Quentin Durward* and *Ivanhoe*.

and twentieth centuries, the musical and video serials nowadays. Themes, narratives and affecting heroes and heroines (Joan of Arc, Wilhelm Tell, Mary Queen of Scots, etc.) move around among printed page, painting, the theatre/opera stage and the screen (silver or digital).

What was attempted in the nineteenth-century three-way intermediality between the historical novel, history writing and history painting, and continued in transferences to different emerging media, is a reconciliation between the textual and the visual, between narrative and spectacle.[24] As we have noted, history paintings showed a gravitation towards the descriptive, anecdotal and narrative. Romantic histories and historical novels often took their readers to scenes set in the past and described as set-pieces, asking the reader to imagine and visualize a setting or situation. These genres were striving to unite the two modalities of art as distinguished by Lessing in his *Laokoon* of 1766: the *Nebeneinander* (one-next-to-another, objects arranged in space) and the *Nacheinander* (one-after-another, events arranged in time). History paintings tended to concatenate into cycles: witness Wislicenus's narrative arrangements of the Goslar Kaisersaal, or Lenepveu's series of scenes from the life of Joan of Arc in the Panthéon, or Mucha's *Slavic Epic*: the narrativity of these scenes episodically arranged into cycles becomes almost that of the graphic novel.

As the canonicity of academic history painting was waning, its way of turning historical narratives into grand spectacle found a new medium of expression, perfectly combining *Nacheinander* and *Nebeneinander*, narrative and spectacle: that of film – 'moving pictures', as they were called. From D. W. Griffith's *Birth of a Nation* to Eisenstein's *Alexander Nevsky*, the cinema screen became the successor to the theatre stage, the canvas, the mural, the diorama, for the projection of a Romantically evoked past. The great epic blockbusters and action movies of the twentieth and twenty-first centuries, which we shall survey in more detail in Chapter 12, in many cases recycle tales and scenes, narratives and spectacles, from the national past as they were rendered canonical by historians, novels and paintings during the Romantic period.

How that perpetuation worked may be illustrated by the telling example of the Norwegian movie *Birkebeinerne* ('Birchlegs', i.e. men with birchbark leggings, 2016; marketed internationally as *The Last King*). It revolves around a historical episode rendered memorable by the Romantic historian Peter Andreas Munch in *Det Norske Folks Historie* (1852–1863) and, following him, by Knud Bergslien's iconic history painting of 1869 (Figure 8.8). That painting was picked up in the 2016 movie poster for *Birkebeinerne* by the contemporary artist Marcell Bandicksson. Norwegian

Figure 8.8 'Birchlegs' Skiing Across the Mountains with the Infant King (Knud Bergslien, 1869; Holmenkollen Ski Museum, Oslo). Wikimedia Commons

historians have moved on from Munch; Norwegian painters have moved on from Bergslien; but Norwegian cultural memory is still deeply informed by their *Birkebeinerne*.

Even in the twenty-first century, Romantic history painting, with its celebration of the nation's colourful past, is alive and kicking in the eco-system of popular cultural memory; and epic still thrives.

CHAPTER 9

In Tune
Concerts, Choirs

How a Wunderkind Became Hungarian

The 1840 painting in Figure 9.1 shows an imagined matinee recital by Franz Liszt. By now the imagery may appear familiar: the enraptured audience listening to an inspired performance is very close to the listeners in the roughly contemporary painting of Rouget de Lisle singing 'La Marseillaise' (Figure 1.3), and the transported gaze of the inspired performer, gazing upwards into the distance, resembles that we have seen in the pictures of Ossian and of the *guslar* (Figures 3.1 and 5.1). Liszt's audience are the *fine fleur* of Parisian Romanticism at the time: swooning on her chair on the left is George Sand, seated next to Alexandre Dumas; standing behind them are fellow composers Berlioz, Paganini and Rossini, looking knowledgeable and appreciative. Reclining next to the piano, and seen from behind, is countess Marie d'Agoult, Liszt's patron and long-term companion. (Although she and Liszt never married, they had three children together, one of whom, Cosima, would later marry Richard Wagner. D'Agoult herself wrote and published under the pen name 'Daniel Stern'.) To add to the clear sense that we are in a locus of concentrated Romanticism, there is a bust of Beethoven on the piano, a portrait of Byron on the wall and a statue of Joan of Arc on the far left.

Besides hinting at the importance of the salon as a hothouse for artistic and intellectual innovation, the painting also documents the flourishing of the Romantic virtuoso as a cultural and social phenomenon. The painting was commissioned by the Viennese piano manufacturer Conrad Graf, an important builder during the time when the grand piano was becoming the instrument for large-scale concerts, with expanded octave range and improved tonal power. Graf built pianos for Beethoven, Chopin and Clara Schumann, and Liszt is here shown (in what is almost a product placement) playing a Graf. Ironically, Liszt's violently passionate performance style is said to have destroyed two Graf pianos in Vienna.[1]

Figure 9.1 *A Matinee Performance by Liszt* (Josef Danhauser, 1840; Alte Nationalgalerie, Berlin). Wikimedia Commons

As the piano evolved into a 'grand' power instrument, the virtuoso piano player became increasingly a public superstar, and Liszt was among the most celebrated of them all. Virtuosi – technically accomplished performers who would give concerts to paying audiences on tour – can be traced back to the early eighteenth century, but the child prodigy Mozart had marked a leap forward, followed by Chopin and the violinist Paganini. Between them, Mozart, Chopin and Liszt mark the onset of the heyday of musical Romanticism, with the definitive emancipation of music from the patronage of nobility and courts and its development into a public and commercially financed art form with superstar celebrities.[2]

Liszt, like Mozart, had started his career as a *Wunderkind.* (The cult of the child prodigy was part of the Romantic fascination with art as something untaught, naturally inborn; it helped young Schubert and Chopin to fame at a very early age.) Born in 1811 near what is now the Hungarian–Austrian border, and having made an early start in Vienna, Liszt moved to Paris with his mother at the age of twelve to pursue his musical training and career. There he soon became part of a network of Romantic musicians and composers; they were of many nationalities (including Italians and Germans), gathered in what was the cultural metropolis not just of

France but of much of Europe. From Paris he would undertake many concert tours. Liszt was, in other words, a wandering cosmopolitan, and the tracks of his lifelong concert tours between 1818 and 1886 enmesh all of Europe like a spider-web (Figure 9.2).

At the time when the painting of his salon performance was commissioned, Liszt had been in Italy for two years, just then parting ways temporarily from his companion Marie d'Agoult. The news of a Danube flood in Budapest had brought Hungary to mind; he travelled to Vienna to perform at a benefit concert for a flood-relief fund and from there moved, for the first time since his early boyhood, into Hungary: by way of Bratislava/Pressburg his journey led to Budapest, where he performed in early January 1840.[3]

The concert was a triumph. As Liszt later wrote, 'Everywhere else I perform for an audience, however in Hungary I address the nation!' The leading national poet Mihaly Vörösmarty dedicated a poem to him after the concert, asking him to awaken once again through his music the spirit of the ancestral tribal leader Árpád. Huge crowds, shouting *Eljen! Liszt Ferenc!* ('Hail, Franz Liszt!', calling him by his Hungarian name-form), greeted him rapturously and welcomed home the most celebrated Hungarian of his day as a long-lost son. Liszt returned the favour: the concert was full of patriotic gestures. Most significantly, Liszt performed the *Rakoczi March*, which, linked as it was to the rebellious nobleman of that name, had been banned by the Austrian censors. He also wore the Hungarian national costume on stage (a tight long-waisted 'Attila' waistcoat fastened with embroidered frogs-and-loops rather than buttons), and to top it all he was presented on-stage with a ceremonial sabre of honour.

Receiving this sabre symbolically inducted Liszt into the Hungarian nobility, and that meant a great deal. At the time, Hungary was still an almost feudal class society with the nobility enjoying and insisting upon its ancient established privileges, not least of which was the 'right to bear arms', symbolized by sword or sabre (still the marker of difference between commissioned officers/gentlemen and the enlisted rank and file). The Hungarian *úriember* (a 'true/fine gentleman' with dignity, bravado and poise) cultivated a sense of aristocratic honour, which during these years began to overlap with a sense of national pride: Hungarian Romantic nationalism was Byronic, chivalric, based on a sense of nobility rather than on (civic) virtue. This affect was powerfully expressed in the great popularity of the sport of fencing, still a 'national sport' among Hungarians, and feeding into that national symbolism was the sabre conferred upon Liszt.[4]

When Liszt gave a speech of thanks – significantly, in French, since his command of Hungarian was insufficient – he showed himself keenly aware of the symbolic import of the moment. He pointed out that of old it had

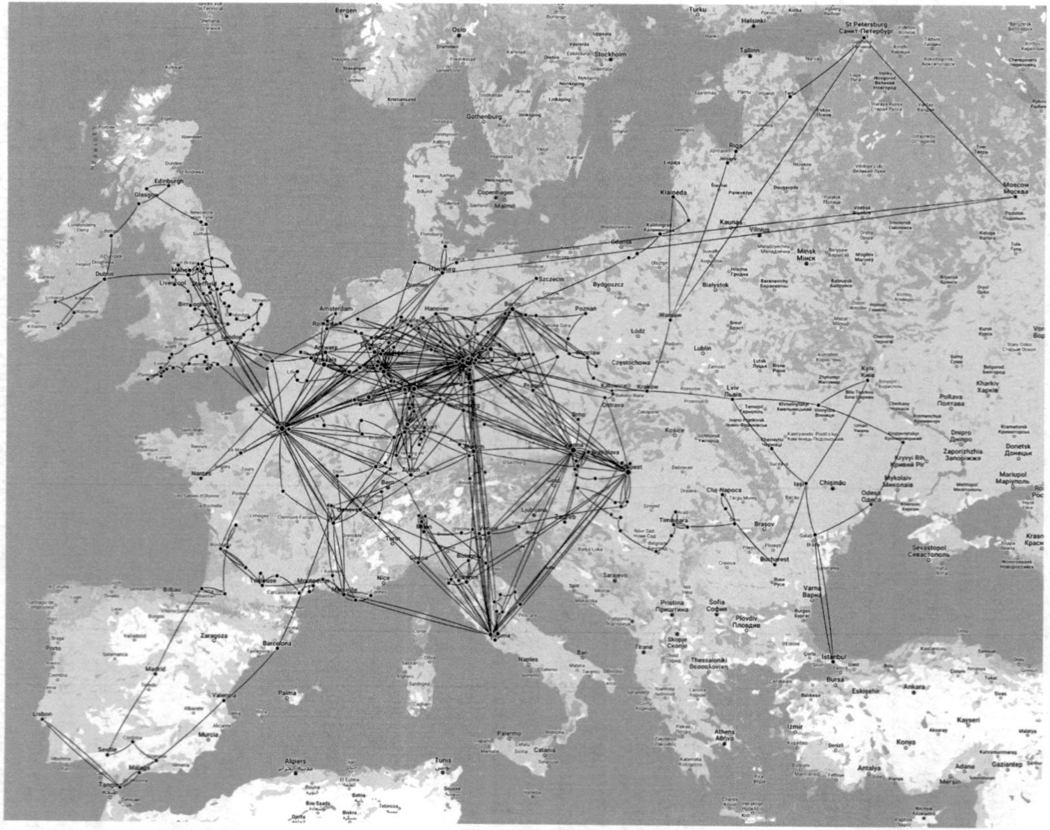

Figure 9.2 Liszt’s concert tours across Europe, 1818–1886 (e-rn.ie/lisztours).

been the warriors and military officers who had buttressed the nation; in these modern days, he suggested, that role was also taken up by the likes of himself, by the arts, literature and science. Even so, he concluded, if the need arose he would be willing to let the sabre 'be drawn again from the scabbard', in readiness to 'let our blood be shed to the last drop for freedom, king and country'.

Pathos and grandstanding; but no doubt sincerely felt both by the audience and by Liszt himself, Romantics one and all. Liszt now placed his art in the service of his rediscovered fatherland and felt that this artistic nationalism was the equivalent of doing battle in arms. Liszt wore the sabre on numerous occasions, but not in 1848, when Hungary was actually rising in arms to assert its independence from the Habsburg crown. The sword that significantly failed to be drawn from the scabbard earned Liszt a withering piece of sarcasm from Heinrich Heine and often featured on caricatures of the performing virtuoso.[5]

But Liszt did henceforth place his art in the service of his country. He did wear the sabre as a symbolic gesture when he performed his *Funérailles* elegy in 1849, turning that piece of musical lyricism into a political statement. The work's subtitle, *October 1849*, referred not only to Chopin's death that month but also to the execution of thirteen Hungarian insurrection leaders. What is more, the piece used the 'gypsy scale' (with augmented seconds) as a marker endorsing Hungarian nationality. Liszt's turn to composing nationally Hungarian music (most prominently, of course, the Hungarian Rhapsodies), was deeply inspired by that remarkable aspect of Hungarian cultural life, the popularity of 'gypsy' music played by bands of Romany performers. Their musical style, with its augmented seconds and fourths and its sprung rhythms and syncopations, lay outside the established, conservatoire-taught classical palette. By incorporating it into his own compositions, Liszt emphasized his national rootedness and at the same time expanded the horizons of his composing technique.[6]

'Gypsies', Rhapsodies and the National Turn

Liszt in fact used the trip (and later return trips) to do fieldwork among Romany musicians, many of whom were employed as occasional providers of entertainment or were (as such) part of the retinue of noblemen. The results of this are noticeable in his later, nationally Hungarian compositions. And he even reflected on this in an extensive essay that was published in book form in 1859, in what was still his primary language: French. The title was *Des Bohémiens et de leur musique en Hongrie*. In it, Liszt tackled the odd circumstance that Hungarian national music was in fact from outside the Magyar cultural tradition, belonging as it did to those wandering Romany communities known variously at the time as Tziganes, Gypsies, Zigeuner or Bohemians.* As Liszt argued, it was only in Hungary that such Romany musicians could enjoy the steady patronage of the sedentary Magyar population, and as a result Hungarian music culture was bicultural, born of the happy integration of Romany music into Magyar society. There is some fond Romanticization in this, and what is also plain is that Liszt personally identifies with his 'bohémiens'. He credits them with temperamental attributes that also apply to himself as a Romantic. He himself was a nomad, only lately adopted by his fellow Magyars. He lived the 'bohemian' lifestyle, spurning the niceties and social conventions of the settled bourgeoisie, living hand-to-mouth, dedicating himself to his own inspiration and wayward emotions. As 'gypsies' were becoming a projection screen for middle-class wanderlust and anti-conformism (to live in a caravan, outside the norms of societies, on a lifelong road trip, hippies *avant la lettre*), Liszt with his *bohémiens* established the link between the allure of cultural exoticism and the Romantic notion of the bohemian artist. (The downside of this idyllic idealization of Romany culture is a strident note of anti-Semitism: wandering and non-territorial like the Romany, and in those respects their counterparts, Jews are, in Liszt's book, culturally noxious, living a life of dour legal observances rather than passionate freedom.[7])

Liszt fitted his 'gypsy' interest into the philological stadialism of his day and age (see Chapter 4). He saw performative Romany culture as something that had not yet crystallized into a proper self-aware and self-reflecting culture, as yet abiding in the preliminary developmental stages of finding its own cultural voice. Like the *guslar*s of the Balkans, the Romany were 'rhapsodes': those wandering pre-Homeric poet-performers whose fragmentary lays required a Homer to be given durable shape and form. This, in short, is what Liszt proposed to do with Romany melodies: his compositions would weld and structure them into a coherent corpus, consolidate them into a robust foundation for a future cultural presence. The use of the word 'rhapsody' is anything but fortuitous: it was deliberately chosen by Liszt in full awareness of the philological implications and the discussions of the literary roots of national self-articulation, involving the Homeric Question and the *guslars* of the Balkans:

> Under the pleasant Grecian sky, wandering rhapsodes gathered around them the inhabitants of towns and hamlets to make them listen to the stories of vanquished nations and toppled kingdoms, or adventurous voyages.

* Those terms have often been used in a stigmatizing discourse and as a result are nowadays mostly deprecated; I mean no disrespect if occasionally I invoke the nineteenth-century usage of the 'gypsy' or 'bohemian' monikers by way of quotation.

> Their chants, once collected into a homogeneous work by old Homer, formed an inimitably perfect monument (Liszt 1859, 5).

After Liszt, the rhapsody emerges as a new musical form. If anything, it is a formless form, a free succession of melodic themes and elaborations – much more fluid than the structured classical forms of concerto, sonata or symphony. In exploring this new, loose and more lyrical musical form, Liszt followed the example of Chopin with his nocturnes, mazurkas and polonaises. Chopin had also used these formal innovations to accommodate the vernacular 'folk' traditions of his homeland: the polonaise was a fast, cheerful Polish dance, and the name of the mazurka echoed its region of origin around the Mazurean Lakes. Following Liszt, the rhapsody would become the premier form for the expression of a sense of nationality in lyrical–musical form. A list of more than ninety of such rhapsodies is included in the Appendix at the end of this chapter (Tables 9.1a, 9.1b and 9.1c), ranging from Aragonese and Armenian to Umbrian and Welsh, and from 1846 (Liszt's prototypical Hungarian ones) to 1940.[8]

The rhapsody was the genre that spearheaded a general 'national turn' in classical music. Much as in academic painting, music had gravitated towards a 'classical' standardization of forms and instruments in the course of the eighteenth century. Gluck aimed for a musical style that would appeal to audiences everywhere 'so as to abolish the ridiculous difference between nations'.[9] Although some national inflection persisted in England and France in the wake of Purcell and Lully, the universal standard became Italian, as we can see from the still prevailing use of Italian for music's technical vocabulary, from *meno piano* and *coda* to *allegro moderato* and *da capo*. From this Italian standard, a Viennese–German tradition branched off from Mozart on; between Beethoven and Brahms, German became the new default for 'classical' music (though less so for opera than for symphonic genres and chamber music). With Chopin and Liszt, we begin to notice a trend where composers seek their inspiration outside the Italo-German classical bandwidth, notably in the vernacular cultures of their native countries. That national turn was often a matter more of presentation than of substance: titles and narrative themes rather than melodic lines or harmonic chord progressions. At best we see a nod to the use of rustic instruments, dance rhythms or the occasional parallel fifth or drone bass. But as with spices in cookery, small doses go a long way to give music a 'national' flavour. The trend persisted and intensified throughout the second half of the century, and affected all of Europe: from Albéniz in Spain to the 'mighty handful' in Russia (Rimsky-Korsakov, Mussorgsky, Borodin), from Elgar in England to Enescu in Romania, from Grieg,

Nielsen and Sibelius in the north to Smetana and Dvořák in the centre. Vaughan Williams and Tchaikovsky drew on native stylistic elements from Anglican and Orthodox plainchant respectively. Others turned to folk music, its modal or pentatonic scales, drone bass and sprung rhythms.[10]

These were all inflections and tentative expansions on the conventions of conservatoire-taught classical music as performed on the established symphonic instruments; but towards the end of the nineteenth-century composers such as Manuel De Falla, Igor Stravinsky and Béla Bartók would go further by using folk elements for avant-garde experimentation. By 1934, Vaughan Williams, in his treatise *National Music*, asserted the need to 'cultivate a sense of musical citizenship. Why should not the musician be the servant of the state and build national monuments like the painter, the writer, or the architect?'[11]

What is remarkable is, here as elsewhere, the universal spread of national particularism. Much as in the Europe-wide genre painting of young peasant women (depicted in standard poses and techniques, and nationalized through the accessories of clothing or background and the painting's title; more on this in Chapter 10), so too music used a fairly common reservoir of 'vernacular' stylistic elements to go national. Here as in history painting, the extent to which 'nationality' can be a generic additive is illustrated by the fact that it often goes in tandem with oriental exoticism: anything 'colourful' from outside the Italo-German classical style is exploited. Grieg inserts a sultry oriental 'Anitra's Dance' in the middle of his *Peer Gynt* suite; Rimsky-Korsakov composed, amidst his more Slavic-style works, a 'Capriccio Espagnol'. The Hispanicism of Ravel is more entangled between exoticism and self-identification: he hailed from the French Basque country, and his Basque mother had grown up in Madrid. National music becoming transnationally entangled is best illustrated by Antonin Dvořák's stint in New York (1892–1895), where he was initially commissioned to write a national American opera. A theme that offered itself for such a work was the *Hiawatha* poem by H. W. Longfellow. As has been mentioned (Chapter 5), *Hiawatha* revolves around the legendary and imperfectly understood Iroquois leader of that name and also drew on Ojibwe traditions as collected by Henry and Jane Schoolcraft. But Dvořák, thanks to his New York encounter with the African-American composer Harry Burleigh, was more deeply inspired by the musical style of spirituals as sung by enslaved Black plantation workers. In the event, the opera never materialized, and Dvořák recycled various 'national' American materials in his ninth symphony *From the New World* (1893).[12]

The metropolitan traditions that had little or no distinct vernacular palette to make use of relied on thematic 'framing' to nationalize their work; one can also think of the Flemish cantatas of Benoît Peeters and the symphony *To My Fatherland* (1888–1890) of the Dutch Wagnerite Bernard Zweers, with its four movements entitled 'In the Forests of the Netherlands', 'In the Countryside', 'At the Beach and at Sea' and 'To the Capital'. Such explicit titles are characteristic of 'programme music', where the composer in programme notes furnishes an explicit guide to what the music is intended to convey and how it is to be listened to. That programme often explicitly imposes a concrete, national frame of reference on abstract melodic lines, harmonic patterns and evolving structure. Smetana programmatically subtitled his famous 'Vltava', a movement of the suite *Ma vlast*, 'My Country', to evoke the course of Bohemia's Vltava (Moldau) river as its bubbles up from its two springs, eddies through picturesque forests and along idyllic meadowlands, elf-haunted at night, foaming through rapids and majestically welcomed to Prague as it flows past the hallowed haunt of the legendary Libuše, the Vyšehrad hill (see Chapter 7).[13]

Audience, Participation, Festivals

Libuše herself was the title heroine of the Czech national opera *par excellence*, also by Smetana (1872); its culminating aria was the princess's prophecy of the future glories of Prague. The opera was used to inaugurate Prague's new National Theatre in 1888. As this case indicates, the most strongly programmatic music, with the greatest nation-building potential, was opera with its libretto. In Hungary, Ferenc Erkel evoked the kingdom's past heroes (*Hunyadi László*, 1844; *Bánk bán*, 1861). In Russia, Glinka (*A Life for the Tsar*, 1836) and Mussorgsky (*Boris Godunov*, 1874, after Pushkin), thematized episodes from the 'Time of Troubles' around 1600; Borodin's *Prince Igor* (1890) set the ancient national epic rediscovered around 1800 to music.[14] French, Italian and German audiences were given operas on strongly national themes by the likes of Giacomo Meyerbeer (*Les Huguenots*, 1836) Giuseppe Verdi (*I Lombardi*, 1843) and Richard Wagner (*Die Meistersinger*, 1868; the *Ring* cycle, 1869–1876).[15] Such grand operas were society events. Audiences could actively intervene in the performance (outside the reverential high-mindedness of Wagner's Festspielhaus in Bayreuth, that is) and in some instances even exploded into national demonstrations. The performance of Auber/Scribe's *La muette de Portici*, with its aria 'Amour sacré de la patrie', sparked off anti-Dutch clashes in Brussels and, ultimately, the Belgian Revolution of 1830. The rejection of Wagner's *Tannhäuser* by Parisian audiences in 1861 was a nail in the coffin of French–German relations.

The case of Verdi deserves special mention. As a composer, his name is linked to the Risorgimento period, when his work was the figurehead of Italian culture before the unification of a sovereign Italy. The 'Va Pensiero' chorus of his *Nabucco* (describing the home-yearnings of the enslaved people of Israel in their Babylonian captivity) became a transnational hymn symbolizing the plight of oppressed people and diasporas everywhere. In 2013, when the opera was performed as a 'national classic' for the 150th-anniversary festivities of the Italian state, the chorus met with frenzied acclaim from the audience, to the extent that director Muti granted an encore, which he prefaced with a speech denouncing the Berlusconi government. During the encore, the audience threw down a confetti of shredded paper from the balconies; that gesture was overtly reminiscent of Visconti's film *Senso* (1954), in which a Verdi opera in Habsburg-dominated Venice becomes the occasion of insurrectionary pamphlets being thrown from the upper balconies.*

This indicates that music was not just the mystical, trance-like affair that the Liszt painting shown at the beginning of this chapter evoked. Certainly in the case of operas, the audience did not sit spellbound as in a séance or religious service, but engaged actively; audience favourites were encored, sung along with; the sheet music was marketed for private or convivial performance. For this was also the great century of amateur music, of parlour and chamber music, and above all the century of the choir. Music was also something that was performed collectively, and the collectivity of the performance created a shared affect and sense of togetherness – often a national one; and as such, music played into the century's festival culture, as outlined further on in this chapter and Chapter 10. In the growth of Hungarian nationalism, the national-historical operas of Ferenc Erkel exercised greater mobilizing power than even the concerts of Liszt.[16]

Convivial singing emerged from religious and pedagogical practices around 1800, in and around churches, masonic lodges and student fraternities.** Two prototypes were the French-style *orphéon* and the German-style *Gesangverein* or *Liedertafel.* From Wales to Catalonia and from the Basque Country to the Balkans choirs proliferated as part of religious, educational,

* The 2013 encore, with Muti's speech, is on YouTube. I have been unable to ascertain whether the scene evoked in Visconti's film is historical or fictional; in any case, the opera in his *Senso* was *Il trovatore* (which premiered in Venice in 1842). Be that as it may, the gesture had obviously become part of a generally current cultural repertoire.

** From the outset, such practices were also seen as pedagogically valuable: training body and mind and instilling the values of harmonious collaboration around an edifying pursuit. As a result, collective musicianship, especially singing, thrived in schools and universities and, later, in the context of workers' organizations.

agricultural, civic or industrial sociability. The spread was 'reticular': local models and activities, usually in towns and cities, inspiring similar ones, franchise-style, in other towns/cities. Choirs were spawned not just by the social conditions of the time but also by each other, by following the example of other choirs, and in turn setting the example for other ones again. In contrast to this 'reticular' spread, with separate, locally distinct but mutually inspired associations and initiatives being sparked off across the map, the repertoire was diffused nationwide: sheet music was available throughout the country as a single, locally undifferentiated corpus.[17]

Patriotic choruses became popular in France after 1789, with composers such as Méhul ('Chant du départ', 1794), Gossec, and Louis Bocquillon (known mainly under his soubriquet 'Wilhem'). In 1806, Bocquillon introduced choral singing as an educational method; the support of the popular songster Béranger allowed him to propagate it as the 'Méthode Wilhem' from the 1820s on. Concert performances by school pupils followed as a matter of course. In 1833 these solidified into a Paris-based performance organization called L'Orphéon. From there, choral societies multiplied across France and the name 'Orphéon' became a generic label for a society of musical amateurs. From the late 1830s onwards, local choirs would also give concerts further afield. The Chanteurs montagnards of Bagnères-de-Bigorre first scored successes in Paris and then went on a tour including Alexandria, Istanbul and Moscow. *Orphéons* manifested themselves in public life on civic occasions and with festivals. A large international festival was held in Asnières in 1850. (Its 'international' nature was exclusively owing to the participation of choirs from Belgium.) By the end of the 1850s, there were 700 *orphéon* associations in France. Provincial festivals proliferated and concerts raised great numbers of spectators; a crowd of 50,000 assembled on the Place de l'Opéra for an open-air concert by a Spanish *tuna* in 1878. In these years, the repertoire seems to have become markedly more French and patriotic; staples were Méhul's old 'Chant du départ' and a composition by Ambroise Thomas entitled 'France! France!' The movement also spread south of the Pyrenees: markedly so in Catalonia (thanks also to the important work by Josep Clavè, Figure 9.3) and Galicia, but also in other parts of Spain, where by 1910 more than twenty *orfeones* were active. English pedagogues translated the Méthode Wilhem into English (1841). Although choral singing in that country had a different origin and social base (Anglican parishes and, later in the century in the industrial areas, trade unions), there was some influence from the French model when it came to the organization of festivals: 137 *orphéons*, with a total of 3,000 members, gave a concert in London's Crystal Palace in 1860.[18]

Figure 9.3 Bust of the choral conductor and composer Josep Clavè in the art nouveau Palace of Catalan Music, Barcelona. Wikimedia Commons: Josep Renalias

Meanwhile, in a parallel development, a no less powerful choral movement had sprung up in Germany. Its reticulating proliferation emanated from two hubs: the bourgeois cultural sociability of 1808 Berlin and the patriotic Protestantism of 1810 Zurich. In the north, the prototype was the private Liedertafel established in Berlin in 1808 by Carl Friedrich Zelter (1758–1832), friend of Goethe, musician and instigator of the German Bach revival. Zelter's Liedertafel was copied within Berlin and in other Prussian and north German cities, as well as in the Prussian Rhineland. In the south, the first such initiative, by the composer and music publisher Hans-Georg Nägeli in Zurich in 1810, prompted widespread dissemination. Like his French counterpart Wilhem, Nägeli was also a musical pedagogue; his educational use of music was inspired directly by Pestalozzi, for whom he published a *Gesangbildungslehre nach Pestalozzischen Grundsätzen* in 1810. Nägeli visited Stuttgart on a lecture tour in 1819–1820, during which he promoted the male choir as the ideal interface between popular sociability (*Volksleben*) and aesthetic education. The choir established in Stuttgart in response to Nägeli's model became a prototype for similar choral societies (initially male-only) in Germany's southern parts, replicating rapidly and widely in the 1820s–1840s. As of the late 1820s the two types began to overlap (especially in Franconia and the Rhineland) and merge. Their success may in part be explained by the fact that they could draw, for their membership, on university alumni who had been introduced to convivial singing as part of the culture of student fraternities (*Burschenschaften*).[19]

The reticulating spread in Germany was two-tiered, involving first a regional and then a federal level. An association between the choirs of Hanover and Bremen formed the nucleus of the League of United North German Choirs in 1831; it attracted other local choirs and organized a series of regional festivals; these intensified in the 1830s–1850s. Similar patterns were at work in Bavaria, Thuringia and Franconia; and these federations in turn entered into a nationwide meta-federative league in 1860. Pan-German festivals were regularly held from the mid-1840s onwards, and officially as *Bundessängerfeste*, for example in Nuremberg in 1860 and in Breslau/Wrocław in 1907. Thus the organizational history of these choirs in a sense offered a template of Germany's political unification. As the choral movement became pan-German, so did, with some delay, Germany itself.

What was also pan-German was the repertoire. The sheet music was printed and sold across all German-speaking lands and states and created a culturally continuous ambience among them. As with students' songbook anthologies (*Commersbücher*), much of the repertoire was nationalistic, expressing patriotic sentiments that at the time were seen as uncontentiously inspirational and uplifting. A *Commersbuch* would contain songs celebrating merry conviviality, nature (including the joys of hiking or hunting), the winsome daughters of innkeepers here, there, and everywhere, and also the higher virtue of patriotic feeling. Those registers could be spliced together: many a song celebrating the communal quaffing of Rhine wine would extol the German fatherlandish qualities of the Rhine region and its vineyards. The song 'Der Jäger Abschied' ('The Huntsmen's Farewell', also known as the 'Waldhymne' or Forest Hymn), by Mendelssohn, had words by Eichendorff and followed that poet's characteristic lyricism, combining religious awe and love of nature; there were few or no overt nationalist connotations. But it was one of the highlights of the 1846 Cologne Song Festival, a fervently nationally minded occasion held in the aftermath of the Rhine Crisis (1840) and the looming of the First Schleswig-Holstein War.* In this context the 'Huntsmen in the Forest' hymn (directed by Mendelssohn himself, who had been engaged

* The galvanizing presence of a Schleswig-Holstein delegation at the Würzburg 1845 feast (Klenke 1998, 55–63) followed a declaration of autonomy of the Holstein Estates (1844) that provoked a Danish centralist backlash and, on the rebound, strong anti-Danish solidarity with Schleswig-Holstein throughout the German lands.

for the occasion) became a figure of Germanity. The song was included in a songbook published 1848 with the telling title 'Germania: A Garland of Liberty Songs for German Singers of All Estates'.[20]

In the years of the Napoleonic hegemony, songs had become a political weapon. Arndt's song 'Was ist des Deutschen Vaterland' and Körner's 'Männer und Buben', effective propaganda in 1813, had become politically suspect in the reactionary 1820s (with Arndt himself dismissed from his university post in Bonn for 'demagoguish' tendencies). It was in this period that the students of the 1814 cohort, after graduating, withdrew into the family life of solid citizenry that would in course become the main recruiting ground for choirs and gymnastic clubs.[21]

The patriotic songs of more radical times were kept alive and ultimately gained new respectability as they entered the repertoire of the German choirs after the Rhine Crisis of 1840; alongside old classics by erstwhile radicals such as Arndt and Maßmann ('Ich hab' mich ergeben', 'I have Dedicated Myself [to the Fatherland]') new patriotic songs were included, such as *Die Wacht am Rhein*, by now familiar to the reader. Nicolaus Becker's 'Der Deutsche Rhein', with its defiant verses ('No, never shall they have it, the free, the German Rhine; even though like greedy ravens they hoarsely clamour for it') inspired what was to become the Flemish national anthem, 'The Flemish Lion' (1847, by Van Peene and Miry): 'No, never shall they tame him, the proud Flemish lion, even though they assail his freedom with fetters and with jeers.' Such songs were *meant* to be sung together, in a rousing chorus and preferably ('All together now!') with the audience joining in.

Composers of note would occasionally throw their weight behind this wave of patriotic song, also as directors. Mendelssohn conducted choral festivals both in the Rhineland and in his second homeland, England. The Bernard Zweers whose name we have encountered as the composer of a symphony 'To the Fatherland' also aided in the production of a Dutch national song-book, *Kun je nog zingen, zing dan mee!* ('If You Can Sing, Then Sing Along!'); its songs celebrated the coastal landscape, the can-do spirit of the great mariners of the seventeenth-century glory days and of the seafaring colonizers, and the stalwart ethnic brethren, the beleaguered Boers in Southern Africa.

The lyrics of those songs, Dutch, German or otherwise, were usually by B-list versifiers: Maßmann, Geibel, Felix Dahn. Their sentiments were hackneyed and combined stridency with the commonplace. As a result such songs could either be anodyne and 'unpolitical' or else fervently nationalistic. The Rhine songs of Schneckenburger and Becker remained on the repertoire long after the subsidence of the Rhine Crisis that had provoked them in 1840. At the National Song Festival of Nuremberg (1861), during a relatively peaceful period, the memories of 1813 (Arndt!) and 1840 (Becker! Schneckenburger!) were channelled when the massed German choirs roared *fortissimo* 'And if the foe approaches, then a united Germany will march to the Rhine, to do battle for the Fatherland!' The chorus line 'Hurrah! We Germans, we march to the Rhine!' was drowned in loud acclamations. The Franco-Prussian War was as yet ten years in the future; but it was foreshadowed and primed in the field of culture through this self-stoking, self-amplifying choral flag-waving.[22]

In Breslau in 1907, another *Bundessängerfest* of the German League of Choral Societies was held. The singers were welcomed by the pan-Germanist poet–professor Felix Dahn with a poem that, in English translation, runs like this:

> To the German people God has given music of richest sonority
> In order that rest and struggle, death and life may be glorified to us in song.
> So sing on, then, German youth, of all things which can swell your heart!
> Of the persistence of true love, of true friendship, gold and ore;
> Of the sacred shivers of pious awe, of the sheen of spring and the joy of
> the forest,
> Of Wanderlust, roving from land to land, and of that darling son of sunshine
> (Do not neglect that!), the golden wine. Yes, sing of all things high
> and lovely,
> But above all cherish one specific song, which should resound inspiring
> and roaring:
> The song of the German heroic spirit! The song of manly duty and honour,
> Of faithfulness uncowed by fear, which jubilantly hurls itself onto the
> foes' spears
> And in death wrests victory! Only he who is willing to die as well as live
> For this song, unlike any other – only he is worthy to intone it:
> The song of the hard-won Reich![23]

Dahn's verse was aimed at middle-class, middle-aged, suburban or small-town German males who once a week indulged in their leisure pursuit of choral singing with a glass or two of beer afterwards. But the self-image that it articulates and celebrates was far less anodyne: it addresses its audience as a convivial *Bildungsbürger* with a slumbering readiness to go berserk for the noble cause of the Fatherland. More importantly, the performativity (and, to be sure, a cheerful and merry performativity it was) rendered these songs uniquely memorable. Great art they were not, but they stuck in the mind. In 1848 Arndt's song 'Was ist des Deutschen Vaterland' earned him, thirty-five years after its composition, a vote of thanks-by-acclamation in the Frankfurt National Assembly.[24] This scene is remarkable not only for the importance of Romantic cultural enthusiasm in the assembly's political deliberations, but also for the total, unargued and self-evident obviousness with which everyone was familiar with Arndt as, first and foremost, the composer of a song that was universally recognized and acknowledged as a potent force in public life. This, it should be noted, was wholly due to its informal popularity at grass-roots level: a bit like 'Auld Lang Syne' or 'O Tannenbaum'.*

A century later again, in another parliament, this time in Bonn, the assembled delegates had at their fingertips another patriotic song that they could use as an impromptu national anthem. By 1949, Hoffmann von Fallersleben's 'Deutschland, Deutschland über alles' had become compromised and even been proscribed; but the delegates, gentlemen with student backgrounds one and all, had learned from their *Commersbücher* Maßmann's 'Ich hab mich ergeben', and that was intoned, as part of an ingrained national repertoire, in the first parliamentary meeting of the new Federal Republic.

The point is not to single out Germany as a uniquely nationalistic special case. Charting the omnipresence of 'La Marseillaise' in French history, or 'The Flemish Lion' in Flanders, or 'A Nation Once Again' in Ireland, or 'Dabrowski's Mazurka' in Poland, would offer an instructive counterweight. And in England, there was the Last Night of the Proms. By 1895 it was felt that English musicianship had at last caught up with that of the Continent and that the general public should profit from its achievements; and to that end a series of informal concerts was established in the newly constructed Albert Hall, the so-called Promenade concerts or Proms. The direction was entrusted to the organist/composer Henry Wood, who had previously produced Gilbert and Sullivan operettas. His patriotic *Fantasia on British Sea Songs* (1905; a medley of traditional shanties arranged orchestrally to celebrate the centenary of the Battle of Trafalgar) became an early fixture of the popular Last Night, which gradually also incorporated other national classics, from Arne's older 'Rule Britannia' to Elgar's 'Pomp and Circumstance' march ('Land of Hope and Glory'). By 1918 the repertoire of nationally inspired and nationally inspiring songs also included 'Onward, Christian Soldiers' and Blake's 'Jerusalem' as set to music by Hubert Parry, and Cecil Spring-Rice's 'I Vow to Thee, My Country', staple of royals weddings and funerals. The melody is so appealing that

* The song had formed part of the *Allgemeines Commers- und Liederbuch* (1818) and had been given a four-part harmonization in 1825. Its mass performance at the Cologne Song Festival of 1846 confirmed its status as the 'clandestine national anthem' (Klenke 1998, 67) of nationally minded Germans, even though it was still suspect to the Metternich-style regimes of the period.

the lyrics, written at the close of the Great War, become secondary, mere syllables to carry the tune, commonplace phrases intoning an ambient patriotic piety.* Yet in all their unpolitical unobtrusiveness they are worth noting for their strident fanaticism, which breathes the same fey battle-readiness we saw in the German case of Felix Dahn.

> I vow to thee, my country, all earthly things above,
> Entire and whole and perfect, the service of my love;
> The love that asks no question, the love that stands the test,
> That lays upon the altar the dearest and the best;
> The love that never falters, the love that pays the price,
> The love that makes undaunted the final sacrifice.
>
> I heard my country calling, away across the sea,
> Across the waste of waters she calls and calls to me.
> Her sword is girded at her side, her helmet on her head,
> And round her feet are lying the dying and the dead.
> I hear the noise of battle, the thunder of her guns,
> I haste to thee my mother, a son among thy sons.[25]

It is this repertoire that has turned each 'Last Night of the Proms' into a massive, festive flag-waving occasion. Flag-waving, literally: at first, Union Jacks were brandished and waved around (with what degree of national earnestness or cheerful irony, it is impossible to tell); during the Brexit debates, a minority of European flags was in evidence (which sparked comments and debates). The point is that convivial cheer can cloak national fervour in good-humoured pleasantry and provides nationalism with the pretext, or antidote, of irony; this makes the Last Night of the Proms a good interpretive lens for viewing the German *Sängerfeste* of the nineteenth century.

The most intriguing cultural transfer in this field occurred in the ethnically mixed territories of Central Europe, especially in the Baltic area. Here, cities with a strong German presence had their choral societies as a matter of course: Königsberg, Breslau/Wrocław, Budapest. In Prague, a Liedertafel der deutschen Studenten was established at the Charles University in 1844. All these sparked off competitive imitations from the non-German (Hungarian, Slavic, Baltic) co-inhabitants of those

* Like Parry's 'Jerusalem', this song gained popularity in the context of casualty commemorations during and after World War I. In 1921, the eminent Gustav Holst set Spring-Rice's words to his hymn tune 'Thaxted' (named after the village where he lived, and also the theme of the 'Jupiter' movement of his orchestral suite *The Planets*). After its first performance in 1925 it became a standard at Armistice Day memorial services. It also became a popular hymn after having been included in Vaughan Williams's collection *Songs of Praise* (1926).

cities. The most extraordinary repercussions took place in the Baltic provinces. Although they had come under Russian rule, city life in Riga, Reval/Tallinn and Dorpat/Tartu was still dominated by German townspeople, their culture and sociability. In 1851, German-style choirs (possibly inspired by the one in Königsberg) were founded in these three cities. The model of cultural-performative conviviality and the 'embodied community' proved ideally suited to the vernacular culture of the Estonian and Latvian populations, among whom consciousness-raising and nation-building processes were just beginning to emerge at that time. A first all-Estonian song festival was held in Tartu in 1869 to commemorate the fiftieth anniversary of the Livonian peasant emancipation, with 845 singers and an audience of 10,000–15,000. The movement gathered in strength with further festivals held in 1879, 1880, 1891, 1894 and 1896; and from 1873 the cue was taken up by Latvians as well. The Baltic Germans had delivered the inspiration, the organizational design and the community-bonding and nation-mobilizing function; the native populations fitted these made-in-Germany vehicles with their own ethnic (Estonian, Latvian, Lithuanian) payload (Figure 9.4).

Figure 9.4 Participants in the Latvian national song festival in traditional dress, 2023. ULD Media / Alamy Stock Photo

Since then, these choral festivals have become huge, drawing thousands of choral singers, dressed in traditional costume, into enormous stadiums, and they have remained a powerful platform for the proclamation of national identity. They can draw on a widespread and deeply rooted cultural praxis: choral singing and the nationwide availability of a shared repertoire have become solidly entrenched in public life. At the end of the Soviet period, such gatherings fulfilled an important role in mobilizing anti-Russian national sentiment and popular resistance, their mobilizing power being so strong that this probably forestalled an armed intervention by Soviet forces in 1989. This 'singing revolution' is now commemorated as the moment when the Baltic republics seized their freedom from Soviet rule. The national character of these festivals is heightened by the wearing of traditional dress (Figure 9.4), by the homeland-celebrating repertoire and by the sheer performative power of joining so many voices into a huge choral whole, an 'embodied community'.[26]

Thus we have traced the power of music from the prestigious ambience of the symphonic concert hall to the grass-roots celebrations of mass festivals. Music was a powerful amplifier of affect, for the audiences both of Liszt and of *Nabucco*, and for the convivially singing performers and participants in Nuremberg, Tartu and the Albert Hall. The power of music can even penetrate into the very fibre of the individual's emotions, as we saw when we discussed the effects of 'Die Wacht am Rhein' and 'La Marseillaise' in Chapter 1: it can make love of the nation overflow, not just among but also within people.

With that, we turn from the Romantic (early to mid nineteenth century) production of knowledge and culture into the mass-entertainment leisure-time culture of the next century. Choral festivals were not a unique phenomenon: as we shall see in Chapter 10, they arose concurrently with literary festivals (the eisteddfod in Wales, the jocs florals in Barcelona) and with sports and athletics festivals, and all of these profited, in drawing the necessary crowds, from increased mobility – railways, a tourism infrastructure. And the nation became not just an inspirational presence but also the enabling ambience and feel-good factor for modern leisure-time entertainment.

Appendix: 'National' Rhapsodies, 1840–1940

Table 9.1a *Chronological list of nationally themed rhapsodies, 1846–1899: Salmen 1966 and interactively accessible at e-rn.ie/rhapsodies*

Year	Title	Composer
1846–1855	Hungarian Rhapsodies	Liszt, Franz
1877	Norwegian Rhapsodies	Svendsen, Johan
1878	Slavonic Rhapsodies	Dvořák, Antonín
1879	Scottish Rhapsody	Mackenzie, Alexander Campbell
1880	Rhapsody on Serbian Folksongs	Hlaváč, Vojtěch
1880	Burns/Scottish Rhapsody no. 2	Mackenzie, Alexander Campbell
1881	Finnish Rhapsodies	Kajanus, Robert
1881	South Slavonic Rhapsody	Bendl, Karel
1882	Swedish Rhapsody nos. 1 and 2	Hallén, Andreas
1882	Romanian Rhapsody	Porumbescu, Ciprian
1883	Bohemian Rhapsody	Ondříček, František
1884	Rhapsody of Auvergne	Saint-Saëns, Camille
1887	Spanish Rhapsody	Albéniz, Isaac
1890	Cambodian Rhapsody	Bourgault-Ducoudray, Louis-Albert
1891	Five Portuguese rhapsodies	Vianna da Mota, José
1891	Russian Rhapsody	Rahmaninov, Sergej Vasil'evič
1891	Three Rhapsodies on Breton Melodies	Saint-Saëns, Camille
1892	Three Rhapsodies on Portuguese Folk Motifs	Hussla, Victor
1893	Polish Rhapsody	Paderewski, Ignacy Jan
1895	Polish Rhapsody	Stojowski, Zygmunt
1895	Armenian Rhapsody on National Themes	Ippolitov-Ivanov, Mihail Mihajlovič
1896	South Slavic Rhapsody	Bendl, Karel
1899	Finnish Rhapsody	Järnefelt, Armas

Table 9.1b *Chronological list of nationally themed rhapsodies, 1900–1913: Salmen 1966 and interactively accessible at e-rn.ie/rhapsodies*

Year	Title	Composer
1900	Béarn Rhapsody	La Tombelle, Fernand de
1901	Piet Hein Rhapsody	Anrooy, Peter van
1901	Aragonese Rhapsody	Granados, Enrique
1901	Six Irish Rhapsodies	Stanford, Charles Villiers
1903	Hebrew Rhapsody	Zolotarëv, Vasilij Andreevič
1903	Indian Rhapsody	Frederic Hymen, Cowen
1903	Romanian Rhapsodies	Enescu, George
1903	Midsummer Vigil (Swedish Rhapsody no. 1)	Alfvén, Hugo
1904	Piedmont Rhapsody	Sinigaglia, Leone
1904	Welsh Rhapsody	German, Edward
1904	Rhapsody for Piano and Orchestra	Bartók, Béla
1905	Rhapsody of Portuguese Folksongs	Rio de Carvalho, João Pedro
1905	Basque Rhapsody	Bordes, Charles
1906	Javanese Rhapsody	Schäfer, Dirk
1906	Lithuanian Rhapsody	Karłowicz, Mieczysław
1906	Norfolk Rhapsodies	Vaughan Williams, Ralph
1907	Spanish Rhapsody	Ravel, Maurice
1907	Brigg Fair: An English Rhapsody	Delius, Frederick
1907	Uppsala Rhapsody (Swedish Rhapsody no. 2)	Alfvén, Hugo
1908	Rhapsody on Ukrainian Themes	Ljapunov, Sergej Mihajlovič
1909	Umbrian Rhapsody	Parelli, Attilio
1909	Rhapsody on Lithuanian Folksongs	Vītols, Jāzeps
1909	Gaelic Rhapsody	Ladmirault, Paul
1909	Italia, Rhapsody for Orchestra	Casella, Alfredo
1910	Irish Rhapsody	Herbert, Victor
1910	Serbian Rhapsody	Bajić, Isidor
1911	Portuguese Songs (Beira Rhapsody)	Silva, Filipe da
1911	Tam o' Shanter/Scottish Rhapsody no. 3	Mackenzie, Alexander Campbell
1912	Portuguese Rhapsody	Figueiredo, Manuel de
1912	Rhapsody of Portuguese Folksongs	Chéu, António Maria
1913	Scottish Rhapsody	Bantock, Granville
1913	Polish Rhapsody	Joteyko, Tadeusz
1913	Polish Rhapsody	Fitelberg, Grzegorz

Table 9.1c *Chronological list of nationally themed rhapsodies, 1915–1940: Salmen 1966 and interactively accessible at e-rn.ie/rhapsodies*

Year	Title	Composer
1915	Hebrew Rhapsody	Lewandowski, Louis
1915	German Rhapsodies	Neal, Heinrich
1918	Rhapsody of Folksongs from the Algarve	Sousa, David de
1919	Finnish Rhapsody	Maasalo, Armas Toivo Valdemar
1919	Norwegian Rhapsodies	Halvorsen, Johan
1920	Moravian Rhapsody	Neumann, František
1920	Italian Rhapsody	Ricci-Signorini, Antonio
1922	Georgian Rhapsody	Čerepnin, Aleksandr Nikolajevič
1923	A Severn Rhapsody	Finzi, Gerald
1924	Romanian Rhapsody	Negrea, Martian
1927	Finnish Rhapsody	Klami, Uuno
1927	Rhapsody Overture: An Imaginary Trip to the Faroe Islands	Nielsen, Carl
1928	Flemish Rhapsody	Absil, Jean
1928	Croatian Rhapsodies	Lhotka, Fran
1928	Rhapsody for Violin and Orchestra	Bartók, Béla
1931	Swedish Rhapsody	Kallstenius, Edvin
1931	Norwegian Rhapsody	Christiansen, F. Melius
1931	Dala Rhapsody (Swedish Rhapsody no. 3)	Alfvén, Hugo
1934	Rhine Rhapsody	Prager, Paul
1935	Hebrew Rhapsody	Pergament, Moses
1935	Flemish Rhapsody	Jong, Marinus de
1940	Russian Rhapsody	Grečaninov, Aleksandr Tihonovič

PART III

Adapting to Modernity

CHAPTER 10

People in the Present

Festive Culture, Urban Reticulation, Embodied Communities

The leisure-time space of the nineteenth-century European city, with its sociability and its café culture, fostered a climate for entertainments that in turn would be platforms for the assertion of national identity. National dances in *cafés-chantants* became a feature from Zagreb (with its tamburica ensembles and kolo dances) to Zaragoza (with its zarzuelas and jota). But city life was, in this century, also internationally enmeshed: the polka, first made popular in Prague in the 1830s as a national Slavic–Bohemian dance, became a veritable craze in mid-1840s Paris and went as global as the Viennese waltz.[1]

Polka and waltz exemplify the matryoshka scalarity that we also encountered when dealing with aggregation levels of language. Leisure-time sociability can oscillate effortlessly between the local and the transnational. The primary ambience for such activities is that of the town or city. As similar cultural leisure pursuits spread from city to city, these can reticulate (as we have seen in the case of choirs) into networks that have a regional or even national function. Leisure activities pursued locally mesh into trends with nationwide or even international outreach and influence.

Sports and athletics follow this same pattern. Football is at the same time global and celebrated in England, where it originated, as a specifically local-cum-national tradition. Some sports are pursued in a powerfully nationalizing context. Events such as the Eleven Cities ice-skating tour in Friesland or cross-country skiing in Sweden and Norway symbolically assert the nation's culture, tradition and identity. The Swedish Vasaloppet and the Norwegian Birkebeinerrennet are both named after nationally legendary historical exploits (see Figure 8.8). Sports associations such as the Gaelic Athletic Association in Ireland and the Sokol athletics clubs in many Slavic lands became nationalistic gathering places, and their sports events functioned as public mass demonstrations of nationalist commitment. Even mountain hiking was undertaken in a nationalizing spirit: for example, Slovak hiking tours in the Tatras or the activities of the Catalan *excursionistas*.[2]

One form of reticulation is competitive imitation – as when Estonians and Lithuanians used the German template of the choral society for their own national agendas. The athletic assertion of nationality had been heralded by the German *Turnvereine*, established in the 1810s by the firebrand nationalist Ludwig Jahn. Their German chauvinism excluded non-Germans from membership; and so Czechs in Prague and Jews in various cities engaged in competitive imitations. The former associated in the Sokol clubs, which became a powerful Austro-Slavic nationalizing platform and reticulated into most Slavic lands under the Habsburg crown. The latter formed Maccabi and Bar Kochba associations, which aimed to develop what Max Nordau called 'muscular Jewry' (*Muskeljudentum*) and which ultimately led to the international Maccabiah Games; these have been held every four years in Israel since 1932. A similar combination of global outreach and national positioning was articulated in the earliest Olympic Games (Athens 1896), developed as an international event but serving as a powerful projecting platform for Greek identity. From the local urban to the global, the national level is somewhere midway, a powerful public validator of leisure culture.[3]

Across urban stepping-stones, a culture of modern, middle-class leisure amusements reticulated and created 'embodied communities' everywhere – with singers joining in a chorus, or dancers dancing together, or athletes competing on the field before a convivial crowd of spectators. The nineteenth century is not only the century of the 'imagined community' but also that of the 'embodied community'. We encountered the *Trachtenvereine* earlier on, as well as the most prominent specimen of embodied sociability, choral singing. The enabling ambience of the embodied community was not restricted to inconsequential leisure-time amusements: the nineteenth century is also the century of the mass demonstration, and any mass event, culturally, could become a political one – as the Baltic 'singing revolution' showed. In the 1820s and 1830s, the Irish agitator for Catholic emancipation Daniel O'Connell harnessed the power of the mass rally to press home political points to an unwilling government; elsewhere, cultural occasions (such as the public funerals we have come across) provided a suitable respectability for assembling together in large numbers in urban squares and thoroughfares. Literary commemorations provided an important crypto-political platform. German commemorations of Schiller's birth and death allowed the celebration of the author who had issued a

Figure 10.1 The spirit of Schiller exhorting a personified Germany to unify as she sits dejected under an oak tree, her imperial regalia cast down (Carl Jäger, 1859). Wikimedia Commons

clarion call for freedom of conscience (*Gedankenfreiheit*) in his *Don Carlos*, and who in his *Wilhem Tell* had celebrated the power of the people, once united beyond their local divisions, to shake off the yoke of tyranny: 'Seid einig! einig! einig!' (Figure 10.1). The Schiller commemorations of 1839, 1845 and especially 1859 (leaving traces in the dozens of Schiller statues and the many hundreds of Schiller Streets in Germany and also in the US) were ostensibly celebrations of a literary giant, and as such wholly unobjectionable, but they carried a potent connotation of ongoing resistance against reactionary politics in the different German statelets.

The impact of the 1859 commemoration in Switzerland was especially noteworthy – and for good reason, because Schiller's *Wilhelm Tell* had canonized that country's foremost national hero. When Schiller was honoured with a monument in 1860, the *Mythenstein*, that occasion led to Gottfried Keller's agenda for a nationally Swiss festivity: the mass-participation cultural *Festspiel*. The fifth centenary of the Battle of Sempach as celebrated in 1886 took the form of such a *Festspiel*: choral tableaux with collectively spoken texts and incidental music evoking important episodes from the national past. After Sempach 1886, *Festspiele* were held with increasing frequency throughout the 1890s and up to 1914. In addition, the Tellskapelle (a fresco-ornamented chapel recently constructed, marking the spot where Tell had made his daring leap into Gessner's boat) became the destination of an official civic pilgrimage, held annually from 1884 on.

Commemorations of national poets carried particular weight in the non-sovereign communities of Central and Eastern Europe: Mickiewicz, Mácha, Gundulić and Prešeren in Poland, Bohemia, Croatia and Slovenia. But also in established states, a tsunami of statues washed over cities' public spaces, each one the focus for wreath-laying, speeches and choral cantatas – from Camões in Lisbon to Runeberg in Helsinki, from Moore in Ireland and Burns and Scott in Scotland to Byron in Athens.[4] A particular type of *Festspiel* had also emerged further west. The Welsh eisteddfod has been mentioned: it had long ago been a poetic gathering and was now reinvigorated from near obsolescence by cultural nationalists around Thomas Price in the 1820s and 1830. Not only did it inspire Bretons and other Celts, but it has developed to become an important annual event in Welsh culture. Cultural revivalists in Ireland and Scotland adopted the template for their Oireachtas and Mòd festivals.[5]

Between the Pyrenees and the Alps something altogether remarkable took shape along literary-historicist lines.[6] During the Bourbon restoration, the city of Toulouse reinvigorated its own, very ancient but somnolescent literary festival, the *jeux floraux* (floral games). The tradition went back to the late Middle Ages as a form of poetic contest (of the type also celebrated in Wagner's *Die Meistersinger von Nürnberg*). Like so many medieval heirlooms it was now Romantically reinterpreted: as a vestigial, urban continuation of the region's underlying troubadour tradition, which itself had of late been rediscovered and celebrated by philologists such as Fauriel. As they saw it, the troubadours had been the earliest to use the Latin-descended vernacular language to express a refined poetic sensibility. Their achievements antedated the development of a literary culture in Paris and Castile. And the city poets competing in their floral games were the civic successors of these chivalric *Ur*-poets. This was the prestige now shedding lustre on the revivified floral games. A youthful and as yet very conservative Victor Hugo made his literary debut by successfully competing in the floral games of 1819 and 1820, and the tradition had gathered steam by the mid-century.

From here, we can see the pattern of urban 'reticulation' setting in, much as in the urban concatenation of choral festivals in Germany: the format spreads from one town to the next. Each town, in adopting the festive format, 'does its own thing' locally as a form of urban sociability, with occasional exchange visits at most; but the repertoire they draw on is translocal and carries a national collective significance. Following the Toulouse example, Barcelonese city culture rediscovered its troubadour roots in the 1850s. When Verdi's opera *Il Trovatore* premiered there in 1854, it was lost on no one that the storyline was based on the successful Spanish play *El trovador* by Antonio García Gutiérrez (1836). Whereas Welsh, Breton and Cornish poets were beginning to see themselves in 'bardic' terms at their eisteddfods and Gorsedds, here, poets were framing themselves as heirs to the troubadours of old. In 1859 Barcelona hosted its own first floral games, involving literary performances and contests and making many references to medieval troubadour and *amour courtois* culture. The successful contestants were given prizes of flowers wrought in precious metal, and pre-eminent writers were given the special title of 'Master of the Joyful Arts' (*Mestre en gai saber*). Barcelona closely followed the Toulouse pattern, and its *Jocs Florals* soon became a huge launchpad for a regionalist, and later nationalist, Catalan literary culture. The driving force was the philologist–poet Antoni de Bofarull, who in 1858 brought out a collection of contemporary poets writing in Catalan under the title *The New Troubadours*. In the same process, the familial relations between the regional Romance languages was renegotiated. Hitherto the regional idioms around Toulouse, Aix-en-Provence and Valencia had been referred to by more or less vague labels such as 'Limousin'; but now their troubadour ancestry and their independent descent from late Latin were asserted (and hence their autonomous standing alongside Spanish and French) and their mutual relations redefined. (Not definitively, or to everyone's satisfaction: the relationships between Occitan and Provençal and between Catalan and Valencian are still sensitive issues.) Catalan was definitively lifted to the A-list of European literary languages as a result of this movement, known as the *Renaixença*.[7]

The Barcelona festival in turn spawned floral games in Valencia, in Galicia (La Coruña and Santiago de Compostela) and in the Basque country, all of them regions that looked back to local feudal autonomy before the centralization of the modern Spanish state. There was also a backwash into France: across the Pyrenees there were joint initiatives, and when Catalan authors took refuge there from political repression, the result was a strengthening of ties and a further reinvigoration of Occitan/Provençal revivalism under the aegis of the Félibrige movement. These encounters inspired formatively influential writers such as Jacint Verdaguer and

Frédéric Mistral, respectively. But the ideological trajectories diverged sharply: the Félibrige in France aligned itself with nostalgic conservative regionalism after 1871, while the Catalan movement remained radical in its pursuit of autonomy from Madrid's reactionary autocratic rule. In both cases, what is nonetheless remarkable is how urban cultural festivals could reticulate, forming networks of mutual inspiration and mutual recognition that were translocal, transregional and indeed transnational as much as national.[8]

The City as Showcase: Modernity, Memory, Belonging

Walter Benjamin's collection of notes and observations known as the *Passagenwerk* or 'Arcades Project' is organized around the covered shopping arcades of Paris, with their girder-and-glass roofs. For Benjamin, these were the new habitat for a modern leisure consumerism. They were places for loitering strollers (*flâneurs*) and chance encounters between strangers. They were also intensely scopic, visual: shops would offer their wares in windows that were like museum showcases or display cabinets; advertisement billboards and columns (the ubiquitous 'Morris columns') dotted Haussmann's boulevards, bedecked with advertisements; even street-walking sex workers would join in this display culture, advertising themselves to lure potential customers. The key word for Benjamin was 'panoramic': named after coin-operated attractions where viewers could gaze at stereoscopic photographs of exotic locations. These commercial attractions formed part of a wider scopic regime that also included dioramas, waxworks, museums, viewing towers, zoos, botanical gardens, trade fairs and, later, the cinema. This display culture affected not only the city's inhabitants and *boulevardiers* but also its visitors and the tourist industry: the modern city becomes an object of sightseeing and becomes itself a display platform. And often the displays would draw into their field of vision the wider world abroad: with its panoramas, botanical gardens and zoos, the city becomes a microcosm capturing global variety.[9]

This turn towards the spectacular *Nebeneinander* was also a turn away from narrative *Nacheinander* (see Chapter 8). As things were arranged visually in side-by-side displays, their historicity, the narrative one-thing-after-another was abolished. In the display cabinet called Paris, all of France and all the world were collapsed into a single location and all of the past was present in the urban here-and-now. That pattern had been initiated by the Paris-based, Cologne-born architect Hittorf, who in the 1830s had redesigned the large square between the Tuileries and the Champs-Elysées into what was called, aspirationally and programmatically, the Place de la Concorde. It had become the locus of multiple incompatible memories palimpsestically inscribed by the country's successive regime changes since 1789: dedicated to Bourbon monarchs but also the place where Louis XVI had been guillotined. In order to retrieve a spatial sense of unity from the divided narratives of history, Hittorf's design abolished all temporal references in favour of geographic ones. Two huge fountains on the oval's focal points evoke the aquatic aspects of France: the country's coastlines and its rivers. In the middle, an Egyptian obelisk was placed in 1836 (donated as a diplomatic gesture by Muhammad Ali Pasha). Its erection was a publicity stunt that demonstrated the tour de force of the French navy bringing it over with its new paddle-steamers and that carried overtones of the country's imperial ambitions in Northern Africa (France was in these years engaged in the colonial conquest of Algeria). Around the square were placed eight statues of personified cities: Bordeaux, Brest, Lille, Lyon, Nantes, Marseille, Rouen and Strasbourg. They function almost as signposts pointing at distant places. The co-presence of these signposts (seated statues of female municipal deities) symbolically draws the various outlying corners of France, like so many spokes in a wheel, into the Place de la Concorde as a unifying hub of the country as a whole. And so Space serves to suspend Time, and Paris becomes a microcosm of the national territory. Hittorf repeated this gesture in his later Gare du Nord, that temple of modern transport, with on its roofline classicist statues representing all the cities now connected by the railways fanning out from that station. The statue of Paris stands in paramount position as the centre of it all, allegorizing what Benjamin would call the 'Capital of the Nineteenth Century'.[10]

This spectacular spatialization was, of course, an overlay on the lingering influence of historicism. Even as Hittorf glorified space, distance and modernity, memorial statues to historical figures sprang up like mushrooms here as in all European cities, recalling a set of historical actors rendered canonical by Romantic historians and placed in public thoroughfares to assert the undiminished presence of the national past. Between 1830 and 1900, the Panthéon developed into the shrine to the great French fatherlanders that it still is today, with on the façade its dedication 'To our great men: the grateful fatherland' (*Aux grands hommes la patrie reconnaissante).* Some seventy-five free-standing statues were erected in Paris alone during this period (including twenty-two historical queens in the Luxembourg Gardens, and three to Joan of Arc), as well as some 300 smaller ones (or busts) that were set in the façade niches of the Hôtel de Ville, the Louvre, the Sorbonne, the Garnier Opera and other prominent public buildings.[11]

In many European cities, neighbourhoods newly constructed post-1870 outside old (formerly walled) city centres were programmatically given historicizing names, so as to provide a sense of continuity in these new streetscapes. Thus Barcelona's Eixample and the expansion belt in Amsterdam, where the streets were named after admirals and painters from the country's seventeenth-century 'Golden Age'. The interplay between modern urban space and national memories is illustrated nowhere better than in the ground plan of the Parisian metro, familiar to anyone who has ever visited that city. The metro, a prime example of the accelerated technological modernity of the nineteenth century, is now a tangled web of linking connections. The stations usually take their names from the streets nearby;[12] these are medieval in the old city centre (Châtelet, Louvre, Temple, Bastille, Notre Dame and many other church names); they evoke glorious events and victorious battles in the immediately adjoining belt (Rivoli, Vosges, Volontaires, Iéna, Alma, Austerlitz, Solférino, Wagram, Campo Formio, Pyramides, Crimée, Sébastopol, Trocadéro, Bir-Hakeim, Stalingrad), far-flung and, deeper in the suburbs, also longer ago (Tolbiac, Alésia). Marshals and generals are in evidence (Ségur, Hoche, Kléber, Daumesnil, Duroc, Drouot, Lourmel, Bizot, Molitor, Mouton-Duvernet, Pelleport and the defiant Waterloo hero Cambronne) as well as statesmen and politicians (Richelieu, Malesherbes, Mirabeau, Robespierre, Félix Faure, Gallieni, Gambetta, Vavin, Clémenceau, Charles de Gaulle, Louis Blanc, Jean Jaurès) and anti-Nazi resistance heroes (Bonsergent, Fabien, Lamarck, Guy Môquet, Gabriel Péri, Léo Lagrange). In the residential areas, we encounter names from arts, learning and literature (Balard, Curie, Jussieu, Mabillon, Monge, Pasteur, Réaumur, Louis Aragon, Victor Hugo, Raymond Queneau, Edgar Quinet, Voltaire, Emile Zola).

These lists give a sense of two things. The first is how many different ideological strands of political life in France are included, from Richelieu to Robespierre – with, to be sure, the radical ones concentrated in the more left-wing quartiers and arrondissements of Paris and the august literati in the more settled bourgeois parts. Second, the ultracanonical sits cheek by jowl with obscure names that by now need explaining (or looking up in Wikipedia, as I have done): the list ranges from celebrated household names to footnotes in specialized history. But even for those who are familiar with French history and culture and with the historical connotations of the more famous station names individually, the condensed and aggregated list may be somewhat startling in showing how very numerous and densely seeded all these names in fact are. The national-mnemonic background noise is much louder than we thought.

To be sure, the effect of a metro trip across Paris cannot amount to a propagandistic history indoctrination: in many cases, the unaware traveller will not even know if a name refers to a locality, a landmark or a person ('Vavin'?). The semantic cloud that is the Parisian metro map is nothing if not diffuse, with many of the references hardly amounting to anything referential at all. But for all its diffuseness, the total effect of this accumulation of mnemonic signals is nonetheless powerful: it does not pedagogically 'inform' the metro traveller (i.e. guide them from ignorance to knowledge), but it offers a constant reaffirmation of the familiarity of these historical names and their *droit de cité* in the public sphere that is Paris (and, by implication, France). These names *belong* here, they are visible like endlessly repeated mantras at every stop and on dozens of signs, and this render the names, if not a concrete national reference, then at least a point of recognizability, a sense of belonging, and a habitual presence in one's experience of public space. Habitual, that is, in the specific sense as defined by Bourdieu: a socio-cultural response that is so steadily and unremittingly present in one's life that it ceases to be perceived as such and becomes unconscious, natural, like drawing breath or blinking one's eyes.[13]

As such, the 'habitual', an ambient and latent presence, is the opposite of something we may call the 'sensational': something that is eminently noticeable, saliently standing out from the ordinary. And in the scopic regime of modern cities, much effort went into making display culture precisely that: noticeable, sensational.

But even as modern cities were developing into an archipelago of display platforms for the sensation of modernity, the countryside with its timeless peasantry was enshrined firmly in how the nation was imagined. That paradox – how in an increasingly urban modernity, the repertoire of the national identity became more rustic – will be addressed in what follows.

Narratives of Timelessness, Rustic Spectacles

The culmination of the nineteenth-century historical novel is Tolstoy's *War and Peace* (1865–1869). It recalls the years 1805–1812. In the hands of a writer such as Tolstoy, the historical novel had outgrown its progenitor, Walter Scott. For one thing, *War and Peace* uses not the single 'privileged witness' protagonist but an entire palette of main characters, all with their own individual personalities and behaviours and together forming the collective tableau of an entire social class. Despite some sentimental vignettes of commoners – most importantly the meek and naively wise cobbler

Platon Karatayev – the class at the centre of the book is firmly aristocratic: the action is set in mansions and among military officers. At the same time, Tolstoy sees the events as collectively experienced and somehow historically fated: great figures such as Napoleon may dream of ordaining, by their might and willpower, the course of events, but what determines the outcome of the war is ultimately the Russian *Volksgeist* as a transcendent instrument of the inexorable course of history – something that is intuited both by the visionary commander-in-chief Kutuzov and the saintly everyman Karataev. The moral tale of *War and Peace* is how an enervated aristocratic elite, conversing in French and pursuing its high-society life, finds its true character in the crucible of war: the Byronic prince Andrej Bolkonsky, the wavering count Pierre Bezukhov, the high-strung adolescent Natasha Rostov.

One celebrated episode revolves around Natasha's winter visit to a relative's country estate. Her uncle, though a nobleman, is rusticated and lives surrounded by his peasant servants. It is here that Natasha witnesses a song-and-dance evening with Russian folk music and is inspired to dance herself. Almost mystically, Tolstoy evokes how the movements of the folk dance come naturally and untaught to Natasha, like a slumbering instinct.

> Where, how and when could this young countess, who had had a French émigrée for governess, have imbibed from the Russian air she breathed the spirit of that dance? … the spirit and the movements were the very ones – inimitable, unteachable, Russian – which 'Uncle' had expected of her. … Her performance was so perfect, so absolutely perfect, that Anisya Fyodorovna [a servant], who had at once handed her the handkerchief she needed to dance, had tears in her eyes, though she laughed as she watched the slender, graceful countess, reared in silks and velvets, in another world than hers, who was yet able to understand all that was in Anisya and in Anisya's father and mother and aunt, and in every Russian man and woman.[14]

As a set piece, this scene has become famous and has furnished the title to an important cultural history study tracing the interaction between elite and folk culture in Russian history, *Natasha's Dance* (Figes 2002). My reason for highlighting it here is related specifically to the Romantic evocation of national character as an innate agency, truly a *Volksgeist*, and how indispensable traditional peasant culture had become by the 1860s as a validator of national authenticity: even in a historical novel and a novelistic philosophy of history. This turn from 'past to peasant' is noticeable both in literature and in painting over the course of the Romantic century (Figure 10.2). Not only does the modern state impose its national

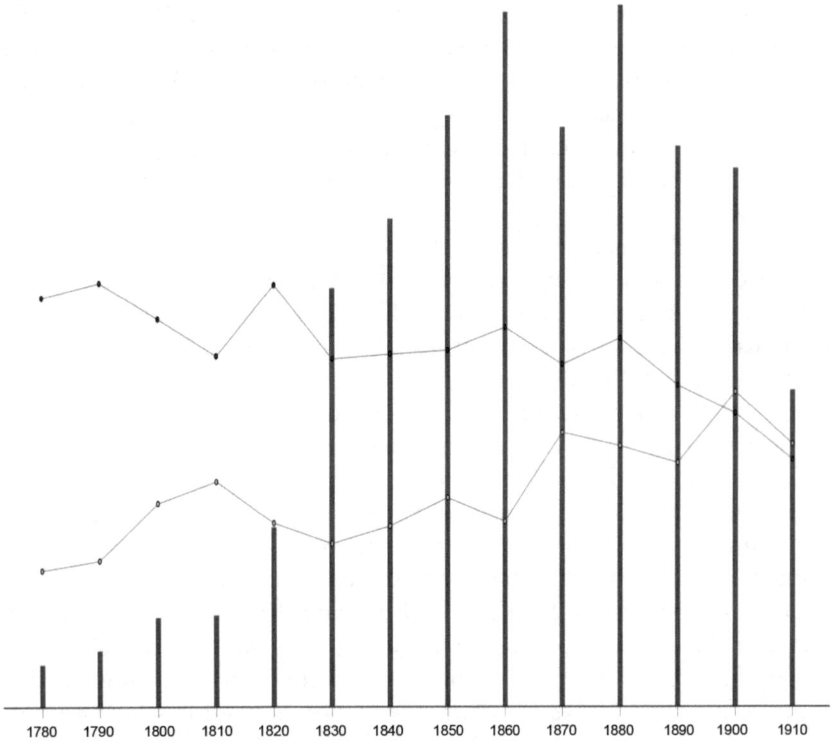

Figure 10.2 Shifting proportions of national-historical themes (upper line graph) and rustic ones (lower line graph) in 4,500 academic paintings, 1760–1910 (e-rn.ie/pastpeasant; vertical bars represent the relative numbers of academic paintings per decade).

state structures on a backward-lagging peasantry (as described in Eugen Weber's classic study *Peasants into Frenchmen*, 1976); the peasantry is at the same time canonized as an enduring, timeless presence at the heart of evolving modernity.

We have come across the sentimental presence of folk culture in Romanticism before, mainly in the Romantics' interest in folksongs and folktales. For Herder, this interest was largely an assertion of the value of spontaneous, untaught art in comparison with the artificial requirements of (classicist) formalism; it dovetailed with Rousseau's cult of innocent childhood and 'noble savages'. The idyllic preference for a simple, rustic life over the stilted conventions of life at court or in high circles is of very long standing indeed, going back all the way to the arcadian and bucolic literature of classical antiquity.[15] With Grimm and the Romantics, the ascendency of spontaneous authenticity over artificial contrivance gains a national-identitarian flavour: popular traditional culture is celebrated for having been unaffected by cosmopolitan or foreign-imposed 'high' culture and for having remained true to the nation's proper, primitive, pre-civilizational origins – in other words, for being *authentic* in the root sense of that word.

Much of the medievalism of Romanticism – the fascination with a chivalric past – is already shot through with a folkloric interest in traditional rustic culture; and rustic idyll becomes increasingly prominent once historicist interest tapers off. Many 'realistic' tales and novels of the mid-century hold up life in the countryside as a wholesome alternative to the modernizing city, or as a sentimental alternative to modern pragmatic soullessness. The opposition systematized in the 1880s by the sociologist Ferdinand Tönnies was already in the air: between the traditional rural community (*Gemeinschaft*) and modern urban society (*Gesellschaft*). Community life, be it among the peasantry or on noble country estates, is evoked in German Biedermeier (post-Romantic) literature by such authors as Annette von Droste-Hülshoff (*Die Judenbuche*, 1842; *Bei uns zulande auf dem Lande*, posthumously published); it is what Dickens's David Copperfield (1850) escapes to when he flees, on foot, from the London slums to his aunt's cottage in Kent. The lure of the traditional countryside is evoked by George Sand (*La Mare au diable*, 1846); and it suffuses, with a cheerful nostalgic glow, Mickiewicz's *Pan Tadeusz* (1834). We see its loving, lingering traces in St Mary Mead (Miss Marple's village) and *Downton Abbey*, in the Provençal tales of Alphonse Daudet and Marcel Pagnol, in the 'Piccolo mondo' of Don Camillo and Peppone.

To be sure, the countryside became the location for tragic and fraught tales as well as idyllic escapism: thus in George Eliot's *The Mill on the Floss* (1860) or Thomas Hardy's *Tess of the D'Urbervilles* (1891), or in Janaček's peasant opera *Jenůfa* (1904). But even in these works, life in the countryside is still represented as 'timeless' and representative of deep ethnographic structures and emotional sincerity; and what is selected for 'comfort viewing' are still adaptations of Eliot's and Hardy's happier-ending tales: *Silas Marner* (1861) and *Far from the Madding Crowd* (1874).

Mass-appeal literature commodified rustic local colour into a comfort zone for undemanding readers. In France, there was the regionalism of the Languedoc. Gounod's opera *Mireille* (1864) was based on Frédéric Mistral's dramatic poem in Occitan, *Mirèio* (1859; Figure 10.3); Mistral also inspired Alphonse Daudet, for example with *L'Arlésienne*, which was

Figure 10.3 Newspaper coverage of Frédéric Mistral's Nobel Prize for literature (1904). Wikimedia Commons

staged as a melodrama with music by Bizet (1872).[16] In Germany, there was the phenomenon of *Heimatliteratur* and, later, the *Heimatfilm*, escapist idylls set in a timeless, unspoilt countryside with picturesque peasants and predictable plotlines (Berthold Auerbach, *Village Tales from the Black Forest*, 1842); this *heile Welt* or 'unmarred world' filled a market need in the suburbs of the modernizing industrial cities of the nineteenth century and in the guilt-burdened and war-ruined Germany of the 1950s. The peasant is here an essentially exoticist presence (not unlike Tolstoy's Anisya Fyodorovna): always described as being alluringly different from the life-world of the readership. *Heimat* literature and the *Dorfgeschichte* ('village tale') accordingly became 'domestic exoticism' for the suburban lower middle classes.[17]

The juxtaposition of traditional countryfolk and rustic landscape gives both an extrahistorical, 'timeless' quality. That effect had already been announced in Wordsworth's 'Solitary Reaper' (1807), in which a singing maiden seen from afar, reaping corn in a wide valley, makes the poet (who cannot understand her, since she sings in Scots-Gaelic) wonder how historical, ancient or timeless her song is. The technique was also used by Thomas Hardy, whose Wessex novels often begin by describing, panorama-style, huge, brooding landscapes with a solitary wandering figure; as that figure is slowly zoomed in upon, the narrative detaches itself from the spectacle. Scott had used similar openings, but whereas he patented the trope of a cavalcade of knights making their way to a distant castle, Hardy's wayfarers are peasants, countryfolk.[18]

In the transition from Wordsworth's Romanticism to Biedermeier sentimentalism and Hardy's naturalism, we see a 'peasant turn' even as Romantic historicism gave way to contemporary concerns. That transition from 'past to peasant' was powerfully affected by a sea-change in painting technique.

The Tube and the Dirndl: *Plein-air* Painting and National Costume

In 1841, John G. Rand patented a squeezable tin (or lead) tube for artist's paint. Oil paint could now be kept from drying out and transported; it need no longer be mixed and used within the confines of the studio but could be taken on field trips, which heretofore had only been used for preliminary sketching or at best water-colour painting. Open-air oil painting had become a possibility.

One of the first to avail himself of this possibility was Gustave Courbet, the harbinger of a new current in painting that he himself called 'Realism'. Rejected for an Academy salon in the mid-1850s, he mounted a private exhibition that he entitled *Le réalisme*. This challenge was all the more resonant because Courbet's Pavillon du Réalisme formed part of a totally new type of display platform: that of the world fair or *exposition universelle*. The first world fair had been held in London – the Great Exhibition of 1851; it was followed by the Parisian Exposition Universelle of 1855. This was the noisy fairground that Courbet sought, bustling with five million visitors seeking a new type of commercial, leisure-time mass entertainment. It was a new ambience for cultural display, as Walter Benjamin was to observe later, expressing itself in commercial concourses such as dioramas, panoramas, zoos and shopping arcades. As the contemporary critic Champfleury noted, Courbet's pavilion represented, for some, an audacious appeal to the public at large, bypassing institutions and selection committees, a sign of liberation; while for others it was an anarchic scandal, sullying art in the mud of fairgrounds. The controversy marked the beginning of an adversarial antagonism between succeeding generations, putting an end to the master–pupil filiations fostered by the academies. A few years later, in 1862, there was a crest in protests against the venerable Academy salon as the official showcase of academically endorsed art, as works by (among others) Courbet and Manet were rejected. As a palliative measure, a 'Salon des refusés' was organized; it included some of the more unconventional new work of the period and became a hatching ground for modern art. The Academy was losing its grip on the visuals arts.[19]

Ironically, these intensely urban, metropolitan developments changed the thematization of, precisely, the countryside. Fontainebleau and its great forest had become accessible by railroad. The railway station at Melun had opened in 1849, and the village of Barbizon was reachable from there; that soon became a haunt of *plein-air* painters armed with lead tubes and portable easels. They mainly did landscape and genre paintings of village scenes and evinced the new taste for 'realism', with its depiction of scenes from ordinary contemporary life. The brushwork became looser, crisp outlines made way for an evocation of shimmering, dappled natural light, and artists began to gather not in the studios at or around academies but in convivial, *bohémien* (and mixed-gender) countryside gatherings. The Barbizon school was the prototype of the artist colonies that would spring up all around Europe, taking over from the academies as the nurseries of great art.[20]

Plein-air painting, almost tautologically, focused on life in the countryside. 'Realism' *à la* Courbet, Cézanne and Van Gogh, or in the style of the Russian *Peredvizhniki* group and their colony at Ambramtsevo, tried to capture the modest, day-to-day essentials of life, often in all their poverty and with implied social criticism. That was a sharply different direction from the celebratory depiction of the nation's historical heroism and glories. But in the process, the depiction of peasant figures in their traditional dress became a fixture, a pictorial icon. They are usually de-individualized, anonymous representatives of a class marginal to the art market but inspiring to artists and their social consciences; they are depicted in their habitual domestic, religious or agricultural pursuits (weddings, processions, milking or harvesting); and, if female, they are usually presented in a flattering light, with their colourful and exotic traditional dress as an eye-catching accessory setting off their elegant bearing to advantage (Figure 10.4).

Those genre paintings of young peasant women in traditional settings are so ubiquitous across Europe, from Brittany and the Basque country to the Baltic and the Bucovina, as to become mere ambient background noise to spectators nowadays. But they represented a new, anti-academic movement in nineteenth-century art that shifted the symbolic representation of the nation's authentic character away from historical grandeur to what was, in the English phrase of that period, 'racy of the soil'. And they also document traditional practices such as markets and fairs, seasonal

Figure 10.4 *The Reaper* (Kanutas Ruseckas, 1844; Lithuanian Art Museum, Vilnius). ERNiE imagebank

feasts and religious processions, lovingly representing the colourful garb in which this all took place.

The depiction of nationally representative costume is not a Romantic invention but goes back to earlier centuries. The earliest examples antedate the invention of print. Maps of the seventeenth century habitually represent, in their margins, figures from various lands in their specific costumes as a display gallery of cultural diversity. Costume books, often depicting colourful sartorial traditions such as those of Spain, the Netherlands and the Scottish Highlands, profited from improved printing techniques and provided a panorama of local colour to armchair travellers, who could enjoy the genres of *Voyages pittoresques* or *Los Españoles pintados por su mismos*; book illustrations added their weight to this ambient tradition.[21]

Costumes themselves acquired the function of signalling a national identity. Romantic German students dressed in an 'Old German' fashion proclaimed by Arndt in 1814 and inspired by Dürer portraits (as in the hairstyle and the outfit of Hoffmann von Fallersleben, Figure 4.4), with tight waistcoasts and open collars: rejecting all the frivolous elegance of French style. Caroline Pichler expressed a hope in 1815 that her Old German dress for ladies would be worn both in Berlin and in Vienna. A military element was added for those in the armed forces. Military uniforms were specific to the armies of different countries and regimes and tended to follow vernacular sartorial traditions (Hussars, Cossacks, Bersaglieri, Highland regiments). In the course of the nineteenth century, these obtained a powerfully national symbolism at a time when formal (civil) dress for men was becoming increasingly transnational and nationally indistinct. George IV wearing a Highland kilt during his Edinburgh visit of 1821 marked an adoption of this vernacular dress code as prestigiously 'national'. The nobility of Hungary prided itself early on its Hussar-style, tight-waisted and heavily embroidered 'Attila' jackets and its tight, embroidered breeches, with the aristocratic accessory of the sabre like the one given to Liszt (Chapter 9). This style was that of the Empress Maria Theresa's Hungarian Guards; it had become fashionable in Vienna and had been worn in the 1780s as an expression of protest against Joseph II's attempts to centralize and Germanize the empire. A similar jacket style was worn by the Polish nobility (the so-called *czamara*), and that frog-and-loop jacket became popular as the *čamara* among Czech supporters of the Polish Uprising of 1831 and again in 1848 among supporters of Hungarian independence. From there it became a pan-Slavic signal, influencing the uniform of the many Sokol athletics clubs that sprang up in Bohemia and other Habsburg–Slavic regions from the mid-century (Figure 10.5).[22]

Thus traditional and 'national' dress began to make its way into the urban middle classes. But the main thrust of that development fanned out from the Alps. The mountain-dwelling population of the Tyrol had gained great sympathy and symbolic prestige following their 1809 insurrection against Napoleonic rule; the leader, the innkeeper Andreas Hofer, was glorified in song and later in painting and statues.[23] Tyrolean garb shared in this prestige: woollen or leather knee-breeches (Lederhosen) and felt hats became the preferred dress code for leisure-time huntsmen and hikers.

Even before Hofer's insurrection, in 1806, the Bavarian agricultural scientist Joseph von Hazzi had compiled a description of peasant dress styles in lower Bavaria as part of the new statistical inventory of state culture (*Trachten aus Niederbayern nach den statistischen Aufschlüssen über das Herzogtum Baiern*). Later, the historian Felix Joseph von Lipowsky published a collection of Bavarian popular costumes, to which he gave the epithet 'national' (*Sammlung Bayerischer National-Costüme*). The various regions of Bavaria (flanked by neighbouring Tyrol, the Black Forest and Switzerland) were at the forefront of this national-traditionalist dress revival under the Romantically minded Ludwig I of Bavaria. In 1842, the wedding of the Bavarian Crown Prince Maximilian with the Prussian Princess Marie featured Bavarian peasants in traditional costume; in 1853,

Figure 10.5 Jindřich Fügner in the Sokol club's national Slavic uniform. ERNiE imagebank

the same Maximilian (by then King Maximilian II) ordained a decree for the 'Encouragement of national feeling and especially of traditional dress' in order to oppose 'general homogenization and levelling'. The first societies with the express aim of cultivating traditional dress (*Trachtenvereine*) were founded (again in Bavaria, more particularly in the Alpine regions) in the 1850s. They joined into a regionwide federative association (*Gauverband*) in 1883; the number of its affiliates grew from fifteen associations in 1891 to sixty-one in 1906. Meanwhile other regional federations were founded, and in 1925 they merged into a Bavarian federation. The motivation was avowedly conservative-national: in 1886 King Ludwig II had ordained a decree to encourage the foundation of such societies 'in order to preserve the beautiful dress of the mountain regions and the old dances … and to foster in these societies a communal feeling and love of the homeland and the fatherland'. Accordingly, such *Trachtenvereine* proclaimed as their aim 'to throw up a barrier against the modern age while cultivating, and preserving for posterity, the dress, mores and traditions of our ancestors'.[24]

While Bavaria and neighbouring Tyrol were the heartlands of the *Trachtenvereine*, the trend spread across the German lands, from the Alps

Figure 10.6 Sigmund and Anna Freud in Austrian country dress. US Library of Congress

to the north Frisian islands and including Austrian and Swiss societies and associations. A generic women's style known as the Dirndl (a blouse under a tight, often low-cut bodice, loose long skirt with apron, white stockings) emerged in the 1870s; it was originally worn by servant girls and as such became known to the urban tourist patrons of rural hotels and inns. Like the Lederhosen it became a popular fashion, also in non-rural settings, in the twentieth century. Having originally been fostered by royal patronage, the success of the Dirndl was mainly commercially carried: the Munich fashion house Wallach, established in 1900, specialized in these dresses and sponsored them being worn by servers at the Munich *Oktoberfest*,* when that event celebrated its centenary in 1910.[25] The success of the Dirndl thus marks the adoption of peasant culture by the urban middle classes, facilitated by festive culture, leisure consumerism and countryside tourism (Figure 10.6).

* The Oktoberfest, like the Dirndl, had started as an exercise in soft power by the Romantic monarchy: it had been instituted to mark the occasion of the wedding of Ludwig I in 1810. Its status as a national feast had been consolidated when a gigantic statue of Bavaria personified and a Hall of Fame of Great Bavarians were added to the festive field in 1843–1850.

A similar pattern is noticeable everywhere in Europe: folk traditions became commodified and an inspiration for middle-class leisure pursuits, although the particulars were very different from country to country. In Sweden and Norway, traditional patterns were used by feminist activists. In Sweden, Hanna Winge and Sophie Adlersparre, founders in 1874 of the still active 'Friends of Manual Craftwork', attempted to create cottage industries for rural women. In Norway, where photographs of peasants in traditional dress became popular from the 1880s, *bunad* (traditional dress) was used in a 1902 performance by the folklorist and folk-dance expert Klara Semb. This inspired the pamphlet *Norsk klædebunad* (1903) by her mentor Hulda Garborg, a social radical and cultural revivalist who was also active in the fields of traditional cookery, amateur theatre and women's rights. We shall encounter this remarkable combination of stylistic traditionalism and social reformism further on, when discussing the Arts and Crafts movement that inspired Garborg.[26]

In the wholly different social context of Central and Eastern Europe, emergent cultural sociability found an outlet in choral singing. As women increasingly participated in mixed choirs, they opted for traditional local dress as a collective stage costume. Some of them may have had inherited specimens of such dresses in their wardrobes; if not, the presence of many *plein-air* paintings in the various local galleries and museums provided patterns from which to work.[27] The fashion caught on in the Slavic portions of the Habsburg Empire and also in western provinces of Russia: the Baltic, Poland and Ukraine. In Lithuania, German Romantics such as the polymath Georg Sauerwein organized festivals where Lithuanians were invited to appear in traditional costume. Photographs were taken on those occasions, and Sauerwein used these as illustrative material in his lectures. Sauerwein also exhorted Lithuanians to maintain or to revive their ancient garments so as to display their nationality.[28]

At his suggestion, the choral director Vydūnas (pseudonym of Wilhelm Storost) had his Tilsit Singers' Society perform in Lithuanian costume (for the women: white aprons, white embroidered shirts, the heads decorated with blue ribbons and green myrtle wreaths). National dress henceforth became a matter of Lithuanian self-identification; and, as in Latvia and Estonia, it was part of collective-performative public presence involving choral singing and amateur theatre. The attire was home-made (possibly after collective consultations).

From the Munich Oktoberfest to the Tilsit choral festival: the adoption of national costume is a veritable performance of national identity. The performers belong to the emerging modest middle classes, sensitized to national identity and traditional culture; the repertoire is that of traditional peasant culture, initially perceived through the 'male gaze' of *plein-air* painters and costume ethnographers, then appropriated by the wearers themselves. And the setting is something that emerges in the context of late-nineteenth-century modernity, along with its proto- or early-feminist undercurrents: that of the leisure-time display platform – festivals and fairgrounds, where town audiences could watch country performances. The countryside with its nationally characteristic traditions was *exhibited*.

Exhibiting the Nation: World Fairs and Nation-Branding

London's Great Exhibition of 1851 was launched out of a pre-existing tradition of public trade and industry fairs. Like them, it displayed the products of agriculture, manufacture, trade and industry (with an emphasis on technologies and design innovation); but it was held in a dedicated new space, the famed Crystal Palace, with its novel girder-and-glass design – made possible by the invention of sheet glass in 1832, which was then widely used for railway stations and large greenhouses in botanical gardens. The Crystal Palace, as the embodiment and prototype of the exhibition platform, became itself a meta-exhibit, both containing the items of display and being one in its own right. This nesting recursivity was to become one of the defining features of world fairs henceforth: they became a telescoping sub-space, a window on the world and at the same time a microcosm of the world, where one could lose oneself among pavilions, and, within the pavilions, among the many exhibits on display there. These displays were often themselves of a compound nature, uniting various elements and performative practices – dances or musical performances with 'authentic' costumes and instruments, or ditto tea ceremonies. The Crystal Palace, copied or imitated in numerous other venues (New York's Crystal Palace, 1853, Amsterdam's Paleis voor Volksvlijt, 1855, Porto's Palacio de Cristal, 1865, the Grand Palais in Paris, 1897), shared its pavilion typology and glass/girder ceiling with the century's great shopping arcades and marked the transition from a fair (in the meaning of 'marketplace for economic exchange') to fairground (in the meaning of 'a venue for multiple spectacular and immersive entertainments'): 'sensational' rather than 'habitual' culture.[29]

The Crystal Palace remained a venue for mass entertainment beyond the immediate occasion of its construction; as we have seen, a large choral festival was held there in 1861. It also heralded a new type of metropolitan landmark. While the fairs themselves were short-lived events, the sites tended to endure, and in some instances for longer, and more prominently, than one might expect. They needed to be constructed, often hastily, under the pressure of a commercial budget and an organizational timeline, and they needed to encapsulate a maximum of space in a minimum of building material; in that respect they were more like circus tents than real 'palaces', as they grandiloquently styles themselves. The term 'pavilion' does their ephemeral and thin, hollow nature greater justice. They could be removed to make place for successor buildings (like the Parisian Palais de l'Industrie, 1855–1897, and Palais du Trocadéro, 1878–1935), and they were prone to accidental destruction by fire. The New York Crystal Palace went up in flames in 1858, the Amsterdam Paleis voor Volksvlijt in 1929, the London Crystal Palace itself in 1936. Or they could just drop out of fashion, lose their function and be demolished. But in a surprising number of instances, things that were conceived as follies, extravaganzas or temporary hangars became fixtures in the cityscape. Besides the flagship examples of the Brussels Atomium (1958) and the Parisian Eiffel Tower and Grand Palais (1889 and 1900), we encounter, also in Paris, the Palais de Tokyo and the Palais de Chaillot (1937); in Prague, the Jugendstil Palace of Industry and the neo-Gothic Tourist Pavilion (1891); in Rome, the Fascist-era Palace of Italian Civilization (1942) and the neo-baroque Pan-Latin lighthouse on the Gianicolo hill (1911, Figure 10.7); in Lisbon, the huge waterfront Monument to the Discoveries (1940); in Barcelona, the waterfront Columbus Monument and the Triumphal Arch leading into the Parc de la Ciutadella (1888); in Seville, the enormous, tilework-embellished Plaza de España (1929) – to name only some prominent examples within Europe.

As these examples show, world fairs played an important role, in tandem with the rise in mass tourism, in turning cities into tourist attractions, studded with places of interest and entertainment spaces. As commercial enterprises, world fairs relied on mass attendance to succeed, and indeed on a larger attendance than the local population could provide. A logic clicked into place whereby the necessary crowds at world fairs would come from far away and stay only for a limited amount of time – the time of a holiday excursion. Their communal presence was, as a result, both numerous and transitory, and their engagement with the spectacle and its exhibits was necessarily and almost by definition superficial; hence also the great number of take-home souvenirs. What was proffered was a sampler of a world of goods and sights, and what was done by the audience was precisely that: they sampled. Heterogeneous cultural products from very different countries were taken in and tried out in quick succession. To be sure, some

Figure 10.7 A landmark left by the 1911 world fair in Rome: lighthouse donated by Argentina to the host city as a 'beacon of the Latin world'. ERNiE imagebank

cultural exhibits could strike a responsive chord (the European interest in Japanese tea, in Indonesian gamelan music and wayang shadow-puppetry, or in Indian raga music are sometimes linked to world fair encounters) and play a role in cultural transfers; but in the majority of cases they left little more impact than a 'flavour', a vague familiarity based on a remembered and confused sense of local colour.

The exhibition tradition had until 1851 been intra-national, aimed at strengthening a country's inner resources. The world fairs added to this a new, mercantilist dimension: that of an international arena in which many nations participated and in which competition and exchange were equally important and equally justified. Not only did nations vie with each other and boast of their own achievements, they also took a mutual interest in each other. What could a country expect from the world as a sphere of operations? What could it expect by way of imports, exports and trade opportunities? For each country to expect interest being taken in what it had to offer, it had to reciprocate by taking an interest in what the others were offering. As manifestations of growing economic internationalism, world fairs were giving the nation a new setting: not the enmity of its Other but its participation (both competitive and collaborative) in an international economic order.

The economic internationalization that world fairs exemplified and encouraged was counterbalanced by national self-positioning. As might be expected, culture provided the repertoire for that. World fairs themselves became an internationally coordinated enterprise, taking place, now in this, then in that metropolis and gradually crystallizing into a fixed system.* But universal and global as they claimed to be, the format very early on explicitly required participants to display themselves also in their local colour and national specificity, with exhibits of traditional lifestyles or cottage industries. And whereas technological progress and the intensification of world trade tended to lead to convergence between modern industries and economies, countries positioned themselves as individually recognizable point of interest – thanks to their cultural traditions.

This led to a triangle of possible registers in which participating nations presented their individuality to the world: either in attractively playful, highly decorated but makeshift pavilions in the style of fairground attractions; or as dynamically modern, internationally engaged and forward-looking (this leading to the great fashion of an almost futuristic 'international modern style' in pavilion design); or, finally, as rooted in authentic traditions that gave each country a national character of its own. These three modalities between them reflect the triangle of 'amusement, modernity and memory' that we have seen at work in the Parisian cityscapes as analysed by Walter Benjamin; and in that triangle, traditional peasant culture, historicism and high modernity are brought together in the nation's international projection of its self-image. The use of vernacular architecture is a key element in the display repertoire, using either historicist pastiches of ancient landmarks or quaint, popular structures: Ottoman kiosks, Byzantine churches, Alpine chalets, American wigwams, rustic villages and traditional Flemish or Merry Old English townscapes. An expo fairground had to be experienced as an architectural zoo; and a specific and authentic culture became a trademark, a 'unique selling point' for participants.[30]

The eclecticism and mixing of registers (something that nowadays counts as the very definition of kitsch) was of course part and parcel of the

* That system was consolidated in the 1928 Convention Relating to International Exhibitions and the establishment of a Bureau international des expositions. Alongside the main canon of 'universal expositions', from London 1951 to Brussels 1958 and beyond, nationally specific, theme-specific, regional or colonial exhibitions were also organized.

format. This was a kermesse, a bazaar. The underlying constant was that the nation's particular identity was here used as an identifying 'brand' in a trade emporium that mashed up the entire world into a welter of economic and cultural encounters and exchanges. In this light, the hoopla-national profiling that world fairs called for may represent the first step in a development that would ultimately lead to the condition of 'banal nationalism'. World fairs came into their own in the century of trade internationalization. Trademarks had come into use around the time of London's Great Exhibition, and by 1891 an attempt was made to regulate their use internationally (the Madrid Agreement Concerning the International Registration of Marks). By this time, nationality itself was beginning to develop into a trademark of sorts. Geographical indications of product provenance were first imposed by the British country-of-origin legislation of 1883, initially a protectionist measure against imports falsely pretending to be British-made. However, the imposition of labels such as 'Made in Germany' or 'Swiss Made' soon became boastful marks of quality; and between 1905 and 1919 France enacted a number of *Appellation d'origine* laws. Thus, as the mesh of international trade grew more tight-knit, a dual necessity took shape: the identification of a product's national point of origin, and at the same time the identifiability of the nationality itself as a recognizable point of origin. Hence the use of national flags as brands and logos on representative 'national' products: watches, pocket knives and chocolate with Swiss flags, tulip bulbs and cheeses with Dutch flags, skiing resorts with Austrian flags. In this bidirectional dynamics – closer involvement of the nation-state in an international mercantile world order; greater need for the nation to set itself apart as recognizably different from the others – world fairs played a leading role.

A national flag on a consumer product such as a pizza box, pocket knife or pickled-herring snack is almost a textbook definition of what Michael Billig (1995) has termed 'banal nationalism'. As with the names of the Parisian metro stations, the effect is one of ambient habituation. The diffuse and trivial carriers (pizza box, pocket knives or herring) turn the nation into a 'hidden persuader', giving to a consumer product a trademark or logo with an instant, automatic feel-good factor. The national brand is used not as a crude exhortation to 'buy this product because it represents an admirable country' but in a more indirect way: 'We who bring this product to your attention do so on the basis of what we think is a shared affect between us and you, the customer: a reliance on the national values symbolized by this flag and applicable to this product.' In advertising terms, the use of the flag is a 'reason to believe': it sends not a message in its own right but a meta-message serving to enhance the message that it accompanies, providing it with a subliminal feel-good factor.[31]

Alongside this 'habitual', unobtrusive nationalization, the display of exotically local-coloured culture has a more 'sensational' effect. The reliance on culture to provide characteristic distinctness and authenticity is now firmly co-opted by the modern state as a self-profiling strategy: for states, with their economic and trading policies, were the institutional participants in world fairs. World fairs, in other words, feed into the increasing instrumentalization of national identity for the benefit of state interests.

To be sure, these were not yet the nation-states that would emerge from the Great War; many of them were empires with colonies worldwide and considerable cultural diversity within their peripheral provinces. As a result, there is a fluid scalarity in their self-presentation. Historicism and technocratic modernity are used to project the metropolitan heartland; but at a sub-imperial level, the rustic provinces and the colonies were used to provide traditionalism, local colour and exoticism. In the cafés, cafeterias and beer gardens, regionally specific food would be served (coffee, tea, lager and sausages), enlivened by national music performances; with 'Gypsy' musicians being a particularly exotic and popular feature for Hungarian and Romanian cabarets (Figure 10.8).[32]

As the presence of those Romany musicians indicates, human subjects themselves were exhibited as local-colour features, in their traditional costumes. Sweden displayed mannequins in traditional peasant clothes and sold postcards depicting these; the Ottoman empire for its Vienna participation provided a sumptuous album of all the local costumes worn in its various provinces, from the Balkans to the Maghreb. Outside the immediate framework of the world fair, the Russian empire would follow that Ottoman template when it brought out a lithographed album of ethnic costumes in order to mark the Empire's millennium; and in 1883 the imperial conspectus of its rich diversity would culminate in the Austro-Hungarian *Kronprinzenwerk*, a twenty-four-volume encyclopedic panorama of minority folk traditions under the benevolent aegis of the Habsburg crown prince. A highly specific development took place in Albania. The Garibaldist insurgent Pietro Marubi took refuge from political persecution in Shkodër and started a photographic studio there, soon specializing in portraits of locals in their traditional costumes. Over the decades, the Marubi studio remained active as the founder's son and grandson took over, and their local postcards became popular among visitors, tourists and soldiers stationed in the area. This sustained production amounts to 150,000 negatives documenting a wealth of traditional

Figure 10.8 Poster for the Romanian cabaret at the 1889 Paris Exposition Universelle (Jules Chéret), showing a waitress in traditional dress and Romany lăutari musicians in the background, with bourgeois patrons seated at the tables. ERNiE imagebank: Minea 2022

costume and culture; it is now incorporated in Albania's Marubi National Museum of Photography.[33]

Meanwhile, back at the fairground, some displays went one better than mannequins in display cases, photographs and lithographs: performers were on display in local-colour settings, employed in traditional handicrafts and wearing traditional apparel. This type of 'folk village' anticipated what would become the many open-air folk museums of Europe, beginning with Sweden's Skansen resort near Stockholm (1891; the staff, like that at the Munich Oktoberfest, were dressed up in folk attire to enhance the sensation of authenticity). A similar performative turn was taken in the display of the trading empires' colonial outposts: Indonesian dance and gamelan music were performed in Dutch exhibits featuring a Javanese folk village, Buffalo Bill displayed the horsemanship of his 'Cowboys and Indians' Rough Riders, and, notoriously, 'primitive' people from the colonies were put on display in 'human zoos'. Thus the scalarity of imperial self-display ranged from the national heartland to the rustic periphery to the outlying colonies.

Used as we are nowadays to the power distribution inherent in 'the gaze', we cannot but consider the reduction of local cultures into an object of metropolitan spectacle as anything other than degrading. The colonial exhibitions held within Europe were part of a Eurocentric exploitation both of the natural resources and of the inhabitants of the colonies and their cultural riches, and as such these exhibitions form a standing reproach, a century later, to this European legacy. The sites that were designed to celebrate European colonialism (such as the ones at Brussels in 1897 and Paris in 1931) have now been refashioned into postcolonial reflections on this problematic heritage: the AfricaMuseum in Tervuren and the Cité de l'Immigration in Paris.

Degrading the 'human zoos' certainly were. The Jardin d'acclimatation in the Bois de Boulogne, where they became a fixture, had originally been a zoo, founded to test the possible domestication of exotic animals. Most of its animals were eaten during the siege of Paris in 1870–1871. In 1877 the management started to mount 'ethnographic spectacles', twenty-two in total over the next decades. These were discontinued in 1931 and the Jardin became the amusement park it is today. 'Acclimatizing' was a misnomer: the subjects were exhibited with insufficient clothing in the uncongenial Parisian temperatures, and thirty-two of them died of exposure.[34] The entire set-up confirmed or expressed existing power relations and was complicit in their underlying injustice. But such exhibitions were the outer end of a sliding imperial centre–periphery scale on which the 'nation' was as yet uncertainly positioned. Nor were all 'existing power relations' necessarily perpetuated or consolidated by these displays; world fairs were reflections and manifestations not only of centre–periphery imbalanc but also of shifts in that balance. Local-colour advertisement was quickly adopted by non-European empires or states to gain access to a new globalized market economy – especially by Japan and the United States, but also by the Ottoman Empire and independent Latin American states. As world fairs came to be hosted outside Europe (Philadelphia 1876, Melbourne 1880, Chicago 1893, St Louis 1904, San Francisco 1915), non-European countries found a platform for self-presentation bypassing the central position that the old continent had arrogated for itself. The careers of the important nation-building artists Raja Ravi Varma of India and Kakuzo Okakura of Japan were launched, tellingly, at the Chicago's World's Fair in 1893, which also provided a global rostrum for the *fin-de-siècle* guru Swami Vivekananda. And the 'colonial' expositions held in Calcutta (1883, 1923) and Hanoi (1902) and in various Australian cities (Sydney 1870 and 1879, Melbourne 1872 and

1888, Adelaide 1887) exhibit a striking difference from the ones in Paris or Brussels. No human zoos there; rather, those events signal colonies taking a more self-focused stance as regards their economic position in the world, announcing a presence in world trade that, at odds with a mere exploitative extraction economy, would later in the century lead into its logical consequence: independence. Autonomous participation in a world fair would also become a newly independent country's manifestation of its place in the twentieth-century's international order, as we can see from the presence of former imperial peripheries – Lebanon, Poland, Ireland and the Baltic states – at the Chicago Century of Progress Expo, 1933, and Paris's Exposition Internationale des Arts et Techniques dans la Vie Moderne, 1937. Europe's Asian and African colonies would follow suit after World War II.

There is a parallel of sorts between the developing presence of extra-European colonies and intra-European imperial peripheries. The large ethnographic exhibition mounted by the Russian empire in Riga in 1896 was to some extent colonial vis-à-vis Russia's inner minority cultures, to some extent also a Slavophile manifestation of pan-Russianism, but not insignificantly an event putting Riga on the map as the empire's most important city after Moscow and St Petersburg, and a boost for Latvian awareness. The Bosnian-Herzegovinian pavilion that the Austro-Hungarian Empire (having annexed that territory) put up in Paris 1900 was designed by Alphonse Mucha, who used his unique combination of art nouveau style and pan-Slavic political sympathies to deliver an oblique message unintended by the imperial rulers. The intense regionalism that was deployed by Spanish designers fed into the localism of Barcelona, which co-hosted the 1929 event together with Seville; the Spanish presence was thus being riven between a Catalan wing at one end and an 'Ibero-American' one at the other.[35]

Late-nineteenth-century regionalism was, if anything, strengthened by a cult of traditional arts and crafts in the empires' rustic peripheries. Patronizingly celebrated as ethnographic infotainment at the world fairs, the local artists and intellectuals nonetheless took strength and inspiration from a sense that Europe, like the world at large, was a transnational palette in which each cultural community could find its own way towards modernity and a coequal standing. What counted as quaint local colour in the fairground ambience became nationally iconic when repatriated into its home country: the Finnish Pavilion in Paris 1900 furnished the baseline design for the Finnish National Museum in Helsinki. Similarly, a Byzantine pavilion at the Paris 1900 Expo, designed by the Frenchman

Lucien Magne, was re-erected, iron columns and girders and all, in Athens where it was consecrated as the church of Agios Sostis, Christ the Saviour. And in many countries, open-air museums of traditional peasant dwellings turned into internal, localized fairs celebrating the country's own identity. Skansen near Stockholm was copied across Europe, with an agenda of internal identity affirmation rather than external local-colour display. Ironically, much as *Heimat* nostalgia is a form of 'domestic exoticism', cultural nationalism in subaltern regions often begins as internalized exoticism.

Europe's imperial peripheries differed from actual colonies in a number of respects. Both lacked self-determination; both were in a subaltern position and had known violent subjection in their past. But the imperial provinces were not, on the whole, subject to an extraction economy; in the local cities and market towns there was an educated class, as well as a petty bourgeoisie and a white-collar working class with sufficient spare time to pursue cultural interests; and cultural interests could enjoy patronage and fostering from a home-grown elite. Scotland, Ireland, Catalonia/Aragon, the Basque country, Poland-Lithuania, Bohemia, Hungary and Croatia all had vestiges of an indigenous feudal past and could look back on their own high-prestige histories, which were frequently invoked as a morale-booster against contemporary subordination.* It is in the context of these sub-imperial peripheries that we see a particular flourishing at the *fin-de-siècle* of a new type of sub-imperial, culture-driven, late-Romantic nationalism, characterized by a new way of combining traditional vernacular culture with progressive politics. The spark-off moments came from the Arts and Crafts movement in London (on which more later in the chapter) and from an amateur theatre in Western Norway.

Henrik Ibsen and the Theatre

In the 1780s, Schiller had hailed the theatre as a 'moral institution' allowing for the development of a public sphere in modern Germany as it had once done in ancient Athens. Certainly the dramatic collaboration between him and Goethe in Weimar had created a rejuvenation of German letters. But for all that, the Romantic generation tended to prefer lyrical poetry and prose fiction to the drama. Goethe's *Faust* (1808/1832) and Shelley's *The Cenci* (1819) had been all but unplayable; theatres tended to provide social

* An intriguing parallel of sorts applies to colonial India, Bengal in particular (see Linden 2024), and to Dutch-dominated Java, weighed down though they were by racist colonial extraction economies.

entertainment rather than exploring new artistic horizons. Even in France, where the advent of Romanticism had been heralded by Hugo's *Hernani* (1830; or rather, its preface–manifesto), the theatres drifted to boulevard amusements with easy-going plays lavishly produced. The point of gravity for theatre productions shifted to musical performances, with grand opera as the prestigious flagship, surrounded by a flotilla of more popular 'variety' entertainments, from operetta to zarzuela and vaudeville. Occasionally a nationalizing impulse could emanate from here, but only incidentally. Thus Kajetan Tyl's operetta *The Shoemakers' Feast* of 1834 featured the nationally sentimental song 'Kde domov můj?' ('Where is My Homeland?'), which grew in popularity to become the Czech national anthem in 1918.[36]

One place where the theatre played a fully national role was Copenhagen, where Adam Oehlenschläger set the tone with his dramatic evocations of the past (starting with his 1809 *Lord Håkon the Rich*). Oehlenschläger's influence radiated out to Christiania (now Oslo), which recently had moved from Danish to Swedish rule but where Danish was still the language of high culture. In Norway, a budding writer, Henrik Ibsen, marked Oehlenschläger's death in 1848 with the elegy 'The Skald in Walhalla'; Ibsen, too, would at the beginning of his career write history plays in the Oehlenschläger mode. Now largely forgotten, they included *Lady Inger of Ostrat* (1855), *The Vikings at Helgoland* (1858) and *Pretenders to the Throne* (1863).

What was formative and innovative in Ibsen's career as a playwright was his work for a small amateur theatre company in the provincial town of Bergen.[37] Ibsen stayed there from 1851 to 1857, then relocating to the Christiania theatre until its closure in 1862. When Ibsen moved abroad (he would not return to Norway until 1891) he abandoned the thematics of semi-legendary heroic warriors. For his *Brand* (1864) and *Peer Gynt* (1867), he turned, tellingly, to the countryside: *Brand* is a moral tragedy set in a rural parish, and *Peer Gynt* relates the tall tales of a larger-than-life strongman (the play is now known mainly for the incidental music that Edvard Grieg composed for it in 1876). But from the mid-1870s on, Ibsen's taste for realism (now no longer just a pictorial but also a literary current) came to the fore, and he turned to the emotional and moral problems of the contemporary middle classes living in post-Romantic and post-religious disenchantment. Plays such as *The Pillars of Society* (1877), *A Doll's House* (1879), *Ghosts* and *An Enemy of the People* (1882) drew on a stagecraft of frugality that he had learned in Bergen but now disseminated globally: the plays premiered in Munich, Copenhagen, Chicago and Oslo respectively. As critics internationally hailed his work, Ibsen became the figurehead of a new approach to drama altogether, 'literary theatre'. Literary theatre eschewed the glitz of the lavish boulevard productions; its audiences were small and the plays that were performed were muted in their production values, relying mainly on the dramatic and literary appeal of the plays' dialogue. Ibsen's unforgiving exposure of the soul-destroying nature of social conventions inspired avant-garde circles in the 1880s; G. B. Shaw and James Joyce were both card-carrying 'Ibsenites', and many small theatre troupes availed themselves gratefully of his sparse, almost spartan production values.

Ibsen's influence took a specific turn in Dublin, where the London-raised Irish poet W. B. Yeats wanted to establish a literary theatre. Yeats's taste (he had pursued his early career among *fin-de-siècle* aesthetes and 'decadents', and he was a snob) did not run to Ibsenite middle-class realism or naturalism; his penchant was more for symbolism, as performed in Parisian theatres staging the rarefied aesthetes Maurice Maeterlinck and Auguste Villiers de l'Isle-Adam. But Yeats's political loyalty lay firmly with Ireland, culturally fallow ground in his view, and a literary theatre in Dublin could make use of amateur companies that had, for their part, certainly been inspired by Ibsen. The resulting Irish Literary Theatre was a hybrid in many senses, uneasily straddling the social radicalism of Ibsenites and Yeats's elitist avant-garde aestheticism. Its use of the term 'national' was in effect glossing over two contradictory meanings of that term: for Yeats, 'national' was the opposite of 'provincial', meaning that Ireland could outgrow its drab vulgarity and take its place in cosmopolitan European modernity; for others, it fitted more in the mold of Douglas Hyde's 'de-anglicisation', meaning that Ireland should abandon alienating foreign influences and return to its native-rooted cultural strength. Cosmopolitan or nativist? The history of the Irish Literary Theatre was marked by vehement altercations between these two wings throughout its existence.[38] The plays in its repertoire similarly oscillate between international avant-garde and de-anglicizing propaganda.

What was beyond doubt was the high quality of the repertoire and of the acting: this theatre was innovative and inspiring, and at its best it managed to draw on Irish themes and settings (both legendary-heroic and contemporary-rustic, past and peasantry) to implement a non-complacent, nonconformist, innovative agenda. The unprofessional background of the actors became an asset: they delivered their lines without 'hamming it up', in a pensive manner that suited the theatre's 'literary' nature. The Irish theatre acquired a high reputation, also in Britain and the US, and deliberately positioned itself as 'artistic inspiration coming from the margins'.

What Bergen was to Swedish-dominated Norway, Dublin was to the English-dominated British Empire.

The Ibsenite turn inspired many grass-roots 'national' theatre companies and playwrights in other sub-imperial cities across Northern Europe: Reykjavík had its Ibsenite moment in 1897 when the Leikfélag Reykjavíkur (Reykjavík Theatre Company) was founded; the instigators were mindful of the work of the Norwegian theatre in Bergen and were influenced, obviously, by impulses from Copenhagen (where the multitalented Sigurður Guðmundsson, painter, costume designer and national activist, had often visited the theatre). In 1908 the Reykjavík Theatre Company produced the first work of Jóhann Sigurjónsson, who would later reach an international audience with his *Eyvind of the Mountains* (1911) and *Loftur the Magician* (1914). In Helsinki, a long-struggling Finnish Theatre Company successfully performed Ibsen's 'A Doll's House' in Finnish, and from the 1890s it staged *Kalevala*-themed plays to increasing public response; it moved to a newly built National Theatre (designed in national-Romantic style) in 1905.[39] A Dublin reverberation also reached the budding Galician movement in Spain, where a Brotherhood of Friends of the Language was founded in 1916 in obvious imitation of the Gaelic League; their founder Antón Villar Ponte translated the most nationalistic of Yeats's plays, *Cathleen Ní Houlihan* (a historical allegory set in a peasant cottage), into Galician in 1921.[40]

In all these cases, the idealism driving these grass-roots companies thrived on an osmosis with manifestations of reformist ideals in other fields, all of these interlinked as communicating vessels. The Irish literary revival drew on Douglas Hyde's Gaelic League (Hyde himself even performing in a production of a one-act farce in Gaelic); and the Gaelic League was more than a mere provider of Gaelic language courses. They also cultivated Irish traditional dance and music, salvaging these art forms in the face of their dwindling demographic base and ensuring their survival among Ireland's urbanized population. Another flanking development was that of a nationally committed women's movement, the Daughters of Ireland. They staged national-allegorical *tableaux vivants*, and among their ranks were playwrights such as Alice Milligan and firebrand activists such as Maud Gonne. From there we see the social mycelium of the literary revival mesh with almost all of the many utopian reform movements that proliferated so widely in the period 1890–1910: anti-alcoholism, vegetarianism, naturism, suffragette feminism including 'rational dress', the co-operative movement, alternative medicine and biodynamic food, Esperantism, Jaeger's woollen clothing and Allinson's bread, and so on.

Shaw was involved in practically all of these; Yeats spent an inordinate amount of his time in occultist pursuits and associations.[41]

The many utopian–reformist pursuits of this period cut a wide swath across Europe. First-wave feminists mentioned in the foregoing pages include Hulda Garborg and Adlersparre; the German-Lithuanian Storost-Vydunas was a vegetarian theosophist. But the influence of William Morris and of the Arts and Crafts movement stands out.

Arts and Crafts in *Fin-de-siècle* Nation-Building

The Arts and Crafts movement was part of the complex legacy of world fair phenomenon. The Great Exhibition in London had set a pattern of showcasing mass-produced utensils, often (as the taste was then) in heavily ornamented style yet cheaply affordable. Later fairs had drawn on the local colour of cottage industries and handcrafted manufacture from the rustic peripheries, while within England, the use of lavish ornamentation for modern mass-produced utensils was rejected as kitsch. And so 'craft' was doubly idealized as the antithetical opposite of industrial mass-production. Small-scale, low-tech and lovingly executed by dedicated, trained labourers, 'craft' shifted from being a form of mere manufacture to something dignified, tasteful and close to artistry. The notion of the 'decorative' and 'ornamental' arts arose alongside the 'fine arts' in these decades, and colleges of design were opened in many European locations. Many of them, such as the Slade School in London, would align themselves with the avant-garde and with reformist utopianism. Progressive spirits criticized, in Marxist terms, the 'alienation' of modern industrial workers from their mode of production, and craftsmanship was therefore both nostalgic and radical: it represented an unalienated, involved and dignified form of manual labour, redolent of tradition and resisting modern capitalism.

No one propounded this ideal of traditional craftsmanship as a progressive radical mobilizer better than William Morris, a socialist visionary, writer and artist steeped in the Romantic tradition of the Pre-Raphaelites. His acolytes and adepts were numerous across Europe – we have already encountered Hanna Winge and Hulda Garborg in Sweden and Norway; like Morris himself, they would design wallpaper, house decorations and books in a post-Pre-Raphaelite style, aiming to bring discerning taste into middle-class households and to restore dignity to the production of household goods.

Morris's post-Pre-Raphaelite style was often medievalist but also drew on natural forms: stylized animals and plants. The repercussion across Europe was twofold: an agenda of integrating artistic design into all

Figure 10.9 Art nouveau posters for national events: the Barcelona Floral Games (left; 1908, Ramón Casas) and the Sokol sports festival in Prague (right; 1912, Alphonse Mucha). ERNiE imagebank

manner of everyday goods and house decorations, ideally in a totalizing form as part of an overall architectural-cum-interior design, and a new formal language opting for gently curved and subtly decorated patterns, austere yet playful. The style was called *Sezession* in Vienna, *art nouveau* in French; *Jugendstil* in German and *modernisme* in Catalan. Its forms could be angular, like those of Rennie Mackintosh in Glasgow, mixing restrained elliptical curves with rectilinearity as in Viennese or Italian neo-baroque (as in the Gianicolo lighthouse, Figure 10.7), or lushly and colourfully curvaceous as in the posters by Alphonse Mucha (Figure 10.9), the glassware of Lalique or the buildings of Gaudí. Over time, the tendency towards a more crystalline, angular linearity became more pronounced; the buildings of Hendrik Berlage in Amsterdam, Victor Horta in Brussels and Henri van de Velde (also in his furniture design) in Ghent and Weimar exemplify this trend. The 1925 Exposition internationale des arts décoratifs et industriels modernes in Paris coined, for the later phase of this stylistic register, the term *art déco*.

From this miniature evocation of so many places, names and trends, it can be seen that a sudden and overwhelming heyday was experienced by the decorative arts in the decades around 1900, all of it, ultimately, a repercussion of Arts and Crafts. Morrisite design and art nouveau design came to the fore when the utopian reformists in Europe's sub-imperial capitals began to make their mark in public affairs, and that also affected the promotion of national ambitions. The art nouveau panorama across Europe shows how new, progressive aesthetics provided a new channel for the expression of national distinctness.[42] In Barcelona, the buildings of the nationally committed bourgeoisie were in an exuberant new style, following the 1878 manifesto of the architect Lluís Domènech i Montaner, *En busca d'una arquitectura nacional*; that search for a national architecture would lead him to Barcelona's *fin-de-siècle modernisme* with his St Paul Hospital (1901–1930) and the landmark Palau de la Música Catalana (1908). Gaudí, too, formed part of this Catalan *modernisme*, although he moved in a very idiosyncratic direction – from the Sagrada Família (started in 1882/1883) to Park Güell (1914), Casa Batlló (1906) and Casa Milà (1910).

In Prague, Mucha designed symbol-heavy tile tableaux in the style of his Parisian advertisement posters; a tile tableau embellished the front of the headquarters of Hlahol, the nationally minded Czech choral movement; Mucha designed posters for the athletic festivals of the Sokol sports clubs (see Figure 10.9) and, later, Czech currency and banknotes.

In Budapest, the Turanian-minded József Huszka advocated the nationalization of Hungarian architecture in his manifesto *Past and Present of our National Architecture* by means of Persian and Central Asian stylistic 'quotations'; this dominated Ödön Lechner's Museum of Applied Arts (1892–1896) and the Postal Savings Bank (1899–1901); the invocation of 'Turanian' formal elements is still obvious in the much more recent Yurt-shaped Millennium Church of Csikszereda/Miercurea-Ciuc, a Romanian town with a Székler-Hungarian majority population (Figure 6.2).

In Riga, to conclude our *tour d'horizon*, a 'Nordic style' was adopted and reached its peak between 1905 and 1910. This style had spread throughout Finland in the late nineteenth century and gained popularity, not only in the other Scandinavian countries but also in the Baltic region.

Traditionalist in form and functional in application, it took inspiration from local nature, the nation's ancient history, folk culture and mythology. As such, it was itself close to the German 'homeland traditional style', *Heimatschutzstil.* Latvian architects sought to manifest their specific national inflection by introducing stylized folk-art motifs, both on facades and in interiors.

The moral of this whirlwind tour of turn-of-the-century-Europe is not meant to say 'Look! This, too, was all nationalistic'. I bring these diverse and heterogeneous pointers together to show how adaptable the repertoire of nationalism was: how the expression of a cultural sense of national distinctness could evolve from the neo-Gothic historicism of early Romanticism to a much modern cultural climate, progressive and emancipationist, anti-imperial and even international in its sense of a Europe-wide avant-garde.

The practice of drawing on folk design and on local traditions, on past and peasants, was not necessarily an exercise in hidebound nostalgia. It could be used as an element of modernity itself, as a liberating force (as it was in the music of Bartók and De Falla) to prompt the exploration of fresh, unconventional sources of inspiration. Even in the modern, forward-looking cultural climate of the pre-1914 decades, with its utopian reformers and artistic innovators, there was still room for that celebration of the nation (defined in its language, history and cultural character) as an inspiring ideal for artistic expression which is part of our definition of nationalism as given in the Introduction to this book. To what extent this facilitated an instrumentalization of that expression in political consciousness-raising (as per the second half of our definition) varied from case to case; it was a possibility, but not an inevitability. But everywhere in Europe's imperial peripheries, the nation could, as it was doing in Dublin, self-distinguish against hegemonic empire in two modes: either by taking recourse inwards to its nativist heritage or by turning outwards in a cosmopolitan ambition.

CHAPTER 11

Culture Mobilized

> Nothing appears more surprising to those who consider human affairs with a philosophical eye, than the easiness with which the many are governed by the few; and the implicit submission, with which men resign their own sentiments and passions to those of their rulers. When we enquire by what means this wonder is effected, we shall find, that, as force is always on the side of the governed, the governors have nothing to support them but opinion. It is therefore on opinion only that government is founded; and this maxim extends to the most despotic and most military governments, as well as to the most free and most popular.
>
> David Hume, 'Of the First Principles of Government', 1742

Public Opinion, Public Rancour

Inter arma silent musae ... well, not quite. The Muses in nineteenth-century Europe did not fall silent amidst warfare: on the contrary, they raised their voices to lend moral support to the fatherland. In returning to the rousing songs and films that we noted in Chapter 1 of this book, we also return to the main geological fault-line in the political landscape of Western Europe: the competing German and French claims on the Rhine – either as a French natural frontier or as a German national artery.

German–French wars since the 1790s have always spawned battle songs, foremost among them 'La Marseillaise' and 'Die Wacht am Rhein'; and we have seen how cultural geopolitics post-Waterloo put Alsace-Lorraine and the Low Countries high on the agenda of intellectuals such as Arndt. Throughout the nineteenth century there is a steady trickle of Romantics cheering on their national causes (Liszt and his sabre) or even intervening proactively in their political activities: Shelley distributing seditious pamphlets from a Dublin lodging-house, Byron joining the Greek War of Independence, Wergeland in Norway and Petőfi in Hungary staging national declamations in public. These poetic interventions, and more specifically their embodied proclamation in the form of songs and anthems, fed into a force that became increasingly powerful in the course of the century: public opinion. The hapless Napoleon III after his defeat stated that it was public opinion that had made the 1870 war inevitable, and this is supported not only by the opening pages of Zola's searing novelistic account *Le Débâcle* (1892; Zola wrote about the Parisian run-up from personal experience) but also by the memoirs of various public figures. General François-Charles du Barail, for instance, in listing the many anti-Prussian parties that lured France into a hasty declaration of war, finishes his list with 'the extreme right-wing chauvinists, who hoped that the war would restore authoritarian rule' and, finally,

> the people in the streets: the workers shouting 'On to Berlin!'; the patrons of brasseries and elegant cafés breaking their glasses of beer or liqueur over the heads of those unfortunates who had the temerity of speaking up for peace; the theatres full of crowds singing the Marseillaise and also shouting 'On to Berlin!'; the ignorant and the learned, from the streetcorner porter to [the journalist] Emile Girardin, laying wagers as to the date when we would march into Berlin.[1]

The mention of 'La Marseillaise' need not surprise us. On the German side, it was this war that lifted the older 'Wacht am Rhein', composed in 1840, to the status of a nationwide battle anthem.[2] The battle songs of earlier conflicts were reprised, as they were to be reprised in their turn during the World Wars of the next century. (We have seen how choirs in the 1860s had already intoned their readiness to do battle over the Rhine). That alone should alert us that the culture of warfare is not an ad hoc accompaniment to the events of the day; it is a constantly available repertoire for the events of the day to dip into should the occasion so require. The successive cross-Rhenian confrontations between Germany and France amply illustrate the formation and persistence of that repertoire, latently quiescent during the intervals of peace, saliently prominent during the succeeding crisis moments – in 1792, in 1813–1814, in 1840, in 1870, in 1914, in 1939–1940. It is, in fact, the persistent availability of that repertoire and that accumulating sedimentation of memory, as much as the long-term foreign policy aims of states, that connects those crises into an echo-chamber of hereditary hostility. The older texts were recalled and amplified at each new occasion, and fresh ones were added to them.[3]

The crushing Prussian victory was compounded by the terrible events around the Parisian Commune, which ripped *fraternité* up into fratricide. The Third Republic drank to the dregs the bitter potion of defeat and, as Wolfgang Schivelbusch has shown in his *Culture of Defeat*, carried a destabilized and dysfunctional public opinion into the fin-de-siècle. Its grievance politics would include various strands of Bourbon, Orléans and Bonapartist restorationism, reactionary ultramontanism (the National Pledge campaign, culminating in the building of the Sacré-Coeur on Montmartre*), paranoid anti-Semitism (the grinding, endless Dreyfus affair) and the seeds of a rancorous nationalism. The word 'nationalism' was coined by the journalist Maurice Barrès (in the writings collected in his *Scènes et doctrines du nationalisme*, 1902); as a political programme, Barrès-style nationalism organized itself into a Ligue de la patrie française that spawned, in 1899, the proto-Fascist *Action française* journal and movement.[4]

Victorious Prussia, for its part, realized that it was now facing a deeply embittered, vengeful neighbour. Peace terms were imposed that aimed to thwart the vanquished foe in future war efforts. 'Reparation' payments were imposed that recalled those imposed by Napoleon on vanquished Prussia in 1810 and that would in turn be remembered when heavy burdens were laid on Germany after 1918. In a back-and-forth of victories and defeats between France and Germany since 1815, the successive iterations of Schivelbusch's *Culture of Defeat* may well be seen as a repeated 'tit-for-tat culture' – witness also the annexations and reannexations of Alsace and Lorraine. In 1871 Alsace and Lorraine were annexed in large part to make sure that future French attacks would have a more distantly removed base of operations than Strasbourg.** Emperor Wilhem I in a letter to Empress Eugénie ruefully acknowledged the likelihood of another, future war, and continued: 'This sad consideration, and not the desire to enlarge my fatherland (whose territory is sufficient in size), forces us to insist upon territorial transfers which are only intended to push back the starting base of such French armies as will want to attack us in the future.'[5] This is in line with the habit among bellicose states to present attack and annexation as a forms of self-defence; but in any case this military geopolitical pragmatism was not how the transfer was sold to the public at

* The site of the construction, Montmartre, had been the heartland of the Commune. The National Pledge emerged among Catholics who considered the defeat of 1871 a divine punishment for the fact that Napoleon III had reneged on his protection of the Papal States. See Rodriguez 1998, Benoist 1992.

** In the event, such measures seem to have inflamed rather than incapacitated the vanquished party: the reparation payments imposed on France were defiantly paid off ahead of schedule and constituted an outstanding debt, called in, together with Alsace and Lorraine, in 1918. In view of Wilhelm I's premonition of wars begetting future wars, it is poignant to see the Great War represented as a 'war to end all wars'; certainly in the light of what the payments imposed on Weimar Germany did to drive its rancorous voters towards Hitler's counter-*revanchisme*.

large. The justification before the court of public opinion was cultural and historicist, in the very same terms that had been used by Arndt: Alsace and Lorraine, it was asserted, culturally belonged to Germany, had seen their political ties with Germany severed by unnatural force, and were now harmoniously reunited with their true fatherland. The Prussian historian Treitschke repeated Arndt's pamphlet 'The Rhine, Germany's River, Not Germany's Border' of 1814 practically verbatim, adding that he had, in fact, very little to add to the masterful arguments that Arndt had put forward half a century previously.

> Were I to marshal the reasons which make it our duty to demand this, I should feel as if the task had been set me to prove that the world is round. What can be said on the subject, was said after the battle of Leipzig, in Ernst Moritz Arndt's glorious tract, 'The Rhine the German river, not the German boundary'; said exhaustively, and beyond contradiction, at the time of the Second Peace of Paris [1815], by all the considerable statesmen of non-Austrian Germany – by Stein and Humboldt, by Münster and Gagern, by the two Crown Princes of Wurtemberg and Bavaria; and confirmed, since that time, by the experience of two generations.[6]

Treitschke's arguments were aimed both at a domestic audience and an international one; his 'What Do We Demand of France?' appeared in 1870 in the *Preussische Jahrbücher* and also as a brochure, and an English translation appeared in London that same year. Another direction was taken by the revered classical historian Theodor Mommsen. He addressed a series of open letters to Italian periodicals, also published in brochure form as *Agli italiani*. Mommsen argued that, much as the Italians had in their Risorgimento lawfully annexed Milan and Venice (and he injected also some anticlerical notes by reminding the Italians how the Papal States had long been kept out of Italy by French interference), so too the Germans were justified in rounding off their unification movement by the incorporation of Alsace and Lorraine.

What was new here was that the justification for the nation was now delivered not in exhortatory poems but in discursive prose; not by poets but by history professors. The intellectual professions were now finding a new role as national apologists; the heyday of the 'political professor' had arrived. After 1918, this 'intellectual nationalism' (Martha Hanna's phrase) would be bitterly denounced by Julien Benda in his *Le trahison des clercs* (1927).[7] But knowledge production and the sphere of intellectual pursuits had never been quite aloof or separate from a commitment to the nation; it merely found a new field of application in the developing medium of war propaganda.

Political Professors: Fichte to Fustel

Treitschke's overt recall of Arndt is significant: the anti-Napoleonic Wars of Liberation (*Befreiungskriege*) of 1813 were remembered as a glorious alliance between military and cultural mobilization, with Arndt, Schleiermacher, Görres and others celebrated as the intellectuals who had prepared the people and the Prussian state for insurgency. Here lay the prototypes of the 'political professors' of the generation of Treitschke and Felix Dahn. Foremost among them was Johann Gottlieb Fichte, he of the *Reden an die Deutsche Nation*. He had enlisted when in 1813 anti-Napoleonic citizen militias were mobilized. The figure he cuts as a fifty-one-year-old, martially brandishing a sabre and carrying holstered pistols in a belt around his portly girth, is not altogether impressive (Figure 11.1); learning and armed combat are, as we can see here, two very different callings. That they converged in the 1813 moment had proved highly memorable.

When, after the Napoleonic wars, academics wanted to prove their usefulness to the fatherland they usually did so as 'brains' rather than 'muscle', and mostly in peacetime deliberations on domestic policy rather than under the direct shadow of actual action in the field. The mobilization of Treitschke and Mommsen manifested the type of public–political leverage that Grimm and the *Germanisten* had tried to obtain in the 1840s; and it shows how a new type of professor had come to wield considerable influence as public intellectuals. A class of 'German mandarins' has even been defined as such by Fritz Ringer in a landmark study.[8]

France responded in kind. If Germany had the *Preussische Jahrbücher*, France by now had the *Revue des Deux Mondes*. Such opinion-making periodicals, independent but semi-official and addressing educated readers, were among the important new platforms of the period. Ernest Renan from the beginning countered German triumphalism by warning them sternly that hubris comes before a fall; Schivelbusch rightly read that as a somewhat pedantic one-upmanship on the part of defeated enemies, part of the see-sawing alternation of boastful victors and peeved losers.[9] Something altogether new and more important crystallized when an academic refugee from Strasbourg arrived in Paris to take the floor: Numa Fustel de Coulanges. Breton by birth and Parisian *normalien* by education, he had taught archaeology and ancient history in the Alsatian capital but left the city and its university when it was annexed into Germany. In Paris he would find employ at his École normale supérieure and ultimately at the Sorbonne, and he would become an inspiring voice from that position. It was Numa Fustel de Coulanges who first tackled the German

Figure 11.1 The philosopher Johann Gottlieb Fichte on parade as a member of the Prussian Landwehr (1862 engraving after Carl Zimmermann, 1813). ERNiE imagebank

justification for the annexation of Alsace and Strasbourg. In his *L'Alsace est-elle allemande ou française? Réponse à M. Mommsen* (1870) he developed what later became such a powerful line of reasoning in Renan's *Qu'est-ce qu'une nation?* (1883): that in deciding the question of national belonging, what should weigh most heavily was the self-identification of the people concerned. Fustel's riposte to Mommsen has been overshadowed by Renan's more famous, indeed classic tract; but it is worth zooming in on because it states things more crisply than Renan and illustrates a telling conjunction of intellectual and political trends.

Fustel was a close colleague of Mommsen. Both had done path-breaking work in the study of Roman institutions (Mommsen's *Römische Geschichte*, 1854–1856; Fustel's *La Cité antique*, 1864). In the course of his own work on ancient history, Fustel had become convinced of two things. One was that the Roman conquest of Gaul had laid the preconditions for the French state by imposing an institutionalized governance on what had been an assemblage of different tribes. In this view, he followed Romantic historians such as Thierry and Michelet. Where he differed from those Romantic forerunners, however, was in his view of the subsequent Frankish conquest of Latinized Gaul. In his view, this had been a matter of gradual infiltration rather than a 'conquest' properly speaking. This neatly subverted the Romantic two-nations view, according to which the conquering Franks had been the ancestors of the nobility, ruling the country by right of conquest; whereas the subjected Gallo-Romans were the ancestors of the Third Estate. In that view, the French Revolution had been the long-awaited reassertion of popular Gaulish rights against the conquering Frankish aristocracy. The two-nations view was certainly appealing; it could draw on eighteenth-century roots, even on a turn of phrase in Sieyès's *What is the Third Estate?*; it had an analogue in the Saxons-and-Normans polarity in English history writing, as propounded in Walter Scott's wildly popular *Ivanhoe*; and it had inspired, in the course of the century, many a popularizing history account by the likes of the historian Henri Martin, and the novelists Alexandre Dumas (*Francs et gaulois*) and Eugène Sue (*Les Mystères du peuple*). But Fustel himself drew from his historical studies a different conclusion, and in the process came to reject the entire ethnohistorical paradigm of *Völkergeschichte*, whereby modern societies were seen as the outflow of the patterns established in ancient tribal warfare.[10]

It must have been particularly irksome to Fustel that this ethnohistorical argument, which he had been at pains to purge from his historical analysis, was precisely the justification that was invoked by the likes of Treitschke and Mommsen, with Treitschke even falling back, overtly, on old Arndt. That was the background to Fustel's feisty rebuttal of Mommsen's *Agli Italiani*. Is Alsace, he asks, German or French?[11]

> Prussia thinks that it can resolve that question by might; but Prussia is not satisfied by force alone, and would like to add Right to that. Thus, while your armies invaded Alsace and bombarded Strasbourg you tried to prove that it was your Right to do so .... Alsace, you assert, is a German region and therefore must belong to Germany. It used to once, and you conclude that it must therefore be given back to you. German is spoken there and you infer that this gives Prussia the right to annex it. ... This you call the nationality principle.

Fustel explodes this in successive stages. He begins by exposing the invocation of the 'nationality principle' as a mere pretext for raw power politics.

> As you see it, that principle would authorize a powerful state to appropriate a province by force because it is inhabited by the same race. Most of Europe, more commonsensically, would understand that principle as authorizing a region or a population to reject the rule of a foreign hegemon. … It may bestow certain rights on Alsace itself, but none on you to overrule it. In invoking that principle regarding Schleswig and Alsace … Prussia is misapplying it. It is a right for the subaltern, not a pretext for expansionism; the nationality principle is not a new way of saying that Might makes Right.

The further argument then sets out to demonstrate that the Fichtean nationality markers of language and descent ('race') are futile.

> If the nationality principle means that Alsace has the right not to be ruled by foreigners, then the question becomes: who is the foreigner here, France or Germany? You assert, Sir, that Alsace is of German nationality. Are you sure about that? … How do you recognize a nationality, a fatherland? You think you have proved the German nationality of Alsace because the population is German by language and race. But it baffles me that a historian like yourself chooses to overlook the fact that neither language nor race makes a nation.

Fustel's demonstration boils down to the points that ethnically similar populations have founded different states, and that states can gather into a shared nationality linguistically mixed populations of diverse (and usually mixed) ethnic descent. This line of reasoning has become familiar: Renan (1883) argued along similar lines in *Qu'est-ce qu'une nation?* But for Fustel in 1870, this is a hard-won fresh insight based on his historical and archaeological work and on his own rejection of the French two-nations model.

From there, like Renan after him, he goes on to locate the true bedrock of national identity, emically, in the nation's act of self-identification.

> Nations are distinguished neither by race nor by language. People feel in their hearts that they belong together once they share ideas, interests, emotions, memories and hopes. That is what constitutes a fatherland. That is why people wish to walk, work, fight together, live and die for each other. A fatherland is what you love. It may be that Alsace is German by race and language, but by nationality and in its sense of fatherland it is French. And do you know what made it French? It was not the conquest by Louis XIV, but our revolution of 1789.

To bolster this case, Fustel asserts that the feelings of the Alsatians are, in fact, pro-French and anti-German, and that the civic legacy of the

French Revolution has left more vivid and important traces in the present than the ancient roots of language and ethnicity. Fustel contradicts German assertions as to the German-mindedness of the population. He states that he himself never experienced anything like the purported reservations against Parisians ('I pride myself on knowing how kindly Alsace receives them') and instead offers numerous examples of the stubborn resistance of the local population to the invading German armies ('they spoke your language, but they did not consider themselves your compatriots'). All this follows to some extent the yea–nay patterns of wartime propaganda – Grimm in 1814 had argued that the Alsatians had remained German-minded despite generations of French rule,[12] and now Fustel argues the opposite. What is the historian to make of it? In asserting the French-mindedness of Alsace, Fustel was to some extent invoking existing French attitudes: as expressed, for example, in the Alsatian-propagandistic *romans nationaux* of the popular novelistic duo Erckmann/Chatrian and the emerging vogue for *brasseries alsaciennes* on the Parisian boulevards.[13] But his assertion of a deep-seated anti-German feeling among the Alsatian population is more believable: the Germans themselves developed an almost phobic mistrust of the figure of the *franc-tireur*, the armed civilian who behind the lines snipes at German troops. For Germans, this was a sign of Gallic treacherousness, and their fear of it was such that in Belgium in 1914 mass executions were carried out among the civilian population on the basis of rumoured *franc-tireur* activities.[14] That phobia cannot have grown out of an open-armed welcome by fraternal fellow Germans in 1870–1871.

Be all that as it may, the most important point is reached when Fustel fundamentally denies that deep historicism as such, *Völkergeschichte*-style, can have any use whatsoever when discussing contemporary issues.

> For Alsace, the fatherland is France, and Germany is foreign. None of your lucubrations will change that. You may invoke ethnography and philology, if you will, but we are not in a university lecture-hall here. … So let us speak no more of nationality and above all stop saying to the Italians that 'Strasbourg belongs to us the way Milan and Venice belong to you'; for the Italians might reply that they never bombarded either Milan or Venice. … You, Sir, are an eminent historian. But when we discuss current affairs, let us not get fixated on history. … History may tell you that Alsace is a German land; but the present proves to you that it is French. It would be childish to argue that it should revert to Germany because some centuries ago it used to form part of it. Are we going to re-establish everything that once used to be? And in that case, if you please, what Europe would that be?

This is truly a new turn in the discussion of national identity. Cultural-historicist arguments, so long dominant (including within France), are now dismissed in favour of a modern, ahistorical approach: a legal one, announcing the idea of international law and the principle of self-determination.

> Let us be of our own time, rather. We have something to guide us that is better than history. We possess in this century a principle of public law which is infinitely clearer and more incontestable than your pretended nationality principle. Our principle is that a population can only be governed by institutions which it freely accepts, and that it should not belong to a state unless by its own will and free consent. ... What is all this talk of 'claims'? Strasbourg belongs to no one. Strasbourg is not an object to be possessed or rendered. Strasbourg is not ours, it is with us. We feel that Alsace should remain a French province, but take note on what basis we do so. Do we say so because it was conquered by Louis XIV? By no means. Do we say so because our defence requires it? No. ... France has only one reason for wanting to keep Alsace, and that is that Alsace has bravely demonstrated that it wished to remain with France. Bretons and Burgundians, Parisians and Marseillais, we fight you over Alsace; but let there be no mistake: we fight, not to maintain a hold over it, but we fight to prevent you from doing so.

Whatever was said, more famously, by Renan a decade later is said much more clearly and pointedly here. When Renan gave his lecture *Qu'est-ce qu'une nation?* at the Sorbonne in 1883, he pointedly avoided any mention of Alsace, Lorraine or Strasbourg, and thus also pre-empted the charge of special pleading: his stance is not that of a champion of his country against Germany but that of a dispassionate philosopher seeking to establish the truth. If Renan refers to Germans at all, it is only as the tunnel-visioned intellectual tradition that deterministically and essentialistically wants to define nationality etically (in terms of its component cultural factors); whereas he, with 'French' clear-sightedness, argues that nationality is defined emically, by how people experience their culture and their allegiance. That disinterested stance has ensured for Renan's analysis a classic status in the theory of national identity, and deservedly so. Much of what he says about the importance of memory in national collective identification (memories glorious and painful, triumphant or grievous, and even memories elided or sanitized) is still authoritative 150 years later. But for his audience, the point, though unstated, was lost on no one, and if Renan called national identity an 'everyday plebiscite' (i.e. an ongoing collective commitment), the challenge to the Germanization imposed from above on Alsace and Lorraine was obvious. And here, again, Renan had the intertext of Fustel's earlier arguments to rely on.

What Renan does in *Qu'est-ce qu'une nation?* is to transmute the political French–German antagonism over Alsace-Lorraine into a philosophical French–German incompatibility between civic voluntarism and ethnic-essentialist determinism. He presents ethnohistorical essentialism, generally and without reference to the contested Alsatian annexation, as 'the German way' of seeing national identity, while presenting democratic, self-choosing voluntarism as 'the French way'. Ever since, this perspective has burdened the debate on the shifting ethnic/civic weightedness of national identity discourse: 'ethnic' nationalism is denounced as a German-obscurantist bad-cop side of the coin as against the French-enlightenment good-cop side of 'civic' nationalism (as if Gobineau, the Dreyfus affair, Barrès's vitriolic xenophobia and the Action française somehow don't count). In the twentieth century Hans Kohn (1950, 1955), writing in the Cold War climate, aligned 'civic' nationalism with 'Western' values and 'ethnic' nationalism with Oriental despotism.* To be sure, German intellectuals in the century after Arndt did themselves no favours by following a *völkisch* sliding scale that led from Felix Dahn to Houston Stewart Chamberlain of unhallowed memory. A discourse continued to hold sway that had been forged when Arndt and his generation repudiated the overpowering might of Napoleonic tyranny; but that discourse was now quite out of date, overtaken by Bismarck's victoriously aggressive expansionist wars of the period 1864–1871. Even in the triumphant, overpoweringly mighty new Reich, its international position continued to be viewed in the ingrained terms of the 1813 moment and through the defensive lens of Arndt's anti-Napoleonism.

This is not lost on Fustel. The victorious Germany of 1871 cannot claim the same position as the underdog Germany of 1813; Treitschke's recycling of Arndt is an incantation, not an analysis. That said, Fustel's rebooting of the nationality debate, shifting it from historicism to international law, is also a little self-serving. He is rather conveniently forgetful of the burden of the past and of the fact that France itself had pursued geopolitical expansionism with strong-arm tactics of the 'Might makes Right' type. Fustel may consider Louis XIV's conquest as being water under the bridge, and he never even mentions Napoleon, but that

* This surreptitiously implied moral bias (civic is 'ours' and OK, ethnic is 'theirs' and not OK) compromises the analytical civic–ethnic distinction. Some critics have overbalanced into a wholesale rejection of the ethnic–civic distinction as such. That may be going too far – after all, the 'nation' structurally defines itself somewhere on a sliding scale between demos and ethnos, political solidarity and cultural familiarity; and its position relative to those two poles is by no means unimportant. See Chapter 12.

was easier for him as a Frenchman than for the Germans remembering the devastations of those wars of conquest. The picturesque ruins dominating the Romantic imagery of the Rhine valley had in most cases been turned into ruins by Louis XIV's rampaging armies. And the justification for Louis's expansionism had in fact not been so very different from that of the Prussian expansionism that Fustel denounces. Louis's marshal Vauban had aimed to consolidate the territory of France by gaining the Rhine as its natural frontier in the east; and that expansionism was maintained, across regime changes, by Danton, by Napoleon, by Thiers (during the 1840 Rhine Crisis). Even a young lieutenant Charles de Gaulle bought into it, if his 1915 correspondence is anything to go by. He optimistically predicted a 'decisive victory' 'which will chase the enemy out of Belgium, which will enable us, if we can muster the necessary audacity, to take their place in that country, and which will yield to us, if we can will it, our natural frontier: the Rhine.'[15] Small wonder that Germans, mindful of their history, were a little defensive about the Rhine, or that French occupation policies in the post-1919 Rhineland touched a raw nerve in Germany.[16] *Il y avait de quoi.*

It makes perfect sense to abandon the stranglehold of historicism in favour of a more 'modern' approach to the nationality principle; but modernity cannot abolish memories. The year 1871 itself turned into such a memory for both warring parties. In 1914, both saw the new war, as Wilhelm I had foreseen, as a rematch of the older one. One thing that had carried over from 1871 to 1914 was the anthropologization of the terms of conflict. In their 1871 defeat, French writers adopted the rancour that Germans such as Arndt had displayed under Napoleon. In no way were the French–German wars seen as state conflicts 'continuing diplomacy by different means'; they were wars between nations with incompatible attitudes and world-views. An ethnotypical opposition clicked into place, schematizing the imputed character traits of the two enemies on ruthlessly binary, incompatible terms (Figure 11.2).*

* The German–French ethnotypical characterizations of 'self' and 'other' have been extensively studied, involving the evidence of many thousands of primary texts over a long time period, by a specialism in comparative literature known as 'imagology' (Dyserinck 1988 and 2015, Beller & Leerssen 2007). These ethnotypes were used initially in dramatic and narrative texts and later also in cultural criticism, ethnography and racial anthropology (McMahon 2009). On French–German ethnotypes: Bollenbeck 2001, Fink 1993 and 2003, Florack 2000a and 2000b, François 1995, Höppel 2001, Jeismann 1992, Lüsebrink & Riesz 1984. MacMillan 2014 (chapter 9, 'What Were They Thinking?') gives an excellent analysis of the role of these 'unspoken assumptions' in the run-up to 1914.

French saw Germans as	Germans saw French as
Impolite	Immoral
Dull, stolid	Untrustworthy
Authoritarian	Vain
Priggish	Superficial
French saw themselves as	**Germans saw themselves as**
Cheerful	Sincere
Gallant	Profound
Socially outgoing	Disciplined
Witty	Reliable

Figure 11.2 French/German ethnotypes around 1914.

Readers will notice how the left-hand column opposes boorish Germans with chivalric Frenchmen. From the time of Herder and Goethe (mid eighteenth century) onwards, a prevailing rejection of aristocratic values and a turn towards middle-class virtues had led to a revalorization of those ethnotypes, as per the right-hand column: French aristocrats were now deprecated, while the land of Kant, Goethe and Beethoven was admired.

In the vertical (top vs. bottom) alignment of these characterizations, the respective self-images (bottom pair) pan out as temperamental opposites. Aligned diagonally, we recognize the positive or negative valorizations of similar behavioural characteristics. What Germans considered, in themselves, as their characteristic sincerity, profundity, sense of discipline and integrity would in a French discourse be represented as signs of boorishness, dullness and an authoritarian and pedantic streak.

We can trace this in the shifting stock figure of the 'German Professor'. Until 1870 he is an eccentric, an object of affectionate irony: the Bible-translating Professor Wittembach in Mérimée's story 'Lokis'; or the Hamburgian Professor Lidenbrock in Jules Verne's *Journey to the Centre of the Earth* (1864). After 1870 he becomes the insufferable Professor Knatschke (Figure 11.3: a caricature created by the artist known as 'Hansi', Jean-Jacques Waltz) throwing his weight around in the annexed Alsace; or the murderous genocidal industrialist Dr Schulze, designer of the cannon-producing 'Stahlstadt' in Jules Verne's *The Begum's Fortune* (1879); Doktor Schulze's evil plans are thwarted by the idealistic French hero Sarrasin and his Alsatian (!) assistant.[17]

Similarly, what Germans denounced in the French as their immorality, untrustworthiness, vanity and superficiality would be seen by the French

Figure 11.3 The pedantic Professor Knatschke as drawn by 'Hansi' (1912). Wikimedia Commons

themselves as their light-heartedness, polite manners, awareness of social appearances and clear-sightedness. It is obvious that these traits aligned thus create polar opposites between the two nations' respective temperaments. They were adroitly and venomously summarized by Ernest Renan when he gave his acceptance speech on becoming a member of the Académie française in 1878. No, he argued, France was not beaten down. Morally, France was still the superior nation it had always been, a beacon of civility that the self-proclaimed victors, still wallowing in their uncouth boorishness, could not hold a candle to. This is how he addressed his fellow *académiciens*:

> You, like me, will mistrust a *Kultur* which fails to make people kinder or better. Nations which to be sure are very serious (for they reproach us our levity) are mistaken if they think that this will ingratiate them to the world. … Pedantic self-obsessed learning, a literature without cheer, a glum political life, an elite without glamour, an aristocracy without wit, a bourgeoisie without politeness: all that will not dispel the memory of

> our traditional French social life, with its glittering brilliance, so courteous, so eager to please. Only when a nation, by means of what it calls its seriousness and its thoroughness, has achieved what we have achieved by means of our frivolousness – better writers than Pascal or Voltaire, more charming women than those who smiled upon our philosophy, an enthusiasm more striking than that of our Revolution, more graceful manners and a more gracious life-style – only when it has become, in short, a more pleasant and spiritual society than that of our ancestors – only then shall we have been vanquished.[18]

I have here translated Renan's *culture* with its German analogue. *Kultur* was becoming a key element in the German self-image as it opposed itself to France. The French had *civilisation*, which implied polite manners and an elegant, harmonious conformity of public standards, but which was also seen as something snobbish and superficial; to this was opposed the German idea of a more profound, deep-rooted *Kultur*, something inherited and naturally spontaneous rather than educationally or socially imposed – witness Fichte's and Grimm's link between love of the fatherland and deep affects such as filial piety, parental solicitude and homesickness from abroad. *Kultur* and *civilisation* became antithetical proxies to capture the incompatibility between the French and German national characters. A similar antithetical homology was that between *Geist* and *esprit*: the German word connoting earnest soulfulness, the other nimble wit.[19] Thomas Mann invoked precisely this discourse in his wartime writings (Chapter 1).

Such ethnotypes had, over the preceding century, slowly become common currency in the world of learning; a *Zeitschrift für Völkerpsychologie und Sprachwissenschaft* had been established in 1860, and since the 1820s anthropologists and ethnographers had come to rely increasingly firmly on the principle of 'national characters'.[20] National stereotyping suffused the oppositional discourse of the decades between 1871 and 1914, when essentialist ethnotypes flourished as never before or since, almost abolishing the distinction between nation and race. They carried with them all the authority of the academics who endorsed them. Much of that discourse was debunked or dismissed in the course of the twentieth century; national clichés are now used more sparingly and back-handedly, often jocularly. But when wielded in earnest, ethnic cliché was best backed up by authors' scholarly or intellectual prestige; and this in turn reinforced the importance of public intellectuals as authorities in the public debates about international frictions and conflicts.

These public intellectuals came out in full force in 1914.

Kultur, War, Propaganda

Wars were increasingly fought before the court of public opinion. The advent of photography and journalism on the battlefields of the Crimean War and the American Civil War had rendered the home front aware of its conduct, as Tennyson's 'Charge of the Light Brigade' (1854) also testifies, and as is indicated by the careers of Florence Nightingale (who rose to fame among the Crimean wounded) and Henri Dunant (who conceived of the Red Cross on the battlefield of Solferino, 1859). Atrocities against civilians, now reported in large-circulation media, became a matter of public outrage; the philhellenic denunciation of the Ottoman-inflicted Massacre of Chios (1822) had been an early sign. The murderous repression of an anti-Ottoman revolt in Bulgaria in 1876 was widely reported and became notorious as the 'Bulgarian horrors'; it led Gladstone to denounce the cruel Turks in ethnotypical terms as congenitally disposed to ruthless sadism and unfit for imperial rule. As a direct result, the Ottoman Empire was ordered to grant self-rule to the Bulgarian exarchate by the western powers at the Conference of Constantinople (1876); this was subsequently enforced by the treaty of San Stefano (which concluded the Russo-Turkish War of 1877–1878).

In these decades, people sought to control the horrors of modern warfare as these became noticeable to the general public. The first Geneva Convention (1864) was to be followed by additional ones in 1907, 1929 and 1947. In the drafting of such conventions, legal scholars found a new application for their expertise. Drawing on earlier texts such as Schmalz's *Europäisches Völkerrecht* (1816), Klüber's *Droit des gens moderne* (1819) and Bluntschli's *Das moderne Völkerrecht* (1868), international law rose to prominence in the post-1871 decades, trying to control Might with Right. In time, legal opinion crystallized into institutions. Frédéric Passy's Ligue permanente et internationale de la paix of 1868 was transformed into a Société française pour l'arbitrage entre nations in 1889. It set up a permanent court of arbitration in The Hague and further buttressed its mission by establishing a first Hague convention in the same year, followed in 1907 by a second one. At that second conference, one influential presence was that of the Institut de droit international, founded in 1873, partly in response to Germany's high-handed annexation of Alsace-Lorraine.[21]

Thus as Europe drifted towards the abyss of 1914, there was at the same time a growing internationalism aimed at preventing war, or at least its worst excesses, and regulating international affairs. It profited from wealthy donors such as Andrew Carnegie (who footed the bill for the

Peace Palace in The Hague, 1907–1913) and Alfred Nobel, who instituted his Peace Prize in 1901. Its first recipients in that year were Henri Dunant and Frédéric Passy, founders of the Red Cross and the arbitration court; in 1904 the Nobel Peace Prize went to the Institut de droit international. An associate of these pacifist individuals and institutions, the activist Bertha von Suttner, won the Nobel Peace Prize in 1905, largely on the strength of her novel *Die Waffen nieder!*

This budding pacifist internationalism formed part of the utopian–reformist climate that we have encountered as the enabling ambience for the spreading the Arts and Crafts movement (Chapter 10). That climate itself should be recalled to understand the shock that was caused by the outbreak of the 1914 war and especially by the fate of neutral Belgium. Yes, the war may have been greeted by fervently patriotic crowds on the streets of the European capitals, each singing their respective national anthems; but what soon came into view was the conduct of the German troops on their way towards Paris, torching the city of Visé and the Louvain university library and executing Belgian citizens in their hundreds. Tellingly, the wholesale executions of Serbian villagers by Austrian troops attracted comparatively little notice.[22] Even though the war had been sparked off in Sarajevo and its conduct in the Balkans was especially murderous, all eyes were on Germany and Belgium. That in itself indicated the importance of publicity and the effectiveness of the aspersions that had been cast upon the German character by French *revanchistes* in the preceding decades. The discourse of propagandistic denunciation had been prepared ever since 1871 and was primed for deployment. How could Germany pride itself on anything like *Kultur* if it violated Belgian neutrality, of which it was itself one of the international guarantors, and behaved as barbarously as it did towards the civilian population?*

Initial reports, bad as they were, were gruesomely exaggerated as they echoed around the outraged media. This was the case on both sides: German justified their retaliatory executions by referring to the sadistic treacherousness of the duplicitous Belgians, women and children not excepted; but setting a medieval university library on fire was definitely not the way to win hearts and minds.

* The first neutral polity to fall victim to the German offensive of August 1914 was not, in fact, Belgium. In crossing the border at Gemmenich, near Aachen, German troops passed through the tiny, undefended, neutral condominium of Moresnet, a mini-statelet left under undivided German–Belgian rule because of its zinc mines. Moresnet locals had attempted to turn this neutral status to profit by printing their own postage stamps, establishing a spa/casino, and eventually opting to become the first officially Esperanto-speaking state of Europe, Amikejo or 'Friendship-land'. This inoffensive instance of utopian internationalism was the first butterfly broken on the wheel of the Great War.

In fact, this war had three fronts: east, west and international public opinion. Germany lost the battle on the third front early on in the war, even though its public intellectuals came to the fore in great numbers. This is how the troops were disposed. Within Germany, there were public lectures and public statements by reputable academics such as Rudolf Eucken, Ernst Haeckel, Friedrich Meinecke, Werner Sombart and Ernst Troeltsch; their lectures came out in collections entitled *Deutsche Reden in schwerer Zeit.*[23] Similarly in France, the Quai d'Orsay (the ministry for foreign affairs) banded leading intellectuals into a committee, led by the highly regarded and fervently nationalist historian Ernest Lavisse, with the aim of directing public opinion through their publications. The Comité Lavisse included Emile Durkheim, Joseph Bédier, Henri Bergson, Ernest Denis and Gustave Lanson. In Britain, a new institution was created, the War Propaganda Bureau; it brought together leading authors to advocate for the British cause in writing.[24]

In most cases, the discourse generated in the war years was largely concerned with the assertion of the rightfulness of the country's war aims,* defensive as they were of course, and the denunciation of the enemy's pernicious, long-plotted aggression and their soldiers' savagery. Cases in point (all from 1915) are the collection *Qui a voulu la guerre?* by Emile Durkheim and Ernest Denis (documents gathered from diplomatic and official sources), Joseph Bédier's *Les crimes allemandes d'après les témoignages allemands* (edited from the field diaries of captured or killed German soldiers), and the notorious *Bryce Report on Alleged German Outrages*, compiled for the British War Propaganda Bureau. These texts were published both for domestic consumption and, on neutral ground

* Governments sought to vindicate their own behaviour in official diplomatic statements and source collections that have become known under colour-coded titles, after the British usage of 'white papers' and 'blue books'. These were, needless to say, self-serving to the point of mendacity. Germany made its case first (early August) in *Das Deutsche Weißbuch über den Ausbruch des deutsch-russisch-französichen Krieges*, which drew responses from Britain (Blue Book, 5 August), Russia (Orange Book, September) and, in late November or early December, France (Martel 2017). France's *Livre jaune* contains one crucial misrepresentation as to the timing of German mobilization orders (before or after the Russian ones? – see Becker 2012 and more generally Becker 1977; but cf. also MacMillan 2014, 565–567, for the tangled timeline of partial and full mobilizations and counter-mobilizations in the last week of July 1914). Among diplomatic historians, that question has become a bit like a 'Cleopatra's nose' issue, partly because it formed part of the harsh guilt assignment laid at Germany's door in the Treaty of Versailles. In public opinion during the early war years, this issue, while by no means ignored, seems to have been wholly overshadowed by other concerns – the breach of Belgian neutrality, the question as to whether the German attack had not required long-premeditated preparation, and the conduct of the German army. In Durkheim's and Denis's *Qui a voulu la guerre?* (1915), the mobilization issue rates only an endnote on the very final page.

such as in the *New York Times*, with the aim of swaying the sympathies of the United States. Bédier's book was published in 400,000 copies, and 25,000 copies in English translation were shipped to the US.

German self-justification before the court of international public opinion started immediately after the invason of Belgium with a declaration by Wilhelm II, which, characteristically overstated and grandstanding, demonstrated not Germany's righteousness but its emperor's self-righteousness.

> Since the foundation of the Reich forty-three years ago, my ancestors and I have done our utmost to preserve peace in the world and in that peace to forcefully promote our development. But there are enemies who begrudge us the fruit of our labour.
>
> We have borne all the open and secret enmity coming from the east, from the west, and from across the sea, aware as we were of our responsibilities and our force. But now we are to be humiliated. We are expected to stand by passively as we watch our foes arm themselves for a treacherous attack, and we are denied the right to support, in steadfast fidelity, our ally [Austria] in its struggle to maintain its position as a major power, and whose humiliation would also destroy our power and our honour.
>
> So let the sword decide. In the midst of peace our foes have assaulted us. To arms, then! Any delay or dithering would be a betrayal of the fatherland.
>
> What is at stake is the existence or annihilation of the Reich that our fathers re-established; the existence or annihilation of German power and the German identity.
>
> We will defend ourselves to the last breath of man and horse. And we will win this struggle, even against a world of foes. Never yet was Germany vanquished if it stood united.[25]

One month later, in September 1914, as the conduct of the German army had provoked widespread outrage, ninety-three prominent German professors and public intellectuals issued an 'Appeal to the Civilized World' (*Aufruf an die Kulturwelt*). Consisting of six brief paragraphs, each containing a single assertion, it followed the lapidary style of the theses that Martin Luther had nailed to the Wittenberg church doors in 1517; but this erudite subtlety may have been lost on readers abroad. The statement declares that 'the undersigned representatives of German learning and culture denounce to the civilized world the slanderous lies with which Germany's enemies have tried to tarnish its just cause in the grievous existential struggle with had been forced upon it'. Then follow the six denials, each paragraph beginning with the large-printed words *Es ist nicht wahr, daß ....* ('It is untrue that ....'). In conclusion, the civilized world (*Kulturwelt*) is once again addressed:

> We cannot defuse our enemies' poisonous mendacious weaponry; we can only proclaim to the world that they bear false witness against us. To you who know us, you who have until now been guardians, together with us, of the most cherished inheritance of humankind, to you we call out: Believe us! Believe, that we will fight this battle to the end as a civilized nation [*Kulturvolk*], which holds the inheritance of Goethe, Beethoven and Kant as sacred as its hearth and home. To this we sign our names and our honour![26]

Many of the signatories are authoritative indeed: eminent writers and artists, prominent scholars from all academic disciplines, including a good few Nobel Prize laureates. Notwithstanding, the overall effect was a tone-deaf rhetorical failure, reminiscent more of Professor Knatschke than of Luther:

> *It is untrue* that our conduct of the war disregards international law … But in the East, the earth is soaked by the blood of women and children butchered by Russian hordes … The claim to defend European civilization is unbecoming for those who have allied themselves with Russians and Serbians and who offer the world the degrading spectacle of turning Mongolians and Negroes loose on the white race.

As Martha Hanna (p. 80) put it, 'the Manifesto of 93 soon became the most vilified document to come out of Germany in the early war'. A rebuttal by French and British intellectuals soon followed, again marked by recrimination, self-righteousness and prestigious signatories. The names on both documents included the luminaries of the day: on the German side Rudolf Eucken, Ernst Haeckel, Karl Lamprecht, Friedrich Naumann, Max Planck, Wilhelm Röntgen, Wilhelm Windelband and Wilhelm Wundt; on the British side Thomas Hardy, G. O. Trevelyan, Arthur Conan Doyle, Rudyard Kipling, J. M. Barrie and H. G. Wells – they had gathered in the preceding week at a conference organized by the War Propaganda Bureau. In a follow-up British statement, 117 prominent scientists and academics signed as well. And that in turn unleashed the massive *Erklärung der Hochschullehrer des Deutschen Reiches*, signed by no less than 3,000 academics. Something like an arms race: a brains race.[27]

Such altercations demonstrate how important the voice of academic scholarship had become as a prestigious support for the state's war efforts; the argument generally turned around the question how Germany could reconcile its belligerence and militarism with its self-image as the nation of *Kultur* and earnest sobriety. Outside Germany, such a notion of *Kultur* was howled down with scorn; as a German loanword in italics, with a hateful Teutonic Knatschke-K belying its Latin derivation, it became a mongrel, an oxymoron, the more so since it was constantly linked to the brutalities (real, exaggerated and imagined) of the German army against their civilian victims. The German scholars, writers, artists and Nobel laureates had hoped to raise their country's reputation by associating their prestige with its war efforts; in the event, they lowered their own prestige by the association.

In the general discourse of French war justification, we see a remarkable prominence of three alumni of the Ecole normale supérieure, Fustel de Coulanges's erstwhile workplace now headed by Ernest Lavisse. One of them, Camille Jullian, an ancient historian like Fustel, we shall encounter further on. The other two were Ernest Denis and Emile Durkheim, both members of the Comité Lavisse; they jointly authored *Qui a voulu la guerre?*, a documentation based on diplomatic and official sources aiming to demonstrate that Germany (despite its protestations that it had been unwillingly forced towards a pre-emptive strike) had been deliberately working towards a premeditated expansionist war.[28]

That 'Who started it?' debate has never quite been laid to rest. The question of Germany's aggressive or defensive war aims resurfaced in 1961 with Fritz Fischer's *Griff nach der Weltmacht*, which itself has continued to feed historiographical controversies up to and including Perry Anderson's *Disputing Disaster* (2024). Political and diplomatic historians who wish to derogate the blame laid exclusively at Germany's door in 1918 (e.g. Christopher Clark's authoritative *The Sleepwalkers*, 2014) tend to discredit evidence of German hawkishness pre-1914, as in the 1907 memorandum by the British diplomat Eyre Crowe warning against appeasement. And, archive-based as their work is, it tends to downplay the importance of published sources (e.g. the tract *Deutschland und der nächste Krieg* by general Friedrich von Bernhardi, 1912) and of press campaigns.[29] But public opinion and press campaigns were by no means inconsequential, and they should be factored into an analysis of the culture of belligerence that was rife in 1914. Public opinion, especially of the hawkish kind, was even more influential in 1914 than it had been in 1870;[30] and the years leading up to 1914 still echoed with the memories of 1871. To ignore that fact, or to argue it away, is as one-sided as to accept the propaganda at face value.

A genre of 'invasion novels' or 'future war novels' had emerged in English literature immediately after the German victory over France in 1871: in that year *The Battle of Dorking* evoked a German landing in England. Notable examples of the genre were *The Riddle of the Sands* (1903), *When William Came: A Study of London under the Hohenzollerns* (1913) and John Buchan's *The Thirty-Nine Steps* (1915). In 1897, William

Le Queux's *The Great War in England* had still imagined the invaders to be the accustomed enemies, France and Russia; but ten years later, in Le Queux's *The Invasion of 1910* (1906), the invading enemy had, as per the conventions of the genre, become Germany. That book came out in a great media blitz, serialized in the *Daily Mail* with newspaper vendors dressed up as Prussian soldiers displaying maps of their armies' progress. The book edition sold a million copies.

That was the public sounding board to Eyre Crowe's diplomatic memorandum of 1907. How intricately the media, fiction and diplomacy were linked is indicated by the fact that Le Queux's book was a fictionalized platform for the war alarmism of Field Marshal Roberts, former commander-in-Chief, whose anti-German speeches of the period appeared in 1907 as *A Nation in Arms*.[31] Indeed the novels created a veritable invasion scare in England, similar to the Napoleonic one of 1803. Matters were stoked up further by Le Queux's sequel, *Spies of the Kaiser: Plotting the Downfall of England* (1909). The resulting moral panic caused members of the public to write to Le Queux about suspected sightings; these communications were placed at the disposal of the nascent bureau of military intelligence. Indeed, one historian suggests that Le Queux himself believed in the veracity of the alarmist tales he put before the public. War propaganda thus *preceded* the outbreak of hostilities by a good few years: historical memories of 1870 (in France and Germany) and imaginative fiction (in England) primed the public for 1914.

Another point of continuity from 1871 to 1914 was the question of the Rhine and Alsace-Lorraine. Camille Jullian, like Fustel de Coulanges an archaeologist and an École normale supérieure alumnus, wrote a number of firebrand pamphlets with juicy titles such as *Pas de paix avec Hohenzollern!* But his most remarkable contribution was a veritable counterpiece to Arndt's old Rhine tract of 1813. It was called *Le Rhin gaulois* (1915) and aimed to demonstrate that since prehistoric and classical times, the population on the banks of that river had been Celtic. He relied heavily on Fustel's view of history to make that case. Yes, even after the incursions of the Germanic tribes, the new settlers adopted the Celtic attitudes of the earlier inhabitants into which they were absorbed and developed an essentially Celtic-rooted, Gaulish relationship with that river, whose Celtic character thus remained unbroken.

Jullian's efforts were amplified by a weightier study published in two volumes in 1916–1917: Ernest Babelon's *Le Rhin dans l'histoire*, which surveyed the long history from Gaulish–Germanic conflicts to French–German ones. The author was the leading numismatist of his generation and a professor at the Collège de France. Both he and Jullian were part of the Comité d'études, consisting of prominent historians, geographers and archaeologists, which had been set up in the closing years of the war to prepare the government's claims to a return of Alsace and Lorraine. Among its members we encounter, unsurprisingly, various members of the Comité Lavisse. The Comité d'études published *L'Alsace-Lorraine et la frontière du nord-est* in 1918; it became an important document during the Paris peace negotiations of 1918–1919, in particular for the annexation of the Saarland. Clémenceau abandoned the principle of self-determination so passionately advanced by Fustel and Renan and applied by the League of Nations in all other contested borderlands in Europe; in 1918–1919 he pushed through a straightforward and immediate French reannexation of Alsace-Lorraine without bothering with a plebiscite.

Emile Durkheim's propaganda efforts are of particular interest. He wrote a long tract denouncing Treitschke and, through Treitschke, a 'German mentality': *L'Allemagne au-dessus de tout: La mentalité allemande et la guerre* (1915). Durkheim constantly dovetails Treitschke's name (redolent of the 1870–1871 confrontation) with that of the notorious warmongering General Friedrich von Bernhardi. His book *Deutschland und der nächste Krieg* is presented by Durkheim as the logical military application of Treitschke's cultural and moral nostrums. In twinning Treitschke and Bernhardi as the 'brain and muscle' of Prussian supremacism, Durkheim clearly betrays his propagandist intent, invoking the ingrained trope of the hateful Knatschke-cum-Junker duo.

Durkheim's tract, obvious war propaganda, is driven by anti-German animus and reifies the 'mentality' it attacks. But like Renan's *Qu'est-ce qu'une nation?*, the argument also rises above its immediate propagandistic pugilism and offers, even beyond its overt anti-German intent, an interesting and insightful analysis of a more general principle: that of a 'might makes right' ethics of the national interest, a self-serving moral exceptionalism in international relations. We may call it by a name that Durkheim had coined in another context: anomie. 'Anomie' can be translated as the more current term 'narcissism' – not just as exaggerated, boastful vanity, but in the pathological sense. As a pathological disorder, narcissism involves self-aggrandizement, a lack of empathy, erratic wilfulness, the inability to admit the relativity of one's own point of view, the self-exemption from the moral standards that one holds up to the rest of the world. All this tallies with what Durkheim called anomie.

Durkheim had identified anomie in certain individuals deviating from general moral normativity. As Dominick LaCapra 1972 has pointed out, that typology of deviant self-righteousness also applies to unilateralist or imperialist states that consider their own national interests to be categorically rightful. Anomie stands for an erosion (linked to social modernity) of one's embeddedness in moral obligations and its replacement by a notion of volition. Durkheim had developed the concept in the 1890s, in his work on labour division and on suicide; it also informed, tacitly, his wartime critique of a specifically 'German' moralistic egotism and self-serving unilateralism. Anomie is what informs that line in Felix Dahn's motto for the *Alldeutscher Verband:* 'a nation's highest good is its right' (*Das höchste Gut des Volkes ist sein Recht*).

Durkheim's 'down with the beastly Germans' reflex is of course mere wartime ire; but his diagnosis of anomie as a facilitator of self-righteous unilateralism is more suggestive. In the course of the nineteenth century, increasing importance is given to the notion of *will* as a moral agency in German thought. Goethe had already juxtaposed *sollen* ('duty', in the classical tragedy of impossible moral obligation) with *wollen* ('will', in the modern tragedy of impossible self-realization). The concept's trajectory thenceforth is suggestive: from Schopenhauer's *Die Welt als Wille und Vorstellung* (1819) by way of Nietzsche's *Wille zur Macht* (posthumously published in problematic editions, 1901 and 1906, but announced in a nutshell in *Also Sprach Zarathustra*) to Leni Riefenstahl's film *Triumph des Willens* (1935). In the run-up to the charismatic leadership so lavishly glorified in Riefenstahl's film, the celebration of willpower is an unmistakable element. Nor is this identification of anomie, as 'Will makes Right', merely an argument of convenience for bashing the Germans. Justifying ruthless aggression from the categorical imperatives of the nation's interest and 'military necessity' went against the fledgling idea of an international legal order and has remained an identifying characteristic of unilateralist states in general. Anomie can be applied to cases such as Putin's Russia (in 2020 Ukraine) or the 'Dahiya' use of disproportionate force by Likud-governed Israel (in various conflicts since 2006); I will return to it in the conclusion of this book.[32]

National Identity at Stake

Thus the intellectuals did their patriotic duty in propaganda battles and provided diplomacy with ammunition. The result of their interventions was also that the war was lifted from a conflict of state interests to a confrontation between incompatible nations, each with their specific characters and temperaments. Character assassination of the enemy has, of course, been a tool of warfare since warfare began; what was new was the fact that the notion of 'national character' had in the preceding century become a thing that philologists, historians, sociologists and ethnographers felt they could discuss with scientific authority; hence their new role as war propagandists.[33]

Poets and versifiers continued to do their patriotic bit as of old. The most interesting altercations took place between Germany and 'England' (that cultural name was habitually used, especially in Germany, to describe the British Empire); it is 'England' that draws the indignation of German apologists, possibly because they had believed in a Germanic–Anglo-Saxon kinship until recently, such as had been experienced in the days of Carlyle and Prince Albert. But Carlyle and Prince Albert were dead. Carlyle's intellectual successor had been Matthew Arnold, who under Renan's influence and with a Cornish mother saw himself as half-Celtic; and the Prince of Wales had married a Danish princess, Alexandra, who was resentfully mindful of the Prussian attack on her country in 1864. After he had ditched Bismarck, Wilhelm II had given free rein to grandiose ambitions for Germany to become a colonial world power with a navy rivalling the British one; that had driven British public opinion away from their German cousin. Britain's Entente Cordiale with France had been concluded in 1904, and the British public was exposed, as described earlier in the chapter, to a steady diet of novels warning of a future German invasion. The sudden swerve of British public opinion and foreign policy away from Germany and towards France, and increasingly belligerent, caught German commentators unaware, and this sudden unpleasant surprise was what most agitated their pens.[34]

The most extreme example is probably the 'Song of Hatred against England' by Ernst Lissauer. It ends as follows:

> Take you the folk of the Earth in pay,
> With bars of gold your ramparts lay,
> Bedeck the ocean with bow on bow,
> Ye reckon well, but not well enough now.
> French and Russian, they matter not,
> A blow for a blow, a shot for a shot,
> We fight the battle with bronze and steel,
> And the time that is coming Peace will seal.
> You we will hate with a lasting hate,
> We will never forego our hate,
> Hate by water and hate by land,
> Hate of the head and hate of the hand,
> Hate of the hammer and hate of the crown,

Hate of seventy millions choking down.
We love as one, we hate as one,
We have one foe and one alone –
ENGLAND![35]

Strong stuff, but by no means unrepresentative. The *Haßgesang* was widely popular; printed as a pamphlet, it was distributed among the troops in the field. The poet (who also coined the slogan 'Gott Strafe England' – 'God punish England' – which went viral) was given Prussian and Bavarian decorations. But while Lissauer's vehemence may have gone down well at home, internationally (the English translation quoted here, by Barbara Henderson, was published in the *New York Times* in October 1915) it served only to demonstrate an embarrassing *furor teutonicus*. Failing to woo international readers, Lissauer left the moral high ground wide open. The one to take it was the venerable Thomas Hardy, august novelist from the previous century, who in his old age was also called to serve the War Propaganda Bureau. This is how he replied:

'O England, may God punish thee!'
– Is it that Teuton genius flowers
Only to breathe malignity
Upon its friend of earlier hours?
– We have eaten your bread, you have eaten ours,
We have loved your burgs, your pines' green moan,
Fair Rhine-stream, and its storied towers;
Your shining souls of deathless dowers
Have won us as they were our own:

We have nursed no dreams to shed your blood,
We have matched your might not rancorously
Save a flushed few whose blatant mood
You heard and marked as well as we
To tongue not in their country's key;
But yet you cry with face aflame,
'O England, may God punish thee!'
And foul in onward history,
And present sight, your ancient name.[36]

And so the mutual sniping at each others' moral character formed part of the hostilities, with the German side from the outset fatally caught in a cleft stick that was partly of its own making. The harsh and ruthless pursuit of war aims meant that 'military necessity' ran afoul of an international climate that in the previous decade had come to place its hope in the pacifist and humane restraints of the Geneva Conferences and the court of arbitration. The apologia that this war had been forced upon a peaceful Germany, which had no other choice than to defend itself, rang hollow in light of the fact that this self-defence was conducted on foreign soil, and also in the light of the ambitious, expansionist war aims that were trumpeted about domestically in triumphalist German media, as if no one else would notice them. The memories of 1870–1871 could not but colour what was universally seen as its 1914 rematch. And finally, there was the toxic ethnotypical frame that had been devised for the German character by French intellectuals since 1871: all too easily could this war be seen as motivated by a *mentalité de boche*, combining egotistal priggishness with a ruthless disregard for the rights and even the viewpoints of others. All that made the propaganda war a lost cause from the outset. Germany fought that war with obsolete weaponry – indeed, it was fighting, as the saying has it, the previous war: Germany's self-definition as a *Kulturnation* was, by 1914, as outmoded as its sense of kinship with England.

The net result of this cultural warfare was to bind intellectuals, as leaders of public opinion, to the national interest. Also, the World War placed the nation, its personality and characteristics, under the aegis of the state; the war as fought on the cultural propaganda front required the robust vindication of the nation's character amidst other nations. The war gave the state the supreme ownership of the nation's sense of identity and a mandate to assert it in the wider world. The end result of that process can be seen in the famous opening paragraph of Charles De Gaulle's memoirs, one World War later, in which he expounds what France (a transcendent France, Michelet-style) means to him:

> All my life I have had a specific idea of what France stands for [*une certaine idée de la France*]. That feeling inspires me as much as my critical judgement. Emotionally I automatically imagine France, like a fairy-tale princess or frescoed Madonna, as being dedicated to a high and exceptional calling. I have the distinct impression that Providence has created her for exemplary achievements or miseries. If occasionally her deeds and experiences should, even so, be marked by mediocrity, this strikes me as an absurd anomaly, due to the shortcomings of Frenchmen, not to the spirit of the fatherland. But even the factual side of my personality convinces me that France is only really herself when she occupies the first rank: that only the greatest enterprises are capable of outweighing the centrifugal ferment which her people carry within themselves; that our country, being as is it – amidst others, being as they are – must, on pains of mortal peril, aim high and stand tall. In short, as I see it, France cannot be France without grandeur.[37]

In this respect (entrusting the state with the ownership and guardianship of the nation's identity) the propaganda of 1914–1918 effected the same thing in wartime that the world fairs had prepared in peacetime. States were now, automatically, about nationality as much as they were about taxation and governance. We may expand Charles Tilly's dictum slightly: States made war, and the war made states national.[38]

Dulce et Decorum

It was, automatically, the state that took charge of its wartime bereavements, acting as chief mourner. The need to keep up morale during the hostilities prevented too much hand-wringing while the war was still going on, but a considerable amount of cultural bandwidth was taken up by public commemorations of the war dead after 1918.[39] The state took charge of the nation's pomp and circumstance (to recall Elgar's tune of 'Land of Hope and Glory'). France's Bastille Day, with its huge military parade between the Arc de Triomphe and the Place de la Concorde, had been fixed as a *fête nationale* in 1880 (the senator in charge of that measure had been the Gaul-obsessed Romantic historian Henri Martin, founding member of the Ligue des patriotes), and in 1894 a Fête nationale de Jeanne d'Arc et du patriotisme was first mooted, to be officially established in 1920 on the official proposal of the Action française leader Maurice Barrès. To this nineteenth-century legacy of state-curated triumphalist remembrance was now added the modality of collective grief. Unknown soldiers were retrieved from dispersed war graves and solemnly reinterred, with eternal flames, under the Arc de Triomphe and in the Vittorio Emmanuele monument in Rome. War cemeteries (a twentieth-century phenomenon in Europe) were arranged from the Alps to Flanders to give an honourable resting place to the millions of casualties. Every village square in France, every parish cemetery in Germany and Austria, every English cathedral has its monument honouring the casualties from the local community. No previous war had had this effect of sublimating grievous loss into a nationwide, all-pervasive public culture of decorous mourning. Decorum: the solemn respect rendered to the dead was linked to the notion that their deaths had been a sacrifice for the fatherland and as such were something heroic and dignified, the fulfilment of a high duty. As of 1915, 'Mort pour la France' became an officially regulated honorific mention in a person's *état civil*, like an academic degree or a title in the nobility; it was appended to the name so distinguished whenever that name was mentioned, and the underage children of someone *mort pour la France* enjoyed some state patronage as 'wards of the nation' (*pupilles de la nation*).

Wards of the *nation*: that word could not have been used thus in previous centuries. Despite the lofty sentiments in *Henry V*'s 'Band of brothers' speech ('For he to-day that sheds his blood with me shall be my brother; be he ne'er so vile, this day shall gentle his condition'), public monuments for fallen soldiers had previously been reserved for commanding field officers; the rank and file were at best honoured collectively, as regiments. Personal military distinctions such as the Médaille militaire and the Victoria Cross (both established during the Crimean War) made glory and social prestige newly available for enlisted men, placing rank and file so decorated at eye level with commanding officers; hence, perhaps, the often-heard saying that the military experience of war acts as a great blender for distinctions within the nation, throwing together people from different regions and walks of life. Jean Renoir's war film *La Grande Illusion* (1937) represents the French soldiery as consisting of carefully chosen representatives of the full palette of French society (as in his *La Marseillaise* of the following year). The aristocratic understanding and well-bred courtesy between two nobly born officers (the German Rauffenstein and the French Boïeldieu) is nullified by the latter's national bond with his French fellow captives: the lieutenants Maréchal (working class) and Rosenthal (a banker's son of Jewish descent). That is what 'nation' comes to mean as reforged in the crucible of war: society at large unified, beyond class and region of origin, by the experience and memory of shared glory and suffering – for so we may summarize Renan.[40]

This usage, with these connotations, may be specific to the French word *nation* and the French history of its usage. Much as it would be difficult to think of a similar usage pre-1800, so it would be difficult to think of an analogous usage in German. The word *die Nation* had fallen into disuse after Fichte (although derivations such as *national* and *Nationalität* remained current) and was by and large replaced by its near-synonym *Volk*. But even the thought experiment of trying to conceive of war orphans to be adopted as *Schützlinge des Volkes* drives home the very different connotations, with *Volk* connoting the specificity of class or ethnicity rather than the all-inclusive societal fraternity that *la nation* can evoke; one would more easily conceive of such patronage being extended on behalf of the *Vaterland* as a moral collective.

Whatever the semantic minutiae, it was the nation or the fatherland that was invoked as the agency that could idealize and sublimate brutal carnage into something that had, in the Latin root sense of the word, decorum.

We know with what bitter sarcasm Wilfred Owen cited Horace's *Dulce et decorum est pro patria mori* when evoking the death-throes of someone dying in a mustard-gas attack; or, in 'Anthem for a Doomed Youth', harshly juxtaposing the decorous rituals of a funeral service with the bestial experiences of 'those who die as cattle'. That traumatized perspective has come to dominate our view of the Great War, and even of warfare as such. Even so, we must not underestimate the consolation that this decorum, and all the pomp and circumstance of commemorative acts, offered to the bereaved families and surviving comrades. We may recall the palliative of the *Chanson de Roland* for 1870s France ('that *douce France* for which one could already die such a good death at Roncesvalles'). Their palliative power rendered the Parry/Elgar setting of 'Jerusalem' and the Holst-scored 'I Vow to Thee, My Country' cherished classics in the public repertoire. They gained their initial popularity during World War I commemorations, but they have featured at royal weddings and the funeral of Margaret Thatcher. The ambivalence of wartime condolence and a generalized cult of the nation is pre-inscribed; we have seen the fey national fanaticism coupled with the stately, pensive melody of Holst's 'Thaxted' hymn. In Laurence Binyon's 'For the Fallen' what we recall is mainly the high-minded stanza that begins 'They shall not grow old', but we overlook that the poem as a whole begins 'With proud thanksgiving, a mother for her children/England mourns for her dead across the sea. Flesh of her flesh they were, spirit of her spirit' – nationality monopolizing the sum total of what the war dead were and stood for.

Decorum cuts both ways. The state can bestow pomp and circumstance, ritual, dignity and decorum on acts of collective mourning, and in return can draw credit from that mourning as the place to turn to when the people are in need of succour. The importance of the function of national decorum can be gauged from the situations where it is in short supply, as tends to be the case when wars are, embarrassingly, lost. In Weimar Germany, the bitterness of war memories was unalleviated, burdened by the 'stab in the back' legend peddled by a self-serving Hindenburg (1920) and expressed in the traumatic art of Otto Dix and Erich Maria Remarque. An analogue of sorts is noticeable in the fraught aftermath of the Algerian war of liberation in France (which was not even officially classified as a 'war' until 1999). In the US, Sylvester Stallone's *Rambo: First Blood* film (1982) thematizes the traumas of an awkwardly non-remembranced Vietnam war. The manic killing spree that Rambo belatedly unleashes on the Vietnamese in *First Blood Part II* (1985) shows the inability to come to terms with defeat ('Do we get to win this time?') and seeks its blood-soaked catharsis in claiming a reciprocity between the soldier's love of country and the country's decorous gratitude. 'I want what … every other guy who came over here and spilt his guts and gave everything he had wants: for our country to love us as much as we love it. That's what I want.'[41] *Rambo: First Blood* was filmed during the Reagan years, while the Thatcherite media in Britain were whipping up jingoistic fervour over the Falkands War. Those years mark an upsurge of strident, chauvinistic nationalism in Hollywood cinema, which will be addressed more closely in Chapter 12. Rambo's traumatized eagerness to re-engage in battle during the post-Vietnam 'culture of defeat' reminds one of the refusal by German war veterans – who organized into so-called *Freikorps* militias – to lay down their arms in 1919, and indeed of the many post-Armistice hostilities that continued to rage around Europe after 1918. It also suggests an interesting side aspect of the 'culture of defeat' as analysed by Schivelbusch: the post-traumatic embitterment disorder that follows lost wars is exacerbated by a perceived lack of proper, official decorum with regard to the sufferings, losses and casualties sustained.[42]

What can we say of the overall impact of the Great War on the cultural history of nationalism in Europe? As a result of the all-devouring belligerence, the culture and cultivation of national identity was rendered both more and less visible. On the one hand, there was the ultra-political stridency of war propaganda, the bitter, mortal national enmity; on the other hand, there was the unpolitical nation as a comfort zone, serene even in its grief, a beleaguered haven of domesticity – the things that soldiers in the trenches pined for; the green fields and unspoilt countryside of the home country, the tender, affective and, yes, peaceful bonds of familial home life and community. Then again, there was the hard-bitten rejection of all that sentimentality, an anti-idyllic and anti-nostalgic look at life. That fed the sensibility of modernist avant-gardism (in the realm of culture), technocratic scientism (in knowledge production) and revolutionary ideologies, mass movements and personality-cult leaders (in politics).

What survived the Great War was the ingrained assumption, both as a political doctrine and as an unpolitical maxim, that the cultural identity of the nation and the political sovereignty of the state are two sides of the same coin. That dogma is what Romantic nationalism has bequeathed to us even in this twenty-first century. That, and the anachronistic belief that the nation, as a permanent, tranquil essence, transcends the turbulent vicissitudes of history.

CHAPTER 12

The Long Tail

Romantic Afterlife in a Modern Century

We began this book with the long tail of Romantic nationalism in post-1918 Europe, from 'Die Wacht am Rhein' to *Alexander Nevsky*, tempered in the fire of wartime experiences; Chapter 11 ended with the war that gave those memories their enduring stature and their ambivalent nature as ultranational and unpolitical at the same time. That war ended with the Paris Peace Treaties, governed by the Wilsonian principle of national self-determination. The assertion of national identity – something that had been aspirational in the century of empires – became a default in the century of nation-states. What had been an agenda became a habit, subsisting in a post-1918 dominated by technological modernity and rejecting Romanticism and its (re-) enchantments.

Even so, a century after the Paris Peace Treaties, nationalism is once again the strongest ideology worldwide, as it was in 1914. These days, it is accompanied by new forces such as neoliberalism and political Islam and proves capable of inflecting both. From Trump's USA to Xi's China, from Putin's Russia to Erdoğan's Turkey, from Modi's India to Netanyahu's Israel, we see how nationalism rides high, regardless of the specifics of states, their histories and local politics.

The way nationalism survived into the twenty-first century is astounding. Across the totalitarian ideologies of Communism, Fascism and Nazism; across a World War that dwarfed even the ruinous frenzy of the first one, with an unprecedented wholesale slaughter of entire populations; across, also, a half-century of liberal internationalism in the West and anticolonial self-liberation in the Global South, nationalism has proved its resilience and adaptability.

The resurgence of nationalism in public culture is aptly illustrated by plotting, on a timeline, the erection of national commemorative monuments (Figure 12.1). The graph visualizes the distribution of around

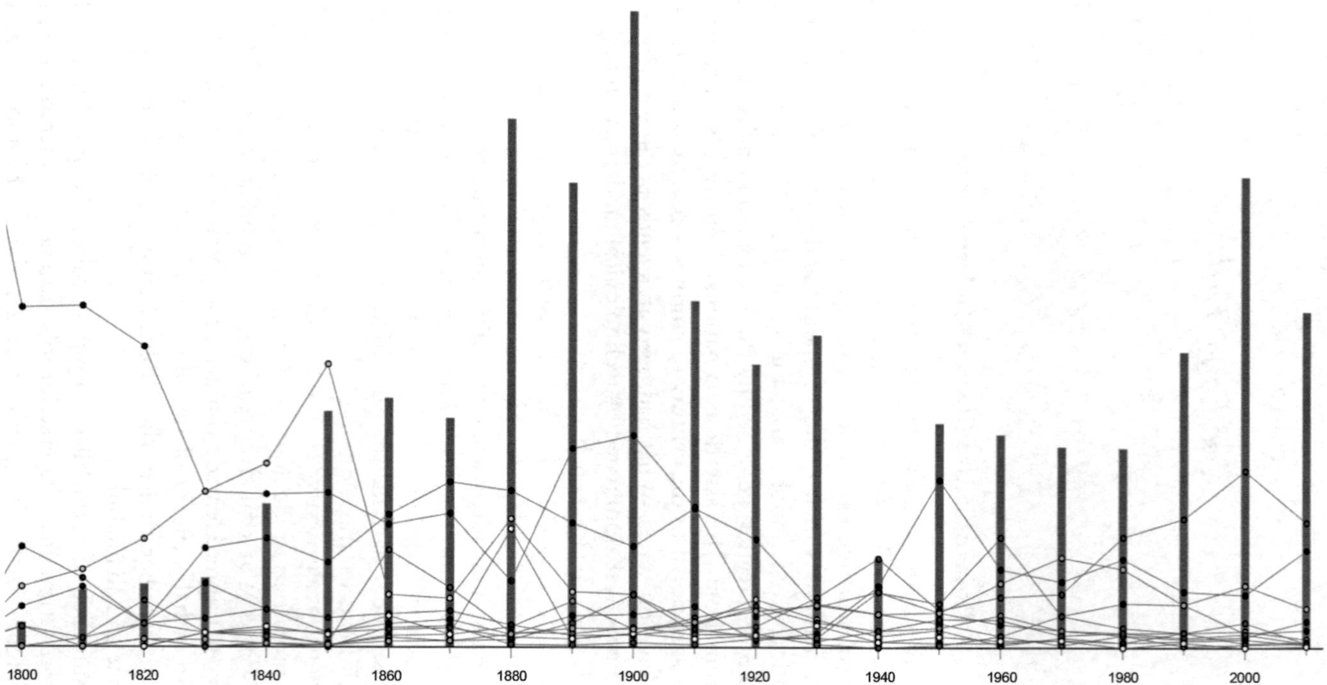

Figure 12.1 National commemorative monuments per decade and country (e-rn.ie/monumentsintime).

7,500 monuments; the bars represent the totals per decade (highest: 841 in 1900–1910, 279 of which in Germany), the lines the proportional share of the various nationalities.

The totals offer a profile something like a suspension bridge. A sudden rise after 1800 peaks between 1880 and 1910; then the curve descends to a low point in the 1940s, followed by restrained productivity into the 1980s; and then a renewed rise into the 2000s and after. Production is dominated in the nineteenth-century heyday by German, Italian and French statues and in the period 1980–2010 by Hungarian, Russian and Polish ones. Obviously, the post-communist countries went through a 'catching up' exercise in public-space historicism when, belatedly, they were in a position to do so, and at a time when the fashion had already passed in Western Europe. That offers a vivid illustration of the often-noted asymmetry between the 'old' and the 'new' Europe, the 'old' being the western half that was liberated from totalitarian dictatorships in 1945 and the 'new' being the eastern half, which would have to endure tyranny until 1989. But there is also a deeper asymmetry between the two halves: in the west, the state system continued much as it had been in 1913; whereas most of the states of Central and Eastern Europe were carved out of dismembered empires in 1919.

The American delegation had come to the 1918 Paris peace conference charged with Wilson's 'Fourteen Points' agenda, stipulating the right of 'peoples' to self-determination. How those 'peoples' could be mapped onto territories had been intensely studied, by way of preparation, by geographers and other scholars (a group known as 'The Inquiry', including Walter Lippmann). We have seen the comments of one of their collaborators, Leon Dominian, concerning Serbia as 'the country of the *gusle*' (Chapter 5). The self-determination principle was applied somewhat selectively: mainly in order to dismember the empires on the losing side (Hohenzollern, Habsburg, and the Ottoman Empire, at least its European portion). The situation was more chaotic for the outlying provinces of Russia (the southern Caucasus, the Baltic lands, Ukraine), which had gone through a revolution and a separate peace treaty with the central powers (Brest-Litovsk, March 1918). Warfare in fact continued after 1918 from Finland to Armenia as new states consolidated themselves under contested regime choices and then tried to stave off incorporation into the new USSR. The states of Western Europe were on the whole left intact; Norway was confirmed in the independence from Sweden that it had peaceably obtained in 1904, the foundations for Icelandic self-government under the Danish crown were laid, and Ireland was engaged in a war of independence that would lead to a self-governing Irish Free State with dominion status in 1922. Cultural minorities in the west, such as Brittany, the

Basque country and Catalonia, continued an agenda of identity-assertion in a spectrum ranging from regionalism to separatism.

The newly sovereign states all asserted their status by proclaiming their national distinctness and authenticity, fully in the mode of the Romantic nationalism of the preceding century, but of course in a drastically modernized climate. Most of them in their new constitutions prefixed a clause affirming that the state was predicated on the nation's identity and established the national language as its language of affairs and education. Indications of how Romantic nationalism was expressed in a modern century can be inferred from the examples of Latvia, Ireland and Poland.

In Latvia, an epic silent film was made in 1930 under the title *Lāčplēsis*. It celebrates the heroic vindication of the national cause in a story set during the recent War of Independence and its aftermath. A wicked German attempts to rape a young woman but is thwarted by a hero-figure, the independence fighter Jānis, who saves the day. That action is presented, however, as the contemporary iteration of a deeply underlying myth: that of the legendary hero Lāčplēsis freeing the medieval heroine Laimdota from the evil Black Knight. The same actors play the mythical and the contemporary roles, and the film creates visual overlays, double-exposure transitions and echoic repetitions between the modern and the mythical. The film made use of the Latvian epic of the same name ('the bear-slayer'), one of those many national epics that had been produced across Europe (Chapter 4); the Latvian author Andrejs Pumpurs had begun his version of *Lāčplēsis* in order to create a counterpart to the Estonian *Kalevipoeg*, and after toying with the idea of a pseudo-ancient counterfeit presented it in 1880 as a modern text based on local legends. Pumpurs's *Lāčplēsis* looks back to the medieval Livonian crusades, when the Teutonic Order subdued the Baltic lands; the incorporation of that tale in the modern anti-German film brings history around full circle. The young hero Jānis, whose imagination has been fired by reading a dog-eared copy of Pumpurs's epic, has magically been made receptive to the spirit of the mythical hero and recognizes in the arrogant Prussian the ancient wicked Black Knight. The epic hero is, in the most literal sense, an *inspiration* for modern freedom fighters. And so a modern melodrama of national independence and evil rapists is calqued onto the Romantic-national epic; this is done, however, in a film drawing heavily on the modern, avant-garde stylistic techniques of German expressionist cinema (*The Cabinet of Dr Caligari*) and Sergey Eisenstein (*Battleship Potemkin*) and intercut with newsreel footage.

This remarkable film is only one example of the many ways in which modern, independent Latvia was channelling the spirit of Lāčplēsis.[1]

Figure 12.2 Latvian postage stamp of 1932, part of a series based on the 1930 film *Lāčplēsis*. ERNiE imagebank

Lāčplēsis memorials dot the country and testify to its historical vicissitudes. One, on the façade of the Riga parliament building, replaced an earlier statue of the Teutonic Landmeister Walter von Plettenberg; it was itself removed under Communist rule in the 1950s and a replica was put up in 2007. Similarly, Lāčplēsis defeating the Black Knight was the subject of a 1932 statue (inscribed 'To the liberators') honouring the Latvian troops that had taken Jelgava in 1919; erected in 1932, it was destroyed in or after World War II and restored in 1992.[2]

A statue of Lāčplēsis was also included in 1935 on the plinth of the remarkable symbolist/art deco 'Freedom Monument' that towers over downtown Riga. Here, the bear-slayer is rendered much as in the film (woollen skullcap, bobbed haircut). He was similarly represented on a postage stamp of 1932, where, as in the film, his face hovers in the clouds above the Riga skyline like a protective spirit (Figure 12.2).* Thus we see the national hero remediated from epic poem to statuary to film and postage stamps. The first step in that progress moves within the established ambit of traditional art forms. Then film and stamps provide new, twentieth-century distribution media.[3] The postage stamp in particular was a ubiquitous platform. Signifying the independence of the state, its currency and its postal service, it habitually featured the nation's semi-official iconography and provided it with possibly the deepest and widest social penetration ever achieved by the graphic arts. The trend started in 1896 when Greece issued classically themed stamps to celebrate the Olympic Games held in Athens. Only in the decades of post-1945 internationalism, when many small countries and newly independent colonies began to make use of stamps as a cheap but popular marker of international presence, do we see an internationalization of philatelic icons – Marie Curie, Leonardo and in the Communist world Karl Marx.[4]

* The magic-realist evocation of ancient spirits making their presence felt in the modern context is widespread. Both Lawrence Olivier's *Henry V* and Powell and Pressburger's *A Canterbury Tale* (1944) use modernist editing techniques to evoke an eternal England as a spiritual presence at the time of the Normandy landings.

Similar dovetailings of historicism and modernity are noticeable at the presence of newly independent states such as Ireland and Poland at world fairs of the interwar period. Both countries considered themselves to be anciently rooted states now restored to their erstwhile sovereignty. Both used the modern, forward-looking and even futuristic platform of the world fair to showcase both their modern viability and their ancient rootedness. The Irish self-presentation was more traditionalist. At the 1933 Century of Progress Exposition in Chicago, a 'Pageant of the Celt' was held, harking straight back at the legendary-historicist repertoire of the Irish Literary Revival (which remained popular anyway among the Irish-American diaspora); more pragmatic was the distribution of an instructive *Handbook of the Irish Free State*, with geographical and statistical information, presented in a sumptuously neo-Celtic design modelled on the country's greatest cultural heirloom, the medieval Book of Kells.[5]

The Polish state, well aware of its parlous position between Germany and the USSR, saw in the world fairs of the 1930s a necessary tool of cultural diplomacy and invested much in its pavilions; it opted for a modernistic pavilion style replete with references to the rich Polish past. On the very eve of Hitler's invasion, in 1939, it marked its presence at the New York World's Fair with a striking flat-roofed prefab building, fronted by an openwork tower constructed out of 1,200 gilded shields and overlooking an old-school, traditionally academic-style equestrian statue of the medieval king Jagiello I brandishing two crossed swords (Figure 12.3). The New York public failed to get the historical reference in this modern building, some people believing that the statue represented the contemporary Polish strongman leader Marshal Piłsudski – as well they might, since some of the material had been transported to New York on a freight ship named *Piłsudski*.[6]

And so world fairs resumed their function after the Great War had ended. The former imperial peripheries of Europe as sovereign state participants continued their Romantic-nationalist identity affirmations

Figure 12.3 Polish pavilion at the 1939 New York World's Fair. Wikimedia Commons

by other means, embedding it in modernist forms and shapes. And it was not only the new states; even the very oldest caught the tide of post-Romantic cultural nationalism. In Lisbon, a World Exhibition was held in 1940 to mark 800 years since the foundation of Portugal and 300 years since the restoration of independence from Spain. The fair was a publicity exercise of the authoritarian regime, the Estado novo; it was opened by Marshal Carmona, the country's nominal president, with de facto dictator Salazar also in attendance. Various streets around the fair grounds were renamed in the following years to evoke the period of colonial discoveries; but the eye-catcher was a large monument glorifying the nation's achievements in the colonial voyages of discovery – perpetuating the triumphalism of the Columbus monument at the Barcelona Universal Exposition of 1880. In 1960 it was replaced by a stone successor, still one of Lisbon's main landmarks (Figure 12.4). Portugal in 1960 still considered itself a colonial empire, and Salazar was still in power.[7]

Figure 12.4 Monument to the Portuguese Discoveries, Belém, Lisbon (António Pardal Monteiro and Leopoldo de Almeida, 1960). Wikimedia Commons

Democracy and Ethnocracy

Names such as Piłsudski and Salazar alert us to the fact that the continuance of Romantic nationalism in the twentieth century was not only affected by a modernist shift in aesthetics and media technology; the political ground was shifting as well. Our view of the interwar years tends to be dominated by the twin juggernauts of Hitler and Stalin, with, as afterthoughts, Mussolini and Franco. But the cases of Poland, Portugal and Latvia alert us to the fact that those dictators were not an anomaly: they represented a general European trend. We have encountered the strong, indeed charismatic leaders of former war commanders in the post-war states, Piłsudski among them. In some cases, they represented a continuity from the imperial pre-1914 days: Hindenburg in Germany, Mustafa Kemal Pasha (Atatürk) in Turkey, Horthy in Hungary. In other cases, they had used their military know-how to ensure their new country's independence: Mannerheim in Finland, Piłsudski in Poland. Mannerheim honourably relinquished power after losing the 1919 elections, but in Poland Piłsudski abolished parliamentary government and became de facto dictator as of 1926. Other coups d'état involving military leaders were those of Primo de Rivera (1923) and Franco (1936) in Spain, Óscar Carmona in Portugal (1926) and Ioannis Metaxas in Greece (1936). We may even include France's Philippe Pétain in that list; his rise to power in Vichy France was dictated by war circumstances, but he undoubtedly used his charisma (having been the heroic defender of Verdun) as a springboard towards running a nationalist dictatorship.[8]

If we add to those generals the other autocratic leaders of nationalist non-democracies, the list grows to dismal proportions. The poet-turned-pilot Gabriele D'Annunzio started the trend by proclaiming himself *duce* of the Istrian city of Fiume/Rijeka; Italy's Mussolini followed suit in 1922. Then came Zogu in Albania (1925, 'King Zog' as of 1928), Antanas Smetona in Lithuania (1926), Engelbert Dollfuß and Kurt Schuschnigg in Austria (1932 and 1934), Konstantin Päts in Estonia and Kārlis Ulmanis in Latvia (both 1934), Boris III in Bulgaria (1935), Carol II in Romania (1938, followed by Ion Antonescu in 1940), Vladko Maček in Yugoslavian Croatia (1939). Hitler's power grab in 1933 was only one in a series. From 1917/1922 (the coups of Lenin and Mussolini) to 1975/1989 (the deaths of Salazar and Ceauşescu), the European twentieth century is mostly one of dictatorships.

That is how the application of the Wilsonian principle of national self-determination derailed. The notion of national self-determination, involving the people's liberation from alien overlordship and imperial oppression, had originally been meant as a democratic gesture. Sieyès, the champion of the *tiers-état* and godfather of its *assemblée nationale* in 1789, would have firmly approved of Wilson's programme. But the newly constituted nation-states, many of them liberated from the rule of imperial overlords, eagerly ditched their democratic freedoms in favour of authoritarianism or dictatorships.* Many countries in Eastern and Central Europe, which subsequently got mangled between Hitler's Third Reich and Stalin's USSR, recall those succeeding tyrannies with anguish but with a historical foreshortening that makes it seem as if this Nazi–Bolshevik double whammy put an end to their recently acquired liberty and self-determination. Not so: almost all of them had already, of their own volition, imposed dictatorships on themselves in the run-up to the Molotov–Ribbentrop Pact.

Many of these anti-democratic movements justified their power grabs by claiming that the imminent threat of a communist revolution had to be averted; we even encounter this, bizarrely, in Ireland's Blueshirt movement. Surely Ireland in 1930, a self-governing, Catholic, agricultural and traditionalist country, was almost as impervious to a communist takeover as the Vatican; in the end, the Blueshirt movement remained quixotic, though it inspired the national poet W. B. Yeats to write anti-democratic 'marching songs' for it, and the spectre of a Bolshevik threat was widely used as a scare tactic. In fact, Ireland is, like Finland, one of the few new (post-1918) countries where democratic stability prevailed and manifested itself in the peaceful transfer of power following general elections – even though both had gone through ruinously divisive internal wars in the early days of their independence. As of 1933, the government of Ireland, though by no means authoritarian, was under the strongly paternalistic leadership of Eamon De Valera. A deeply committed Irish nationalist, he had been an anti-British separatist insurgent and was prone to a type of Catholic integralism also practised in Spain and Portugal. Still, that was not ipso facto anti-democratic: a similar national paternalism characterized

* Authoritarianism (generally Hermet 1985) was discussed in a characteristically thoughtful and incisive way by Hannah Arendt (1957). She has been preceded by Erich Fromm's *Die Furcht vor der Freiheit* (1941), which concentrated in Marxist–Freudian terms on people's susceptibility to authoritarianism (rather than on its function in the leadership persona; see also McLaughlin 1996). Another Marxist critique of society's drift towards ethnic nationalism is contained in György Lukács's *Die Zerstörung der Vernunft* ('The Destruction of Reason', 1954), a very problematic book that shows how rigidly doctrinaire and intolerant Lukács could be. Unreason, for Lukács, is anything outside the true, scientific understanding of the world as vouchsafed by dialectical materialism, and his ire is hurled at liberals and Fascists alike. The book certainly has not aged well, but Lukács's sharp powers of observation come through in his identification of a philosophical idealism gone rampant among a bourgeoisie heedlessly buying into hero-worship and charismatic leadership. In that respect, Lukács's *Zerstöring der Vernunft* can be placed side by side with Karl Popper's *The Open Society and its Enemies*, both books (*bien étonnés de se trouver ensemble*) targeting the same problematics but from diametrically opposite political standpoints. The two differ sharply in their assessment of Hegel; Popper's view (seeing Hegel as the mainspring of obscurantist and historicist nationalism) has been largely discredited (see Avineri 1962, Stewart 1996, Pinkard 2000).

anti-Fascist leaders such as Charles De Gaulle, Winston Churchill and Queen Wilhelmina of the Netherlands, strong-willed personalities who all believed in their transcendentally imposed (rather than democratically mandated) stewardship of the nation.*

Not all nationalists, then, were authoritarians; but all authoritarians (west of Stalin, that is) were nationalists. The B-list of European dictators of the interwar years all invoked a mission to vouchsafe the survival of the nation and the fatherland. Overtly so, as we can tell by the names and mottos of the movements they headed: the Patriotic Union for Primo de Rivera, the falangists with their shouted call-and-response *España: una – España: grande – España: libre*, the Lithuanian Nationalist Union for Smetona, the Fatherland Front for Dollfuß and Schuschnigg, the Action française and so on. From the days of the Ligue des patriotes to the Front national, the invocation of the nation and the flag-waving assertion of national identity is massively overrepresented on the right wing of the political spectrum. It is among the political right that that national flag is the most sought-after cloak to wrap one's politics in.[9]

The track record of post-imperial European nation-states in the 1920s in retrospect appears like a prefiguration of the more recent drift (usually linked to the notion of 'populism') towards strongman authoritarian leaders with a charismatic media presence and a nationalist agenda. Once liberated from foreign-imposed tyranny, the newly independent Central European governments turned, as Spain, Portugal and Italy had done, to homegrown nativism and xenophobic nationalism, invoking it if necessary to derogate the powers of parliament, the independence of the judiciary, the international rule of law as established by treaties and the freedom of the press. All this was rationalized by the categorical imperative of national identity, and the legacy of Romantic historicism was heavily drawn on, instrumentalizing a national past as canonized by nineteenth-century historians and artists.

That inter-war trend has been echoed across Europe in recent decades, Italy under Berlusconi leading the way to Boris Johnson and Victor Orbán and their ilk. What this parallel across the intervening decades suggests is that there may well be an inherent instability in the very concept of the 'nation-state', even though now it is often accepted as the default model for a democracy.

* Catholicism itself went through a cult-of-personality mass mobilization of the faithful under Pius X and his successors (the Legion of Mary, 1921, the post-1918 Eucharistic Congresses, the cult of Christ the King as of 1925). This easily converged with the political culture of Fascism or authoritarianism in Catholic countries; Mussolini himself gained considerable goodwill among Catholics worldwide

Scholars in nationalism studies are keenly aware of the heuristic distinction between civic and ethnic nationalism. It has been overworked in the past but is nevertheless an indispensable distinction since, as we have repeatedly seen in the foregoing pages, the very concept of the nation hovers between two connotations: the nation as the common society that derives a sense of shared purpose and solidarity from being co-responsible for the state and its governance; and the nation as the cultural community that derives its sense of joint identity from a shared descent and inherited culture (language and memories). In most cases, the two are intermingled; but the proportion in which the two are commingled can be established only if we have a sense of the ideal-typical, civic versus ethnic nature of the ingredients that make up the mix. Those components are habitually called by the two Greek names for 'the people' in a political or a cultural sense: demos and ethnos. The shifting emphases with which nationalism presents itself as civic or ethnic reflects the way in which the nation is defined, or self-defines, as demos (the citizen stakeholders of a state) or ethnos (the people sharing the same culture).

The ambivalence in the very concept of the nation-state is a direct consequence of the vacillation in the self-definition of the nation as demos or ethnos. As stated before, the Wilsonian self-determination of peoples was initially meant as a democratic principle. It is for that very reason that Churchill, an old school imperialist, resisted its readoption, post-1945, in the Atlantic charter and by the United Nations: it could be invoked by colonially subjected peoples and Churchill, as a British imperialist, was not prepared to allow that.

Although the idea of national self-rule was meant democratically, as citizens' freedom from foreign overlordship, we note that in many cases it gravitated in a direction we may call *ethnocratic*: the rule not of the demos (the people as a social body) but of the ethnos (the people as a cultural community). The rhetoric of contemporary populism oscillates between demotically motivated anti-elitism and ethnically motivated nativism. The denunciation of over-educated, smugly liberal elites, out of touch with the worries that affect the common people, can always emerge out of, or shade into, the warnings against swarms of immigrants or unassimilated denizens from a culturally hostile world, aided and abetted by those cosmopolitan elites.[10]

for his treaty with Pius XI over the sovereignty of the Vatican (1929). On integralism generally: Chappel 2018 and Buchanan & Conway 1996. In Spain: Elzora 1995, Urigüen 1986 (on nineteenth-century antecedents); in Portugal: Costa Pinto 1982.

The nation-state may be inherently vulnerable to a gravitation from democracy towards ethnocracy. And despite the intervening totalitarian dictatorships and a World War, and despite the horrified recoil from totalitarianism in post-1945 internationalism, that ethnocratic gravitation, away from democracy, affects the nation-state today as much as it did a century ago.

Nationalism after Decolonization

Studying the 'afterlife' of Romantic nationalism after 1918 would require a multi-volume work rather than this single chapter – given the seismic intensity, the magnitude and the ongoing duration of the political turbulence in the century since the Treaty of Versailles. Globalization, and the decentring of Europe's position in the world, had been announced in the world's trading economy (witness the world fairs) and was now vastly amplified by the end of the European empires. The break-up of the Romanov, Habsburg, Hohenzollern and Ottoman Empires in 1917–1919 was accompanied in Western Europe by the imperial breakdown of Spain (Cuba and the Philippines, 1898), Britain (Ireland 1922, South Africa 1931, India and Pakistan 1947, Kenya 1964), Denmark (Iceland 1944), the Netherlands (Indonesia 1948), Belgium (Congo 1960), France (Indochina 1954, Algeria 1962) and Portugal (Angola and Mozambique, 1975). Each of those dates (and the list is only indicative) represents a hugely complex process. Remarkably, that imperial break-up was a process that spanned across the worst and most ruinous war in human history.

Nationalism in Europe's former colonies was, on the whole, driven less by a 'cultivation of culture' than by political and economic independence. Asserting the right to self-determination among disenfranchised colonials is primarily a struggle against political and economic injustice rather than Romantic identity assertion as in nineteenth-century Europe. Identity-driven, nativist nationalism can, however, be encountered globally: a drift towards ethnocracy was as noticeable outside Europe as it was within Europe's new nation-states. By way of example (random but telling) I point readers to places as far apart as South Africa, Israel and India. In South Africa, a mythology emerged during the Boer Wars of stalwart, biblically devout Boer intransigence, exemplified and commemorated in events such as the 'Great Trek' and the exodus of the Boers in trains of ox-drawn wagons to a new home in the Transvaal. Afrikaner nationalism was the result; it combined post-defeat grievance politics with equal measures of fundamentalist Calvinism and white supremacism. Afrikaner nationalism found a radical champion in Oswald Pirow, a Nazi sympathizer who in 1940 published a ground plan for a 'New Order' in South Africa, ambiguously inspired by

Salazar's Estado novo and/or by Nazi Germany. The political figurehead of Afrikaner nationalism, the Calvinist preacher Daniel François Malan, leader of a Reunited National Party, formalized South Africa's system of apartheid in 1948. In 1958, Pirow acted as chief prosecutor in the 'treason trials' that saw Nelson Mandela arraigned for the first time, accused not of just of sedition but of high treason against the South African republic. In Israel, the two-state Zionism of David Ben-Gurion vied with the Jewish supremacist revisionist Zionism of Ze'ev Jabotinsky, the Mussolini-inspired intellectual godfather first of the Hatzohar and Herut movements and ultimately, indirectly, of Likud. In India, Gandhi's anticolonialism was accompanied by a wide palette of Hindu nationalist movements. Many of these were inspired by the Hindutva ('Hindu-ness') nationalism of Vinayak Damodar Savarkar, who after 1938 became an admirer of Hitler; the Bharatiya Janata Party eventually issued from that Hindutva-inspired tradition.[11]

Within the European heartlands of the former empires, post-imperial nostalgia took hold. The loss of colonies and of trans-European power coincided with, or amplified, a more general nostalgic undercurrent under the surface of high modernity. Miguel de Unamuno's journeys inwards to the various regions and villages of the Spanish heartland (recounted in *Paisajes*, 1902; *De mi país*, 1903; *Andanzas y visiones españolas*, 1922) were part of a cultural reaction to the calamitous colonial losses of the (proverbially traumatic) year 1898. In Germany, the tradition of the idyllic *Dorfgeschichte* continued in force after 1918 and engendered the rustic tales of 'blood and soil' as well as the first cinematic versions of rustic idylls.* These *Heimatfilms* became all-dominant in the post-1945 period of defeat and *Wiederaufbau* ('economic reconstruction').[12]

In Britain, the nostalgic mode of 'Englishness' similarly drew on nineteenth-century sentimental idyll, continued in the downmarket fiction of the 1920s known as 'love and loamchild', as well as the magic realism of John Cowper Powys and various Powell and Pressburger films, hinting at the lingering presence of ancient memories encoded within the English landscape itself.[13] An eternal England, remembered from childhood and

* Witness the posthumous fame of Hermann Löns (1866–1912), a regionalist poet and novelist celebrating the north German moorlands around Lüneburg. His sentimental verse, set to music, has remained popular and inspired conservationists and idyllic *Heimatfilms* throughout the century; but he also penned a grim tale set in the Thirty Years' War, *Der Wehrwolf* (1910), in which a moorland community, still breathing the warrior spirit of pagan Germanic antiquity, sets up a guerrilla defence against marauding Swedish soldiers. Löns, a fervent nationalist, volunteered for military duty in 1914 and fell in the opening weeks of the Great War; his corpse was repatriated and reinterred in 1934–1935 in a Nazi propaganda stunt. The *Wehrwolf* book (which had sold 865,000 copies by 1945) inspired a campaign of warfare behind enemy lines in 1944–1945 (Radler 1987, Biddiscombe 1998). A common archaic-Germanic cultural repertoire (*Wolfsangel* runes, raging battle fury, etc.) made it possible for Löns's book to be appropriated by the Nazi regime (Watt 1997).

outlasting history and the Empire itself, was evoked by Conservative Prime Minister Stanley Baldwin in his famous lecture to the English nationalist Society of St George in 1924:

> The sounds of England, the tinkle of hammer on anvil in the country smithy, the corncrake on a dewy morning, the sound of the scythe against the whetstone, and the sight of a plough team coming over the brow of a hill, the sight that has been in England since England was a land, and may be seen in England long after the Empire has perished and every works in England has ceased to function, for centuries the one eternal sight of England.[14]

That evocative, practically verbless conspectus of sights and sounds leads naturally enough to the conclusion that 'The love of these things is innate and inherent in our people.' Fichte would have approved. The sentiments were echoed (with some sarcasm, but still) in George Orwell's reflection on the war effort, *The Lion and the Unicorn* (1941), from which Conservative Prime Minister John Major cherry-picked one soundbyte in 1993 and inserted it in a neo-Baldwinesque context:

> Fifty years from now Britain will still be the country of long shadows on county grounds, warm beer, invincible green suburbs, dog lovers and pools fillers and – as George Orwell said – 'old maids bicycling to Holy Communion through the morning mist' and if we get our way – Shakespeare still read even in school.[15]

Reading Shakespeare in school: that sting in the tail is, of course, a dog-whistle to a national, traditionalist educational policy. It also circles back to the fountainhead of this type of English nationalism: Thomas Carlyle's celebration of Shakespeare as a cornerstone of English identity in *On Heroes and Hero-Worship*.

National nostalgia is still with us, and it, too, alternates between salience and dormancy. The *Heimatfilm* dropped steeply out of fashion in Germany in the mid-1960s, to the point of becoming proverbial as the nadir of kitsch after 1968. As such it was evoked in 1984, with ironic back-handedness, as a point of departure for Edgar Reitz's experimental film/TV series *Heimat* (with sequels in 1992 and 2004), which combined a coming-of-age story with a regionalist exploration of the communal and generational memories of a fraught German century. Since then, the layered ironies of the 1980s have evaporated, and the *Heimatfilm* has become once again, straightforwardly, a romance genre for undemanding mass consumption (now, of course, featuring strong female characters). Such are the alternations and dialectics of cultural taste.

Similarly, in France, after the *nouvelle vague* had trashed the *cinéma de papa* (their term for the complacent commercial movies of the 1950s) and had produced, across the 1960s and 1970s, an edgy, urban avant-gardism, the 1980s saw mellow regionalism return in force: the twin films *Jean de Florette* and *Manon des Sources* (1986, based on works by the regionalist author and film-maker Marcel Pagnol). A similar resurgence of nostalgic comfort viewing occurred around the same time in British cinema: after the 'swinging sixties', period costume drama returned in the 1980s, lovingly evoking Victorian or Edwardian England (*Chariots of Fire*, 1981), with at best some vestigial ironies inherent in the source material (the Merchant-Ivory productions of E. M. Forster's *A Room with a View*, 1985, and *Howards End*, 1992). The BBC produced many idyllic costume dramas, drawing on canonical works of Victorian vintage (George Eliot, Charles Dickens, Elizabeth Gaskell, Anthony Trollope), and serialized the rural memoirs of Flora Thompson (*Lark Rise to Candleford*, published 1939–1943, broadcast 2008–2011). In the 2010s, marked by austerity and leading up to Brexit, there was the remarkable vogue of *Downton Abbey* (TV series 2010–2015, film spin-offs 2019, 2022 and 2025), with its mellow afterglow of a Baldwin-style harmony of squires and servants, castles and cottagers.*

These examples, few and somewhat randomly chosen as they are, do have indicative value and offer food for thought. For one thing, the dates of *Heimat*, *Chariots of Fire* and *Jean de Florette* suggest that a return to a nostalgically national cultural repertoire preceded the downfall of communism in 1989, coinciding with the Falklands War and the growth of Rambo-style martial action-hero movies in the US; and that therefore it is problematic to explain the revival of nationalism at the end of the twentieth century purely and simply as a response to '1989'. The new nationalism is often represented as a palliative to the agoraphobia of globalization and the disintegration of a bipolar world system post-1989; but the cultural material suggests the gestation a new nationalism starting in the 1980s. When communism vanished from the political landscape as an ideological presence, and well before globalization went into overdrive by the end of the century, the feel-good factor of national identity was already there, poised, standing by.

* Post-imperial nostalgia was accompanied in some European countries in the 1970s and 1980s by an equally nostalgic evocation of former colonial times. While the guilt of systemically imposed racism and tyrannical exploitation could not be wholly denied or ignored, the 'Raj Revival' in Britain and the *tempo doeloe* ('Olden Times') vogue in the Netherlands tended to sugarcoat remorse in wistfulness and attractive period detail. Cases in point are M. M. Kaye's *The Far Pavilions* (1978, with TV and musical spin-offs), the 1984 TV adaptation of Paul Scott's *The Jewel in the Crown*, and David Lean's 1984 film version of E. M. Forster's *A Passage to India*. These adaptations sacrificed some of the anticolonial critique in the literary originals to a more exoticist visual presentation. The same can be said of the 1992 adaptation of Marguerite Duras's autobiographical, Saigon-set *L'amant* (1984) and the Dutch TV serialization (1974) of Louis Couperus's *De Stille Kracht* (1900).

The Nation at the Movies

In flagging the post-1918 alternating dormancy/salience cycles of national nostalgia, I have drawn on examples from cinema and television, the twentieth-century's new media *par excellence*. Those particular new media proved their power in many genres: documentaries, love stories, adventure romance, psychological drama and so on. Among all those things, it was highly suitable for dramatizing and visualizing the nation, uniting the narrative and the spectacle of national identity, either as a foregrounded theme or as an underlying frame. As such, cinema offered a new platform for Romantic nationalism in a technological, post-Romantic age.

Given that function, we can use film history data as an Ariadne's thread through the mixed, mashed-up track record of the twentieth century. Instead of attempting, in these closing pages, an exhaustive conspectus of cultures of nationalism in twentieth-century Europe, I trace instead a single cultural tradition through the labyrinth, tracking post-Romantic nationalism in its cinematic articulation. Cinema, the century's standout new art form, has been encountered numerous times across the pages of this book, from *Casablanca* to *Birkebeinerne*. Of all narrative genres, cinema was and is truly representative of the twentieth century: high-tech, mass-audience, global, reaching from downmarket commercialism to art-house aesthetics.[16]

We have seen how the Latvian film *Lāčplēsis* recycled national-Romantic legends in the new medium of film, even with its avant-garde aesthetics. Even before 1918, cinema had proved its suitability for patriotic, Romantic-historical narratives, largely in the mode of the dramatization of

Table 12.1a *National-heroic movies in Europe, 1909–1914*

Year	Country	Theme/title	Notes
1909	Russia	*Mazeppa*	On the cossack leader thematized by Pushkin, Byron and Verdi
1910	Russia	*Peter the Great*	Reprised in Soviet Russia in 1937
1910	Denmark	*Holger Danske*	On the legendary warrior
1911	Serbia	Karađorđe	—
1912	Germany	*Theodor Körner*	Reprised in 1932
1913	Germany	Queen Louise	Reprised in 1929, 1931 and 1957
1913	Germany	Wilhelm Tell	Reprised in 1923, 1934, 1956, 1960 and 2007
1914	Hungary	*Bank Bán*	On the heroic Ban (viceroy) Bank thematized in Jozsef Katona's 1819 play and Erkel's 1861 opera

Table 12.1b *National-heroic movies in Europe, 1918–1929*

Year	Country	Theme/title	Notes
1918	Britain	*Nelson*	—
1919	'Yugoslavia'	*Matija Gubec*	On the insurgent thematized in the novel *Seljačka buna* ('The Peasant Revolt', 1877) by August Šenoa; reprised in 1975
1921	Czechoslovakia	*Jánošík*	On the heroic outlaw; reprised in 1935
1923	Germany	*Friedrich Schiller*	Reprised in 1940
1923	Germany	*Wilhelm Tell*	See 1913 and 1934
1923	Hungary	*The Stars of Eger Fortress*	Based on the novel *Egri csillagok* (1899) by Géza Gardonyi, with the hero Gergely Bornemissza; reprised in 1968
1924	Germany	*Nibelungen / Siegfried*	Fritz Lang's expressionist version, based on Hebbel's dramatization of 1861; in two parts
1924	Germany	The Battle of Teutoburg Forest	On the hero Arminius the Cheruscan
1924	Sweden	*Frithiof's Saga*	Based on Esaias Tegnér's version of 1825
1926	USSR	*Taras Shevchenko*	On the Ukrainian national poet/painter as a working-class hero
1927	Britain	*Boadicea*	—
1927	France	*Napoleon*	Abel Gance's large-scale epic
1928	France	Joan of Arc	French production directed by the Danish Carl Theodor Dryer, based on the trial records edited by Quicherat in 1841–1849
1928	USSR	Kastus Kalinovsky	On the Belarusian insurgent/writer executed in 1864, based on the historical novels by V. V. Krestovsky
1928	Sweden	*Gustav Vasa*	In two parts
1929	Germany	*Queen Louise*	See 1913, 1931 and 1957
1929	Germany	*Andreas Hofer*	On the leader of the Tyrolean rebellion of 1809; see 1932

great national figures. Tables 12.1a, 12.1b and 12.1c indicate a productivity that is fairly evenly distributed across Europe.*

A few striking patterns emerge from this list. The production spread was pan-European (albeit skewed towards Germany, Central–Eastern Europe and Italy). The themes are almost invariably of nineteenth-century

* A full searchable checklist and dataset of the films mentioned here and in the following pages is online at e-rn.ie/heroicmovies.

Table 12.1c *National-heroic movies in Europe, 1930–1939*

Year	Country	Theme/title	Notes
1931	USSR	The Koliivščyna Uprising	On an insurgency, based on Shevchenko's epic poem *Hajdamaky* ('The Outlaws') of 1841
1931	Germany	*Louise, Queen of Prussia*	See 1913 and 1929
1932	Germany	*The Rebel*	The protagonist is based on Andreas Hofer (see 1929); allegory of refusal to abide by the terms of the Versailles Treaty; highly appreciated by the Nazi leadership
1932	Germany	*Theodor Körner*	See 1912
1934	Germany	*Wilhelm Tell*	See 1913 and 1923
1934	Netherlands	*William of Orange*	—
1934	Italy	*Villafranca*	Risorgimento-themed film based on a play by Mussolini
1934	Italy	*The 1,000-Man Army of Garibaldi*	—
1935	Czechoslovakia	*Jánošík*	See 1921
1935	Belgium	*Ulenspieghel Still Lives*	On the abiding spirit of the trickster folk hero (celebrated in Charles de Coster's 1867 novel) in the Flemish character
1935	Italy	*Ettore Fieramosca*	After the 1833 novel by Manzoni
1936	Britain	*Rhodes of Africa*	Celebrating the imperialist Cecil Rhodes
1937	USSR	*Peter the Great*	See 1910; in two parts
1938	Poland	*Kosciuszko at the Battle of Racławice*	—
1938	France	*The Marseillaise*	On the anthem's nation-building effect in 1792
1938	Italy	*Giuseppe Verdi*	—
1938	USSR	*Alexander Nevsky*	—
1939	USSR	*Minin and Pozharsky*	On two anti-Polish resistance heroes in 1611–1612

vintage. Even when themes or heroes from an earlier period are thematized, the film versions tend to follow the canonized version of events as laid down by Romantic writers and historians (Schiller being the main conduit for Wilhelm Tell). In that sense, most of these films are remediations of nineteenth-century Romantic historicism in a new, high-tech medium. What is also noticeable is the thematic repetitiveness: many of these films return to the themes of earlier ones. That is partly due to the technical innovations of the medium. Sound film would return to topics covered previously in silent movies, now obsolete, and the later advent of colour or extra-large formats would stimulate similar recyclings.

On the other hand, that pattern is also characteristic of canonicity as such. Whatever enjoys canonical status is, almost by definition, a repeatedly reactivated – not a dormant or inert – cultural presence: like repeated performances of Shakespeare plays or reprints of *Les Misérables*. What is more, canonicity seems to project these repetitions and reactivations across different media and makes use of new media as they emerge: operas and films based on Shakespeare plays; graphic-novel renderings of *Les Misérables* as well as audio books and films and musicals, and musicals turned into films. And so we can phrase the principle both ways: film is a new habitat for classics of Romantic-nationalist vintage; and also the cultural canon established by Romantic nationalism was successfully remediated into the emerging new media of cinema and television.

In the present century, DVD and then streaming video have become the dominant platforms for viewing, eroding the centralized distribution of the twentieth century (cinemas, broadcasting corporations); at the same time, this more diffused mode of home-viewing distribution has been counterbalanced by a collectivized, internet-based mode of reviewing (websites, blogs, discussion channels, social media). But 'cloudification' (domestic consumption, online discussion) affects only the distribution and reception patterns of cinematic drama. Production costs have remained high, and studios and broadcasting corporations remain important producers.

Even in the 1920s and 1930s, the signs of globalization were there. In India, a film was produced about the nation-building King Harishchandra as early as 1913. Post-1918, the foundations were laid for what later would become the largest film industry worldwide. Some early films are already national consciousness-raisers invoking the subcontinent's proud past and rich heritage. *Bhakta Vidur* ('The devotion of Vidura', 1921) dramatized an episode from the classic Mahabharata epic, but it was banned by the British authorities because they felt it to be an allegorical endorsement of Gandhi. Gandhi's presence was also noticeable in the first Indian talking movie in Tamil and Telugu, *Kalidas* (1931, now lost), which celebrated the Sanskrit poet of that name but included publicity songs of the Congress Party and in praise of Gandhi. The first Marathi talkie, *The King of Ayodhya* (1931, with a Hindi-language version in 1932) returned to the figure of King Harishchandra. The 1933 historical drama *Sinhagad* was an adaptation of a 1903 historical novel by Hari Narayan Apte celebrating the inspiring figure of the Marathi warrior-monarch Shivaji, a widespread *lieu de mémoire* in modern India's developing national consciousness; he would be thematized again in films in 1952, 2018 and 2019. The 1936 biopic of the seventeenth-century Saint Tukaram (Marathi, again) marked the breakthrough of Indian cinema on the international scene: it won high praise at the 1937 Venice film festival. Inside India it was seen as an exemplification of the non-violent values of Gandhi-style nationalism.

And there was, of course, Hollywood. The films discussed here are from a period that is bracketed by two American classics. The earlier one was D. W. Griffiths's *Birth of a Nation* (1915), a landmark of American cinema and, be it added, a diatribe of southern states resentment, white supremacism and Ku Klux Klan glorification (it was based on Thomas Dixon's racist novel *The Clansman*, 1905). The American south was also the setting of the period's later-date bookend: *Gone With the Wind* (1939), in which cinema exploded into full-colour large-screen spectacle. The premiere took place in Atlanta, the city whose burning marks the film's dramatic high point midway; a screening was held in 1961 to mark the centenary of the Civil War's outbreak. In successive reissues, its format was enlarged to widescreen and then to 70mm. Its status as a national classic stands at odds with the middlebrow book that provides the screenplay: Margaret Mitchell's 1938 novel was typical of the bodice-ripping romances into which the Scott format of the historical novel had declined. No *War and Peace* this; yet it aptly caught the most incisive crisis in American history in a passionate combination of private, feminine-focused romance and national historical epic. Its enduring persistence in post-war American culture was compounded and reinforced by a similarly constructed television series, *North and South* (1985–1994), based on the 1980s trilogy by John Jakes.*

The cases of India and the US indicate strong lines of continuity across World War II. Within Europe, the years 1940–1945 marked a caesura.

* Another 1930s movie that occupies a 'nodal' position was *The Thirty-Nine Steps* (1935), by the young Alfred Hitchcock. It trademarked the Hitchcock style, deftly manipulating tension by innovative techniques combined with debonair storytelling; but it also drew on the tradition of Great War propaganda. The screenplay was based on one of the Richard Hannay novels by John Buchan, an important voice in the British propaganda machine. Buchan, later to become Governor-General of Canada, patented the nationally propagandistic pulp-fiction 'secret agent' genre: the pluck and daring of British heroes was put to the test in a clever and exciting showdown with evil foreign adversaries. The end of the Great War made the further production of this type of tales strategically superfluous, but they remained in circulation (as *The Thirty-Nine Steps* shows) and the genre as such had a lasting audience appeal. Espionage thrillers remained wildly popular. James Bond would in due course become the new Richard Hannay, but (as Hitchcock's own transfer to Hollywood illustrates) in a Western alignment of Atlantic countries against the communist East.

Cold-War Asymmetries

The years 1940–1945 saw some historicist propagandistic films in the 'Great Men' mode: Soviet films on the Cossack hetman Khmelnitsky (1941), on the victorious general Suvorov (1941), on the Armenian hero Davit Bek (1944). The Third Reich produced films on Schiller and Bismarck (both 1940) and – embracing Dutch/Afrikaans – Rembrandt (1936) and the Boer leader Kruger (1941); Portugal chipped in with a biopic on Camões (1941).

The most notable nationalist film to come out of the war years was Goebbels's massive pet project *Kolberg* (1945), a lavish full-colour production completed even as the Third Reich was collapsing. Its storyline, set in the days of Napoleonic hegemony, was meant to encourage the German public in its dire straits: how a town held out against overwhelming odds, mobilizing the population one and all, until as if by a magic dispensation the fortunes of war turned and the mighty foes were vanquished. The anti-Napoleonic wars of liberation were a favourite point of reference for Goebbels, with frequent references to the verse of Theodor Körner.* But the film, like the Reich itself, sank in ruination.

The years of the Cold War show a remarkable asymmetry in production on the two sides of the Iron Curtain. Much propagandistic English-language movie entertainment, increasingly enmeshed in a Hollywood-dominated anglosphere, celebrated the heroism of the bygone war effort, first during the war years and afterwards as well. Wartime propaganda continued to be produced well after the war had actually ended and became a form of popular celebratory remembrance. In the Netherlands, the 1971 memoirs of a resistance hero were filmed by Paul Verhoeven, first as film (*Soldier of Orange*, 1977) and then as a television miniseries (*For Queen and Country*, 1979). The film in turn was made into a musical that premiered in 2010; *Soldaat van Oranje* has been on an uninterrupted run since then, with 3.5 million tickets sold, and is arguably the country's most important mnemonic platform in its remembrance of the Nazi occupation.

War commemoration was couched and made popular in dramatic action tales – also, in the G. A. Henty tradition, for boys, witness the 'Biggles' series by Captain W. E. Johns, and comic strips with such titles as *Commando*,

* As noted in Chapter 3, Goebbels had channelled the spirit of 1813 in the Sports Palace speech he held in early 1943, two weeks after the defeat at Stalingrad. On that occasion, he proclaimed a 'total war' (a phrase brought into general circulation by WWI general Ludendorff's book of 1935; meaning a complete subordination of civilian life, the national economy and public opinion to the war effort). The mounting frenzy of Goebbels's rhetoric culminated in a concluding quotation from Körner: 'Then, *Volk*, arise, and storm, break loose!'.

Warlord and *Battle Picture Weekly* – pulp comics that rendered shouts of *Achtung!* and *Schnell, schnell, Schweinhund!* widely familiar.[17] For Johns, the war never really ended: to the initial Biggles stories, set in the Great War, were added tales of the plucky pilot battling first the Nazis and then, after 1945, international communists and criminals. The timeline of military-hero comics also gravitates from the 1960s to the 1980s: *War Picture Library* ran from 1958 to 1984, *Commando* from 1961 to the present, *Warlord* from 1974 to 1986 and *Battle Picture Weekly* from 1975 to 1988. As those dates indicate, this mass-produced cartoon view of history continued right up to the moment when cinema took up the cue, Indiana Jones snarled his 'Nazis! I hate those guys!' and Rambo 'got to win this time'.

Throughout these Cold War decades, John Wayne starred multifunctionally, either as a sheriff in the Wild West or as an officer fighting the Nazis or the Japanese; British cinema evoked the exploits of navy vessels under their benign paternalist captains, from *In Which we Serve* (1942) and *We Dive at Dawn* (1943) to *The Cruel Sea* (1953). World War II movies morphed into heroic action in the 1960s (*The Guns of Navarone*, 1961; *The Longest Day*, 1962; *The Great Escape*, 1963; *The Dirty Dozen*, 1967). The genre then moved into the cheaper domain of television serials (the comedy *Dad's Army*, 1968–1977; *Colditz*, 1972; *Secret Army*, 1977–1979; the spoof *'Allo 'allo*, 1982–1992). National self-glorification in the epic pre-1940 mode took a back seat to a simple scheme of 'we the heroes' versus 'them the villains'. At best these productions deployed, seriously or comically, standard ethnotypes to characterize heroes and villains in the national-characterological clichés of 1914 vintage: sadistic, technocratic or rigidly unimaginative Germans versus mercurial French charm, quietly courageous English 'pluck' and energetic American 'can-do'.

In the West, war movies such as these largely supplanted the patriotic-heroic epic of earlier decades. Still, a steady trickle of Romantic-historicist dramas continued in Western Europe after 1945, with Franco's Spain as an added production area (see Tables 12.2a and 12.2b). The genre subsided into ambient unobtrusiveness.

The decline of French cinematic productivity after the end of the Fourth Republic in 1958 is striking – coinciding with the vehement rejection of the *cinéma de papa*. The temporal dynamics here are almost exactly in tandem with the periodicity of the decline and revival of idyllic rusticism as noted earlier, reaching a low ebb in the 1960s and 1970s and reviving in the 1980s with a shift towards TV. Heroic historicism goes into an almost total eclipse in the 1970s, which may perhaps be correlated with the coming of age of a baby-boom cohort that combined anti-authoritarianism with an anti-historicist

Table 12.2a *National-heroic movies in Western Europe, 1950–1960*

Year	Country	Title	Notes
1950	Spain	*Agustina de Aragón*	On Aurora Batista, heroine of the anti-Napoleonic wars
1951	Spain	*Dawn over America*	On Columbus
1952	Italy	*Red Shirts*	On Garibaldi
1953	Italy	*Verdi, Tragedy and Triumph*	—
1954	France	*Versailles, a Story*	*Si Versailles nous était conté*: *lieu-de-mémoire* compilation by Sacha Guitry
1955	France	*Napoleon*	Sacha Guitry version
1956	Austria	*Wilhelm Tell*	—
1956	France	*Paris, a Story*	*Si Paris nous était conté*: *lieu-de-mémoire* compilation by Sacha Guitry
1957	Germany	*Love and Sufferings of Queen Louise*	Remake of 1913, 1929, 1931; the theme of female royalty romance would switch to the *Sissi* franchise
1959	Spain	*Where To Now, Alfonso XI?*	Royalty glamour romance
1960	Switzerland	*Wilhelm Tell*	—
1960	France	*Austerlitz*	Late work by Napoleon-worshipper Abel Gance

Table 12.2b *National-heroic movies in Western Europe, 1961–1987*

Year	Country	Title	Notes
1961	Italy	*Viva l'Italia!*	On Garibalidi, by Rosselini
1964	Scotland	*Culloden*	Dramatized documentary
1965	Sweden	*Gustav Vasa*	—
1966	Germany	*Nibelungen*	In the sword-and-sandals style; in two parts
1967	Spain	*The Adventures of Cervantes*	—
1967	Germany	*Arminius the Cheruscan*	—
1969	Britain	*Alfred the Great*	—
1973	Britain	*Bequest to the Nation*	Romantic drama about Nelson's relationship with Lady Hamilton
1980	Basque country	*Sabino Arana*	Now possible in the post-Franco years
1981	Spain	*Cervantes*	—
1981	Britain	*Chariots of Fire*	Pan-British 'band of brothers' win medals at Parisian Olympics of 1924

Table 12.2b (*cont.*)

Year	Country	Title	Notes
1982	Italy	*Verdi*	TV miniseries
1983	Wales	*Owain Glendower*	Made for Welsh television (Channel 4 Cymru)
1984	Germany	*The Battle of the Teutoburg Forest*	TV production of Kleist's *Die Hermannsschlacht* (1808)
1984	Flanders	*The Lion of Flanders*	After the 1838 historical novel by Hendrik Conscience, *De Leeuw van Vlaenderen*; produced both as film and as TV miniseries
1984	Netherlands	*William of Orange*	TV miniseries
1987	Italy	*Garibaldi*	TV miniseries

turn. There is, however, an emergence of sub-national, regionalist films on Basque, Scottish, Welsh and Flemish themes, extolling the subaltern. And here as in the case of rusticism, a pronounced revival of patriotic history films begins in the 1980s, drawing markedly on the medium of television.*

As the mention of the *nouvelle vague* indicates, there was a general shift in tastes. Westerns and war movies were receding as well, overtaken by contemporary-set drama, thrillers, romantic comedies both urban and rustic-idyllic, and magic realism and science fiction. Even the war movies, dedicated to heroism in the national service, situated this heroism in a struggle not against other nations but against Nazism. In Western Europe's post-1945 ideological landscape, nationalism was, for once, a weak force – as we can also see from the steep drop in national commemorative monuments around this time (Figure 12.1). Internationalism thrived instead. The trend for multinational co-productions and multinational all-star casts became pronounced, and politically international relations were dominated by multilateralist organizations such as the United Nations, the European Economic Community and NATO – for the main enemy was now the Communist bloc.

The cinema of the Communist eastern bloc presents a different aspect, with a more intensive and sustained productivity that patently continues the cinematic remediation of Romantic nationalism (nineteenth-century heroes, and themes made familiar by nineteenth-century novels). For the Cold War years, Tables 12.3a, 12.3b and 12.3c list a lone Albanian film

* This trend was in sync with American developments: the *North and South* series of the mid-1980s was preceded in 1977 by the TV-series remake of the epic *How the West was Won*, originally a 1962 film.

Table 12.3a *National-heroic movies in Central and Eastern Europe, 1946–1962*

Year	Country	Title	Notes
1946	USSR	*Glinka*	Composer
1952	Poland	*The Youth of Chopin*	Composer
1952	Hungary	*Erkel*	Composer
1952	USSR	*The Composer Glinka*	Composer
1953	Albania	*The Great Warrior Skanderbeg*	USSR–Albanian co-production
1954	Poland	*Nicholas Copernicus*	Reprised in 1973
1954–1957	Czechoslovakia	*Jan Hus / Jan Žižka / Alone Against the World*	The so-called Hussite Trilogy
1956	USSR	*Ilya Muromets*	Based on *byliny* ballads about a legendary *bogatyr* (knight)
1960	Poland	*The Teutonic Knights*	Based on the 1900 novel by Henryk Sienkiewicz
1962	USSR	*The Hussar Ballad*	Romantic musical on the cross-dressing, gender-fluid cavalry officer Nadezhda Durova during the Napoleonic campaign, based on their autobiography

Table 12.3b *National-heroic movies in Central and Eastern Europe, 1966–1979*

Year	Country	Title	Notes
1966	USSR	*War and Peace*	Tolstoy's novel in Bondarchuk's dramatization; in four parts
1967	Romania	*The Dacians*	Decebalus's resistance against imperial Rome
1968	Hungary	*The Stars of the Eger Fortress*	Remake of the 1923 version
1969	Bulgaria	*Hristo Botev*	On the national poet, freedom fighter and martyr
1969	USSR (Estonia)	*The Last Relic*	On a popular rebellion; based on Eduard Bornhöhe's 1893 tale 'Prince Gabriel or The Last Days of Pirita Monastery'
1969–1999	Poland	*Sienkiewicz Trilogy*	The three canonical nationalist-historical novels – *By Fire and Sword*, 1884, *The Deluge*, 1886 and *Squire Wołodyjowski*, 1888 – were filmed in reverse order in 1969, 1974 and 1999

Table 12.3b (*cont.*)

Year	Country	Title	Notes
1970	Hungary	*Franz Liszt*	Composer
1970	Romania	*Michael the Brave*	On the sixteenth-century Wallachian voivode
1973	Romania	*Ciprian Porumbescu*	Composer
1973	Poland	*Copernicus*	See 1954
1975	Romania	*Stephen the Great and the Battle of Vaslui, 1475*	—
1974	Poland	*Janosik*	TV miniseries; Czechoslovak films on this outlaw had been made in 1921 and 1935
1975	Yugoslavia	*The Peasants' Revolt of 1573*	On the rebellion thematized in the novel *The Peasant Revolt* by August Šenoa (1877); already thematized in 1919
1979	Romania	*Vlad the Impaler*	Celebrating the Wallachian voivode

Table 12.3c *National-heroic movies in Central and Eastern Europe, 1980–1989*

Year	Country	Title	Notes
1980	Romania	*Burebista*	On the Dacian king
1980	Romania	*Nicolae Bălcescu*	On the 1848 revolutionary
1981	Yugoslavia	*Strahinja Banović*	On the legendary hero at the eve of the 1389 Battle of Kosovo
1982	USSR (Azerbaijan)	*Nizami*	On the Persian (Azeri?) poet
1982	USSR	*Yaroslav the Wise*	—
1983	GDR	*Martin Luther*	On the occasion of his 500th birthday; the communist view
1983	Czechoslovakia	*The Wanderings of Jan Amos*	On Comenius
1983	Yugoslavia	*Karađorđe's death*	On the leader of the Serbian uprising of 1804–1813
1983	Hungary	*Heroic Times*	Animated film based on Arany's 1846 three-part epic poem about Miklos Toldi
1984	Hungary	*King Stephen*	Filmed version of the 1983 rock opera about the medieval king
1986	USSR	*Lermontov*	On the Romantic writer
1986	USSR	*Primeval Rus'*	After the historical novel by Valentin Ivanov (1960)

Table 12.3c (*cont.*)

Year	Country	Title	Notes
1987	Yugoslavia	*Vuk Karadžić*	TV series
1987	Hungary	*Bank the Viceroy*	Made for TV; on the heroic Ban (viceroy) Bank thematized in Jozsef Katona's 1819 play and Erkel's 1861 opera
1988	Bulgaria	*Time of Violence*	On Ottoman oppression; based on Anton Donchev's 1864 novel
1989	Yugoslavia	*The Battle of Kosovo*	Marking the 600th anniversary of that event

(on the nation's über-hero Skanderbeg) and a single East German one, two films from Bulgaria, four from Czechoslovakia (including a bizarre trilogy where Jan Hus appears to be motivated by a Stalinist class consciousness), five from Yugoslavia, six each from Hungary and Romania, eight from Poland and ten from the USSR (including the Soviet republics of Estonia and Azerbaijan). That total of forty-two national-heroic film productions is fifty per cent higher than that of Western Europe during the same period.

Again, in many cases, the screenplays were based on pre-1914 novels or history books (Sienkiewicz, Bornhöhe, Šenoa, Arany, Donchev). The heroes represent a peculiar sociological selection: monarchs/warlords, proletarian outlaws/revolutionaries, and a slew of composers, poets and intellectuals.

Readers are probably bewildered by this array, some of whose names (Chopin, Copernicus) stand out amidst the numerous unfamiliar ones. But none of the names in Tables 12.3(a-c) are obscure. The monarchs, warlords, insurgents and artists/intellectuals: all have monuments and thoroughfares named after them in their countries' capitals, and they appear on banknotes and postage stamps. The films merely add to the commemorative cult that for each and every one of them had begun in the Romantic historicism of the nineteenth century. Much more remarkable is their sociological background, which emphatically includes and celebrates the elite, and which follows in the footsteps of a canon established by pre-socialist, 'bourgeois-liberal' authors, lacking class consciousness. That wholesale adoption by the communist regimes is puzzling. To account for this apparent anomaly, we should realize that in Marxist literary and cultural criticism 'bourgeois patriotism' was seen as an unobjectionable albeit obsolete stage in society's historical progress towards class consciousness and class struggle. These 'bourgeois-patriotic' productions apparently were acceptable enough for the communist regimes to be recycled as entertainment, if necessary draped in some class-consciousness or as prefigurations of the present-day leaders. Many of these films became popular and were fixtures, broadcast annually on TV on public holidays. (And a turn towards TV production is noticeable here, as elsewhere, in the 1980s.) Some of the productions were instrumentalized by post-1968 communist leaderships (gestures towards youth culture during the later Kadar regime in Hungary; Ceauçescu's Romanian exceptionalism and his leadership cult). Others laid the foundations for what after the fall of communism would become foregrounded preoccupations in the new cultures of nationalism, for example the Kosovo myth in Serbia or the Polish sense of being surrounded by enemies on all sides (the dominant self-image in Sienkiewicz's novels).

The ongoing cultural presence of post-Romantic national historicism during the Cold War years stands in contrast to the genre's decline in the West in the decades of the baby-boomers' counter-culture. The sudden resurgence of nationalism as the leading ideology after the downfall of communism in Eastern Europe cannot be seen in isolation from the latent persistence of 'bourgeois patriotism' and the ongoing affirmation of the nation as a feel-good factor under communist rule. While in the West between 1945 and 1989 nationalism was frowned upon, or at best ambient and 'banal', it remained discreetly influential in communist Eastern Europe.[18]

Meanwhile, outside Europe

In India, now an independent country, cinematic nationalism was neither dormant nor latent but very much present. Here the film industry was burgeoning, and the dominance of patriotic content continued in the early post-independence decades.[19] This persisted without much discontinuity across the 1989 divide and intensified after 2000 in a climate of growing Hindu nationalism (Tables 12.4a and 12.4b).

These films from various parts of India celebrate a mix of historical nation-builders (from ancient and more modern periods) and anticolonial activists. Production seems to have stagnated somewhat in the decades 1970–2000 (six noteworthy productions in thirty years). This period was marked by the Congress Party's decline (first election loss in 1977, the assassinations of Indira and of Rajiv Gandhi in 1984 and 1991). Post-2000, another surge in production occurred: fifteen noteworthy productions

Table 12.4a *National-heroic movies in India, 1949–1991*

Year	Title	Notes
1949	*Maharana Pratap*	On Maharana Pratap Singh (1540–1597); see 2012
1952	*Chhatrapati Shivaji*	On the heroic Marathi ruler (seventeenth century); see 2018
1952	*Anand Math*	Based on the canonical Bengali novel *Anandamath* (1882) by Bankim Chandra Chatterjee; set during the late-eighteenth-century Sannyasi Rebellion
1953	*Queen of Jhansi*	On the 1857 rebel queen; the first Technicolor film made in India; see 2019
1959	*Veerapandiya Kattabomman*	On the eighteenth-century south Indian rebel against the East India Company; first Tamil film in Technicolor
1959	*Samrat Prithviraj Chauhan*	On the legendary Rajput king; see 1962, 2006
1960	*Ranadheera Kanteerava*	On the Mysore emperor; made in Karnataka in the Kannada language
1961	*Kappalottiya Thamizhan*	on V. O. Chidambaram Pillai (1872–1936)
1962	*Raani Samyuktha*	On the wife of Prithviraj Chauhan (1959)
1963	*Chitor Rani Padmini*	On the legendary Queen Padmini; see 1959, 1964, 2018
1964	*Maharani Padmini*	See 1963, 2018
1965	*Shaheed*	On the freedom fighter Bhagat Singh, executed by the British authorities in 1931
1970	*Sri Krishnadevaraya*	On the monarch of the Vijayanagara Empire
1979	*Meera*	On Mirabai (1502–1556), mystic poet and Krishna devotee
1981	*Kranti*	Historical epic on a variety of activists in the independence movement, 1825–1875
1986	*Tandra Paparayudu*	In Telugu, on the seventeenth-century military leader who resisted French colonial expansion
1990	*Tipu Sultan*	On the nineteenth-century ruler of Mysore; based on a novel by Bhagwan Gidwani and broadcast on Indian national TV in 1990
1991	*Chanakya*	Hindu-nationalist 47-part epic-historical television drama the ancient political thinker Chanakya (a.k.a. Kauṭilya)

in twenty years, culminating in 2022 with the extravaganza *RRR*, which received worldwide fame through Netflix. In the panoply of glorified national heroes, old monarchs and modern insurgents alike, the post-2000 production was able to pick up from the pre-1970 tradition: there were remakes of the films dedicated to Shivaji, Maharana Pratap Singh, Prithviraj Chauhan and the fighting Queen Lakshmibai of Jhansi.

Table 12.4b *National-heroic movies in India, 2000–2022*

Year	Title	Notes
2000	*Bharati*	On the Tamil-language nationalist writer Subramania Bharati (1882–1921)
2001	*Aśoka*	On the emperor who ruled most of the Indian subcontinent in the third century BC; also broadcast as a TV miniseries
2005	*Magnal Pandey: The Rising*	Celebrating the soldier who sparked the Indian Rising ('Mutiny') in 1857
2006	*Dharti ka Veer Yodha Prithviraj Chauhan*	TV serial, see 1959
2010	*Khelein Hum Jee Jaan Sey*	On the 1930 Chittagong armoury raid masterminded by Surya Sen (executed 1933)
2011	*Chandragupta Maurya*	TV series, revived in 2018, on the founder of the ancient Maurya empire
2012	*Maharana Pratap*	See 1949
2012	*Krantiveera Sangolli Rayanna*	On the military leader executed by the British in 1831; made in Karnataka in the Kannada language
2015	*Rudhramadevi*	On the thirteenth-century queen; made in Telangana in the Telugu language; also thematized in a 100-part TV series (2021)
2015	*Bajirao Mastani*	On founder of the Maratha Empire, Baji Rao I (1700–1740), and his Muslim concubine; based on a Marathi-language novel by N. S. Inamdar (1972)
2018	*Farzand*	On epic warfare during the reign of Shivaji; see 1952, 2019
2018	*Padmaavat*	On Padmavati; see 1963, 1964
2019	*Fatteshikast*	On epic warfare during the reign of Shivaji; see 1952, 2018
2019	*Queen of Jhansi*	See 1953
2020	*Marakkar: Arabikadalinte Simham*	Made in Kerala in the Malayalam language; on the naval defence against Portuguese colonial encroachment
2022	*RRR*	On the anticolonial activists Alluri Sitarama Raju (1897–1924) and Komaram Bheem (1901–1940)

RRR, for all its intensely Indian, Hindutva content, achieved global fame on a newly burgeoning, transnational video streaming platform; it deserves a brief extra comment. A lavish action-hero extravaganza, the film fictionalizes the imagined interaction between two historical figures, anticolonial activists from the 1920s. A Telugu production (the initials in the title stand for *Raudraṁ Raṇaṁ Rudhiraṁ*, 'Rage, War, Blood'), but co-produced by companies from various parts of India, the film focuses on the plight and resistance of the Adivasi tribal communities of Southern India. The film portrays the representatives of British rule as cartoonishly evil; the resistance triumph is almost literally an apotheosis, as one of the heroes takes on the looks and guise of the mythical Rama, hero of the *Ramayana* epic. The finale celebrates a selection of personalities as a veritable lineage, from various parts of India, in the tradition of anti-British resistance: twentieth-century activists such as Subhas Chandra Bose, Vallabhbhai Patel and Bhagat Singh, and canonical historical figures such as Queen Lakshmibai and Chhatrapati Shivaji. That *tableau de la troupe* is set to a song-and-dance exhortation to honour the national flag. The flag that is featured visually is the 1907 flag of Indian independence, emblazoned with the long-standing nationalist *Vande Mataram* mantra/slogan, which is repeatedly chanted in the course of the film.[20]

The visual spectaculars and song-and-dance interludes are pure Bollywood (stretching that term to include Telugu 'Tollywood' and other production hubs in the subcontinent outside Mumbai); and the heroes and historical memories are as homegrown Indian as the Bollywood production style. Even so, I would venture to suggest that *RRR* is also an example of what Bob van der Linden has termed 'Romantic nationalism in India'.[21] It displays all the hallmarks: linking together a series of activists from different periods and regions into a transcendental lineage asserting *une certaine idée de l'Inde* (for what is Hindutva other than such an ideal essence of cultural identity?); the invocation of national myth (Rama and the *Ramayana*) as the ultimate validator of national authenticity; the positioning of culture and its *lieux de mémoire* as an inspirational and motivating force in the resistance against foreign rule – and doing so, to boot, in a movie that tightly dovetails narrative and spectacle. In all those respects *RRR* answers to the very definition of Romantic nationalism. It would be simplistic to reduce *RRR* to 'the influence of Walter Scott and Jules Michelet'; but it would be equally wrong to deny that influence altogether. The Romantic historicism of Scott and the national idealism of Michelet entered not only into a European circulation of ideas but into a global one, and it reached not only Latvia and Iceland but also the US and India, inflected meanwhile by a multitude of local and global circumstances. Specific to India were the repertoire of a prestigious historical culture native to the subcontinent and a lineage of Indian intellectual and artistic activists with an anticolonial agenda. But inflected and assimilated as it was, the mode of Romantic nationalism forms part, and recognizably so, of the style and substance of such films as *RRR*. Romantic nationalism after the century of globalization can no longer be studied in European isolation.

Epic Nationalism: Outrage into Charisma

Plotting a timeline of the worldwide production of nationally themed entertainment cinema offers a curve that is highly reminiscent, albeit on a different timescale, to the one illustrating the production of commemorative statues (Figure 12.1): a sudden onset, a mid-twentieth-century dip, and a remarkable resurgence post-1990 (Figure 12.5).

'Romantic nationalist' cinema comes in a variety of styles and genres. There are the reverent recyclings of national classics; the historicist celebrations of the lives of national heroes (such as Queen Lakshmibai of Jhansi, or Winston Churchill, or Napoleon); the fictionalized/narrative evocations of critical turning points in the nation's history (often based on classics in the Walter Scott tradition). There is also a much more 'unpolitical' genre, where the nation is unobtrusively present only as a mellow feel-good factor, as in period dramas (*Chariots of Fire*), royalty glamour

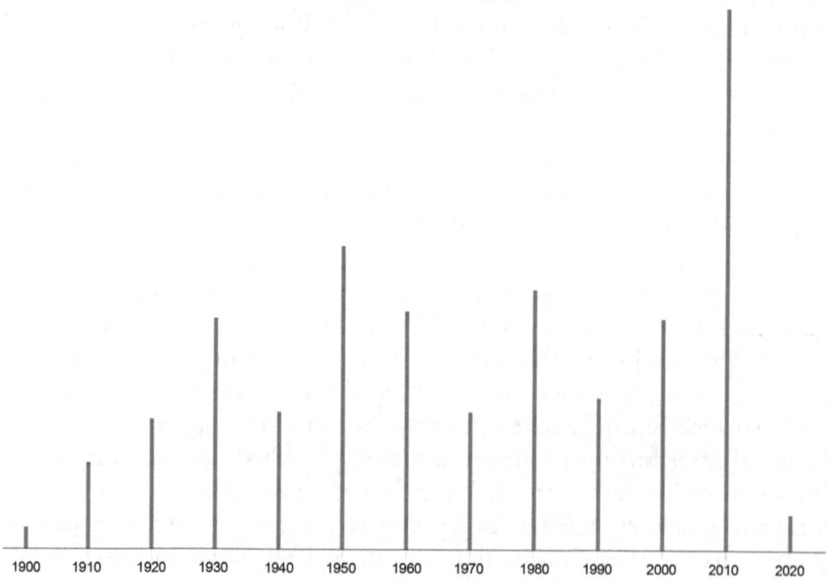

Figure 12.5 Production of films with national-heroic content per decade (e-rn.ie/moviesovertime; the vertical bars represent the relative numbers of films).

(the various *Queen Louise* iterations) and the rustic-idyllic register (*Jean de Florette*). And finally, there is the strident genre of the national action-hero movie. That, I would suggest, is the way in which national epic is nowadays presented to mass audiences. In many cases, epic lies at the heart of it: not only through cinematic versions of the *Nibelungenlied* or *Beowulf*, but also in that an entire sub-genre is dedicated to Hegelian hero-figures and how they brought the nation into being (Gustav Vasa and Wilhelm Tell) or ensured its survival at a critical juncture (King Stephen of Hungary).

The sheer number of these films post-1989 is overwhelming. From 1991 (yet another Alexander Nevsky version, Russian) to 2020 (yet another thematization of Arminius the Cheruscan in the German Netflix series *Barbaren*), the total comes to something like seventy-five (excluding almost twenty Indian productions). Many of the post-1989 instances revert to canonical figures already celebrated in earlier thematizations. Between them, they are a heterogeneous lot,* but all of them exemplify the enduring power of hero-worship almost two centuries after Carlyle. National epics share a small twenty-first-century world, with DVDs marketed through Amazon and streaming services wrapping the globe in a single cloud, pooling the heroic resources of all nations into a single entertainment market.

Small wonder, then, that despite the huge cultural and geographic span of these national epics, there should be a strong stylistic family likeness between all these action movies. A certain global convergence of the format is noticeable, favouring similar production values and marketing strategies for similar products. The posters, for instance, tend to follow a highly standardized iconography. A stern, defiant figure is foregrounded against a stormy sky or scenes of battle, symbolizing both the heroic stature of the protagonist and the crisis in which his (or in some cases her) heroism manifests itself. The hero's facial expression is aggressively battle-ready to match the occasion.

More importantly, perhaps, similarities can be explained from a common thematic DNA. We can trace these common elements through the focusing lens of Mel Gibson's *Braveheart* (1995). Gibson came out of a generation of masculine action stars in a genre that, following *Rambo*, had already begun to make use of patriotism and family values to motivate and ethically justify their blood-soaked violence. William Wallace, title hero of *Braveheart*, is marked as a 'good guy' by his tender attachment to his fiancée and his

* In 1996 we encounter Yermak Timofeyevich, Robert the Bruce and Michael Collins; in 1997 Jinnah (founding father of Pakistan) and Aśoka; in 2012 Mehmet II and Abraham Lincoln; in 2016 Robert the Bruce (again) and the proto-Kazakh Queen Tomiris.

happily integrated life in his home community; the rape and murder of that fiancée are what drive him into berserker mode, painting his face blue and inspiring his armies with the roar of 'Freedom!' It is in fact a remarkable dramatic transmutation: the cruel depiction of outraged and violated women is transmuted into righteous anger against invading armies, and the spoliation of the home community provokes a nationwide war to cleanse the country as a whole. Private affect is evoked in painful, lingering detail; the horribly evil villains, the heart-rendingly innocent and vulnerable victims and the admirable, outraged heroes are depicted in stark black-and-white contrast. Epic meets melodrama: neither does 'subtle', and mixed feelings and moral dilemmas are left to more high-minded genres. Black-and-white contrast is also applied to the happy, harmonious and familial scenes of the homeland community and its hideous disruption by sadistic invaders. The technique of the *fête interrompue* is frequently applied: scenes of cheerful festivity precede the sudden disaster that interrupts them. The powerful, primary emotions that are depicted are easily empathized with by popcorn-snacking audiences; these passions then trigger and motivate a revenge campaign, in which the private becomes political and the agitated viewer shares the heroes' anguish and glory.[22]

All this emotive sound and fury cloaks a political sleight of hand. The communitarian man of the people, even as he takes up the banner of freedom, becomes an authoritarian leader. 'Freedom' becomes a battle cry for commanders barking orders and imposing discipline. Moral outrage about individual fates morphs into a territorial strategy about a fatherland. The innocent victims may or may not be individually avenged on the actual perpetrators, but the anger at their fate serves to invest their self-appointed avenger with the authority of righteousness and the power to command his followers in the territorial crusade to cleanse the country. Outrage is transfigured into charisma.

That rhetoric is not exclusively cinematic, of course; readers will have no trouble thinking of examples from populist politics. And *Braveheart* did not invent it – we can find the tropes already in the epic followers of Walter Scott, such as Sienkiewicz and Conscience, and in early epic films such as *The Birth of a Nation* and *Alexander Nevsky*. In the former, liberated slaves (played by actors in blackface) chase and rape terrified young women (white, of course); in the latter, morose Teutonic Knights ritually throw toddlers into a fire. The screams of the innocent are transmuted into roars of vengeance: raised by the Ku Klux Klan in Griffiths's film, by the title hero in Eisenstein's (liberating *Russkaya Zemlya*, the Russian Land). Braveheart's rousing call to 'Freedom!' segues into a roared *Alba gu bragh* ('Scotland for ever').

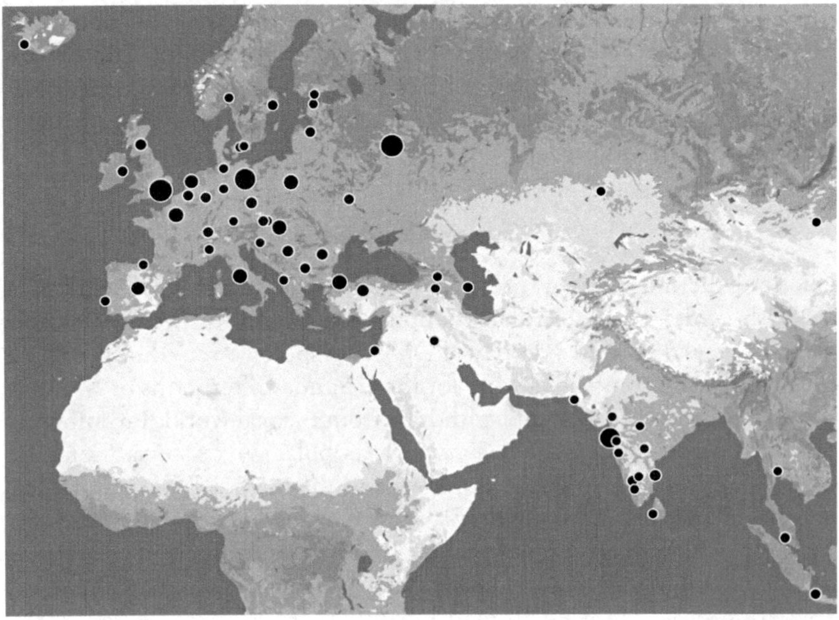

Figure 12.6 Eurasian geographic distribution by production location of 100 epic-heroic national action movies since 1990 (e-rn.ie/movies).

The dramatic scheme is crude (as it is in epic by nature) but effective, and post-*Braveheart* it is applied again and again in the national action movie. The ERNiE checklist gives close to 100 titles post-1990 answering to this description, with a worldwide distribution concentrated in Britain, Russia and India and in a forked belt reaching from Turkey to the Baltic (Figure 12.6).

Like statues, such films are expensive to produce but cheap to get access to; in their distribution they are as 'unrestricted' as postage stamps or banknotes (to recall Bourdieu's terms as discussed in the Introduction). On the whole, they target not art-houses but large audiences seeking entertainment, and they rely on a commercial investment-and-return model rather than on cultural subsidies.

All this turns commercial mass-entertainment cinema into a congenial habitat for popularized nationalism. In noticing the worldwide prevalence of nationalism in the twenty-first century, it is impossible not to take account of this widespread, sustained and deeply penetrative cinematic presence. These films are not in themselves remarkable – they do not often figure in the film festivals and awards presentations; outside their country of origin they are often marketed direct-to-DVD or by streaming services, and their cultural presence is unobtrusive. That unobtrusiveness has been described as 'banal' by Michael Billig. Such terms have been used across the pages of this book to hint at that unobtrusiveness of nationalism: diffuse, unpolitical, latent. It is now time to focus more sharply on this aspect.

Diffusion Condensed

I noticed the most 'banal' presence of cinematic nationalism in 2018 in a British garden centre. In that shopping emporium for the comfortable middle classes, I spotted a display of DVDs on special offer. They promised cheap, domestic comfort viewing for those Sunday afternoons or Monday evenings when we cocoon and withdraw from the real world. Prominently displayed were *Upstairs, Downstairs* (a popular 1970s social/domestic drama series set in Edwardian London) and the many BBC costume dramas based on Jane Austen, the Brontës, Charles Dickens and Anthony Trollope, with lashings of local-colour Englishness and period feel. In the next stand, targeting the male rather than the female customers, there was a selection of war movies; Roman Polanski's *The Pianist* was flanked by *The Great Escape*, *The Bridge over the River Kwai* and *Dad's Army*; there were generous helpings of Churchill and gung-ho military stuff, all of it recalling Britain's finest hour when she proudly stood alone. Remaindered DVDs in a garden centre: it doesn't get much more banal, or trivial, than this. But here, I felt, I came face to face with the deep cultural undercurrents that delivered Brexit when nobody was expecting it. By that time, the Falklands War of 1982 had become yesterday's news, submerged and unrecalled, superseded by so many new crises and conflicts. Forgotten, too, was how that conflict had instantaneously resuscitated the Dunkirk Spirit in a jingoistic publicity blitz from the red-top press, unleashing waves of flag-waving belligerence in a country that the year before had mellowed out over *Chariots of Fire*.[23] Latent nationalism is to be found not even in new productions but in the ongoing, cheap, 'unrestricted' availability of half-forgotten older ones.

Much of this book was, in a way, a pre-history of this trickled-down cultural residue. Walter Scott, Jacob Grimm, Franz Liszt, Jules Michelet, Hermann Wislicenus and Max Müller have come to this. The nation is still an operative factor, but homeopathically diluted down from its actual political meaning; an unpolitical cliché, like 'family values', to tell the Good Guys from the Bad Guys – a far cry indeed from Sieyès and Fichte. Can this unpolitical nation in mass consumer culture have any mobilizing force at all?

The way in which political nationalism (the 'politics of the nation') interacts with cultural nationalism (the 'culture of the nation') is in itself a diffuse and widely ramifying topic. It covers knowledge production (linguistics, history writing, philology) and artistic production (literature, painting, music); and while political nationalism manifests itself in a specific country or society, the culture of the nation can spread across borders and eventually diffuse itself across the globe. In addition, we have seen how this culture of the nation can move from celebrated artists and scholars to the general public (like the Grimms's fairy tales or Walter Scott's *Ivanhoe*). Diffusion across fields, across countries, across the social spectrum. To trace all that diffusion – to, in a word, *condense* it all into historical data – is like retro-engineering the vapour of criss-crossing contrails in the sky into flight paths and airplanes and the history of aviation. The massive undertaking of the *Encyclopedia of Romantic Nationalism in Europe* made it possible for me to attempt such as condensation, to see the forest through the many, many trees.

The pattern that stands out in the twentieth century, which brings this book to its close, is a dynamics of alternating states that I call latency (or dormancy) and salience. Nationalism has manifested itself in culture, sometimes as a fervently professed political ideal, sometimes unpolitically as a general feel-good factor or an background noise, sometimes not at all.

The re-emergence of fervently professed, foregrounded nationalism after 1989 happened both in politics and in cultural production; and at that time, after the Cold War and two World Wars, it appeared (at least within the narrowly European purview) to come out of nowhere. How did it rise from oblivion? Many commentators saw it as an anomaly, an erratic response to unprecedented social change. The answer I suggest here is that the intervening 'oblivion' was not all that absolute; a nationalistic affect had persisted in a latent state, as an inert, deactivated but still available repertoire, in the ambient camouflage of everyday culture as an unpolitical feel-good factor. As cinematic evidence shows, that national affect was rising again in intensity from around 1980 on, reactivated in movies either rustic-nostalgic or action-heroic. One can liken the alternation between latency and salience to the progress of a dolphin. It startles us and attracts our attention when it rises above the water's surface, glistening in the sunlight, briefly. Now you see it – and then you don't. But wherever it surfaces, it is always the same dolphin; its trajectory is defined by the underwater periods between the moments of its salient visibility. Similarly, we need to understand nationalism, crucially, when it is submerged, becomes unnoticeable (Figure 12.7).

Figure 12.7 A visual metaphor for the alternating states of latency and salience in the cultural history of nationalism.

These submerged, unnoticeable states could be called 'banal' or 'trivial', but they are neither. Something that can exercise such a powerful ideological influence without even being noticeable deserves a better terminology. I prefer, therefore, the notions of 'salient' and 'latent' cultural nationalism; more or less what Billig calls 'hot'and 'banal' in political nationalism. The alternation of latency and salience corresponds also to the two-way traffic between cultural memory and what Aleida Assmann has called 'archival memory': the cultural repertoire that is not actively present in society but is on standby, available in books and cultural products, passively ready for activation.[24] This also explains the fact that much of cultural nationalism works by way of reappropriation, recall, recycling and remediation, in ever more 'unrestricted' formats: from manuscripts found on forgotten library shelves to outdated nineteenth-century novels recycled into action movies. To trace the history of cultural nationalism is like following the forward-moving trajectory of a rearview mirror, constantly catching new things in the past as it moves into the future.

Nationalism is a highly flexible, adaptable ideology. That poses a challenge to those who want to establish a specific typology or periodization. Our survey has followed how it bobbed and weaved in and out of political force fields, sometimes virulent, sometimes anodyne, how it swirled around the political and social crisis moments of the last two centuries, how it spread among highly dissimilar societies, art forms and communicative media, always molding itself into its changing surroundings. It is thanks to that plasticity and adaptability that nationalism has survived the twentieth century to become, once again, the most powerful ideology worldwide. But beneath the shifting shapes and hues, the cultural historian can detect that the new nationalism is not so very new after all; it plays on the same affects, uses the same tropes and principles, as what began around 1800 along the grinding edges of Europe's empires.

Summing Up

The Wave and the Turbulence

Over the preceding pages we have seen how the culture of nationalism ran its course from a sudden onset in the decades around 1800 to its many manifestations in the artistic and intellectual fields and to its steady, soft influence in how people envisioned states and their sovereignties. We have seen how its long, tapering aftermath was capable of infusing popular leisuretime culture as this emerged after 1850, and capable also of generating strident war propaganda after 1870 and political discourse in 1914, surviving the upheavals of the twentieth century in the sanctuary of popular culture. The pattern reminds us of a wave, cresting and crashing with foaming violence in its onset, then levelling off but leaving turbulence in its wake. It is during such a period of renewed turbulence that I am finishing this book. A newly virulent nationalism has carried over from the realm of a popular culture still breathing the spirit of wartime propaganda into the field of domestic politics and international relations. At the same time, this ultra-political virulence is counterbalanced by a sentimental celebration of the home nation in terms of the long continuance of its historical traditions and its idyllic communitarianism. These tropes are so ambient and all-pervasive that it required a long hard look at them to see that they all originated in the decades around 1800: the war propaganda, the traditionalism and the idyllic sentimentalism, which celebrates the nation as a political extension of familial domesticity, tranquil, benign and utterly inoffensive, yet capable of rousing its citizens into righteous battle fury. To render visible this ambient, diffuse ideological force, I had to note its manifestations in diverse fields of knowledge production (linguistic history and philosophy, philology, ethnography and folklore, history writing, mythological studies) and in art forms in different media (textual, musical, visual, performative); and I also had to trace how these cultural manifestations could be encountered in societies all over Europe, despite their considerable differences as regards economy, class relations and governance.

After exploring this complex turmoil, we must ask ourselves if any patterns can be extrapolated by way of conclusion. What are the takeaways?

Shape-Shifting, Thin-Centred, Soft-Powered

Complexity and turbulence are in themselves features of nationalism, thrown into sharp relief as we traced its cultural manifestations – those would be far less multifarious if we traced the art forms inspired by communism or Fascism. This is partly because of the greater longevity of nationalism, but then again, that longevity is itself an interesting characteristic. We have seen how nationalism was a revolutionary force challenging the might of empires in Odessa and Belfast; how it had become a state-affirming, reactionary force by the time of Treitschke and Barrès; how the nation allowed border-straddling minorities ('non-dominant ethnic groups') to develop a unified political ideal, feeding into emancipationism and separatism among its various constituents; how it could inspire the progressive, utopian reformism around the Arts and Crafts movement as well as the intolerant authoritarianism of illiberal states in the 1920s and 2000s. Nationalism is, among the political ideologies, the ultimate shape-shifter. It is chimerical, almost, and weaves in and out of near-invisibility, ranging from a mere feeling to a fully fledged social movement.[1]

Throughout this book, we have traced the latent and salient states of nationalism: now anodyne, 'unpolitical', cultural; now strident, confrontational, ultra-political; sometimes a mere feel-good flavour, sometimes a resounding call to arms. In those shimmering alternations, the culture of nationalism has over the centuries spread across the European landmass and across cultural fields and media. In all that mobility, nationalism has adapted itself to different circumstances: whether the country was at peace or at war; whether an economy was agricultural and serf-based or rapidly industrializing; whether there was an advanced public sphere carried by print capitalism and a dense media distribution, or a society with low literacy-rates and largely lacking printed matter; whether the cultural centres gravitated to courts, monasteries or middle-class urban sociability; regardless of religion (Protestant, Catholic, Orthodox, Jewish, Muslim or secularist): across all those divides nationalism could adapt itself, survive by shape-shifts and mutations.

This adaptability appears to be typical of nationalism. For this reason, nationalism has been called 'thin-centred' – a characterization also, interestingly, applied to populism (on which more in what follows).[2] Nationalism is, to be sure, an ideology properly speaking, in that it 'consists of a body of tenets and prejudices constituting both a world-view and a value system',[3] but it seems capable of attaching itself to any other political doctrine on the political right or left. There are nationally tinged inflections not only in its siblings on the far right but also in the political middle ground – conservatism, (neo-)liberalism, Christian democracy – and even in social democracy, socialism and communism. The epithet 'thin' may carry a misleading connotation of weakness and inconsequence with it, but that is certainly not the point. I take the notion of 'thinness' to connote precisely this flexible adaptability. Nationalism is almost a meta-ideology, an inflection of other political doctrines, and something that can camouflage itself as being unpolitical, merely an extension of family values.

Thinness does not mean weakness. But it does mean that we cannot measure its importance in terms of power, the capacity to enforce social change despite opposition or inertia. Compared to the power of the state, certainly pre-1914, the power of nationalism is indeed weak – as weak as a fishbone lodged in the throat of a champion weightlifter. As we have seen, direct confrontations with the power of the state almost invariably panned out in favour of the state; but the repeated defeats of national movements eventually led to their political ascendancy in the century after 1918. Nationalism has exercised, over a long period of time, influence rather than raw power. It has vested the nation, against the oppression of tyrants and the perceived danger coming from foreigners, with a lasting reservoir of soft power. It has given the nation its charisma: that is to say, the power to inspire and to nudge political developments at moments of crisis and political dissolution.

This brings us back to the longevity of nationalism. Although my periodization of nationalism brands me a 'modernist', we must realize that this 'modern' history of nationalism by now spans fully a quarter of a millennium. Its sustained survival along such a long time-span reminds us of the endurance of culture, which displays the same adaptability and shape-shifting flexibility in the remediating presence of its canonical works, surfing in self-perpetuation from books to operas to streaming video. And this also leads me to conclude that we cannot understand nationalism unless we understand it historically, as a persistent influence in modern history.

The Presence of the Past

Scattered across the preceding pages are the many traces left by Romanticism. From glamourized queens and empresses to patriotic verse echoing in the minds of post-1945 politicians (even Boris Johnson could not stop himself from muttering Kipling's 'Mandalay' while on a state visit to Myanmar), such traces may each individually have opened a single sight-line, an anecdotal anachronism, a trailing presence of the Then in the Now. Between them these individual threads form a web, something coherent and significant. Medieval epics and Romantic novels adapted to streaming video; anthems sung across the centuries with undiminished fervour; heavy metal bands recycling Germanic runes and sagas; Viktor Orbán's turanism allowing him access to a post-communist Eurasian support network; Slavophilia in the policies of Vladimir Putin; juvenile-Romantic national-imperial chauvinism in the thought of conservative politicians such as John Major, Michael Gove and Jan-Peter Balkenende; modern cityscapes suffused with national-historicist street names and monuments.

When I set out to trace the typology, manifestations and repertoire of Romantic nationalism, I envisaged this initially as an almost antiquarian project, dealing with neo-Gothic buildings and bourgeois medievalism; I soon discovered that many of those neo-Gothic buildings were dedicated to modern, technological purposes and that the statues, paintings and historical novels of nineteenth-century vintage had obtained a fresh lease of life on banknotes and postage stamps and in films. While the erection of national monuments went through a noticeable dip in the twentieth century, the resurgence of that type of cultural production since 1990 was unmistakable (Figure 12.1). The ongoing recycling and availability of the Romantic-historicist nineteenth-century repertoire in new, mass-diffused and unobtrusive media seemed to span the mid-century dip and to connect the nationalist heydays of 1910 and 2020. It is then that I saw the 'bump-dip-bump' shape of those graphs as the trajectory of that metaphorical dolphin that visibly surfaces, dives into invisibility and elsewhere surfaces again.

The power of nationalism to condense time and to abolish historical distance is remarkable. The culture of nationalism has become the great enabler of anachronism. It creates short-cuts of memorability, recognizability and identification across decades and centuries of changing circumstances, adding up to the most potent anachronism of all: that of 'timeless nations' with their abiding national identities.[4] National memories have an enormous power and presence in the here and now, and whoever would study nationalism only within the temporal parameters of a given social situation or a political moment would lose sight of that cardinally important potency. Nationalism can invoke memories and traditions spanning many centuries; it can pack all that temporality into a mighty ideological punch. Culture spans many centuries, but its national cultivation is concentrated in a handful of decades.

National Culture Transnationally Pursued

The cultural manifestations of nationalism take a similar form in highly dissimilar societies. Architecture, choral singing, the mural, amateur theatre and the decorative arts develop in parallels modes from Riga to Barcelona, Dublin to Iaşi. Academic scholars were aware of what was going on internationally in their field of expertise. Modern entrepreneurial formats such as the world fair developed standardized modes of showcasing the national individuality of the participants. The historical novel, academic history painting, the collecting of folktales were vogues enveloping all of Europe in their spread. Taken together, all this adds up to a strong counter-argument to the common wisdom that culture develops as a response to its surrounding societal conditions. The parallels are too numerous, too patently evident in various cultural fields, too diverse as to their societal backgrounds to be explained infrastructurally – certainly in the light of the many documented instances of communicative transfer. Culture has responded not just to 'this society over here' but also to 'those other cultures over there'.

Nationalism is capable of spanning geographical distances. To illustrate a pattern that is visible all over this book, I recall only two instances: oral epic echoing back and forth between Ossianic Scotland and the Balkans, with ricochets reaching Goethe, Grimm, Mérimée and Pushkin; and a Parisian edition of Greek popular poetry by the philhellene Fauriel (1824) inspiring the Irish antiquarian Hardiman to publish Gaelic anti-English ballads in 1831, with an introduction stating that the relationship between London and Dublin is like that between Istanbul and Athens. We have repeatedly seen the culture of nationalism leapfrog across the European continent in two or three great bounds. Culturally, the European space is tightly and densely entangled. In the field of knowledge production, Europe was a single, homogeneous space: the Republic of Philology. The world of academic learning heaved with 'Grimm Ripples' (as Terry Gunnell has called them, 2022). We have seen the visualizations of dense epistolary networks.

In the fields of literature and the arts, we have encountered the remarkable paradox of 'universal exceptionalism': national authenticity was celebrated as being 'different from the rest' for each nation separately, but this was asserted by all nations in highly similar ways. The cultural thought of Herder, the historical novels of Scott, the philology and folktales of the Grimms, the rhapsodies of Liszt, the aesthetics of national-history painting, the agendas of language revivalism: these were taken up everywhere in Europe from Reykjavík to Tbilisi, Helsinki to Santiago de Compostela. Parallel movements occurred across huge cleavages. The cultures are all distinct, but their cultivation is a transnational process. *Rien de plus international que le nationalisme.*[5]

Cultural Entanglement, Political Localism

This transnational fluidity of cultural patterns stands in contrast to the more society- or state-specific workings of national movements as forms of activism. Activism characterizes what Miroslav Hroch has termed the 'B' and 'C' phases of national movements; cultural consciousness-raising commences in (but is not restricted to) his 'A' phase.[6]

The 'cultivation of culture' that I consider fundamental to national consciousness-raising (Figure I.3) takes shape as part of Hroch's Phase A, in three successive and intensifying modes: 'recollection', 'production' and 'propaganda'. These continue beyond phase A to inspire and accompany the social demands and the activist mobilization phases of national movements – and, I may add, in the nationalism of sovereign states. What is unmistakable in the successive chronological overlays of Hroch's phases is a change in spatiality. The social and political action that characterizes phases B and C takes place in the context of a specific society or state. Cross-national patterns here became more anomalous, certainly after 1848. As national movements assert their social demands and mobilize their followers, they do so in a particular place in specific circumstances. By the time people start petitioning their governments or waging publicity campaigns, the transnational fluidity of everyone reading Herder or Walter Scott, or listening to Liszt becomes irrelevant.

And so, as the cultivation of culture moves across its stages of intensification, and as Hroch's phase model moves from A to B to C, an initially diffuse condition of communicative transnationalism crystallizes into the specificity of localized action. This is represented schematically in Figure 13.1.

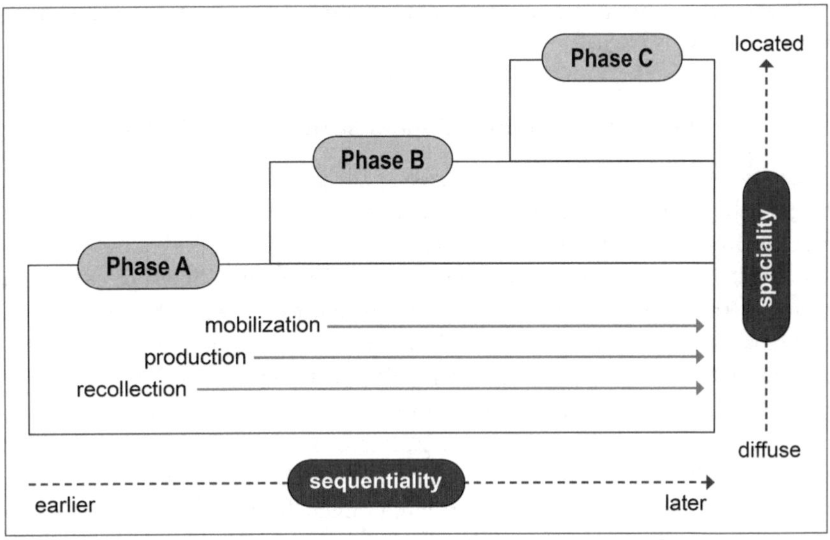

Figure 13.1 Phases of national movements between communicative diffusion and localized activism.

This suggests another type of historical dynamics: between diffusion and condensation. Culture diffuses, activism condenses. Ideas and cultural fashions can be spread far and wide by books, songs, music: in short, by cultural communication. This form of 'broadcasting' is untargeted, a bit like the sower sowing his seeds in the biblical parable: only a portion of the indiscriminately scattered seeds yields a harvest, while others land on fallow or rocky ground.[7] Models for cultural organization and manifestation (choirs, sports associations, festivals, Matica book clubs) likewise proliferate, but in a slightly different mode, which I have termed 'reticulation': imitatively spreading from city to city across the European map, as often as not across cultural boundaries, with local associations often linking up in federative associational networks. But the social and political mobilization that is inspired by this, such as the Slavic Congress in 1848, or the choral mass demonstrations in the Baltic countries, or Patrick Pearse proclaiming Irish independence from Dublin's General Post Office: each of these is concentrated in a specific society, subject to its social and political conditions, often occurring in urban spaces. And in turn those activist moments can resonate far and wide, like the Galician Irmandades da Fala emulating the Irish Gaelic League in 1916, or Catalan activists setting up a human chain across the land in 2013 in imitation of the Baltic one of 1989.[8]

Transnational and Intimate: Scalarity and Affect

The wide span of these processes across space and time has been contrasted repeatedly with their immediacy in the here and now. But where is here? The culture of nationalism can be sensed and registered at many levels. It can affect a far-flung aggregate such as the self-defining 'Slavs' of 1848; or a country (the Irish programme of de-Anglicization by way of Gaelic sports and language revivalism), a region (the Flemish-speaking part of Belgium) or a city (Valencia asserting its stature alongside Barcelona).[9] How exactly the units are spaced on that scale is moot. Are Wales and Brittany regions or countries? And when the Slavs gathered at their 1848 Congress, was that event affecting their entire community, or the city of Prague, or both at the same time? And if the latter, what effect did that have on the communitarian tensions between Prague's German and Czech inhabitants? In factoring in such scalar complexities, this book has moved beyond a comparative approach to a transnational one. The comparative method has traditionally tended to juxtapose nations as modular country-by-country units. A transnational approach has allowed me to take the multiscalarity of nesting levels of aggregation into account. A city or region is part of a country but may itself be culturally hybrid (Anglo-Irish Dublin, Spanish–Catalan Barcelona, German–Czech Prague, Danish–German Schleswig). Differences run within as well as between the aggregates we compare, and the smaller aggregation level may be as complex as the larger, outer ones. Even the single individual may go through changes, or feel conflicted, as to the culture(s) they feel they belong to, or the name they should call themselves (Douglas Hyde or Dubhghlas de h-Íde, Friedrich Tirsch or Miroslav Tyrš). And those scalar levels and juxtaposed units overlap and interpenetrate, as in the case when nationally-minded philologists from different regions and countries met in Vienna at the *Stammtisch* of Jernej (or Bartholomäus) Kopitar; or when Christian Bunsen and Max Müller, Britain-based Germans, drew Dwarkanath Tagore, as a 'fellow-Aryan', into the ambit of a Welsh eisteddfod.

And so nationality is also a yo-yo, bobbing up and down the gradations of scalarity from large, far-flung associations (Aryans, Slavs, Celts, Germans) to small, local ones. Languages can be lumped together or split into particularist component variants. Valencian revivalism sometimes distinguishes its culture, together with the Catalan *Renaixença*, against

Madrid; and sometimes distinguishes its local culture from its Catalan-hegemonic neighbour Barcelona.*

Amidst all that scalar fluidity, a heuristic end-point in the here and now is reached within the bosom of the individual affected emotionally by the culture of nationalism. Its emotive power comes to the fore prominently in the performative arts as they affected 'embodied communities' and participants – lyrical-poetic declamation, oratory, music. The ecstatic upward gaze encountered in so many instances is a form of secular religion, or rather a response to the nation's charisma. That selfsame gaze had traditionally, in baroque religious art, been a sign of mystical fervour; it was now transplanted to the realm of national culture. To recall this book's opening pages, and the powerful affect inspired by communally singing 'Die Wacht am Rhein' or 'La Marseillaise': nationalism, before it becomes an explicit political doctrine or ideology, is experienced as a private feeling; and even at the heart of the fully fledged ideology, that emotive state remains quite, quite powerful.[10]

Charisma, Disenchantment, Narcissism

There is a sliding slope from seeing the nation as a sovereign subject rationally pursuing its goals towards seeing it as the bearer of a transcendent world-historical mission. This 'charismatic supercharging of the idea of nationality'[11] was noticeable in the German 'conservative revolution' and as such formed part of that country's 'culture of defeat' post-1918, in which bitterness and rancour were rife and people turned to the extraordinary appeal of charismatic leaders. That appeal is by no means specific to Weimar Germany, nor even to countries in defeat (although it has been pointed out that charismatic leadership is better suited to 'states of exception' than to routine governance[12]) – but there is, I argue, a meaningful correlation between the new political force of charisma and the decline of the two other forms of Weberian authority, dynastic and institutional, a decline accelerated as a result of the Great War.

* Nowhere are the transnational and multiscalar complexities more pronounced than in the case of Jewish nationalism, which played out in sometimes similar, sometimes different forms amongst Europe's Jewish communities from Paris to the Pale of Settlement and Odessa, with some favouring a Zionist exodus to a new Palestinian state, others prioritizing civic empowerment within their state of residence, some wishing to revive Hebrew, others relying on Yiddish or on the language of their state of residence; and all this affected, from around 1870 on, by intensifying anti-Semitism everywhere in Europe and by the public opinion of a growing Jewish-American diaspora population. Some elements are surveyed in e-rn.ie/jewish. On Odessa as a multiscalar node in Jewish history: King 2011.

In addition, we have seen a general, long-term alternation between the Weberian notion of disenchantment (as a concomitant of the modernizing process) and the Romantic appeal of the nation, which I have linked to Romanticism's poetics of re-enchantment. I have drawn attention to the renewed presence, in European culture, of a thematics of disenchantment as the power of Romanticism, and the Romantic re-enchantment of the world, declines, and with the rise of realism and naturalism. Romanticism and lyricism were rejected scornfully by the post-1918 avant-garde (subsisting only in downmarket comfort reading); but the charisma of the nation, and the derived charisma of the new type of leaders who spoke for the nation, remained a political force that became increasingly important in the 1920s. People whom the events of 1914–1918 had robbed of many a fond illusion bought into the enthusiasm of a new nationalism under charismatic leadership, fervently attended huge rallies and dedicated themselves to the cause of their nationality. The nation's charisma became, in other words, a palliative to the disenchantment of twentieth-century modernity. It could be that it still functions as such. The nation, as a tranquil, serene, communitarian essence transcending the unpredictable sound and fury of a conflicted world, uniting the people across society and uniting the generations across history, is a powerful antidote to a modern sense of disorientation and deregulation. It gives modern people in a secular world something to believe in, something to cherish and to adore – the political equivalent of football fans devoted to their home teams. Hence the upward-gazing ecstasies that the nation can inspire. This may explain how nationalism, as the power of the nation's charisma, has survived across revolutions and regime changes from empires to restored monarchies to republics and nation-states to dictatorships and back; it is still thriving, in its ethnopopulist form, in a globalized neoliberal world order.

There is a downside to this. Whether the nation is a sovereign subject rationally pursuing its goals or the bearer of a transcendent world-historical mission, it may become a moral validator of the goals the state chooses to pursue. As the state's national interest is underwritten by a transcendent, charismatic nation, it obtains a specious moral-categorical justification: 'My country, right or wrong'. Yes, that facile phrase was memorably exploded by G. K. Chesteron, who sarcastically likened it to 'My mother, drunk or sober'. But Chesteron's ridicule had a serious undertone. The question of whether one's mother takes to drink, or whether one's country is in the right or in the wrong, should be a matter of grave concern, not of 'gay indifference'.[13]

The state cannot do whatever it finds expedient on the grounds that it does so on behalf of a cherished nation. What Chesterton is driving is it that the jingoistic cult of 'My country, right or wrong' suspends the higher criteria of morality and lawfulness in a national narcissism. We have noted how a similar narcissism in Germany (Dahn's phrase that 'a nation's highest good is its rightful entitlement') was denounced by Emile Durkheim as a form of anomie: the idea that the will to realize the nation's needs constitutes a rightful justification, surpassing international laws and treaties. In other words: the more fervently we buy into the nation's charisma, the more prone we are to unilateralism and reckless self-righteousness. 'Anomie' was coined by Durkheim from the Greek word for 'lawlessness', a replacement of rules and regulations by willpower and self-interest.[14] The applicability of that principle to post-1989 manifestations of ruthless, self-righteous nationalism is obvious, both within the state and in the field of international relations. Narcissism is a possible side effect of the nation's charisma.

Small Government, Big Flags

While this book does not set out to analyse contemporary politics, it does furnish an explanatory background – by no means an all-explaining one, but relevant nonetheless. To understand the ethnopopulist turn that has dominated politics in the first quarter of the twenty-first century, we must see its reliance on the culture of nationalism not as an incidental proclivity that happens to affect populist politicians, like a case of bad breath, but as an intrinsic core element of their political repertoire and discourse. Nationalism is not an occasional feature of populism; populism is the new carrier of nationalism.

Seen in this light, populism is not a political novelty emerging in a realigning social order; it is the latest manifestation of a shape-shifting phenomenon with long, deep historical roots, and this book has demonstrated how deep and widely-ramified those roots run. Anti-immigrant xenophobia amidst the resurgent hard right in European politics is just not a symptom of generic bigotry; Donald Trump's desire to annex Canada or Greenland is not just a mark of his flippant eccentricity; these things are, very pointedly, motivated by the nationalist commitment to expand the nation's territory, to keep it unsullied by foreign admixture, to maintain the body politic's cultural line of descent. The heaving gestures of populist rhetoric draw on a centuries-old, ingrained discourse. The mobilizing power of Donald Trump on 6 January 2021 was not mere rancorous rabble-rousing but involved – could not possibly have done without – the ubiquitous inspirational invocation of nationalist symbols and a patriotism so fervent and yet so ambient as to be unquestionable and almost unnoticeable in the sound and fury of the events. The rune-tattooed Capitol-storming 'QAnon Shaman' (Figure 5.3) was filmed marching along, *Braveheart*-style, with shouts of 'Freedom!' Footage shows that he, too, like Rouget de Lisle, Ossian, Liszt and the Serbian guslar (Figures 1.3, 3.1, 5.1 and 9.1), had his eyes fervently turned heavenwards and must have felt his commitment intensely, privately, while tapping into into global internet memes to obtain his neopagan tattoo designs. Those were not just decorative anecdotal ornaments or incidental whimsies: they are the internalized insignia, bodily indentured into his skin, of an ethnicist challenge to the political order. The meme is the message.

Populism insistently and consistently draws on the congenial rhetoric and symbols of nationalism. The proliferation of national flags in the public appearances of populist leaders is an indicator. This is all the more remarkable since many of those politicians (Silvio Berlusconi, Donald Trump, British Conservatives of recent vintage) are avowedly neoliberal and in favour of 'small government'. As the regulatory and fiscal powers of the state are being steadily whittled away, the symbolic emblems of the state's nationality are being multiplied and magnified. As the government is made small, the nation is 'Made Great Again'.[15] In the neoliberal view of the nation-state, the 'nation' and the 'state' are in direct inverse proportionality, like the opposite ends of a see-saw. The 'state' is being diminished and relinquished to market forces, the 'nation' with its symbols and pomp and emotive appeal to our loyalty is bombastically enlarged. Illiberal and authoritarian states are equally dedicated to the inflation of the symbols of nationhood; and so the nation is proclaimed fervently everywhere, by every sort of state, while everywhere its democracy is deregulated and ceding to autocracy or ethnocracy.

Stating that ethnopopulism draws its water from the well of nationalism raises the question of how it differs from nationalism's earlier iterations.[16] One important novelty is the shift from experts (Michael Gove: 'the people of this country have had enough of experts'[17]) to influencers. In public opinion, a radical epistemic intransigence has taken hold, denying evidence-based, institutionally scrutinized authority and relying, instead, on the swarm knowledge of the internet. The importance of social media in political debate marks a deep paradigm shift in societal relations, fundamentally altering the workings of the public sphere and the production of public opinion. It is difficult, and still too early in the current century's erratic developments, to tell how these new media affect, specifically, the culture of nationalism. First impressions suggest that in the lapidary brevity and ephemeral transience of social media, the repertoire of that culture is becoming more formulaic, selective and abbreviated, like headlines or the ten-second digests of football matches showing only the goals (including slow-motion replays) and the cheers.

The historical dynamics I have summarized so far tend to be of a bistable nature, oscillating between latency and salience, diffusion and condensation, wider and narrower scalarities or temporalities. If these phase changes are triggered by anything specific, it would be the 'culture of defeat'. To the cases analysed by Schivelbusch (2004) we can add the various instances of loss of empire: for example Spain in 1898 and the defeats of Austria, Turkey and Russia in 1866, 1878 and 1904 as experienced in those empires' heartlands; and in that context also, perhaps, the evaporation of the nation-state's sovereignty in a globalizing world. The Dutch intellectual Menno ter Braak, when discussing National Socialism in the 1937, spoke of an 'ideology of rancour' (*rancuneleer*, Braak 1937); *mutatis mutandis*, defeats appear to have something to do with the politics of rancour, resentment, grievance.[18]

What seems steadily unidirectional in all this is the shift from restricted to unrestricted cultural production: the culture of nationalism appears to have relied increasingly, over the past century and a half, on popular rather than 'high' culture. That slow, steady shift has been driven by the emergence of new mass-diffusion media and seems to have gone into overdrive now that communication, and what we may call 'recreational opinioneering', are produced in the cloud by self-replicating viral memes, by influencers and possibly even by bots and troll-farms. What is also unidirectional is the tendency for the nation-state to gravitate from democracy to ethnocracy; we saw it happen in the 1920s and 1930s and it is happening again in these decades. The cry of 'Freedom!' intoned by Mel 'Braveheart' Gibson and the QAnon Shaman has shifted away from democratic to populist usage; it had been originally raised by the insurrectionists of 1789, 1830 and 1848 as the nation tried to wrest sovereignty from haughty monarchs. After 1848, nationalism has increasingly allied itself with the political right, and since the days of George W. Bush and Boris Johnson, the cry of 'Freedom!' has been appropriated by the far right. It is now used in an exclusivist and exclusionary sense: freedom is claimed only, exclusively, for one's own nation, to the exclusion of foreigners and minorities. This shift from democratic solidarity towards populist intolerance, the gravitational slide from democracy to ethnocracy, seems unidirectional and appears to occur in tandem with the shift towards 'unrestricted' cultural production.

That may be a glum note on which to end this book; but the book has studied the culture of nationalism not to celebrate it but to diagnose it – in the Greek root sense of that word: to 'see through it'. Once we see how it works, what its appeal is and what its foibles are, we can perhaps also work out how, while opposing its intellectual complacency, its political narcissism and its bigoted intolerance, we can salvage its message of communitarianism, social cohesion and civic solidarity.

Notes

Introduction

1. In the ambit of that cultural history, I include intellectual history and the history of ideas as well as conceptual history (*Begriffsgeschichte*). As Koselleck 1986 argued, such a *Begriffsgeschichte*, tracing the historical usage and evolving semantics of societal and political concepts, constitutes an important interface between cultural and social history. Another such interface is the study of public opinion, which, more than being just an ambient condition like the weather, or one's hormones, can exercise a nudging influence on state policies. As I show in Chapter 11, public opinion constitutes a point where culturally conceived and culturally platformed ideas and attitudes can exercise leverage on political developments.
2. In this approach I follow Anderson 2006, e.g. his identification of 'print capitalism' and far-flung readerships as a precondition for establishing 'imagined communities' at a translocal, nationwide level. An excellent analysis of the national role of the writer is Thiesse 2019. For case studies on intellectuals and nation-building in various countries (neigbouring Russia), see Suny & Kennedy 2001. I emphatically include 'popular culture', as per Edensor 2020.
3. The historical agency of objects has been advanced in the actor–network theory of Bruno Latour (2005). In addition, I take from Latour the crucial insight that agency should not be misinterpreted as intentionality. On the idea that texts in their capacity to inspire other texts are 'procreative', see Rigney 2012, esp. chapter 2, 'Procreativity: Remediation and *Rob Roy*'.
4. Hroch 2009, chapter 6 ('The Players: Speaking in the Name of the Nation'; summarizing his earlier research, Hroch 1995), gives a fine-meshed grid depicting the social origin of nationally active university-educated German, Czech, Slovak, Norwegian, Finnish and Lithuanian intellectuals, ranging across nine social strata from peasants to large landowners and high officials. That social spread is differently distributed in the different areas examined. This may, as Hroch argues, have coloured the extent to which these intellectuals stressed social or economic issues in their social demands. How decisive these differerentiations are for determining the course of national movements as such is, however, open to some doubt, for various reasons. (1)

The distribution is given in percentages, which means that the patterns for smaller national populations (Lithuanians) are given a massively overstated equivalence to those for larger ones (Germans). (2) These data all concern activists in, specifically, Hroch's Phase B, which means precisely those who were, by his definition, involved in raising social demands. While this may throw interesting light on the distribution of conservatism or radicalism in national movements, or on the importance of cohorts such as country doctors or country clergymen, or (as Hroch suggests) on the wider mobilizing appeal of protagonists in different countries, it remains unclear what the applicability is for Phase A. The one insight that does stand from Hroch's model is how great is the social spread of protagonists' backgrounds, as we see represented in the nationally minded intelligentsia Europe-wide; this suggests that the elite/masses distinction did not play a determining role.

5. Bourdieu 1993 (on restricted vs. unrestricted cultural production). Studying both restricted and unrestricted cultural production allows me to take account of the 'popular culture and everyday life' addressed by Edensor 2020.
6. Bourdieu 1979 (on distinction and prestige), Rigney 2012 (on remediation), Erll & Rigney 2009 (on canonicity and remediation).
7. On complex systems, see, besides Latour 2005, also Luhman 1984. Complexity (the systemic prominence of iterative and nesting input–output feedback loops) generates 'autopoiesis', the ability for systems to self-stabilize and become more than mere 'output' derived from underlying factors. On positing cultural history as, precisely, the history of complexity: Sirinelli 1997.
8. On habitus: Bourdieu 1980; more on this in Chapter 12.
9. *Fremderfahrung*: Dyserinck 2015, 43–47, Connor 1967, also Connor 1973 and 1994. On the importance of Connor's work in nationalism studies: the editorial introduction of Conversi 2002, 1–23.
10. The model was first proposed in Leerssen 2006a and formed the basis of the material collected in ERNiE 2022.
11. As one characteristic example of the reluctance among social historians to see culture in any other terms than as a mere emanation or indicator of socio-political patterns, see Haupt & Tacke 1996. Their discussion of 'Die Kultur des Nationalen' (the culture of the nation) opens with a stricture that 'Although cultural-historical questions have opened innovative fields for modern nationalism studies and may yield a greater political relevance, they do not render the social-historical analysis of the national phenomenon superfluous. *On the contrary*' (255, my emphasis). The rest of the article reduces 'the culture of the nation' to a social and political analysis of groups and actors evincing a cultural interest. The work of Pierre Nora and Mona Ozouf is presented as an extension into 'cultural anthropology'; the study of historical monuments (by the likes of Maurice Agulhon and Thomas Nipperdey) presents a possible slide towards mere iconography – unless analysed as to their social 'Trägergruppen' (carrier groups). Not a single publication from the disciplines of literary history, music history or art history is taken into account.

12. Here I follow John Hutchinson's thoughtful discussion of cultural nationalism (which, to be sure, is not quite the same thing as the culture of nationalism or the cultural history of nationalism: Hutchinson 2013).
13. I take my cue from Wimmer & Schiller 2002, since then also inspiringly applied to nationalism studies by Storm 2024.
14. For the phase model: Hroch 1968. Hroch has since then elaborated and refined his theory in numerous other publications, notably Hroch 2015, with various articles collected in Hroch 2015. On the whole, the present book accords quite closely with *European Nations* (Hroch 2015), which enriches our understanding of the period with valuable and thoroughly researched socio-historical insights and examples and deeply informed discussions of the *status quaestionis* and the secondary literature. Because my approach is so deeply beholden to Hroch, I should specify the three points where this book takes up a different position from his.

    The most superficial one is Hroch's disapprobation of the term 'nationalism', which for him specifally denotes national chauvinism ('an excessive worshipping of one's own nation, connected with overvaluing it and placing it above other nations', Hroch 2015), and which he therefore does not wish to see heedlessly applied to the protagonists of national movements. While chauvinism certainly is a frequent component of nationalism, in the English-speaking world the -ism in 'nationalism' (analogous to that in 'liberalism', 'socialism' or 'feminism') merely denotes the ideology or set of ideals driving a social or political movement.

    Secondly, Hroch (like Smith 1978) has shown himself very critical of diffusionist models, which I here unashamedly espouse. Cultural/communicative diffusion is particularly important for the understanding of Phase A, while most of Hroch's attention is focused on Phases B and C. And *pace* Hroch, diffusion models need not presuppose a 'ground zero' from where the diffusion process originates. My 'ground zero', such as it is, I locate in the political friction zones of destabilized European states and empires around 1800, and in the anti-Napoleonic intelligentsia's response to accelerated (largely Napoleonic) modernization. I am mindful of the many political, institutional and intellectual factors that converged during this period to precipitate the rise of Romantic historicism and Romantic nationalism.

    Thirdly, Hroch as a social historian situates historical developments in the context of state-governed societies, which means that it is important for him to distinguish typologically between established and aspirational states, nations and 'non-dominant ethnic groups', and regions with or without an indigenous elite. To me, as a cultural and intellectual historian, such distinctions are of less importance, since all these polities and societies, irrespective of their undeniable socio-political differences, were affected by the culture of nationalism. More on this in the conclusion to this book.
15. Hroch 1968, 2005, Thiesse 1999; for 'cultural transfer': Espagne & Werner 1990, 1994, 1996, Breuilly 2013, 2020, Dyserinck 1988. A pioneering transnational compilation of relevant data was Pearson 1994.

16. The reconfiguration of the historian's working field and the availability of archivally ordered data during the *Sattelzeit* is well illustrated in Peter Burke's long-term history of knowledge production, Burke 2012. During the presentation of that book at the University of Göttingen in 2012, Burke described how as a result of post-1800 changes the emerging discipline of history morphed into 'the archive-based study of changes imposed from above'.
17. This was cogently argued, against Anthony Smith, by Connor 2004.
18. The 'invention of tradition' concept (Hobsbawm & Ranger 1983) emerged around the same time as the *lieux de mémoire* approach (see Nora 1997), soon followed by the formalization of memory studies (see Jan Assmann 1992, Aleida Assmann 1999). On Romantic historicism and medievalism as intellectual enablers of national identity cultivation: Bák, Geary & Klaniczay 2014, Geary 2002, Thiesse 1999.
19. On cultural memory studies: Rigney 2001, 2012.
20. Deutsch 1969: 3.
21. Ethno-symbolism: Smith 2006, 2009. Irish cultural nationalism: Hutchinson 1987. Groupism: Brubaker 2004a. Dyserinck's original: 'im Raum der Geschichte vorübergehend verwirklichte Denkmodelle', Dyserinck 2015, 25.
22. Hutchinson 2013.
23. Brubaker 1996, 16.
24. This is not meant to supplant other definitions, only to give them a practical application in the context of this book's scope.
25. Leerssen 2013, ERNiE 2022.
26. Further elaborated in Leerssen 2018 and ERNiE 2022. It is my contention that the 'circulation of ideas' within this polygon was markedly more dense and intense than in contacts with the world outside.
27. Schivelbusch 2004.
28. Connor 1967.
29. These shifting states recall the axis of intensity as identified by Jonathan Hearn (2006), who sees nation-awareness as ranging from a mere 'feeling' by way of 'identity' and 'ideology' to 'social movement'. Breuer 2005 distinguishes between *Weltanschauung* (world-view), *Gesinnung* (mindset, attitude) and *Ideologie*. To distinguish sharply between these semantic clouds is problematic, but in all cases a sliding scale of ideological intensification is implied, which tallies with the stages of political/activist intensification registered by Hroch in his phase model. To clarify the terms: for 'feeling', see the useful examples in François 1995. I myself have distinguished between 'national thought' (much in the sense as Breuer uses 'Nationalbewußtsein') and its more intensified, ideologically programmatic manifestation 'nationalism' (Leerssen 2018). The notion of 'identity', let alone 'national identity', is notoriously vexed; in this book, I use it in the imagological sense ('a consciously experienced national self-image': Beller & Leerssen 2007, see under 'Identity/alterity'). I use 'ideology' in the sense defined by Gérard Genette as 'a body of tenets and prejudices constituting both a world-view and a value system' (Genette 1969, 73).

1 The Romantic Spell

1. On the monument: Alings 1996. Quotation: Hitler 1939 (1925–1927): 213–214, with thanks to Paul Stevens for alerting me to it. On war enthusiasm: generally Konrad 2016 and Kieft 2015, Silbey 2005 (Britain), Verhey 2000, Bruendel 2003, 70, Hoeres 2004 (Germany).
2. On that tradition from Arndt into the twentieth century: Leerssen 2017a. Arndt's seminal text is online in English translation at ERNiE (e-rn.ie/arndt rhine), as are the poems by Schneckenburger and Hoffmann von Fallersleben.
3. Langemarck: Unruh 1986, Dithmar 1992, Krumeich 2001.
4. *Casablanca*: Harmetz 2002.
5. The Michelet quotations are online at e-rn.ie/micheletmarseillaise. On Michelet and his idealization of history as the self-realization of France: Rigney 1990. On 'La Marseillaise': Vovelle 1997, Richard n.d.
6. On the making of Olivier's *Henry V*: Aldgate & Richards 2007.
7. Nevsky dedications: e-rn.ie/nevsky. Eisenstein and the film: Goodwin 1993. Alexander Nevsky as a memory figure in Russian history: Schenk 2004.
8. Rousseau 1762 Livre IV cap. 8: 'De la religion civile'. Burke 1790 paragraphs 154, 158, 165.
9. Sparta as Rousseauesque ideal: Shklar 1966; for Robespierre; Cartledge 2002; generally Rawson 1969. Cult of personalilty: Dikötter 2020.
10. Hegel 1857, Introduction (Sibree's translation). The 1837 German edition (by Gans) did not include Hegel's Introduction; Sibree follows the 1840 edition (by Karl Hegel). Hegel's life and thought are masterfully outlined by Pinkard 2000.
11. On Carlyle's views on history: Rigney 1990, 2001.
12. Carlyle 1841, chapter 3.
13. See Leerssen 2006b and 2019a.
14. On 'cultural saints': Dović & Helgason 2016. The iconography on banknotes and statues is collected at e-rn.ie/currency.
15. Krumeich 1989, Winock 1997.
16. 'Merkmale der charismatischen Herrschaft', in Weber 1922 section 1 chapter 3 para 10. Weber had floated the idea previously in the *Archiv für Sozialwissenschaft und Sozialpolitiek* and in his *Politik als Beruf*. For a conceptual history, see Derman 2011. The passages quoted here follow the English translation by A. M. Henderson & Talcott Parsons (Weber 1924).
17. E.g. Lepsius 1986; Breuer 2011, esp. chapter 2 ('Charismatische Herrschaft'), 25–79. Some historians have argued that Bismarck may have been a prototype; but the great cult of personality surrounding Bismarck flourished only after his resignation as chancellor in 1890, and rested not on his authority as a statesman (he had become increasingly unpopular in that capacity) but on his reputation as the architect of the new Reich. For a map of more than 250 Bismarck monuments and Bismarck towers erected between 1869 and 1934 from Königsberg to Metz and from Kiel to Konstanz, see e-rn.ie/bismarck. Only ten of these predate 1891.

18. Breuilly 2011 applies the notion of charismatic leadership to anticolonial leaders and to European Fascists (notably Hitler); he sees the latter as stepping into a void created by Weberian disenchantment, but is predominantly concerned with a juxtaposition of their charisma with 'routinized' and often impersonal power in the state's social fabric (as per Weber's notion that charisma is fundamentally *außeralltäglich*, non-commonplace, extra-ordinary). Breuilly sees a contradiction between Weber's archaic (pre-modern, non-rational) charisma principle and the fact that it is re-enabled by the precondition of modernization; the intellectual lineage of the concept from Hegel by way of Carlyle and the vestiges of palingenetic Romantic thought in modern totalitarian leaders suggest a mode in which the two could be ideologically reconciled. In this book, I shift the locus of charisma away from modern political leaders towards the idealized nation itself, with charismatic leaders deriving their authority from being the nation's champions.
19. On Hindenburg: Hoegen 2007, Goltz 2009. Of the two German wartime leaders, Ludendorff is usually seen as the main continuity towards National Socialism, with which he actively sympathized; but Ludendorff never achieved Hindenburg's charismatic status. On the cult of Hinderburg as charismatic in nature: Pyta 2007, 285–295. Once Hindenburg's rule was 'routinized', disenchantment set in and his stature suffered.
20. On them: Mango 1999, Deák 1996, Sakmyster 1983, Papacomsa 2007 (and generally Fischer 2007), Garlicki 1995, Vergez-Chaignon 2014, Screen 1970–2000.
21. On them: Soubigou 2002, Huntford 1997, Zamoyski 1982.
22. Readers may be reminded of the title of Stefan Breuer's book *Der charismatische Staat* (2014). That book deals with ancient states rather than modern nations and with archaic periods of early state foundation; his argument is that before institutional and dynastic authority were established, the nascent state had to rely on charismatic authority. Breuer is the foremost expert on Max Weber and his authority model, and I gratefully rely on him throughout this book; but I am not altogether convinced that his approach here is fundamentally different from Durkheim's notion that in the religions of early polities, what was really revered was society's own enduring permanence (Breuer 2014 chapter 1 note 2; Durkheim 1912).
23. Leerssen 1996, 2016a, 2020. The swerve from politics to culture in Irish nationalism after Parnell's death may be less categorical than contemporaries, such as the nationalist poet Yeats, asserted (see Foster 1997–2003); but the impact of Hyde's lecture was nonetheless momentous.
24. Hyde 1892. Yes, the word 'race' is used – as a mere throwaway, a metaphorical synonym for 'nation', but twice over. As such it does reflect the ambient ethnicizing, racialist discourse of the 1890s; see also McMahon 2009.
25. Mann 2012, Pross 1967. On Mann's own later assessment of German nationalism, see his open letter to *Common Sense*, 1940, responding to Viereck's *Metapolitics*, and quoted in Viereck 2004, li–lxi ('Thomas Mann on Metapolitics').
26. See also Anderson 2006 and Reed 2018.

2 Becoming Something, Unmaking Empires

1. This chapter, in some passages, summarizes the more extensive treatment of these developments that appears in Leerssen 2018, 2023a and 2023b. Analytically, Breuilly 1992 stands out as a classic in the field; his focus is more on power relations and on nationalism as a political movement, arguing that 'political analysis provides the key to a general understanding of nationalism' (xii). Breuilly 2009 summarizes the dialectics between Germany and Napoleonic France. To complement Breuilly's state-political focus, the reader can fruitfully turn to Peter Watson's admirable surveys of German and French socio-cultural and intellectual history, Watson 2010 and 2022. Specifically on Germany in these transition years: Langewiesche 2000, Sheehan 1992, Hewitson 2014. On empires challenged by nationalities after 1800: Berger & Miller 2015, Connelly 2020, Storm 2024.
2. The continuity principle holds that states maintain their identity as legal entities across territorial changes, regime changes and occupation, their rights and obligations devolving to their successor states. Marek 1954 contends that an 'ideal legal notion' of statehood suffices to establish such continuity. Witness the German *Reichsidee* of the period 1806–1871; Louis-Philippe's invocation of a transcendent 'France' subsuming both his royal rule and the imperial one of Napoleon; and the idea that the independence of the Baltic States proclaimed in 1989 was the resumption of a sovereignty suspended, but not abolished, in 1938.
3. Schiller, unpublished note (1797) quoted by Dann 1995, 68.
4. On Metternich and the congress system: Schroeder 1962, Ghervas 2019 and Wilson 2003. On Haxthausen: Schupp 2004; on the demagogue persecutions generally: Tyrichter 2019. Studies of the individuals concerned give information by way of context: e.g. Reetz 2002 (on Schleiermacher) and Richter 1992 (on Hans Ferdinand Maßmann).
5. Frost 1867 gives a journalistic but useful conspectus of secret societies. For the Wartburg Feast: Brandt 1988. Decembrists: Raeff 1966, Rabow-Edling 2007 and Trigos 2009. Accounts of the Philomaths and Philarets are in Weeks 2015 and in biographies of Lelewel and Mickiewicz (Skurnowicz 1981 and Koropeckyj 2008); also, more generally, Eile 2000 and Walicki 1982. The Filikia Eteria: Panagiōtopoulos 2003.
6. Rath 1964, Santuccio 2020. On Garibaldi: Riall 2007. On Mazzini: Mack Smith 1994; on Mazzini's international influence: Bayly & Biagini 2009. For the French Charbonnerie: Spitzer 1971, Lambert 1995. Young Germany: Estermann 1972. Young Turks: Gorgeon 1995, Hanioğlu 2001, Uzer 2016.
7. Lehming 2011, Vinke 1980: 112.
8. Philhellenism generally: Noe 1984, Konstantinou & Wiedenmann 1989, Dimakis 1992, St Clair 2008, Heß Agazzi & Décultot 2009. Franco-German: Maufroy 2011. German: Quack-Eustathiades 1984, Meyer 2013. Italian: Pécout 2004. Dutch/Flemish: Wagner-Heidendal 1972. In painting: Athanassoglou-Kallmyer 1989, Constans, Lambraki-Plaka & Ribemont 1996. Byron: Raizis 1988.

9. 1830 Uprising: Church 1983; 1863 Uprising: Leslie 1969.
10. Burgdorf 2006, Dann 1995, Langewiesche 1992 and 2008.
11. Ribhegge 1998, Engehausen 2023, Engehausen & Kohnle 1998, Vick 2002, Fitzpatrick 2008.
12. Palacký's letters of 1848 refusing to take a Frankfurt seat and convoking a Slavic Congress at Prague are online at e-rn.ie/palackyfrankfurt and e-rn.ie/palackyprague. On him: Zacek 1970. On the Slavic Congress: Orton 1978. The documentation on that event has been collected in Žáček 1958.
13. Dowe 2000. Clark 2023, though exemplary in its transnational scope, sees the revolutions as purely socially driven and downplays their nationalist 'springtime of nations' aspect; for which, see Jaworski 1998.
14. Albrecht-Carré 1968, Sédouy 2009. Generally, Schroeder 1972 and Wilson 2003.
15. On Scandinavism and its post-1864 decline: Glenthøj & Nordhagen Ottosen 2021, Gerven 2022. On Barrès and the coinage and emergence of nationalism in France: Bell 2001, Girardet 1958, Weber 1985, and quoting Francesca Zantedeschi's ERNiE article 'Nationalism and Politics: France', e-rn.ie/frn-1.
16. More extensively covered in Leerssen 2021a.

3 Romantic Prophets: Inspired Poets Inspiring People

1. Original genius: Monk 1960, 101–133, Simonsuuri 2010. On Vico and this delayed impact, see Leerssen 2012a. Eighteenth-century reassessments of northern antiquity: Parker 2015.
2. From amidst the great body of Ossian scholarship I highlight Stafford's biography of Macpherson (Stafford 1988), the text edition by Gaskill 1996, 2004, Gaskill & Stafford 1998, Gaskill & Bär 2012.
3. Iconography and engravings: Macdonald 2013. The vignette on the British title page by Wale and Taylor was re-engraved by Antonio Baratti for Cesarotti's Italian edition.
4. Gaskill 1996, 197–198.
5. Monk 1960.
6. Liminality: my contribution to Gaskill & Stafford 1998; Aeolian harp: as per M. H. Abrams's classic essay (1957).
7. Uhland 1807, Novalis 1797 nr. 37. For the related concept, in English, of 'enthusiasm': Mee 2003. On the metaphysics of Romanticism, the classical survey remains Deugd 1966. Generally also Schanze 2018.
8. Hugo, 'La fonction du poëte', in his *Les rayons et les ombres*, online at wikisource, w.wiki/CdRN.
9. Lange 1954, 260. See generally also Verschoor 1928.
10. Quoted in Watson 2022, 298.
11. Carl 2000, Planert 2007; for the patriotic verse of the period, and its public impact: Ernst Weber 1991.
12. Fetscher 1988. Nazi propaganda, especially in the less successful phase of the war, frequently invoked the anti-Napolonic resistance.

13. Ferguson's lament is online at e-rn.ie/lamentdavis; an interactive survey of 570 national monuments to post-1800 poets is online at e-rn.ie/poetmonuments.
14. See the title of the collection Hemans 1834: *National Lyrics, and Songs for Music*.
15. See Leerssen 2023c.
16. Thorslev 1962, Poole 2010, Raizis 1988, Leerssen 2023d.
17. Scott 1805, Rigney 2012.
18. Embodied communities: Rigney 2001; commemorations: Leerssen & Rigney 2014; Němcová and Borovský: Nekula 2012, Reinfeld 1982, Morava 1985, generally, e-rn.ie/poetmonuments.

4 Manuscripts Found in the Attic

1. The classic discussion of antiquarianism as a forerunner of modern disciplines is Momigliano 1950.
2. Antiquarianisms's confused use of oriental sources: Droixhe 1978, Vance 1981, Leerssen 1996; reliance on the imagination to construct images of the past: Rigney 2001 and 2012.
3. Bodmer 1757, VI–VIII. Generally Parker 2015; for the European impact: Gaskill 2004.
4. See Henrikson 2002, Hulle & Leerssen 2008, Schäfer-Hartmann 2009. On the paradigmatic case of G. G. Gervinus: Ansel 1990.
5. On the role of Cesarotti's Ossian in the European rediscovery of Vico and in preparing, through Herder's reading of Ossian, the Homeric Question: Gillies 1933, Clark 1947, Berlin 1976 as reviewed by Scouten 1978 (with a blustering but not altogether convincing rejoinder by Berlin) and Leerssen 2012a.
6. Aretin 1803, 3–4.
7. Joseph Görres, 'Ankündigung der Bibliotheca Vaticana: Subskriptions-Anzeige (1812)', in Görres 1955, 109–110. The text is online at e-rn.ie/goerres.
8. In Schlegel 1988 4: 7–9.
9. 'New philology' carries a double meaning. On the one hand it stands as a counterpart to classical philology and refers to the linguistic-textual investigation of the vernacular 'modern' languages of Europe and their literatures. On the other hand (and it is used thus by Tom Shippey 2005, whom I follow) it refers to a new cohort of scholars working in a new paradigm in the humanities, dominated by such names as Jacob Grimm (see Bluhm 1997). On the developing notion of the 'philologist': Hummel 2003 and Turner 2014. Schlegel's advocacy of a comparative historical linguistics in *Über die Sprache und Weisheit der Indier* (1808) was materially indebted to the work of Sir William Jones on Sanskrit (Aarsleff 1967). August Boeckh's *Enzyklopädie der Philologie* defined philology as 'the understanding of what is understood' – unconsciously echoing Vico (see Rodi 1979, Leerssen 2012a).
10. On the transformation from familial and private networks into academic-professional ones, and the role of correspondence: Leerssen 2019b. ERNiE

was kindly assisted in incorporating the metadata of the Grimm correspondence by the Arbeitsstelle Grimm-Briefwechsel at Humboldt University, Berlin (grimmbriefwechsel.de).

11. Hroch 1968; see also Hroch 2015 (and the Introduction to this book).
12. Willems 1834, my shortened trl.; full original at e-rn.ie/willems.
13. Gautier 1872, cc–cci, dated 8 December 1870. My trl. On Lenient and Paris: Ridoux 2001, 116.
14. Quoted in Ridoux 2001, 414. Online at e-rn.ie/ancienstextes.
15. Verhandlungen 1847 and 1848. Generally Fürbeth et al. 1999 and Netzer 2006.
16. Biographies: Gerstner 1952, Denecke 1971, Peppard 1971, Martus 2009. Grimm as philologist: Bluhm 1997, Wyss 1979; international influence: Gunnell 2022, Heilfurth, Denecke & Greverus 1963; politics: Storost 1988, See 1999, Norberg 2022.
17. On these cultural transfers: Espagne & Werner 1990, 1994, Espagne & Dmitrieva 1996, Thiesse 1999.
18. The paragraphs that follow summarize Leerssen 2011a and 2011b.
19. He wrote a piece of verse celebrating their conviviality: Pogačnik 1978, 31.
20. Hoffmann 1838.
21. Ibid., xxviii–xxix; note the shift from *Niederdeutsch* to *Plattdeutsch*, the Low-German variant of German as spoken in Northern and Coastal Germany, as opposed to *Oberdeutsch* (the German variants spoken in the inland and Southern German lands).
22. For the early history of this entanglement: Von der Dunk 1966, Leerssen 2011a. The later stages are exhaustively documented in the digital *Encyclopedie van de Vlaamse Beweging*, encyclopedievlaamsebeweging.be.
23. The notion of 'portable monuments' I take from Rigney 2012.
24. Generally on philological *Beowulf* appropriations: Shippey & Haarder 1998. The quoted passage from Simrock 1859 is online in the original at e-rn.ie/simrock.
25. Anglo-Saxonism: MacDougall 1982, Frantzen & Niles 1997, Scragg & Weinberg 2000. Manifest destiny: Horsman 1981.
26. The following account of competing appropriations of the Reynard fable summarizes my Dutch-language study Leerssen 2011a.
27. Lutz-Hensel 1975, Timpanaro 1963, Bein 2011, Lange & Schubert 2023.
28. Grimm, 'Über das Finnische Epos' (1845), in Grimm 1864–1890, 5:112.
29. On Willems: Stynen 2012.
30. England: Macoff 1995, Parker 2014; English–German comparison: Oergel 1998. Specifically on Germany: Ehrismann 1975, Gentry et al. 2002; also Saalfeld 1977.
31. Grimm 1864–1890: 5, 75.

5 Ancestral Voices

1. On Vuk Karadžić: Wilson 1970; on his contacts with Grimm: Bojić 1977, Mojašević 1990. On Kopitar: Bonazza 1984, 1995, Hafner 1957, Lukan 1995,

2000, Merchiers 2007, Pogačnik 1978. The correspondence between Kopitar and Grimm has been edited by Vasmer (1938). Kopitar's given name is variously rendered in its Slovenian or German forms as Jernej or Batholomäus.

2. On the Bökendorf and Wollzeiler Circles and their use of circular letters and questionnaires: Leerssen 2019b. Documentation on the relations between Haxthausen and Laßberg and a persisting aristocratic orientation: Schupp 2004. The circular letters of Brentano (1806) and Grimm (1814) are online at e-rn.ie/wunderhornletter and e-rn.ie/wollzeilerletter. The Wollzeiler questionnaire pointedly inquired about animal fable material – Reynard was already on Grimm's mind, apparently.
3. On Fauriel: Ibrovac 1966, Espagne & Schöning 2014. On Hardiman: Leerssen 1996. Hardiman invoking Fauriel in his preface to his *Irish Minstrelsy* is online at e-rn.ie/hardimanfauriel.
4. On the *hajduk* figure: Neubauer et al. 2010 – more culturally comparatist than Hobsbawm's class-fixated *Bandits* (1981). The quotation is from Dominian 1917, 321; see also Kedourie 1960, 122–123. On Dominian: Joerg 1936.
5. Wolff 2001. In what follows, I also discuss materials covered in Leerssen 2012b.
6. The 'Homeric Question' came to a head in Friedrich Wolf's *Prolegomena ad Homerum* of 1795 and has sprawlingly dominated Homeric studies ever since. A good survey is Nesselrath 2011. See also Chapter 4 of this book.
7. Sgoff 1994 and Neubauer 2006.
8. On Mérimée's *La guzla*: Yovanovitch 1911. On Hoffmann von Fallersleben: Leerssen 2011a.
9. Wlhelm Grimm, in his 1831 Göttingen lectures on the *Nibelungenlied*, distinguishes between two types of medieval epic poetry: of Romance origin and of German. The former works were created by named, celebrated (*nahmhaft*) poets working in a courtly environment. The latter are authorially unspecific. 'These appear to belong to the entire nation and merely to have been articulated by an individual.' And while the courtly poems are often confused, the native ones (*Nationalgedichte*) have a solid, well-defined content and stand on a straightforward footing. Wilhelm Grimm 1985, 13.
10. On Rybnikov and *bylyny*: Sokolov & Sokolov 1932; see Gruel-Apert 1998 (also on Afanas'ev). On Northern European reverberations: Gunnell 2022.
11. Generally Sihvo 2009, Fewster 2006; on Lönnrot and the *Kalevala*: Anttonen 2014. On the nationalizing function of folklore studies in Finland: Hautala 1969, Harvilahti 2018. *Kalevala* as a mythological text: Pentikäinen 1999.
12. Grimm 1864, 113.
13. See the communication by H. J. Holmberg, graduate student (candidatus) in Helsingfors/Helsinki, in the *Verhandlungen der gelehrten estnischen Gesellschaft zu Dorpat* (Tartu), 1 (1846): 25–37; Laugaste 1990, Thiesse 1999, Hasselblatt 2016.
14. On Jane Schoolcraft: Noori 2008, reviewing Schoolcraft's writings as edited by Robert Dale Parker (2007). On historical and poetic Hiawatha figures: Thompson 1922. On the relationship between Hiawatha and the *Kalevala*: Nyland 1950.

15. Dvořák: Hamm 1983, Tibbets 1993; Sibelius: Goss 2009; Gallen-Kallela: Jackson & Wagemann 2006.
16. Grimm and mythology: Kellner 1994, also Shippey 2005b. Grimm and legal antiquities: Schmidt-Wiegand 1987.
17. In what follows I draw on Leerssen 2016b and 2021c.
18. The Saussurean *langue/parole* model was applied to folktales by Bogatyrev & Jakobson (1929). Motif research in folklore studies led in 1910 to Antti Aarne's *Verzeichnis der Märchentypen* which, translated by Stith Thompson in 1928 as *Types of the Folktale*, has become the great Aarne/Thompson Motif Index. For Grimm's extrapolation from folktale motifs into mythology, see Kellner 1994.
19. On mythology and the reception of myths in modern Europe: Detienne 1981 and Feldman & Richardson 1972.
20. On the Nordic starting-point for the new mythology: Roesdahl & Meulengracht Sørensen 1996, Wawn 2005, Ross 2018, Bønding, Kølle Martinsen & Stahl 2021. On Grundtvig and his impact on Danish nation-building: Hall, Korsgaard & Pedersen 2015.
21. On the shape-shifting invocation of myth, see Williamson 2004 and Lincoln 1999; the latter also addresses the *muthos–logos* duality.
22. Generally Carpenter 1977. On Tolkien as a philologist in the Grimm tradition, the leading authority is Tom Shippey (2005a and 2005b, in the latter work esp. his introductory chapter, pp. 1–28, 'A Revolution Reconsidered: Mythography and Mythology in the Nineteenth Century').
23. See Junginger 1999, Puscher & Vollnhals 2012, Goodrick-Clark 2003 (exploring also the esoteric fringe) and 2019. Many scholars in Ancient Germanic philology were sympathetic to *völkisch* or Nazi politics, e.g. the Amsterdam professor and Nazi collaborator Jan de Vries; on him: Henkes 2005, 121–193. In France, Indo-European studies as an academic discipline were infiltrated by sympathizers of the alt-right GRECE movement during the 1980s, see Demoule 2017; for a wholesale critique of the Indo-European mythological paradigm, Arvidsson 2006. Ahnenerbe: Kater 2006. Widukind: Lambert 2014. Recycling of Ahnenerbe material: e.g. Gilst 2009, a hostile popularizing biography of Charlemagne. On neopaganism: Glünder 2008, Schnurbein 2016 and sources there. On paganism in the alt-right: Puschner & Großmann 2009. Heavy metal music: Goodrick-Clarke 2003, 193–212, Gardell 2003, Lohmann & Wanders 2002. Runic symbols: Birkett 2021; a checklist of these symbols is at imagologica.eu/altrightsymbols.
24. On the influence of Arndt in this idea: Krügel 1914. The international influence of Savigny's *Volksgeist* in legal theory: Ramathian 2007. On *Germanistik* as a branch of historical jurisprudence: Dilcher & Kern 1984. On the Hegelian line of conceptual development: Mährlein 2000. Stocking 1996 registers the later sedimenation of the *Volksgeist* idea in ethnographical anthropology; see also Kalmar 1987. On the rise of organicist historicism, Rothacker 1923 remains a classic.
25. Vienna lectures, 1812 (Schlegel 1961, 14).

26. Humboldt 1973, 6, my trl. Generally on Romantic language theories: Auroux et al. 2000–2001, Caussat, Adamski & Crépon 1996.
27. Humboldt's 1836 treatise was the introduction to his three-volume investigation of the Javanese Kawi language (Humboldt 1907, and see Solleveld 2020). A full scholarly edition of his linguistic writings is still in progress, see Mueller-Vollmer & Messling 2024. This and other linguistic writings are collected in Humboldt 1973. Humboldt's *ergon/energeia* dualism is elucidated in Mueller-Vollmer & Messling 2024; see also Lyandra-Geller 2016. For the Sapir–Whorff hypothesis, see also Gipper 1972, Miller 1968, Koerner 1992. More generally on *Volksgeist* and post-Herderian language philosophy: Bunzl 1996 and Forster 2010.
28. Van Duyse, 'Aen België' (1834). Buffon's dictum appeared in his *Discours sur le style* of 1753.
29. *Volk* as language community: Grimm in his presidential speech at the 1846 Germanisten congress (Verhandlungen 1847); see Habermas 1999. Grimm on Belgium and the Frenchification of Flanders: *Kleinere Schriften*, 5:112, echoing points already made by Fichte in the *Reden an die deutsche Nation*. Generally also Leerssen 2025.
30. Davis 1845.
31. Viale 1857, my trl.
32. In the original: 'Das höchste Gut des Mannes ist sein Volk. / Das höchste Gut des Volkes ist sein Recht. / Des Volkes Seele lebt in seiner Sprache. / Dem Volk, dem Recht und seiner Sprache treu / Fand uns der Tag, wird jeder Tag uns finden.' On the *Alldeutscher Verband* and on Dahn: Puschner Schmitz & Ulbricht 1996.
33. Ireland: Leerssen 2016a. Hungary: quoting Sándor Hites's contribution to ERNiE on 'Language Interest: Hungarian', e-rn.ie/language-hun.
34. The Slovak national movement stressed its Slavic roots and connections in response to the Magyar centralization policies of the Kingdom of Hungary. See generally Brock 1976.

6 Languages, States, Races

1. Grimm 1864–1890, 4: 84–93. Online at e-rn.ie/grimmdanish. On Grimm and the Schlewig-Holstein question: Storost 1988. On the linguistic nationalism of Grimm and Arndt: Leerssen 2025.
2. The attempts of the Jacobin French Republic to centralize and direct the nationwide use of (exclusively) French are notorious: Balibar & Laporte 1974, Certeau, Julia & Revel 2002, Schlieben-Lange 1996. More generally on language and class/power/prestige relations: Bourdieu 1982.
3. ABC war: Juvan 2015.
4. Sijs 1999 gives a general survey of language purisms; see also Thomas 1992.
5. Quoted in Behland 1967, 341–342. Campe had already written a treatise on German language purification in 1794, 'Über die Reinigung und Bereicherung

der deutschen Sprache', and had followed through with a *Wörterbuch zur Erklärung und Verdeutschung der unserer Sprache aufgedrungenen fremden Ausdrücke* (1801–1813). Quak 1999.

6. Grimm 1848; Grimm notes the Frisians and the Catti (with whom Grimm, hailing from Hessia, personally identified) as non-migratory tribes, already noted by Tacitus in his *Germania* in the locations they still occupy today. On the *Wörterbuch*: Kirkness 1980, Kochs 1967.
7. Grimm 1864–1890, 6: 411–418, online at e-rn.ie/grimmdesiderio, together with the English translation by J. J. Schlicher (1935). In what follows I summarize Leerssen 2015b.
8. Grimm's motion to pursue war against Denmark has been discreetly passed over by his admiring biographers, but it can be found in the minutes of the Nationalversammlung (*Stenographischer Bericht* 1:289–290), online at e-rn.ie/grimmdanish. It is preceded by a somewhat rambling speech invoking the scholarly work he had just published as the *Geschichte der deutschen Sprache*. The quotation given here is from Grimm 1848, 836–837; discussed in more detail in Leerssen 2025.
9. Arndt's writings are online at ERNiE, e-rn.ie/EMA (tab 'Writings').
10. See Storey 2011.
11. The opposition between 'splitters' and 'lumpers' is widespread colloquially; for the application to linguistic taxonomy I am indebted to Alexander Maxwell.
12. Arndt 1834, 9. Given the contorted language, the original needs to be quoted: 'das ganze Deutschland sollte in einem verjüngten verwandelten Zustande so hergestellt werden, daß sie wenigstens, wenn sie auch nicht sogleich mit voller Liebe hineingingen, doch sich billig nicht sträuben könnten, anzuerkennen, daß sie vernünftiger Weise solcher Einladung folgen müßten. Denn das müßte beiden allenfalls mit der Degenspitze gewiesen werden dürfen, daß die Schweizer hinfort nicht mehr als Söldner fremder Tyrannei zur Befehdung oder gar Unterjochung ihrer deutschen Landsleute sich verkaufen, noch daß die Holländer die deutsche Lebensader, den Rhein, zubinden und sperren dürfen.' For the context: Leerssen 2011a, 96–100.
13. On political Scandinavism: Glenthøj & Nordhagen Ottosen 2021; on cultural Scandinavism: Gerven 2022. Generally on Scandinavism as a form of macro-nationalism: Hemstad & Stadius 2023. On the 'united kingdoms' model as a template for state-driven pan-nationalism: Alvin Jackson 2023.
14. On the dialect-with-an-army meme: Maxwell 2018.
15. The text is online at e-rn.ie/viennadeclaration. In what follows, I summarize Leerssen 2024.
16. Newly introduced in the Montenegrin Latin alphabet were <ś> and <ź>, and in the Cyrillic alphabet corresponding new characters were composed by placing an acute accent over <с> and <з>. Bosnian linguistic particularism expresses itself stylistically rather than formally: Alexander 2006.
17. See also Flere 2018.

18. For the coemerging and competing notions of a Bulgarian and a Macedonian ethnolinguistic identity, see Sampimon 2006 and Marinov 2006.
19. Generally Kohn 1960 (Herkel's quotation on p. 332); also (for South-Slavism) Lord 1963, Milojković-Djurić 1994.
20. Arendt 1976, chapter 8: 'The Pan-movements', note 1. The congress had not, *pace* Arendt, been called by the victorious Russians but by the defeated Bulgarians, trying to escape from their Axis opprobrium and isolated position, and currying favour with the Soviet Union; see Petrov 2016. Many primary sources on mid-century Pan-Slavism under Soviet hegemony are given by Kohn 1960.
21. On Dobrovský, Rask and Kopitar: Blom 2013, Fryščák 1982, Hjelmslev 1966, Lukan 1995, Pogačnik 1978, Wirtz 1999.
22. Greek and Irish Gaelic language debates: Mackridge 2009, Crowley 2008.
23. See Pereira González 2017. Leach 2009 indicates how post-1945, Pan-Celtic associations and platforms were established in Ireland by Bretons who had taken refuge there following their Nazi collaboration during the occupation.
24. On Celticism following the Price/Le Gonidec axis: Leerssen 2019a, Löffler 2006, Ellis 1993; on the eisteddfod: e-rn.ie/wls-10; on La Villemarqué and Wales: Constantine 2007; on German interest in the eisteddfod: Gruber 2014. On the British Foreign Bible Society: Howsam 1991.
25. Fraser 1966 and 1968, Gurden-Williams 2008, Price 1854. On Bunsen: Höcker 1951.
26. Lennon 2007 and (more generally) 2008, Grant 2001. On Renan and Arnold: Leerssen 2006b.
27. On Müller: Bosch 2002, Davis & Nicholls 2018, Nicholls 2015; writings are anthologized in Stone 2002.
28. On the growing racialism of comparative ethnographic philology in the nineteenth century: Snyder 1939, Poliakov 1987, Hutton 1988, MacMahon 2016 and 2019, Harpham 2009. On Gobineau and Chamberlain: Fortier 1967, Biddiss 1970 and 1997; on Chamberlain: Field 1981.
29. As quoted by MacDougall 1982, 121.
30. Müller 1994, 2: 408, 410.
31. Müller 1854, 1855.
32. On Hungarian Turanism: Ablonczy 2022. On Vambéry: Alder & Dalby 1979. On Turkish Turanism: Landau 1995, Meyer 2014.
33. Translation thanks to Ayşenur Korkmaz. For another rendering and for additional poetic productions from Turkish Turanism in the period 1900–1914, see Grigoriadis & Opçin-Kıdal 2020. On Ziya Gökalp: Heyd 1950, esp. p. 105 for the poem. On Akçura: Gorgeon 1980. I am also indebted to personal information from Usman Ahmedani and to his Turkish-themed contributions to ERNiE.
34. Laruelle 2007. Tengrism is an informing presence in the Turkish TV action series *Deliler* (2018).
35. Sisa 2016.

36. Enver Pasha and the Basmachi Rebellion: O'Kearney 2008, Zenkovsky 1967. On the place of the Grey Wolves and their ideology in the Turkish political landscape: Poulton 1997. TV series: e.g. *Diriliş: Ertuğrul* (2014) and its sequel *Kuruluş: Osman* (2019); also the film *Direnis Karatay* (2019). Nomadic Games: w.wiki/CnCj. For the cultural re-emergence of Hungarian Turanism in a Eurasianist frame: Kremmler 2023.

7 History Related

1. On the post-Ossianic and Romantic trope of being 'the last of the race', Stafford 1994.
2. Scott 1805.
3. Rigney 2012. As Rigney has also pointed out, Scott, the master of historical evocation, was in no way a nostalgic: he embraced modernity and innovation wholeheartedly while celebrating the allure of the past.
4. On Romantic historicism: Rigney 2001 and Leerssen 2012a. Entries on historicism will be found in most handbooks of history, philosophy of history and history of ideas; see also Jäger & Rüsen 1992, or, more generally, Tollebeek, Ankersmit & Krul 1996. For repercussions on literary history and literary history writing, see Wellek 1941, Laan 1997 and Spiering 1999.
5. Scott 1814, Chapter XXII, ('Highland Minstrelsy').
6. On romance: Scott 1824. Waverley, addled by wayward reading, as a Romantic Quixote: Scott 1814, Chapter IV ('Education') and the opening to Chapter V ('Castle-Building').
7. For a narratological analysis of history writing, and for Scott's influence on the Romantic historians, see Rigney 1990. Also Berger, Eriksonas & Mycock 2008.
8. On the professionalization of history writing: Boer 1989, highlighting Guizot. More generally: Porciani & Tollebeek 2012. On the historical profession in the century of nation-building: Berger & Conrad 2015, Berger, Donovan & Passmore 1999, Berger & Lorenz 2010. On the historicist reframing of national identity: Baar 2010 (Central Europe), D'Auria 2020 (France).
9. On the Bohemian manuscripts and their impact: Dobiaš 2014, 2019. On the ongoing 'arms race' between forgers and philologists: Grafton 2019.
10. On *lieux de mémoire:* Nora 1997, especially Nora's introduction, 'Entre histoire et mémoire'. On the funeral at Vyšehrad: Nekula 2012. On Havliček: Morava 1985, Reinfeld 1982.
11. Stafford 1994.
12. Libuše: Höhne 2013; Wanda: Degen & Dzikowska 2015; Amaya: Juaristi 1987 and Yoeli-Rimmer 2018.
13. Rigney 2001.
14. On Conscience: Humbeeck, Absillis & Weiermars 2016; on Sienkiewicz: Lednicki 1960. Generally on the international influence of Scott: Pittock 2007. Historical novels in Estonia/Finland: Kaljundi, Laanes & Pikkanen

2015; in Belgium: Bemong 2007. On historicism generally: Furtado 2012, Mathijsen 2013.

15. On George IV's Edinburgh visit: Scott 1822, Prebble 2000. Kilt and Highland dress: the saturnine treatment by Hugh Trevor-Roper in *The Invention of Tradition* (Hobsbawm & Ranger 1983) overstates the case badly.
16. Conscience 1838, final sentence.
17. Aleš Žužek, 'Janšev Beli panter razkriva skrivnost izvora Slovencev', Siol.net, 19 December 2014, siol.net/novice/slovenija/jansev-beli-panter-razkriva-skrivnost-izvora-slovencev-281833. Lily Baier, 'Panther Pandemonium Polarizes Slovenia Ahead of EU Presidency', Politico, 17 May 2021, politico.eu/article/slovenia-panther-pandemonium-eu-presidency-janez-jansa/.
18. See Frech 1996.
19. This drift to the less prestigious periphery of the literary marketplace is exhaustively documented for the Dutch case in Streng 2020.
20. Leerssen 2021a.
21. Henty and imperialist juvenile fictuion in Britain: Arnold 1980, Castle 1996. Dutch case: Wagenaar 2004.
22. Handelingen der Staten-Generaal 2006–2007, 6 (session of 28 Sept 2006), 272–294. See w.wiki/CnCq.
23. In a lecture to the Berlin Academy of Sciences: Schoof 1961, 357.
24. Michelet 1847–1853, book 2, Chapter 4: on the night of 4 August 1789.
25. 'Nos ancêtres les Gaulois': Viallaneix & Ehrard 1982, Dietler 1994. Historians as nation-builders: Deletant, Hanak & Seton-Watson 1988, Porciani & Tollebeek 2012, Berger & Conrad 2015, Berger & Lorenz 2010. On Michelet: Mitzman 1990, Rigney 1990. On Herculano: Bernstein 2013, Melo 2013. On Palacký: Kořalka 2007, Zacek 1970. Popular vs. academic history in Ireland: Leerssen 1996. Dutch commemorations and religious rifts: Zeijden 2002.
26. On Scott's afterlives outside the fields of the novel and history writing: Rigney 2012.
27. On Arminius: Kösters 2009; on Barbarossa: Kaul 2007. Also: Dann 1983 and Klein 1980 on Cologne Cathedral. Generally on German historical myths: Wülfing, Bruns & Parr 1991, Münkler 2009. French myths are covered in the *lieux de mémoire* collection (Nora 1997). On German historicist architecture and monuments: Storm-Rusche 1990, Werquet 2010. Vittorio Emmanuele monument: Atkinson & Cosgrove 1998. An English example: Vandrei 2018 on Queen Boudicca. Flacke 1998 is a Europe-wide conspectus. On commemorative feasts in Germany and elsewhere: Hansen 1976, Leerssen & Rigney 2014, McCrone & McPherson 2009, Quinault 1998.
28. e-rn.ie/jeanne and e-rn.ie/panoramas.
29. Quoted in Ian Cruse, Library Note for the House of Lords debate on 20 October 2011: 'Teaching History in Schools' (London: House of Lords, 2022), parliament.uk/globalassets/documents/lords-library/Library-Notes/2011/LLN-2011-030-TeachingHistorySchoolsFP2.pdf. Similar sentiments were voiced during the centre-right government coalition talks of 2017 in the Netherlands.

30. Tollebeek, Boone & Van Nieuwehuyse 2022.
31. Jan-Frederik Abbeloos, 'Het subsidieverhaal van Vlaanderen', *De Standaard* (7 January 2023).
32. Huizinga 1929. On 'proper' and 'improper' history (the latter including 'hyphenated' history such as art history and literary history, heritage studies and memory studies): Rigney 2007. On cultural memory: Jan Assmann 1992, Aleida Assmann 1999. On the history–memory relationship: Cubitt 2007.

8 The Image and the Presence

1. On the sublime: Monk 1960.
2. Harding 1979, Wolf 2012, Schoonenboom 2015.
3. Haskell 1993. The emergence of 'ancient history' as a historiographical field fissioning out of antiquarianism together with archaeology has been memorably discussed by Arnaldo Momigliano (1950).
4. Smiles 1994.
5. Delaroche: Ziff 1977; Gérôme: Ackerman 1986, Christoper Allan Scott 2010; generally: Bann & Paccoud 2014, Sérié 2014, Picon 2012.
6. On the Düsseldorf school and the Belgian influence: Jenderko-Sichelschmidt 1979; on Aman: Florea 2010. This chapter relies on a corpus of 3,500 European history paintings made between 1780 and 1914, online at e-rn.ie/historypaintings.
7. Danish artists' community in Rome: Rohde 1982. Nazarenes: Bachleitner 1976, Benjamin 2002, Gossman 2003 (accessed 14 March 2024), Mitchell 2001.
8. *Düsseldorfer Malerschule* 1979; Hütt 1995. On Cornelius: Büttner 1980.
9. A searchable checklist is online at e-rn.ie/murals. Maclise: Murray 2008; Leys in Antwerp: Baetens 2012, Cleaver 1955; Belgian murals generally: Ogonovszky 1999; Rethel: Koetschau 1929, Oellers 1987; Piloty: Baumstark & Büttner 2003. Murals: Monika Arndt 1976, Arnold 2006, Rommé 1996, Gräf & Tacke 2004.
10. Prendergast 1997.
11. Constans, Lambraki-Plaka & Ribemont 1996, Athanassoglou-Kallmyer 1989.
12. Schäfer 1985.
13. For what follows: Monika Arndt 1976 and Leerssen 2017b.
14. Gallen-Kallela: Jackson & Wageman 2006; and see (for Estonia) Pütsep 1990.
15. See Grijzenhout 1996.
16. A hundred years after its completion, the painting was made famous by Roy Strong in his pioneering vindication of Victorian art (Strong 1978). See also Morris & Milner 1992 and Sanders 2013.
17. See Bann 2012.
18. Repin: Fan Parker & Parker 1980; Panoramas and waxworks: Hess 2011, Melman 2012, e-rn.ie/panoramas; Mucha's *Slavic Epic*: Bydžovská & Srp 2011. On earlier history painting in the Czech lands: Huig 2005, also Cooper 2010.
19. Salviati mosaics: Barr 2008.

20. On Varma: Neumayer & Schelberger 2003, Linden 2024.
21. Dusza 2012; Zariņš: Ducmane 2016, Pourchier-Plasseraud 2015. An inventory of national icons on banknotes and postage stamps is online at e-rn.ie/currency.
22. Bourdieu 1993, Billig 1995, Lowenthal 2012.
23. Rigney 1990, 2001.
24. On spectacle versus narrative in Romantic history writing: Rigney 1990. On *Nebeneinander* vs. *Nacheinander*: Lessing 1766.

9 In Tune: Concerts, Choirs

1. In Paris, Liszt tended to play Erard pianos. Gibbs 2006. Generally on Liszt: Walker 1983–1996 and 2005.
2. On Liszt as Romantic virtuoso: L. Kramer 2002, Leppert 2002, Quinn 2014. Specifically on Liszt's combination of virtuoso showmanship and Romantic inspiration: Samson 2007.
3. On Liszt's Hungarian reconnection and the events related here: Legány 1983 and 1992, Hamburger 1987, all following Schober 1843. The Vörösmarty poem is at e-rn.ie/vorosmarty. Liszt responded to Vörösmarty's Hungarian praise with his symphonic poem *Hungaria* (1854).
4. On the sabre symbolism and the *úriember*: Lajosi 2022.
5. 'Hungary is bleeding to death, but Franz the knight has escaped unscathed; so has his sabre, kept safely in the cupboard' ('Ungarn blutet sich zu Tode – Doch unversehrt blieb Ritter Franz, Sein Säbel auch – er liegt in der Kommode'; Heine, 'Im Oktober 1849').
6. Hamilton 2005 and Walker 1983–1996, 2: 58–73.
7. Liszt 1859, 18–49. The anti-Semitism is sometimes blamed on Liszt's mistress Carolyne Sayn-Wittgenstein, but the first 1859 edition, which Liszt published under his own name, is as every bit as anti-Semitic as the posthumous, expanded one of 1881. The German translation (Leipizg 1861, by Peter Cornelius) shortened the anti-Semitic passages, but it is not Liszt's original.
8. Salmen 1966.
9. As quoted in Salmen 1966, 95: 'Ich habe eine allen Nationen gleich ansprechende Musik vor Augen, um den lächerlichen Unterschied der National-Musiken aufzuheben.'
10. What follows summarizes Leerssen 2014 and is much indebted to Samson 2002, Samson 2007, White & Murphy 2001.
11. Vaughan Williams 1934, 17.
12. Beckerman 2003, Hamm 1983, Tibbets 1993.
13. Kregor 2015, 233 (generally chapter 8, 'Programming the Nation').
14. Lajosi 2018, Frolova-Walker 2007, Helmers 2014.
15. On Wagner and the quest for a German national opera: Kooten 2019.
16. Verdi: Gossett 1990 and more generally 2012; Kimbell 1981, Martin 2005, Parker 1997. Erkel and the unified-singing effect of the opera chorus: Lajosi 2018.

17. The following relies on the case studies in Lajosi & Stynen 2015 and summarizes my introduction to that volume. For a full bibliography, see e-rn.ie/musicassociations.
18. Gumplowitz 1987, Narváez Ferri 2005.
19. Blommen 1960 (zooming in on the Lower Rhine); Elben 1887. The standard work in critical history is Klenke 1998; also Düding 1984 and Minor 2012.
20. Klenke 1998, 66. Original title: *Germania: Ein Freiheitsliederkranz für deutsche Sänger aller Stände* (ed. T. Täglichsbeck; Stuttgart 1848).
21. On festival culture in nineteenth-century Germany: Düding 1984, Düding Friedemann & Münch 1998 and (more sociologically) Hettling & Nolte 1993. Specifically in Schleswig-Holstein: Unverhau 2000. Festival culture in France: Ozouf 1988, Corbin, Gérôme & Tartakowsky 1994.
22. On the massed-choir programme of the Nürnberg Festival, with its fervently anti-French militarism, see Klenke 1998, 110–115. The quotation is on p. 114. In the visual arts, too, the image of a Germania vigilantly guarding the Rhine was constantly reproduced: e.g. Lorenz Clasen's painting *Germania auf der Wacht am Rhein* (1860) and Hermann Wislicenus's of the same name (1873). e-rn.ie/germanias.
23. Klenke 1998, 170.
24. *Stenographischer Bericht* 1848–1850, 1, 27.
25. e-rn.ie/vowtothee.
26. Estonian choral festivals: Tall 1985, Brüggemann & Kasekamp 2014; embodied communities: Rigney 2011.

10 People in the Present

1. On the Zarzuela: Doppelbauer & Sartingen 2010. Polka: Stavělová 2015.
2. Gaelic Athletic Association: Cronin Duncan & Rouise 2009, Mandle 1987. Sokol: Blecking 1991, Blecking & Waic 2008, Nolte 2002, Balikić, Newman & Pojar 2023.
3. Turnvereine and Jahn: Illig 1998 (on Bavaria, but giving wider context); Düding 1984, Bartmuß, Kunze & Ulfkotte 2008. Sokol: see note 2. Jewish sports clubs, Maccabiah Games: Brenner & Reuveni 2006, Friedler 1998, Wildmann 2009. Nordau's call for 'muscular Jewry' is online at e-rn.ie/muskeljudentum.
4. On the Schiller 1859 commemorations: Logge 2014. On the power of literary commemorations generally: Leerssen & Rigney 2014 (chapter 2 on Schiller). Swiss *Festspiele*: e-rn.ie/sws-4.
5. On the eisteddfod: e-rn.ie/wls-10; on Price: Price 1854.
6. What follows summarizes Leerssen 2015a.
7. On the Catalan Renaixença and the Barcelona Jocs Florals: Domingo 2011, Ginebra 1988, Miracle 1960.
8. On the Félibrige: Berjoan 2011, Martel 1997 and 2010. On the Occitan movement: Ripert 1917, Zantedeschi 2013; on Catalan–Occitan crosscurrents: Ginebra 1989, Zantedeschi 2019.

9. Benjamin 2002. These pages summarize Leerssen 2022b.
10. *Nebeneinander/nacheinander*: Lessing 1766. Hittorf: Kiene 2011.
11. Panthéon: Ozouf 1997. The statues are online in the ERNiE collection of landmarks.
12. Milo 1997, Bouvier 2007.
13. Bourdieu 1980 chapter 3 defines habitus as 'a system of stable and generalized attitudes, shaped by experience but capable of shaping experience in that they form a template for generating and organizing social action and representations'.
14. Tolstoy 1869 book 7 chapter 7. The scene is set in 1810–1811.
15. Lovejoy & Boas 1997.
16. On *Mireille*: Ellis 2012. On regionalism in French literature: Thiesse 1991.
17. Höfig 1973, Leerssen 1992.
18. Scott's cavalcades: Rigney 2012. Hardy openings: see *The Return of the Native*, *The Mayor of Casterbridge*, *Two on a Tower*, *Tess of the D'Urbervilles*.
19. Champfleury 1857, 270. On Benjamin and spectacle platforms as part of the world fairs paradigm, Leerssen 2022b. On the Salon des refusés: Boime 1969, Dunlop 1972.
20. Thiesse 2022.
21. Dutch costume books: Koolhaas-Grosveld 2010. On 'panoramatic literature' and the Spanish mode of costumbrismo: Krantz 2012, Kuijk 2018, Peñas Ruiz 2012.
22. 'Old German' dress: Eva Maria Schneider 2002. Hungarian, Austrian: Maxwell 2019, Houze 2015. Generally: Maxwell 2014.
23. For the Hofer iconography: e-rn.ie/AH0.
24. Höflein 1988 (concentrating on Baden). Dirndl fashion: Egger 2008, Weissengruber 2004 (post-1945). Bavarian institutionalization under the Wittelsbachs: Wartelsteiner 2015.
25. Ständecke 2007.
26. On Norway: Bjørnholt 2005, Oxaal 1998. On Garborg: Obrestad 1992. Adlersparre's 'Friends of Handicraft', still active, maintain a website at handarbetetsvanner.se.
27. Schubert 1992.
28. On Sauerwein: Masalski 2003, Vistdal 2000. On traditional Lithuanian dress: Šidiškienė's article in e-rn.ie/lit-6.
29. What follows draws substantially on the studies collected in Leerssen & Storm 2022, as well as the survey articles by Gimeno Martínez and by Storm in ERNiE: e-rn.ie/survey-12 and e-rn.ie/survey-13. Generally: Greenhalgh 2010; for regional-to-international scalarity: Schwarz 2012. See also Stoklund 1994.
30. Storm 2022. On the Swiss chalet: Cieraad 2018.
31. Feige 2012, Fernandez 2022. 'Hidden Persuaders' as per the classic Packard 1957.
32. Minea 2022.

33. Ottoman costumes: Osman Hamdi Bey & Launay 1873; interesting light on Osman Hamdi Bey is thrown by Uslu 2015. On the *Kronprinzenwerk*: Fikfak & Johler 2008. On Marubi: Elsie in ERNiE, e-rn.ie/alb-4.
34. Bergougniou, Clignet & David 2001, Bancel et al. 2011.
35. Radiņš et al. 2016, Hlavačka, Orliková & Štembera 2002.
36. On theatre history in the context of various national movements: Mäkinen, Wilmer & Worthen 2001, Senelick 2008, Wilmer 2004 and 2008.
37. On Ibsen: Figueiredo 2019, Fulsås & Rem 2021.
38. The conflict between these two poles has been brought into sharp focus by Philip O'Leary 1994. On the Irish Literary Theatre: Leerssen 1996. On Yeats: Foster 1997–2003.
39. Generally Einarsson 2006 (Iceland), Pikkanen 2010 and 2012; Mäkinen, Wilmer & Worthen 2001 (Finland).
40. Leerssen 2021b.
41. Milligan: Morris 2013; Gonne and the Daughters of Erin: Coxhead 1985, Trotter 2001, esp. 73–100 ('Women's Work and the Irish Nationalist Actress: Inghinidhe na hEireann'). Shaw: Holroyd 1989–1993, esp. vol. 2. Yeats and occultism: Foster 1997–2003. Generally also Foster 2014.
42. What follows draws on the relevant ERNiE articles on design and architecture, by Sidó (Hungarian, e-rn.ie/hun-11), Villaverde (Spanish-Catalan, e-rn.ie/spa-8), Grīnvalde (Latvian, e-rn.ie/lat-9). For Czech developments: Filipová 2019.

11 Culture Mobilized

1. Du Barail 1898, 149. Generally on belligerent public opinion in 1870: Stengers 1956.
2. See the republication Schneckenburger 1870.
3. The accumulating repertoire is online at e-rn.ie/rhine and in the appendix to Beller & Leerssen 2017 ('Literary Appropriations of the Rhine', 262–345). What follows is based in part on my contribution to that volume, Leerssen 2017a.
4. Schivelbusch 2004. From amidst the wealth of literature on nationalism, Barrès and the Action française I mention Weber 1959 and 1985 and Sternhell 1972. On revanchism and the *Ligue des Patriotes*: Rutkoff 1981.
5. Quoted in Reinach 1920, 193.
6. Treitschke 1870. The article appeared in the *Preussische Jahrbücher*, in brochure form, and in English translation (London: Macmillan; here quoted).
7. Hanna 1996 addresses the complex entanglements in French intellectual patriotism. Benda 1927 is a classic denunciation of the failure among intellectuals to remain critically aloof from the discourse of nationalism.
8. Ringer 1990. Ringer focuses on the political economists of the 1890s and after, and as such his survey is less than representative of the 'German Academic Community' mentioned in the book's subtitle. Political economists were

heavily outnumbered by other disciplines in the apologetic writings that we see around the wars of 1870 and 1914.

9. Schivelbusch 2004 summarizes this as the 'Vae victoribus' mode.
10. The two-nations view of French history: Poliakov 1987; see also chapter 7. Fustel as a historian: Hartog 1988, Herrick 1954.
11. Fustel de Coulanges 1870 for the following extracts. See generally also Jurt 2013.
12. Grimm 1814. This contribution to Görres's *Rheinischer Merkur* appeared anonymously; Grimm's authorship was established by Friemel 1995.
13. On this duo of popular–patriotic novelists from the Lorraine region: Grandhomme 2021, Marotin 1999.
14. Well documented in Bisschoff 2018.
15. Quoted in Lacouture 1984–1986, 1: 66. Generally Beller & Leerssen 2017, Leerssen 2018.
16. French annexations and hegemonism in the Rhineland post-1918 provoked millennial commemorations of the region's medieval ties with the empire; see Cepl-Kaufmann 2009.
17. Loetscher & Scheibling 2006.
18. Renan 1878.
19. Bollenbeck 2001. The opposition *Geist/esprit* was made by Wechssler 1927, see Schmidt 2012.
20. Kalmar 1987, McMahon 2009 and 2016.
21. Ghervas 2014, Koskenniemi 2001.
22. Rodolphe Reiss's *Report upon the Atrocities Committed by the Austro-Hungarian Army During the First Invasion of Serbia* appeared only in 1917. On Belgium and war propaganda: Horne & Kramer 2001, Alan Kramer 2007, more generally Paddock 2014.
23. Online at wikisource: w.wiki/Cmsm.
24. Generally: Mommsen 1996. Germany: Flasch 2000, Bruch 2006; France: Hanna 1996, Morton 1990, Prochasson & Rasmussen 1996, also Gephart 1996 (on Durkheim), Krumeich 1996 (on Lavisse). Britain: Andrew 1981, Buitenhuis 1987, Sanders & Taylor 1982. On Lavisse as nationalist historian: Bourdon 2017.
25. Wilhelm II, 'To the German Nation' (6 August 1914), online in the original at https://w.wiki/Cj$V. The final sentence echoed a line by Max Schenkendorf from 1813 that had become a widespread motto: 'Never will the Reich be vanquished if ye are united and faithful'. That line also featured on a 1919 medal protesting the Treaty of Versailles and was used by the NSDAP as an election slogan in 1933.
26. The full text is online in the original at w.wiki/CgSD.
27. Hanna 1996, 80. The *Erklärung* is online at wikisource, w.wiki/CfjZ, and related materials at e-rn.ie/greatwar. See also Ungern-Sternberg & Ungern-Sternberg 1996.
28. Durkheim & Denis 1915.

29. On Crowe: Dunn 2013 and Rose 2017, also the relevant portions in Clark 2014. I argue the case in more detail in Leerssen 2022a with particular reference to Rose 2017 and Mommsen 1973. Many discussions of the Fischer thesis concentrate on the representativity of his documentation and on the moral–political shortcomings of his life in the Third Reich. What is more relevant here is the fact that Fischer's book, rather than perpetuating the Entente's vilification of Germany at Versailles, broke through a German historiographical complacency rooted in the country's self-vindications of the period 1914–1919. Also, its very title identified an important driving force in the run-up to 1914: Germany's ambition to rise from the rank of a European power (which it had achieved in 1871) to that of a world power, hegemonic within Europe and with colonial possessions globally. On *Weltpolitik*, the ambition to become a world power, in the run-up to 1914: Mommsen 1981, Fröhlich 1994. Since the days of the Fischer controversy, a consensus has been reached that extra-European colonial imperialism is inextricably entangled with, and cannot be seen separately from, the jostling for primacy within Europe; see Anderson 2024.
30. See Clarke 1992, Firchow 1986, Jeismann 1992, Kennedy 1980, Melby 2019, Scully 2012. For the generalized culture of belligerence: Kieft 2015, MacMillan 2014, and note 1 in this chapter.
31. See James 1954, 424, Sladen 1938, Andrew 1981. On Le Queux: Rose 2017, 51–58. Also Kennedy 1980, chapter 19 ('The Impulse and Orchestration of Public Opinion').
32. Goethe on ancient and modern tragedy: in his *Shakespeare und kein Ende*, 1815:

> Ancient tragedy is based on an inexorable 'this must be' [*Sollen*], which is only imposed more sharply and swiftly if it is opposed by one's will [*Wollen*]. Here is the locus of all those oracular dooms, those fateful themes presided over by the figure of Oedipus … But all that *Sollen* is despotic … Willpower [*Wollen*] is or appears as something free, something that favours the individual. Thus, willpower is winsome and will be embraced by those who get to know it. It is the God of modern times. We turn to it as we shrink from its opposite, and this is the reason why our modern art and mentality will always be different from that of antiquity.

For anomie in Israeli counterterrorism, see Byman 2011, woefully borne out by Israel's genocidal response to the terrorist Hamas attacks of 7 October 2023.
33. See Hoeres 2004.
34. Kennedy 1980, Firchow 1986 (tracing the recoil from the 'cousinship' described in Mander 1974), Stibbe 2001. Generally on literary jingoism in Britain: Eby 1987.
35. Online in German and English at e-rn.ie/lissauer.
36. Online at e-rn.ie/hardylissauer.
37. De Gaulle 1954, Volume I, opening.
38. Tilly 1975 famously quips that 'War made the states, and the states made war'. On Tilly as a theorist of nationalism: Brubaker 2010. In charting the impact of modern warfare on nationalism I take my cue from the classic study in the field, Hutchinson 2017; his comments on Tilly: 13–18.

39. Generally Winter 1998.
40. The Waterloo monument proposed in 1815 was a novelty in that it honoured rank-and-file troops as well as officers: see Castlereagh's address to the House of Commons, 29 June 1815, Hansard's parliamentary debates 31 (1815): 1049–1057. For the public veneration of fallen soldiers in France and Germany post-1871: Maas 1995. Also Hutchinson 2017, 62–63.
41. Hindenburg 1920. Algeria: Valensi 1999. *Rambo: First Blood Part II*, ending transcribed from the excerpt online at YouTube (in many versions and copies), remarkable also for the patriotic and hero-worshipping comments appended by the YouTube viewers. See Hutchinson 2017, 66–68.
42. Continued hostilities after November 1918: Gerwarth 2016; Culture of defeat: Schivelbusch 2004.

12 The Long Tail

1. On the importance of myth in independent Latvia: Ķencis 2012.
2. Generally, Pourchier-Plasseraud 2015.
3. On historicist mass media in the twentieth century: Landsberg 2015.
4. e-rn.ie/stampslist and, for a chronological network visualization of their meshing canonicities, e-rn.ie/stampscloud.
5. On the 'Pageant of the Celt': Carew 2014. The design of the 'Official Handbook' (e-rn.ie/handbookirishfreestate) was by Art O'Murnaghan, who exemplified the overlap between the Irish revival movement and the decorative arts; see Figgis 1985.
6. Dziewanowski-Stefańczyk 2022.
7. Sapega 2007, Corkill & Pina Almeida 2009.
8. For the run-up to ethnocracy in independent Poland: Böhler 2018, Porter 2002; on Smetona in neighbouring Lithuania: Eidintas 2015.
9. The transition from nationalism to Fascism had been exhaustively studied in the French case by Zeev Sternhell, e.g. Sternhell 1972, 1978; the capacity of Fascist movements to ingest a source tradition of extreme nationalism is discussed for three countries (France, Italy and Germany) by Breuer 2005. Also Frantz, Geddes & Wrights 2018. Roger Griffin 1991 characterizes Fascism as 'palingenetic ultranationalism'. In sum, John Breuilly's contention that Fascism is a heightened form of nationalism is incontrovertible (Breuilly 2011, 2020).
10. Mudde 2007, 2019.
11. South Africa: Duffy 2006, Marx 1998, Moody 1975. Israel: Kaplan 2005, Tress 1984; for cross-currents with Piłsudski's Poland: Heller 2017, for Jabotinsky, see also King 2011, 167–176. India: Bhakle 2024, Sharma 2011, Chaturvedi 2022, Graham 1990.
12. On *Blut und Boden*: Dupke 1994, Bramwell 2003, Schärli 2007. On *Heimat* movies: Höfig 1973, Moltke 2005.
13. Cavaliero 1977, Lowenthal 1991, Short 1992, Colls & Dodd 1986, Giles & Middleton 1995, Matless 1998.

14. Baldwin, 'What England Means to Me', speech to the Royal Society of St George, 6 May 1924, online at e-rn.ie/baldwin.
15. Speech to the Conservative Group for Europe, 22 April 1993, online at johnmajorarchive.org.uk/1993/04/22/mr-majors-speech-to-conservative-group-for-europe-22-april-1993/.
16. The surveys are all based on the 'Cinema and TV' project in the *Encyclopedia of Romantic Nationalism in Europe*, interactively accessible at e-rn.ie/FilmTV. For the Indian material I am particularly grateful to Bob van der Linden.
17. Generally Riches 2009.
18. For a thoughtful typological comparison between pre- and post-Communist forms of nationalism in Eastern/Central Europe, see Hroch 1996.
19. See also Linden 2024.
20. See screenrant.com/rrr-movie-ending-explained-in-detail/. Also: Abrams 2022, Babu 2022, Dore 2021.
21. Following the cue of Linden 2024.
22. In highlighting these characteristics of melodrama, I follow Brooks 1995.
23. Harris 1983.
24. Jan Assmann 1992, Aleida Assmann 1999. The idea of ideas 'on standby', archivally encapsulated in books and media and potentially present and retrievable for reactivation even during periods of inert dormancy, was implied by Karl Popper's notion of a 'World-3', an intermediate zone between the ontological worlds of material objects and mental notions (Popper 1972).

Summing Up

1. Hearn 2006.
2. Freeden 1998, Stanley 2008; on populism generally: Mudde 2007, Mudde & Rovira Kaltwasser 2017. For a strenuous critique of applying the qualification 'thin' to populism: Schroeder 2020.
3. Genette 1969, 73.
4. Connor 2004.
5. The motto is from Anne-Marie Thiesse, whose classic work (1999) broke significant new ground, and inspired as well as informed this book, in tracing the importance of 'cultural transfers'.
6. See the comments in the Introduction of this book. It is generally accepted (and it was never intended otherwise by Hroch himself) that Phases A, B and C are not like carriages in a train, neatly separate periods characterizing discrete paradigms of a national movement. The cultural consciousness-raising that characterizes Phase A does not cease once social demands are being raised or mass movements are being mobilized, but remains an operative agent throughout. Later phases are overlays on earlier ones, not their replacements. That seemed to warrant a more sustained history of Phase A consciousness-raising, and much of this book is just that: tracing Phase A

even as it interacted with the social and political shifts and revolutions of the nineteenth and twentieth centuries.

7. There may be different incubation periods in different areas before a cultural broadcast 'takes root' (e.g. the genre of the rhapsody or the historical novel, or the fashion for folktale-collecting). Why, Hroch (2009, 44) asks, was the French message of 'national' popular sovereignty influential in Bohemia well before it took root in Catalunya, which was located much closer to France? To begin with, geographical distance does not count for much in the communicative diffusion of ideas. Moreover, the diffusion of culture does not take place wholesale from one 'national' space to another one, but moves piecemeal from hub to hub, between cities. Cities, with their bookshops, post offices, newspapers, sociability and institutions are the main relay points for the exchange of ideas. (There are also more decentred channels of diffusion: the 'peer-to-peer' networks of letter-writing artists and intellectuals, and the travels of individuals.) We may assume, then, that the emission and diffusion of culture and ideas takes places at a more or less even speed in all directions, like the sower sowing his seed, along a plurality of ramifying conduits in different directions. The asynchronicity of when the seeds take root would result either from contingent happenstance (some conduits may be more propitious than others in the conveyance of ideas) or from the fact that institutional or 'social preconditions' (I here gratefully avail myself of Hroch's phraseology) are, indeed, less propitious for their successful adoption in one society than in another. This is less a historical 'given' than a historical problematics, and should be addressed in future research.
8. w.wiki/Ch4Q and w.wiki/Ch4T. The feedback of political activism into cultural consciousness-raising is the subject of Ann Rigney's project ReAct, 'Remembering Activism'; rememberingactivism.eu and see Rigney 2025.
9. On Valencia vis-à-vis the Spanish state and the Catalan movement: Archilés 2001, Martínez Roda 2000, Villanueva 2017.
10. For the span from 'feeling' to ideology: Hearn 2006. What I am addressing here concerns the pragmatics of how people experience cultural phenomena as they encounter them; I am not addressing the putative emotional motivations of national thought as conjecturally discussed by social psychologists.
11. As analysed by Arcan Gossler 2001, 74, discussing Stefan Breuer 1993, 187.
12. Breuilly 2011 and note 11 in the Introduction of this book. I am mindful of the arguments of Hannah Arendt (1976) and Giorgio Agamben (2005) that it is in 'states of emergency' or 'states of exception' that democracy tends to founder, along with the rule of law and civil rights.
13. Chesterton 1902.
14. Durkheim 1992, Mestrovic 1989.
15. Durkheim himself linked anomie to market deregulation in his *Leçons de sociologie* (Durkheim 1992); see also Burgi 2014.
16. On populism: Anselmi 2018, Brubaker 2020, Mudde 2007, 2009, Rovíra Kaltwasser et al. 2017. For the systemic connection between populism and

recent forms of authoritarianism: Applebaum 2020, 2024. For the alt-right *nouvelle droite* and identitarian movements, and their reliance on Fascist ideas: Griffin 2000.

17. Interview with Faisal Islam on Sky News, 3 June 2016, www.skygroup.sky/article/eu-in-or-out-faisal-islam-interview-with-michael-gove-30616-8pm.
18. Braak 1937. For the sociological and politological discussion of contemporary European ethnopopulism in terms of 'resentment' and 'grievance' politics: Betz 1990 and 1993, Ivarsflaten 2008, Heitmeyer 2018.

Bibliography

ä, ö, and ü have been alphabetized as ae, oe, ue; Dutch ij as y; þ as th.
Space constraints necessitated the omission of most subtitles.
Older, frequently re-issued texts are referred to in reputable online versions. In addition to the sources explicitly referred to here, it is understood that information has been garnered from general reference works such as the Encyclopaedia Britannica, *the* Allgemeine deutsche Biographie *and the* Encyclopedia of Romantic Nationalism in Europe.

Aarsleff, Hans (1967). *The Study of Language in England, 1780–1860* (Princeton, NJ: Princeton University Press).

Ablonczy, Balázs (2022). *Go East: A History of Hungarian Turanism* (Bloomington: Indiana University Press).

Abrams, M. H. (1957). 'The Correspondent Breeze: A Romantic Metaphor', *Kenyon Review* 19.1: 113–130.

Abrams, S. (2022). 'How the Indian Action Spectacular "RRR" Became a Smash in America', *New York Times*, 3 August 2022.

Ackerman, Gerald M. (1986). *The Life and Work of Jean-Léon Gérôme* (London: Sotheby's Publications).

Agamben, Giorgio (2005). *State of Exception* (trl. Kevin Attell; Chicago: University of Chicago Press).

Agulhon, Maurice (1988). *Histoire vagabonde* (Paris: Gallimard).

Albrecht-Carrié, R. (1968). *The European Concert* (London: Palgrave Macmillan).

Alder, Lory & Richard Dalby (1979). *The Dervish of Windsor Castle* (London: Bachman and Turner).

Aldgate, Anthony & Jeffrey Richards (2007). *Britain Can Take It: The British Cinema in the Second World War* (3rd ed.; London: Tauris).

Alexander, Ronelle (2006). *Bosnian, Croatian, Serbian, a Grammar* (Madison: University of Wisconsin Press).

Alings, Reinhard (1996). *Monument und Nation. Das Bild vom Nationalstaat im Medium Denkmal* (Berlin: De Gruyter).

Anderson, Benedict (2006). *Imagined Communities* (new ed.; London: Verso).

Anderson, Perry (2024). *Disputing Disaster* (London: Verso).

Andrew, Christopher (1981). 'The Mobilization of British Intelligence for the Two World Wars', in *Mobilization for Total War*, ed. N. F. Dreisziger (Waterloo, ON: Wilfrid Laurier University Press), 87–110.

Ansel, Michael (1990). *G.G. Gervinus' 'Geschichte der poetischen National-Literatur der Deutschen'* (Frankfurt: Lang).

Anselmi, Manuel (2018). *Populism* (London: Routledge).

Anttonen, Pertti J. (2014). 'The Kalevala and the Authenticity Debate', in *Manufacturing a Past for the Present*, ed. J. M. Bak, P. J. Geary & G. Klaniczay (Leiden: Brill), 56–80.

Applebaum, Anne (2020). *Twilight of Democracy* (New York: Doubleday).

Applebaum, Anne (2024). *Autocracy, Inc.* (New York: Doubleday).

Archilés, Ferran & Manuel Martí (2001). 'Ethnicity, Region and Nation', *Ethnic and Racial Studies* 24.5: 779–797.

Arendt, Hannah (1957). 'Was ist Autorität?', in id. *Fragwürdige Traditionsbestände im politischen Denken der Gegenwart: Vier Essays* (Frankfurt: Europäische Verlagsanstalt), 117–168.

Arendt, Hannah (1976). *The Origins of Totalitarianism* (new ed.; New York: Houghton Mifflin).

Aretin, Johann Christoph von (1803). *Älteste Sage über die Geburt und Jugend Karls des Grossen* (Munich: Scherer).

Arndt, Ernst Moritz (1813a). *Der Rhein, Teutschlands Strom, aber nicht Teutschlands Gränze* (Leipzig: Rein). Online at e-rn.ie/arndtrhine

Arndt, Ernst Moritz (1813b). *Noch ein Wort über die Franzosen und über uns* (Leipzig: Rein). Online at e-rn.ie/arndtwort

Arndt, Ernst Moritz (1834). *Belgien und was daran hängt* (Leipzig: Weidmann).

Arndt, Ernst Moritz (1934). *Deutsche Volkwerdung*, ed. Carl Petersen & Paul Hermann Ruth (Breslau: Hirt).

Arndt, Monika (1976). *Die Goslarer Kaiserpfalz als Nationaldenkmal* (Hildesheim: Lax).

Arnold, Alice Laura (2006). *Poetische Momente der Weltgeschichte* (doctoral thesis; Munich: Ludwig-Maximilians-Universität).

Arnold, Guy (1980). *Held Fast for England: G.A Henty, Imperialist Boys' Writer* (London: Hamish Hamilton).

Arvidsson, Stefan (2006). *Aryan Idols* (Chicago: University of Chicago Press).

Assmann, Aleida (1999). *Erinnerungsräume* (Munich: Beck).

Assmann, Jan (1992). *Das kulturelle Gedächtnis* (Munich: Beck).

Athanassoglou-Kallmyer, Nina Maria (1989). *French Images from the Greek War of Independence 1821–1830* (New Haven, CT: Yale University Press).

Atkinson, David & Denis Cosgrove (1998). 'Urban Rhetoric and Embodied Identities', *Annals of the Association of American Geographers* 88.1: 28–49.

Attridge, Steve (2003). *Nationalism, Imperialism, and Identity in Late Victorian Culture* (London: Palgrave Macmillan).

Auroux, Sylvain et al. (eds.) (2000–2001). *History of the Language Sciences* (2 vols.; Berlin: De Gruyter).

Avineri, Shlomo (1962). 'Hegel and Nationalism', *Review of Politics* 24.4: 461–484; also in Stewart 1996, 109–128.

Baár, Monika (2010). *Historians and Nationalism* (Oxford: Oxford University Press).

Babu, R. (2022). 'RRR is an Incredible Action Movie with Seriously Troubling Politics', vox.com, 20 July 2022, vox.com/23220275/rrr-netflix-tollywood-hindutva-caste-system

Bachleitner, Rudolf (1976). *Die Nazarener* (Munich: Heyne).

Badiou, Alain (2005). *Metapolitics* (London: Verso).

Baetens, Jan Dirk (2012). 'Voor vorst en vaderland', *Belgisch tijdschrift voor filologie en geschiedenis* 90.2: 513–539.

Bak, János M., Patrick J. Geary & Gábor Klaniczay (eds.) (2014). *Manufacturing a Past for the Present* (Leiden: Brill).

Bakhle, Janaki (2024). *Savarkar and the Making of Hindutva* (Princeton, NJ: Princeton University Press).

Balibar, Renée & Dominique Laporte (1974). *Le français national* (Paris: Hachette).

Balikić, Lukija, John Paul Newman & Vojtěch Pojar (2023). *The Sokol Movement between State and Society in Interwar East-Central Europe* (East Central Europe special issue, 50.2–3; Leiden: Brill).

Bancel, Nicolas et al. (eds.) (2011). *Zoos humains et exhibitions coloniales* (Paris: La Découverte).

Bann, Stephen (1997). *Delaroche: History Painted* (London: Reaktion).

Bann, Stephen (2006). 'Paul Delaroche's Early Work in the Context of English History Painting', *Oxford Art Journal* 29.3: 341–369.

Bann, Stephen (2012). *The Clothing of Clio* (new ed.; Cambridge: Cambridge University Press).

Bann, Stephen & Stéphane Paccoud (eds.) (2014). *L'invention du passé, vol 2: Histoires de coeur et d'épée en Europe, 1802–1850* (Paris: Hazan).

Barnard, A. (2002). 'Emic and Etic', in *Encyclopedia of Social and Cultural Anthropology*, ed. A. Barnard & J. Spencer (London: Routledge), 180–182.

Barr, Sheldon (2008). *Venetian Glass Mosaics, 1860–1917* (Woodbridge: ACC Art Books).

Bartels, Larry (2023). *Democracy Erodes from the Top* (Princeton, NJ: Princeton University Press).

Bartmuß, Hans-Joachim, Eberhard Kunze & Josef Ulfkotte (eds.) (2008). *'Turnvater' Jahn und sein patriotisches Umfeld* (Cologne: Böhlau).

Baumstark, Reinhold & Frank Büttner (eds.) (2003). *Großer Auftritt: Piloty und die Historienmalerei* (Munich: Pinakothek-Dumont).

Bayly, C. A. & Eugenio F. Biagini (eds.) (2009). *Giuseppe Mazzini and the Globalization of Democratic Nationalism, 1830–1920* (Oxford: Oxford University Press).

Bayrisch Land (1976). *Bayrisch Land, bayrisch Gwand* (Traunstein: Chiemgauer Verlagshaus – Eigenverlag Vereinigte Bayerische Trachtenverbände).

Becker, Jean-Jacques (1977). *1914: Comment les Français sont entrés dans la guerre* (Paris: Fondation Nationale des Sciences politiques).

Becker, Jean-Jacques (2012). 'Le mensonge en histoire', *Écrire l'histoire* 10: 37–45.

Beckerman, Michael B. (2003). *New Worlds of Dvořák: Searching in America for the Composer's Inner Life* (New York: Norton).

Bein (2011). 'Karl Lachmann', in *Neugermanistische Editoren im Wissenschaftskontext*, ed. R. S. Kamzelak, R. Nutt-Kofoth & B. Plachta (Berlin: De Gruyter), 1–16.

Bell, David A. (2001). *The Cult of the Nation in France* (Cambridge, MA: Harvard University Press).

Beller, Manfred & Joep Leerssen (eds.) (2007). *Imagology* (Amsterdam/Leiden: Rodopi/Brill). Online at imagologica.eu/ethnotypology.

Beller, Manfred & Joep Leerssen (eds.) (2017). *The Rhine* (Leiden: Brill).

Bemong, Nele (2007). Vormen en functies van de Belgische historische roman (1827–1850) (doctoral thesis; Leuven: Katholieke Universiteit).

Benda, Julien (1927). *La Trahison des clercs*. Online at classiques.uqac.ca/classiques/benda_julien/trahison_des_clercs/trahison_des_clercs.html

Benjamin, Walter (1963). 'Das Kunstwerk im Zeitalter seiner technischen Reproduzierbarkeit', in id., *Drei Studien zur Kunstsoziologie* (Frankfurt: Suhrkamp), 7–63.

Benjamin, Walter (2002). *The Arcades Project* (ed./trl. H. Eiland & K. McLaughlin; Cambridge, MA: Belknap Press).

Benoist, Jacques (1992). *Le Sacré Coeur de Montmartre* (2 vols.; Paris: Editions ouvrières).

Berger, Stefan & Christoph Conrad (eds.) (2015). *The Past as History* (Basingstoke: Palgrave Macmillan).

Berger, Stefan, Mark Donovan & Kevin Passmore (eds.) (1999). *Writing National Histories* (London: Routledge).

Berger, Stefan, Linas Eriksonas & Andrew Mycock (eds.) (2008). *Narrating the Nation* (New York: Berghahn).

Berger, Stefan & Chris Lorenz (eds.) (2010). *Nationalizing the Past* (Basingstoke: Palgrave Macmillan).

Berger, Stefan & Alexei Miller (eds.) (2015). *Nationalizing Empires* (Budapest: CEU Press).

Bergougniou, Jean-Michel, Rémi Clignet & Philippe David (2001). *Villages noirs et autres visiteurs africains et malgaches en France et en Europe, 1870–1940* (Paris: Karthala).

Berjoan, Nicolas (2011). 'L'idée latine du Félibrige', *Revue d'histoire du XIXe siècle*, 42.1: 121–136.

Berlin, Isaiah (1976). *Vico and Herder: Two Studies in the History of Ideas* (New York: Viking).

Bernstein, Harry (2013). *Alexandre Herculano, 1810–1877* (Paris: J. Touzot).

Betz, Hans-Georg (1990–93). 'Politics of Resentment', *Comparative Politics* 23.1: 45–60, 25.4: 413–427.

Biddiscomble, Perry (1998). *Werwolf! The History of the National Socialist Guerrilla Movement, 1944–1946* (Toronto: University of Toronto Press).

Biddiss, Michael D. (1970). *Father of Racist Ideology: The Social and Political Thought of Count Gobineau* (London: Weidenfeld & Nicholson).

Biddiss, Michael D. (1997). 'History as Destiny: Gobineau, H.S. Chamberlain and Spengler', *Transactions of the Royal Historical Society* 7: 73–100.

Billig, Michael (1995). *Banal Nationalism* (London: Verso).

Birkett, Tom (2021). 'Why Far-Right Groups Co-opt Norse Symbols', *Fast Company* 13 January 2021, fastcompany.com/90593544/why-far-right-groups-co-opt-norse-symbols

Bischoff, Sebastian (2018). *Kriegsziel Belgien* (Münster: Waxmann).

Bjørnholt, Margunn (2005). 'Hvorfor er folkedrakt så viktig i Norge og marginalt i nabolandene?', *Nordisk kulturpolitisk tidsskrift*, 8.2: 34–50.

Blecking, Diethelm (ed.) (1991). *Die slawische Sokolbewegung* (Dortmund: Forschungsstelle Ostmitteleuropa an der Universitat Dortmund).

Blecking, Diethelm & Marek Waic (eds.) (2008). *Sport, Ethnie, Nation* (Baltmannsweiler: Schneider).

Blix, Göran (2008). *From Paris to Pompeii: French Romanticism and the Cultural Politics of Archaeology* (Philadelphia: University of Pennsylvania Press).

Blom, Alderik H. (2013). 'Rasmus Rask and Romanticism', *Beiträge zur Geschichte der Sprachwissenschaft*, 23: 241–274.

Blommen, Heinz (1960). Anfänge und Entwicklung des Männerchorwesens am Niederrhein (doctoral thesis; Cologne: University of Cologne).

Bluhm, Lother (1997). *Die Brüder Grimm und der Beginn der Deutschen Philologie* (Hildesheim: Weidmann).

Bodmer, Johann Jacob (1757). *Chriemhilden Rache, und die Klage*. Online at collections.library.yale.edu/catalog/2046591

Böhler, Jochen (2018). *Civil War in Central Europe, 1918–1921* (Oxford: Oxford University Press).

Boer, Pim den (1989). *History as a Profession* (Princeton, NJ: Princeton University Press).

Bogatyrev, Pyotr & Roman Jakobson (1929). 'Die Folklore als eine besondere Form des Schaffens', in *Donum natalicium Schrijnen* (Utrecht: Dekker & Van der Vegt), 900–913.

Boime, Albert (1969). 'The Salon des Refusés and the Evolution of Modern Art', *Art Quarterly* 32: 411–426.

Bojić, Vera (1977). *Jacob Grimm und Vuk Karadžić: Ein Vergleich ihrer Sprachauffassungen und ihre Zusammenarbeit auf dem Gebiet der serbischen Grammatik* (Munich: Otto Sagner).

Bollenbeck, Georg (2001). 'Selbstbilder, Fremdbilder, Feindbilder: "Kultur" und "civilisation"', in *France, Allemagne, passions croisées*, ed. K. H. Götze & M. Vanoosthuyse (special issue of *Cahiers d'Études Germaniques*, 41): 19–34.

Bonazza, Sergio (1984). 'Austro-Slavism as the Motive of Kopitar's Work', *Slovene Studies* 5.2: 155–164.

Bonazza, Sergio (1995). 'Bartholomäus Kopitar', *Welt der Slaven* 40: 285–303.

Bønding, Sophie, Lone Kølle Martinsen & Pierre-Brice Stahl (eds.) (2021). *Mythology and Nation Building* (Aarhus: Aarhus University Press).

Bonfiglio, Thomas Paul (2010). *Mother Tongues and Nations* (Berlin: De Gruyter).

Bonikowski, Bart (2017). 'Ethno-Nationalist Populism and the Mobilization of Collective Resentment', *British Journal of Sociology* 68. Suppl: 181–213.

Bosch, Lourens P. van den (2002). *Friedrich Max Müller* (Leiden: Brill).

Bourdieu, Pierre (1979). *La distinction: Critique sociale du jugement* (Paris: Seuil).

Bourdieu, Pierre (1980). *Le sens pratique* (Paris: Seuil).

Bourdieu, Pierre (1982). *Ce que parler veut dire* (Paris: Fayard).

Bourdieu, Pierre (1993). *The Field of Cultural Production* (Cambridge: Cambridge University Press).

Bourdon, Etienne (2017). *La forge gauloise de la nation: Ernest Lavisse et la fabrique des ancêtres* (Lyons: ENS).

Bouvier, Jean-Claude (2007). *Les noms de rues disent la ville* (Paris: Bonneton).

Braak, Menno ter (1937). *Het nationaal-socialisme als rancuneleer* (Assen: Van Gorcum). Online at dbnl.org/tekst/braa002natio1_01

Bramwell, Anna (2003). 'Blut und Boden'. in *Deutsche Erinnerungsorte*, ed. Étienne François & Hagen Schulze (Munich: Beck), 3: 380–391.

Brandt, Peter (1988). 'Das studentische Wartburgfest vom 18./19. Oktober 1817', in Düding, Friedemann & Münch (1988), 89–112.

Braw, J. D. (2007). 'Vision as Revision: Ranke and the Beginning of Modern History', *History and Theory* 46.4: 45–60.

Brenner, Michael & Gideon Reuveni (eds.) (2006). *Emancipation through Muscles: Jews and Sports in Europe* (Lincoln, NE: University of Nebraska Press).

Breuer, Stefan (1993). *Anatomie der konservativen Revolution* (Darmstadt: Wissenschaftliche Buchgesellschaft).

Breuer, Stefan (2005). *Nationalismus und Faschismus* (Darmstadt: Wissenchaftliche Buchgesellschaft).

Breuer, Stefan (2011). *'Herrschaft' in der Soziologie Max Webers* (Wiesbaden: Harassowitz).

Breuer, Stefan (2014). *Der charismatische Staat* (Darmstadt: Wissenschaftliche Buchgesellschaft).

Breuilly, John (2009). 'The Response to Napoleon and German Nationalism', in *The Bee and the Eagle: Napoleonic France and the End of the Holy Roman Empire, 1806*, ed. Alan Forrest & Peter H. Wilson (Basingstoke: Palgrave Macmillan), 256–283.

Breuilly, John (2011). 'Max Weber, Charisma and Nationalist Leadership', *Nations and Nationalism* 17.3: 477–499.

Breuilly, John (2020). 'Nationalism', in *The Globalization of World Politics*, ed. J. Baylis, S. Smith & P. Owens (8th ed.; Oxford: Oxford University Press), 402–417.

Breuilly, John (ed.) (2013). *The Oxford Handbook of the History of Nationalism* (Oxford: Oxford University Press).

Brewer, David (2001). *The Greek War of Independence* (New York: Overlook).

Bridge, Roy & Roger Bullen (2004). *The Great Powers and the European State System, 1814–1914* (2nd ed.; London: Routledge).

Brock, Peter (1976). *The Slovak National Awakening: An Essay in the Intellectual History of East Central Europe* (Toronto: University of Toronto Press).

Brooks, Peter (1995). *The Melodramatic Imagination* (New Haven, CT: Yale University Press).

Broomans, Petra et al. (eds.) (2008). *The Beloved Mothertongue* (Leuven: Peeters).

Brubaker, Rogers (1996). *Nationalism Reframed* (Cambridge: Cambridge University Press).

Brubaker, Rogers (2004a). *Ethnicity without Groups* (Cambridge, MA: Harvard University Press).

Brubaker, Rogers (2004b). 'In the Name of the Nation: Reflections on Nationalism and Patriotism', *Citizenship Studies* 8.2: 115–127.

Brubaker, Rogers (2010). 'Charles Tilly as a Theorist of Nationalism', *American Sociologist* 41: 375–381.

Brubaker, Rogers (2020). 'Populism and Nationalism', *Nations and Nationalism* 26.1: 44–66.

Bruch, Rüdiger vom (2006). 'Geistige Kriegspropaganda', online at *Themenportal Europäische Geschichte*, www.europa.clio-online.de/essay/id/fdae-1363

Brüggemann, Karsten & Anders Kasekamp (2014). '"Singing Oneself into a Nation?": Estonian Song Festivals as Rituals of Political Mobilisation', *Nations and Nationalism* 20: 259–276.

Bruendel, Steffen (2003). *Volksgemeinschaft oder Volksstaat* (Berlin: De Gruyter).

Buchanan, Tom & Martin Conway (eds.) (1996). *Political Catholicism in Europe, 1918–1965* (Oxford: Oxford University Press).

Büttner, Frank (1980). *Peter Cornelius* (Wiesbaden: Franz Steiner).

Buitenhuis, Peter (1987). *The Great war of Words: British, American and Canadian Propaganda and Fiction, 1914–1933* (Vancouver, BC: University of British Columbia Press).

Bunzl, Matti (1996). 'Franz Boas and the Humboldtian Tradition', in *Volksgeist as Method and Ethic*, ed. George W. Stocking (Madison, WN: University of Wisconsin Press), 17–78.

Burgdorf, Wolfgang (2006). *Ein Weltbild verliert seine Welt: Der Untergang des Alten Reiches und die Generation von 1806* (Munich: Oldenbourg).

Burgi, Noëlle (2014). 'Societies Without Citizens', *European Journal of Social Theory* 17.3: 290–306.

Burke, Edmund (1790). *Reflections on the Revolution in France*. Online at wikisource, w.wiki/CdRT

Burke, Peter (2012). *A Social History of Knowledge 2: From the Encyclopédie to Wikipedia* (Cambridge: Polity).

Burke, Peter (2013). 'Nationalism and Vernaculars, 1500–1800', in *The Oxford Handbook of the History of Nationalism*, ed. John Breuilly (Oxford: Oxford University Press), 21–35.

Bydžovská, Lenka & Karel Srp (eds.) (2011). *Alfons Mucha: Slovanská Epopej* (Prague: Galerie Hlavního Města Prahy).

Byman, David (2011). *A High Price: The Triumphs and Failures of Israeli Counterterrorism* (New York: Oxford University Press).

Camus, Jean-Yves (2019). 'Alain de Benoist and the New Right', in *Key Thinkers of the Radical Right*, ed. Mark Sedgwick (Oxford: Oxford University Press), 73–90.

Carbonell, Charles-Olivier (1976). *Histoire et historiens: Une mutation idéologique des historiens français, 1865–1885* (Toulouse: Privat).

Carew, Mairéad (2014). 'The "Pageant of the Celt": Irish Archaeology at the Chicago World's Fair, 1933–34', *Archaeology Ireland* 28.1: 9–12.

Carl, Horst (2000). 'Der Mythos des Befreiungskrieges: Die "martialische Nation" im Zeitalter der Revolutions- und Befreiungskriege, 1792–1815', in *Föderative Nation*, ed. Dieter Langewiesche & Georg Schmidt (Munich: Oldenbourg), 63–82.

Carlyle, Thomas (1841). *On Heroes and Hero-Worship*. Online at wikisource, w.wiki/CdRV

Carpenter, Humphrey (1977). *Tolkien* (New York: Ballantine).

Cartledge, Paul (2002). 'To Die For?', *History Today*, 52.8: 19–25.

Castle, Kathryn (1996). *Britannia's Children* (Manchester: Manchester University Press).

Caussat, Pierre, Dariusz Adamski & Marc Crépon (eds.) (1996). *La langue source de la nation* (Sprimont: Mardaga).

Cavaliero, Glen (1977). *The Rural Tradition in the English Novel 1900–1939* (Basingstoke: Macmillan).

Cepl-Kaufmann, Gertrude (ed.) (2009). *Jahrtausendfeiern und Befreiungsfeiern im Rheinland* (Essen: Klartext).

Certeau, Michel de, Dominique Julia & Jacques Revel (eds.) (2002). *Une politique de la langue* (new ed.; Paris: Gallimard).

Champfleury (i.e. Jules François Fleury-Husson) (1857). *Le réalisme*. Online at archive.org/details/ChampfleuryRealismeGoogoo

Chappel, James (2018). *Catholic Modern* (Cambridge, MA: Harvard University Press).

Chaturvedi, Vinayak (2022). *Hindutva and Violence: V. D. Savarkar and the Politics of History* (New York: SUNY Press).

Chaudonneret, Marie-Claude (1980). *Fleury Richard et Pierre Révoil: La peinture troubadour* (Paris: Arthena).

Chesterton, G. K. (1902). 'A Defence of Patriotism', in id., *The Defendant* (new ed. London: R. Brimley Johnson). Online at gutenberg.org/cache/epub/12245/pg12245-images.html#A_DEFENCE_OF_PATRIOTISM

Church, Clive H (1983). *Europe in 1830* (London: Routledge).

Cieraad, Irene (2018). 'Bringing Nostalgia Home: Switzerland and the Swiss Chalet', *Architecture and Culture* 6.2: 265–288.

Clark, Christopher (2014). *The Sleepwalkers* (London: HarperCollins).

Clark, Christopher (2023). *Revolutionary Spring* (London: Allen Lane).

Clark, Robert T. (1947). 'Herder, Cesarotti and Vico', *Studies in Philology* 44.4: 645–671.

Clarke, I. F. (1992). *Voices Prophesying War* (2nd ed.; Oxford: Oxford University Press).

Cleaver, Dale G. (1955). Henri Leys (doctoral thesis; Chicago, IL: University of Chicago).

Colls, Robert & Philip Dodd (eds.) (1986). *Englishness* (London, Croom Helm).

Connelly, John (2020). *From Peoples into Nations* (Princeton, NJ: Princeton University Press).

Connor, Walker (1967). 'Self-Determination: The New Phase', *World Politics* 20.1: 30–53.

Connor, Walker (1973). 'The Politics of Ethnonationalism', *Journal of International Affairs* 27.1: 1–21.

Connor, Walker (1978). 'Ethno-National versus Other Forms of Group Identity', in *Intergroup Accommodation in Plural Societies*, ed. N. Rhoodie & W. C. Ewing (London: Palgrave Macmillan), 53–83.

Connor, Walker (1994). *Ethnonationalism* (Princeton, NJ: Princeton University Press).

Connor, Walker (2004). 'The Timelessness of Nations', *Nations and Nationalism* 10.1–2: 35–47.

Conscience, Hendrik (1838). *De Leeuw van Vlaenderen* (Antwerpen: De Cort). Online at dbnl.org/tekst/conso001leeu01_01/

Constans, Claire, Marina Lambraki-Plaka & Francis Ribemont (eds.) (1996). *La Grèce en révolte* (Paris: Réunion des Musées Nationaux).

Constantine, Mary-Ann (2007). *The Truth against the World: Iolo Morganwg and Romantic Forgery* (Cardiff: University of Wales Press).

Conversi, Daniele (ed.) (2002). *Ethnonationalism in the Contemporary World* (London: Routledge).

Cooper, David L. (2010). *Creating the Nation* (DeKalb: Northern Illinois University Press).

Corbin, Alain, Noëlle Gérôme & Danielle Tartakowsky (eds.) (1994). *Les usages politiques des fêtes aux XIXe–XXe siècles* (Paris: Sorbonne).

Corkill, David & José Carlos Pina Almeida (2009). 'Commemoration and Propaganda in Salazar's Portugal', *Journal of Contemporary History* 44.3: 381–399.

Costa Pinto, António (1982). 'A formação do Integralismo Lusitano (1907/17)', *Análise Social* 18.72: 1409–1419.

Coxhead, Elizabeth (1985). *Daughters of Erin* (Gerrard's Cross: Colin Smythe).

Cronin, Mike, Mark Duncan & Paul Rouse (eds.) (2009). *The Gaelic Athletic Association, 1884–2009* (Dublin: Irish Academic Press).

Crowley, Tony (2008). *Wars of Words: The Politics of Language in Ireland 1537–2004* (Oxford: Oxford University Press).

Cubitt, Geoffrey (2007). *History and Memory* (Manchester: Manchester University Press).

Daly, Nicholas (2020). *Ruritania: A Cultural History* (Oxford: Oxford University Press).

Dann, Otto (ed.) (1983). *Religion-Kunst-Vaterland: Der Kölner Dom im 19.* Jahrhundert (Cologne: J.P. Bachen).

Dann, Otto (1995). 'Nationale Fragen in Deutschland', in *Nation und Emotion*, ed. Etienne François (Göttingen: Vandenhoeck & Ruprecht), 66–82.

D'Auria, Matthew (2020). *The Shaping of French National Identity* (Cambridge: Cambridge University Press).

Davis, John R. & Angus Nicholls (eds.) (2018). *Friedrich Max Müller and the Role of Philology in Victorian Thought* (London: Routledge).

Davis, Thomas (1845). 'Our National Language', in id., *Prose Writings* (London: The Walter Scott Publishing Co.), 158–165. Online at e-rn.ie/davisnationallanguage

De Gaulle, Charles (1954). *Mémoires de guerre* (Paris: Plon).
Deák, István (1996). 'Admiral and Regent Miklós Horthy', *Hungarian Quarterly* 37.143: 78–89.
Degen, Andreas & Elżbieta Dzikowska (2015). 'Wanda: Femme polonaise', in *Deutsch-Polnische Erinnerungsorte*, ed. Hans-Henning Hahn & Robert Traba (5 vols.; Munich: Schöningh), 1: 524–526.
Deletant, Dennis, Harry Hanak & Hugh Seton-Watson (eds.) (1988). *Historians as Nation Builders* (Basingstoke: Macmillan).
Demoule, Jean-Paul (2017). *Mais où sont passés les Indo-Européens?* (new ed.; Paris: Seuil).
Denecke, Ludwig (1971). *Jacob Grimm und sein Bruder Wilhelm* (Stuttgart: Metzler).
Derman, Joshua (2011). 'Max Weber and Charisma', *New German Critique* 113: 51–88.
Detienne, Marcel (1981). *L'invention de la mythologie* (Paris: Gallimard).
Deugd, Cornelis de (1966). *Het metafysisch grondpatroon van het romantische literaire denken: De fenomenologie van een geestesgesteldheid* (Groningen: Wolters).
Deutsch, Karl W. (1953). *Nationalism and Social Communication* (Boston, MA: Massachusetts Institute of Technology).
Deutsch, Karl W. (1969). *Nationalism and it Alternatives* (New York: Knopf).
Díaz-Andreu, Margarita & Timothy Champion (eds.) (1996). *Nationalism and Archeology in Europe* (Boulder, CO: Westview).
Dietler, Michael (1994). '"Our Ancestors the Gauls"', *American Anthropologist* 96.3: 584–605.
Digeon, Claude (1959). *La Crise allemande de la pensée française, 1870–1914* (Paris: Presses universitaires de France).
Dikötter, Frank (2020). *Dictators: The Cult of Personality in the Twentieth Century.* (London: Bloomsbury).
Dilcher, Gerhard & Bernd-Rüdiger Kern (1984). 'Die juristische Germanistik des 19. Jahrhunderts und die Fachtradition der Deutschen Rechtsgeschichte', *Zeitschrift für Rechtsgeschichte* 101 (Germ. Abt.): 1–46.
Dimakis, Jean (1992). *'Philhelléniques'* (Athens: Kardamitsa).
Dithmar, Reinhard (ed.) (1992). *Der Langemarck-Mythos in Dichtung und Unterricht* (Neuwied: Leuchterhand).
Dobiáš, Dalibor (ed.) (2014). *Rukopisy královédvorský a zelenohorský a česká věda* (Prague: Academia).
Dobiáš, Dalibor (ed.) (2019). *Rukopisy královédvorský a zelenohorský v kultuře a umění* (2 vols.; Prague: Academia).
Domingo, Josep Maria (2009). 'Renaixença: El mot i la idea', *Anuari Verdaguer*, 17: 215–234.
Domingo, Josep Maria (ed.) (2011). *Barcelona i els Jocs Florals, 1859* (Barcelona: Museu d'Història de Barcelona).
Dominian, Leon (1917). *The Frontiers of Language and Nationality in Europe* (New York: American Geographical Society).
Doppelbauer, Max & Kathrin Sartingen (eds.) (2010). *De la zarzuela al cine* (Munich: Meidenbauer).

Dore, B. (2021). 'The Player: Akshay Kumar's Role as Hindutva's Poster Boy', *The Caravan*, 1 February 2021, caravanmagazine.in/amp/reportage/akshay-kumar-role-hindutva-poster-boy
Dović, Marijan & Jón Karl Helgason (eds.) (2016). *National Poets, Cultural Saints* (Leiden: Brill).
Dowe, Dieter (ed.) (2000). *Europe in 1848* (London: Berghahn).
Droixhe, Daniel (1978). *La linguistique et l'appel de l'histoire (1600–1800)* (Genève: Droz).
Du Barail, François-Charles (1898). *Mes souvenirs* vol. 3 (1864–1879) (11th ed.; Paris; Plon). Online at gallica.bnf.fr/ark:/12148/bpt6k209912r/f1.item
Ducmane, Kristīne (2016). *Rihards Zariņš* (Riga: Neptuns).
Düding, D. (1984). *Organisierter gesellschaftlicher Nationalismus in Deutschland (1808–1847)* (Munich: Beck).
Düding, D., P. Friedemann & P. Münch (eds.) (1998). *Öffentliche Festkultur* (Reinbek: Rowohlt).
Düsseldorfer Malerschule (Die) (1979). (Künstmuseum Düsseldorf & Mainz: Philipp von Zabern).
Duffy, Joanne L. (2006). *The Politics of Ethnic Nationalism: Afrikaner Unity, the National Party, and the Radical Right in Stellenbosch, 1934–1948* (London: Routledge).
Dumont, Hervé (2009). *L'antiquité au cinéma* (Paris: Nouveau Monde).
Dunk, H. W. von der (1966). *Der deutsche Vormärz und Belgien, 1830–1848* (Wiesbaden: Steiner).
Dunlop, Ian (1972). 'The Salon des Refusés (1863)', in id., *The Shock of the New* (New York: American Heritage Press).
Dunn, J. S. (2013). *The Crowe Memorandum* (Newcastle: Cambridge Scholars).
Dupke, Thomas (1994). *Mythos Löns* (Wiesbaden: Deutscher Universitätsverlag).
Durkheim, Emile (1912). *Les Formes élémentaires de la vie religieuse* (Paris: Presses universiteires de France).
Durkheim, Emile (1915). *'L'Allemagne au-dessus de tout': La mentalité allemande et la guerre* (Paris: Armand Colin). Online at wikisource, w.wiki/CdRY
Durkheim, Emile (1992). *Professional Ethics and Civic Morality* (trl. Cornleia Brookfield; 2nd ed.; London: Routledge).
Durkheim, Emile & Ernest Denis (1915). *Qui a voulu la guerre?* (Paris: Armand Colin). Online at wikisource, w.wiki/CdRa
Dusza, Erin M. (2012). Epic Significance: Placing Alphonse Mucha's Czech Art in the Context of Pan-Slavism and Czech Nationalism (doctoral thesis; Atlanta: Georgia State University).
Dyserinck, Hugo (1988). 'Komparatistische Imagologie', in *Europa und das nationale Selbstverständnis*, ed. H. Dyserinck and K. U. Syndram (Bonn: Bouvier), 13–38.
Dyserinck, Hugo (2015). *Ausgewählte Schriften zur Vergleichenden Literaturwissenschaft*, ed. Elke Mehnert (Berlin: Frank & Timme).
Dziewanowski-Stefańczyk, Bartosz (2022). 'World Fairs as Tools of Diplomacy: Interwar Poland', in Leerssen & Storm 2022, 300–328.

Eby, Cecil D. (1987). *The Road to Armageddon* (Durham, NC: Duke University Press).

Edensor, Tim (2020). *National Identity, Popular Culture and Everyday Life* (London: Routledge).

Egger, Simone (2008). *Phänomen Wiesntracht* (Munich: Utz).

Ehrismann, Otifrid (1975). *Das Nibelungenlied in Deutschland* (Munich: Fink).

Eidintas, Alfonsas (2015). *Antanas Smetona and his Lithuania* (Leiden: Brill).

Eile, Stanislaw (2000). *Literature and Nationalism in Partitioned Poland, 1795–1918* (Basingstoke: Palgrave Macmillan).

Einarsson, Sveinn (2006). *A People's Theatre Comes of Age* (Reykjavík: University of Reykjavík Press).

Eiranen, Reetta (2019). 'Emotional and Social Ties in the Construction of Nationalism', *Studies on National Movements*, 4: 1–38.

Elben, Otto (1887). *Der volksthümliche deutsche Männergesang* (Tübingen: Laupp).

Ellis, Katharine (2010). 'Paris, 1866: In Search of French Music', *Music and Letters* 91: 536–554.

Ellis, Katharine (2012). 'Mireille's Homecoming?', *Journal of the American Musicological Society* 65: 463–509.

Ellis, Peter Berresford (1993). *The Celtic Dawn* (London: Constable).

Ellis-Petersen, Hannah (2023). 'India Invokes Emergency Laws to Ban BBC Modi Documentary. Government Accused of "Censorship" over Ban on Film about PM's Role in Violence during 2002 Gujarat Riots', *The Guardian*, 23 January.

Elorza, Antonio (1995). *Los integrismos* (Madrid: Historia).

Engehausen, Frank (2023). *Werkstatt der Demokratie* (Frankfurt: Campus).

Engehausen, Frank & Armin Kohnle (eds.) (1998). *Gelehrte in der Revolution* (Ubstadt-Weiher: Regionalkultur).

Erll, Astrid & Ann Rigney (eds.) (2009). *Mediation, Remediation, and the Dynamics of Cultural Memory* (Berlin: De Gruyter).

ERNiE (2022). *Encyclopedia of Romantic Nationalism in Europe*, ed. J Leerssen (2nd ed., 2 vols.; Amsterdam: Amsterdam University Press). Online at e-rn.ie

Espagne, Geneviève & Udo Schöning (eds.) (2014). *Claude Fauriel et l'Allemagne: Idées pour une philologie des cultures* (Paris: Champion).

Espagne, Michel & Michael Werner (eds.) (1990). *Philologiques I* (Paris: Maison des sciences de l'homme).

Espagne, Michel & Michael Werner (eds.) (1994). *Philologiques III* (Paris: Maison des sciences de l'homme).

Espagne, Michel & Katia Dmitrieva (eds.) (1996). *Philologiques IV* (Paris: Maison des sciences de l'homme).

Estermann, Alfed (ed.) (1972). *Politische Avantgarde 1830–1840* (2 vols.; Frankfurt: Athenäum).

Feige, Stefan (2012). 'Die Marke Schweiz: Schweizer Stereotypen als Element einer Marketing- und Verkaufsstrategie', in *Wir und die Anderen*, ed. Baltz Engler (Fribourg: Fribourg Academic Press), 245–260.

Fernandez, Nichole (2022). 'Nation Branding', State of Nationalism, stateofnationalism.eu/article/nation-branding/

Feldman, Burton & Robert D. Richardson (eds.) (1972). *The Rise of Modern Mythology, 1680–1860* (Bloomington: Indiana University Press).

Fetscher, Iring (1988). *Joseph Goebbels im Berliner Sportpalast 1943* (Hamburg: Europäische Verlagsanstalt).

Feuer, Kathryn B. (2008). *Tolstoy and the Genesis of War and Peace* (Ithaca, NY: Cornell University Press).

Fewster, Derek (2006). *Visions of Past Glory* (2nd ed.; Tampere: Tammer-Paino).

Fichte, Johann Gottlieb (1808). *Reden an die deutsche Nation*. Online at zeno.org/Philosophie/M/Fichte,+Johann+Gottlieb/Reden+an+die+deutsche+Nation

Field, Geoffrey G. (1981). *Evangelist of Race: The Germanic Vision of Houston Stewart Chamberlain* (New York: Columbia University Press).

Figes, Orlando (2002). *Natasha's Dance: A Cultural History of Russia* (London: Macmillan).

Figgis, Peter (1985). 'Remembering Art O'Murnaghan', *Irish Arts Review* 2.4: 41–44.

Figueiredo, Ivo de (2019). *Henrik Ibsen* (trl. Robert Ferguson; New Haven, CT: Yale University Press).

Fikfak, Jurij & Reinhard Johler (eds.) (2008). *Ethnographie in Serie* (Vienna: Institut für Europäische Ethnologie der Universität Wien).

Filipová, Marta (2011). 'Peasants on Display: The Czechoslavic Ethnographic Exhibition of 1895', *Journal of Design History*, 24.1: 15–36.

Filipová, Marta (2019). *Modernity, History and Politics in Czech Art* (New York: Routledge).

Filipová, Marta (2025). *Czechoslovakia at the World's Fairs* (Budapest: CEU Press).

Fink, Gonthier-Louis (1993). 'Réflexions sur l'imagologie', *Recherches germaniques* 23: 3–31.

Fink, Gonthier-Louis (2003). 'Prolégomènes à une histoire des stéréotypes nationaux franco-allemands', *Francia* 30.2: 141–157.

Firchow, Peter Edgerly (1986). *The Death of the German Cousin* (Lewisburg, PA: Bucknell University Press).

Fischer, Bernd Jürgen (ed.) (2007). *Balkan Strongmen* (West Lafayette: Purdue University Press).

Fitzpatrick, M. P. (2008). *Liberal Imperialism in Germany* (New York: Berghahn).

Flacke, Monika (ed.) (1998). *Mythen der Nationen* (2nd ed.; Munich: Koehler & Amelang).

Flasch, Kurt (2000). *Die geistige Mobilmachung* (Berlin: Fest).

Flere, Sergej (2018). 'Slovenes: "A Nation of Owners of One of the Three Original European Languages"?', *Nationalities Papers* 46.3: 441–459.

Florack, Ruth (ed.) (2000a). *Nation als Stereotyp* (Tübingen: Narr).

Florack, Ruth (ed.) (2000b). *Tiefsinnige Deutsche, Frivole Franzosen* (Stuttgart: Metzler).

Florea, Vasile (2010). *Theodor Aman* (Bucharest: Monitorul oficial).

Forster, Michael N. (2010). *After Herder* (Oxford: Oxford University Press).

Fortier, Paul (1967). 'Gobineau and German Racism', *Comparative Literature* 19.4: 341–350.

Foster, R. F. (1997–2003). *W.B. Yeats* (2 vols.; Oxford: Oxford University Press).

Foster, R. F. (2014). *Vivid Faces: The Revolutionary Generation in Ireland, 1890–1923* (New York: Norton).

François, Etienne (1995). *Nation und Emotion* (Göttingen: Vandenhoeck & Ruprecht).

Frantz, Erica, Barbara Geddes & Joseph Wrights (2018). *How Dictatorships Work* (Cambridge: Cambridge University Press).

Frantzen, Allen J. & John D. Niles (eds.) (1997). *Anglo-Saxonism and the Construction of Social Identity* (Gainesville: University Press of Florida).

Fraser, Maxwell (1966). 'Sir Benjamin and Lady Hall in the 1840s, 1: 1840–1845', *National Library of Wales Journal*, 14: 35–42.

Fraser, Maxwell (1968). 'Lady Llanover and Her Circle', *Transactions of the Honourable Society of Cymmrodorion*, 170–196.

Frech, Kurt (1996). 'Felix Dahn', in Puschner, Schmitz & Ulbricht 1996, 685–698.

Freeden, Michael (1998). 'Is Nationalism a Distinct Ideology?', *Political Studies* 46: 748–765.

Friedler, Eric (1998). *Makkabi Chai, Makkabi lebt* (Vienna: Brandstätter).

Friemel, Berthold (1995). 'Unpreußische Ansichten: Dokumente und Tatsachen zum politischen Engagement der Brüder Grimm 1813–1815', *Brüder Grimm Gedenken* 11, 250–275.

Frist, Thomas (1876). *The Secret Societies of the European Revolution* (2 vols.; London: Tinsley).

Fritzsche, Peter (2004). *Stranded in the Present: Modern Time and the Melancholy of History* (Cambridge, MA: Harvard University Press).

Fröhlich, Michael (1994). *Deutsche Kolonial- und Weltpolitik 1880–1914* (Munich: DTV).

Frolova-Walker, Marina (2007). *Russian Music and Nationalism* (New Haven: Yale University Press).

Fryščák, Milan (1982). 'Kopitar and Dobrovský', *Papers in Slavic Philology* 2: 41–54.

Fürbeth, Frank et al. (eds.) (1999). *Zur Geschichte und Problematik der Nationalphilologien in Europa* (Tübingen: Niemeyer).

Fulsås, Narve & Tore Rem (eds.) (2021). *Ibsen in Context* (Cambridge: Cambridge University Press).

Furtado, Peter (ed.) (2012). *Histories of Nations: How Identities Were Forged* (London: Thames & Hudson).

Fustel de Coulanges, Numa (1870). *L'Alsace est-elle allemande ou française? Réponse à M. Mommsen* (Paris: Dentu). Online at e-rn.ie/fustel

Gardell, Mattias (2003). 'Hail Loki! Hail Satan! Hail Hitler! Darkside Asatrú, Satanism and Occult National Socialism', in id., *Gods of the Blood: The Pagan Revival and White Separatism* (Durham, SC: Duke University Press), 284–324.

Garlicki, Andrzej (1995). *Józef Piłsudski* (Aldershot: Ashgate).

Gaskill, Howard (ed.) (1996). *The Poems of Ossian and Related Works* (Edinburgh: Edinburg University Press).

Gaskill, Howard (ed.) (2004). *The Reception of Ossian in Europe* (London: Thoemmes).

Gaskill, Howard & Fiona Stafford (eds.) (1998). *From Gaelic to Romantic: Ossianic Translations* (Amsterdam: Rodopi).

Gaskill, Howard & Gerald Bär (eds.) (2012). *Ossian and National Epic* (Frankfurt: Lang).

Gautier, Léon (ed.) (1872). *La chanson de Roland* (Tours: Mame). Online at wikisource, w.wiki/CdRc

Geary, Patrick J. (2002). *The Myth of Nations* (Princeton, NJ: Princeton University Press).

Geddes, Barbara. (1999). 'What Do We Know about Democratization after Twenty Years?' *Annual Review of Political Science* 2:115–144.

Gellner, Ernest & Anthony D. Smith (1996). 'The Warwick Debates', *Nations and Nationalism* 2.3: 357–481.

Genette, Gérard (1969). 'Vraisemblance et motivation', in id., *Figures II* (Paris: Seuil), 71–100.

Gentry, Francis et al. (2011). *The Nibelungen Tradition* (new ed.; Abingdon: Routledge).

Georgeon, François (1980). *Aux origines du nationalisme Turc: Yusuf Akçura (1876–1935)* (Paris: ADPF).

Georgeon, François (1995). *Des Ottomans aux Turcs* (Istanbul: Isis).

Gephart, Werner (1996). 'Die französische Soziologie und der Erste Weltkrieg', in Mommsen 1996, 49–64.

Gerstner, Hermann (1952). *Die Brüder Grimm: Ihr Leben und Werk in Selbstzeugnissen, Briefen und Aufzeichnungen* (Ebenhausen bei München: Wilhelm Langewiesche-Brandt).

Gerven, Tim van (2022). *Scandinavism* (Leiden: Brill).

Gerwarth, Robert (2016). *The Vanquished: Why the First World War Failed to End* (London: Penguin).

Ghervas, Stella (2014). 'Antidotes to Empire: From the Congress System to the European Union', in *EUtROPEs: The Paradox of European Empire*, ed. John W. Boyer & Berthold Molden (Chicago: University of Chicago Press), 49–81.

Ghervas, Stella (2019). 'From the Balance of Power to a Balance of Diplomacy?', in *Securing Europe after Napoleon*, ed. B. de Graaf, I. de Haan & B. Vick (Cambridge: Cambridge University Press), 95–113.

Gibbs, Christopher Howard (2006). '"Just Two Words. Enormous success": Liszt's 1838 Vienna Concerts', in *Liszt and His World*, ed. Chr. H. Gibbs & D. Gooley (Princeton, NJ: Princeton University Press), 167–230.

Giles, Judy & Tim Middleton (eds.) (1995). *Writing Englishness 1900–1950* (London: Routledge).

Gillies, Alexander (1933). *Herder und Ossian* (Berlin: Juncker & Dünnhaupt).

Gilst, Aat van (2009). *Karel de Grote* (Soesterberg: Aspekt).

Gimeno-Martínez, Javier (2016). *Design and National Identity* (London: Bloomsbury).

Ginebra, Jordi (1988). *Antoni de Bofarull i la Renaixença* (Reus: Associació d'Estudis Reusencs).

Ginebra, Jordi (1989). 'Renaixença catalana i llengua occitana', in *Actes del Vuitè Colloqui Internacional de Llengua i Literatura Catalanes*, ed. A. M. Badia I. Margarit & M. Camprubí (Barcelona: Abadia de Montserrat), 1: 141–158.

Gipper, Helmut (1972). *Gibt es ein sprachliches Relativitätsprinzip?* (Frankfurt: Fischer).

Girardet, Raoul (1958). 'Pour une introduction à l'histoire du nationalisme français', *Revue française de science politique*, 8.3: 505–528.

Glenthøj, Rasmus & Morten Nordhagen Ottosen (2021). *Union eller undergang: Kampen for et forenet Skandinavien* (Copenhagen: Gads).

Glünder, René (2008). *Germanisches (Neu-)Heidentum in Deutschland* (Berlin: Logos).

Görres, Joseph (1955). *Geistesgeschichtliche und literarische Schriften II (1808–1817)* (Gesammelte Schriften, 4; ed. Leo Just; Paderborn: Schöningh).

Goethe, Johann Wolfgang (1815). *Shakespeare und kein Ende*. Online at zeno .org/Literatur/M/Goethe,+Johann+Wolfgang/Theoretische+Schriften/Shake speare+und+kein+Ende!/2.+Shakespeare,+verglichen+mit+den+Alten+und+ Neusten

Goldsworthy, Vesna (1998). *Inventing Ruritania* (London: Hurst).

Goltz, Anna von der (2009). *Hindenburg* (Oxford: Oxford University Press).

Goodrick-Clarke, Nicholas (2003). *Black Sun: Aryan Cults, Esoteric Nazism, and the Politics of Identity* (New York: NYU Press).

Goodrick-Clarke, Nicholas (2019). *The Occult Roots of Nazism* (new ed.; London: Tauris).

Goodwin, James (1993). *Eisenstein, Cinema, and History* (Urbana, IL: University of Illinois Press).

Goss, Glenda Dawn (2009). *Sibelius* (Chicago: University of Chicago Press).

Gossett, Philip (1990). 'Becoming a Citizen: The Chorus in "Risorgimento" Opera', *Cambridge Opera Journal*, 2.1: 41–64.

Gossett, Philip (2012). 'Giuseppe Verdi and the Italian Risorgimento', *Proceedings of the American Philosophical Society* 156.3: 271–282.

Gossler, Arcan (2001). *Publizistik und konservative Revolution* (Münster: Lit).

Gossman, Lionel (2003). 'Unwilling Moderns: The Nazarene Painters of the Nineteenth Century', *Nineteenth-Century Art Worldwide* 2.2 (Autumn), 19thc-artworldwide.org/autumn03/273-unwilling-moderns-the-nazarene-painters-of-the-nineteenth-century

Gräf, Holger & Andres Tacke (eds.) (2004). *Preussen in Marburg* (Darmstadt: Hessische Historische Kommission).

Grafton, Anthony (2019). *Forgers and Critics* (new ed.; Princeton, NJ: Princeton University Press).

Graham, B. D. (1990). *Hindu Nationalism and Indian Politics* (Cambridge: Cambridge University Press).

Grandhomme, Charles (2021). *Littérature et société au XIXe siècle: Erckmann-Chatrian devant l'histoire* (Metz: CRULH).

Grant, Kevin (2001). 'British Suffragettes and the Russian Method of Hunger Strike', *Comparative Studies in Society and History* 53.1: 113–143.

Greenhalgh, Paul (2010). *Fair World: A History of the World's Fairs and Expositions from London to Shanghai, 1851–2010* (Winterbourne: Papadakis).

Griffin, Roger (1991). *The Nature of Fascism* (London: Pinter).

Griffin, Roger (2000). 'Between Metapolitics and Apoliteia: The Nouvelle Droite's Strategy for Conserving the Fascist Vision in the "Interregnum"', *Modern and Contemporary France* 8: 35–53.

Grigoriadis, Ioannis N. & Arzu Opçin-Kıdal (2020). 'Imagining Turan', *Middle Eastern Studies* 56.3: 482–495.

Grimm, Jacob (1814). 'Die Elsässer', *Rheinischer Merkur* 98 (6 August 1814). Online at e-rn.ie/alsacegrimm

Grimm, Jacob (1848). *Geschichte der deutschen Sprache* (new ed.; Leipzig: Hirzel).

Grimm, Jacob (1864–90). *Kleinere Schriften* (8 vols.; Berlin/Gütersloh: Dümmler/Bertelsmann).

Grimm, Wilhelm (1985). *Nibelungenkolleg* (1831; ed. Else Ebel; Marburg: Elwert).

Gruber, Edith (2014). King Arthur and the Privy Councillor: Albert Schulz as a Cultural Mediator (doctoral thesis; Bangor: Bangor University).

Gruel-Apert, Lise (1998). *La tradition orale russe* (Paris: Presses Universitaires de France).

Gruel-Apert, Lise & Tatiana Grigorevna Ivanovna (2011). *Du côté des frères Grimm et d'Alexandre Afanassiev* (Paris: Bibliothèque nationale de France).

Grijzenhout, Frans (1996). 'La patrie réinventée: L'art hollandais dans la période française', in *Remous révolutionnaires*, ed. Annie Jourdan (Amsterdam: Amsterdam University Press), 138–158.

Gumplowitz, Philippe (1987). *Les travaux d'Orphée: 150 ans de vie musicale amateur en France* (Paris: Aubier).

Gunnell, Terry (ed.) (2022). *Grimm Ripples: The Legacy of the Grimms' 'Deutsche Sagen' in Northern Europe* (Leiden: Brill).

Gurden-Williams, Celyn (2008). Lady Llanover and the Creation of a Welsh Cultural Utopia (doctoral thesis; Cardiff: Cardiff University).

Habermas, Jürgen (1999). 'Was ist ein Volk? Bemerkungen zum politischen Selbstverständnis der Geisteswissenschaften im Vormärz', in *Zur Geschichte und Problematik der Nationalphilologien in Europa*, ed. Frank Fürbeth (Tübingen: Niemeyer), 23–39.

Hafner, Stanislaus (1957). 'August Heinrich Hoffmann von Fallersleben und Bartholomäus Kopitar', *Die Welt der Slaven* 2: 183–200.

Hagen, Friedrich Heinrich von der (ed.) (1807). *Der Nibelungen Lied* (Berlin). Online at e-rn.ie/nibelungenhagen

Hall, John A., Ove Korsgaard & Ove K. Pedersen (eds.) (2015). *Building the Nation* (Montreal: McGill-Queen's University Press).

Hamburger, Klára (1987). *Liszt* (Budapest: Corvina).

Hamilton, Kenneth (2005). 'Liszt's Early and Weimar Piano Works', in *The Cambridge Companion to Liszt*, ed. K. Hamilton (Cambridge: Cambridge University Press).

Hamm, Charles (1983). *Music in the New World* (New York: Norton).

Hanioğlu, M. Şükrü (2001). *Preparation for a Revolution: The Young Turks, 1902–1908* (Oxford: Oxford University Press).

Hanna, Martha (1996). *The Mobilization of Intellect: French Scholars and Writers During the Great War* (Cambridge, MA: Harvard University Press).

Hansen, Wilhelm (1976). *Nationaldenkmäler und Nationalfeste im 19. Jahrhundert* (Lüneburg: Niederdeutscher Verband für Volks- und Altertumskunde).

Harding, James (1979). *Artistes Pompiers* (New York: Rizzoli).

Hardtwig, Wolfgang (1999). 'Historismus als ästhetische Geschichtsschreibung: Leopold von Ranke', *Geschichte und Gesellschaft* 23.1: 99–114.

Harmetz, Aljean (2002). *The Making of 'Casablanca'* (New York: Hyperion).

Harpham, Geoffrey Galt (2009). 'Roots, Races, and the Return to Philology', *Representations* 106.1: 34–62.

Harris, M. (1976). 'History and Significance of the Emic–Etic Distinction', *Annual Review of Anthropology* 5, 329–350.

Harris, Robert (1983). *GOTCHA! The Media, the Government and the Falklands Crisis* (London: Faber and Faber).

Hartog, François (1988). *Le XIXe siècle et l'histoire: Le cas de Fustel de Coulanges* (Paris: Presses universitaires de France).

Harvilahti, Lauri (ed.) (2018). *Visions and Traditions* (Porvoo: Folklore Fellowship Communications).

Haskell, Francis (1993). *History and Its Images* (New Haven, CT: Yale University Press).

Hasselblatt, Cornelius (2016). *Kalevipoeg Studies* (Vantaa: Hansaprint).

Haupt, Heinz-Gerhard & Charlotte Tacke (1996). 'Die Kultur des Nationalen', *Geschichte und Gesellschaft* 16 (special issue on 'Kulturgeschichte heute'), 255–283.

Hautala, Jouko (1969). *Finnish Folklore Research, 1828–1919* (Helsinki: Societas Scientiarum Fennica).

Hearn, Jonathan (2006). *Rethinking Nationalism* (Basingstoke: Palgrave).

Hegel, G. W. F. (1857). *Lectures on the Philosophy of History* (trl. John Sibree). Online at marxists.org/reference/archive/hegel/hisindex.htm

Heilfurth, G., L. Denecke & I.-M. Greverus (eds.) (1963). *Brüder Grimm Gedenken 1963* (Marburg: Elwert).

Heitmeyer, Wilhelm (2018). *Autoritäre Versuchungen* (Frankfurt: Suhrkamp).

Heller, Daniel Kupfert (2017). *Jabotinsky's Children* (Princeton, NJ: Princeton University Press).

Helmers, Ruther (2014). *Not Russian Enough? Nationalism and Cosmopolitanism in Nineteenth-Century Russian Opera* (Rochester, NY: University of Rochester Press).

Hemans, Felicia (1834). *National Lyrics, and Songs for Music* (Dublin: Curry). Online at wikisource, w.wiki/9NfJ

Hemstad, Ruth & Peter Stadius (eds.) (2023). *Nordic Experiences in Pan-Nationalisms* (London: Routledge).

Henkes, Barbara (2005). *Uit liefde voor het volk. Volkskundigen op zoek naar de Nederlandse identiteit 1918–1948* (Amsterdam: Atheneum).

Henrikson, Paula (2002). 'Kampen om litteraturhistorien: Romantikerna som filologer', in *Text och tradition: Om textedering och kanonbildning*, ed. Lars Burman & Barbro Ståhle Sjönell (Stockholm: Svenska Vitterhetssamfundet), 42–58.

Hermet, Guy (1985). 'L'Autoritarisme', in *Traité de science politique*, ed. Madeleine Grawitz & Jean Leca (Paris: Presses universitaires de France), 2: 269–312.

Herrick, Jane (1954). *The Historical Thought of Fustel de Coulanges* (Washington, DC: Catholic University of America Press).

Heß, Gilbert, Elena Agazzi & Elisabeth Décultot (eds.) (2009). *Graecomania: Der europäische Philhellenismus* (Berlin: De Gruyter).

Hess, Günter (2011). *Panorama und Denkmal* (Würzburg: Köningshausen & Neumann).

Hettling, Manfred & Paul Nolte (1993). *Bürgerliche Feste* (Göttingen: Vandenhoeck & Ruprecht).

Hewitson, Mark (2000). *National Identity and Political Thought in Germany* (Oxford: Oxford University Press).

Hewitson, Mark (2014). 'On War and Peace: German Conceptions of Conflict, 1792–1815', *Historical Journal* 57.2: 447–483.

Heyd, Uriel (1950). *Foundations of Turkish Nationalism* (London: Luzac).

Hindenburg, Paul von (1920). *Aus meinem Leben.* Online at archive.org/details/ausmeinemlebenoohind

Hitler, Adolf. (1939). *Mein Kampf* (trl. not named; Boston: Houghton Mifflin).

Hjelmslev, Louis (1966). 'Commentaires sur la vie et l'oeuvre de Rasmus Rask', in *Portraits of Linguists*, ed. T. A. Sebeok (Bloomington, IN: Indiana University Press), 179–199.

Hlavačka, Milan, Jana Orliková & Petr Štembera (2002). *Alfons Mucha – Paříž 1900: Pavilon Bosny a Hercegoviny na světové výstavě* (Prague: Obecní dům).

Hobsbawm, Eric (1981). *Bandits* (new ed.; New York: Pantheon).

Hobsbawm, Eric & Terence Ranger (eds.) (1983). *The Invention of Tradition* (Cambridge: Cambridge University Press).

Höcker, Wilma (1951). *Der Gesandte Bunsen als Vermittler zwischen Deutschland und England* (Göttingen: Musterschmidt).

Hoegen, Jesko v. (2007). *Der Held von Tannenberg* (Cologne: Böhlau).

Höfig, Willi (1973). *Der deutsche Heimatfilm, 1947–1960* (Stuttgart: Enke).

Höflein, Ulrike (1988). *Vom Umgang mit ländlicher Tracht* (Frankfurt: Lang).

Höhne, Steffen (2013). 'Libussa: Konstruktion und Transformation eines böhmischen Staatsgründungsmythos im 19. Jahrhundert', in *Weibliche Mythen in Musik, Literatur und bildender Kunst*, ed. Helen Geyer & Maria Stolarzewic (Vienna/Jena: Institut für Musikwissenschaft), 126–136.

Höppel, Thomas (2001). *Deutschlandbilder – Frankreichbilder 1700–1850* (Leipzig: Leipziger Universitätsverlag).

Hoeres, Peter (2004). *Krieg der Philosophen* (Paderborn: Schöningh).

Hoffmann von Fallersleben, August Heinrich (1838). 'Einleitung', in id., *Altniederländische Schaubühne* (Breslau: Aderholz). Online at e-rn.ie/hvf-flemishbelgium

Holroyd, Michael (1989–93). *Bernard Shaw* (4 vols.; London: Chatto and Windus).

Horne, John & Alan Kramer (2001). *German Atrocities, 1914: A History of Denial* (New Haven, CT: Yale University Press).

Horsman, Reginald (1981). *Race and Manifest Destiny* (Cambridge, MA: Harvard University Press).

Houze, Rebecca (2015). *Textiles, Fashion, and Design Reform in Austria–Hungary before the First World War* (Farnham: Ashgate).

Howsam, Leslie (1991). *Cheap Bibles* (Cambridge: Cambridge University Press).

Hroch, Miroslav (1968). *Die Vorkämpfer der nationalen Bewegung bei den kleinen Völkern Europas* (Praha: Universita Karlova).

Hroch, Miroslav (1995). 'Das Bürgertum in den nationalen Bewegungen des 19. Jahrhunderts', in *Bürgertum im 19 Jahrhundert*, ed. Jürgen Kocka (Göttingen: Vandenhoeck & Ruprecht), 3 (*Verbürgerlichung, Recht und Politik*), 197–219.

Hroch, Miroslav (1996). 'Nationalism and National Movements', *Nations and Nationalism* 2.1: 35–44.

Hroch, Miroslav (2009). 'Learning from Small Nations', *New Left Review* 58: 41–59.

Hroch, Miroslav (2015). *European Nations: Explaining their Formation* (London: Verso).

Hütt, Wolfgang (1995). *Die Düsseldorfer Malerschule, 1819–1869* (Leipzig: Seemann).

Huig, Michael (2005). Tot eer van Bohemen (doctoral thesis; Amsterdam: University of Amsterdam).

Huizinga, Johan (1929). 'Over een definitie van het begrip geschiedenis', in id., *Cultuurhistorische verkenningen* (Haarlem: Tjeenk Willink), 156–168.

Humbeeck, Kris, Kevin Absillis & Janneke Weiermars (eds.) (2016). *De grote onleesbare: Hendrik Conscience herdacht* (Gent: Academia).

Humboldt, Wilhelm von (1907). 'Über die Verschiedenheit des menschlichen Sprachbaues', *Gesammelte Schriften*, ed. A. Leitzmann (Berlin: Behr), VI.1: 111–303.

Humboldt, Wilhelm von (1973). *Schriften zur Sprache* (ed. M. Böhler; Stuttgart: Reclam).

Hummel, Pascale (2003). *Philologus auctor: Le philologue et son oeuvre* (Bern: Lang).

Huntford, Roland (1997). *Nansen* (London: Duckworth).

Hutchinson, John (1987). *The Dynamics of Cultural Nationalism: The Gaelic Revival and the Creation of the Irish Nation State* (London: Allen & Unwin).

Hutchinson, John (2013). 'Cultural Nationalism', in *The Oxford Handbook of the History of Nationalism*, ed. John Breuilly (Oxford: Oxford University Press), 75–94.

Hutchinson, John (2017). *Nationalism and War* (Oxford: Oxford University Press).

Hutton, Christopher M. (1988). *Linguistics and the Third Reich* (London: Routledge).

Hyde, Douglas (1892). *The Necessity for de-Anglicising Ireland.* Online at e-rn.ie/HydeNecessity

Ibrovac, Miodrag (1966). *Claude Fauriel et la fortune européenne des poésies populaires Grecque et Serbe* (Paris: Didier).
Illig, Stefan (1998). *Zwischen Körperertüchtigung und nationaler Bewegung* (Cologne: SH).
Ivarsflaten, Elisabeth (2008). 'What Unites Right-Wing Populists in Western Europe?', *Comparative Political Studies* 41.1: 3–23.
Jackson, Alvin (2023). *United Kingdoms* (Oxford: Oxford University Press).
Jackson, David & Patty Wageman (eds.) (2006). *Akseli Gallen-Kallela* (Rotterdam: NAi Publishers).
Jäger, Friedrich & Jörn Rüsen (1992). *Geschichte des Historismus* (Munich: Beck).
Jäger, Wolfgang (1984). *Historische Forschung und politische Kultur in Deutschland* (Göttingen: Vandenhoeck & Ruprecht).
James, David (1954). *The Life of Lord Roberts* (London: Hollis & Carter).
Jaworski, Rudolf (1998). 'Völkerfrühling 1848', in *Demokratiebewegung und Revolution 1847 bis 1849*, ed. D. Langewiesche (Heidelberg: Springer).
Jeismann, Michael (1992). *Das Vaterland der Feinde* (Stuttgart: Klett-Cotta).
Jenderko-Sichelschmidt, Ingrid (1979). 'Die profane Historienmalerei, 1826–1860', in *Die Düsseldorfer Malerschule* (Künstmuseum Düsseldorf & Mainz: Philipp von Zabern).
Joerg, W. L. G. (1936). 'Memoir of Leon Dominian', *Annals of the Association of American Geographers* 26.4: 197–198.
Juaristi, Jon (1987). *El linaje de Aitor: La invención de la tradición vasca* (Madrid: Taurus).
Junginger, Horst (1999). *Von der philologischen zur völkischen Religionswissenschaft* (Stuttgart: Steiner).
Jurt, Joseph (2013). 'Langue et nation: Le débat franco-allemand entre Renan, Fustel de Coulanges et David Friedrich Strauss et Mommsen en 1870 et 1871'. Online at etudes-romantiques.ish-lyon.cnrs.fr/wa_files/Langues-Jurt.pdf.
Juvan, Marko (2015). 'In the Background of the "Alphabet War"', *Interlitteraria* suppl. 1: 148–158.
Kaljundi, Linda, Eneken Laanes & Ilona Pikkanen (eds.) (2015). *Novels, Histories, Novel Nations: Historical Fiction and Cultural Memory in Finand and Estonia* (Helsinki: Finnish Literature Society – SKS).
Kalmar, Ivan (1987). 'The "Völkerpsychologie" of Lazarus and Steinthal and the Modern Concept of Culture', *Journal of the History of Ideas* 48: 671–690.
Kamusella, Tomasz & Motoki Nomachi (eds.) (2024). *Languages and Nationalism Instead of Empires* (London: Routledge).
Kaplan, Eran (2005). *The Jewish Radical Right* (Madison: University of Wisconsin Press).
Kater, Michael H. (2006). *Das 'Ahnenerbe' der SS 1935–1945* (4th ed.; Munich: Oldenbourg).
Kaul, Camilla G. (2007). *Friedrich Barbarossa im Kyffhäuser* (Cologne: Böhlau).
Kedourie, Elie (1960). *Nationalism* (New York: Praeger).
Keenan, Edward L. (2003). *Josef Dobrovský and the Origins of the Igor′ Tale* (Cambridge, MA: Harvard University Press).

Kellner, Beate (1994). *Grimms Mythen* (Frankfurt: Lang).
Ķencis, Toms (2012). A Disciplinary History of Latvian Mythology (doctoral thesis; Tartu: University of Tartu).
Kennedy, Paul M. (1980). *The Rise of the Anglo-German Antagonism, 1860–1914* (London: Allen & Unwin).
Kieft, Ewoud (2015). *Oorlogsenthousiasme* (Amsterdam: De Bezige Bij).
Kiene, Michael (2011). *Jakob Ignaz Hittorff, précurseur du Paris d'Haussmann* (Paris: Éditions du Patrimoine).
Kimbell, David (1981). *Verdi in the Age of Italian Romanticism* (Cambridge: Cambridge University Press).
King, Charles (2011). *Odessa* (New York: Norton).
Kirkness, Alan (1980). *Geschichte des Deutschen Wörterbuches, 1838–1963* (Stuttgart: Hirzel).
Klein, Adolf (1980). *Der Dom zu Köln* (Cologne: Wienand).
Klenke, Dietmar (1998). *Der singende 'deutsche Mann'* (Münster: Waxmann).
Kochs, Theodor (1967). 'Nationale Idee und nationalistisches Denken im Grimmschen Wörterbuch', in *Nationalismus in Germanistik und Dichtung*, ed. B. v. Wiese & R. Henß (Berlin: Schmidt), 273–284.
Koerner, E. F. Konrad (1992). 'The Sapir-Whorf Hypothesis', *Linguistic Anthropology* 2.2: 173–198.
Kösters, Klaus (2009). *Mythos Arminius* (Münster: Aschendorff).
Koetschau, Karl (1929). *Alfred Rethels Kunst vor dem Hintergrund der Historienmalerei seiner Zeit* (Düsseldorf: Kunstverein für die Rheinlande und Westfalen).
Kohn, Hans (1945). 'Treitschke: National Prophet', *Review of Politics* 7.4: 418–440.
Kohn, Hans (1950). 'Romanticism and the Rise of German Nationalism', *Review of Politics* 12: 443–470.
Kohn, Hans (1955). *Nationalism: Its Meaning and History* (Princeton, NJ: Nostrand).
Kohn, Hans (1960). *Pan-Slavism* (New York: Vintage).
Konrad, Maxilian (2016). 'The European War Enthusiasm of 1914', in *Bellicose Entanglements 1914*, ed. Maximilian Lakitsch, Susanne Reitmair-Juárez & Katja Seidel (Vienna: Lit), 15–42.
Konstantinou, Evangelos & Ursula Wiedenmann (eds.) (1989). *Europäischer Philhellenismus* (Neuried: Hieronymus).
Koolhaas-Grosfeld, Eveline (2010). *De ontdekking van de Nederlander in boeken en prenten rond 1800* (Zutphen: Walburg).
Kooten, Kasper van (2019). '*Was deutsch und echt…*': *Richard Wagner and the Articulation of a German Opera, 1798–1876* (Leiden: Brill).
Kořalka, Jiří (2007). *František Palacký, 1798–1876* (Vienna: Österreichische Akademie der Wissenschaften).
Koropeckyj, Roman (2008). *Adam Mickiewicz* (Ithaca, NY: Cornell University Press).
Koselleck, Reinhart (1986). 'Sozialgeschichte und Begriffsgeschichte', in *Die Sozialgeschichte innerhalb der Geschichtswissenschaft*, ed. W. Schieder (Göttingen: Vandenhoeck & Ruprecht), 89–109.

Koselleck, Reinhart (1988). *Vergangene Zukunft: Zur Semantik geschichtlicher Zeiten* (Frankfurt: Suhrkamp).

Koskenniemi, Martti (2001). *The Gentle Civilizer of Nations: The Rise and Fall of International Law, 1870–1960* (Cambridge: Cambridge University Press).

Kramer, Alan (2007). *Dynamic of Destruction: Culture and Mass Killing in the First World War* (Oxford: Oxford University Press).

Kramer, Lawrence (2002). 'Franz Liszt and the Virtuoso Public Sphere', in *Musical Meaning: Toward a Critical History* (Berkeley: University of California Press), 68–99.

Kranz, Isabel (2012). 'Medium und Genre: Panoramatische Literatur als historiographisches Material in Walter Benjamins Passagenarbeit', *Interférences littéraires* 8: 27–41.

Kregor, Jonathan (2015). *Program Music* (Cambridge: Cambridge University Press).

Kremmler, Katrin (2023). '"Eurasian Magyars"', in *Digging Politics: The Ancient Past and Contested Present in East-Central Europe*, ed. James Koranyi & Emily Hanscam (Berlin: De Gruyter Oldenbourg), 181–216.

Krügel, Rudolf (1914). *Der Begriff des Volksgeistes in Ernst Moritz Arndts Geschichtsanschauung* (Langensalza: Beyer).

Krumeich, Gerd (1989). *Jeanne d'Arc in der Geschichte* (Sigmaringen: Thorbecke).

Krumeich, Gerd (1996). 'Ernest Lavisse und die Kritik an der deutschen "Kultur"', in Mommsen 1996, 143–150.

Krumeich, Gerd (2001). 'Langemarck', in *Deutsche Erinnerungsorte*, ed E. François & H. Schulze (3 vols.; Munich: Beck), 3: 292–309.

Kuitenbrouwer, Vincent (2012). *War of Words: Dutch Pro-Boer Propaganda and the South African War (1899–1902)* (Amsterdam: Amsterdam University Press).

Kuijk, Leonoor (2018). Knitting the Nation: A Comparative Analysis of National Type Collections in Europe around 1840 (doctoral thesis; Gent).

Laan, Nico (1997). *Het belang van smaak* (Amsterdam: Historisch Seminarium).

LaCapra, Dominick (1972). *Emile Durkheim* (New York: Cornell University Press).

Lacouture, Jean (1984–86). *De Gaulle* (3 vols.; Paris: Seuil).

Lajosi, Krisztina (2018). *Staging the Nation* (Leiden: Brill).

Lajosi, Krisztina (2022). 'Fencing as a National Sport in Hungary', in ERNiE 2022: e-rn.ie/fencing-hun

Lajosi, Krisztina & Andreas Stynen (eds.) (2015). *Choral Societies and Nationalism in Europe* (Leiden: Brill).

Lambert, Peter (2014). 'Widukind or Karl der Große?', in *Mass Dictatorship and Memory as Ever Present Past*, ed. J.-H. Lim, B. Walker & P. Lambert (Palgrave Macmillan), 139–161.

Lambert, Pierre-Arnaud (1995). *La charbonnerie française, 1821–1823* (Lyon: Presses Universitaires de Lyon).

Landau, Jacob M. (1995). *Pan-Turkism* (Bloomington: Indiana University Press).

Lange, Fritz (ed.) (1954). *Neithart von Gneisenau* (Berlin: Rütten & Loening).

Landsberg, Alison (2015). *Engaging the Past: Mass Culture and the Production of Historical Knowledge* (New York: Columbia University Press).

Lange, Judith & Martin Schubert (2023). *Geschichte der altgermanistischen Edition* (Berlin: De Gruyter).

Langewiesche, Dieter (1992). 'Reich, Nation und Staat in der jüngeren deutschen Geschichte', *Historische Zeitschrift* 254: 341–381.

Langewiesche, Dieter (2000). *Nation, Nationalismus, Nationalstaat in Deutschland und Europa* (Munich: Beck).

Langewiesche, Dieter (2008). 'Zum Überleben des Alten Reiches im 19. Jahrhundert', in *Das Jahr 1806 im europäischen Kontext*, ed. A. Klinger, H. Hahn & G. Schmidt (Cologne: Böhlau), 123–134.

Laruelle, Marlène (2007). 'Religious Revival, Nationalism and the "Invention of Tradition"', *Central Asian Survey* 26.2: 203–216.

Latour, Bruno (2005). *Reassembling the Social: An Introduction to Actor-Network Theory* (Oxford: Oxford University Press).

Laugaste, Eduard (1990). 'The Kalevala and Kalevipoeg', in *Religion, Myth, and Folklore in the World's Epics*, ed. L. Honko (Berlin: De Gruyter), 265–285.

Lawrence, Paul (2005). *Nationalism: History and Theory* (London: Longman).

Leach, Daniel (2009). *Fugitive Ireland* (Dublin: Four Courts).

Lednicki, Wacław (1960). *Henryk Sienkiewicz* (The Hague: Mouton).

Leerssen, Joep (1992). 'Identity and Self-Image', in *Komparatistik und Europeaforschung*, ed. H. Dyserinck & K. U. Syndram (Bonn: Bouvier), 117–136.

Leerssen, Joep (1996). *Remembrance and Imagination* (Cork: Cork University Press).

Leerssen, Joep (2006a). 'Nationalism and the Cultivation of Culture', *Nations and Nationalism*, 12.4: 559–578.

Leerssen, Joep (2006b). 'Englishness, Ethnicity and Matthew Arnold', *European Journal of English Studies*, 10: 63–79.

Leerssen, Joep (2011a). *De bronnen van het vaderland* (2nd ed.; Nijmegen: Vantilt).

Leerssen, Joep (2011b). 'Viral Nationalism', *Nations and Nationalism* 17.2: 257–271.

Leerssen, Joep (2012a). 'The Rise of Philology', in *The Making of the Humanities 2: From Early Modern to Modern Disciplines*, ed. R. Bod, J. Maat and T. Weststeijn (Amsterdam: Amsterdam University Press), 23–35.

Leerssen, Joep (2012b). 'Oral Epic', in *Folklore and Nationalism during the Long Nineteenth Century*, ed. T. Baycroft and D. Hopkin (Leiden: Brill), 11–26.

Leerssen, Joep (2013). 'Notes towards a Definition of Romantic Nationalism', *Romantik: Journal for the Study of Romanticisms*, 2.1: 9–25.

Leerssen, Joep (2014). 'Romanticism, Music, Nationalism', *Nations and Nationalism*, 20.4: 606–627.

Leerssen, Joep (2015a). 'The Nation and the City', *Nations and Nationalism*, 21.1: 2–20.

Leerssen, Joep (2015b). 'Latinitas Goes Native', in *Bilingual Europe*, ed. J. Bloemendal (Leiden: Brill), 187–200.

Leerssen, Joep (2015c). 'Knotenpunkte', in *Literarische Transnationalität*, ed. K. Hoff, A. Sandberg & U. Schöning (Würzburg: Königshausen & Neumann), 127–145.

Leerssen, Joep (2016a). 'Cuchulain in the General Post Office', *Journal of the British Academy* 4: 137–168.

Leerssen, Joep (2016b). 'Gods, Heroes and Mythologists', *History of Humanities* 1: 71–100.

Leerssen, Joep (2016c). 'Imagology: On Using Ethnicity to Make Sense of the World', *Iberic@l* 20: 13–31.

Leerssen, Joep (2017a). 'The Never-Ending Stream: Cultural Mobilization over the Rhine', in Beller & Leerssen 2017, 224–261.

Leerssen, Joep (2017b). 'Once upon a Time in Germany', in *The Making of Medieval History*, ed. G. Loud & M. Staub (Woodbridge: Brewer), 101–126.

Leerssen, Joep (2018). *National Thought in Europe* (3rd ed.; Amsterdam: Amsterdam University Press).

Leerssen, Joep (2019a). *Comparative Literature in Britain, 1800–2000* (Oxford: MHRA/Legenda).

Leerssen, Joep (2019b). 'Mit wem arbeiteten die Grimms zusammen?', in *Über Nachtfliegen, Zaunkönige und Meisterdiebe*, ed. H. Ehrhardt et al. (Kassel: Kassel University Press), 277–299.

Leerssen, Joep (ed.) (2020). *Parnell and His Times* (Cambridge: Cambridge University Press).

Leerssen, Joep (2021a). 'Romancing the Monarchy', in *Cosmopolitan Conservatisms*, ed. M. Lok, F. Pestel & J. Reboul (Leiden: Brill), 283–304.

Leerssen, Joep (2021b). 'Cultural Mobility and Political Mobilization', in *The First World War and the Nationality Question in Europe*, ed. Xosé Manoel Núñez Seixas (Leiden: Brill), 17–36.

Leerssen, Joep (2021c). 'Intuiting Archetypes', in Bønding, Kølle Martinsen & Stahl 2021, 43–66.

Leerssen, Joep (2022a). 'Enmity, Identity, Discourse', in *New Perspectives on Imagology*, ed. Katharina Edtstadler, Sandra Folie & Gianna Zocco (Leiden: Brill), 49–69.

Leerssen, Joep (2022b). 'Trademarking the Nation', in Leerssen & Storm 2022, 31–55.

Leerssen, Joep (2023a). 'Beginning with Culture', in *The Cambridge History of the European Union*, ed. Mathieu Segers & Steven Van Hecke (Cambride: Cambridge University Press) 2: 561–590.

Leerssen, Joep (2023b). 'The Rise of the Charismatic Nation', in *The Cambridge History of Nationhood and Nationalism*, ed. Cathie Carmichael, Matthew D'Auria & Aviel Roshwald (Cambridge: Cambridge University Press) 2: 231–255.

Leerssen, Joep (2023c). 'Heart to Heart', *Interlitteraria* 28.1: 8–19.

Leerssen, Joep (2023d). 'Honour and Violence', in *European Modernity and the Passionate South*, ed. Xavier Andreu-Muralles & Mónica Bolufer-Peruga (Leiden: Brill), 92–107.

Leerssen, Joep (2023e). 'Quixotic? Not Quite', in Hemstad & Stadius 2023, 19–34.

Leerssen, Joep (2024). 'Language or Dialect?', in Kamusella & Nomachi 2024, 10–23.

Leerssen, Joep (2025). 'Ethnophilology', *History of Humanities*, 10.1: 15–38.

Leerssen, Joep & Ann Rigney (eds.) (2014). *Commemorating Writers in Nineteenth-Century Europe* (Basingstoke: Palgrave Macmillan).

Leerssen, Joep & Eric Storm (eds.) (2022). *World Fairs and the Global Moulding of National Identities* (Leiden: Brill).

Legány, Dezső (1983). *Ferenc Liszt and His Country, 1869–1873* (Budapest: Editio Musica).

Legány, Dezső (1992). *Ferenc Liszt and His Country, 1874–1886* (Budapest: Occidental Press).

Lehmann, Hartmut (2009). *Die Entzauberung der Welt* (Göttingen: Wallstein).

Lehming, Malte (2011). 'McCarthy in Deutschland', *Tagesspiegel* 11 January 2011, p. 4.

Lennon, Joseph (2007). 'Fasting for the Public', in *Enemies of Empire*, ed. Eóin Flannery & Angus Mitchell (Dublin: Four Courts), 19–51.

Lennon, Joseph (2008). *Irish Orientalism* (Syracuse, NY: Syracuse University Press).

Leppert, Richard (2002). 'Cultural Contradiction, Idolatry, and the Piano Virtuoso: Franz Liszt', in *Piano Roles*, ed. J. Parakilas & E. D. Bomberger (New Haven, CT: Yale University Press) 252–281.

Lepsius, M. Rainer (1986). 'Charismatic Leadership', in *Changing Conceptions of Leadership*, ed. C. F. Graumann and S. Moscovici (New York: Springer), 53–66.

Leslie, Robert Frank (1969). *Reform and Insurrection in Russian Poland, 1856–1865* (Westport, CT: Greenwood).

Lessing, Gotthold Ephraim (1766). *Laokoon oder Über die Grenzen der Malerei und Poesie*. Online at projekt-gutenberg.org/lessing/laokoon/laokoon.html

Lévi-Strauss, Claude (1963). *Structural Anthropology* (trl. C. Jacobson & B. Grundfest; New York: Basic).

Lincoln, Bruce (1999). *Theorizing Myth* (Chicago: University of Chicago Press).

Linden, Bob van der (2024). *Romantic Nationalism in India* (Leiden: Brill).

Liszt, Franz (1859). *Des Bohémiens et de leur musique en Hongrie* (Patis: Librairie Nouvelle Bourdilliat).

Löffler, Marion (2006). 'Pan-Celticism around 1900', in *Celtes et Gaulois dans l'histoire, l'historiographie et l'idéologie moderne*, ed. Sabine Rieckhoff (Glux-en-Glenne: Collection Bibracte), 143–151.

Loetscher, Michel & Yannick Scheibling (2006). *Hansi: Une vie pour l'Alsace* (Strasbourg: La nuée bleue).

Logge, Thorsten (2014). *Zur medialen Konstruktion des Nationalen: Die Schillerfeiern 1859 in Europa und Nordamerika* (Göttingen: V&R unipress).

Lohmann, Johannes & Hans Wanders (2002). 'Evolas Jünger und Odins Krieger', in *RechtsRock*, ed. C. Dornbusch & J. Raabe (Hamburg/Münster: Unrast), 287–311.

Lord, Alfred B. (1963). 'Nationalism and the Muses in the Balkan Slavic Literature in the Modern Period', in *The Balkans in Transition*, ed. Barbara & Charles Jelavich (Berkeley, CA: University of California Press), 258–296.

Lovejoy, Arthur O. & George Boas (1997). *Primitivism and Related Ideas in Antiquity* (new ed.; Baltimore, MD: John Hopkins University Press).

Lowenthal, David (1991). 'British National Identity and the English Landscape', *Rural History* 2.2: 205–230.

Lowenthal, David (2012). *Possessed by the Past* (Cambridge: Cambridge University Press).

Lüsebrink, Hans-Jürgen & János Riesz (eds.) (1984). *Feindbild und Faszination* (Frankfurt: Diesterweg).

Luhman, Niklas (1984). *Soziale Systeme* (Frankfurt: Suhrkamp).

Lukan, Walter (ed.) (1995). *Bartholomäus (Jernej) Kopitar* (Vienna: Böhlau).

Lukan, Walter (ed.) (2000). *Bartholomäus Kopitar und die europäische Wissenschaft im Spiegel seiner Privat-bibliothek* (Ljubljana: Narodna in univerzitetna knjižnica v Ljubljani).

Lutz-Hensel, Magdalene (1975). *Prinzipien der ersten textkritischen Editionen mittelhochdeutscher Dichtung* (Berlin: Erich Schmidt).

Lyandra-Geller, Olga (2016). 'Herder's Philosophy of Language and its Influence on the Concept of "Inner Form" in German and Russian Thought', in *J. G. Herder*, ed. Beate Allert (Heidelberg: Synchron), 275–289.

Maas, Annette (1995). 'Der Kult der toten Krieger', in François 1995, 215–213.

Macdonald, Murdo (2013). 'Ossian and Italian art', *Cesarotti Project*, University of Padua. Online at murdomacdonald.wordpress.com/ossian-and-italian-art/

MacDougall, Hugh (1982). *Racial Myth in English History* (Hanover, NH: University Press of New England).

MacMillan, Margaret (2014). *The War That Ended Peace* (London: Profile).

Mackrell, Alice (1998). 'Dress in Le Style Troubadour', *Costume* 32.1: 33–44.

Mackridge, Peter (2009). *Language and National Identity in Greece, 1766–1976* (Oxford: Oxford University Press).

Mack Smith, Denis (1994). *Mazzini* (New Haven: CT: Yale University Press).

Mährlein, Christoph (2000). *Volksgeist und Recht* (Würzburg: Königshausen & Neumann).

Mäkinen, Helka, S. E. Wilmer & W. B. Worthen (eds.) (2001). *Theatre, History and National Identities* (Helsinki: Helsinki University Press).

Malešević, Siniša (2004). '"Divine Ethnies" and "Sacred Nations"', *Nationalism and Ethnic Politics* 10: 561–593.

Mancoff, Debra N. (1995). *The Return of King Arthur* (New York: Harry N. Abrams).

Mander, John (1974). *Our German Cousins* (London: John Murray).

Mandle, W. F. (1987). *The Gaelic Athletic Association and Irish Nationalist Politics, 1884–1924* (Dublin: Gill & Macmillan).

Mango, Andrew (1999). *Atatürk* (London: John Murray).

Mann, Thomas (2012). *Betrachtungen eines Unpolitischen* (5th ed.; Frankfurt: Fischer).

Marek, Krystyna (1954). *Identity and Continuity of States in Public International Law* (Genève: Droz).

Marinov, Tchavdar (2006). *L'Impasse du passé* (Paris: Ecole de Hautes Etudes en Sciences Sociales).

Marotin, François (ed.) (1999). *Erckmann-Chatrian entre imagination, fantaisie et réalisme* (Phalsbourg: Musée de Phalsbourg).

Martel, Gordon (2017). *The Month That Changed the World: July 1914* (Oxford: Oxford University Press).

Martel, Philippe (1997). 'Le Félibrige', in Nora 1997, 3: 3515–3553.

Martel, Philippe (2010). *Les félibres et leur temps* (Pessac: Presses Universitaires de Bordeaux).
Martin, George (2005). 'Verdi, Politics, and "Va, pensiero"', *Opera Quarterly*, 21.1: 109–132.
Martínez Roda, Federico (ed.) (2000). *Historia de Lo Rat Penat* (Valencia: Lo Rat Penat).
Martus, Steffen (2009). *Die Brüder Grimm* (Berlin: Rowohlt).
Marx, Christoph (1998). *Im Zeichen des Ochsenwagens* (Münster: LIT).
Masalskis, Hans (2003). *Das Sprachgenie: Georg Sauerwein* (Oldenburg: Igel).
Mathijsen, Marita (2013). *Historiezucht* (Nijmegen: Vantilt).
Matless, David (1998). *Landscape and Englishness* (London: Reaktion).
Maufroy, Sandrine (2011). *Le philhellénisme franco-allemand, 1815–1848* (Paris: Belin).
Maxwell, Alexander (2014). *Patriots against Fashion* (Basingstoke: Palgrave Macmillan).
Maxwell, Alexander (2018). 'When Theory Is a Joke', *Beiträge zur Geschichte der Sprachwissenschaft* 28.2, 263–292.
Maxwell, Alexander (2019). *Everyday Nationalism in Hungary, 1789–1867* (Berlin: De Gruyter).
McCrone, David & Gayle McPherson (eds.) (2009). *National Days* (Basingstoke: Palgrave Macmillan).
McLaughlin, Neil (1996). 'Nazism, Nationalism, and the Sociology of Emotions', *Sociological Theory* 14.3: 241–261.
McMahon, Richard (2009). 'Anthropological Race Psychology 1820–1945', *Nations and Nationalism* 15.4: 575–596.
McMahon, Richard (2016). *The Races of Europe* (London: Palgrave Macmillan).
McMahon, Richard (ed.) (2019). *National Races* (Lincoln: University of Nebraska Press).
Mee, Jon (2003). *Romanticism, Enthusiasm, and Regulation* (Oxford: Oxford University Press).
Melby, Christian K. (2019). 'Empire and Nation in British Future-War and Invasion-Scare Fiction, 1871–1914', *Historical Journal*, online ed. DOI: 10.1017/S0018246X19000232.
Melman, Billie (2012). 'That Which We Learn with the Eye', in *Popularizing National Pasts, 1800 to the Present*, ed. B. Melman, S. Berger & Chr. Lorenz (London: Routledge), 75–101.
Melo, Daniel (2013). 'O intelectual no seu labirinto', *Romance Studies*, 31.2: 123–135.
Merchiers, Ingrid (2007). *Cultural Nationalism in the South Slav Habsburg Lands in the Early Nineteenth Century* (Munich: Sagner).
Mestrovic, Stjepan (1989). 'Durkheim's Conception of Political Anomie', *Research in Political Sociology* 4: 1–26.
Meyer, Anne-Rose (ed.) (2013). *Vormärz und Philhellenismus* (Forum Vormärz Forschung, Jahrbuch vol. 18; Bielefeld: Aisthesis).
Meyer, James H. (2014). *Turks Across Empires* (Oxford: Oxford University Press).
Michelet, Jules (1847–1853). *Histoire de la Révolution française*. Online at wikisource, w.wiki/CdRf

Miller, Robert L. (1968). *The Linguistic Relativity Principle and Humboldtian Ethnolinguistics* (Berlin: De Gruyter).
Milo, Daniel (1997). 'Le nom des rues', in Nora 1997, 2: 1887–1918.
Milojković-Djurić, Jelena (1994). *Panslavism and National Identity in Russia and in the Balkans, 1830–1880* (Boulder, CO: Columbia University Press).
Minea, Cosmin (2022). 'Roma Musicians, Folk Art and Traditional Food from Romania at the Paris World Fairs of 1889 and 1900', in Leerssen & Storm 2022, 144–169.
Minor, Ryan (2012). *Choral Fantasies* (Cambridge: Cambridge University Press).
Miracle, Josep (1960). *La restauració dels Jocs Florals* (Barcelona: Aymà).
Mitchell, Benjamin Frank (2001). *Romantic Painting Redefined* (Aldershot: Ashgate).
Mitzman, Arthur (1990). *Michelet, Historian* (New Haven, CT: Yale University Press).
Mojašević, Miljan (1990). *Jacob Grimm und die serbische Literatur und Kultur* (Marburg: Hitzeroth).
Moltke, Johannes von. (2005). *No Place Like Home* (Berkeley: University of California Press).
Momigliano, Arnaldo (1950). 'Ancient History and the Antiquarian', *Journal of the Warburg and Courtauld Institutes* 13.3/4: 285–315.
Mommsen, Wolfgang J. (1973). 'Domestic Factors in German Foreign Policy Before 1914', *Central European History* 6.1: 3–43.
Mommsen, Wolfgang J. (1981). 'Triebkräfte und Zielsetzungen des deutschen Imperialismus vor 1914', in *Kultur und Gesellschaft in Deutschland von der Reformation bis zur Gegenwart*, ed. Klaus Bohnen, Sven-Aage Jørgensen & Friedrich Schmöe (Munich: Fink), 118–135.
Mommsen, Wolfgang J. (ed.) (1996). *Kultur und Krieg* (Berlin: De Gruyter).
Monk, Samuel H. (1960). *The Sublime* (new ed.; Ann Arbor, MI: University of Michigan Press).
Moody, T. Dunbar (1975). *Afrikanerdom* (Berkeley: Univeristy of California Press).
Morava, Georg J. (1985). *Der k.k. Dissident Karel Havlíček 1821–1856* (Vienna: Österreichischer Bundesverlag).
Morris, Catherine (2013). *Alice Milligan and the Irish Cultural Revival* (Dublin: Four Courts).
Morris, E. & F. Milner (1992). *And When Did You Last See Your Father?* (Liverpool: Walker Art Gallery).
Morton, Jean-Claude (1990). 'L'organisation centrale des services d'information et de propagande du Quai d'Orsay pendant la Grande guerre', in *Les sociétés européennes et la guerre de 1914–1918*, ed. J.-J. Becker & S. Audouin-Rouzeau (Nanterre: Centre d'Histoire de la France contemporaine), 125–143.
Mosse, George (1964). *The Crisis of German Ideology* (New York: Grosset & Dunlap).
Motzkin, Gabriel (2005). 'On the Notion of Historical (Dis)continuity: Reinhart Koselleck's Construction of the "Sattelzeit"', *Contributions to the History of Concepts* 1.2: 145–158.

Mounk, Yascha (2018). *The People vs. Democracy* (Cambrudge, MA: Harvard University Press).

Mudde, Cas (2007). *Populist Radical Right Parties in Europe* (Cambridge: Cambridge University Press).

Mudde, Cas (2019). *The Far Right Today* (Cambridge: Polity Press).

Mudde, Cas & Cristobal Rovira Kaltwasser (2017). *Populism* (Oxford: Oxford University Press).

Münkler, Herfried (2009). *Die Deutschen und ihre Mythen* (Berlin: Rowohlt).

Müller, Friedrich Max (1854). *Letter to Chevalier Bunsen on the Classification of the Turanian Languages* (London: Spottiswoode).

Müller, Friedrich Max (1855). *The Languages of the Seat of War in the East* (London: Williams and Norgate).

Müller, Friedrich Max (1994). *Lectures on the Science of Language* (orig. 1861–64; intr. Roy Harris; 2 vols.; London: Routledge/Thoemmes).

Mueller-Vollmer, Kurt & Markus Messling (2024). 'Wilhelm von Humboldt', *Stanford Encyclopedia of Philosophy*, ed. Edward N. Zalta & Uri Nodelman. Online at plato.stanford.edu/archives/win2023/entries/wilhelm-humboldt/ (11 March 2024).

Murray, Peter (2008). *Daniel Maclise, 1806–1870* (Cork: Crawford Art Gallery).

Narváez Ferri, M. (2005). L'Orfeó Català, cant coral i catalanisme, 1891–1951 (doctoral thesis; Barcelona: Universitat de Barcelona).

Nekula, Marek (2012). 'Constructing Slavic Prague', *Bohemia*, 52: 22–36.

Nesselrath, Heinz-Günther (2011). 'Geschichte der Homerforschung', in *Homer-Handbuch*, ed. Antonios Rengakos & Bernhard Zimmermann (Stuttgart: Metzler), 175–199.

Netzer, Katinka (2006). *Wissenschaft aus nationaler Sehnsucht: Verhandlungen der Germanisten 1846 und 1847* (Heidelberg: Winter).

Neubauer, John (2006). 'Rhetorical Uses of Folk Poetry in Nineteenth-Century East-Central Europe', in *Studying Transcultural Literary History*, ed. Gunilla Lindberg-Wada (Berlin: De Gruyter), 88–97.

Neubauer, John (2010). 'Figures of National Poets', in *History of the Literary Cultures of East-Central Europe*, ed. M. Cornis-Pope & J. Neubauer (4 vols.; Amsterdam/Philadelphia: Benjamins) 4: 11–18.

Neubauer, John et al. (2010). 'The Rural Outlaws of East-Central Europe', in *History of the Literary Cultures of East-Central Europe*, ed. M. Cornis-Pope & J. Neubauer (4 vols.; Amsterdam/Philadelphia: Benjamins) 4: 407–440.

Neumayer, Erwin & Christine Schelberger (2003). *Raja Ravi Varma and the Printed Gods of India* (New Delhi: Oxford University Press).

Nicholls, Angus (2015). 'Max Müller and the Comparative Method', *Comparative Critical Studies*, 12.2: 213–234.

Noe, Alfred (ed.) (1984). *Der Philhellenismus in der westeuropäischen Literatur 1780–1830* (Amsterdam: Rodopi).

Nolte, Claire E. (2002). *The Sokol in the Czech Lands to 1914* (New York, NY: Palgrave Macmillan).

Noori, Margaret (2008). 'The Complex World of Jane Johnston Schoolcraft', *Michigan Quartely Review* 47.1. Online at hdl.handle.net/2027/spo.act2080.0047.121

Nora, Pierre (ed.) (1997). *Les lieux de mémoire* (Quarto ed.; 3 vols.; Paris: Gallimard).

Norberg, Jakob (2022). *The Brothers Grimm and the Making of German Nationalism* (Cambridge: Cambridge University Press).

Novalis (1797). 'Fragmente und Studien', in id., *Werke*, ed. G. Schultz (Munich: Beck, 1981).

Nyland, Waino (1950). 'Kalevala as a Reputed Source of Longfellow's Song of Hiawatha', *American Literature* 22.1: 1–20.

Obrestad, Tor (1992). *Hulda* (Oslo: Gyldendal).

Oellers, Adam C. (1987). *Alfred Rethel* (Aachen: Museum Burg Frankenberg).

Oergel, Maike (1998). *The Return of King Arthur and the Nibelungen* (Berlin: De Gruyter).

Ogonovszky, Judith (1999). *La peinture monumentale d'histoire dans les édifices civils en Belgique, 1830–1914* (Brussels: Acad. Royale de Belgique).

Ó hÓgáin, Dáithí (1982). *An file* (Dublin: Oifig an tSoláthair).

O'Kearney, Donna (2008). 'Enver Pasha and the Basmachi Rebellion', *Crossroads* 3.1: 98–105.

O'Leary, Philip (1994). *The Prose Literature of the Gaelic Revival, 1881–1921* (University Park, PA: Pennsylvania State University Press).

Olivier de Sardan, J.-P. (1998). 'Émique', *Homme* 147: 151–166.

Orton, Lawrence (1978). *The Prague Slav Congress of 1848* (Boulder, CO: East European monographs).

Osman Hamdi Bey & Marie de Launay (1873). *Les Costumes populaires de la Turquie en 1873*. Online at digitale-sammlungen.de/de/details/bsb11135044

Oxaal, Anne (1998). 'Bunaden', in *Jakten på det norske*, ed. Øystein Sørensen (Oslo: Gyldendal).

Özkirimli, Umut (2000). *Theories of Nationalism* (Basingstoke: Palgrave).

Ozouf, Mona (1988). *La fête révolutionnaire* (Paris: Gallimard).

Ozouf, Mona (1997). 'Le Panthéon' in Nora (1997), 1: 155–178.

Packard, Vance (1957). *The Hidden Persuaders* (Philadelphia, PA: David McKay).

Paddock, Troy R. (ed.) (2014). *World War I and Propaganda* (Leiden: Brill).

Panagiōtopoulos, Vasilīs (2003). 'Ī Filikī Etaireia', in id. (ed.), *Istoria tou neou Ellīnismou 1770–2000* (Athens: Ellinika grammata), 8–32.

Papacomsa, Victor (2007). 'Ioannis Metaxas and the Fourth of August Dictatorship in Greece', in Bernd Jürgen Fischer 2007, 165–199.

Parker, Fan & Stephen Jan Parker (1980). *Russia on Canvas: Ilya Repin* (Old Main, PA: Pennsylvania State University Press).

Parker, Joanne (2014). *'England's Darling': The Victorian Cult of Alfred the Great* (Manchester: Manchester University Press).

Parker, Joanne (ed.) (2015). *The Harp and the Constitution: Myths of Celtic and Gothic Origin* (Leiden: Brill).

Parker, Roger (1997). *'Arpa d'or dei fatidici vati': The Verdian Patriotic Chorus in the 1840s* (Parma: Istituto nazionale di studi Verdiani).

Pearson, Raymond (1994). *The Longman Companion to European Nationalism, 1789–1920* (London: Longman).

Pécout, Gilles (2004). 'Philhellenism in Italy', *Journal of Modern Italian Studies* 9.4: 405–427.

Peñas Ruiz, Ana (2012). 'Artículos de costumbres y fisiologías literarias', in *Literatura i espectacle/Literatura y espectáculo*, ed. R. Alemany Ferrer & F. Chico Rico (San Vicente del Raspeig: Universitat d'Alacant), 433–447.

Pentikäinen, Juha (1999). *Kalevala Mythology* (Bloomington, IN: Indiana University Press).

Peppard, Murray B. (1971). *Paths through the Forest* (New York, NY: Holt, Rinehart & Winston).

Pereira González, Fernando (2017). *Nas orixes do celtismo galego* (A Coruña: Fernando Pereira González).

Petrov, Bisser (2016). 'Slavianskiat Săbor v Sofia v 1945 g.', *Balkani* 5: 63–73.

Picon, Guillaume (ed.) (2012). *Cent tableaux à clef de l'histoire de France* (Paris: Hazan).

Pikkanen, Ilona (2010). 'Theatre Histories and the Construction of National Identity', in Berger & Lorenz 2010, 209–232.

Pikkanen, Ilona (2012). Casting the Ideal Past (doctoral thesis; Tampere: Tampere University).

Pinkard, Terry (2000). *Hegel: A Biography* (Cambridge: Cambridge University Press).

Pittock, Murray (ed.) (2007). *The Reception of Sir Walter Scott in Europe* (London: Continuum).

Planert, Ute (2007). *Der Mythos vom Befreiungskrieg: Frankreichs Kriege und der deutsche Süden 1792–1841* (Paderborn: Schöningh).

Pogačnik, Jože (1978). *Bartholomäus Kopitar* (Munich: Trofenik).

Poliakov, Léon (1987). *Le mythe aryen* (2nd ed.; Brussels: Complexe).

Poole, Gabriele (2010). 'The Byronic Hero, Theatricality and Leadership', *Byron Journal* 38.1: 7–18.

Popper, Karl (1972). *Objective Knowledge* (Oxford: Clarendon Press).

Porciani, Ilaria & Jo Tollebeek (eds.) (2012). *Setting the Standards: Institutions, Networks, and Communities of National Historiography* (Basingstoke: Palgrave Macmillan).

Porter, Brian (2002). *When Nationalism Began to Hate* (Oxford: Oxford University Press).

Poulton, Hugh (1997). *The Top Hat, the Grey Wolf, and the Crescent: Turkish Nationalism and the Turkish Republic* (New York: NYU Press).

Pourchier-Plasseraud, Suzanne (2015). *Arts and a Nation* (Leiden: Brill).

Prebble, John (2000). *The King's Jaunt: George IV in Scotland, August 1822* (new ed; Edinburgh: Birlinn).

Prendergast, Christopher (1997). *Napoleon and History Painting* (Oxford: Oxford University Press).

Price, Thomas (1854). *Literary Remains*, ed. J. Williams (2 vols.; Llandovery: Rees).

Prochasson, Christophe & Anne Rasmussen (1996). *Au nom de la patrie* (Paris: La Découverte).

Pross, Harry (1967). 'On Thomas Mann's Political Career', *Journal of Contemporary History* 2.2: 65–80.

Pütsep, Ervin (1990). 'Estnische Kunststudenten in St. Petersburg Anfang des 20. Jahrhunderts', in *Kunst und Geschichte im Ostseeraum*, ed. Erich Böckler (Kiel: Martin-Carl-Adolf-Böckler-Stiftung).

Puschner, Uwe & Ulrich Großmann (eds.) (2009). *Völkisch und national* (Darmstadt: Wissenschaftliche Buchgesellschaft).

Puschner, Uwe, Walter Schmitz & Justus H. Ulbricht (eds.) (1996). *Handbuch zur 'Völkischen Bewegung', 1871–1918* (Munich: Saur).

Puschner, Uwe & Clemens Vollnhals (eds.) (2012). *Die völkisch-religiöse Bewegung im Nationalsozialismus* (Göttingen: Vandenhoeck & Ruprecht).

Pyta, Wolfram (2007). *Hindenburg* (Berlin: Siedler).

Quack-Eustathiades, Regine (1984). *Der deutsche Philhellenismus während des griechischen Freiheitskampfes, 1821–1827* (Munich: Oldenbourg).

Quak, Aat (1999). 'Purisme in Duitsland', in Sijs 1999, 91–96.

Quinault, Roland (1998). 'The Cult of the Centenary, c. 1784–1914', *Historical Research* 71.176: 303–324.

Quinn, Erika (2014). *Franz Liszt: A Story of Central European Subjectivity* (Leiden: Brill).

Rabow-Edling, Susanna (2007). 'The Decembrists and the Concept of a Civic Nation', *Nationalities Papers* 35.2: 369–391.

Radiņš, Arnis et al. (eds.) (2016). *1896: Latvian Ethnographic Exhibition* (Riga: Neptuns).

Radler, Rudolf (1987). 'Löns, Hermann', in *Neue Deutsche Biographie* 15: 51–54. Online at deutsche-biographie.de/pnd118573853.html#ndbcontent

Raeff, Mark (1966). *The Decembrist Movement* (Englewood Cliffs, NJ: Prentice-Hall).

Raizis, Marius Byron (ed.) (1988). *Lord Byron* (Athens: Ministry of Culture and Sciences).

Ramathian, Andreas (2007). 'Friedrich Carl von Savigny's "Beruf" and "Volksgeistlehre"', *Journal of Legal History* 28.1: 1–29.

Ranke, Leopold von (1906). *Über die Epochen der neueren Geschichte* (Leipzig: Duncker & Humblot).

Rath, John (1964). 'The Carbonari', *American Historical Review*, 69.2: 353–370.

Rawson, Elizabeth (1969). *The Spartan Tradition in European Thought* (Oxford: Clarendon Press).

Reed, Maci (2018). '"A Singing Army Is a Fighting Army"', *Voces novae* 8.6. Online at digitalcommons.chapman.edu/vocesnovae/vol8/iss1/6

Reetz, Dankfried (2002). *Schleiermacher im Horizont preussischer Politik* (Recklinghausen: Spenner).

Reinach, Joseph (1920). 'Le rôle de l'impératrice Eugénie en septembre et octobre 1870', *La Révolution de 1848 et les révolutions du XIXe siècle*, 17.85: 192–200.

Reinfeld, Barbara (1982). *Karel Havlíček (1821–1856)* (New York, NY: Columbia University Press).

Renan, Ernest (1878). 'Inaugural speech at the Académie française,' in Renan 1947–61, 1: 727–728. Online at e-rn.ie/renankultur

Renan, Ernest (1883). 'Qu'est-ce qu'une nation?', in Renan 1947–61. Online at e-rn.ie/nationrenan

Renan, Ernest (1947–61). *Oeuvres Complètes*, ed. H. Psichari (4 vols.; Paris: Calmann-Lévy).

Riall, Lucy (2007). *Garibaldi* (New Haven, CT: Yale University Press).

Ribhegge, Wilhelm (1998). *Das Parlament als Nation* (Düsseldorf: Droste).

Richard, Bernard (n.d.). 'La Marseillaise, chant de guerre, chant de liberté'. Online at cheminsdememoire.gouv.fr/fr/la-marseillaise-chant-de-guerre-chant-de-liberte

Richards, Robert J. (2018). 'The Foundations of Archetype in Evolutionary Biology', *Republics of Letters* 6.1: 1–15.

Riches, Adam (2009). *When the Comics Went to War* (Edinburgh: Mainstream).

Richter, Joachim Burkhard (1992). *Hans Ferdinand Maßmann* (Berlin: De Gruyter).

Ridoux, Charles (2001). *Evolution des études médiévales en France de 1860 à 1914* (Paris: Champion).

Rigney, Ann (1990). *The Rhetoric of Historical Representation* (Cambridge: Cambridge University Press).

Rigney, Ann (2001). *Imperfect Histories: The Elusive Past and the Legacy of Romantic Historicism* (Ithaca, NY: Cornell University Press).

Rigney, Ann (2007). 'Being an Improper Historian', in *Manifestos for History*, ed. S. Morgan, K. Jenkins & A. Munslow (London: Routledge), 149–159.

Rigney, Ann (2011). 'Embodied Communities: Commemorating Robert Burns, 1859', *Representations* 115: 71–101.

Rigney, Ann (2012). *The Afterlives of Walter Scott* (Oxford: Oxford University Press).

Rigney, Ann (2025). *Remembering Hope: The Cultural Afterlife of Protest* (Oxford: Oxford University Press).

Ringer, Fritz (1990). *The Decline of the German Mandarins* (new ed.; Hanover, CT: University Press of New England).

Ripert, Emile (1917). *La renaissance provençale, 1800–1860* (Paris: Champion).

Rodi, Frithjof (1979). '"Erkenntnis der Erkannten" – August Boeckhs Grundformel der hermeneutischen Wissenschaften', in *Philologie und Hermeneutik im 19. Jahrhundert*, ed. Hellmut Flashar, Karlfried Gründer & Axel Horstmann (Göttingen: Vandenhoeck & Ruprecht), 68–73.

Rodriguez, Miguel (1998). 'Du voeu royal au voeu national', *Cahiers du centre de recherches historiques* 21, doi.org/10.4000/ccrh.2513

Roesdahl, Else & Preben Meulengracht Sørensen (eds.) (1996). *The Waking of Angantyr: The Scandinavian Past in European Culture* (Aarhus: Aarhus University Press).

Rohde, Peter (1982). *Danske kunstnere i Rom* (Viborg: Rosenkilde og Bagger).

Rommé, Barbara (1996). *Moritz von Schwind* (Ostfildern-Ruit: Hatje).

Roobol, W. H. (1998). 'Notities over de natiestaat', *Theoretische Geschiedenis* 25: 370–381.

Rose, Andreas (2017). *Between Empire and Continent* (trl. Rona Johnston, intr. Christopher Clark; London: Berghahn).

Ross, Margaret Clunies (2018). *The Pre-Christian Religions of the North* (2 vols.; Turnhout: Brepols).

Rothacker, Erich (1923). 'Savigny, Grimm, Ranke', *Historische Zeitschrift* 128.3: 415–445.

Rousseau, Jean-Jacques (1762). *Du contrat social.* Online at wikisource, w.wiki/CdRk

Rovira Kaltwasser, Cristóbal et al. (2017). *The Oxford Handbook of Populism* (Oxford: Oxford University Press).

Rutkoff, Peter M. (1981). *Revanche and Revision: The Ligue Des Patriotes and the Origins of the Radical Right in France, 1882–1900* (Athens, OH: Ohio University Press).

Saalfeld, Lerke von (1977). *Die ideologische Funktion des Nibelungenliedes in der preussisch-deutschen Geschichte von seiner Wiederentdeckung bis zum Nationalsozialismus* (Berlin: Freie Universität Berlin).

Sahlins, M. (2017). 'In Anthropology, it's Emic All the Way Down', *Hau: Journal of Ethnographic Theory* 7: 91–128.

Sakmyster, Thomas (1983). 'From Habsburg Admiral to Hungarian Regent', *East European Quarterly* 17.2: 129–148.

Salmen, Walter (1966). *Geschichte der Rhapsodie* (Zürich: Atlantis).

Sampimon, Janette (2006). *Becoming Bulgarian* (Amsterdam: Pegasus).

Samson, Jim (2002). 'Nations and Nationalism', in *The Cambridge History of Nineteenth-Century Music*, ed. J. Samson (Cambridge: Cambridge University Press), 568–600.

Samson, Jim (2007a). *Virtuosity and the Musical Work: The Transcendental Studies of Liszt* (Cambridge: Cambridge University Press).

Samson, Jim (2007b). 'Music and Nationalism', in *Nationalism and Ethnosymbolism*, ed. Athena S. Leoussi & Steven Grosby (Edinburgh: Edinburgh University Press), 55–67.

Sanders, Andrew (2013). *In the Olden Time* (New Haven, CT: Yale University Press).

Sanders, Michael & Philip M. Taylor (1982). *British Propaganda during the First World War, 1914–18* (Basingstoke: Macmillan).

Santuccio, Salvatore (2020). *Uno Stato nello Stato* (Acireale: Bonanno).

Sapega, Ellen W. (2007). '"E, se mais mundo houvera, lá chegara": Discourses of Empire in Lisbon's 1940 Exposition of the Portuguese World', in *Postcolonial Theory and Lusophone Literatures*, ed. P. de Medeiros (Utrecht: Portuguese Studies Center).

Schäfer, Marie (1985). Historienmalerei und Nationalbewusstsein in Russland 1860–1890 (doctoral thesis; Cologne: University of Cologne).

Schäfer-Hartmann, Günter (2009). *Literaturgeschichte als wahre Geschichte* (Frankfurt: Lang).

Schärli, Franziska (2007). Die Entwicklung des Bauernromans zur Blut-und-Boden-Literatur und das Interesse des Dritten Reiches an Jeremias Gotthelf (Bern: Universität Bern, Lizenziatsarbeit).

Schanze, Helmut (2018). *Erfindung der Romantik* (Stuttgart: Metzler).

Schenk, Frithiof Benjamin (2004). *Aleksandr Nevskij* (Cologne: Böhlau).

Schenk, Irmbert (2006). 'The Cinematic Support to Nationalist(ic) Mythology: The Italian Peplum 1910–1930' in *Globalization, Cultural Identities and Media Representations*, ed. N. Gentz & S. Kramer (Albany, NY: State University of New York Press).

Schivelbusch, Wolfgang (2004). *Culture of Defeat: On National Trauma, Mourning, and Recovery* (London: Picador).

Schlegel, Friedrich (1988). *Geschichte der Alten und Neuen Literatur*, ed. H. Eichner (Werke, vol. 6; Paderborn: Schöningh).

Schlieben-Lange, Brigitte (1996). *Idéologie, révolution et uniformité de la langue* (Liège: Mardaga).

Schmidt, Georg (2014). 'Friedrich Meineckes Kulturnation', *Historische Zeitschrift* 284.1: 597–622.

Schmidt, Horst (2012). 'Imagotype Philologie', in *Imagologie Heute*, ed. D. Dukić (Bonn: Bouvier), 319–335.

Schmidt-Wiegand, Ruth (1987). 'Das sinnliche Element des Rechts', in *Kasseler Vorträge in Erinnerung an den 200. Geburtstag der Brüder Jacob und Wilhelm Grimm*, ed. L. Denecke (Marburg: Elwert), 1–24.

Schneckenburger, Max (1870). *Deutsche Lieder: Auswahl aus seinem Nachlaß* (Stuttgart: Metzler).

Schneider, Eva Maria (2002). Herkunft und Verbreitungsformen der 'Deutschen Nationaltracht der Befreiungskriege' als Ausdruck politischer Gesinnung (doctoral thesis; Bonn: Friedrich-Wilhelms-Universität).

Schnurbein, Stephanie von (2016). *Norse Revival: Transformations of Germanic Neopaganism* (Leiden: Brill).

Schober, Franz von (1843). *Briefe über F. Liszt's Aufenhalt in Ungarn* (Berlin: Schlesinger).

Schoof, Wilhelm (1961). *Jacob Grimm: Aus seinem Leben* (Bonn: Dümmler).

Schoonenboom, Merlijn (2015). *De nimf en de bunny* (Amsterdam: Atlas Contact).

Schroeder, Paul W. (1962). *Metternich's Diplomacy at its Zenith, 1820–1823* (Austin, TX: University of Texas Press).

Schroeder, Paul W. (1972). *Austria, Great Britain, and the Crimean War* (Ithaca, NY: Cornell University Press).

Schroeder, Ralph (2020). 'The Dangerous Myth of Populism as a Thin Ideology', *Populism* 3: 13–28.

Schubert, Gabriella (1992). 'Von den "Nationaltrachten" zur europäischen Stadtkleidung', in *Die Volkskultur Südosteuropas in der Moderne*, ed. K. Roth (Munich: Südosteuropa-Gesellschaft), 197–234.

Schupp, Volker (2004). 'Vitae parallelae. Kettenbrüder: Joseph von Laßberg und Werner von Haxthausen', *Badische Heimat* 3: 354–369.

Schwarz, Angela (2012). 'The Regional and the Global: Folk Culture at World's Fairs and the Reinvention of the Nation', in *Folklore and Nationalism in Europe during the Long Nineteenth Century*, ed. T. Baycrift & D. Hopkin (Leiden: Brill), 99–111.

Scott, Christopher Allan (ed.) (2010). *Reconsidering Gérôme* (Los Angeles: J. Paul Getty Museum).

Scott, Walter (1805). *The Lay of the Last Minstrel.* Online at wikisource, w.wiki/9Nf4

Scott, Walter (1814). *Waverley; or, 'tis Sixty Years Since.* Online at the Internet archive, archive.org/details/waverleyortissi09scotgoog

Scott, Walter (1822). *Hints Adressed to the Inhabitants of Edinburgh, and Others, in Prospect of His Majesty's Visit* (Edinburgh: Blackwood/Robertson). Online at e-rn.ie/visitscott

Scott, Walter (1824). 'An Essay on Romance', in id., *Misellaneous Prose Works 6: Chivalry, Romance, the Drama*, 127–215. Online at archive.org/details/essaysonchivalr01scotgoog

Scouten, Arthur H. (1978). Review of Isaiah Berlin, 'Vico and Herder: Two studies in the history of ideas', *Comparative Literature Studies* 15: 336–340.

Scragg, Donald & Carole Weinberg (eds.) (2000). *Literary Appropriations of the Anglo-Saxons from the Thirteenth to the Twentieth Century* (Cambridge: Cambridge University Press).

Screen, John E. O. (1970–2000). *Mannerheim* (2 vols.; London: Hurst).

Scully, Richard (2012). *British Images of Germany* (Basingstoke: Palgrave Macmillan).

Sédouy, J.-A. de (2009). *Le Concert européen* (Paris: Fayard).

See, Klaus von (1999). 'Jacob Grimm und die Göttinger Protestation von 1837', in *Zur Geschichte und Problematik der Nationalphilologien in Europa*, ed. Frank Fürbeth (Tübingen: Niemeyer), 277–286.

Senelick, Laurence (ed.) (2008). *National Theatre in Northern and Eastern Europe* (Cambridge: Cambridge University Press).

Sérié, Pierre (2014). *La peinture d'histoire en France 1860–1900: La lyre ou le poignard* (Paris: Arthena).

Sgoff, Brigitte (1994). Claude Fauriel und die Anfänge der romanischen Sprachwissenschaft (doctoral thesis; Munich: Ludwig-Maximilians-Universität).

Sharma, Jyotirmaya (2011). *Hindutva* (3rd ed.; New Delhi: Penguin Books India).

Sheehan, J. J. (1992). 'State and Nationality in the Napoleonic Period', in *The State of Germany*, ed. J. Breuilly (London: Longman), 47–59.

Shippey, T. S. (1994). 'Local Patriotism and the Early Interpretation of Beowulf', in *Traditions and Innovations*, ed. F. G. Andersen & L. O. Sauerberg (Odense: Odense University Press), 303–318.

Shippey, T. S. (2005a). *The Road to Middle-Earth* (new ed.; London: HarperCollins).

Shippey, T. S. (ed.) (2005b). *The Shadow Walkers. Jacob Grimm's Mythology of the Monstrous* (Tempe, AZ: Center for Medieval and Renaissance Studies).

Shippey, T. S. (2009). 'Kemble, Beowulf, and the Schleswig-Holstein Question', in *The Kemble Lectures on Anglo-Saxon Studies*, ed. Alice Jorgensen et al. (Dublin: School of English, Trinity College), 64–80.

Shippey, T. S. & A. Haarder (eds.) (1998). *Beowulf: The Critical Heritage* (London: Routledge).

Shklar, Judith N. (1966). 'Rousseau's Two Models: Sparta and the Age of Gold', *Political Science Quarterly* 18.1: 25–51.

Short, Brian (1992). *The English Rural Community* (Cambridge: Cambridge University Press).

Sieyès, Emmanuel-Joseph (1789). *Qu'est-ce que le tiers-état?* Online at wikisource, w.wiki/CdRn

Sihvo, Hannes (2009). *L'image de la Carélie* (Helsinki: Arator Oy).

Silbey, David (2005). *The British Working Class and Enthusiasm for War, 1914–1916* (London: Frank Cass).

Simonsuuri, Kristi (2010). *Homer's Original Genius* (Cambridge: Cambridge University Press).

Simrock, Karl (1859). *Beowulf: Das älteste deutsche Epos* (Stuttgart: Cotta).

Sirinelli, Jean-François (1997). 'Éloge de la complexité', in *Pour une histoire culturelle*, ed. Jean-Pierre Rioux & J.-F Sirinelli (Paris: Seuil), 433–444.

Sisa, József (ed.) (2016). *Motherland and Progress: Hungarian Architecture and Design 1800–1900* (Basel: Birkhäuser).

Skurnowicz, Joan S. (1981). *Romantic Nationalism and Liberalism: Joachim Lelewel and the Polish National Idea* (New York: Columbia University Press).

Sladen, N. St. Barbe (1938). *The Real Le Queux* (London: Nicholson & Watson).

Smiles, Sam (1994). *The Image of Antiquity* (New Haven: Yale University Press).

Smith, Anthony D. (1978). 'The Diffusion of Nationalism', *British Journal of Sociology* 29: 238–239.

Smith, Anthony D. (2006). 'Ethnicity and Nationalism' in *The SAGE Handbook of Nations and Nationalism*, ed. G. Delanty and K. Kumar (London: SAGE), 169–181.

Smith, Anthony D. (2009). *Ethno-Symbolism and Nationalism* (London: Sage).

Snyder, Louis L. (1939). 'Count Arthur de Gobineau and the Crystallization of Nordicism', in *Race: A History of Modern Ethnic Theories* (London: Longmans, Green & Co.).

Sokolov, Boris & Jurij (1932). 'La recherche des bylines', *Revue des Études Slaves* 12: 202–215.

Solleveld, Floris (2020). 'Expanding the Comparative View: Humboldt's "Über die Kawi-Sprache" and Its Language Materials', *Historiographica linguistica* 47.1: 49–78.

Solomos, John (2014). 'Stuart Hall: Articulations of Race, Class and Identity', *Ethnic and Racial Studies* 37.10: 1667–1675.

Soubigou, Alain (2002). *Thomas Garrigue Masaryk* (Paris: Fayard).

Spiering, Menno (ed.) (1999). *Nation Building and Writing Literary History* (Amsterdam: Rodopi).

Spitzer, Alan Barrie (1971). *Old Hatreds and Young Hopes: The French Carbonari against the Bourbon Restoration* (Cambridge, MA: Harvard University Press).

St Clair, William (2008). *That Greece Might Still be Free* (Cambridge: OpenBook).

Ständecke, Monika (2007). *Dirndl, Truhen, Edelweiss* (Munich: Jüdisches Museum).

Stafford, Fiona (1994). *The Last of the Race* (Oxford: Oxford University Press).

Stafford, Fiona (1988). *The Sublime Savage* (Edinburgh: Edinburgh University Press).

Stanley, Ben (2008). 'The Thin Ideology of Populism', *Journal of Political Ideologies* 13.1: 95–110.

Stavělová, Daniela (2015). 'The Polka versus the Waltz', *Traditiones* 44.2: 91–111.

Stengers, Jean (1956). 'Aux origines de la guerre de 1870', *Revue Belge de Philologie et d'Histoire* 34.2: 701–747.

Stenographischer Bericht über die Verhandlungen der Deutschen Constituirenden National-versammlung zu Frankfurt am Main 1848–50 (9 vols.; Frankfurt: Sauerländer).

Sternhell, Ze'ev (1972). *Maurice Barrès et le nationalisme français* (Paris: Colin).

Sternhell, Ze'ev (1978). *La droite révolutionnaire, 1885–1914* (Paris: Seuil).

Stewart, Ian (2025). *The Celts: A Modern History* (Princeton, NJ: Princeton University Press).

Stewart, Jon (1996). *The Hegel Myths and Legends* (Evanston, IL: Northwestern University Press).

Stibbe, Matthew (2001). *German Anglophobia and the Great War, 1914–1918* (Cambridge: Cambridge University Press).

Stocking Jr., George W. (ed.) (1996). *Volksgeist as Method and Ethic* (Madison, WN: University of Wisconsin Press).

Stoklund, Bjarne (1994). 'The Role of International Exhibitions in the Construction of National Culture in the Nineteenth Century', *Ethnologia Europaea*, 24: 35–44.

Stone, Jon R. (ed.) (2002). *The Essential Max Müller* (New York: Palgrave Macmillan).

Storey, David (2011). *Territories: The Claiming of Space* (London: Routledge).

Storm, Eric (2022). 'The Transnational Construction of National Identities', in Leerssen & Storm 2022, 53–83.

Storm, Eric (2024). *Nationalism: A World History* (Princeton, NJ: Princeton University Press).

Storm-Rusche, Angelika (1990). 'Personendenkmäler', in *Heimat*, ed. Susanne Althoetmar-Smarczyk (Bonn: Bundeszentrale für Politische Bildung), 706–743.

Storost, Jürgen (1988). 'Jacob Grimm und die Schleswig-Holstein-Frage', *Brüder Grimm Gedenken* 8: 64–80.

Streng, Toos (2020). *De roman in de negentiende eeuw* (Hilversum: Verloren).

Strong, Roy (1978). *And When Did You Last See Your Father? The Victorian Painter and British History* (London: Thames and Hudson).

Stynen, Ludo (2012). *Jan Frans Willems* (Antwerpen: De Bezige Bij).

Suny, Ronald Grigor & Michael D. Kennedy (eds.) (2001). *Intellectuals and the Articulation of the Nation* (Ann Arbor: University of Michigan Press).

Sunyer, Magí (2006). *Els mites nacionals catalans* (Vic: Eumo).

Sunyer, Magí (2014). *Mites per a una nació* (Vic: Eumo).

Sijs, Nicoline van der (ed.) (1999). *Taaltrots* (Amsterdam: Contact).

Tall, Johannes (1985). 'Estonian Song Festivals and Nationalism in Music toward the End of the Nineteenth Century', in *National Movements in the Baltic*

Countries during the Nineteenth Century, ed. A. Loit (Uppsala: Almqvist & Wiksell), 449–454.

Teitelbaum, Benjamin (2019). 'Daniel Friberg and Metapolitics in Action', in *Key Thinkers of the Radical Right*, ed. Mark Sedgwick (Oxford: Oxford University Press), 259–275.

Thiesse, Anne-Marie (1991). *Ecrire la France* (Paris: Presses Universitaires de France).

Thiesse, Anne-Marie (1999). *La création des identités nationales: Europe, XVIIIe-XXe siècles* (Paris: Seuil).

Thiesse, Anne-Marie (2019). *La fabrique de l'écrivain national: Entre littérature et politique* (Paris: Gallimard).

Thiesse, Anne-Marie (2022). 'A Network in Search of an Alternative Modernity: Artists' Colonies in Europe (1870–1914)', in *Networks, Narratives and Nations*, ed. M. Brolsma et al. (Amsterdam: Amsterdam University Press), 97–104.

Thomas, George (1992). *Linguistic Purism* (London: Longman).

Thompson, Stith (1922). 'The Indian Legend of Hiawatha', *PMLA* 37: 128–140.

Thorslev, Peter L. (1962). *The Byronic Hero* (Minneapolis: University of Minnesota Press).

Tibbets, John C. (ed.) (1993). *Dvořák in America: 1892–1895* (Portland: Amadeus Press).

Tilly, Charles (1975). 'Reflections on the History of European State-Making', in *The Formation of National States in Western Europe*, ed. Ch. Tilly (Princeton, NJ: Princeton University Press), 3–83.

Timpanaro, Sebastiano (1963). *La genesi del metodo del Lachmann* (Firenze: Le Monnier).

Tollebeek, Jo, Frank Ankersmit & Wessel Krul (eds.) (1996). *Romantiek en historische cultuur* (Groningen: Historische Uitgeverij).

Tollebeek, Jo, Marc Boone & Karel van Nieuwenhuyse (2022). *Een canon van Vlaanderen* (Brussel: KVAB).

Tolstoy, Leo (1869). *War and Peace* (trl. Constance Garnett). Online at gutenberg.org/files/2600/2600-h/2600-h.htm

Treitschke, Heinrich von (1870). 'Was fordern wird von Frankreich?', *Preussische Jahrbücher*, 26: 250–275.

Tress, Madeleine (1984). 'Fascist Components in the Political Thought of Vladimir Jabotinsky', *Arab Studies Quarterly* 6.4: 304–324.

Trigos, Ludmilla (2009). *The Decembrist Myth in Russian Culture* (London: Macmillan).

Trotter, Mary (2001). *Ireland's National Theater* (Syracuse, NY: Syracuse University Press).

Turner, James (2014). *Philology* (Princeton, NJ: Princeton University Press).

Tyrichter, Jean Conrad (2019). *Die Erhaltung der Sicherheit* (Frankfurt: Klostermann).

Uhland, Ludwig (1807). *Über das Romantische*. Online at zeno.org/Literatur/M/Uhland,+Ludwig/%C3%84sthetische+Schriften

Ungern-Sternberg, Jürgen von & Wolfgang von Ungern-Sternberg (1996). *Der Aufruf 'An die Kulturwelt!'* (Stuttgart: Steiner).

Unruh, Karl (1986). *Langemarck: Legende und Wirklichkeit* (Koblenz: Bernard & Graefe).

Unverhau, Henning (2000). *Deutsche Liedertafeln, Sängerfeste, Volksfeste und Festmähler und ihre Bedeutung für das Entstehen eines nationalen und politischen Bewußtseins in Schleswig-Holstein 1840–1848* (Frankfurt: Lang).

Urigüen, Begoña (1986). *Orígenes y evolución de la derecha española* (Madrid: Departamento de Historia de la Iglesia).

Uslu, Günay (2015). Homer, Troy and the Turks (doctoral thesis; Amsterdam: University of Amsterdam).

Uzer, Umut (2016). *An Intellectual History of Turkish Nationalism* (Salt Lake City, UT: University of Utah Press).

Vaillant, André (1939). 'Vuk Karadžić et l'Hasanaginica', *Revue des Études Slaves* 19: 87–98.

Valensi, Lucette (1999). 'Traumatic Events and Historical Consciousness: Who is in Charge?', in *Historians and Social Values*, ed. J. Leerssen & A. Rigney (Amsterdam: Amsterdam University Press).

Vance, Norman (1981). 'Celts, Carthaginians and Constitutions: Anglo-Irish Literary Relations, 1780–1820', *Irish Historical Studies* 22.87: 216–238.

Vandrei, Martha (2018). *Queen Boudica and Historical Culture in Britain* (Oxford: Oxford University Press).

Van Hulle, Dirk & Joep Leerssen (eds.) (2008). *Editing the Nation's Memory: Textual Scholarship and Nation-Building in Nineteenth-Century Europe* (Amsterdam: Rodopi).

Vasmer, Max (ed.) (1938). *B. Kopitars Briefwechsel mit Jakob Grimm* (Berlin: Akademie der Wissenschaften).

Vaughan Williams, Ralph (1934). *National Music* (Oxford: Oxford University Press).

Venturi, Franco (1971). *Utopia and Reform in the Enlightenment* (Cambridge: Cambridge University Press).

Verdaguer, M. Àngels (2004). *Verdaguer i els Jocs Florals de Barcelona* (Barcelona: Ajuntament de Barcelona).

Vergez-Chaignon, Bénédicte (2014). *Pétain* (Paris: Perrin).

Verhandlungen (1847). *Verhandlungen der Germanisten zu Frankfurt am Main* (1846) (Frankfurt: Sauerländer). Online at e-rn.ie/germanisten1846

Verhandlungen (1848). *Verhandlungen der Germanisten zu Lübeck* (1847) (Lübeck: Boldemann). Online at e-rn.ie/germanisten1847

Verhey, Jeffrey (2000). *The Spirit of 1914* (Cambridge: Cambridge University Press).

Verschoor, Andries David (1928). *Die ältere deutsche Romantik und die Nationalidee* (Amsterdam: H.J. Paris).

Viale, Salvatore (1857). 'Dell'uso della lingua patria in Corsica', *Archivio Storico Italiano*, NS 6: 25–37. Online at e-rn.ie/vialecorsica

Viallaneix, Paul & Jean Ehrard (eds.) (1982). *Nos ancêtres les Gaulois* (Clermont-Ferrand: Université de Clermont-Ferrand II).

Vick, B. (2002). *Defining Germany: The 1848 Frankfurt Parliamentarians and National Identity* (Cambridge: Cambridge University Press).

Vidan, Aida (2003). *Embroidered with Gold, Strung with Pearls: The Traditional Ballads of Bosnian Women* (Cambridge, MA: Milman Parry Collection of Oral Literature).

Viereck, Peter (2004). *Metapolitics* (new ed.; New Brunswick: Transaction).

Villanueva, Pepita (2017). Le nationalisme valencien au début du XXIe siècle (doctoral thesis; Paris: Université Paris–Nanterre).

Vinke, Hermann (1980). *Das kurze Leben der Sophie Scholl* (Ravensburg: Maier).

Virgil (1916). *Eclogues. Georgics. Aeneid: Books 1–6* (Loeb ed.; trl H. Rushton Fairclough, rev. G. P. Goold; Cambridge, MA: Harvard University Press).

Viroli, Maurizo (1995). *For Love of Country: An Essay on Partiotism and Nationalism* (Oxford: Clarendon Press).

Vistdal, Oskar (2000). *Georg Sauerwein, europear og døl* (Bergen: Norsk bokreidingslag).

Voss, Ernst & J. J. Schlicher (1935). 'Jacob Grimm's De Desiderio Patriae', *Monatshefte für den deutschen Unterricht*, 27.5: 177–183.

Vovelle, Michel (1997). 'La Marseillaise', in Nora 1997, 1: 107–152.

Wagenaar, Henk (2004). 'Een canon van historische kennis voor de basisschool', in *Dat moet je gelezen hebben*, ed. H. van Lierop-Debrauwer, Piet Mooren & Harry Bekkering (Leidschendam: Biblion), 80–91.

Wagner-Heidendal, Lutgard (1972). *Het Filhellenisme in het Koninkrijk der Nederlanden 1821–1829* (Brussel: Paleis der academiën).

Walicki, Andrzej (1982). *Philosophy and Romantic Nationalism* (Oxford: Oxford University Press).

Walker, Alan (1983–96). *Franz Liszt* (3 vols.; New York, NY: Cornell University Press).

Walker, Alan (2005). *Reflections on Liszt* (New York, NY: Cornell University Press).

Wartelsteiner, Daniela (2015). *Bayerische Tracht* (Documentary, Bayerischer Rundfunk). Online at br.de/s/1WCM9nP

Watson, Peter (2010). *The German Genius* (London: Simon & Schuster).

Watson, Peter (2022). *The French Mind* (London: Simon & Schuster).

Watt, Roderick H. (1997). 'Wehrwolf or Werwolf?', *Modern Language Review* 87.4: 879–895.

Wawn, Andrew (2005). 'The Post-Medieval Reception of Old Norse and Old Icelandic Literature', in *A Companion to Old Norse-Icelandic Literature and Culture*, ed. R. McTurk (Oxford: Blackwell), 320–337.

Weber, Ernst (1991). *Lyrik der Befreiungskriege, 1812–1815* (Stuttgart: Metzler).

Weber, Eugen (1959). *The Nationalist Revival in France, 1905–1914* (Berkeley, CA: Berkeley University Press).

Weber, Eugen (1976). *Peasants into Frenchmen* (Stanford, CA: Stanford University Press).

Weber, Eugen (1985). *L'action française* (Paris: Fayard).

Weber, Max (1922). *Wirtschaft und Gesellschaft*. Online at zeno.org/Soziologie/M/Weber,+Max/

Weber, Max (1924). *The Theory of Social and Economic Organization* (trl. A. M. Henderson & Talcott Parsons; New York: Free Press).

Wechssler, Eduard (1929). *Esprit und Geist* (Bielefeld: Velhagen & Klasing).

Weeks, Theodore R. (2015). *Vilnius between Nations* (DeKalb, IL: Northern Illinois University Press).

Weissengruber, Thekla (2004). *Zwischen Pflege und Kommerz: Studien zum Umgang mit Trachten in Österreich nach 1945* (Münster: LIT).

Wellek, René (1941). *The Rise of English Literary History* (Chapel Hill, NC: University of North Carolina Press).

Werquet, Jan (2010). *Historismus und Repräsentation: Die Baupolitik Friedrich Wilhelms IV. in der preußischen Rheinprovinz* (Berlin: Deutscher Kunstverlag).

White, Harry & Michael Murphy (eds.) (2001). *Musical Constructions of Nationalism* (Cork: Cork University Press).

Whyte, Max (2008). 'The Uses and Abuses of Nietzsche in the Third Reich', *Journal of Contemporary History* 43.2: 171–194.

Wildmann, Daniel (2009). *Der veränderbare Körper* (Tübingen: Mohr Siebeck).

Willems, Jan Frans (1834). *Reinaert de Vos naer de oudste beryming* (Eecloo: Van Han).

Williamson, George S. (2004). *The Longing for Myth in Germany* (Chicago: University of Chicago Press).

Williamson, George S. (2018). *Retracing the Sattelzeit* (Cambridge: Cambridge University Press).

Wilmer, S. E. (2004). *Writing and Rewriting National Theatre Histories* (Iowa City, IA: University of Iowa Press).

Wilmer, S. E. (ed.) (2008). *National Theatres in a Changing Europe* (Basingstoke: Palgrave Macmillan).

Wilson, Duncan (1970). *The Life and Times of Vuk Stefanović Karadzić, 1787–1864: Literacy, Literature and National Independence in Serbia* (Oxford: Clarendon).

Wilson, Keith M. (ed.) (2001). *The International Impact of the Boer War* (Abingdon: Routledge).

Wilson, Keith M. (2003). *Problems and Possibilities: Exercises in Statesmanship, 1814–1918* (Stroud: Tempus).

Wimmer, Andreas & Nina Glick Schiller (2002). 'Methodological Nationalism and Beyond', *Global Networks* 2.4: 301–334.

Winckelmann, Johann Joachim (2011). *Letter and Report on the Discoveries at Herculaneum* (orig. 1762 and 1764; trl. Carol C. Mattusch; Los Angeles: J. Paul Getty Museum).

Winock, Michel (1997). 'Jeanne d'Arc', in Nora 1997, 3: 675–733.

Winter, Jay (1998). *Sites of Memory, Sites of Mourning: The Great War in European Cultural History* (new ed.; Cambridge: Cambridge University Press).

Wirtz, Markus (1999). *Josef Dobrovský und die Literatur* (Dresden: Dresden University Press).

Wolf, Norbert (2012). *The Art of the Salon* (London: Prestel).

Wolff, Larry (2001). *Venice and the Slavs* (Stanford, CA: Stanford University Press).

Wülfing, Wulf, Karin Bruns & Rolf Parr (1991). *Historische Mythologie der Deutschen, 1798–1918* (Munich: Fink).

Wyss, Ulrich (1979). *Die wilde Philologie: Jacob Grimm und der Historismus* (Munich: Beck).

Yoeli-Rimmer, Neah (2018). 'Jewish Villains and Basque Heroes: Ethnic Identities and National Narratives in Francisco Navarro Villoslada's "Amaya, o los vascos del siglo VIII"', *Bulletin of Spanish Studies* 95.7: 795–813.

Yovanovitch, Voyslav M. (1911). *'La Guzla' de Prosper Mérimée* (Paris: Hachette).

Zacek, Joseph Frederick (1970). *Palacký* (The Hague: Mouton).

Žáček, Václav (ed.) (1958). *Slovanský Sjezd v Praze roku 1848* (Prague: Nakladatelství Československé Akademie Věd).

Zacharasiewicz, Waldemar (1977). *Die Klimatheorie in der englischen Literatur und Literaturkritik* (Vienna: Braumüller).

Zamoyski, Adam (1982). *Paderewski* (New York: Scribner).

Zantedeschi, Francesca (2013). *Une langue en quête d'une nation* (Puylaurens: Institut d'Estudis Occitans).

Zantedeschi, Francesca (2019). *The Antiquarians of the Nation* (Leiden: Brill).

Zeijde, Albert van der (2002). *Katholieke identiteit en historisch bewustzijn* (Hilversum: Verloren).

Zenkovsky, Serge A. (1967). *Pan-Turkism and Islam in Russia* (Cambridge, MA: Harvard University Press).

Ziff, Norman David (1977). *Paul Delaroche* (New York, NY: Garland).

Index

Page numbers in **bold** refers to figures and tables.

1745 rebellion (Scotland), 161–162

Aachen Congress (1818), 52–53
Abbotsford, 84
ABC war (Ljubljana, 1820s), 134–135
academic scholars. *See also* German professor (stock figure); philology/philologists; writers/intellectuals
  as political professors, 267–273
  as propagandists, 283–284, 287–288
academicism, 184, 186–190
Académie des beaux-arts (Academy of Fine Arts) (Paris), 183, 186
academies of art, 183, 187–188
activism
  Flemish, 99
  national movements and, 45, 93, 338–340, **339**
  repressive measures against, 52, 59
  self-renamings as, 130–132
Adlersparre, Sophie, 246
Aeneid (Virgil), 68
Afanas'ev, Alexander, 116
Afrikaans language, 138, 141–142
Agli italiani (Mommsen), 267, 270
Ahnenerbe, 124
Ajuda library (Lisbon), 87
Akçura, Yusuf, 155
L'Alsace est-elle allemande ou française? Réponse à M. Mommsen (Fustel de Coulanges), 269–275
Albania, 61, 252, 302, 318
Albanian language, 144
Albert, Prince consort of the United Kingdom, 101
Alexander Nevsky (film) (Eisenstein), 34, 201, 328
Alexandra of Denmark, Queen consort of the United Kingdom, 288
Alldeutscher Verband, 287
L'Allemagne au-dessus de tout (Durkheim), 286
all-Estonian song festival, 220
Allgemeines Commers- und Liederbuch, 218
Alma-Tadema, Lawrence, 184
Alsace-Lorraine
  in general, 264
  territorial debate about
    anti-German feelings and, 271–272
    Arndt on, 267
    Clémenceau and, 286
    Fustel de Coulanges on, 268–273
    in general, 22, 59, 140, 175
    legal approach to, 272–273
    Mommsen on, 267
    propaganda and, 285
    Renan on, 273–274
    Treitschke on, 267
L'Alsace-Lorraine et la frontière du Nord-Est (Comité d'Études), 286
Aman, Theodor, 187, 196
Amaya o los vascos en el siglo VIII (Navarro Valloslada), 169
amor patriae, 53, 136
An mein Volk (manifesto of Friedrich Wilhelm III), 74
Ancient French Texts Society (*Société des anciens textes français*), 94, 96
And When Did You Last See Your Father? (Yeames), 195, **196**
Anderson, Benedict, 81
Anderson, Perry, 284
Andrej Bolkonsky (character in *War and Peace*), 236
Angélique (S. and A. Golon), 173
Anglo-Saxon language, 100–101
Anglo-Saxon world empire, 101
Anisya Fyodorovna (character in *War and Peace*), 236
Annals of the Four Masters (Irish chronicles), 89
anomie, 286–287, 343, 370, 373

'Anthem for a Doomed Youth' (Owen), 293
anthems. *See* national anthems
antiquaries, 83–84
  professionalization of. *See* philology/philologists
The Antiquary (Scott), 83–84
antiquity
  biblical and classical, 85, 184–185, 238
  historicism and, 159
  legal, 95, 125
  Northern European, 84–86, 151
  primordial, 118
anti-Semitism, 59, 208, 266, 341, 365
Antonescu, Ion, 302
Appeal to the Civilized World (*Aufruf an die Kulturwelt*), 282–283
Appellation d'origine laws, 251
Apte, Hari Narayan, 313
Arbo, Peter Nicolai, 187
archaeology, 84, 86–88
architecture, 262–263. *See also* monuments
archival materials, 86–88, 165–167
archives, 178. *See also* archival materials; libraries
Arendt, Hannah, 303
Aretin, Johann Christoph von, 88
L'Arlésienne (Daudet/Bizet), 238
Arminius monument (Detmold), 179
Army Comrades Association (Blueshirts), 303
Arndt, Ernst Moritz
  on Alsace-Lorraine, 267
  anti-French stance of, 128
  correspondence networks of, 103
  on German language, 128
  on a greater Germany, 139
  political agenda of, 137–138
  songs of, 77, 128, 138, 216–218
  status of, 78
  works of, 29
  mention of, 52, 175, 216
Arnim, Achim von, 109
Arnold, Matthew, 39, 151
art
  academies of, 183, 187–188
  Arts and Crafts movement, 260–262, 280
  classicist repertoire, 183–184
  colonies, 241
  Nazarenes, 185, 188–190, 197
  salons, 240–241
  styles in
    academicism, 184, 186–190
    art déco, 262
    art nouveau/Jugendstil, 261–262, **261**
    history painting. *See* history paintings
    plein-air painting, 240–242
art colonies, 241
art déco, 262
art nouveau/Jugendstil, 261–262, **261**
art salons (France), 240–241
artists, national authority of, 73–76
Arts and Crafts movement, 260–262, 280
Aryan, use of term, 153–154
Assemblée nationale (France), 49
Assmann, Aleida, 332
Atatürk (Mustafa Kemal Pasha), **42**, 43, 302
Atomium (Brussel), 248
atrocities, against civilians, 279–280
audiences, 6–7, 211–212
Aufhebung (sublation), 171
Aufruf an die Kulturwelt (*Appeal to the Civilized World*), 282–283
Austen, Jane, 173
Austria. *See also* Austro-Hungarian Empire; Habsburg Empire
  atrocities in Serbia, 280
  autocratic leaders in, 302
  culture of defeat in, 59
  traditional costumes in, 243, **245**
Austro-Hungarian Empire, 60, 252, 255. *See also* Austria; Habsburg Empire
authenticity, 236–237, 325, 337–338
authoritarianism, 303. *See also* dictatorships
authority. *See* charismatic leadership; cult of personality
Les aventures du maître Renard (Paris), 102

Babelon, Ernest, 285
Badiou, Alain, 47
Baldwin, Stanley, 307
Balkans. *See also under individual countries*
  fictitious states and monarchs from, 60
  geopolitical wars on, 55, 61
  nationalism in, 57
  regime changes in, 51
Balkenende, Jan-Peter, 174
ballads, 76. *See also* oral poetry
Balmoral Castle (Scotland), 171
banal nationalism, 198, 251
Bandicksson, Marcell, 201, 202
'The Baptism on the River Savica' ('Krst pri Savici') (Prešeren), 108, 169
Bar Kochba associations, 228
Baratashvili, Nikoloz, 80
Barbizon school, 241
Barcelona, **214**, 231, 248, **261**, 262, 301
Les bardes bretons du VIe siècle (La Villemarqué), 150
bards. *See* minstrels/bards/troubadours
Barrès, Maurice, 60, 266, 291
Barrie, J. M., 283
Basques, 62, 298

Bastille Day (France), 291
The Battle of Dorking (Chesney), 284
Battle of the Golden Spurs (painting) (Wappers), 170
battle songs, 264–265. *See also under individual battle songs*
Bavaria, 41, 243–244
'The Bear-Slayer' ('Lāčplēsis') (Pumpurs), 298
Becker, Nicolaus, 216
Bédier, Joseph, 281
The Begum's Fortune (Verne), 276
Belarusian language, 145
Belgium. *See also* Flanders; Low Countries; Southern Netherlands
  establishment of, 56
  Flemish national movement in, 172
  Frenchification of, 128–129
  German atrocities in, 280
  philology in, 96
  rejection of francophone dominance in, 105
  secession of, 104–5
Beli panter (*The white panther*) (Janša), 172
Belle époque, 60–61
Bellini, Vincenzo, 169
Bellum civile (Lucan), 68
Benda, Julien, 267
Benedictine order, 87
Ben-Gurion, David, 131, 307
Benjamin, Walter, 5, 232, 240, 250
Ben-Yehuda, Eliezer, 131
Beowulf
  in literary history books, 89
  philological appropriation of
    Danish, 100
    English, 100–101
    German, 100–101
  sole surviving copy of, 87
Béranger, Pierre, 77–78
Bergen, 257, 259
Bergman, Ingrid, 43
Bergslien, Knud, 201, **202**
Bergson, Henri, 281
Berlage, Hendrik, 262
Berlioz, Hector, 203
Berlusconi, Silvio, 1, 212, 304, 344
Bernhardi, Friedrich von, 284, 286
Bernhardt, Sarah, 106
Betrachtungen eines Unpolitischen (Observations of an Unpolitical Man) (Mann), 45
Bezukhov, Pierre, 54
BFBS (British Foreign Bible Society), 149–150
Bhakta Vidur (The devotion of Vidura) (film) (Rathod), 313
Bharatiya Janata Party (BJP), 307
Bible translations, 149–150
Biblioteca Laurentina (Florence), 86
Bibliotheca palatina, 88
Bibliothèque de l'Arsénal (Paris), 87
Bibliothèque du roi (Paris), 86–87
Bibliothèque mazarine (Paris), 87
Biefve, Édouard de, 187
'Big Bang' theory of Vico, 67, 86
Biggles (Johns), 315–316
Billig, Michael, 198, 251
Binyon, Laurence, 293
Birkebeinerne (*The Last King*) (film), 201, **202**
Birkebeinerrennet (ski marathon), 227
Birth of a Nation (film) (Griffith), 201, 314, 328
Birutė (pagan priestess-princess), 108, 169
Bismarck, Otto von, 59, 351
Bizet, Georges, 239
Bjørnson, Bjørnstjerne, 140
Blair, Hugh, 69
Blueshirts (Army Comrades Association), 303
Bocquillon, Louis (Wilhelm), 213
Bodleian library (Oxford), 89
Bofarull, Antoni de, 231
Bogart, Humphrey, 44, 80
Bohemia, 58–59, 166, 177
bohémiens, 5, 208, 241
Des Bohémiens et de leur musique en Hongrie (Liszt), 207
Bökendorf Circle, 109
Book of Kells, 300
Boris III, Tsar of Bulgaria, 302
Borodin, Aleksandr, 211
Borovský, Karel Havlíček, 82, 167
Botev, Hristo, 79, **319**
Bouguereau, William, 197
Bourdeau, Louis, 178
Bourdieu, Pierre, 5–6, 198, 235
'bourgeois patriotism', 321–322
Brand (Ibsen), 257
brands, national identity as, 250–252
Braveheart (film) (Gibson), 327–329
'Breathes There the Man' (Scott), 76–77
Brentano, Clemens, 109
Breton language, 149
Bretons/Brittany, 62, 297
Breton–Welsh kinship, 149–151
Breuer, Stefan, 352
Breuilly, John, 352, 353
Bridgerton (Quinn), 173
British Foreign Bible Society (BFBS), 149–150
British Museum library (London), 87
Brizeux, Auguste, 80
Brown, Ford Madox, 189
Brubaker, Rogers, 17–18

Bryce Report on Alleged German Outrages (British War Propaganda Bureau), 281
Buchan, John, 284, 314
Bulgaria, 279, 302, 321. *See also* Balkans
Bulgarian language, 144–145
bunad (traditional dress), 246
Bundessängerfest Breslau (1907), 217
Bundessängerfeste, 215
Bunsen, Christian, 151–152, 340
Bureau international des expositions (Paris), 250
Burke, Edmund, 35–36, 71
Burleigh, Harry, 210
Burns, Robert, 77, 81
Burschenschaften, 215
Bute, John Stuart, Lord, 114
Byron, Lord, 55, 79–80, 264
Byron statue (Athens), **56**

Cancioneiro da Ajuda, 87, 89
canonicity, 6, 105–6, 177–178, 312–313
canons, 180–181
A Canterbury Tale (film) (Powell & Pressburger), 299
Capitol riots (2021) (USA), 124
Capriccio Espagnol (Rimsky-Korsakov), 210
Carbonari (nationalist society), 54
Carlyle, Thomas, 38–39, 74, 308
Carmona, Óscar, 301–302
Carnegie, Andrew, 279
Carol II, King of Romania, 302
Casablanca (film) (Curtiz), 31, 43–44, 80, 176
Casas, Ramón, 261
Castro, Rosalía de, **79**
Catalan language, 80, 141, 231
Catalans/Catalonia
  activists in, 339
  in general, 51, 62, 298
  language of, 80, 141, 231
  modernisme in, 262
  Renaixença movement in, 231, 340
Cathleen Ní Houlihan (Yeats), 259
catholicism, 304
Celtic languages, 149
Celticism, 149
Cesarotti, Melchiorre, 70, 84, **85**, 86, 114
Chamberlain, Houston Stewart, 152
Champfleury (Jules François Felix Fleury-Husson), 240
Chansley, Jacob (QAnon Shaman), 124, 344
La Chanson de Roland, 89, 94, 293
Chansons nationales (Debraux), 78
'Chant du départ' (Méhul), 213
Chanteurs montagnards (choir), 213
Chants populaires de la Grèce moderne (Fauriel), 112
charisma, 40–41, 328
charismatic fervour, 33
charismatic leadership. *See also* cult of personality; hero-worship
  former war commanders and, 302
  in general, 41–42
  in Ireland (Parnell), 44
  post-1918, 42–43, 287, 341–342
  theory of, 41
charismatic nations, 44, 342–343
Der charismatische Staat (Breuer), 352
Charlemagne, 88
Charles X, King of France, 55
Chéret, Jules, **253**
Chesterton, G. K., 342
choirs. *See also* singing/songs
  in general, 212–213
  patriotic
    in Baltic area, 219–221
    in England, 213
    in France, 213
    in Germany, 214–219
    in Spain, 213
  traditional dress and, 246
Chopin, Frédéric, 204, 209, **319**
Churchill, Winston S., 101, 304
cinema. *See* films/television
cinéma de papa, 308, 316
cities. *See also* architecture; monuments; statues
  display cultures in, 232, 235
  historicizing street names in, 233–234
  leisure-time activities and, 227
  literary festivals in, 230
  as microcosm of national territory, 232–233
  as tourist attractions, 248–249
civilians, atrocities against, 279–280
civilizations, 67, 278
The Clansman (Dixon), 314
Clark, Christopher, 284
classical music, 209–211. *See also* opera
classicism, 85
classics. *See* vernacular classics
Clavè, Josep, 213, **214**
Clémenceau, George, 286
Cold-War period, 314–322
Cologne Song Festival (1846), 215
colonialism
  degradation of folk culture and, 253–254
  of the Netherlands, 174
  sugarcoating/remorse, 309
  world fairs and, 253–255
Columbus Monument (Barcelona), 248, 301
Comburg Abbey, 102
Comité d'études, 286
Comité Lavisse, 281, 284, 286

commemorations. *See also* monuments; statues
in general, 177
literary
in France, 230
in general, 230
in Germany, 228–229
spread of, 230–232
in Switzerland, 229–230
in Wales, 150–151, 230
of lost wars, 293–294
on postage stamps, 299, **299**
of wars
bereavements, 291–292
in comic strips, 315–316
in films, 315–316
in literature, 315–316
palliative effects of, 293
Commersbücher, 215
Committee of Union and Progress (Turkey), 155
communism, 303, 309, 321–322
communities
embodied, 81–82, 220–221, 228–229, 341
imagined, 81, 228, 347
competitive imitation, 228
condensation (counterpart to diffusion), 29–30, 35, 336–337, 339
Conference of Constantinople (1876), 279
Congress Party (India), 313, 323
Connor, Walker, 9
Conscience, Hendrik, 50, 128, 170–172, 176
consumerism, 232
Cooper, James Fenimore, 168
Cornelius, Peter von, 188, 191
Cornwall, 151
Corpus Christi College library (Cambridge), 87
correspondence networks. *See* networks
Corsica, 129
costume books, 242, 252
costume dramas, 309
costumes. *See* traditional costumes
Cotton, Robert, 87
countryside. *See also* cities; folk/peasant culture; imperial peripheries
in Ibsen's plays, 257
as location for tragedy, 238
mass-appeal literature commodifying of, 238–239
plein-air painting and, 241–242
as rustic idyll, 80, 238
Couperus, Louis, 309
Courbet, Gustave, 192–194, 240–241
court of arbitration (The Hague), 279
crafts/craftsmanship, 260–263
Crimean War (1853–1856), 59, 279
Les crimes allemandes d'après les témoignages allemands (Bédier), 281
Critical Dissertation on the Poems of Ossian, the Son of Fingal (Blair), 69
Croatia, 145
Croatian language, 142, 145
Croker, Thomas Crofton, 116
Crowe, Eyre, 284–285
Crystal Palace (London), 247–248
Crystal Palace (New York), 247–248
cult of personality. *See also* charismatic leadership; hero-worship
of Bismarck, 351
in general, 36
of Hindenburg, 42
military authority and, 42–43
cult of uniforms, 43
cultivation of culture
art. *See* art
dual timescale of, 15–17
in general, 9–10
languages. *See* language(s)
modes of, 338
performative culture. *See* fairy tales, folktales; films/television; myths/mythologies; oral literature
schema of, 10–12, **10**
text based culture. *See* historical novels; history-writing; philology/philologists
transnationality of, 92, 337–338
cultural heritage, 85, 100, 109, 196
cultural history, theories of, 86
cultural organization, models for, 339–340
cultural productions. *See also under individual productions*
artists and intellectuals, 4–5
dissemination of, 5
in general, 3–4
high vs. low, 5–6
restricted vs. unrestricted, 5, 345–346
schematization of, **4**
symbolic value of, 5
culture. *See also* cultivation of culture; cultural productions; culture of nationalism
audiences of, 6–7
definition of, 2–3
longevity of, 9
reflective self-awareness of, 8
Culture and Anarchy (Arnold), 39
culture of defeat
in Austria, 59
charismatic leadership and, 42
in Denmark, 59
in France, 22, 59, 94, 265

culture of defeat (cont.)
in general, 345
in Germany, 22, 62
in Hungary, 62
post-traumatic embitterment disorder and, 294
in Turkey, 62
after Vietnam War, 294
Culture of Defeat (Schivelbusch), 265
culture of nationalism. *See also* nationalism
artists and intellectuals, 5
definition of, 19
in general, 1–2, 333–334
pretended continuity and, 16
schematization of, 7–8, **7**
spread of, 334
currencies, 197
St Cyril, 107
Czech history, 166
Czech language, 144–145
Czech names, 131
Czechoslovakia. *See also* Prague
films/television in, 321
history of, 166
languages in, 144–145

d'Agoult, Marie Comptesse, 203, 205
Dahiya (Israeli military doctrine), 287, 370
Dahn, Felix, 123, 130, 172, 217, 287
Dalio, Marcel, 31
Danhauser, Josef, 203, **204**
Danish language, 133, 137
D'Annunzio, Gabriele, 302
Dante Alighieri, 7, 38, 68, 83, 93, 200
Darwin, Charles, 152
Daude, Alphonse, 238
Daughters of Ireland (women's movement), 259
David, Jacques-Louis, 186, 190
David Copperfield (Dickens), 238
Davis, Thomas, 75–76, 79, 129
De Leeuw van Vlaenderen (The Lion of Flanders) (Conscience), 50, 128, 170–172
De Quincey, Thomas, 37
De Valera, Eamon, 131, 303
De Valera, Sinéad, 131
the dead, respect to, 291
de-anglicisation, 44–45, 258
The Death of General Wolf (West), 185
Le Débâcle (Zola), 265
Debraux, Émile, 78
Decembrist revolt (1825) (Russia), 53–54
Declaration of Human and Civil Rights (France), 49
decorative arts, 156, 178, 181, 196–197, 262
decorum, 292–294
Deirdre/Cuchulain tales, 89
Delacroix, Eugène, 55, 190–191
Delaroche, Paul, 186, 200
democracies, 305, 345–346
Denis, Ernest, 281, 284
Denmark
culture of defeat in, 59
mythology of, 121
national canon of, 180
royal historiography of, 67
territorial debates of. *See* Schleswig-Holstein
theatre in, 257
Les déracinés (Barrès), 60
Det Norske Folks Historie (Munch), 201
Deutsche Grammatik (J. Grimm), 96, 139
Deutsche Mythologie (J. Grimm), 119, 122, 140
Deutsche Rechtsaltertümer (German Legal Antiquities) (J. Grimm), 95, 125
Deutsche Reden in schwerer Zeit, 281
'Der Deutsche Rhein' (Becker), 216
Deutsche Sagen (Brothers Grimm), 95
Deutsches Wörterbuch (German Dictionary) (Brothers Grimm), 95, 136
'Deutschlandlied' (Hoffmann von Fallersleben), 28–29, 218
Deutschland und der nächste Krieg (Bernhardi), 284, 286
The devotion of Vidura (*Bhakta Vidur*) (film) (Rathod), 313
dialects, 141–143
dictatorships
European trend in, 302
justification of, 303
nationalism and, 303–304
self-determination and, 302–303
Diez, Friedrich, 96
diffusion, 331, 339, 373
Dirndl costumes, 245. *See also* traditional costumes
disenchantment, 162, 257, 342
Disney Princesses, 61
Disputing Disaster (Anderson), 284
dissolution of the monasteries (1536–1541), 86
Dix, Otto, 293
Dixon, Thomas, 314
Dobrovský, Josef, 107, 144, 146
Doktor Schulze (character in *The Begum's Fortune*), 276
Dollfuß, Engelbert, 302, 304
Domènech i Montaner, Lluís, 262
Dominian, Leon, 112–113, 297
Don Carlos (Schiller), 54, 229
Dorpat (Tartu), 220

Downton Abbey (films/TV series), 309
Doyle, Arthur Conan, 283
Drost, Aarnout, 169
Droste-Hülshoff, Annette von, 238
Droste-Hülshoff, Jenny von, 110
Du Barail, François-Charles, 265
Du contrat social (Rousseau), 35
dual monarchy, 60
dualis (grammatical feature), 143
dualism, temperamental, 69
Dublin, 258–259
Duff, William, 67
Dumas, Alexandre (père), 203, 270
Dunant, Henri, 279–280
Duras, Marguerite, 309
Durkheim, Emile, 281, 284, 286
Düsseldorf art academy, 187–188
Dutch language, 137–138
Dvořák, Antonin, 118, 210
Dyserinck, Hugo, 9, 17

Easter Rising (1916, Ireland), 44
Eco, Umberto, 195
Ecole normale supérieure (Paris), 268, 284
Edda (mythological work), 67, 121–123
editions of ancient texts. *See* philology/philologists
Eichendorff, Josepf Freiherr von, 215
Eiffel Tower (Paris), 248
Eisenstein, Sergey, 34
Eisner, Kurt, 41
Eisteddfod (Wales), 150–151, 230
Elementa universalis linguae Slavicae e vivis dialectis eruta (Herkel), 144
Eliot, George, 238
Elisabeth, Queen of Austria-Hungary (Sissi), 173
Elnon manuscript, 98–100
embodied communities, 81–82, 220–221, 228–229, 341
emic and etic, 140–142, 145, 271, 273
enchantment/disenchantment, 162
Encyclopaedia Britannica, 163
Encyclopedia of Romantic Nationalism in Europe, 91, 331
England. *See* United Kingdom
'England and Spain, or: Valour and Patriotism' (Hemans), 77
Enlightenment, 67
Entente Cordiale (1904), 288
Enver Pasha, 156
epiphany, in Romanticism, 74
Erasmus, Desiderius, 184
Erdoğan, Recep Tayyip, 157, 295
Erkel, Ferenc, 211–212, **319**
Erklärung der Hochschullehrer des Deutschen Reiche, 283
Ernest Augustus, King of Hannover, 96
esprit, vs. *Geist*, 278
Essay on the Inequality of the Human Races (Gobineau), 152
Estates General (France), 49
Estonia, 117, 219–221, 321
ethnocracies, 305–306, 345–346
ethnohistory (*Völkergeschichte*), 91, 125, 175–176, 270
ethnotypes
  in general, 46, 278
  German vs. French, 275–278, **276**
  German vs. others, 46–48, 128, 273–274
  in post-WW II films, 316
  temperamental dualism and, 69
  Volksgeist and, 130
etic and emic, 140–142, 145, 271, 273
Eucken, Rudolf, 281, 283
Eugénie, Empress consort of the French, 266
Europe. *See also under individual countries*
  conflicts after World War I, 62
  democratic aspirations and, 52
  dismemberment of empires in, 61–62
  in general, 20
  independence of states after WW I, 297–298
  influence of national movements in, 57
  influence of the Grimm brothers in, 116
  Metternich system and, 52–53, 57, 59
  Napoleonic upheaval of, 51–52
  nationalist uprisings/revolts in, 55–61
  reactionary trends in, 52–55
  regime changes/internal conflicts in, 50–51
  Republic of Learning in, 86, 91–92
  sons of German dynasties on thrones in, 60
Everyman Karatayev (character in *War and Peace*), 236
exoticism, 161, 190–191, 210
experts, 344
Exposition Universelle (1855) (Paris), 240

fairy tales, 95, 122. *See also* folktales; oral literature; oral poetry
Falklands War (1982), 294
family names, 130–132. *See also* names
Fantasia on British Sea Songs (Wood), 218
Far from the Madding Crowd (Hardy), 238
Faroese language, 138
fatherland
  Arndt on, 77, 128
  death as sacrifice to, 35, 291
  love for one's, 35–36, 53, 136–137
Fauriel, Claude, 55, 112, 230

Félibrige movement (France), 231
female characters, 168–169
female nudity, 185
Fennomans (Finland), 45
Ferguson, Samuel, 75–76
festive cultures, 81–82
Festspiele, 229
Feszty, Árpád, 196
Fichte, Johann Gottlieb, 50, 268, **269**
Le Figaro (newspaper), 60
filial piety, 35
Filiki Eteria ('Friendly society'), 54–55
La Fille de Roland (play), 106
films/television
  Alexander Nevsky, canonized war leader in, 34
  distribution of, 313, 327
  in France, 308, 316
  in Germany, 239, 298, 307–308, 315
  Heimatfilm, 239, 307–308
  Heimatliteratur, 239
  in India, 313–314
  internationalism in, 318
  narration and spectacle, 201, 310
  national-heroic. *See* national-heroic films/ television
  peplum movies, 175
  posters for, 201, **202**, 327
  post-romantic nationalism and, 309–310
  remediation of the past in, 201–202
  in UK, 308–309
Fingal (Macpherson), 70
Finland
  culture in, 116–117
  Fennicization of, 45, 118, 131
  mythology of, 121
  oral poetry collecting in, 116–117
Finnish language, 154
Fischer, Fritz, 284
Flanders
  language of, 138
  national canon of, 180
  national movement in, 99, 128, 172
  Reynard versions and, 105
Die Fledermaus (operetta) (Strauss), 60
'The Flemish Lion' (van Peene & Miry), 216
Flemish language, 138
Fleury-Husson, Jules François Felix (Champfleury), 240
Flora MacIvor (character in *Waverley*), 161–162, 169
Floral Games (Jocs Florals) (Barcelona), 231, **261**
Floral Games (Toulouse), 230
folk/peasant culture
  in Austro-Hungarian Empire, 252
  commodification of, 245–246, 253–254
  dress. *See* traditional costumes
  Grimm on, 238
  Herder on, 237–238
  modernity and, 263
  national authenticity and, 236–237
  vs. urban society, 238
folk villages, 253
folklore, use of term, 119
folktales, 121, 237. *See also* fairy tales; myths/ mythologies; oral literature
football, 227
'For the Fallen' (Binyon), 293
forgeries, 115, 165–167. *See also* Ossian
Forster, E. M., 309
Fortis, Alberto, 113
The Foundations of the Nineteenth Century (Chamberlain), 153
foundational texts, 105–106, 114–115. *See also* vernacular classics
Fragments of Ancient Poetry Collected in the Highlands of Scotland (Macpherson), 68
frame stories, 160
France. *See also under individual heads of state*
  academy art salons in, 240–241
  anti-cosmopolitanism in, 59–60
  anti-restoration revolt in, 55
  Assemblée nationale of, 49
  culture of defeat in, 59, 94, 265
  De Gaulle on, 290
  display cultures in, 232
  establishment of republic in, 59
  Estates General of, 49
  ethnotype of, 46–48
  expansionism of, 274–275
  fêtes nationales in, 291
  film/television in, 308, 316
  language of, 99–100, 128–129
  libraries in, 87–88
  literary festivals in, 230–232
  minorities in. *See* Basques; Bretons/Brittany; Occitan/Provençal
  monuments in, 179
  national anthem of. *See* 'La Marseillaise'
  new philology in, 96
  nostalgia in, 308
  as old enemy of Germany, 30
  patriotic choirs in, 213
  political professors in, 268–273
  regionalism in, 238–239
  territorial debates. *See* Alsace-Lorraine; Rhine/Rhineland, territorial debates about
  theatre in, 257
  Third Estate and, 49
  war propaganda of, 280, 284, 286–287

'France! France!' (Thomas), 213
Francis I, King of France, 134
Franco, Francisco, 302
Franco-Prussian War (1870), 265–266
francs-tireurs, 272
Frankfurt, 57–58, 188
Frederick II, King of Prussia, 41
Freeden, Michael, 47
'Freedom!' (battle cry), 328, 344–346
freedom of conscience (*Gedankenfreiheit*), 229
freedom of thought, 54
Fremderfahrung, 9
French language, 99–100, 128–129
French Revolution, 36, 74
frescos, 188
Freud, Anna, **245**
Freud, Sigmund, **245**
Friedrich Barbarossa, Holy Roman Emperor, 179, 192
Friedrich Wilhelm III, King of Prussia, 74–75
Friends of Manual Craftwork (Swedish association), 246
From the New World (Dvořák), 210
Fromm, Erich, 303
The Frontiers of Language and Nationality In Europe (Dominian), 112
Fügner, Jindřich, **244**
Fundgruben (Hoffmann von Fallersleben), 97
Funérailles (Liszt), 207
funerals, 82, 167, 228, 293
Fuseli, Henry, 186
Fustel de Coulanges, Numa
  on Alsace-Lorraine, 268–275
  biographical sketch, 268
  on French two-nations model, 269–270

Gaelic languages, 44, 68, 134, 151. *See also* Irish language
Gaelic League (Ireland), 44–45, 259
Galician movement, 259, 339
Gallait, Louis, 187
Gallen-Kallela, Akseli, 118, 131, 194
Ganander, Christfried, 121
Gandhi, Mohandas, 307, 313
Garrett, Almeida, 79
Garborg, Hulda, 246, 260
Gaudí, Antoni, 262
Gaul, 270
Gaulle, Charles de, 275, 290, 304
Gautier, Léon, 94
'Die Gedanken sind frei' (song), 54
Geist, vs. *esprit*, 278
Geneva Conventions, 279
George IV, King of United Kingdom, 171, 243
George, Stefan, 41
German Dictionary (*Deutsches Wörterbuch*) (Brothers Grimm), 95, 136
German dynasties, 60
German language. *See also* Germanic languages
  Arndt on, 128
  Belgium and, 99
  Campe on, 135
  Danish language and, 133, 137
  Dutch language and, 137
  Fatherland and, 77
  French laguage and, 99–100
  German nationality and, 135–136
German League of Choral Societies, 217
German Legal Antiquities (*Deutsche Rechtsaltertümer*) (J. Grimm), 95
German professor (stock figure), 276
Germania (Veit), 188
Germania monument (Niederwald), 27–28, **28**
Germanic languages, 138–140. *See also* German language
Germanisten
  conferences of, 95, 105, 125
  scholarly fields of, 125
  Widukind and, 123
Germanness, 29
Germany. *See also under individual heads of state*
  Anglo-Saxon kinship and, 288
  anti-absolutism in, 54–55
  choirs and choral festivals in, 214–219
  claims on disputed borderlands, 22, 95, 101, 175
  culture of defeat in, 62
  ethnotype, 46–48
  films/television in, 239, 298, 307–308, 315
  France as old enemy of, 30
  Holy Roman Empire's abolition and, 57
  language of. *See* German language
  libraries in, 87–88
  literary commemorations in, 228–229
  Low Countries and, 99
  monuments in, 179
  nostalgia in, 307–308
  political bitterness of, 42
  political professors in, 268
  statues in, 27, **28**
  territorial debates. *See* Alsace-Lorraine; Rhine/Rhineland, territorial debates about; Schleswig-Holstein
  theatre in, 256
  traditional costumes in, 242–245
  trial by jury in, 95
  Turnvereine in, 228
  war propaganda of, 46, 280–283, 288–289
Gérôme, Jean-Léon, 186
Gerwarth, Robert, 62

Gesangbildungslehre nach Pestalozzischen Grundsätzen (Nägeli), 214
Geschichte der deutschen Sprache (J. Grimm), 96, 137, 140
Geschichten der germanischen und romanischen Völker (Ranke), 175
Gezelle, Guido, 79
Gianicolo lighthouse, 248, **249**, 261
Gibson, Mel, 327–328
Girardin, Emile, 265
Gladstone, William Ewart, 279
Glinka, Michail, 211
Gloeckle (librarian), 88
Gneisenau, Count August von, 74
Gobineau, Arthur de, 152
'God Save the King' (British national anthem), 33
The Goddess Saraswati (Ravi Varma), **198**
Goebbels, Joseph, 75, 315
Goethe, Johann Wolfgang von, 71, 113, 287
Gökalp, Ziya, 156
Golden Spurs, Battle of (1302), 170
Gone With the Wind (film) (Fleming), 314
Gonne, Maud, 80
Görres, J. J., 88
Gorsedd, 150
Die Götter Griechenlands (Schiller), 162
Göttingen University, 96
Gove, Michael, 180, 344
Graf, Conrad, 203
Grammatica Celtica (Zeuss), 151
Grammatik der Slavischen Sprache in Krain, Kärnten und Steyermark (Kopitar), 143
Grand Palais (Paris), 247–248
La Grande Illusion (Renoir), 292
Great Britain. *See* United Kingdom
Great Exhibition (1851) (London), 240, 247
Great War. *See* World War I (1914–1918)
The Great War in England (Le Queux), 285
Greece, 55, 57, 299
Grey Wolves, 156
Grieg, Edvard, 257
Griff nach der Weltmacht (Fischer), 284
Griffiths, D. W., 314
Grimm, Jacob. *See also under individual works*
  collecting of popular songs by, 109–110
  correspondence networks of, **92**, 109–110
  critical editing of, 102
  on disputed borderland, 175
  on epic and folklore, 118
  on folk culture, 238
  on German vs. Danish, 133
  Germanisten congresses, 95
  historical-comparative methodology of, 119–121
  inaugural lecture (1830), 136
  on *Kalevala* vs. Serbian ballads, 117
  on linguistic tenacity, 135–136
  on love of fatherland, 136–137
  mention of, 95, 146
  on nation and language, 128–129
  on national epics, 106
  Reynard fable and, 102, 104
  study of language and law, 125
  on *Völker*, 175
Grimm, Wilhelm, 95, 109, 357
Grimm brothers, 116
Gros, Antoine-Jean, 186
groupism, 17
Grundtvig, N. F. S., 121
Die Gründung Prags (Brentano), 169
Grünwald, Battle of (1410), 170
Guðmundsson, Sigurður, 259
guslars (traditional singers), 112–113
Gutiérrez García, Antonio, 231
La guzla (Mérimée), 115

Ha'am, Ahad, 131
Habsburg Empire, 59, 61, 144, 166. *See also* Austria; Austro-Hungarian Empire
habitus, 8–9, 235, 251, 367
haček (diacritical hook), 134
Haeckel, Ernst, 281, 283
Hagen, Friedrich Heinrich von der, 93–94
Hajdamaky (*The Outlaws*) (Shevchenko), 108
Halide Edib Adıvar, 155
Hanka, Václav, 166–167
Hansi (Jean-Jacques Waltz), 276
Hanusch, Ignaz Johann, 122
Hardiman, James, 112, 337
Hardy, Thomas, 238, 240, 283, 289
Harishchandra (legendary king), 313
'*Hasanaginica*' (Serbian song), 115
'*Hasanaginica*' (South-Slavic ballad), 113–114
Hasan-Aga (warlord), 113
Haskell, Francis, 185
'*Haßgesang*' ('Song of hatred against England') (Lissauer), 288–289
Haxthausen, Werner von, 52, 110
Hazzi, Joseph von, 243
heavy metal rock music, 124
Hegel, Georg Wilhelm Friedrich, 36–37
Heimat (film/TV series) (Reitz), 308
Heimatfilm, 239, 307–308
Heimatliteratur, 239
Heine, Heinrich, 12
Helmers, Jan Frederik, 107
Helsinki, 118
Hemans, Felicia, 77, 79

Henderson, Barbara, 289
Henreid, Paul, 43
Henry V (film) (Olivier), 6, 33, 299
Henry V (play) (Shakespeare), 6, 33–34
Henry VIII, King of England, 86, 134
Henty, G. A., 173
Herculano, Alexandre, 177
Herder, Johann Gottfried von. *See also under individual works*
  on folk culture, 237–238
  on language of diversity, 127, 135
  on Ossian, 114
  works of, 113
Herkel, Jan, 144
Hermingard van de Eikenterpen (Drost), 108, 169
heroes/supermen, 36–37
hero-worship. *See also* charismatic leadership; cult of personality
  Carlyle on, 38–39
  enduring power of, 327
  men vs. women, 40
  of Viktor Laszlo, 43–44
  of writers, 38–39
Heusler, Andreas, 123
Heyer, Georgette, 173
Hiawatha (Native American leader), 118, 210
Hindenburg, Paul von, 42, 293, 302
Hindu deities, 197
Hindutva, 307, 324
L'histoire et les historiens: Essai critique sur l'histoire considérée comme science positive (Bourdeau), 178
historical novels
  becoming school reading, 174
  for boys, 172–174
  colonialism in, 173–174
  of Conscience, 170–172
  decline of, 195–196
  as epic, 172
  film adaptations of, 175
  gaps in the historical documentation and, 169–170
  historicist dualism in, 194–195
  history painting and, 199–201
  nation in, 175
  of Scott. *See* Scott, Walter
  set in ancient Rome, 174
  of Sienkiewicz, 170
  of Tolstoy, 235
  for women, 172–173
historicism
  antiquity and, 159
  definition of, 106
  exoticism and, 190
  national, 95, 180
  romantic, 21, 160, 167–169, 178, 194–195, 199
  in Russia and Finland, 194
  sentimental, 195–196
history. *See also* ethnohistory (*Völkergeschichte*)
  as civic pedagogy, 176–177
  as national history, 176–177
  as unfinished business, 171–172
history of the French Revolution (Carlyle), 38
history paintings
  academic mode of, 184–186
  classical thematic repertoire in, 183–185
  decline of, 194, 196
  as decorative art, 196–197
  domestic settings in, 195
  influence of, 191
  international thematic repertoire in, 200
  legacy of, 197–198
  national thematic repertoire in, 184–186, 191–192
  Orientalism and, 190–191
  in Russia and Finland, 194
  spread of, 186–187
  state-sanctioned application of, 190
  textual historicism and, 199–201
history-writing
  history painting and, 199–201
  professionalization of, 200
Hitchcock, Alfred, 314
Hitler, Adolf, 27–30, 302
Hittorf, Jacques Ignace, 232–233
Hlahol choral society, 262
Hochdeutsch, 99, 139
Hofer, Andreas, 243, **311**
Hoffmann von Fallersleben, August Heinrich, 29, 96, 99, **97**, 115, 139
De Hollandsche Natie (Helmers), 107
Holli, Jan, 107
Hollywood, 314
Holy Roman Empire, 50, 52, 57–58, 87
Homer, 67, 114
homesickness, 76–77, 136
Horae Belgicae, 98
Horta, Victor, 262
Horthy, Miklós, 43, 302
Hôtel des Invalides, 36, 179
Hroch, Miroslav
  on intellectuals, 4, 347
  phase model of, 14, 92, 338, 349–350, 372–373
Hrolf Krake (Oehlenschläger), 107
Hugo, Victor, 74, 230
Huizinga, Johan, 181

human zoos, 253–254
Humboldt, Wilhelm von, 127
Hume, David, 264
Hungarian language, 108, 154
Hungary
architecture in, 262
culture of defeat in, 62
films/television in, 321
language of, 108, 154
Magyarization of family names in, 131
romantic nationalism in, 205
traditional costumes of, 243
Turanism in, 156–157, 336
hunger strikes, 151
Hus, Jan, 134
Huszka, József, 262
Hutchinson, John, 17–18
Hyde, Douglas, 44–45, 131, 258–259, 340

'I Vow to Thee, My Country' (Holst & Spring-Rice), 218–219, 293
Ibsen, Henrik, 257–258
Iceland, theatre in, 259
'Ich hab mich ergeben' (Maßmann), 218
idealism, 73, 127
ideologies, 13
idylls, of the countryside, 80
If you can sing, then sing along! (Kun je nog zingen, zing dan mee!) (Dutch national songbook), 216
imagined communities, 81, 228, 347
Imagined Communities (Anderson), 81
imitation, competitive, 228
Imperial Manor (Goslar), 191–192, 201
imperial peripheries, 256
independence, of European states after WW I, 297–298
India, 306–307, 313–314, 325–326
Indo-European languages, 141, 143, 151, 154
Indo-Europeans, 152–153
influencers, 344
Ingres, Jean-Auguste-Dominique, 186
The Inquiry (study group), 297
inspiration, 37–38, 72–73
instability, of states, 36
Institut de droit international (Institute of International Law), 279–280
intellectuals. *See* writers/intellectuals
international law, on warfare, 279
internationalization, economic, 249–250
The Invasion of 1910 (Le Queux), 285
invasion/future war novels, 284–285
invasion scares, 285
Ireland
anti-English popular histories in, 177
Blueshirt movement in, 303
de-Anglicisation of, 258
democratic stability in, 303
Gaelic League in, 44–45, 259
Gaelicization of names in, 131
language of. *See* Irish language
process of cultural nationalism in, 44–45
republican rebellion in, 51
romantic nationalism in, 44–45, 300
theatre in, 258–259
at world fairs, 299–300
women's movements, 259
Irish language
ban on, 134
decline of, 44
in general, 151
standardization of, 148
Irish Literary Theatre (Ireland), 258–259
Irish Minstrelsy (Hardiman), 112
Irish War of Independence (1919–1921), 44
Israel, 307
Italy. *See also* Rome
monuments in, 179
Risorgimento period in, 59, 179, 212
secret societies in, 54
united statehood of, 59
Ivanhoe (Scott), 163–164, 175–176, 195

Jabotinsky, Ze'ev, 307
Jacob, Therese von (Talvj), 113
Jacobite rising 1745 (Scotland), 161–162
Jacques-Louis, David, 186
Jäger, Carl, **229**
'Der Jäger Abschied' ('The Huntsmen's Farewell') (Mendelsohn), 215
Jagiello I, King of Poland, 300
Jahn, Friedrich Ludwig, 52, 228
Jakes, John, 314
Janaček, Leoš, 238
Janis (character from film *Lāčplēsis*), 298
Janša, Janez, 172
Japikx, Gysbert, 7
Jardin d'acclimatation (Paris), 254
Jean de Florette (film) (Berri), 309
Jeanne d'Arc (Joan of Arc), 40, 50, 179, 184, **311**, **312**
Jenůfa (Janaček), 238
'Jerusalem' (Parry & Elgar), 218, 293
Jesuit order, 87
Jewish names, 131
Jewish nationalism, 341
Joan of Arc (Jeanne d'Arc), 40, 179, 184
Joan of Arc in Armour at the Siege of Orléans (Lenepveu), **189**, 201
Jocs Florals (Floral Games) (Barcelona), 231, **261**

Johns, Capt. W. E., 315–316
Johnson, Boris, 1, 304, 336, 344
Joseph II, Holy Roman Emperor, 87, 243
Journey to the Centre of the Earth (Verne), 276
Joyce, James, 40
Jugendstil/art nouveau, 261–262, **261**
Jullian, Camille, 284–285
Die Jungfrau von Orléans (Schiller), 40

Kačić-Miošić, Andrija, 144
Kaiserpfalz (Goslar), 191–192, 201
Kalevala (Lönnrot), 50, 116–118
Kalevipoeg (Kreutzwald), 117
Kalidas (film) (Patankar), 313
Ein Kampf um Rom (Dahn), 172
Karadžić, Vuk, 109–110, **111**, 142, 150, **323**
Kashubian language, 144
Kaye, M. M., 309
Kayssarow, Andrej von, 121
'Kde domov můj?' ('Where is my homeland?') (Tyl), 257
Keller, Gottfried, 229
Kemble, John Mitchell, 96
Kervyn de Lettenhove, Joseph, 176
Kim (Kipling), 173
Kinder- und Hausmärchen (Grimm Bros.), 95, 109
The King of Ayodhya (film) (Shantaram), 313
The King's Threshold (Yeats), 151
Kipling, Rudyard, 173, 283
Des Knaben Wunderhorn (Arnim & Brentano), 54, 109
The Knights of the Cross (*Krzyżaci*) (Sienkiewicz), 170
Kohn, Hans, 274
Koidula, Lydia, 75, 79
Kollár, Jan, 80, 107, 144
Konrad Wallenrod (Mickiewicz), 108
Kopitar, Jernej, 97, 109, 134, 143, 146
Körner, Theodor, 74–75, 77, 216, **310**, **312**, 315
Kossuth, Lajos, 59
Krek, Gregor, 122
Kronprinzenwerk, 252
Krst pri Savici (The Baptism on the River Savica) (Prešeren), 108
Krzyżaci (The Knights of the Cross) (Sienkiewicz), 170
Kultur, vs. civilization, 278
Kun je nog zingen, zing dan mee! (If you can sing, then sing along!) (Dutch national songbook), 216
Kutuzov, Michael, 236
Kyffhäuser monument, 179

La Villemarqué, Théodore Claude Henri, vicomte Hersart de, 150
LaCapra, Dominick, 286
Lachmann, Karl, 102
'Lāčplēsis' ('The Bear-Slayer') (Pumpurs), 298–299
Lāčplēsis (film) (Rusteiķis), 298, **299**, 310
'Lament for Thomas Davis' (Ferguson), 75–76
Lamprecht, Karl, 283
'Land of Hope and Glory' ('Pomp and Circumstance' march) (Elgar), 218
Landnahme (Feszty), 196
landscapes, in literature, 239–240
Langemarck, Battle, 30
language(s). *See also* vernacular languages; *under individual languages*
  function and status of, 133–135
  German vs. Danish, 133
  historicist views on, 147
  linguistic descent of, 141, 143
  as logos, 127
  of minorities, 146
  mother's milk and, 133, 135
  nationalism and, 125–126
  nations and. *See* nations/nation-states
  philologists as masters of, 146–147
  primary functions, 89
  race and, 153–154
  scalarity of, 143–146
  society-specific views on, 147–148
  spelling reforms, 134–135
  standardization of, 135, 148–149
  territorialization of, 138, 149
The Languages of the Seat of War in the East, with a Survey of the Three Families of Language, Semitic, Arian and Turanian (Müller), 154
Lanson, Gustave, 281
Laokoon (Lessing), 201
Lark Rise to Candleford (TV series), 309
Larsson, Carl, 196
Laßberg, Joseph von, 110
The Last King (*Birkebeinerne*) (film), 201, **202**
Last Night of the Proms, 218–219
Last of the Mohicans (Cooper), 168
latency, of nationalism, 331, **332**
Latium und Hellas (Humboldt), 127
Latvia, 219–221, 262–263, 298–299, **299**. *See also* Riga
Lavisse, Ernest, 281
'*Lay of Prince Igor's Campaign*' (epic poem), 89
'Lay of the Last Minstrel' (Scott), 76, 81, 168
Le Gonidec, Jean-François, 149–150
Le Queux, William, 284–285

League of Nations, 286
League of United North German Choirs, 215
League of Virtue (Tugendbund), 53–54
Lean, David, 309
Lebeau, Madeleine, **31**, 43, 176
Lechner, Ödön, 262
Lectures on the Philosophy of History (Hegel), 36
Lectures on the Science of Language (Müller), 153
Legend of Saint Servatius, 89
Leikfélag Reykjavíkur (Reykjavík Theatre Company), 259
leisure-time activities. *See also* choirs
  cities and, 227, 232
  embodied communities and, 228–229
  international character of, 227–228
  national character of, 227–228
  sports, 227–228
Lelewel, Joachim, 53, 122
Lenepveu, Jules, **189**, 201
Lenient, Charles, 94
The Leopard (Tomasi de Lampedusa), 195
Lessing, Gotthold Ephraim, 201
Leys, Henri, 189
Liberty Leading the People (Delacroix), 190
libraries, 86–88. *See also under individual libraries*
Libuše (legendary Czech princess), 168, 176, 211
Libuše (Smetana), 211
Das Lied der Deutschen (Hoffmann von Fallersleben), 28–30
Liedertafel (choral societies), 214
Liedertafel der deutschen Studenten (Prague), 219
lieu de mémoire, 167, 314
Likud party, 287, 306
liminality, 71–72
Linden, Bob van der, 325
linguistic family tree, 143
linguistic laws, 96
linguists, 146–147
The Lion and the Unicorn (Orwell), 308
The Lion of Flanders (*De Leeuw van Vlaenderen*) (Conscience), 128, 170–172, **318**
Lipowsky, Felix Joseph von, 243
Lippmann, Walter, 297
Lisbon, 87, 248, 301
Lissauer, Ernst, 288
Liszt, Franz
  concert tours of, 205, **206**
  in Hungary
    Budapest concert, 205
    ceremonial sabre, 207
    nationally Hungarian music, 207–209
  painting of imagined matinee performance of, 203, **204**
  start of career of, 204–205
literary archaeology, 86–88
literary festivals. *See* commemorations
literary histories, rewriting of, 86, 88–89
Lithuania. *See also* Vilnius
  conflict with Poland, 61–62
  language of, 141
  patriotic choirs in, 219–221
  traditional costumes in, 246
Llanover, Augusta Hall, Lady, 110, 150
locus amoenus, 71
Lohengrin (chivalric romance), 88–89
Lokis (Mérimée), 150, 152, 276
London, 87, 196, 240, 247–248
Longfellow, Henry Wadsworth, 117, 210
Lönnrot, Elias, 116–117
Löns, Hermann, 307
The Lord of the Rings (Tolkien), 123
Louis XIV, King of France, 274–275
Louis XVI, King of France, 49
Louise, Queen of Prussia, 173, 192, **310–312**, **317**, 327
Louis-Philippe I, King of the, French, 56, 59
love of country. *See also* patriotism
  filial piety and, 35
  in general, 53, 136–137
  religious element in, 35
  stability of the state and, 35–36
Low Countries, 99, 139–140, 175, 264
Lowenthal, David, 198
Ludwig I, King of Bavaria, 59, 182, 243, 245
Ludwig II, King of Bavaria, 61, 244
Ludwigslied, 98
Lukács, György, 303
lumpers, of language variants, 139–140, 148–149, **148**. *See also* splitters, of language variants
Luther, Martin, 282
Luxembourgish, 138, 141–142
Lyrical Ballad (Wordsworth), 73

Má vlast (Smetana), 211
Maccabi associations, 228
Maccabiah Games, 228
Macedonian language, 144–145
Maček, Vladko, 302
Mácha, Karel Hynek, 79, 82, 167
Mackintosh, Rennie, 261
Macpherson, James, 68, 83, 114, 166
macro-nationalism, 138–140, 146–147
Madame Tussauds (wax museum) (London), 196

Madrid Agreement Concerning the International Registration of Marks (1891), 251
Maeterlinck, Maurice, 258
magic realism, 299
Magne, Lucien, 256
Magyars, 154
Mahabharata, 313
Major, John, 180, 308
Makovecz, Imre, **156**
Malan, Daniel François, 307
Mallet, Paul-Henri, 85
'Mandalay' (Kipling), 336
Mandela, Nelson, 307
Manifesto of 93, 282
Mann, Thomas, 45–48, 278
'Männer und Buben' (Körner), 216
Mannerheim, Gustaf, 43, 302
Manon des Sources (film) (Berri), 309
manuscripts, 100. *See also under individual manuscripts*
Manx language, 151
Manzoni, Alessandro, 75
Marcus Aurelius, 184
Maria Theresa, Holy Roman Empress, 243
'La Marseillaise' (French national anthem)
  in *Casablanca*, 31–32, 44
  creation of, 31–32
  Franco-Prussian War and, 265
  mention of, 50, 264, **312**
  Michelet on, 32–33
Martin, Henri, 176, 270, 291
Marubi, Pietro, 252
Masaryk, Thomas, 43
masculinity code, 173
mass demonstrations/events, 228
mass production, 260
Massacre of Chios (1822), 279
Maßmann, Hans Ferdinand, 52, 216, 218
Matejko, Jan, 170
Matthew Arnold, 288
Maud Gonne, 259
Maximilian II, King of Bavaria, 160, 244
Médaille militaire, 292
medievalism, 85–86
Méhul, Étienne Nicolas, 213
Mein Kampf (Hitler), 27–28
Meinecke, Friedrich, 281
melodramas, 239, 298, 328
memories, 89, 270–271, 275
Mendelssohn, Felix, 215–216
Menno ter Braak, 345
Méon, Dominique Martin, 102
Mérimée, Prosper, 103, 115, 150
metapolitics, 47
Metaxas, Ioannis, 43, 302
St Method, 107
Méthode Wilhem, 213
methodological nationalism, 14
metro map, 234–235
Metternich, Clemens von, 52
Metternich system, 52–53, 57, 59
Meyerbeer, Giacomo, 211
Michel, Francisque, 89
Michelet, Jules, 32–33, 40, 74, 176
Mickiewicz, Adam, 53, 79, 82, 108, 238
Midvinterblot (Larsson), 196
military distinctions, 292
military uniforms, 243
military-hero comics, 315–316
The Mill on the Floss (Eliot), 238
Millennium Church (Csikszereda), **156**
Milligan, Alice, 259
minority languages, 146, **148**
minstrels/bards/troubadours. *See also* Ossian
  as chivalric *Ur*-poets, 230
  literary festivals and, 230–231
  in work of Scott, 80–81, 158–159
'Mirèio' (poem) (Mistral), 238
Les Misérables (Hugo), 313
Mistral, Frédéric, 79, 232, 238, **239**
Mitchell, Margaret, 314
mnemonics, 235
modern historians
  disregard of national history by, 179–180
  national canons and, 180
  professionalization of, 178–179
  romantic history writing and, 178
modernism, 12–13, 262
Modi, Narendra, 295
Mommsen, Theodor, 267, 270
monastic libraries
  in England, 86–87
  in Europe, 87
Montenegrin language, 145
Montmartre, 266
Monument to the Discoveries (Lisbon), 248, 301
monuments. *See also* statues; *under individual monuments*
  distribution of, 295, **296**, 297
  for fallen soldiers, 292
  in France, 179
  in Germany, 27–28, **28**, 179
  increase in erection of, 336
  in Italy, 179
  in Netherlands, 179
Monuments de la mythologie et de la poésie des Celtes, et particulièrement des anciens Scandinave (Mallet), 85

Moore, Thomas, 77, 82
Moresnet, 280
Morris, William
in general, 260
influence of, 262
post-Pre-Raphaelite style of, 260–262
Mozart, Wolfgang Amadeus, 204
Mucha, Alphonse, 167, 196–197, 255, **261**, 262
La muette de Portici (Auber & Scribe), 211
Muhammad Ali Pasha, 233
Muiderslot (Muiden), 179
Müller, Friedrich Max
on Aryan races, 153
in general, 152
mythology and, 152
Turanian language family of, 154, 156
use of term Aryan, 153
mention of, 96, 340
Munch, Peter Andreas, 201
Munich, 187–188
Munich court library, 87–88
murals, 188–194, 196
Murguía, Manuel, **79**
muse-figures, 80
music. *See also* choirs; singing/songs; *under individual musical pieces and composers*
classical, 209–211
in general, 221
opera, 211–212
Mussolini, Benito, 302, 304
Mussorgsky, Modest, 211
Mustafa Kemal Pasha (Atatürk), **42**, 43, 302
Muti, Riccardo, 212
Myslbek, Josef Václav, 166
The Myth of Hiawatha (Schoolcraft), 118
Mythologia Fennica (Ganander), 121
Mythologie in alphabetischer Ordnung (Kayssarow), 122
myths/mythologies
as artistic inspirations, 122–123
as cultural archetype, 122, 124–125
Danish, 121
definition of, 121
Finnish, 121
German, 119
Müller and, 152
provenance of, 121–122, 167–169
religious and moral worldviews in, 123
Slavic, 121–122
as validator of national authenticity, 67, 325

Nabucco (opera) (Verdi), 211–212
Nacheinander vs. Nebeneinander, 201, 232
The Name of the Rose (Eco), 195
names
in general, 130
of girls, 169
nativization of, 130–131, 340
on Paris metro map, 234–235
self-renaming, 131
of streets, 233–234
Nansen, Fridtjof, 43
Napoleon Bonaparte, Emperor of the French, 36, 74–75, 179, 190, **311, 317**
Napoleon III, Emperor of the French, 265–266
Narbutt, Teodor, 122
narcissism, 287, 342–343
narrative and spectacle, 164–165, 192, 200–201, 240, 310, 325
narrative strategies, 160–162, 164–165
Naruszewicz, Adam, 122
Natasha Rostov (character in *War and Peace*), 236
A Nation in Arms (Roberts), 285
national anthems
charisma and, 33
chronology of, 33
Czech, 257
Dutch, 33
Flemish, 216
French. *See* "La Marseillaise' (French national anthem)
Polish, 57
UK, 33
National Assembly (1848) (Frankfurt), 57–58, **57–58**, 95, 137, 139, 188, 217
national epics, 105–108
national heroic movies, 312
national history
back in school curricula, 180
commemorative events and public holidays and, 177
cultural memory and, 181–182
disregard by modern historians, 179–180
in general, 176–177
greatest figure in history election, 180–181
legacy of romantic historians on, 181
national canons and, 180–181
in school curricula, 177
national identity/character (*Volksgeist*)
as brands, 250–252
coining of, 125
emanations of, 125
emic or etic, 273
essence of, 125
ethnotypes and, 130
as innate, 236
native language and, 127–130
political articulation of, 9–10
Renan on, 273

states and, 290–291, 295
in Tolstoy's *War and Peace*, 236–237
world fairs and, 250–252
national memories, 89, 234, 336–337
national movements, 44–45, 338–340, **339**. *See also* Hroch, Miroslav
national music, 209–211. *See also* national anthems
National Music (Vaughan Williams), 210
national past, 169
National Pledge campaign (Voeu national), 266
National Socialism, 123–124, 345
National Song Festival (Latvia), **220**
National Song Festival of Nuremberg (1861), 217
National Theatre (Prague), 211
national-heroic films/television
Central/Eastern European, 318, 321–322, **321**
European, 312–322, **312**
in general, 326–327
India, 313, 322–325, **324**
post-1989
in general, 327–329
as mass medium, 330
production of, **326**, 329–330, **329**
stylistic similarities in, 327–328
USA, 314
Western Europe, **318**
nationalism. *See also* patriotism
adaptability of, 334–335
ambivalence in, 48
as cult of the dead, 167
cultural history and, 12–13
definition of, 19
diffusion vs. condensation, 29–30, 35, 336–337, 339
emotive power, 341
ethnic or civic, 304–305
ethno-symbolist approach, 17
in general, 12–13
influence of, 57, 62–63
internationality in, 337–338
Jewish, 341
longevity of, 335
methodological, 14
modernists and, 12–13
multinational phenomenon, 14
in new nation-states, 62
populism and, 343–345
post-1989, 331–332
power of, 335
print capitalism and, 81
resurgence of, 295
romantic. *See* romantic/cultural nationalism
romanticism and, 19
scalarity of, 340–341
traditionalists and, 13
World War I's impact on, 294
nationality principle, 273
Nationalversammlung (National Assembly Frankfurt), 57–58, **57–58**, 95, 137, 139, 188, 217
nations/nation-states. *See also* states; *under individual countries*
ambivalence in concept of, 305
authoritarian leaders and, 304
charisma of, 342–343
concept of, 304
definition of, 9, 19
democracy and, 345–346
distinctness of. *See* national identity/character (*Volksgeist*)
emergence of, 49–50
formed after World War I, 62
French usage of term, 292
Fustel on forming of, 271
language and
Humboldt on, 127
in general, 126–127, 140–141
in Germany. *See* German language
threat to language and, 128–130
national memories and, 89
neoliberal view of, 344
as unpolitical, 44–48
wartime bereavements and, 291–292
Naumann, Friedrich, 283
Navarro Valloslada, Francisco, 169
Nazarenes (German Romantic painters), 185, 188–190, 197
Nebeneinander vs. *Nacheinander*, 201, 232
'The Necessity for De-Anglicising Ireland' (lecture) (Hyde), 44–45
Němcová, Božena, 82, 167
neopaganism, 123–124
Netanyahu, Benjamin, 295
Netherlands. *See also* Low Countries; Southern Netherlands; *under specific heads of state*
break-up of (1830). *See* Belgium
colonialism of, 173–174
film industry in, 315
language of, 137–138
monuments in, 179
national anthem of, 33
National Canon of, 180
revolt against Spain, 177
networks
of Arndt, 103, **104**
in general, 337
of Grimm, 91, **92**, 109–110
of Mérimée, 103, **103**
of philologists, 91, 97

Neuschwanstein Castle, 61
Nevsky, Alexander, 34
Nibelungenlied (epic poem), 89, 93–94, 106
Nibelungentreue, 95
Nibelungentreue: Kriegsgesänge, 106
Niederdeutsch, 99
Niederwalddenkmal, 27–28, **28**
Nietzsche, Friedrich, 194, 287
Nightingale, Florence, 279
Nobel, Alfred, 280
Nobel Prize, **239**, 280
Noli, Fan, 150
Nora, Pierre, 167
Nordau, Max, 228
Nordens Mytologi (Grundtvig), 121
Norma (character in Bellini opera), 108, 169
Normandy Landings, 33–34
Norsk klædebunad (Garborg), 246
Norske Folkeæventyr (Asbjørnsen & Moe), 116
North and South (TV series) (Heyes), 314
Norway, 140, 227, 245–246, 257–258
Norwegian language, 138
nostalgia, 307–309
'Not Yet is Poland Lost' (Polish national anthem), 57
Novalis, 72–73
Nyerup, Rasmus, 121

obelisks, 233
Oberdeutsch, 99
Observations of an Unpolitical Man (*Betrachtungen eines Unpolitischen*) (Mann), 45
Occitan/Provençal, 141, 231–232
O'Connell, Daniel, 228
Odessa, 51, 53, 341
Oehlenschläger, Adam Gottlob, 107, 257
'Of the First Principles of Government' (Hume), 264
Oghuz Khan, 156
Ojibwe material, 117
Okakura, Kakuzo, 254
Oktoberfeste (Munich), 245, 253
Old Mortality (Scott), 160
Olivier, Lawrence, 6, 33, 299
Olympic Games, 228, 299
Om Odin og den hedniske Gudelære og Gudstjeneste udi Norden (Suhm), 121
O'Murnaghan, Art, 371
On Heroes and Hero-Worship (Carlyle), 38–39, 308
On Literature in its Relations to Social Institutions (de Staël), 69
'On the Romantic' (Uhland), 72
'On the Use and Abuse of History for Life' (Nietzsche), 194
'Onward, Christian Soldiers' (Sullivan), 218
open-air museums, 253, 256
opera, 211–212
oral culture, 118–119, **120**
oral epics, 115
oral literature, 114–116. *See also* fairy tales; folktales; oral poetry
oral poetry
  collecting of
    in Finland, 116–117
    by Grimm, 109–110
    by Karadžić, 109–111
    in North America, 117–118
  European spread of, 113–114
  image of performer and, 111–112
  inspirational values of, 118
  national aspirations and, 112–113
  as precursor of foundational epics, 114–115
  remediation of, 118
  shift from sentimental to national, 115
Orbán, Viktor, 295, 304, 336
Ordinance of Villiers-Cotterêts (1539), 134
Orientalism, 190–191, 210
original geniuses, 67–70, 82
Orkhon inscriptions, 155
Orphéon (singing societies), 213
Orwell, George, 308
Ossian
  as antiquarian discovery, 84
  Cesarotti's Italian edition of, 84, **85**
  in general, 68
  Hasanaginica and, 113–114
  iconography of, 69–71, **70**
  influence of, 71–72, 84
  last elegy of, 70–71
  Napoleon Bonaparte and, 74
  oral sources and, 114
  as original genius, 68–70
  tale of his retrieval, 83
Ottoman Empire
  Bulgaria and, 279
  dismemberment of, 61
  resistance against, 51, 55
  rivalry with Russia, 53, 59
  secret societies against, 51
  Tanzimat reforms in, 59
Outlander (Gabaldon), 173
'The Outlaws' (*Hajdamaky*) (Shevchenko), 108
outrage, 328. *See also* melodramas
Owen, Wilfred, 293

pacifism, international, 279–280
Paderewski, Ignacy, 43

Paganini, Niccolò, 203–204
Pagnol, Marcel, 309
painting. *See* history paintings; plein-air painting
Palace of Catalan Music (Barcelona), **214**
Palace of Industry (Prague), 248
Palace of Italian Civilization (Rome), 248
Palacio de Cristal (Porto), 247
Palacký, František, 58, 166–167
Palais de Chaillot (Paris), 248
Palais de Tokyo (Paris), 248
Paleis voor Volksvlijt (Amsterdam), 247–248
Pan-Celticism, 149–152
panoramic, use of term, 232
Pan-Slavic Congress (1848) (Prague), 59, 144, 167
Pan-Slavic Congress (1867) (Moscow), 145
Pan-Slavic Congress (1945) (Sofia), 145
Pan-Slavic Congress (1946) (Belgrade), 145
Pan-Slavism, 144–146
Pan-Turkism (Turanism), 155–157, 336
Paris
  art academies in, 183, 186
  exhibition palaces in, 247–248
  Jardin d'acclimatation in, 254
  metro map of, 234–235
  Panthéon in, 233
  Place de la Concorde in, 232–233
  shopping experience in, 232
  statues in, 233
  world fairs in, 240, **253**, 255
Paris, Gaston, 94
Paris, Paulin, 94, 102
Paris Commune, 265–266
Paris Peace Conference (1919–1920), 61–62, 112
Parker, Matthew, 87
Parnell, Charles Stewart, 44
Parry, Hubert, 218
A Passage to India (film) (Lean), 309
Passagenwerk (Arcades Project) (Benjamin), 232
Passy, Frédéric, 279–280
patriotism. *See also* love of country
  bourgeois, 321–322
  choirs and. *See* choirs
  in films, 34. *See also* national-heroic films/television
  in Shakespeare's plays, 6
  in war propaganda. *See* war propaganda
Päts, Konstantin, 302
Paulskirche (Frankfurt), 188
Peace Conference (Paris), 297–298
Peace Palace (The Hague), 280
Pearse, Patrick, 339
peasant culture. *See* folk/peasant culture
peasants, 236–237, 239, 241–242
Peer Gynt (Ibsen), 257
Peer Gynt suite (Grieg), 210
Peeters, Benoît, 211
peplum movies, 175
performers, images of
  iconicity of, 112
  Rouget de Lisle, **32**, 111
  in *Srpske narodne pjesme*, 111–112, **111**
Pestalozzi, Johann Heinrich, 214
Pétain, Philippe, 43, 302
Petőfi, Sándor, 59, 79, 131, 264
philhellenism, 55, 77, 80
philology/philologists. *See also under individual philologists*
  diplomatic vs. critical editing of, 102–103
  in Europe, 95–97
  historicist views of, 147
  as masters of language, 146–147
  networks of, 91, 97
  oral culture and, 118–119
  origin of term, 89
  professionalization of, 95
Philomaths and Philarets ('Friends of science'/'Friends of virtue'), 53–54
pianos, 203–204
Pichler, Caroline, 242
Pierre Bezukhov (character in *War and Peace*), 236
Piłsudski, Józef, 43, 300, 302
Pirow, Oswald, 306
Pius X, Pope, 304
pjesme, 112–113
Place de la Concorde (Paris), 232–233
Planck, Max, 283
Plato, 73, 125, 127
Platon Karatayev (character in *War and Peace*), 236
Plattdeutsch, 99
Plaza de España (Seville), 248
plein-air painting, 240–242
La poésie des races celtiques (Renan), 151–152
poetry/poetical themes, 76–77, **79**. *See also* oral poetry
poets, 72–73, 75–82. *See also* writers/intellectuals
'The Poet's Function' (Hugo), 74
Poland
  conflict with Lithuania, 61–62
  films/television in, 321
  language of, 108, 145
  national anthem of, 57
  secret societies in, 53
  traditional costumes in, 243
  uprisings in, 53, 57, 62, 144, 243
  at world fairs, 300, **300**
Polish language, 108, 145
Polish Uprisings (1831 & 1863), 53, 57, 62, 144, 243
Polish-Lithuanian University (Vilnius), 53

political nationalism, vs. cultural nationalism, 330–331
political professors, 267–273
Polonaise (dance), 209
'Pomp and Circumstance' march ('Land of Hope and Glory') (Elgar), 218
Pompeii, 84
Popper, Karl, 73, 303
popular culture, 333
popular song. *See* oral poetry
popular sovereignty, 51
populism, 343–344
A Portrait of the Artist as a Young Man (Joyce), 40
portraits, historically reimagined, 185
Portugal, 87, 96, 177, 301. *See also* Lisbon
postage stamps, 299, **299**
posters
  for films/television, 201, **202**, 327
  of Mucha, 197, 262
  for national events, **261**
  for propaganda, 198
potenzieren (raising to a higher degree), 73
Powell and Pressburger films, 299, 307
Powys, John Cowper, 307
Prague
  cemeteries in, 167
  exhibition palaces in, 248
  foretelling greatness of, 168
  founding of, 166
  memorials in, 167
  Mucha and, 262
  Pan-Slavic Congress, 59, 144, 167
  theatre in, 211
  Tourist Pavilion in, 248
Prešeren, France, 79, 82, 108, 131, 169
Preussische Jahrbücher, 267–268
Price, Thomas, 149–150
Primo de Rivera, Miguel, 302, 304
Prince Igor (Borodin), 211
Princess Turandot (character in *Turandot*), 153
print capitalism, 81
The Prisoner of Zenda (Hope), 60
Professor Knatschke (caricature by Hansi), 276, **277**
Professor Lidenbrock (character in *Journey to the Centre of the Earth*), 276
Professor Wittembach (character in *Lokis*), 150, 152, 276
Promenade concerts (Proms), 218–219
propaganda posters, 198
Prussia, 59, 74–75, 268, **269**, 270–271. *See also* Franco-Prussian War (1870)
public opinion. *See also* war propaganda
  culture of defeat and, 265–266
  Franco-Prussian War and, 265
  new media and, 344–345
  warfare and, 279
  World War I and, 280–283
Pumpurs, Andrejs, 298
pupilles de la nation (wards of the nation), 292
Pushkin, Alexander, 54
Putin, Vladimir, 145, 287, 295, 336
Puvis de Chavannes, Pierre, 196

QAnon Shaman (Jacob Chansley), 124, 344
queens, 60–61
Qu'est-ce que le Tiers État (*What is the Third Estate?*) (Sieyès), 49, **50**
Qu'est-ce qu'une nation? (Renan), 8, 269, 273–274
Qui a voulu la guerre? (Durkheim & Denis), 281, 284
quiz election shows, 180–181

race, use of term, 152–153
Rambo: First Blood (film) (Kotcheff), 293–294
Rambo: First Blood Part II (film) (Cosmatos), 293–294
Rand, John G., 240
Ranke, Leopold von, 160, 175, 178
Rask, Rasmus, 133, 146
Ravel, Maurice, 210
Ravi Varma, 197, **198**, 254
realism
  in literature, 194–195, 257
  in painting, 240–241
The Reaper (Ruseckas), **242**
recycling, 336
Red Cross, 279
Reden an die deutsche Nation (Fichte), 50, 268
re-enchantment, 162, 167, 169, 342
Reflections on the Revolution in France (Burke), 36
reform movements, 259–260
reformism, utopian, 260, 262, 280, 334
Regensburg, **182**
Reineke Fuchs (Goethe), 101
Reinhart Fuchs (Grimm), 102, 105, 120
Reitz, Edgar, 308
religion, love of one's country and, 35
religious devotionals, 197
Remarque, Erich Maria, 293
remediations
  canonicity, 6, 312–313
  in films, 312
  in general, 6
  of romantic evocations of the past, 200–202
Renaixença movement, 231, 340
Renan, Ernest, 8, 151–152, 268–269, 273–274, 277–278
Renoir, Jean, 292

reparation payment, 266
repertoire
in art, 183–184
of German patriotic choirs, 215–216
in history paintings. *See* history paintings
of Promenade concerts, 218–219
'Die Wacht am Rhein' on, 216–217
repetitiveness, thematic, 312–313
Repin, Il'ja, 196
Republic of Learning, 86, 91–92
restricted vs. unrestricted cultural productions, 5, 345–346
Reval (Tallinn), 220
revolutions. *See* uprisings/revolutions
revolutions of 1848, 57–59, 144
Revue des Deux Mondes, 268
Reykjavík, 259
Reynard fable, 88, 94, 97
diplomatic vs. critical editing of, 102–103
Franco-German appropriation of, 103
in literary history books, 89
philological appropriation of
Flemish, 104–105
French, 101–102
in general, 101–102
German, 102
rhapsodies, 208–209, **222–224**
Le Rhin dans l'histoire (Babelon), 285
Le Rhin gaulois (Jullian), 285
Rhine (river), 27, 29
Rhine/Rhineland, territorial debates about, 30, 87, 215–217, 264, 275, 285–286
The Rhine, Germany's River, but Not Germany's Border (Arndt), 29–30, 267
Rhine Crisis (1840), 215–217, 275
Richard Hannay (character in *The Thirty-Nine Steps*), 314
Rick Blaine (character in *Casablanca*), 44, 80
The Riddle of the Sands (Childers), 284
Riefenstahl, Leni, 287
Riga, 220, 255, 262–263, 299
Rigney, Ann, 81, 159
Rig-Veda (Hindu scriptures), 152–153
Rimsky-Korsakov, Nikolaj, 210
Der Ring des Nibelungen (Wagner), 106, 123
Risorgimento period, 59, 179, 212, 267
Rizal, José, 82
Rob Roy (Scott), 161
Roberts, Frederick Sleigh, 1st Earl, 285
Robespierre, Maximilien de, 36
Robin Hood, 164
role models, 79–81
Roman de Renard (Méon), 102
Romania, 321
Romanian cabaret, poster for, **253**
romantic/cultural nationalism
in twentieth century, 298–301
connections between cultural fields within, **126**
after decolonization, 305–307
dictatorship and, 302
in general, 19–20, 336
in Hungary, 205
in India, 325–326
in Ireland, 44–45, 300
in Latvia, 298–299
in Poland, 300
in Portugal, 300
as unpolitical, 44–45
vs. political nationalism, 330–331
romantic historians/history-writing
grip on public imagination, 179
inspired by Scott, 164–165
later historians' disavowal of, 178–179
legacy of, 181
narrative strategies of, 164–165
professionalization of their trade, 165
as public intellectuals/nation builders, 177
romanticism. *See also* poets
epiphany in, 74
in general, 19–20
Ossian's effect on, 71–73
poetic philosophy of history, 37–38
poets as nationalist role models, 79–81
as re-enchantment, 162, 342
Romany culture, 207–208, 252, **253**
Rome, 82, 187–188, 248, **249**
Roncesvalles, Battle of (1813), 94–95, 293
Röntgen, Wilhelm, 283
Rossini, Gioachino, 203
Rouget de Lisle, Claude Joseph, **32**, 111, 203
Rousseau, Jean-Jacques, 35
RRR (film) (Rajamoudi), 323–325
'Rule Britannia' (Arne), 218
Runeberg, Johan Ludvig, 79
Ruritania (fictitious kingdom), 60–61
Ruseckas, Kanutas, **242**
Russia/USSR
Decembrist revolt in, 53–54
films/television in, 321
languages in, 145
revolution of 1917 in, 61
rivalry with Ottoman Empire, 53–54, 59
secret societies in, 53–54
statues in, 40
traditional costumes in, 252
war propaganda, 34
Russian language, 145
Russian Orthodox Church, 34, 145
Rusyn language, 144, 146
Rybnikov, Pavel, 116

Šafárik, Pavol, 131, 134, 144
Salazar, António de Oliveira, 301
salience, of nationalism, 331, **332**
Salon des refusés, 241
Sand, George, 203, 238
Sattelzeit, 15
Sauerwein, Georg, 246
Savarkar, Vinayak Damodar, 307
Savigny, Carl von, 110, 125
Saxonism, 101
Scandinavia, 51
Schiller, Friedrich, 40, 50, 54, 82, 162, 228–229, **311**
Schivelbusch, Wolfgang, 22, 42, 265–266, 268
Schlegel, Friedrich, 89–90, 127, 175
Schleiermacher, Friedrich, 52
Schleswig-Holstein, 95, 101, 133, 137, 139–140, 175
Schleswig-Holstein Wars, 215
Schlözer, August, 144
Schneckenburger, Max, 29
Schnorr von Carolsfeld, Julius, 191
Scholl, Sophie, 55
Schoolcraft, Henry and Jane, 117–118
Schoonenboom, Merlijn, 197
Schopenhauer, Arthur, 287
Schottelius, Justus Georg, 135
Schuschnigg, Kurt, 302, 304
Schwarzenegger, Arnold, 175
Scienza nuova (Vico), 67, 89
Scotland. *See also* Scott, Walter
  ancestral antiquity, 85
  festive culture in, 81
  Gaelic language in, 68
  Highland dress, 243
  Jacobite rising of 1745, 161–162
Scott, Paul, 309
Scott, Walter
  afterlives of, 177–178
  historians inspired by, 164–165
  managing royal visit, 171
  as poet and novelist, 161
  on Romance, 163
  works of
    The Antiquary, 83–84
    enchantment/disenchantment in, 162
    ethnic conflicts in, 176
    Hegelian sublation and, 171
    historicist dualism of, 195
    hybridity of, 162–164
    Ivanhoe, 163–164, 176, 195
    'Lay of the Last Minstrel', 76–77, 81, 158–159, 168
    minstrels in, 80–81, 158–159
    narrative strategies in, 159–162
    nation in, 175
    Old Mortality, 160
    Ossianic influence in, 161
    Rob Roy, 161
    Waverley, 161–163, 169
Scottish Gaelic, 151
Scottish Society of Antiquaries, 84
secret societies, 51, 53–54, 57
secularization, 38–39
self-determination
  colonialism and, 306
  as democratic principle, 305
  dictatorship and, 302–303
  in general, 273
  in imperial peripheries, 256
  at Paris Peace Conference, 61, 112, 286, 295, 297
self-renaming, 131
Semb, Klara, 246
Sempach, Battle of (1386), 229
Senso (Visconti), 212
sentimentalism, 195
Serbia, 280. *See also guslars* (traditional singers)
Serbian language, 110, 142, 145, 148
Serbo-Croatian language, 142
Seville, 248
Shakespeare, William, 38–39, 82, 158, 180, 308, 313
sheet music, 212–213
Shelley, Percy Bysshe, 37
Shevchenko, Taras, 79, 108, 172, **311**, **312**
Shippey, Tom, 355, 358
Shivaji I, Indian ruler, 313
The Shoemakers' Feast (Tyl), 257
shopping arcades, 232, 247
Sibelius, Jean, 118
Sienkiewicz, Henryk, 170, **319**
Sieyès, Emmanuel, 49, 58, 270
Sigurjónsson, Jóhann, 259
Silas Marner (Eliot), 238
Simrock, Karl, 101
singing/songs. *See also* choirs; opera; *under individual songs*
  emergence of convivial, 212–213
  French nationalistic, 77–78
  in general, 76
  German nationalistic, 77
  inspired by remembered glories, 28
  of national anthem of France, 31–32
  of national anthem of Germany, 29
  as politically suspect, 216
  of semi-national anthem of Germany, 27–28
Sinhagad (film) (Shantaram), 313
Skandinavernes hedenske Gudelære (Nyerup), 121
Skansen resort (Sweden), 253, 256
Skiing Birchlegs Crossing the Mountain with the Royal Child (Bergslien), **202**
Slade School (London), 260
Slavic Epic (Mucha), 196, 201
Slavic languages, 134–135, 143–146

Slavín memorial (Prague), 167
Slavophilia, 336
Slavy Dcera (Kollár), 108
The Sleepwalkers (Clark), 284
Slovak language, 107, 144–145
Slovak names, 131
Slovene language, 108, 142–143, 145
Slovenec, 143
Smetana, Bedřich, 168, 211
Smetona, Antanas, 302, 304
Smith, Anthony, 17
Smith, Joseph, 41
social media, 344–345
Société des anciens textes français (Ancient French Texts Society), 94, 96
Society of Antiquaries, 83
'Society of True and Loyal Sons of the Fatherland', 54
Sokol athletic clubs, 228, 243, **244**, **261**, 262
Soldaat van Oranje (*Soldier of Orange*) (film) (Verhoeven), 315
'Solitary Reaper' (Wordsworth), 73, 239
Sombart, Werner, 281
'Song of hatred against England' ('*Haßgesang*') (Lissauer), 288–289
'The Song of Hiawatha' (Longfellow), 117, 210
Sorbian language, 144–145
Sorrows of Young Werther (Goethe), 71
source criticism (*Quellenkritik*), 160
South Africa, 306
Southern Netherlands, 51, 56. *See also* Belgium
souvenirs, **182**
Spain. *See also* Barcelona
  architecture in, 262
  Galician movement in, 259
  minorities in. *See* Basques; Catalans/ Catalonia; Galician movement
  new philology in, 96
  patriotic choirs in, 213
  post-imperial nostalgia in, 307
spectacular writing, 164
spelling reforms, 134–135
Spies of the Kaiser: Plotting the Downfall of England (Le Queux), 285
splitters, of language variants, 140, 148–149, **148**. *See also* lumpers, of language variants
sports, 227–228. *See also* Sokol athletic clubs
Srpske narodne pjesme (Vuk Karadžić), 109–110, **111**
St Amand des Eaux (monastery), 98–99
stability, of states, 35–36
Staël, Madame de, 69, 75
Stalin, Joseph, 34
Stallone, Sylvester, 293–294
standardization, of language(s), 135, 148–149
states. *See also* nations/nation-states
  independence of, 297–298
  instability of, 36
  national identity and, 290–291
  order-changing supermen and, 36–37
  rejection of rule of, 50–51
  stability of, 35–36
  wartime bereavements and, 291–292
statues. *See also* monuments
  equestrian, 184
  in general, 184
  of Germania, 27, **28**
  of historical figures, 233
  of Jagiello I, 300
  of Lāčplēsis, 298–299
  in Paris, 233
  in Russia, 40
  of writers/intellectuals, **56**, 82
stereotyping, national. *See* ethnotypes
Stern, Daniel, 203
Stevenson, Robert Louis, 173
Stimmen der Völker in Liedern (Herder), 113
Stollwerck (chocolate manufacturer), 27
Storost, Wilhelm (Vydūnas), 246, 260
Strasbourg, 273
streaming services, 327
Stuart, John, 3rd Earl of Bute, 114
'The Study of Celtic Literature' (Arnold), 151
Štúr, Ľudovit, 79, 131
sublation (*Aufhebung*), 171
the Sublime, 71
Sue, Eugène, 176, 270
Suhm, Peter Frederik, 67, 121
suicides, 71
supernatural beings, 122
superstitions, 122
Surikov, Vasilij, 191
Suttner, Bertha von, 280
Sweden, 227, 245–246
Switzerland, 229–230

De taal is gansch het volk (Willems), 98
Tagore, Dwarkanath, 151, 340
Tallinn (Reval), 220
Tannhäuser (Wagner), 211
Tartu (Dorpat), 220
Tegnér, Esaias, 107, **311**
television. *See* films/television
Tell, Wilhelm. See Wilhelm Tell
Tengrism, 156
Tengström family, 110
territorial debates. *See* Alsace-Lorraine; Rhine/ Rhineland, territorial debates about; Schleswig-Holstein
Tess of the D'Urbervilles (Hardy), 238

Teutoburg Forest, Battle of the (9 AD), 179, 190
text editions. *See* philology/philologists
Thatcher, Margaret, 293
theatre(s)
  in general, 256–257
  grassroots national, 259–260
  Ibsen's influence on European, 258–260
  literary, 257–258
Thierry, Augustin, 176
Thiesse, Anne-Marie, 14
thin-centred ideology, nationalism as, 335
Third Estate (France), 49
The Thirty-Nine Steps (Buchan), 284
The Thirty-Nine Steps (film) (Hitchcock), 314
Thomas, Ambroise, 213
Thompson, Flora, 309
Thorkelin, Grímur Jónsson, 87, 100
The Three Musketeers (Dumas), 174
Tilly, Charles, 291
Tilsit Singers' Society, 246
Tito, Josip Broz, 145
To my fatherland (Zweers), 211
Tolkien, J. R. R., 123, 174
Tolstoy, Leo, 54, 195, 235
Tomasi di Lampedusa, Giuseppe, 195
Tönnies, Ferdinand, 238
Toulouse, 230
tourist gift shop, **182**
Tourist Pavilion (Prague), 248
Trachtenvereine, 244
trademarks, 251
traditional costumes
  in Albania, 252–253
  in Austria, 243–245, **245**
  in Bavaria, 243–244
  as collective stage costumes, 246
  in general, 242
  in Germany, 242–243
  in Hungary, 243
  in Lithuania, 246
  national identity and, 242–243, 246–247
  in Norway, 246
  in paintings, 241–242
  in Poland, 243
  in Russia, 252
  in Scotland, 243
  at world fairs, 252, **253**
Le trahison des clercs (Benda), 267
transnationality
  of classicist repertoire, 184
  in cultivation of culture, 92, 337–338
  of manuscripts, 100
Travels in Central Asia (Vámbéry), 155
Travels into Dalmatia (Fortis), 114
Treitschke, Heinrich Gotthard Freiherr von, 267, 274, 286
Trevelyan, G. O., 283
tribal history. *See* ethnohistory (*Völkergeschichte*)
Tristan and Iseult (chivalric romance), 88
Triumph des Willens (film) (Riefenstahl), 287
Troeltsch, Ernst, 281
troubadours. *See* minstrels/bards/troubadours
El trovador (Gutiérrez García), 231
Il Trovatore (Verdi), 231
Trump, Donald, 295, 343–344
Tugendbund (League of Virtue), 53–54
Saint Tukaram, 314
Turan, Hüseyinzade Ali, 155
Turanian language family, 154
Turanism
  in Hungary, 156–157, 336
  in Turkey, 155–157
Türk Yurdu (newspaper), 155
Turkey
  Turanism in, 155–157
  Young Turk reformers, 155–156
Turkish-Hungarian connections, 154–155
Turnvereine, 228
two-nations view in history, 270
Tyl, Kajetan, 257
Tyrol, 51, 139
Tyrš, Miroslav, 131, 340

'Über das finnische Epos' (J. Grimm), 117
Uhland, Ludwig, 72
Ukrainian language, 108, 145
Ulmanis, Kārlis, 302
Unamuno, Miguel de, 307
'Union of Prosperity', 54
'Union of Salvation', 54
United East India Company (VOC) (Verenigde Oost-Indische Compagnie), 174
United Kingdom. *See also* London
  ethnotype, 46–48
  films/television in, 308–309
  invasion scares in, 285
  libraries in, 86
  national anthem of, 33
  national nostalgia in, 308–309
  patriotic choruses in, 213
  post-imperial nostalgia in, 307–308
  Promenade concerts in, 218–219
  war propaganda of, 33–34, 289
United States of American (USA), 314
universal exceptionalism, 337–338
'unpolitical' status of nations, 44–48
uprisings/revolutions
  anti-Ottoman, 55
  in Europe, 55–61
  in France, 36, 74
  in Russia, 53–54
Urtexts, 102, 160

USSR. *See* Russia/USSR
utopian reformism, 260, 262, 280, 334

'Va Pensiero' chorus (Verdi), 211–212
Valencian revivalism, 340
Valenciennes, library of, 98–99
Vámbéry, Ármin, 155
Vasaloppet (ski race), 227
Vatican Library, 88
Vauban, Marquis of, 275
Vaughan Williams, Ralph, 210
Vaulundur's Saga (Oehlenschläger), 107
Veit, Philipp, **188**, 189
Velde, Henri van de, 262
Verdaguer, Jacint, 79, 80, 231
Verdi, Giuseppe, 211–212, 231, **312**, **317**
Verenigde Oost-Indische Compagnie (United East India Company) (VOC), 174
Verhoeven, Paul, 315
vernacular classics. *See also* foundational texts
  in general, 88–89
  nationalizing effect of, 93–95
  rediscovery of, 86–88, 90–91
  textual re-editions of, 91
  timeline of text editions of, **90**
vernacular languages
  nation and, 126–130
  national identity and, 127–130
vernacular music, 209
Viaggio in Dalmazia (Fortis), 113
Viale, Salvatore, 129
Vico, Giambattista, 67, 86, 89
Victoria, Queen of the United Kingdom, 101, 171
Victoria Cross (British decoration), 292
Vielvölkerstaat (multi-ethnic empire), 60
Vienna, 187
Vienna Congress (1814), 52
Vienna Literary Agreement (1850), 142–143
Viereck, Peter, 73
Viktor Laszlo (character in *Casablanca*), 43–44
Villar Ponte, Antón, 259
Villiers de l'Isle-Adam, Auguste, comte de, 258
Vilnius, 53, 61–62
virtuosi, 203–204
Vyšehrad cemetery (Prague), 167
Višnjić, Filip, 112
the visually impaired, 112
Vittorio Emmanuele II, King of Italy, 59, 179
VOC (Verenigde Oost-Indische Compagnie) (United East India Company), 174
VOC-mentaliteit, 174
Volk/*Völker*, use of terms, 175, 292
Völkergeschichte (ethnohistory), 91, 125, 175–176, 270, 272
Volksgeist (national identity). *See* national identity/character (*Volksgeist*)
Vörösmarty, Mihaly, 108
Vydūnas (Wilhelm Storost), 246, 260

'Die Wacht am Rhein' (Schneckenburger)
  in *Casablanca*, 31
  creation of, 29
  Franco-Prussian War and, 265
  in *Mein Kampf*, 27–28
  mention of, 264
  reactivations of, 30
  on repertoire, 216–217
Die Waffen Nieder! (von Suttner), 280
Wagner, Richard, 7, 106, 123, 211
Wales
  Breton connections with, 149–151
  language in, 151
  literary commemorations in, 150–151, 230
Waltz, Jean-Jacques (Hansi), 276
Wanda (Polish princess), 169
Wappers, Gustaaf, 170
war alarmism, 285
War and Peace (Tolstoy), 54, 195, 235
war enthusiasm, 28
war films, 315–316
war propaganda. *See also* public opinion
  academic scholars and, 283–284, 287–288
  cultural productions and, 34–35
  in general, 333
  World War I and
    allied, 281–284
    British, 289
    French, 280, 284, 286–287
    in general, 289–290
    German, 46, 280–283, 288–289
    invasion/future war novels and, 284–285
    Rhineland and Alsace-Lorraine in, 285
  World War II and
    British, 33–34
    films as celebratory remembrance, 315
    Russian, 34
War Propaganda Bureau (UK), 281, 283
wards of the nation (*pupilles de la nation*), 292
warfare, 279–280. *See also under individual wars*
'Was ist des Deutschen Vaterland' ('What is the German's Fatherland') (Arndt), 77, 128, 138, 216–218
Waverley (character in *Waverley*), 171
Waverley (Scott), 161–163, 169
Wayne, John, 316
Weber, Max, 40–41, 162
Weihenstephan Abbey, 88
Weimar Germany, 30
Weisthümer (J. Grimm), 125
Wells, H. G., 283

Welsh language, 151
Wergeland, Henrik, 82, 264
Werner, Anton von, 190
Wessex (fictional landscape), 240
West, Benjamin, 185
'What Do We Demand of France?' (Treitschke), 267
'What is the German's Fatherland' ('Was ist des Deutschen Vaterland') (Arndt), 77, 128, 138, 216–218
What is the Third Estate? (*Qu'est-ce que le Tiers État?*) (Sieyès), 49, **50**
When William Came: A Study of London under the Hohenzollerns (Saki), 284
'Where is my homeland?' ('Kde domov můj?') (Tyl), 257
The White Panther (*Beli panter*) (Janša), 172
Widukind, 123
Wilfred of Ivanhoe (character in *Ivanhoel*), 171
Wilhelm, Prince of Albania, 61
Wilhelm I, German emperor, 192, **193**, 266, 275
Wilhelm II, German emperor, 46, 282, 288
Wilhelm Tell (legendary hero), 54, 229–230, **310**, **312**, **317**
Wilhelm Tell (Schiller), 229
Wilhelmina, Queen of the Netherlands, 304
Wilhelmus (Dutch national Anthem), 33
will, willpower, 287, 370
Wille zur Macht (Nietzsche), 287
Willem I, King of the Netherlands, 56
Willems, Jan Frans, 94, 96–98, 105
William Wallace (character in *Braveheart*), 327
Wilson, Woodrow, 61
Winckelmann, J. J., 84
Windelband, Wilhelm, 283
Winge, Hanna, 246, 260
Wislicenus, Hermann, 191–194, **193**, 201
Wissenschaft als Beruf (Weber), 162
Wollzeiler Circle, 110
women, convivial/domestic learned circles, 110
women's movements, 259
Wood, Henry, 218
Wood, Robert, 67
Wordsworth, William, 73, 76, 80, 239
world fairs
  (1851) (London), 240, 247
  (1855) (Paris), 240
  (1880) (Barcelona), 301
  (1889) (Paris), **253**
  (1893) (Chicago), 27
  (1896) (Riga), 255
  (1900) (Paris), 255
  (1911) (Rome), **249**
  (1933) (Chicago), 255, 300
  (1939) (New York), **300**
  (1940) (Lisbon), 301, **301**
  colonialism and, 253–255
  diorama pavilions in, 196
  economic internationalization and, 249–250
  folk villages at, 253
  mass-production and, 260
  national identity and, 250–252, 255–256
  newly independent countries and, 255, 299–300
  outside Europe, 254–255
  power relations and, 254–255
  tourism and, 248–249
  traditional costumes at, 252, **253**
  venues for, 247–248
World War I (1914–1918). *See also* war propaganda
  commemorations of, 291–292
  governments vindications of own behaviour, 281
  impact of, 294
  outbreak of, 280
  public opinion and, 280–283
  as rematch of older wars, 275
  reminiscences about, 27
  'Who started it?' debate, 284
World War II. *See* war propaganda
writers/intellectuals. *See also* academic scholars
  Arnold on, 39
  Carlyle on, 38–39
  funerals of, 82
  national importance of, 39–40
  as original geniuses, 82
  poets, 72–73, 75–82
Wundt, Wilhelm, 283
Württemberg Library (Stuttgart), 88

Yeames, William Frederick, 195, **196**
Yeats, W. B., 80, 151, 258, 303
Yeni Turan (Halide Edib Adıvar), 155
Yermak's Conquest of Siberia (Surikov), 191
Yugoslavia, 142–143, 145, 321
Yvonne (character in *Casablanca*), 31, 43–44

Zalan's Flight (*Zalan futása*) (Vörösmarty), 108
Zariņš, Rihards, 197
Zeitschrift für Völkerpsychologie und Sprachwissenschaft, 278
Zelter, Carl Friedrich, 214
Zeuss, Johann Caspar, 151
Zionism, 306, 341
Zog I, King of Albania, 302
Zola, Émile, 265
Zweers, Bernard, 211, 216

Printed in the United Kingdom by TJ Clays Ltd.